The Family Experience
A Reader in Cultural Diversity

Fourth Edition

Mark Hutter
Rowan University

PEARSON

Boston   New York   San Francisco
Mexico City   Montreal   Toronto   London   Madrid   Munich   Paris
Hong Kong   Singapore   Tokyo   Cape Town   Sydney

*To the memory
of my parents
and in-laws*

Executive Editor: *Jeff Lasser*
Editor in Chief, Social Sciences: *Karen Hanson*
Editorial Assistant: *Andrea Christie*
Marketing Manager: *Krista Groshong*
Editorial Production Service: *Whitney Acres Editorial*
Manufacturing Buyer: *JoAnne Sweeney*
Cover Administrator: *Kristina Mose-Libon*
Electronic Composition: *Omegatype Typography, Inc.*

For related titles and support materials, visit our online catalogue at www.ablongman.com.

Library of Congress Cataloging-in-Publication Data

DATA NOT AVAILABLE AT THE TIME OF PUBLICATION

ISBN: 0-205-38920-1

Printed in the United States of America

10   9   8   7   6   5   4   3   2   1   08   07   06   05   04   03

Contents

Chapter 2   **The Family, Kinship, and the Community   63**

technologies, and how this technology affected the amount of contact and support exchanged with members of their distant social networks.

This study examines qualitative aspects of mother/child relationships and the strengths in these relationships. Boundary issues and role shifts between children and their divorced mothers are particularly emphasized.

Arendell examines how men's conceptualizations of their gender identity is highly influential in their attitudes and behavior regarding marriage, parenthood, and divorce.

The high divorce rate among African Americans is examined through an analysis of the impact of divorce on fatherhood, custody issues and visitation, children as a factor in remaining married, children's reactions to divorce, telling children, and fathers' perceptions of children's reactions. Other issues looked at include child custody, visitation and child supports, interracial children, noncustodial fathering, and the future of Black fathering.

Building on the theme that there are insufficient institutional supports and guidelines to ensure optimal success of remarriages after divorce, the authors examine the problems that are confronted by stepparents and their stepchildren in everyday family encounters.

The authors review changes in family law over the last 30 years and the role that the social sciences have had in the family law revolution. The following areas are examined: marriage, divorce, child custody, remarriage and stepfamilies, unwed fathers, third-party visitation, nontraditional partnership, assisted reproduction, and adoption. The authors speculate about future changes in the family and the role that the social sciences will play in legal reforms.

Preface

In this the beginning of the twentieth-first century, academia is still engaged in the great debate begun more than a quarter of a century ago regarding the nature and quality of the college curriculum, and what, if any, place "outsiders"—people of color, ethnic groups, and recent immigrant groups—should have in it. In many ways this debate is a continuation of the major redirection of historical study that began about the same time. The "new social history" stressed day-to-day experiences of ordinary people. It sensitized us to the importance of studying women, children, the elderly, as well as the poor, working people, and racial and ethnic minorities in order to have a better understanding of our past, our present, and our future. No longer would history be restricted to the study of great men and of epochal events that emphasized the powerful and neglected the rest of us.

During this time period, we have witnessed global change that has had dramatic effects on all our lives. Our country has become more multicultural and, in addition, new types of living-together arrangements, marriages, and families are emerging that require us to understand the varieties of the family experience.

Reflecting these changes, colleges and universities have become concerned with the integration of issues regarding gender, race, class, and ethnicity into the curriculum. Often the resolution of this concern is to try to achieve a balance between the traditional core curriculum, which emphasized white, male-dominated Western culture, and the more recent diversified curriculum that reflects global concerns, the study of non-Western cultures, and the inclusion of women, minorities, and persons of color.

Sociology has recognized the importance of internationalizing the curriculum and integrating issues of gender, race, class, and ethnicity. Increasingly, we have seen more and more courses that have become sensitive to curriculum inclusion. The study of the family is becoming one of the areas that has incorporated a greater awareness of gender studies. Matters of ethnicity, race, and class are now being given greater recognition, but for the most part, they are separated from the "mainstream" curriculum and are either not discussed or are relegated to peripheral study topics. The result is that a major characteristic of the American family—its class and cultural diversity—is omitted from discussion.

The fourth edition of this anthology addresses contemporary issues regarding the cultural diversity of today's American family. The coverage of race-ethnicity, gender issues, and social class variations is integrated throughout the topic sections. The selections are representative of the diversity of families in the United States. There are also selections that focus on historical background patterns that will foster an increased understanding of the dynamics of contemporary family patterns. The anthology is designed to broaden student awareness on the increased heterogeneity of families in the United States. At the same time, the anthology is designed to discuss social policy and legal issues and trends that impact on and transcend the concerns of particular variants of the American family.

This edition contains 32 readings, five more than the previous edition, while it keeps the same organizational framework. Eighteen selections are new to this edition and reflect the most current thinking on important family topics. The 14 carry-over selections reflect the best of the old editions. The selections discuss germane topics that are very pertinent to the current understanding of families. These include readings by the most influential current thinkers on family and community involvements, kinship interaction patterns, teenage pregnancy, homeless families, family violence, generational relationships, and economic matters. Also explored are such topics as the Internet and its impact on family and community involvements and the Internet and teenage dating patterns; public policy issues, the depiction of the family in the popular media, and how gender roles operate in different family settings.

These readings reflect an ethnographic, qualitative approach to understanding the dynamics of gender, race, class, and ethnicity as they pertain to marriage and the family patterns and structures. The selections do not require familiarity with sophisticated statistical techniques nor are they "number-crunching." They avoid unnecessary terminology and are jargon-free. These readings were chosen for their scholarly content *and* to be informative and interesting so that they will capture the reader's attention.

The organizational structure follows the standard format of sociology of the family courses. Each part of the book contains an introductory essay that outlines the major issues and concerns to be discussed in the readings. For each reading, these essays provide an overview to orient the reader and highlight its sociological significance. The goal is an anthology that can be used with or without an accompanying textbook.

ACKNOWLEDGMENTS

Rowan University and its students, faculty, and administration have fostered the viewpoints expressed in this book. Their emphasis on the integration of gender, ethnicity, race, and class into the curriculum and their openness to interdisciplinary studies has enriched my worldview. Administrative and teaching involvement in Rowan University's Honors Program has been especially rewarding. Members of the Family Research Committee of the International Sociological Association and members of the National Council on Family Relations have broadened my understanding of the global diversity of the family.

Over the years I have benefitted from participation in a number of National Institute of the Humanities Summer Institutes and Seminars and I am most appreciative to the directors and fellow participants for sharing their perspectives with me. Also, and most importantly, through professional involvements with Alpha Kappa Delta, the International Sociology Honors Society, and the Society for the Study of Symbolic Interaction, I have been able to extend my understanding of curriculum matters and pedagogical concerns.

The sociology editor at Allyn and Bacon, Jeff Lasser, and the entire Allyn and Bacon production staff provided the support necessary to ensure the completion of this edition. Much thanks is expressed to past reviewers and to Cathy Petrissanes, Clarion University of Pennsylvania, the reviewer of this edition.

The authors and publishers of these articles are thankfully acknowledged for granting permission to reprint their works. My wife, Lorraine, and my children, Daniel and Elizabeth have made my life emotionally and intellectually meaningful. My parents and my parents-in-law taught me to value and understand the immigrant-ethnic family experience, and, by so doing, have enriched my life.

General Introduction

The average man—or woman—of fifty years or more ago had the greatest respect for the institution called the family, and wished to learn nothing about it. According to the Victorian ideology, all husbands and wives lived together in perfect amity; all children loved the parents to whom they were indebted for the gift of life; and if these things were not true, they should be, and even if one knew that these things were not true, he ought not to mention it. Everything that concerned the life of men and women and their children was shrouded, like a dark deed, from the light.

Today all that is changed. Gone is the concealment of the way in which life begins, gone the irrational sanctity of the home. The pathos which once protected the family from discussion clings to it no more. Now we do not want to be ignorant about the family; we want to learn as much about it as we can and to understand it as completely as possible. We are engaged in the process of reconstructing our family institutions through criticism and discussion (Waller 1938, p. 13).

Willard Waller was one of the most prominent American family sociologists of the mid-twentieth century. These words, written more than sixty years ago in his seminal work, *The Family: A Dynamic Interpretation,* are reflective of his gadfly status in American sociology. His contemporaries did not agree with his critical—some would say scathing—look at the middle-class American family. Most had a much more sanguine view of the American family system that reflected their own middle-class biases. They saw harmony and concord, not tension and discord. Their perspective was shared by the popular media, which typified the American family as exclusively Caucasian, affluent, and residing in suburban and rural areas in peaceful harmony.

Indeed, American sociology was so uncritical of the family that it failed to foresee the revolution that swept across the United States beginning in the early 1960s and continues to the present. Social protest movements called for equality and civil rights for all those "forgotten" in affluent America. These movements, led by "outsiders"—people of color, ethnic groups, feminists, and gays—ushered in a wave of new thought in the study of the family that stressed the diversity of the American experience. These outsiders led American sociology to at last follow the call made by Willard Waller to engage "in the process of reconstructing our family institutions through criticism and discussion."

New conceptual frameworks allowed us to "see" family phenomena formerly hidden from view. We began to understand patterns and dynamics of family violence that we once did not even know existed. Further, new family structures—including dual-career families, single-parent families, and families reconstituted by divorce and remarriage—increases in the rates of desertion and divorce, teenage pregnancy, abortion, singlehood, voluntary child-lessness, and the feminization of poverty underwent sociological scrutiny and analysis.

The nature of marriage, family, and kinship systems in American society has under-gone a new examination. Conventional assumptions about the necessity of maintaining kin-ship relations and the role of the nuclear family in today's world are being questioned: What are the proper gender roles for women and men? Is parenthood an inevitable and desirable consequence of maturation? A new, more permissive sexual morality led to the re-examination of previously held beliefs and attitudes regarding premarital and extramarital sexual relations, out-of-wedlock pregnancies, and abortions.

Family structures have fluctuated considerably in the last thirty years. More couples than ever before have voluntarily chosen to have fewer children. Many have voluntarily chosen childlessness. Still others have reconsidered that decision and opted to have children in later years. Divorce rates that were accelerating in the 1970s have leveled off and stabi-lized but remain at a higher rate than ever before in U.S. history.

New family patterns have emerged. That cohabitation has, for many, become an Amer-ican way of life comments not only on premarital or nonmarital relationships but has implication for marital relationships as well. For those who eventually marry, the full impli-cation of cohabitation as a facilitator for, or a hindrance to, marital adjustment and happi-ness is still unknown. Singlehood is accepted by many. Media discussion of the "marriage squeeze" raises questions on whether singlehood is a voluntary permanent option, or a state caused principally by the relatively low number of eligible men for "career" women. Regardless, singlehood involves a different series of life commitments than marriage and family.

Women have been particularly affected by and have affected family life. The number of single-parent families headed by women has been steadily growing. Much of this increase was caused by the rising divorce rate, but another major factor was the rising ille-gitimacy rate, especially among poor teenage females. These trends have led to the femini-zation of poverty. Women's labor force participation has been constantly rising in the last fifty years. Further, a significant number of working wives have children, especially young children. Because mothers are generally the primary caretakers, women have had to juggle their career aspirations and family responsibilities. This has led to the demand for increased day-care facilities and to talk of a "mommy-track" career ladder depending on the ages of children and the husband's occupational and familial career patterns.

The legitimacy of abortion has become the crystallizing issue in reaction to changes in family behavior. Passions ignite over the issue. A polarization has developed between "pro-choice" and "pro-life" advocates that has as its fundamental basis the nature of family values and individual options. Homosexuality is yet another area that has become a debating ground for issues regarding changes in the family. The debate on the acceptability of homosexuality as a legitimate alternative family lifestyle has been exacerbated by the deadly disease AIDS. Fear of AIDS has been used to incite the expression of homophobia and the rejection of gay rights.

The controversy surrounding sexuality, marriage, and the family has entered the world of politics and public policy more than ever before. Laws regarding abortion and homosexuality are continually argued, challenged, and changed. Laws regarding illegitimacy, and regulations regarding welfare for single-parent households, are being written, argued, rewritten, and reargued. Politics continues to intrude on the government's responsibility to provide public support for child-care facilities. Arguments and counterarguments continue on this issue between traditionalists, who seek to preserve "natural" family values, and proponents of individual options in a family system more amicable to family diversity. The divorce revolution brought about by no-fault legislation has had the unintended consequence of dramatically improving the economic situation of divorcing husbands/fathers while at the same time leading to the povertization of wives/mothers and children. Economic discrimination of women justified by a traditional belief in women's "natural" role in the family and the inappropriateness of their participating in the workplace still exists. Although increased attention has recently been given to parallel concerns regarding men's roles, this has not generated nearly the same attention and controversy as women's commitments and options.

In recent years, biological knowledge has increased tremendously and the implications of the applications of this knowledge—cloning, genetic engineering, reproductive technology—are seen to have profound ramifications for the family. Further, a revolution in the technology of electronic communications—the Internet, cyberspace, dot.coms—has so dramatically impacted on our lives that it is hard to think how we ever lived without the personal computer. Here too, the future implications on family relations remain to be seen.

As a result of all these changes, debates, and controversies, there has been great discussion about the future of the family. A widespread view declares that the family is a dying institution and expresses much concern about the implications for the "American way of life." A counter view holds that the "family" itself is not dying, but rather that one form of the family is declining and being replaced by new types of families that are supportive of individuals of both sexes and of all ages. These new family forms will usher in emancipatory and egalitarian transformations in gender relations that include, but are not limited to, marital and family relations.

To understand the contemporary status of the American family, and to be able to predict its future, is vital. Unfortunately, American sociology has only recently recognized the importance of studying the historical and cultural diversity of family systems. In the last fifteen years, American sociology has increasingly realized that comparative and multicultural analysis can frequently help in understanding things that are so near to us they are difficult to see. Ignoring such diversity, in fact, distorts analysis of the American family; diversity in American families is the very essence of the American family.

The aim here is to develop understanding of the causes, conditions, consequences, and implications of American family diversity for individual, family, and society. This book looks at the diversity of the family experience through time. A multicultural approach is the best way to answer questions about family processes and structures and their relationship to other societal institutions. The family is a prime reflector of the major societal changes experienced in the twentieth century and into the twenty-first. The study of the family experience allows us to see the impact of broader patterns of societal change on individuals and their everyday lives. The rapid economic, political, and social changes characteristic of present times make such a comparative perspective crucial.

Reference

Waller, Willard. 1938. *The Family: A Dynamic Interpretation.* New York: Dryden.

Part I

Multicultural Perspectives

As we begin the first decade of the first century of the new millennium, we can look back at more than two centuries of continual economic, religious, political, and social upheavals throughout the world. Massive modifications and breakdowns of social structures and cultural values have been associated with social and individual crises in which everyday experiences could no longer be taken for granted. Conventional assumptions regarding gender role relationships, marriage, and the family have been under scrutiny and challenge. The sociological perspective is vital to understand these social forces that have affected people's lives.

Throughout history, the family has been the social institution that has stood at the very center of society. For most people, the family is the most important group to which they belong throughout their lives. The family provides intimate and enduring relationships and acts as a mediator between its members and the larger society. It transmits the traditional ways of a culture to each new generation. It is the primary socializing agent and a continuing force in shaping people's lives. Through the family women and men satisfy most of their interpersonal, emotional, and sexual needs. Children are raised in families, providing a tangible link among past, present, and future generations. The family provides the setting in which individuals are socialized and motivated for integration into occupational, religious, political, and social positions that ensure the continuation of societal institutions and structures.

These prefatory remarks suggest why the family is vital to the society and to the individual. It should, therefore, be apparent that changes in the family will have serious ramifications for a given society and its people. Sociology as a discipline developed in the early nineteenth century as a response to the major changes that occurred first in Western Europe and the United States and then rapidly spread through the rest of the world as a consequence of Western colonization. The sociological perspective on marriage and the family was to view it in terms of the social forces that affect people's lives.

Prior to the nineteenth century, Western thought generally held to a biblical belief in the origins of the family stemming from God's creation of the world, including Adam and Eve. Although there was a recognition of relatively minor familial changes over time, the biblical family form and its underlying patriarchal ideological precepts were seen as continuing intact into the nineteenth century. Western thought clung to uniformity throughout the world in terms of family structures, processes, and underlying familial beliefs and values. These governed the behavior of men, women, and children in families.

This belief in the worldwide uniformity of the family underwent severe challenge and was finally discarded as a result of a number of important factors. Western societies were industrializing and urbanizing at a rapid rate, destroying the old societal class systems as a new social class structure developed. Individual rights, duties, and obligations were redefined, and the relationships of the individual to the family and the family to the larger community were reworked. Western colonial expansionism and imperialism fostered a new economic system that had global implications for all cultures. Contacts were being made with people whose systems of family life were markedly different from each other. The recognition of worldwide family diversity led to the overthrow of the belief that there was a single family form. What was needed was an alternative theoretical perspective to reevaluate the origins of the family. This alternative perspective took the form of evolutionary theory.

The theory of evolutionary change developed by Charles Darwin in his *Origin of Species* in 1859 was the culmination of an intellectual revolution begun much earlier that promoted the idea of progressive development. As the theory of evolution became the dominant form in explaining biological principles, social scientists of the nineteenth century developed belief that there was a link between biological and cultural evolution. These social scientists were called Social Darwinists. Their basic tenet was that since biological evolution proceeded through a series of stages (from the simple to the complex), the same process would hold for cultures.

Henry Sumner Maine, Lewis Henry Morgan, J. J. Bachofen, and Herbert Spencer were among those who applied evolutionary theories to the study of the human family. Social Darwinists seemingly dealt with such nonimmediate concerns as the origins and historical development of the family, yet their theories had social and political implications. Social Darwinism provided "scientific" legitimation for Western colonization and exploitation of "primitive" peoples through the erroneous belief that Western culture represented "civilization" and non-Western cultures, particularly among nonliterate, low-technology societies, represented a primeval state of savagery or barbarity. And through its advocacy of evolutionary progress, Social Darwinism provided laissez-faire guidelines that supported neglect of the poorer classes of American and Western European societies. It also had implications for the roles of men and women in nineteenth-century family systems. By arguing for a patriarchal evolutionary theory of male supremacy and dominance over females, Social Darwinists gave implicit support to the Victorian notions of male supremacy and female dependency.

An important rebuttal to Social Darwinism that in part also developed out of evolutionary theory was made by Friedrich Engels ([1884]1972) in *The Origins of the Family, Private Property, and the State*. Concerns for gender role egalitarianism, as opposed to patriarchy and male sexual dominance, achieved their fullest evolutionary theory expression in this work. Engels' evolutionary theory saw economic factors as the primary determinants of social change and linked particular technological forms with particular family forms. Echoing Lewis Henry Morgan, Engels depicted the stage of savagery as one with no economic inequalities and no private ownership of property. The family form was group marriage based on matriarchy. During the stage of barbarism, men gained economic control over the means of production. In civilization, the last stage, women became subjugated to the male-dominated economic system and monogamy. This stage, in Engels' view, rather than representing the apex of marital and familial forms, represented the victory of private property over common ownership and group marriage. Engels speculated that the coming of socialist revolution would usher in a new evolutionary stage marked by gender equality and by common ownership of property.

Engels' main achievement was in defining the family as an economic unit. This has become a major focus in much of the subsequent historical research on the family and is of great theoretical importance in the sociology of the family. But, insofar as Engels' Marxist view constituted a branch of evolutionary thought, it was subject to many of the same objections (see below) raised against other evolutionary theories.

By the end of the nineteenth century, the popularity of Social Darwinism was rapidly declining. Contributing to the decline were the methodological weaknesses of the approach (data obtained by nontrained, impressionistic, and biased travelers and missionaries) and growing rejection of both its explicit value assumptions on the superiority of Western family forms and its belief in unilinear evolutionary development of the family. More importantly, the shift in the focus of the sociology of the family was at least in part precipitated by the sweeping changes in U.S. and European societies during the nineteenth century. There was a dramatic increase of awareness to such conditions as poverty, child labor, desertions, prostitution, illegitimacy, and abuse of women and children. Social scientists were appalled by the excesses of industrial urban society and the calamitous changes in the family system.

The Industrial Revolution dramatically changed the nature of economic and social life. The factory system developed, and with its development there was a transformation from home industries in rural areas to factories. Rural people were lured by the greater economic opportunities that the city promised. The domestic economy of the preindustrial family disappeared. The rural- and village-based family system no longer served as a productive unit. The domestic economy had enabled the family to combine economic activities with the supervision and training of its children; the development of the factory system led to a major change in the division of labor in family roles.

Patriarchal authority was weakened with urbanization. Previously, in rural and village settings, fathers reigned supreme; they were knowledgeable in economic skills and were able to train their children. The great diversity of city life rendered this socialization function relatively useless. The rapid change of industrial technology and the innumerable forms of work necessitated a more formal institutional setting—the school—to help raise the children. Laws came into existence to regulate the amount of time children were allowed to work and their work conditions. Laws also required that children attend school. These legal changes reflected the change in the family situation of the urban setting; families were no longer available or able to watch constantly over their children.

The separation of work from the home had important implications for family members. Increasingly, men became the sole provider for the family and the women and children developed a life centered around the family, the home, and the school. Their contacts with the outside world diminished, and they were removed from community involvements. The family's withdrawal from the community was characterized by its hostile attitude toward the surrounding city. The city was thought of as a sprawling and planless development bereft of meaningful community and neighborhood relationships. The tremendous movement of a large population into the industrial centers provided little opportunity for the family to form deep or lasting ties with neighbors. Instead, the family viewed neighbors with suspicion and wariness. Exaggerated beliefs developed on the prevalence of urban poverty, crime, and disorganization.

Social scientists began to see the decline in the importance of kinship and community involvements and the changes in the makeup of the nuclear family as more important areas of investigation than the study of the evolutionary transformations of the family. Their research and theories focused on the causal connections relating family change to the larger industrial and urban developments occurring in the last two centuries. Much attention has also been given to theoretical analyses of the effects these changes have had on the individual, on women, men, and children, on the family, on kinship structures, and on the larger community and the society.

For almost 200 years sociologists have wrestled with these concerns. The readings in the first part of this book focus on the relationship between societal change and the family. By necessity, this examination must be informed by the desire to understand these changes in the context of immigration and ethnic family experiences in the United States.

Chapter One opens with Stephanie Coontz's (Reading 1) social historical examination of the family in the United States. With a broad historical brush stroke, Coontz compares the contemporary family to the realities and myths of the family in the past. She is particularly sensitive to the diversity of the American family both in terms of structure and ethnicity. Of particular interest is her examination of the 1950s, which is seen as a benchmark era for the "traditional" norms of the two-parent family with husband as "breadwinner" and wife as "breadbaker." This is the family depicted on such television shows as "Father Knows Best" and "Ozzie and Harriet." Coontz observes that the 1950s was the most atypical decade in the history of American marriage and family life. To understand marriage and family life we must examine it in its historical and economic context. By so doing, not only will we get a better grasp of that family type but also such analysis is invaluable in understanding today's marriage and family patterns. We should not be misled by our myths of the past and the "way we never were" in trying to understand the present.

In the late nineteenth and early twentieth centuries there was mass immigration to the United States largely in response to the massive industrial growth of American cities. In Reading 2, "Immigrant Families in the City," by Mark Hutter, the editor of this anthology, there is an examination of the urban ways of life of some of these immigrant family groups.

Immigrants from these areas concentrated in the industrial cities of the Northeast and the Midwest, where job opportunities were plentiful and chances of success were greatest. The ultimate success of an immigrant group depended in large part on its ability to re-establish a normal pattern of family life in the United States. However, popular as well as sociological opinion saw the emerging immigrant ghettos as settings of social disorganization, with alienation, anomie, social isolation, juvenile delinquency, crime, mental illness, suicide, child abuse, separation, and divorce as inherent characteristics of urban life. The social reform movement that developed during this time period saw family disorganization as pervasive and as a consequence arising from governmental nonsupervision of industrial and urban institutions. In Reading 2, the nature of the social organizational patterns that were developing among these immigrant groups is examined.

The history of the African American family in the United States reflects to a large degree many of the historical turning points and changes experienced by the American family of European origin. However, the African American family experience also has unique characteristics that stem from its African origins as well as from the extraordinary historical experience it has had in the United States. The study of the African American family's historical experience has been influenced by a discussion on the relative importance of the African cultural heritage on African American family organization. Niara Sudarkasa (Reading 3) provides an overview of African family and Black American family structure as it developed in the political and economic context of U.S. history. The cultural and historical importance placed on the extended consanguineal kinship relationship over the importance of the marital or conjugal relationship is seen to distinguish the African American family from the American family of European origin.

The concluding selection for this chapter, "Setting the Clock Forward or Back?: Covenant Marriage and the Divorce Revolution," (Reading 4) by Laura Sanchez and her colleagues, examines "covenant marriage" in the larger context of the societal debate regarding "family values" and "culture wars." For many, the decline or "breakdown of the family" is seen as a primary factor for the rise of a host of social ills including the extensive use of drugs, startling increases in teenage pregnancies, family violence and child neglect, the decline in educational standards, and the overall decline in societal morality and ethics.

Covenant marriage refers to a more traditional form of marriage *and* divorce. It views marriage as a lifetime commitment and in the event that divorce is contemplated it can only be granted on fault-based criteria that includes infidelity, physical or sexual abuse, a felony conviction, or long-term separation. Covenant marriage legislation has passed in Arizona and Louisiana and 20 other states are considering similar legislation. In this reading, covenant marriage is contrasted with what has become the more conventional form of marriage which allows for its dissolution on the basis of "irreconcilable differences" and is usually accompanied by no-fault divorce provisions. Sanchez and her colleagues are interested in the role of the state in trying to influence marriage and divorce trends by legislating marital and divorce reforms. Three diverse groups, covenant couples, feminists, and public-housing residents, were studied and all were concerned with the quality of contemporary marriage and how to handle the myriad problems that accompany marital failure.

Issues raised in this reading can be seen as linked with "decline of community" and "self-centered" or "self-development" arguments. This perspective argues that close-knit bonds of moral reciprocity have declined and have been replaced in its stead with a vocabulary of individualism. As a consequence, the middle class finds itself without a language of commitment in which to create its moral discourse (Bellah et al., 1985).

Robert Bellah and his associates (1985) emphasize that one theme has been of central concern to sociologists since the nineteenth century: the debate about individualism versus social commitment and individual rights versus civic responsibility. America's moral dilemma is seen to revolve around the conflict between the desire for fierce individualism on the one hand and the need for community and commitment on the other. Bellah and his colleagues find that the failure of contemporary Americans is in their weakening of motivational commitments to collective purposes of families, communities, and the nation. The unchecked growth of individualism, "inside the family as well as outside it," is the cause of the society's general decline (Bellah et al., 1985:90). An all-powerful market economy is seen to have fostered individualism and achieved its first manifestation in the family by allowing its members to freely choose love matches. More recently, individualism appears in the form of the quest for personal growth that is not necessarily associated with commitment and emotional bonds. As a consequence, the security of lasting relationships and of stable marriages is in jeopardy as individuals seek self-knowledge and self-realization. The meaning of one's life is no longer seen to be anchored or derived from one's relationships with one's parents or children.

Bellah's assessment of the decline of American character is echoed by "family value" proponents who see that decline echoed in the decline of the American family. Sanchez et al., in Reading 4, believe that proponents of covenant marriage legislation see it as one form of necessary social policy that needs to be taken to restore the traditional family. Advocates against the restoration of the traditional family believe that the social changes that have occurred in the family including alternative family forms and a greater independence of partners in intimate relationships are responses to new post-industrial realities.

The counter-argument to the conservative position is that the changes in the American family that have occurred in the last thirty years do not represent a decline of the family but rather the opportunity for the empowerment of women. The decline is not of the family, but rather of a particular form of family life based on traditional nineteenth-century notions of father as the good provider and mother as the moral guardian of the home. Critics of the conservative viewpoint believe that increased attention to underlying family processes, particularly in terms of how the family deals with new stresses, reaches out for assistance, adopts new roles, alters patterns of courtship and sexuality, and satisfactorily adapts to social change, is needed. Also, the difficulties for family members associated with family change must be investigated to better understand them and deal with them. This, in their view, is more constructive than bemoaning the loss of traditional gender roles in the family.

The readings in Chapter Two, "The Family, Kinship, and the Community," focus on the relationship of the nuclear family to both the extended family and the larger community. Family historians have emphasized that changes in Western society resulted in the gradual separation of the public institution of work and the community from the private sphere of the family. Middle-class family life since the nineteenth century has been distinguished by this removal from the community setting. And the American suburb has continued to foster this privatizing process.

Many sociologists see the privatization of the middle-class family as antithetical to women's independence. More specifically, the spatial segregation of residence from home and the development of the single-family house led to the increased dependence of women on income-earning husbands. In addition, and most significantly, the house became the setting that required the full involvement of women. As Ruth Schwartz Cowan (1983) and Susan Strasser (1982) have demonstrated, women's domestic labor paradoxically increased with the development of mechanized techniques, e.g., vacuum cleaners and sewing, washing, and dishwashing machines that were designed supposedly for efficiency's sake but in fact have set new housekeeping standards. In addition, the automobile fostered the end of home delivery services for all kinds of goods and services, thus requiring that families own an automobile to perform these services. These new tasks included driving spouses to commuter transportation stations, picking up and delivering children to school and after-school activities, and taking sick family members to doctors, who no longer made house calls.

One technological advance that ran counter to the prevailing "more work for mother" pattern was the residential telephone (Fischer, 1988). Historically, the residential telephone has been used by women to foster gender-linked social relationships and involvements. Often, women used the telephone for what Micaela di Leonardo (Reading 5) calls "kin-work." Kin-work involves kinship contact across households and is as much a part of domestic labor as housework. It includes maintaining kinship ties, organizing holiday gatherings, and the creation and sustaining of kinship relationships. Kin-work is seen to fuse both the labor perspective and the domestic network categories of female work. The concern of di Leonardo's article is examining kin-work in the context of the interrelationships between women's kinship and economic lives of Italian American women who work in the labor market and at home.

In contrast to the relative separation of the nuclear family from extended kinship ties and community involvement with middle-class suburbia, is the family life of working class and ethnic groups. Di Leonardo's article provides one such illustrative example. So does Reading 6, "Mexican American Women Grassroots Community Activists: 'Mothers of East Los Angeles.'" In this article, Mary Pardo discusses the community activities of a group called the Mothers of East Los Angeles (MELA). It demonstrates how women use their family networks and family roles as the basis for political action that includes the building of new schools and safe work sites.

Pardo's work, as well as the research by Mark Hutter (Reading 2), demonstrates that the family structures of many immigrant and ethnic family groups in the United States are characterized by a developed social network comprising extended kin and neighbors. This social support structure is often an important mediating factor in a given family's involvement with the larger community.

Reading 7 is concerned with how women among the Muscogee (Creek) Native American group of central Oklahoma perceive the dual effects of ethnicity and gender on their work choices and their success as workers. Barbara B. Kawulich's research supports earlier studies that women from matrilineal tribes were guided in their personal and professional lives by their ethnic identities that had developed within their tribal cultures. Of particular interest to us is how they perceived the influence of their extended families on their sense of personal, gender, and ethnic identity.

The concluding reading for this part of the book, is an examination of the impact that the newest technology, home computers and the Internet, has on family, kinship and community involvements, and relationships. Let's return to our earlier discussion regarding individualism, the family, and the community to set the context for this reading. Robert Putnam (2000) has been one of the leading advocates that see a predominant characteristic of contemporary life in the decline of community involvements. The title of his book, *Bowling Alone,* both literally and figuratively summarizes his position. Putnam reports that nearly every kind of political, cultural or recreational activity that involves personal contact—church-going, card-playing, dinner parties, neighborhood get-togethers, and even family members having dinner together—has declined in the last 50 years. Activities that have increased involve minimal social interaction and many are solitary. They include watching television, going to the movies and playing video games. In recent years, playing home computer games and "surfing the Net" have become increasingly popular.

Putnam believes that the consequence of the increase of solitary activities at the expense of more social undertakings, is the shrinking access of "social capital"—the trust and reciprocity with others—that is the reward of communal activity and community sharing. Social capital can be thought of as the social networks and reciprocal norms of social trust that contribute to the functioning of a strong community. The consequence of the decline in social engagement is civic apathy that is ultimately a threat to both civic and personal health.

Putnam places the blame in part to the demand of financial pressures that result in two income families that hinders the time available for civic engagement. For example, women's employment often results in less involvement with family, friends, neighbors, and with community organizations like school-parent associations. Suburbanization is partly responsible in that it demands considerable time spent commuting; people live in one suburb, work in another and shop at malls in a third location. Electronic home entertainment, particularly television watching, consumes large amounts of time and offers little socially redeeming value.

The role of the computer and the Internet is one form of new technology that has raised questions on whether or not it is an enhancement of social capital or a deterrent. Putnam rejects the belief that the Internet holds the promise of developing a viable "virtual" community. Putnam concedes that while the Internet makes it possible to be in touch with more people, it has not fostered social and political awareness. It has not led to greater organizational involvement, nor has it stimulated personal action and interaction. Putnam would argue that social capital is primarily generated by face-to-face communal interactions.

Barry Wellman is a much-cited sociologist on the study of social networks. He is particularly interested in the investigation of the social uses and development of the computer and social "networking." In Reading 8, he along with a colleague, Keith N. Hampton, examine the experiences of the residents of "Netville," a suburban neighborhood with access to some of the most advanced new communications technologies available. They are concerned how this technology affects the amount of contact and support exchanged with members of their distant social networks. They look at relatives and friends who live outside of Netville. "Community" is analyzed as relations that provide a sense of belonging rather than as a group of people living near each other. They find that through "networking," ties that were "just out of reach" geographically are increased and supported as a result of access to computer-mediated communication. Hampton and Wellman's research suggests that the Internet can provide new opportunities for family and social relationships and engagements with the community. It leads to speculation that as the emerging electronic technology becomes more and more part of our everyday life it may influence the nature of family as well as community relationships in ways that may lead once again to "bowling together."

References

Bellah, Robert N., Richard Madsen, William M. Sullivan, Ann Swidler, and Steven M. Tipton. 1985. *Habits of the Heart: Individualism and Commitment in American Life.* New York: Perennial Library, Harper & Row.

Cowan, Ruth Schwartz. 1983. *More Work for Mother: The Ironies of Household Technology from the Open Hearth to the Microwave.* New York: Basic Books.

Engels, Friedrich. 1972. *The Origins of the Family, Private Property, and the State.* New York: Pathfinder Press. (Originally published in 1884.)

Fischer, Claude S. 1988. "Gender and the Residential Telephone: 1890–1940." *Sociological Forum* 3(2):211–233.

Putnam, Robert. 2000. *Bowling Alone: The Collapse and Revival of American Community.* New York: Simon & Schuster.

Strasser, Susan. 1982. *Never Done: A History of American Housework.* New York: Pantheon.

Chapter

1

The Changing Family: History and Politics

Reading 1   Where Are the Good Old Days?

STEPHANIE COONTZ*

The American family is under siege. To listen to the rhetoric of recent months, we have all fallen down on the job. We're selfish; too preoccupied with our own gratification to raise our children properly. We are ungrateful; we want a handout, not a hand.

If only we'd buckle down, stay on the straight and narrow, keep our feet on the ground, our shoulder to the wheel, our eye on the ball, our nose to the grindstone. Then everything would be all right, just as it was in the family-friendly '50s, when we could settle down in front of the television after an honest day's work and see our lives reflected in shows like *Ozzie and Harriet* and *Father Knows Best*.

But American families have been under siege more often than not during the past 300 years. Moreover, they have always been diverse, both in structure and ethnicity. No family type has been able to protect its members from the roller-coaster rides of economic setbacks or social change. Changes that improved the lives and fortunes of one family type or individual often resulted in losses for another.

A man employed in the auto industry, for example, would have been better off financially in the 1950s than now, but his retired parents would be better off today. If he had a strong taste for power, he might prefer Colonial times, when a man was the undisputed monarch of the household and any disobedience by wife, child, or servant was punishable by whipping. But woe betide that man if he wasn't born to property. In those days, men without estates could be told what to wear, where to live, and whom to associate with.

His wife, on the other hand, might have been happier in the 1850s, when she might have afforded two or three servants. We can be pretty sure, though, that the black or Irish servants of that day would not have found the times so agreeable. And today's children, even those scarred by divorce, might well want to stay put rather than live in the late 19th century, when nearly half of them died before they reached their late teens.

A HISTORY OF TRADEOFFS

These kinds of tradeoffs have characterized American family life from the beginning. Several distinctly different types of families already

*Coontz, Stephanie. 1996. "Where Are the Good Old Days?" *Modern Maturity* (May/June): 36–43. Reprinted by permission of the author.

coexisted in Colonial times: On the East Coast, the Iroquois lived in longhouses with large extended families. Small families were more common among the nomadic Indian groups, where marital separation, though frequent, caused no social stigma or loss of access to group resources. African-American slaves, whose nuclear families had been torn apart, built extended family networks through ritual coparenting, the adoption of orphans, and complex naming patterns designed to preserve links among families across space and time.

White Colonial families were also diverse: High death rates meant that a majority spent some time in a stepfamily. Even in intact families, membership ebbed and flowed; many children left their parents' home well before puberty to work as servants or apprentices to other households. Colonial family values didn't sentimentalize childhood. Mothers were far less involved in caring for their children than modern working women, typically delegating the task to servants or older siblings. Children living away from home usually wrote to their fathers, sometimes adding a postscript asking him to "give my regards to my mother, your wife."

A REVOLUTION OF SORTS

Patriarchal authority started to collapse at the beginning of the Revolutionary War: The rate of premarital conception soared and children began to marry out of birth order. Small family farms and shops flourished and, as in Colonial days, a wife's work was valued as highly as her husband's. The revolutionary ferment also produced the first stirrings of feminism and civil rights. A popular 1773 Massachusetts almanac declared: "Then equal Laws let custom find, and neither Sex oppress: More Freedom give to Womankind or to Mankind give less." New Jersey women had the right to vote after the Revolution. In sev-

eral states slaves won their freedom when they sued, citing the Declaration of Independence.

But commercial progress undermined these movements. The spread of international trade networks and the invention of the cotton gin in 1793 increased slavery's profits. Ironically, when revolutionary commitment to basic human equality went head-to-head with economic dependence on slavery, the result was an increase in racism: Apologists now justified slavery on the grounds that blacks were *less* than human. This attitude spilled over to free blacks, who gradually lost both their foothold in the artisan trades and the legal rights they'd enjoyed in early Colonial times. The subsequent deterioration in their status worked to the advantage of Irish immigrants, previously considered nonwhite and an immoral underclass.

Feminist ideals also faded as industrialization and wage labor took work away from the small family farms and businesses, excluding middle-class wives from their former economic partnerships. For the first time, men became known as breadwinners. By the post-Civil War era of 1870–90, the participation of married women in the labor force was at an all-time low; social commentators labeled those wives who took part in political or economic life sexual degenerates or "semi-hermaphrodites."

WOMEN LOSE; CHILDREN LOSE MORE

As women left the workforce children entered it by the thousands, often laboring in abysmal conditions up to ten hours a day. In the North, they worked in factories or tenement workshops. As late as 1900, 120,000 children worked in Pennsylvania's mines and factories. In the South, states passed "apprentice" laws binding black children out as unpaid laborers, often under the pretext that their parents neglected them. Plantation owners (whose wives and daughters encased themselves in corsets and grew their fingernails long) accused their former female slaves of "loaferism" when they resisted field labor in order to stay closer to home with their children.

So for every 19th-century middle-class family that was able to nurture its women and children comfortably inside the family circle, there was an Irish or German girl scrubbing floors, a Welsh boy mining coal, a black girl doing laundry, a black mother and child picking cotton, and a Jewish or Italian daughter making dresses, cigars, or artificial flowers in a sweatshop.

Meanwhile, self-styled "child-saver" charity workers, whose definition of an unfit parent had more to do with religion, ethnicity, or poverty than behavior, removed other children from their families. They sent these "orphans" to live with Western farmers who needed extra hands—or merely dumped them in a farm town with a dollar and an earnest lecture about escaping the evils of city life.

THE OUTER FAMILY CIRCLE

Even in the comfortable middle-class households of the late 19th century, norms and values were far different from those we ascribe to "traditional" families. Many households took in boarders, lodgers, or unmarried relatives. The nuclear family wasn't the primary focus of emotional life. The Victorian insistence on separate spheres for men and women made male-female relations extremely stilted, so women commonly turned to other women for their most intimate relationships. A woman's diary would rhapsodize for pages about a female friend, explaining how they carved their initials on a tree, and then remark, "Accepted the marriage proposal of Mr. R. last night" without further comment. Romantic friendships were also common among young

middle-class men, who often recorded that they missed sleeping with a college roommate and laying an arm across his bosom. No one considered such relationships a sign of homosexuality; indeed, the term wasn't even invented until the late 19th century.

Not that 19th-century Americans were asexual: By midcentury New York City had one prostitute for every 64 men; the mayor of Savannah estimated his city had one for every 39. Perhaps prostitution's spread was inevitable at a time when the middle class referred to the "white meat" and "dark meat" of chicken to spare ladies the embarrassment of hearing the terms "breast" or "thigh."

THE ADVENT OF THE COUPLE

The early 20th century brought more changes. Now the emotional focus shifted to the husband and wife. World War I combined with a resurgence of feminism to hasten the collapse of Victorian values, but we can't underestimate the role the emergence of a mass consumer market played: Advertisers quickly found that romance and sexual titillation worked wonders for the bottom line.

Marriage experts and the clergy, concerned that longer lifespans would put a strain on marriages, denounced same-sex friendships as competitors to love; people were expected to direct all their emotional, altruistic and sensual impulses into marriage. While this brought new intimacy and sexual satisfaction to married life, it also introduced two trends that disturbed observers. One was an increased dissatisfaction with what used to be considered adequate relationships. Great expectations, social historian Elaine Tyler May points out in her book of the same name, could generate great disappointments. It's no surprise that the U.S. has had both the highest consumption of romance novels and the highest divorce rates in the world since the early part of the 20th century.

The second consequence of this new cult of married bliss was the emergence of an independent and increasingly sexualized youth culture. In the late 19th century, middle-class courtship revolved around the institution of "calling." A boy was invited to call by the girl or her parents. It was as inappropriate then for a boy to hint he'd like to be asked over as it was in the 1950s for a girl to hint she'd like to be asked out. By the mid-1920s, calling had been almost totally replaced by dating, which took young people away from parental control but made a girl far more dependent on the boy's initiative. Parents especially worried about the moral dangers the automobile posed—and with reason: A middle-class boy was increasingly likely to have his first sexual encounter with a girlfriend rather than a prostitute.

The early part of the century brought a different set of changes to America's working class. In the 1920s, for the first time, a majority of children were born to male-breadwinner, female-homemaker families. Child labor laws and the spread of mass education allowed more parents to keep their children out of the workforce. Numerous immigrant families, however, continued to pull their offspring out of school so they could help support the family, often arousing intense generational conflicts. African-American families kept their children in school longer than other families in those groups, but their wives were much more likely to work outside the home.

THERE GOES THE FAMILY

In all sectors of society these changes created a sense of foreboding. *Is Marriage on the Skids?* asked one magazine article of the times; *What Is the Family Still Good For?* fretted another. Popular commentators harkened back to the "good old days," bemoaning the sexual revolution, the

fragility of nuclear-family ties, the cult of youthful romance, and the threat of the "emancipated woman."

The stock market crash, the Great Depression, and the advent of World War II moved such fears to the back burner. During the '30s and '40s, family trends fluctuated from one extreme to another. Depression hardship—contrary to its television portrayal on *The Waltons*—usually failed to make family and community life stronger. Divorce rates fell, but desertion and domestic violence rose sharply; economic stress often translated into punitive parenting that left children with emotional scars still apparent to social researchers decades later. Murder rates in the '30s were as high as in the 1980s; rates of marriages and births plummeted.

WWII started a marriage boom, but by 1946 the number of divorces was double that in 1941. This time the social commentators blamed working women, interfering in-laws and, above all, inadequate mothers. In 1946, psychiatrist Edward Strecker published *Their Mothers' Sons: The Psychiatrist Examines an American Problem,* which argued that women who were old-fashioned "moms" instead of modern "mothers" were emasculating American boys.

Moms, he said disapprovingly, were immature and unstable and sought emotional recompense for the disappointments of their own lives. They took care of aging parents and tried to exert too much control over their children. Mothers, on the other hand, put their parents in nursing homes and derived all their satisfaction from the nuclear family while cheerfully urging independence on their children. Without motherhood, said the experts, a woman's life meant nothing. Too much mothering, though, would destroy her own marriage and her son's life. These new values put women in an emotional double-bind, and it's hardly surprising that tranquilizers, which came on the scene in the '50s, were marketed and prescribed almost exclusively to housewives.

THE '50s: PARADISE LOST?

Such were the economic and cultural ups and downs that created the 1950s. If that single decade had actually represented the "tradition" it would be reasonable to argue that the family has indeed collapsed. By the mid 1950s, the age of marriage and parenthood had dropped dramatically, divorce rates bottomed out and the birthrate, one sociologist has recently noted, "approached that of India." The proportion of children in Ozzie-and-Harriet type families reached an all-time high of 60 percent.

Today, in contrast, a majority of mothers, including those with preschool children, work outside the home. Fifty percent of children live with both biological parents, almost one quarter live with single parents and more than 21 percent are in stepfamilies. Three quarters of today's 18–24-year-olds have never been married, while almost 50 percent of all first marriages—and 60 percent of remarriages—will end in divorce. Married couples wait longer to bear children and have fewer of them. For the first time there are more married couples without children than with them. Less than one quarter of contemporary marriages are supported by one wage earner.

Taking the 1950s as the traditional norm, however, overstates both the novelty of modern family life and the continuity of tradition. The 1950s was the most atypical decade in the entire history of American marriage and family life. In some ways, today's families are closer to older patterns than were '50s families. The median age at first marriage today is about the same as it was at the beginning of the century, while the proportion of never-married people is actually lower. The number of women who are coproviders and the proportion of children living in step-

families are both closer to that of Colonial days than the 1950s. Even the ethnic diversity among modern families is closer to the patterns of the early part of this century than to the demographics of the 1950s. And the time a modern working mother devotes to childcare is higher than in Colonial or Revolutionary days.

The 1950s family, in other words, was not at all traditional; nor was it always idyllic. Though many people found satisfactions in family life during that period, we now know the experiences of many groups and individuals were denied. Problems such as alcoholism, battering, and incest were swept under the rug. So was discrimination against ethnic groups, political dissidents, women, elders, gays, lesbians, religious minorities and the handicapped. Rates of divorce and unwed motherhood were low, but that did not prevent 30 percent of American children from living in poverty, a higher figure than at present.

IT'S ALL RELATIVE

Why then, do many people remember the 1950s as so much easier than today? One reason is that after the hardships of the Depression and WWII, things *were* improving on many fronts. Though poverty rates were higher than today, they were falling. Economic inequality was also decreasing. The teenage birthrate was almost twice as high in 1957 as today, but most young men could afford to marry. Violence against African-Americans was appallingly widespread, yet many blacks got jobs in the expanding manufacturing industries and for the first time found an alternative to Southern agriculture's peonage.

What we forget when politicians tell us we should revive the 1950s family is that the social stability of that period was due less to its distinctive family forms than to its unique socio-economic and political climate. High rates of unionization, heavy corporate investment in manufacturing, and generous government assistance in the form of public-works projects, veterans' benefits, student loans and housing subsidies gave young families a tremendous jump start, created predictable paths out of poverty, and led to unprecedented increases in real wages. By the time the "traditional male breadwinner" reached age 30, in both the 1950s and '60s, he could pay the principal and interest on a median-priced home on only 15–18 percent of his income. Social Security promised a much-needed safety net for the elderly, formerly the poorest segment of the population. These economic carrots combined with the sticks of McCarthyism and segregation to keep social dissent on the back burner.

THE NEW TRENDS

Because the '60s were a time of social protest, many people forget that families still made economic gains throughout the decade. Older workers and homeowners continued to build security for their retirement years. The postwar boom and government subsidies cut child poverty in half from 1949 to 1959. It was halved again, to its lowest levels ever, from 1959 to 1969. The high point of health and nutrition for poor children came in 1970, a period that coincided with the peak years of the Great Society, not the high point of the '50s family.

Since 1973, however, a new phase has emerged. Some things have continued to improve: High school graduation rates are at an all-time high; minority test scores rose steadily from 1970 to 1990; poverty rates among the elderly have continued to fall while life expectancy has risen.

Other trends show mixed results: The easy availability of divorce has freed individuals from oppressive or even abusive marriages, but many divorces have caused emotional and economic suffering for both children and adults. Women have found new satisfaction at work, and there's considerable evidence that children can benefit from having a working mother, but the failure of businesses—and some husbands—to adjust to working mothers' needs has caused much family stress and discord.

In still other areas, the news is quite bleak. Children have now replaced seniors as the poorest segment of the population; the depth and concentration of child poverty has increased over the past 20 years so it's now at 1965 levels. Many of the gains ethnic groups made in the 1960s and '70s have been eroded.

History suggests that most of these setbacks originate in social and economic forces rather than in the collapse of some largely mythical traditional family. Perhaps the most powerful of these sources is the breakdown of America's implicit postwar wage bargain with the working class, where corporations ensured labor stability by increasing employment, rewarding increased productivity with higher wages, and investing in jobs and community infrastructure. At the same time, the federal government subsidized home ownership and higher education.

Since 1973, however, real wages have fallen for most families. It increasingly requires the work of two earners to achieve the modest upward mobility one could provide in the 1950s and '60s. Unemployment rates have risen steadily as corporations have abandoned the communities that grew up around them, seeking cheap labor overseas or in nonunionized sectors of the South. Involuntary part-time work has soared. As Time magazine noted in 1993, the predictable job ladders of the '50s and '60s have been sawed off: "Companies are portable, workers are throwaway." A different article in the same issue found, "Long-term commitments…are anathema to the modern corporation."

During the 1980s the gap between the rich and middle-class widened in 46 states, and each year since 1986 has set a new postwar record for the gap between rich and poor. In 1980 a CEO earned 30 to 40 times as much as the average worker; by 1994 he earned 187 times as much. Meanwhile, the real wages of a young male high school graduate are lower today than those earned by his 1963 counterpart.

These economic changes are not driven by the rise in divorce and unwed motherhood. Decaying wage and job structures—not changing family structures—have caused the overwhelming bulk of income redistribution. And contrary to what has been called a new bipartisan consensus, marriage is not the solution to poverty. According to sociologist Donald J. Hernandez, Ph.D., formerly with the U.S. Census Bureau, even if every child in America were reunited with both biological parents, two thirds of those who are poor today would still be poor.

OUR UNCERTAIN FUTURE

History's lessons are both positive and negative. We can take comfort from the fact that American families have always been in flux and that a wide variety of family forms and values have worked well for different groups at different times. There's no reason to assume that recent changes are entirely destructive. Families have always been vulnerable to rapid economic change and have always needed economic and emotional support from beyond their own small boundaries. Our challenge is to grapple with the sweeping transformations we're currently undergoing. History demonstrates it's not as simple as returning to one or another family form from the past. Though there are many precedents for successfully reorganizing family life, there are no clear answers to the issues facing us as we enter the 21st century.

Reading 2   Immigrant Families in the City

MARK HUTTER*

The period of time from 1880 to 1924, when immigration laws placed severe limitation on movement into the United States, witnessed a massive exodus of people from southern and eastern Europe. This "new" immigration was from countries like Austria-Hungary, Greece, Italy, Poland, Rumania, Russia, and Serbia (now a part of Yugoslavia). Immigrants from these countries were joined by others from China and Japan, Mexico, French Canada, and the West Indies. It contrasts with the peoples of the "old" immigration, those who arrived between 1820 (when federal statistics of origin were first recorded) and 1880. That was made up almost entirely of northwest Europeans who came from countries such as England, Ireland, Scotland, France, Germany, Norway, and Sweden.

Total immigration in the three decades before the Civil War totaled five million. Between 1860 and 1890 that number doubled, and between 1890 and the beginning of the first world war in 1914, it tripled. The peak years of immigration were in the early twentieth century, with over a million people entering annually in 1905, 1906, 1907, 1910, 1913, and 1914. The main explanation for this massive movement of people to the United States was that the countries of origin of the "new" immigrants were experiencing population explosions and dislocations. By the later part of the nineteenth century, the

pressures of overpopulation, combined with the prospects of economic opportunity in the United States and the availability of rapid transportation systems that included railroads and steamships, set the wheels of world migration moving. Maldwyn Allen Jones, whose study *American Immigration* (1960) has been a standard work on the subject, comments on the shared motives of the culturally diversified immigrants for coming to America:

> *The motives for immigration...have been always a mixture of yearning— for riches, for land, for change, for tranquillity, for freedom, and for something not definable in words.... The experiences of different immigrants groups...reveal a fundamental uniformity. Whenever they came, the fact that they had been uprooted from their old surroundings meant that they faced the necessity of coming to terms with an unfamiliar environment and a new status. The story of American immigration is one of millions of enterprising, courageous folk, most of them humble, nearly all of them unknown by name to history. Coming from a great variety of backgrounds, they nonetheless*

*Hutter, Mark. 1986–1987. "Immigrant Families in the City." *The Gallatin Review* 6(Winter): 60–69.

resembled one another in their willingness to look beyond the horizon and in their readiness to pull up stakes in order to seek a new life. (Jones 1960, pp. 4–5)

There was a great deal of variation in immigrant family migration arrangements. Some immigrant groups coming from Scandinavian societies and from Germany came as nuclear families responding to America's needs to settle and farm the vast lands of middle western America. For these groups settlement often meant the almost complete reconstitution of Old World rural village life and family patterns in rural America (Hareven and Modell 1980). One extreme example of this practice were the Hutterites, a German religious group that lived in Russia and migrated to the United States in the late nineteenth century. They settled in isolated rural agricultural sections in order to maintain their distinctive family patterns. These include early marriage, exceptionally high fertility, and near universal remarriage after widowhood. The Hutterite community was a highly cooperative family economy ruled by a family patriarch that operated through kinship affiliations created by the high fertility and strict laws of intermarriage. This isolated group could and has maintained itself until today because of its ability to find marriage partners within the group.

As agricultural opportunities in rural America declined and as the demand for skilled and especially unskilled urban workers grew, the "new" immigrations from southern and eastern Europe concentrated in the industrial cities of the Northeast and the Midwest. It was in these urban areas where job opportunities were plentiful and where the chances of success were greatest. Young unattached males became the mainstay of the migration population. The ethnic historian Thomas J. Archdeacon (1983) reports that, in the decades between 1840 and 1899,

males constituted 58 to 61 percent of the arrivals. By contrast, the importance of single males accounts for the statistic that 70 percent of the newcomers between 1900 and 1909 and that two out of every three between 1910 and 1914 were males. The proportion of males to females did not take place evenly across the immigrant nationalities. Jews displayed the best balance with an almost fifty-fifty split. Southern Italians, on the other hand, had more than three times as many males as females. The sex ratio among Greeks, the most extreme group, indicated that for every one Greek female there were 11 Greek men. Such sex ratio imbalances obviously set limits on the possibility of family life during this time period.

The ultimate success of an immigrant group depended in large part on its ability to reestablish a normal pattern of family life in America. This initially proved quite difficult. Severe problems confronted the immigrant families in America. The huge influx of immigrants to the American cities gave new meaning and visibility to urban poverty. Ghetto housing was awful; inadequate buildings were cheaply and quickly built to meet immediate needs, which proved to be inadequate. People lived in overcrowded, dirty, unsanitary, and poorly ventilated and poorly heated apartment dwellings that were still expensive because of the demand. Boarders and lodgers were numerous and helped provide some of the needed monies to pay the rent. It was not uncommon for beds to be used around the clock, with day-shift workers using them at night and night-shift workers using them during the day.

The horrible living conditions were dramatically exposed in the muckraking works of such novelists as Upton Sinclair, whose famous novel *The Jungle* exposed the grinding poverty in the Slavic communities in Chicago located within the stench of the blood and entrails of cattle being slaughtered in the neighborhood stockyards, and also of the journalistic accounts of newsmen like Lincoln Steffens whose book, *The Shame of the Cities,* refers to the ghetto slums as literally looking like hell. The journalist Jacob Riis, himself an immigrant from Denmark, wrote and photographed the urban poverty of New York's ghetto life in his classic work, *How the Other Half Lives.* His graphic descriptions of the barren and filthy firetraps of New York's tenements startled the nation. The following passage from his book is typical of what life was like in one of these buildings:

—Cherry Street. Be a little careful please. The hall is dark and you might stumble over the children. . . . Not that it would hurt them; kicks and cuffs are their daily diet. They have little else. Here where the hall turns and dives into utter darkness is a step, and another, another. A flight of stairs. You can feel your way, if you cannot see it. Close? Yes! What would you have? All the fresh air that ever enters these stairs comes from the hall-door that is forever slamming, and from the windows of dark bedrooms that in turn receive from the stairs their sole supply of the elements God meant to be free, but man deals out with such niggardly hand. . . . The sinks are in the hallway, that all the tenants may have access—and all be poisoned alike by their summer stenches. . . . Hear the pumps squeak! It is the lullaby of tenement house babies. In summer, when a thousand thirsty throats pant for a cooling drink in this block, it is worked in vain. But the saloon, whose open door you passed in the hall, is always there. The smell of it has followed you up. Here is a door. Listen! That short hacking cough, that

tiny, helpless wail—what do they mean? They mean . . . a sadly familiar story—before the day is at an end. The child is dying with measles. With half a chance it might have lived; but it had none. That dark bedroom killed it. (Riis, 1890/1957, pp. 33–34).

A common theme in the popular literature of that time were stories of wives forgotten in the old country and of families torn asunder by the clash of the old ways of life with the new. The editorial columns of the immigrant press frequently reported on the life struggles of its readers. Many newspapers had "advice" columns with its editors serving as lay clergy, social worker, friend, and relative to those who had nowhere else to turn. The "Bintel Brief" ("Bundle of Letters") of the *Jewish Daily Forward* has become the most famous of these advice columns. Through it, readers wrote of their marital and family problems, the impact of poverty on their lives, religious conflicts in terms of attitudes and behavior, and other life concerns. The following two letters, the first from 1906 and the second from 1910, were reprinted in *A Bintel Brief* (Metzker 1971) and are illustrative of such advice columns:

1906

Worthy Mr. Editor,

   I was married six years ago in Russia. My husband had not yet been called up for the military service, and I married him because he was an only son and I knew he would not be taken as a soldier. But that year all originally exempted men were taken in our village. He had no desire to serve Czar Nickolai and since I didn't want that either, I sold everything I could and sent him to London. From there he went to America:

   At first he wrote to me that it was hard for him to find work, so he couldn't send me anything to live on. I suffered terribly. I couldn't go to work because I was pregnant. And the harder my struggles became, the sadder were the letters from my husband. I suffered from hunger and cold, but what could I do when he was worse off than I?

Then his letters became fewer. Weeks and months passed without a word.

In the time I went to the rabbi of our town and begged him to have pity on a deserted wife. I asked him to write to a New York rabbi to find out what had happened to my husband. All kinds of thoughts ran through my mind because in a big city like New York anything can happen. I imagined perhaps he was sick, maybe even dead.

A month later an answer came to the rabbi. They had found out where my husband was but didn't want to talk with him until I could come to America.

My relatives from several towns collected enough money for my passage and I came to New York, to the rabbi. They tricked my husband into coming there too. Till the day I die I'll never forget the expression on my husband's face when he unexpectedly saw me and the baby.

I was speechless. The rabbi questioned him for me, sternly, like a judge, and asked him where he worked and how much he earned. My husband answered that he was a carpenter and made twelve dollars a week.

"Do you have a wife, or are you single?" the rabbi asked. My husband trembled as he answered, "I have committed a crime," and he began to wipe his eyes with a handkerchief. And soon a detective appeared in the rabbi's house and arrested my husband, and the next day the story appeared in the Jewish newspapers. Then some good women who had pity on me helped me. They found a job for me, took me to lectures and the-

aters. I began to read books I had never realized existed.

In time I adjusted to life here. I am not lonely, and life for me and my child is quite good. I want to add here, too, that my husband's wife came to me, fell at my feet and cried, but my own problems are enough for me.

But in time my conscience began to bother me. I began to think of my husband, suffering behind bars in his dark cell. In dreams I see his present wife, who certainly loves him, and her little boy living in dire need without their breadwinner. I now feel differently about the whole thing and I have sympathy for my husband. I am even prepared, when he gets out of jail, to wish him luck with his new life partner, but he will probably be embittered toward me. I have terrible pangs of conscience and I don't know what I can do. I hope you will print my letter, and answer me.

Cordially,
Z.B.

Answer:

In the answer to this letter, the woman is comforted and praised for her decency, her sympathy for her husband and his second wife. Also it is noted that when the husband is released he will surely have no complaints against her, since he is the guilty one in the circumstances, not she.

1910

Worthy Editor

My husband [here the name was given] deserted me and our three small children, leaving us in desperate need. I was left without a bit of bread for the children, with debts in the grocery store and the butcher's and last month's rent unpaid.

I am not complaining so much about his abandoning me as about the grief and suffering of our little children, who beg for food, which I cannot give them. I am young and healthy. I am able and willing to work in order to support my children, but unfortunately I am tied down because my baby is only six months old. I looked for an institution which would take care of my baby, but my friends advise against it.

The local Jewish Welfare Agencies are allowing me and my children to die of hunger, and this is because my "faithful" husband brought me over from Canada just four months ago and therefore I do not yet deserve to eat our bread.

It breaks my heart but I have come to the conclusion that in order to save my innocent children from hunger and cold I have to give them away.

I will sell my beautiful children to people who will give them a home. I will sell them, not for money, but for bread, for a secure home where they will have enough food and warm clothing for the winter.

I, the unhappy young mother, am willing to sign a contract, with my heart's blood, stating that the children belong to the good people who will treat them tenderly. Those who are willing and able to give my children a good home can apply to me.

Respectfully,
Mrs. P [The full name and address are given]
Chicago

Answer:

What kind of society are we living in that forces a mother to such desperate straits that there is no other way out than to sell her three children for a piece of bread?

Isn't this enough to kindle a hellish fire of hatred in every human heart for such a system?

The first to be damned is the heartless father, but who knows what's wrong with him? Perhaps he, too, is unhappy. We hope, though, that this letter will reach him and he will return to aid them.

We also ask our friends and readers to take an interest in this unfortunate woman and to help her so that she herself can be a mother to her children. (Metzker 1971, pp. 50–52, 104–105).

In the late nineteenth and early twentieth century as a result of the public outcry generated by the exposures by social-minded individuals like Sinclair, Steffens and Riis, and such tragedies as the Triangle Shirtwaist Factory fire that claimed the lives of one hundred and forty-six people, reforms were directed to change the living and working environments of immigrants. These movements included tenement-house reforms, workmen's compensation, the abolition of child labor, and the protection of women and children in industry.

However, the pervasive poverty in rapidly growing industrial cities led many to the erroneous conclusion that it was the immigrants themselves who were to blame for their poverty. Blame was not placed on the economic circumstances that the immigrants had to confront. This belief led to the development of a wide number of social programs aimed directly at changing the immigrant families themselves. Social reformers created both private and public welfare agencies to help alleviate the problems of the sick, the poor, and the delinquent or criminal. Immigrant families and especially their children became the major targets for discipline and reformation, and programs were designed to intervene in the affairs of immigrant families. The concern was to Americanize them into what they saw as the great American melting pot where the cultural variations of the given immigrant group would be altered to the standard American way of life.

The settlement house, a private social welfare agency, is a typical example of how some of these practices became articulated. The term "settlement" meant giving the immigrant newcomers the wherewithal to survive in a modern industrial city. Located right in the heart of the immigrant communities, it sought to help the immigrant families cope with poverty and improve their living standards. Settlement house workers tried to teach English, American social customs, and, when necessary, the rudiments of household management, health care, and sanitation. They encouraged family member involvement in work and household roles that often conformed to their own middle class standards of family morality. When successful, as in the case of Jane Addams of Chicago's Hull House, they integrated their work without undermining the immigrant's native culture. Unfortunately, much too frequently, workers saw as their primary task the eradication of "non-American" cultural points of view as to family traditions regarding marital roles and parent child relationships.

Education was seen as the key institution to eradicate immigrant cultures and to achieve Americanization. For example, in the years before World War I Henry Ford required all of his foreign workers to attend English school. For a five year period, 1915–1920, the federal Bureau of Education subsidized a Division of Immigrant Education, which encouraged school districts throughout the nation to establish special Americanization programs. The response was favorable and many state governments provided funds for the education of immigrants. During this period and continuing afterwards, numerous public school systems instituted night classes in which foreign students could learn English and gain knowledge of American government to acquire citizenship (Archdeacon 1983).

For the Americanization of immigrant children, the school system became the prime vehicle to help accomplish this task. Education meant more than simply teaching proper English and the three "Rs" of reading, "riting," and "rithmetic," but also meant socializing children to "American" ways of life, habits of cleanliness, good housekeeping, nutrition, and social graces. Children were also graded on their level of acculturation to American values, as measured by behavior in school. State legislation was passed making compulsory attendance laws more stringent to help ensure that children were adequately exposed to the assimilative influences of the schools. Settlement house workers also played a role here by assisting in the supervision of school attendance and observance of child labor laws.

However, it was the immigrants themselves, especially the immigrant family system that was primarily responsible for the success of the "new" immigration in "making it" in America. Let's see how this came about. By 1920 almost sixty percent of the population of cities of more than 100,000 inhabitants were first or second generation ethnic Americans (Sellers 1977). The immigrant settled in ethnic enclaves which people referred to as "Little Italys," "Polanias," "Little Syrias," and "Jewtowns." Each enclave reflected its distinctive ethnic flavor with its own church, stores, newspapers, clothing, and gestural and language conventions. The Chicago newspaper journalist, Mike Royko, reminiscing on his own Slavic community background recalls that you could always tell where you were "by the odors of the food stores and the open kitchen windows, the sound of the foreign or familiar language, and by whether a stranger hit you in the head with a rock" (Seller 1977, p. 112).

The establishment of immigrant "ghettos" in cities reflects a stage in the development of American cities where there was a great need for occupational concentration as a result of the expansion of the industrial economy in the late 19th century (Yancey, Ericksen, and Juliani 1976). Low-paid industrial immigrant workers were forced by economic pressures to live close to their places of work. The particular choice of residence and occupation was strongly influenced by the presence of friends and relatives in a process that has been called "chain migration." Chain migration refers to the connections made between individuals in countries of origin and destination in the process of international migration and to the process in which choices of residence and occupation were influenced by friends and relatives.

Networks of friends and relatives established in America maintained their European kinship and friendship ties and transmitted assistance across the Atlantic. Relatives acted as recruitment, migration, and housing resources, helping each other to shift from the often rural European work background to urban industrial work. A number of social historians (Anderson 1971; Hareven 1975; Yans-McLaughlin 1971) have observed that nineteenth as well as twentieth century migrants chose their residential and occupational destinations in large part because of the presence of kin group members in the new area.

Chain migration can be seen as facilitating transition and settlement. It ensured a continuity in kins contacts, and made mutual assistance in cases of personal and family crises an important factor in the adjustment of immigrants to the new urban American environment. Workers often migrated into the new industrial urban centers keeping intact or reforming much of their kinship ties and family traditions. As previously mentioned, a prevalent practice was for unmarried sons and daughters of working age, or young

childless married couples to migrate first. After establishing themselves by finding jobs and housing they would tend to send for other family members. Through their contacts at work or in the community they would assist their newly arrived relatives or friends with obtaining jobs and housing.

The fact that so many single individuals came to America alone accounts for the fact that turn of the century urban households of immigrants often included people other than the nuclear family. These people were not kinship related but were strangers. These strangers were boarders and lodgers who for various reasons came to America alone and for a period of time lived with fellow immigrants. This practice of taking in boarders and lodgers proved extremely valuable in allowing new migrants and immigrants to adapt to urban living (Hareven 1983).

The family can be seen as being an important intermediary in recruitment of workers to the new industrial society. Family patterns and values often carried over to the urban setting, and provided the individual with a feeling of continuity between one's rural background and new industrial city. Initially, selected individuals migrated, then families migrated in groups, and often entire rural communities reconstituted themselves in ethnic enclaves. They helped recruit other family members and countrymen into the industrial work force. Migration to industrial communities, then, did not break up traditional kinship ties; rather the family used these ties to facilitate their own transition into industrial life. Tamara Hareven (1983) after examining the historical evidence concludes that it is grossly incorrect to assume that industrialization broke up traditional kinship ties and destroyed the interdependence of the family and the community.

In summary, the 50 year dramatic growth period of 1876–1925 of the industrial urban centers of the Northeast and Midwest can be attributed to the social and family organization of the newly arriving immigration groups. Rather than view this period in terms of social disorganization we would argue that insufficient attention has been placed on the nature of social interac-

tional patterns that were developing among the immigrant groups in American cities. We owe the spectacular rise of world cities like New York City to the vitality of the immigrants and their social support structures.

Reading 3 Interpreting the African Heritage in Afro-American Family Organization

NIARA SUDARKASA*

Many of the debates concerning explanations of Black family organization are waged around false dichotomies. The experience of slavery in America is juxtaposed to the heritage of Africa as *the* explanation of certain aspects of Black family structure. "Class" versus "culture" becomes the framework for discussing determinants of household structure and role relationships. Black families are characterized either as "alternative institutions" or as groups whose structures reflect their "adaptive strategies," as if the two viewpoints were mutually exclusive.

Just as surely as Black American family patterns are in part an outgrowth of the descent into slavery (Frazier, 1939 [1966]), so too are they partly a reflection of the archetypical African institutions and values that informed and influenced the behavior of those Africans who were enslaved in America (Herskovits, 1941 [1958]). With respect to "class" and "culture," it is indeed the case that the variations in historical and contemporary Black family organization cannot be explained without reference to the socioeconomic contexts in which they developed (Allen, 1979). But neither can they be explained without reference to the cultural contexts from which they derived (Nobles, 1974a, 1974b, 1978). Whereas Black families can be analyzed as groups with strategies for coping with wider societal forces (Stack, 1974), they must also be understood as institutions with historical traditions that set them apart as "alternative" formations that are not identical to (or pathological variants of) family structures found among other groups in America (Aschenbrenner, 1978).

After more than a decade of rethinking Black family structure (see, for example, Billingsley, 1968; Staples, 1971, 1978; Aschenbrenner, 1973; English, 1974; Sudarkasa, 1975a; Allen, 1978; Shimkin et al., 1978), it is still the case that a holistic theory of past and present Black family organization remains to be developed. Such a theory or explanation must rest on the premise that political-economic variables are *always* part of any explanation of family formation and functioning, but that the cultural historical derivation of the formations in question helps to explain the nature of their adaptation to particular political-economic contexts.

Author's note: I wish to thank Tao-Lin Hwang for his assistance with the research for this chapter, and Bamidele Agbasegbe Demerson for his helpful comments.

Obviously, it is beyond the scope of this chapter to try to set forth such a holistic explanation of Black family organization. Its more modest aim is to take a step in this direction by laying to rest one of the false dichotomies that stand in the way of such an explanation. This review seeks to show how an understanding of African family structure sheds light on the form and functioning of Black American family structure as it developed in *the context of slavery* and later periods. It seeks to elucidate African institutional arrangements and values that were manifest in the family organization of Blacks enslaved in America, and suggests that some of these values and institutional arrangements continue to be recognizable in contemporary formations.

The relationships of causality, correlation, and constraint that exist between the political-economic sphere and that of the family cannot be dealt with here. What the chapter seeks to clarify is why Black familial institutions embrace certain alternatives of behavior and not others. It suggests a cultural historical basis for the fact that Black family organization differs from that of other groups even when political and economic factors are held relatively constant.

Thus, it is suggested that it cannot suffice to look to political and economic factors to explain, for example, the difference between lower-class Anglo- or Italian-American families and lower-class Afro-American families. One has to come to grips with the divergent culture histories of the groups concerned. In other words, one is led back to the institutional heritage stemming from Western Europe on the one hand and from West Africa on the other. Knowledge of the structure and functioning of kinship and the family in these areas helps to explain the structure and functioning of families formed among their descendants in America.

It might appear that this is too obvious a point to be belabored. However, when it comes to the study of Black American families, the scholarly community has historically taken a different view. Whereas it is generally agreed that the history of the family in Europe is pertinent to an understanding of European derived family organization in America (and throughout the world), many—if not most—scholars working on Black American families have argued or assumed that the African family heritage was all but obliterated by the institution of slavery. This view has retained credence, despite the accumulation of evidence to the contrary, in large measure because E. Franklin Frazier (1939), the most prestigious and prolific student of the Black American family, all but discounted the relevance of Africa in his analyses.

This chapter takes its departure from W. E. B. DuBois (1908[1969]), Carter G. Woodson (1936), and M. J. Herskovits (1958), all of whom looked to Africa as well as to the legacy of slavery for explanations of Afro-American social institutions. Herskovits is the best-known advocate of the concept of African survivals in Afro-American family life, but DuBois was the first scholar to stress the need to study the Black American family against the background of its African origins. In his 1908 study of the Black family, DuBois prefaced his discussions of marriage, household structure, and economic organization with observations concerning the African antecedents of the patterns developed in America.

> *In each case an attempt has been made to connect present conditions with the African past. This is not because Negro-Americans are Africans, or can trace an unbroken social history from Africa, but because there is a distinct nexus between Africa and America which, though broken and perverted, is nevertheless not to be neglected by the careful student [DuBois, 1969: 9].*

Having documented the persistence of African family patterns in the Caribbean, and of African derived wedding ceremonies in Alabama, DuBois noted:

> Careful research would doubtless reveal many other traces of the African family in America. They would, however, be traces only, for the effectiveness of the slave system meant the practically complete crushing out of the African clan and family life [p. 21].

With the evidence that has accumulated since DuBois wrote, it is possible to argue that even though the constraints of slavery did prohibit the replication of African lineage ("clan") and family life in America, the principles on which these kin groups were based, and the values underlying them, led to the emergence of variants of African family life in the form of the extended families which developed among the enslaved Blacks in America. Evidence of the Africanity to which DuBois alluded is to be found not only in the relatively few "traces" of direct *institutional transfer* from Africa to America, but also in the numerous examples of *institutional transformation* from Africa to America.

No discussion of the relevance of Africa for understanding Afro-American family organization can proceed without confronting the issue of the "diversity" of the backgrounds of "African slaves" (read "enslaved Africans") brought to America. Obviously for certain purposes, each African community or each ethnic group can be described in terms of the linguistic, cultural, and/or social structural features which distinguish it from others. At the same time, however, these communities or ethnic groups can be analyzed from the point of view of their similarity to other groups.

It has long been established that the Africans enslaved in the United States and the rest of the Americas came from the Western part of the continent where there had been a long history of culture contact and widespread similarities in certain institutions (Herskovits, 1958: chs. 2 and 3). For example, some features of kinship organization were almost universal. Lineages, large co-resident domestic groups, and polygynous marriages are among the recurrent features found in groups speaking different languages, organized into states as well as "segmentary" societies, and living along the coast as well as in the interior (Radcliffe-Brown, 1950; Fortes, 1953; Onwuejeogwu, 1975).

When the concept of "African family structure" is used here, it refers to those organizational principles and patterns which are common to the different ethnic groups whose members were enslaved in America. These features of family organization are known to have existed for centuries on the African continent and are, therefore, legitimately termed a part of the African heritage.

AFRICAN FAMILY STRUCTURE: UNDERSTANDING THE DYNAMICS OF CONSANGUINITY AND CONJUGALITY

African families, like those in other parts of the world, embody two contrasting bases for membership: *consanguinity,* which refers to kinship that is commonly assumed or presumed to be biologically based and rooted in "blood ties," and *affinity,* which refers to kinship created by law and rooted "in-law." *Conjugality* refers specifically to the affinal kinship created between spouses (Marshall, 1968). Generally, all kinship entails a dynamic tension between the operation of the contrasting principles of consanguinity and affinity. The comparative study of family organization led Ralph Linton (1936: 159–163) to observe that in different societies families tend to be built either around a conjugal core or around a consanguineal core. In either case, the other principle is subordinate.

According to current historical research on the family in Europe, the principle of conjugality appears to have dominated family organization in the Western part of that continent (including Britain) at least since the Middle Ages, when a number of economic and political factors led to the predominancy of nuclear and/or stem families built around married couples. Certainly for the past three or four hundred years, the conjugally based family has been the ideal and the norm in Western Europe (Shorter, 1975; Stone, 1975; Tilly and Scott, 1978). Whether or not the European conjugal family was a structural isolate is not the issue here. The point is that European families, whether nuclear or extended (as in the case of stem families), tended to emphasize the conjugal relationship in matters of household formation, decision making, property transmission, and socialization of the young (Goody, 1976).

African families, on the other hand, have traditionally been organized around consanguineal cores formed by adult siblings of the same sex or by larger same-sex segments of patri- or matrilineages. The groups which formed around these consanguineally related core members included their spouses and children, and perhaps some of their divorced siblings of the opposite sex. This co-resident *extended family* occupied a group of adjoining or contiguous dwellings known as a compound. Upon marriage, Africans did not normally form new isolated households, but joined a compound in which the extended family of the groom, or that of the bride, was already domiciled (Sudarkasa, 1980: 38–49).

African extended families could be subdivided in two ways. From one perspective, there was the division between the nucleus formed by the consanguineal core group and their children and the "outer group" formed by the in-marrying spouses. In many African languages, in-marrying spouses are collectively referred to as "wives" or "husbands" by both females and males of the core group. Thus, for example, in any compound in a patrilineal society, the in-marrying women may be known as the "wives of the house." They are, of course, also the mothers of the children of the compound. Their collective designation as "wives of the house" stresses the fact that their membership in the compound is rooted in law and can be terminated by law, whereas that of the core group is rooted in descent and is presumed to exist in perpetuity.

African extended families may also be divided into their constituent conjugally based family units comprised of parents and children. In the traditional African family, these conjugal units did not have the characteristics of the typical "nuclear family" of the West. In the first place, African conjugal families normally involved polygynous marriages at some stage in their developmental cycle. A number of Western scholars have chosen to characterize the polygynous conjugal family as several distinct nuclear families with one husband/father in common (Rivers, 1924: 12; Murdock, 1949: 2; Colson, 1962). In the African conception, however, whether a man had one wife and children or many wives and children, his was *one* family. In the case of polygynous families, both the husband and the senior co-wife played important roles in integrating the entire group (Fortes, 1949: chs. III and IV; Sudarkasa, 1973: ch. V; Ware, 1979). The very existence of the extended family as an "umbrella" group for the conjugal family meant that the latter group differed from the Western nuclear family. Since, for many purposes and on many occasions, *all* the children of the same generation within the compound regarded themselves as brothers and sisters (rather than dividing into siblings versus "cousins"), and since the adults assumed certain responsibilities toward their "nephews" and "nieces" (whom they term sons and daughters) as well as toward their own offspring, African conjugal families did not have the rigid boundaries characteristic of nuclear families of the West.

The most far-reaching difference between African and European families stems from their differential emphasis on consanguinity and con-jugality. This difference becomes clear when one considers extended family organization in the two contexts. The most common type of European extended family consisted of two or more nuclear families joined through the parent-child or sibling tie. It was this model of the stem family and the joint family that was put forth by George P. Murdock (1949: 23, 33, 39–40) as the generic form of the extended family. However, the African data show that on that continent, extended families were built around consan-guineal cores and the conjugal components of these larger families differed significantly from the nuclear families of the West.

In Africa, unlike Europe, in many critical areas of family life the consanguineal core group rather than the conjugal pair was paramount. With respect to household formation, I have already indicated that married couples joined existing compounds. It was the lineage core that owned (or had the right of usufruct over) the land and the compound where families lived, farmed, and/or practiced their crafts. The most important properties in African societies—land, titles, and entitlements—were transmitted through the lin-eages, and spouses did not inherit from each other (Goody, 1976).

Within the extended family residing in a single compound, decision making centered in the consanguineal core group. The oldest male in the compound was usually its head, and all the men in his generation constituted the elders of the group. Together they were ultimately respon-sible for settling internal disputes, including those that could not be settled within the sepa-rate conjugal families or, in some cases, by the

female elders among the wives (Sudarkasa, 1973, 1976). They also made decisions, such as those involving the allocation of land and other resources, which affected the functioning of the constituent conjugal families.

Given the presence of multiple spouses within the *conjugal* families, it is not surprising that decision making within them also differed from the model associated with nuclear family organization. Separate rather than joint decision making was common. In fact, husbands and wives normally had distinct purviews and responsibili-ties within the conjugal family (Sudarkasa, 1973; Oppong, 1974). Excepting those areas where Islamic traditions overshadowed indigenous Afri-can traditions, women had a good deal of control over the fruits of their own labor. Even though husbands typically had ultimate authority over wives, this authority did not extend to control over their wives' properties (Oppong, 1974; Robert-son, 1976; Sudarkasa, 1976). Moreover, even though women were subordinate in their roles as wives, as mothers and sisters they wielded con-siderable authority, power, and influence. This distinction in the power attached to women's roles is symbolized by the fact that in the same society where wives knelt before their husbands, sons prostrated before their mothers and seniority as determined by age, rather than gender, gov-erned relationships among siblings (Sudarkasa, 1973, 1976).

Socialization of the young involved the en-tire extended family, not just the separate conju-gal families, even though each conjugal family had special responsibility for the children (theirs or their relatives') living with them. It is impor-tant to note that the concept of "living with" a conjugal family took on a different meaning in the context of the African compound. In the first place, husbands, wives, and children did not live in a bounded space, apart from other such units. Wives had their own rooms or small dwellings, and husbands had theirs. These were not necessarily adjacent to one another. (In some matrilineal societies, husbands and wives resided in separate compounds.) Children ordinarily slept in their mothers' rooms until they were of a certain age, after which they customarily slept in communal rooms allocated to boys or girls. Children usually ate their meals with their mothers but they might also eat some of these meals with their fathers' co-wives (assuming that no hostility existed between the women concerned) or with their grandmothers. Children of the same compound played together and shared many learning experiences. They were socialized by all the adults to identify themselves collectively as sons and daughters of a particular lineage and compound, which entailed a kinship, based on descent, with all the lineage ancestors and with generations unborn (Radcliffe-Brown and Forde, 1950; Uchendu, 1965; Sudarkasa, 1980).

The stability of the African extended family did not depend on the stability of the marriage(s) of the individual core group members. Although traditional African marriages (particularly those in patrilineal societies) were more stable than those of most contemporary societies, marital dissolution did not have the ramifications it has in nuclear family systems. When divorces did occur, they were usually followed by remarriage. Normally, all adults other than those who held certain ceremonial offices or who were severely mentally or physically handicapped lived in a marital union (though not necessarily the same one) throughout their lives (for example, Lloyd, 1968). The children of a divorced couple were usually brought up in their natal compound (or by members of their lineage residing elsewhere), even though the in-marrying parent had left that compound.

Several scholars have remarked on the relative ease of divorce in some traditional African societies, particularly those in which matrilineal descent was the rule (for example, Fortes, 1950:

283). Jack Goody (1976: 64) has even suggested that the rate of divorce in precolonial Africa was higher than in parts of Europe and Asia in comparable periods as a corollary of contrasting patterns of property transmission, contrasting attitudes toward the remarriage of women (especially widows), and contrasting implications of polygyny and monogamy. If indeed there was a higher incidence of divorce in precolonial Africa, this would not be inconsistent with the wide-ranging emphasis on consanguinity in Africa as opposed to conjugality in Europe.

Marriage in Africa was a contractual union which often involved long-lasting compassionate relationships, but it was not expected to be the all-encompassing, exclusive relationship of the Euro-American ideal type. Both men and women relied on their extended families and friends, as well as on their spouses, for emotionally gratifying relationships. Often, too, in the context of polygyny women as well as men had sexual liaisons with more than one partner. A woman's clandestine affairs did not necessarily lead to divorce because, in the absence of publicized information to the contrary, her husband was considered the father of all her children (Radcliffe-Brown, 1950). And in the context of the lineage (especially the patrilineage), all men aspired to have as many children as possible.

Interpersonal relationships within African families were governed by principles and values which I have elsewhere summarized under the concepts of respect, restraint, responsibility, and reciprocity. Common to all these principles was a notion of commitment to the collectivity. The family offered a network of security, but it also imposed a burden of obligations (Sudarkasa, 1980: 49–50). From the foregoing discussion, it should be understandable that, in their material form, these obligations extended first and foremost to consanguineal kin. Excepting the gifts that were exchanged at the time of marriage, the material obligations entailed in the conjugal relationship and the wider affinal relationships created by marriage were of a lesser magnitude than those associated with "blood" ties.

AFRO-AMERICAN FAMILY STRUCTURE: INTERPRETING THE AFRICAN CONNECTION

Rather than start with the question of what was *African* about the families established by those Africans who were enslaved in America, it would be more appropriate to ask what was *not* African about them. Most of the Africans who were captured and brought to America arrived without any members of their families, but they brought with them the societal codes they had learned regarding family life. To argue that the trans-Atlantic voyage and the trauma of enslavement made them forget, or rendered useless their memories of how they had been brought up or how they had lived before their capture, is to argue from premises laden with myths about the Black experience (Elkins, 1963: 101–102; see also Frazier, 1966: ch. 1).

Given the African tradition of multilingualism and the widespread use of lingua francas (Maquet, 1972: 18–25)—which in West Africa would include Hausa, Yoruba, Djoula, and Twi—it is probable that many more of the enslaved Africans could communicate among themselves than is implied by those who remark on the multiplicity of "tribes" represented among the slaves. As Landman (1978: 80) has pointed out:

> *In many areas of the world, individuals are expected to learn only one language in the ordinary course of their lives. But many Africans have been enculturated in social systems where multiple language or dialect acquisition have been regarded as normal.*

The fact that Africans typically spoke three to five languages also makes it understandable why they quickly adopted "pidginized" forms of European languages as lingua francas for communicating among themselves and with their captors.

The relationships which the Blacks in America established among themselves would have reflected their own backgrounds *and* the conditions in which they found themselves. It is as erroneous to try to attribute what developed among them solely to slavery as it is to attribute it solely to the African background. Writers such as Herbert Gutman (1976), who emphasize the "adaptive" nature of "slave culture" must ask what it was that was being adapted as well as in what context this adaptation took place. Moreover, they must realize that adaptation does not necessarily imply extensive modification of an institution, especially when its structure is already suited (or "preadapted") to survival in the new context. Such an institution was the African extended family, which had served on that continent, in various environments and different political contexts, as a unit of production and distribution; of socialization, education, and social control; and of emotional and material support for the aged and the infirm as well as the hale and hearty (Kerri, 1979; Okediji, 1975; Shimkin and Uchendu, 1978; Sudarkasa, 1975b).

The extended family networks that were formed during slavery by Africans *and their descendants* were based on the institutional heritage which the Africans had brought with them to this continent, and the specific forms they took reflected the influence of European-derived institutions as well as the political and economic circumstances in which the enslaved population found itself.

The picture of Black families during slavery has become clearer over the past decade, particularly as a result of the wealth of data in Gutman's justly heralded study. Individual households were normally comprised of a conjugal pair, their children, and sometimes their grandchildren, other relatives, or non-kin. Marriage was usually monogamous, but polygynous unions where the wives lived in separate households have also been reported (Gutman, 1976: 59, 158; Blassingame, 1979: 171; Perdue et al., 1980: 209).

Probably only in a few localities did female-headed households constitute as much as one-quarter of all households (Gutman, 1976: esp. chs. 1–3). The rarity of this household type was in keeping with the African tradition whereby women normally bore children within the context of marriage and lived in monogamous or polygynous conjugal families that were part of larger extended families. I have tried to show elsewhere why it is inappropriate to apply the term "nuclear family" to the mother-child dyads within African polygynous families (Sudarkasa, 1980: 43–46). In some African societies—especially in matrilineal ones—a small percentage of previously married women, or married women living apart from their husbands, might head households that were usually attached to larger compounds. However, in my view, on the question of the origin of female-headed households among Blacks in America, Herskovits was wrong, and Frazier was right in attributing this development to conditions that arose during slavery and in the context of urbanization in later periods (Frazier, 1966; Herskovits, 1958; Furstenberg et al., 1975).

Gutman's data suggest that enslaved women who had their first children out of wedlock did not normally set up independent households, but rather continued to live with their parents. Most of them subsequently married and set up neolocal residence with their husbands. The data also suggest that female-headed households developed mainly in two situations: (1) A woman whose husband died or was sold off the plantation might head a household comprised of her children and perhaps her grandchildren born to an unmarried daughter; (2) a woman who did not marry after having one or two children out of wedlock but continued to have children (no doubt often for the "master") might have her own cabin built for her (Gutman, 1976: chs. 1–3).

It is very important to distinguish these two types of female-headed households, the first being only a phase in the developmental cycle of a conjugally headed household, and the second being a case of neolocal residence by an unmarried female. The pattern of households headed by widows was definitely not typical of family structure in Africa, where normally a widow married another member of her deceased husband's lineage. The pattern of neolocal residence by an unmarried woman with children would have been virtually unheard of in Africa. Indeed, it was also relatively rare among enslaved Blacks and in Black communities in later periods. Before the twentieth-century policy of public assistance for unwed mothers, virtually all young unmarried mothers in Black communities continued to live in households headed by other adults. If in later years they did establish their own households, these tended to be tied into transresidential family networks.

The existence during slavery of long-lasting conjugal unions among Blacks was not a departure from African family tradition. Even with the relative ease of divorce in matrilineal societies, most Africans lived in marital unions that ended only with the death of one of the spouses. In the patrilineal societies from which most American Blacks were taken, a number of factors, including the custom of returning bridewealth payments upon the dissolution of marriage, served to encourage marital stability (Radcliffe-Brown, 1950: 43–54). Given that the conditions of slavery did not permit the *replication* of African families, it might be expected that the husband and wife as elders in the household would assume even greater importance than they had in

Africa, where the elders within the consanguineal core of the extended family and those among the wives would have had major leadership roles within the compound.

When the distinction is made between family and household—and, following Bender (1967), between the composition of the co-resident group and the domestic functions associated with both households and families—it becomes apparent that the question of who lived with whom during slavery (or later) must be subordinate to the questions of who was doing what for whom and what kin relationships were maintained over space and time. In any case, decisions concerning residence per se were not always in the hands of the enslaved Blacks themselves, and space alone served as a constraint on the size, and consequently to some extent on the composition, of the "slave" cabins.

That each conjugally based household formed a primary unit for food consumption and production among the enslaved Blacks is consistent with domestic organization within the African compound. However, Gutman's data, and those reported by enslaved Blacks themselves, on the strong bonds of obligation among kinsmen suggest that even within the constraints imposed by the slave regime, transresidential cooperation—including that between households in different localities—was the rule rather than the exception (Gutman, 1976: esp. 131–138; Perdue et al., 1980: esp. 26, 256, 323). One might hypothesize that on the larger plantations with a number of Black families related through consanguineal and affinal ties, the households of these families might have formed groupings similar to African compounds. Certainly we know that in later times such groupings were found in the South Carolina Sea Islands and other parts of the South (Agbasegbe, 1976, 1981; Gutman, 1976; Johnson, 1934: ch. 2; Powdermaker, 1939: ch. 8).

By focusing on extended families (rather than simply on households) among the enslaved Blacks, it becomes apparent that these kin networks had many of the features of continental African extended families. These Afro-American groupings were built around consanguineal kin whose spouses were related to or incorporated into the networks in different degrees. The significance of the consanguineal principle in these networks is indicated by Gutman's statement that "the pull between ties to an immediate family and to an enlarged kin network sometimes strained husbands and wives" (1976: 202; see also Frazier, 1966: pt. 2).

The literature on Black families during slavery provides a wealth of data on the way in which consanguineal kin assisted each other with child rearing, in life crisis events such as birth and death, in work groups, in efforts to obtain freedom, and so on. They maintained their networks against formidable odds and, after slavery, sought out those parents, siblings, aunts, and uncles from whom they had been torn (Blassingame, 1979; Genovese, 1974; Gutman, 1976; Owens, 1976). Relationships within these groups were governed by principles and values stemming from the African background. Respect for elders and reciprocity among kinsmen are noted in all discussions of Black families during slavery. The willingness to assume responsibility for relatives beyond the conjugal family and selflessness (a form of restraint) in the face of these responsibilities are also characteristics attributed to the enslaved population.

As would be expected, early Afro-American extended families differed from their African prototypes in ways that reflected the influence of slavery and of Euro-American values, especially their proscriptions and prescriptions regarding mating, marriage, and the family. No doubt, too, the Euro-American emphasis on the primacy of marriage within the family reinforced conjugality among the Afro-Americans even though the "legal" marriage of enslaved Blacks was prohibited. As DuBois noted at the turn of the century, African corporate lineages could not survive intact during slavery. Hence, the consanguineal core groups of Afro-American extended families differed in some ways from those of their African antecedents. It appears that in some of these Afro-American families membership in the core group was traced bilaterally, whereas in others there was a unilineal emphasis without full-fledged lineages.

Interestingly, after slavery, some of the corporate functions of African lineages reemerged in some extended families which became property-owning collectivities. I have suggested elsewhere that "the disappearance of the lineage principle or its absorption into the concept of extended family" is one of the aspects of the transformation of African family organization in America that requires research (Sudarkasa, 1980: 57). Among the various other issues that remain to be studied concerning these extended families are these: (1) Did members belong by virtue of bilateral or unilineal descent from a common ancestor or because of shared kinship with a living person? (2) How were group boundaries established and maintained? (3) What was the nature and extent of the authority of the elder(s)? (4) How long did the group last and what factors determined its span in time and space?

CONCLUSION

At the outset of this chapter it was suggested that a holistic explanation of Black family organization requires discarding or recasting some of the debates which have framed discussions in the past. I have tried to show why it is time to move beyond the debate over whether it was slavery *or* the African heritage which "determined" Black family organization to a synthesis which looks at institutional transformation as well as institutional transfer for the interplay between Africa and America in shaping the family structures of Afro-Americans.

Obviously, Black families have changed over time, and today one would expect that the evi-dence for African "retentions" (Herskovits, 1958: xxii–xxiii) in them would be more controvertible than in the past. Nevertheless, the persistence of some features of African family organization among contemporary Black American families has been documented for both rural and urban areas. Although this study cannot attempt a full-scale analysis of these features and the changes they have undergone, it is important to make reference to one of them, precisely because it impacts upon so many other aspects of Black family organization, and because its connection to Africa has not been acknowledged by most contemporary scholars. I refer to the emphasis on consanguinity noted especially among lower-income Black families and those in the rural South. Some writers, including Shimkin and Uchendu (1978), Agbasegbe (1976; 1981), Aschenbrenner (1973; 1975; 1978; Aschenbrenner and Carr, 1980) and the present author (1975a, 1980, 1981) have dealt explicitly with this concept in their discussions of Black family organization. However, without labelling it as such, many other scholars have described some aspects of the operation of consanguinity within the Black family in their discussions of "matrifocality" and "female-headed households." Too often, the origin of this consanguineal emphasis in Black families, which can be manifest even in households with both husband and wife present, is left unexplained or is "explained" by labelling it an "adaptive" characteristic.

In my view, historical realities require that the derivation of this aspect of Black family organization be traced to its African antecedents. Such a view does not deny the adaptive significance of consanguineal networks. In fact, it helps to clarify why these networks had the flexibility they had and why they, rather than conjugal relationships, came to be the stabilizing factor in Black families. The significance of this principle of organization is indicated by the list of Black family characteristics derived from it.

Scrutiny of the list of Black family characteristics given by Aschenbrenner (1978) shows that 12 of the 18 "separate" features she lists are manifestations of the overall strength and entailments of consanguineal relationships.

Some writers have viewed the consanguineally based extended family as a factor of *instability* in the Black family because it sometimes undermines the conjugal relationships in which its members are involved. I would suggest that historically among Black Americans the concept of "family" meant first and foremost relationships created by "blood" rather than by marriage. (R. T. Smith [1973] has made substantially the same point with respect to West Indian family organization.) Children were socialized to think in terms of obligations to parents (especially mothers), siblings, and others defined as "close kin." Obligations to "outsiders," who would include prospective spouses and in-laws, were definitely less compelling. Once a marriage took place, if the demands of the conjugal relationship came into irreconcilable conflict with consanguineal commitments, the former would often be sacrificed. Instead of interpreting instances of *marital* instability as prima facie evidence of family instability, it should be realized that the fragility of the conjugal relationship could be a consequence or corollary of the *stability* of the consanguineal family network. Historically, such groups survived by nurturing a strong sense of responsibility among members and by fostering a code of reciprocity which could strain relations with persons not bound by it.

Not all Black families exhibit the same emphasis on consanguinity relationships. Various factors, including education, occupational demands, aspirations toward upward mobility, and acceptance of American ideals concerning marriage and the family, have moved some (mainly middle- and upper-class) Black families toward conjugally focused households and conjugally centered extended family groupings. Even when such households include relatives other than the nuclear family, those relatives tend to be subordinated to the conjugal pair who form the core of the group. This contrasts with some older type Black families where a senior relative (especially the wife's or the husband's mother) could have a position of authority in the household equal to or greater than that of one or both of the spouses. Children in many contemporary Black homes are not socialized to think in terms of the parent-sibling group as the primary kin group, but rather in terms of their future spouses and families of procreation as the main source of their future emotional and material satisfaction and support. Among these Blacks, the nuclear household tends to be more isolated in terms of instrumental functions, and such extended family networks as exist tend to be clusters of nuclear families conforming to the model put forth by Murdock (1949: chs. 1 and 2).

For scholars interested in the heritage of Europe as well as the heritage of Africa in Afro-American family organization, a study of the operation of the principles of conjugality and consanguinity in these families would provide considerable insight into the ways in which these two institutional traditions have been interwoven. By looking at the differential impact of these principles in matters of household formation, delegation of authority, maintenance of solidarity and support, acquisition and transmission of property, financial management, and so on (Sudarkasa, 1981), and by examining the political and economic variables which favor the predominance of one or the other principle, we will emerge with questions and formulations that can move us beyond debates over "pathology" and "normalcy" in Black family life.

Reading 4   Setting the Clock Forward or Back?

Covenant Marriage and the "Divorce Revolution"

LAURA SANCHEZ*   STEVEN L. NOCK
JAMES D. WRIGHT   CONSTANCE T. GAGER

In 1997, Louisiana codified a new family form by becoming the first state to pass covenant marriage legislation. Soon after, Arizona and Arkansas followed suit. This act created two marriage types with substantially different marital and divorce provisions. In spring 1998, the authors conducted qualitative interviews with focus groups consisting of covenant married couples, feminist activists, and poor women living in public housing, examining their views on marriage and divorce trends, divorce consequences, and covenant marriage. All groups were concerned about the effects of divorce on children's well-being. Beyond that, the authors found little commonality in the discourse. Instead, they found major disagreements about whether family life is in decline and whether marriage law reinforcement will improve it. Covenant married couples and feminists polarized along familiar traditionalist-feminist axes; low-income women combined feminist, liberal, and conservative views in their understanding of contemporary family trends and the perceived necessity of covenant marriage.

Louisiana's passage of a covenant marriage act in August 1997 marked a momentous change in domestic relations law in the United States. Since then, Arizona has passed covenant marriage legislation, and at least 20 other states have considered similar acts. Couples in Louisiana now choose between two forms of marriage: the conventional form with standard no-fault divorce provisions and the newer covenant marriage, which is both harder to enter and to exit. A key provision of covenant marriage is that divorce requires proof of fault. This pendular swing back to fault-based divorce comes at a volatile time in our history, following on the heels of the 1996 Hawaiian Supreme Court gay marriage case, *Baehr et al. v. Lewin* (1993), and the recent 1996 Federal Defense of Marriage Act.

Academics and policy makers debate the meaning of these and other family changes, often in terms of larger "culture wars," "family values wars," and even "welfare wars" (Cohen & Katzenstein, 1988; Donovan, 1998; Folbre, 1984; Fraser, 1989; Fraser & Gordon, 1994; Howard, 1993; Kozol, 1995). Thus, covenant marriage is

Authors' Note: *This research was supported by National Science Foundation Grant No. 98-03736 from the National Science Foundation.*

part of an ongoing debate about the meanings of marriage and the actions, if any, that legislators should take to reduce high rates of divorce, cohabitation, nonmarital fertility, and nonfamily living arrangements. Some scholars view recent trends as evidence that Americans are becoming more selfish and hedonistic and less family oriented (Davidson, 1990; Gilder, 1989; Goldberg, 1989; Popenoe, 1993; Popenoe, Elshtain, & Blankenhorn, 1996; Whitehead, 1997), whereas others think we are simply changing in response to new postindustrial realities (Hochschild, 1997; Stacey, 1990, 1993, 1996). Regardless, evidence documents a growing acceptance of alternative family forms and greater independence between adults in intimate relationships (Goldscheider & Waite, 1991; Stacey, 1993).

This article examines popular discourse concerning the role of the state in trying to influence marriage and divorce trends by legislating marital and divorce reforms. We conducted focus groups to explore Louisiana residents' views about divorce and covenant marriage. We chose groups with divergent characteristics and experiences who are stakeholders in the outcomes of any marriage or divorce reforms. Each group expressed concerns about the nature and quality of contemporary American marriage and what could or should be done to address problems caused by marital failures.

Our study reveals three principal axes of contention about contemporary marriage and marriage reform efforts. First, we find considerable disagreement across and within our focus groups about whether the institution of marriage is ailing. Second, we observe contradictory views about the nature of contemporary obligations and responsibilities in marriage, with some very sharp disagreements about whether the institution of marriage is weaker today and how society experiences the social consequences of relatively high nonmarriage and divorce rates. However, we find a common theme of concern about the

well-being of children and the harm that marital breakdown can do to their self-esteem, ability to trust and commit; and material security. This seems to be the central point of agreement among our groups. Last, we also find disagreement about whether covenant marriage is even a partial solution to problems in marriage.

Based on these interviews, we argue that covenant marriage will certainly escalate political debates about marriage reform in the United States. Our selected interest blocs—as represented by our different focus groups—are quite knowledgeable about the perspectives of their opponents and attuned closely to the "family values" debates. But they hold divergent opinions about the necessity of covenant marriage or of marriage reform in general. In the following sections, we describe the provisions of covenant marriage legislation, then address the focus groups' views on whether contemporary marriage is "in trouble" and whether covenant marriage is a useful reform.

DATA AND METHOD

In April and May 1998, with support from the National Science Foundation, we conducted three focus groups of approximately 12 participants each. We selected participants to represent a range of views on marriage, divorce, and legal reform. We examined the language used by participants to describe their views, the common themes within and across groups, and how discussions highlighted consent or dissent about covenant marriage. One of the advantages of focus group research is the ability to observe collaborative interactions, debates, and discussions about a topic in a group setting (Wilkinson, 1998). In this case, we explored how focus group participants advanced controversial views about marriage and marriage reform, debated problems in marriage and divorce, and shared their views about the utility of covenant marriage. We asked general questions about marriage and divorce trends, the purpose of marriage, and whether they had ever heard of covenant marriage. We also described the actual covenant marriage law and then explored their opinions about whether covenant marriage will improve marriage and family life and how covenant marriage might change the terms of the family values debate in contemporary America.

Covenant-Married Couples

We interviewed 6 conservative Christian couples who had converted their marriages into covenant marriages on Valentine's Day 1998, along with approximately 70 other couples in their congregation. These couples were all White and had been married from 11 to 56 years, with most in the third decade of their marriage. We selected this constituency for two reasons. First, they are the very first people to avail themselves of this new marriage option. Second, a few of them were political lobbyists for the covenant marriage law, and they all are members of a church that is influential in propounding the covenant marriage option to the community.

Feminist Activists

To represent a nontraditional, feminist constituency, we interviewed 12 middle-class, White feminists who were either members of the Louisiana National Organization for Women (NOW) (9 participants) or else employees, volunteers, or members of feminist women's agencies in the New Orleans area (3 participants). The group consisted of 11 White women and 1 White man, with ages ranging from the early 20s to the early 50s. Several were cohabiting, 2 were married, and some were single noncohabitors.

We could have interviewed members from a number of different types of feminist organizations, but we selected and invited this group because the membership included a number of sea-

soned lobbyists for women's issues with the Louisiana state legislature and, more important, a few that had actually lobbied against the covenant marriage legislation. Their lobbying efforts, along with help from other political action groups, encouraged the legislators to add spouse and child abuse as a fault-based reason for terminating divorce under the covenant marriage law.

PUBLIC-HOUSING RESIDENTS

We interviewed 10 low-income residents of public housing to represent yet a third constituency with possibly divergent views. This group consisted of 9 Black women and 1 White woman. Their ages ranged from the early 20s through early 50s. Several were never married, a few cohabited, and some maintained discontinuously cohabiting long-term relationships. A few of the women were divorced. Two women were married for 18 and 26 years each.

We selected this constituency for two reasons. First, local and national social welfare debates focus great attention on the problems faced by low-income minority communities. Many of these debates address whether marriage can be promoted to reduce the economic insecurities and social isolation caused by female-headed families. Second, Louisiana has both high poverty rates and a large minority population. Of Louisiana residents, 24% are poor, and 56% of Louisiana's Black children are poor (U.S. Bureau of the Census, 1990). Thus, the views of low-income and minority women with family obligations are an important component of our understanding of the perceived utility of covenant marriage.

WHAT IS COVENANT MARRIAGE?

Since the early 1970s, most states have adopted virtually unrestricted no-fault divorce legislation

(Buehler, 1995). Much of 20th-century marriage and family legislation aims to protect nuclear families from state and community interference and preserve and expand family privacy (McIntyre, 1995). Beginning in 1967 with *Loving v. Virginia,* the U.S. Supreme Court has consistently elaborated and reaffirmed a constitutional right to marry, thereby limiting states' abilities to impose limits. Although Loving declared Virginia's attempt to forbid interracial marriages unconstitutional, the decision became an important precedent for issues beyond race. In general, limitations on the right to marry are now based more on contractual capacity than on social-engineering concerns (e.g., minimum ages for marriage are the same as minimum ages for contractual capacity) (Krause, 1995; McIntyre, 1995). The no-fault divorce component of this marriage liberalization movement was motivated in part by beliefs that the former marriage regime trapped many women and children in difficult, abusive, or otherwise unsatisfactory marriages and was enabled by shifting cultural values about divorce, remarriage, cohabitation, and life course commitments.

The covenant marriage movement of the late 1990s grew out of wide-spread concern that no-fault divorce laws have threatened the institution of marriage. Covenant marriage sets stricter terms for both entering and exiting marriage, including required premarital counseling; submission of a signed affidavit acknowledging that marriage is a lifetime commitment and that the partners have revealed everything about their personal histories that might adversely affect the marital relationship; agreement to an extended, monitored legal separation before divorce; and required marital counseling before a divorce could be granted. Covenant marriage allows only limited fault-based criteria for divorce, including substantiated infidelity, physical or sexual abuse, a felony conviction, or long-term abandonment.

Critically, irreconcilable differences, general incompatibility, or irretrievable breakdown of the marriage are not acceptable grounds for divorce. A no-fault option is still available for covenant marriages, but the new law requires that the couple live separately for 2 years (vs. 6 months under the standard Louisiana marriage regime) or be legally separated for 18 months. Newly marrying couples must choose between the conventional and covenant options; currently married couples may convert their existing marriages into covenant marriages.

The evident intent of the covenant marriage law is to make marriage an enduring, lifelong commitment by requiring couples to receive counseling both before marriage and afterward, if difficulties arise, and by making divorce a more difficult, restricted process. The legislators and advocates intended to promote a more sober, considered understanding of the commitments and obligations that marriage entails.

Louisiana's marriage innovation raises a number of interesting questions. What do proponents and opponents say about the possible effects? Does covenant marriage spell the death of no-fault divorce, perhaps even the end of the "Divorce Culture," to invoke Whitehead's (1997) term? Will covenant marriages be healthier, happier, or more stable than conventional marriages? Will the covenant marriage option make young couples more reflective about the obligations marriage entails?

Is the institution of marriage "in trouble"?

Marriage Suffers Because of Our Hedonistic Culture

Our first question addresses the focus groups' perspectives on whether marriage as an institution is suffering and why. The covenant-married couples gave the clearest, most forceful argument that our culture faces a severe breakdown in the quality of and values in marriage. These couples believe very strongly in Christian values, heterosexual marriage, and traditional gender roles. One wife said that a husband "should be the godly leader for the family, the one who is there to reflect the Lord for our children." Another felt that "the husband should be the head of the family." One wife described the differing gender responsibilities as follows: "There's a clear distinction—that's my feeling. The husband's major job is being the protector, provider, and leader of the family. The wife's is more nurturing, taking care of the home and children." Another added, "We're all in agreement here that the man is the head of the home.... I think that my role—what I can teach my children is that their father is the head of the house. That can show them how I respect that position. And that teaches them to respect authority in general." The husbands' comments were generally quite similar, stressing their leadership responsibility in the family.

These couples felt strongly that traditional marriage faces severe challenges. They blamed the decline of traditional two-parent families on a society-wide moral failure, arguing that individuals no longer value commitment, respect, and trust and are no longer willing to subordinate their own hedonistic interests to the needs of their spouses and children. This exchange clearly exemplifies this view:

> *I think there's a lack of commitment in a broad range of marriages, you know. In marriages represented here, I think each spouse is strongly committed, but I don't think that's the general view of marriage because they're [failing] or giving up too easily. You know, there's not a commitment to one another or the commitment to the Lord that you made a covenant to stay married.*

> *I think a big problem is the focus on self and self-centered[ness], rather than putting somebody else's interests first. I think that's going to be a hallmark of all successful marriages, the spouse who is willing to put the other spouse's interests first. So, when you put two people together that are very "me-centered," I think it's doomed to fail eventually—and sooner rather than later. If you have the mindset to put other people's interests first, you're certain to put the spouse first and usually the kids before either spouse. You know, I think that's the hallmark of a successful family and a successful marriage.*

The covenant couples tied the inability to commit to marriage (and the ensuing willingness to divorce) to a false pursuit of one's own enjoyment. One of these women referred to the notion that "the pursuit of happiness is the most important goal" as "a lie" and added that successful couples are "willing to go through the tough times that every marriage has because [they see that] commitment to the family is more important than their happiness—temporary happiness."

The covenant couples also perceived marriage to suffer because of changes in gender roles. Specifically, they argued that society and women no longer perceive homemaking and mothering as "callings." Some covenant men indicated that husbands encouraged wives' employment out of a selfish pursuit of an improved standard of living and that women and children suffered. A number of the covenant wives agreed with this argument, to a point, but also indicated that some families needed a wife's income and that families and marriages only suffered if the wife took her job too seriously as a "career" and tried to compete with her husband or required too much of his domestic help. The following comments first by a covenant wife and second by a covenant husband illustrate:

> *I think society doesn't hold a mother and a woman staying at home in very high esteem. I think they're held in real low esteem. In my personal belief, that's one of the greatest jobs you can do is mold young minds and raise children who grow up with good character, good morals, people that'll be an asset to society rather than a liability. And I think it now happens that so many mothers aren't taking that job and that role seriously. And, you know, you reap what you sow.*

> *As men, we have in many cases abdicated the leadership throne, if you will. Allowed our wives to assume positions of responsibility that they really shouldn't have to assume. And, in fact, many times have required them to do that. Deciding that we need a standard of living that's above where we are, so that if a wife would take a job, that would create a position… where she is trying to balance family and work and, therefore, she is not giving her commitment to the marriage and to her children.*

These couples expressed a traditional Christian perspective of wives as nurturers and homemakers and of husbands as breadwinners, protectors, and leaders of families. They endorsed the belief that a vow of marriage was a sacred, irrevocable trust. The covenant-married couples uniformly felt that contemporary wives and husbands were "falling really short" in their obligations and responsibilities to one another and to society as a whole.

People Suffer Because of an Anachronistic, Patriarchal, and Capitalist Institution

In stark contrast, our feminist focus group participants felt that the question of whether society suffers from a general decline in the institution of marriage was completely beside the point. These feminists argued that marriage, as currently structured, harms women, men, and children in numerous ways. They perceived the concern about family and marriage decline as simply a scheme of conservative interest groups to buttress fundamentalism, capitalism, patriarchy, and other social ills, and they emphasized that rather than lament the decline of marriage, the public would be better served by altering the institution's inherently sexist, debilitating qualities.

Their arguments fell into three broad categories. First, they argued that historically, marriage has had negative consequences for women's independence and legal and social citizenship and that marriage is inherently patriarchal. Second, they held a lively, vivid discussion about how marriage and the wedding ceremony itself are examples of "conspicuous consumerism," a mega-industry devoted to selling women their own subjugation. Third, they argued that marriage sets unreasonable and demeaning expectations of women and men. This group was strongly and consistently opposed to the viewpoints elaborated by the covenant couples, and in fact, the covenant couples routinely referred to feminists and the National Organization of Women as their political and cultural enemies.

The theme of women's legal disempowerment via marriage was nearly universal.

> *It's a little too harsh to say that I think marriage is the enslavement of women, but it's pretty close to that. I think that women are made to feel like they're inadequate or "other," if*

they don't conform to the paradigm of marriage. So, it's a way to continually keep women in a position of not being able to fully explore their equality and autonomy.

My impulse is to denigrate marriage … as creating, making women chattel…. For me, what's important is how it is actualized in contemporary [society], at least within my contemporary society, just in Western U.S. society. And I think it really sucks. I think it institutionalizes and legitimates heterosexuality. I think it creates for women a false, false—underlined and italicized—sense of security. I think that it legitimates domestic violence, rape, battery of children. I think it really sets up a lot of—it facilitates a lot of acting out of sexism. And even in the best of intentions.

I think, above all, the major purpose of marriage in American culture is to keep women in the place that they've been historically, which is enslaved or in modified enslavement to men, whether that's their fathers or their husbands. If you do read the history of marriage, it's very clear and it's not up for debate that marriage has been—up until very recent history in some states and some countries—has been male ownership of female bodies…. It's a total denial of a woman's personhood or individuality.

I think that if all women made a point of being students of history, not the history of the victors but the history of women's enslavement, that they would be nauseated by the rituals that we find so appealing.

Rather than "strengthen marriage," these women would prefer to do away with it altogether. Thus, they were unwilling to discuss the decline of marriage and rise of divorce as a problem of political or social consequence, except when women's, men's, and children's economic and personal security were endangered. They elaborated knowledgeably about the changes in marriage and divorce patterns, even across race and class, but did not typify any of these changes as problematic. And they certainly did not raise any discussion of an overall decline in values or morality as a consequence or cause of marriage breakdown.

A strong second theme was that courtship, wedding rituals and celebrations, and marriage itself were examples of a destructive, coercive capitalism that makes women compete for men and celebrate their "victories" with conspicuous consumerism. Contemporary society defines a woman's success as her ability to improve or maintain her class standing by marrying well. As one young feminist said, "[Marriage] is a middle-class institution…. You nab some marriageable guy, which means a guy that has some economic viability. *That's your badge of success* [emphasis added]. Another said that "success for a female in our culture is to be sexually attractive to men so that one will marry you," "in a big ceremony," as an "homage to conspicuous consumerism." In this view, being sexually attractive to be marriageable is part of "an enormous industry" in which "people make billions of dollars talking you into subjugating yourself legally and probably emotionally." They believed that the practices surrounding marriage cannot be separated from "the beauty myth" and from ideologies that women "are mothers and should be mothers and *essentially* mothers." Their lengthy dialogue about the capitalist, consumer-oriented packaging of weddings and marriage in the United States interwove with their views on the sexist nature of marriage and the social control of women and men through prefabricated, unrealistic expectations.

A number of the feminists who were currently or previously married were troubled that even their own strongly held feminist principles did not shelter them from the cult of consumerism. As one middle-aged feminist poignantly noted,

> [When I married] I learned the limited agency of individuals, that in spite of your politics and your strength and your discussions amongst each other, as soon as you interact with culture, including your mom, his mom, and [him], everyone is going to work very hard to make the marriage go in a very traditional way. It's really tiring.

Another said, "I'm in a relationship right now, and there's this massive internal struggle between the intellectual feminist and the consumer in me trying to consume American culture and who wants to 'win the game.'" The feminists were less concerned about a decline in family values and morality in American culture than by how capitalism perverts sexuality and love so as to prohibit egalitarian forms of intimacy. They perceived the courtship and marriage systems to be ones of socialized, internalized subjugation.

Last, these feminists believe that contemporary marriage sets unreasonable, rigid, hierarchical, and gender-stereotypical expectations for women and men. When asked about the purpose of marriage in our society, they quickly replied, "to keep women down," "to perpetuate stereotypes," and "to put people in their place."

Accordingly, although the covenant couples perceived gender-stereotyped marital obligations as strengthening family life, the feminists were troubled by what they perceived as lingering, pervasive, and powerful gender roles in intimate relationships. The following exchange documents the feminists' views on how modern women simply incorporated new gender-stereotyped obligations into the older nurturant responsibilities.

> Legally, it's very clear-cut what the obligations in marriage are for men and for women. But, yeah, culturally, what messages are people getting as to what their obligations are? I think, in contemporary American culture, women are getting the idea that it's their obligation to be sexually attractive, and now, economically viable. Educated, caring, nurturing, smart, sexy.

> Not too smart [interrupting and overlapping]!

> [Laughing] Warm and caring, yet strong and tough. And to do everything from wearing lingerie and high heels to really enjoying football. [Laughter, agreement] Really raise children, but really be a high-powered, you know, career woman. And the set of expectations that, really, I think many women and men think are obligations, really, you know, because of the cultural messages they're getting, are totally unrealistic for women. And yet, when I think of the same set of expectations slash obligations for men, they seem very reasonable. Men are expected to have a job. [Laughter.] And, in many cases expected to be monogamous, which, you know, I assume many are able to do. And to impregnate the wife at some point. I do not see a lot of perceived obligations that men supposedly have in marriage, I don't see a lot of cultural pressure on men to do anything other than have a job.

When you listen to the rhetoric surrounding marriage, it's the man who's giving something up and the woman who's gaining something.

A Practical Eye on American Family Troubles

Public-housing residents' views on contemporary marriage were more inclusive and less ideological than the other two groups. These women combined the Christian vision of covenant couples with a far more practical understanding of the everyday problems that families face. Also, unlike the feminists, their discussion focused on the disadvantages to women of not being married. They addressed a broader range of family problems than marital strain and divorce and seemed far more comfortable discussing both micro-level problems influencing family breakdown such as declines in personal values, commitments, and communication skills and macro-level forces such as poverty, lack of government support of families, and changes in legal, economic, and social conditions.

These women felt that "if the husband is true to what he's supposed to be doing, obligations come naturally to the woman. They know what they're supposed to do, as far as cooking, cleaning, keeping, nurturing, and keeping the kids clean." Uniformly, the low-income women felt that husbands should be breadwinners and provide moral, spiritual, and role-model leadership for the family. But they also argued that homemaking has to be shared, with husbands appreciating wives' efforts and offering to pitch in when necessary. The following exchange shows this sense of mutual responsibility for home life:

I personally feel that it's my obligation, like "B" said, the house, the cooking, the cleaning, but also it's the man's obligation to see, if I'm tired and worn out from a hard day at work, it's his obligation also to take over and to say, "Okay, baby, now you rest tonight and I'll do the cooking and I'll do the cleaning and I'll take care of the kids."

[General consent] Now, that's true. … That's right.… It's got to be a two-way thing.

The pragmatism of these women shaped their opinions about whether marriage was in trouble. They agreed that the institution of marriage is ailing but noted a far greater range of reasons. They talked about some women's mistreatment of men, the lack of appreciation women and men sometimes show each other, the problems caused by poor communication between wives and husbands, the necessity of listening with a full heart to one's spouse, and the tension between being strong and independent versus overly independent and too autonomous.

Many discussed how women's employment was a necessity for families and for women's security against male abandonment but noted that this necessity may strain marriages.

When you have women in the workforce, a lot of moms are there because of necessity. So, there has to be a sharing there. Because if you have to go out and work 8 hours and then come home and everybody can veg, except you, at nighttime, it sometimes builds up animosity. It's a slow process. So, I can see why, if the woman can stay home, and the man is really committed to her, after she's been home taking care of the family for 20 years and now they're grown, that he does not walk out on her and leave her in a bad situation. And for that reason, I see why there are so many women today who do work. Who have to be independent. But when they take that home that—because of the rockiness of the marriage, then the family suffers, especially children.

Another responded,

But there are women who treat their men badly. They have good husbands who provide. And when the husband comes home, there's nothing on that stove and that house is dirty and the children are too. [General agreement: "Yes, indeed. Yes, indeed."] And that's a terrible thing.

This discussion lasted a long time, as the women explored the mutual "lack of appreciation" and "lack of communication" facing many couples and how some men suffered because they "don't have a strong woman." They felt that "a reason for most divorces is that they don't communicate. You need a bond to be set. They need to find their foundation. And most young couples, they don't have that."

The discussion was fascinating particularly because these women, unlike our other respondents, did not have any pat solutions about how marriage should be structured. Consider the following exchange concerning independence versus interdependence in relationships:

You know, the husband comes home and he's had a bad day and you're so busy, you can't listen to what he has to say. Well, then he's going to find someone who will [lots of affirmations]. And you could lose him.

It's like me, I used to fix my faucets and change the oil in my car, and somehow he felt that he wasn't needed to do that. Now, I don't do that anymore.... I used to get under the sink and fix things, you know. But

I find that now, I let him do these things, and he does them.

My daddy taught me those things to be independent. And, you know, I maybe made a mistake, but I'm trying to teach my daughter to be independent but not overly. We are complete without males, male partners, and males are complete without us. But together, you see, we fit.

These women emphasized infidelity and divorce as a "chain reaction of dumping" because of people's unhappiness. They argued that no-fault divorce facilitated this process, and that "people are taking advantage of it." Like the covenant couples, they felt that "people just don't want to be bothered" with marital obligations, so they leave relationships with relative ease. But unlike the covenant couples, they showed a greater tolerance for the problems of falling out of love, growing apart, and modern strains on women and men in marriage. And unlike the feminists, they felt that despite the problems of miscommunication, infidelity, and dysfunctional valorization of personal happiness over commitment, marriage was still an ideal, a valued state to which both men and women should aspire. As one said, "I think that it's right for a woman to be married.... I'm not saying you shouldn't live with anyone, because I have. But I know that, spiritually, that's not right. You're supposed to be married."

Is Covenant Marriage a Solution to Problems in Marriage and Divorce?

How did these three interest groups perceive the new covenant marriage legislation? The divergent views of our focus groups illustrate the forces shaping public dialogue about marriage and divorce reform, family values, and the relationship between the state and family. Of the three groups, not surprisingly, the covenant couples were the most supportive of covenant marriage. They saw nothing negative in the legislation and felt that the law itself could reinforce important community values such as commitment, trust, integrity, fidelity, and maturity. The feminists, also not surprisingly, were the most strongly opposed to covenant marriage. Although they debated the utility of some of the particulars (such as required counseling), they primarily felt that this legislation was a cynical, hypocritical attempt by conservative politicians to draw attention away from real social problems facing Americans in general and women in particular, by casting blame on individuals for the decline of marriage and rise in divorce. The public-housing residents presented the most even-handed, evaluative view of the three groups. They were circumspect about the law but willing to discuss some of its likely positive and negative features. They considered a wider variety of issues about the legislation than the covenant couples or feminists. In comparison to the covenant couples and feminists, the low-income women fused both conservative and liberal attitudes about marriage and divorce reform; the current social, political, and economic climate; and personal liberties and responsibilities.

Covenant Marriage as a First Step Toward Reinforcing Traditional Marriage and Family Values

The covenant couples expressed concern about the effects of divorce on children. They talked in passionate detail about how a culture of divorce emphasized to children that their own personal interests were more important than family interests and that families and authority figures could not be trusted. These couples expressed alarm about their perceptions of the younger generation; they worried that children, adolescents, and young adults were fearful of commitment, low in self-esteem, and fragile in confidence and willingness to sacrifice personal gain for family and community goals. They felt this state of affairs arose directly from the breakdown in marriage and rise in divorce. The following exchanges highlight these concerns:

I don't think people realize what it's doing to this generation of children. And I don't think they care. They're worried about themselves. And they're just going to ignore and deny what it's doing to their children. My daughter has a good friend whose parents just divorced and the dad remarried just recently. We were having dinner and his [the friend's] whole topic of conversation all night was that he would never get married. That marriage was just a terrible thing. I think he was just consumed with that. That's all he talked about, he was just miserable. And I think parents just don't realize that when they're divorced, it's just so much stress on children.

I'm afraid it's just going to be a downward spiral that does not stop. Because these kids are being subjected to divorces and remarriages so early that they're going to think that that's the lifestyle.

It's normal. I just don't know what will happen to our kids when they get older and start marrying. Will it turn around because they know how much hurt they had and they'll be more committed, or are they even just gonna wonder why you even would get married?

Say you've got an 8-year-old boy whose father decides he's going to take off. If you can't trust your own father to stick around, then what other authority figure in your life are you going to trust? You know. Your employer? Law enforcement people? That's got to affect your ability to see other people as having your best interests at heart.

Right. That's an excellent point. If you can't trust your dad, who can you trust?

When asked whether politicians should do something to reduce divorce and strengthen marriage, a covenant husband replied, "Yeah, I think the state has a compelling reason and an obligation to strengthen marriage, if for no other reason than economic." They approved of covenant marriage wholeheartedly and discussed their support of "tax incentives to [promote] long-term marriages." The couples held an animated discussion about how "the country is built on strong families," thus the government has a vested interest to protect, promote, and strengthen traditional families.

In their view, covenant marriage performs an important public service. These couples want some sort of political, cultural, or legal mechanism that will get young people to think about their selfishness, their motives, and their willingness to commit and accept their vows.

A covenant is a strong commitment, and I just think the concept of covenant should be brought back into marriage, which is what we all should be doing anyhow. But I'm not sure everyone does when they're first getting married. So, it'll make'em stop and think.

I look forward to the days that I can counsel my boys and younger daughter as they decide how they will choose a spouse for life. So, I look forward, as I encourage them to opt for

covenant marriage, to tell them that as soon as we could get that, we did.

I run across a lot of my secular-world friends and I say, "Are you going to get your marriage, you going to make a covenant marriage?" "Oh, no. I want to keep my options open." That's the self-centered approach. That's the core problem, in my mind, as I've said many times, the core problem for most of what ails us in this country. "No, I'm going to keep my options open." A marriage contract is unenforceable from day one. A marriage contract should be the most important covenant of all, and it's worthless in a no-fault divorce situation. I mean—this is how absurd it is—the person that breaches [his vows], the husband who runs off with the secretary, can walk back in to the nonbreaching wife and say, "I'm out of here. There's nothing you can do about it. I'm gone." No excuse. "I'm gone." No sanction or penalty. And, I mean, even business will give you better than that.

These couples spoke knowledgeably and candidly about the practical and symbolic reasons for their support of covenant marriage, and they took care to situate their view against liberal and feminist views on marriage reform.

It's amusing to me. The liberal mantra is you can't legislate morals, therefore, this is kind of a moral issue, so we're not going to do this. But it's the same people that want to regulate guns and they want to regulate tobacco and regulate all these other things. But, yet, when it comes to family matters, well, then that's some-

thing that the government shouldn't be involved in.

Yeah, for us that have been married for a long time, the overriding long-term important thing [about covenant marriage] is just forcing that one question before you get married. I mean, even though it's optional, this is what threatens the NOW gang and the rest of them. If you're going to get married in Louisiana, you have to answer the question to your spouse, to your future spouse, "Do you want to have a covenant marriage?" If it does nothing else, [covenant marriage] is fine because it's going to force the couple to answer that question.

It changes the focus from a 2- or 3-year date to a lifetime, you know?

Young, bright-eyed couples don't feel like they'll ever need it.... You know, nobody gets married if they expect to get divorced. But the fact is they run on the rocks. And it does bring up a fundamental problem. If a couple that's about to get married consciously said, "I don't want to do this" (i.e., get a covenant marriage), I think that's probably a good time for the relationship to end. If two people who want to get married were not willing to make a covenant marriage, I'd say, "Well, go get another boyfriend, you know, this is not a husband."

Although the covenant-married couples liked every aspect of the legislation, from the premarital counseling to the lengthened waiting periods for divorce, they seemed less concerned with the practical changes toward fault-based divorce and more enamored by the symbolic function of this

legislation. They perceived covenant marriage as their chance to inspire confidence in marriage in their children, make a statement to their wider communities about the value of family commitment, and raise the terms of the debate with liberal interest groups whom they perceived as undermining family values.

Covenant Marriage as a Cynical Political Backlash

The feminists proved a strong counterpoint to the covenant married couples. They seemed uniformly suspicious of covenant marriage and the motives of covenant marriage legislators. At core, the feminists felt that political innovations in marriage reform were doomed. As one young, never-married woman said,

> *I can really relate to people wanting to reinvent marriage, so I can relate to people who might be working on this covenant marriage thing, though they are taking it to a difference place than I might take it if I tried to reinvent marriage. But that urge to make [marriage] something different than what it currently is, I can really relate to that.*

Her older, married colleague replied, "I don't have a lot of faith in anyone's ability to be inventive as long as we live within the context of patriarchy.... I think, fundamentally, we need to inscribe ways to respect women and value women, and reinventing marriage seems, to me, real dated."

The feminists felt that focusing so strongly on preserving marriage and reducing divorce was a misspecification of the real social problems facing American families.

> *I'm not sure it's necessarily bad to have easy divorce.... I think that the justification behind it [covenant marriage]*

was that there are all these bad social problems attached to divorce, but I don't think that divorce is necessarily a problem. And I think that there are definitely other ways of addressing those social problems than attacking divorce.

I don't care how many people or women get divorced. I care about how many women are happy and are leading healthy lives that are good for themselves and the children and the other people that they're involved with. I think the divorce rate, in and of itself, is nothing; it doesn't indicate healthy or unhealthy relationships. It only represents failure at a set of expectations that we all question.

And I think that just because it's maybe legally a lot easier to get divorced than it used to be, does not mean that getting divorced is easy.... For my friends and relatives that I've seen get divorced, it seems like a heart-wrenching, devastating experience.... They make it sound like women are just running off and getting divorced, and I kind of equate it to the way that some people talk about women running off getting abortions. Well, getting an abortion is not easy either. These are complex, complicated decisions about people's entire lives, and they don't need to have it made more difficult by some law.

For these feminists, divorce itself is not a problem requiring a legislative fix. Instead, society should focus on child poverty, domestic abuse, and economic and social inequalities. As one noted, "[Covenant marriage] presumes that mar-riage is inherently a good thing that must be preserved. And I don't buy that at all."

Many felt that proponents of covenant marriage are "oppressors of women and deniers of women's autonomy and women's choices." One feminist lobbyist felt that "the legislature, at least in Louisiana, feels like they can define and enforce morality. They do it with teen pregnancy. They do it with sexuality education. They think they can do it with marriage." These feminists see covenant marriage as a regressive step for a number of constituencies, including heterosexual women, children, gays, and lesbians. One young woman said, "I see covenant marriage as 'let's give patriarchy some reinforcement here.'" And another said,

Women get hurt in our culture by our legal system and by the men who vowed to love them, whether you have fault divorce or no-fault divorce. Each one has a set of variable ways in which the man is able to victimize or abuse the woman, but neither cures the misogyny or the subjugation of women.

Just as one covenant husband asserted, "I think this group would say there's absolutely no negative costs of covenant marriage," a young woman from the feminist group said, "To me there's basically nothing good about covenant marriage. Not a thing."

The feminists' disdain of covenant marriage was especially vivid in their critique of the counseling requirements. "You know, the knee-jerk reaction is [that] counseling is a good thing. Well, counseling with whom? You know, a lot of psychiatrists molest their patients!" Some reported concerns about the possibility of a sudden growth in the cottage industry of "quickie" counseling, but more were concerned about counseling as provided by religious leaders:

"Counseling that is—what?—Indoctrination 101!" Another said,

> Pastors are individuals with ideologies and…the idea of using someone as a sounding board is an excellent, excellent idea, but there's nothing that truly protects either spouse from getting bad counseling or biased counseling. And…in most situations, women are going to be at a disadvantage in counseling situations that [are] religious.

One woman felt very negatively about religious counseling, saying, "A lot of Catholic priests tell women, 'You should quit your job and serve your husband like it says in the Bible, and divorce is not an option.'" Later, a woman who worked on a crisis line at a battered women's shelter said, "I've heard this a million times from a million women, their preacher's telling her not to leave and it's her duty to stay in the relationship."

Covenant Marriage as an Option to Consider, Although Not Wholeheartedly Endorse

Again, the public-housing residents held the most wide-ranging, probing, and mixed discussion about the likely effects of covenant marriage. These women acknowledged problems in society and the quality of family life and saw both individual and societal causes for the decline in marriage and rise in divorce. They felt circumspect about covenant marriage and were divided in opinions, exchanging ideas actively and playing devil's advocate with each other. They willingly engaged the debate about the utility of covenant marriage from a number of ideological points of view. And they felt more even-handed about the motives of the legislators and elements of the legislation than the feminist group. Last, they expressed innovative views on covenant marriage, as well as ideas that over-

lapped with both the covenant-married couples' and feminists' opinions.

Concerning the costs of divorce and weakened marriage on American families, public-housing residents tended to echo the sentiments of the covenant couples. One single mother said, "When the parents get divorced, it hurts everybody." And a long-time married grandmother argued that the United States did not compare well to other countries, such as Sweden, in its care of families and respect for the institution of marriage. She said, "We have a system now that's like, it's not ours, us, or we anymore, it's mine, me." She noted that Swedes "have day care automatically…[and a] system where they take care of the family." Another mother felt that the divorce rate was high because of lack of education. In her view,

> You need a driver's license and you have to take a test to get a driver's license—for a nurse, just to do sitting. But there's no class to tell you how you should react in marriage. How do you raise your children, you know? What classes do you have to teach you how to do that?

And, like the covenant couples, these low-income women uniformly felt that children were harmed because of the rise of single-mother families, divorce, and remarriage. They felt that men needed to take a more active role in their children's lives. They talked at length about how "desperately" fathers were needed by both daughters and sons. One said, "These days, women are trying to raise boys, but it's not going to work. I don't care how hard you try. It's not going to work. You've got to have a strong male figure." Another added,

> That's right, and if the fathers are a strong male figure in the family, then the daughter will want a husband just

like her dad. And you don't have to be validated by the opposite sex because you are significant for what you are.

These women examined a constellation of issues facing children's relationships with residential parents, nonresidential parents, and stepparents and were very careful to widen the conversation beyond simply divorced families. Ultimately, though, they regretted the passing of what they saw as a better time for families. One married woman said,

The nuclear family, we had it, you know, where the grandmother lived in the house with them, and the extended family. But now where does the grandmother live? In Timbuktu or China or Kalamazoo. And so you don't have that connection, where, you know, that Grandma and Ma live down the street and they can babysit, and you can all come together for Sunday dinner.

These women wanted a wider range of initiatives to strengthen marriage and family than either the covenant couples or feminists. They saw roles for government, families, and communities. From the government, they favored legislation making both divorce and marriage harder to get. And they endorsed the idea that the government should offer more resources, such as free or low-cost counseling and legal services, to married couples. The women also believed that extended families should support married relatives more, encouraging them to stick out their troubles.

Well, when I decided that I was going to walk away, leave my house and everything, I took my clothes and went to my mother. She looked at me and said, "What was that?" And I said,

"It's my clothes. I'm leaving." She said, "You're crazy. You do not walk away from your house. That is your house. That is where your child belongs and you decided that you wanted to marry this man. ["You had a good mom. Work it out."] You can stay here tonight, but you're going home tomorrow." ["Umm hmm."]

Thus, unlike the covenant couples who cast blame on personal irresponsibility and micro-level reasons for divorce and unlike the feminist activists who focused primarily on macro-level ideological processes, the low-income women interwove both perspectives, acknowledging problems at both levels.

The low-income women were also more even-handed about the counseling requirements in covenant marriage, noting both positive and negative features. Some felt that the new provisions were beneficial because "it makes a person think twice," makes a couple "try to work it out, instead of just jumping into divorce court." As one woman said,

For me, [covenant marriage is] a positive because you're going to think more about your situation. And when you get to talking about everything in [your] past that you've done that you're supposed to tell this person, that's going to be a stopper right there."

Another stated, "We need to get more people to think about this marriage stuff anyway." One woman advocated

sessions for you to go to, you know, so if you decide you want to go and file for divorce or something, that person should give you or tell you, "Look, before you file for this divorce,

*go to this place and seek help to tell
you how to make a marriage healthy
or help you back off or do something
about it."*

Others were even more positive, as this woman's
statement shows:

*I'd say that it would help, especially
the family structure as a whole, because people would have to think
about their commitment and their responsibility because there is a responsibility when you walk down that aisle
and you stand and you say, "I do."*

And, like the covenant couples, some women
felt that counseling may be especially beneficial
for youth. "For a younger couple, it might make
them think about it before they get into it, really
think about what they're doing."

Yet, others were negative or ambivalent.
One woman asked, "What about if he or she
kicks against [counseling]? They don't want to
go at all?" Another woman agreed, saying,

*Counseling will give you a little time.
If you decide you want to get divorced, you can get counseling, you
both get counseling and you can
come together, then it's good. But
then if you have one person who's
just going to say, "I don't want to be
here, I don't care what you do," it's
not going to do any good.*

This led to a discussion about whether counseling people who truly fell out of love or grew
apart was useful—whether it made any sense to
counsel people to stay in loveless, dispassionate
marriages in which both partners lived essentially separate lives.

What most distinguished the low-income
women's views from the other two groups was
their continued preoccupation with the effectiveness of covenant marriage in the face of circum-
spection about people's heart-felt willingness to
make marriage work, no matter what. They
talked pragmatically, even poetically, about how
a law can only work if it is accepted by people
and endorsed with full spirit. One woman said,

*If you can set a law that affects a per-
son's heart then you can do this...
because that's something within a
person that has to be changed. That's
like the covenant marriage or any
other marriage. If you don't change it
in here, what you feel about the person, no matter what laws are set up.
Laws are set up because somebody
did something wrong. Laws are set up
after something's been broken.*

Another argued, "If you don't change their
hearts, you can make all the laws you want, it
ain't going to help. It ain't going to stop." Another agreed, asking,

*If you drive without a license, there is
a penalty. If you break the [covenant
marriage] law, what is the penalty? If
you decide, "I'm going to walk out on
her, I'm not going to counseling, I'm
not going to take care of the kids, I'm
not going to pay the alimony," where
is the deterrent? There isn't. I don't
see anything here.*

Overall, the low-income women felt something
should be done to improve the quality of contemporary family life and gave great consideration to covenant marriage, but they finally concluded on a note of ambivalence.

*In some ways, it will work and it's
good, but in some ways, I think if it's
not in your heart, no matter what a*

piece of paper says, it's not going to do any good.

Well, it takes two. And, if they can't make it work, I don't see how the covenant is going to make it work neither. It takes two people to make it work. ("That's right. Umm, hmm.")

Ain't nobody make you love nobody. You have to have that relationship going on between the two of y'all. And ain't no law going to give you no love that you need. But, legally, it might work. They really need it because they're married today, divorced tomorrow. And they really need to stick them down and make them be married.

The Hardening of Lines in the Marriage Debate?

Clearly, the covenant couples believe strongly that covenant marriage will reduce divorce rates and strengthen family life. They supplied a rich abundance of prosocial reasons for why covenant marriage was right for them and the larger society. They want to show their abiding love for each other, demonstrate to their children that they need not despair of making lasting commitments in their own lives, be models of respect and trust for their community, and underscore that marriages can last through difficulties with perseverance, to name a few. But, in their case, covenant marriage is literally "preaching to the choir." Will covenant marriage work for the rest of the poor souls mucking about in the trials and tribulations of daily married life? Will covenant marriage create problems for other groups in our society who want our legal and social systems to move toward greater liberties and privileges rather than greater restrictions? As McIntyre (1995) said,

Traditionally, the courts have extended…protection to a limited vari-

ety of relationships—the two-parent household surrounded by a picket fence comes to mind here. Yet, as individuals within society, freed from normative and legal controls to an unprecedented degree, continue to explore new ways of constituting family life, new and complex issues of law emerge. (p. 27)

Hunt and Hunt (1982) argued that the rise in child-free dual-working couples would create great social inequalities as these wealthier couples used their lobbying power to accrue privileges at the expense of traditional single-earner families with children. Now, we may see the backlash and a further cleavage in our society as the latter faction pursues legal and social protections for traditional family life, whereas other groups continue to explore liberalist policies. Therefore, we may very well experience an escalating polarization in the rhetoric surrounding family values.

A number of conservatives assert that extended families and heterosexual nuclear families are the core of a civil society and that, distressingly, this foundation has been undermined by a host of attacks to traditional values, via a liberal popular culture, secularism, illegitimacy, sexual revolutions, no-fault divorce reform, father absence, and other social problems (Davidson, 1990; Gilder, 1989). They argue that "very little attention is being paid to what makes for marital success. It's every couple on its own bottom, without a compass, often without a goal" (Kass, 1997, p. 40). Some scholars report that American attitudes about the permanence of marriage have changed in such a way that married individuals simply no longer feel committed to their spouses. Glenn (1991) said,

Although many contemporary marriage ceremonies include traditional marriage vows, such as "till death do

us part" and "as long as we both shall live," it is doubtful that most brides and grooms mean what they say. More honest vows would often be "as long as we both shall love" or "as long as no one better comes along." (p. 268)

As a result, many conservatives and some moderate centrists are the main outspoken proponents of covenant marriage. They perceive a social necessity in strengthening marriage. Kass (1997) illustrated this view with the following:

Under present democratic conditions, with families not what they used to be, anything that contributes to promoting a lasting friendship between husband and wife should be cultivated. A budding couple today needs even better skills at reading character and greater opportunities for showing it, than was necessary in a world that has lots of family members looking on. (p. 62)

Conservatives lead the lobbying effort for premarital and marital counseling as well as greater church involvement in marriage, family, and community, and they encourage legislators to "elevate marriage in public policy" and "valorize marital toughness" (Mattox, 1995, p. 53). They contend that no-fault divorce fosters a model of marriage as a contract in which the state acts as a neutral enforcer of bargains struck between self-interested parties, with negative consequences including women's economic vulnerability, harm to children, undermined social welfare, and corrupted family values. Other conservatives argue that no-fault divorce transformed marriage into an illusory contract that provides no remedy for breach of the marriage vows. In this view, no-fault divorce encourages opportunistic behavior by husbands and threatens wives' marital investments.

Although multiple feminist perspectives address domestic relations law, "They all agree …that existing law contributes to the relative impoverishment of many women and children and that even when the rules purport to be gender-neutral, they are administered in systematically biased ways" (Carbone, 1994, p. 183). Feminists usually express cautious reservations about family legal and policy reform because they perceive U.S. history to be rife with "numerous examples of law-sanctioned discrimination against women (i.e., the right to vote, to enter all occupations, to serve on juries, to hold public office, to contract, and to conduct business)" (Weisberger, 1986, p. 205). They often point out that this discrimination also included laws that regulated poor women's family lives and social welfare through "man in the house," "midnight raid," and "illegitimacy" clauses in the enactment and implementation of welfare programs (Abramowitz, 1988; Fraser & Gordon, 1994).

With respect to family law, feminists argue that the implementation of marriage and divorce law reforms has not alleviated women's disproportionate share of child-rearing responsibilities (in or out of marriage) or their disproportionate poverty (Fraser, 1989). Some feminists point to men's exclusion from child-rearing through marital arrangements or custody awards as a significant social problem (Folbre, 1994). Feminists argue that a truly democratic society cannot be achieved without a fundamental restructuring of inequalities in gender relations in both public and private arenas, especially not without a focused effort to eliminate unequal gender socialization of children. For example, Okin (1989) asked, "How much do we want the just families that will produce the kind of citizens we need if we are ever to achieve a just society?" (p. 186). Generally, feminists want to more equitably divide the costs of divorce between women and men.

Feminist critics of covenant marriage raise important questions. Do covenant marriage laws revalorize gender-stereotypical marital roles? Is traditional religious counseling a good thing? Will covenant marriage create great difficulties for battered women trying to exit abusive relationships? Will covenant marriage adversely affect rulings on custody and support that disadvantage women? Does covenant marriage signal the beginning of a retrogression in public policy that undermines women's recent political and economic empowerment?

The views expressed by our covenant-married couples and feminists hewed closely to common public understandings. The covenant couples wholly endorsed covenant marriage by stating their interests in preserving traditional marriage and family life. The feminist activists wholly denounced covenant marriage, citing concerns about women's unfair treatment in public and private arenas throughout history. We found little, if any, convergence in their views about covenant marriage, and they even mentioned each other as political rivals. That each group's discourse about and analysis of the political and social implications of covenant marriage are so vastly different probably should not be surprising, except that both groups believe that current generations of children face harsh insecurities, both emotional and financial, and that "something should be done."

Concerning this latter point, we note a difference in how covenant couples, feminists, and public-housing residents talked about children's well-being, and we place this difference along a continuum representing "private" and "public" conceptions of political interests. The covenant couples talked at length about the importance of modeling traditional gender roles as a parental obligation and how divorce harms children permanently. They situated children's well-being centrally within the context of a two-parent married family. Covenant couples avoided talking about children within the framework of the rise of cohabitation, single parenthood, and alternative family arrangements, mentioning diverse family arrangements only obliquely through a brief reference to unwed teen motherhood and problems with the welfare state. Their discussions of children were personal, with many illustrations coloring a perspective in which children's well-being is a personal, familial matter best left to married husbands and wives and that the state only recently needed to intervene because marriage has been assailed.

On the other hand, the feminists we interviewed spoke about children largely from a more distant, macro-level perspective. They rarely offered examples from their own childhood experiences or mentioned real mothers, fathers, or children in their personal networks. Instead, they talked mainly about how societal roles—particularly roles that define women essentially as mothers—harm women, men, and children. They discussed social policies that would benefit children as a group but did not mention personal parenting practices, intentions, desires, or beliefs. The feminists wanted societal-level changes to improve children's conditions. Thus, they situated children's well-being squarely as a public domain concern, worrying less about personal, familial parenting failures (i.e., except battery and abuse) and more about spurring social equality.

As noted previously, the low-income women talked about children's well-being from both micro- and macro-level perspectives. They talked about their own childhoods, their children's lives, their children's children, and children as a political interest group. They had numerous macro-level examples of assaults to children's well-being, discussing differences in family policy in the United States and Sweden, problems facing multiracial and ethnic children throughout the world, and the social violence plaguing children via poverty. They advocated a number of political reforms to improve children's economic well-being but also felt that only strong families and loving caretakers could really assure healthy lives for children. Thus, far more clearly than either the covenant couples or feminists, they presented children's well-being as both a public- and private-domain social issue.

We do not know whether the differences in the groups' discourse about children are an artifact of our interview guide and sample selection procedures. Our focused interview asked respondents to consider the obligations and responsibilities of wives and husbands and whether divorce harms children and was therefore a social problem. Hence, both the covenant couples and feminists saw the discussion as a request to present a thumbnail sketch of their more political sensibilities about marriage reform. They may have opted to address the real division between how "family" is defined as either a public- or private-domain issue for their constituencies. The low-income women did not face this interview problem, as they were not necessarily representing a clearly defined political advocacy group. Bound less by an imperative to present a coherent political view, they were able to talk more freely about multiple views on children's well-being. Last, the covenant couples and low-income women were, by and large, older than the feminists and had more children. Many of the younger feminists were neither parents nor had very many social contacts with children. Thus, they by necessity would have offered fewer personal examples of how marriage and marriage reform affect children's well-being.

We do not wish to overdraw this latter point because at the close of their interview, several of the feminists bemoaned the feeling that they always had to talk about their political interests in a socially palatable way. In this case, they resented the expectation that women should be "natural" proponents of children's interests first and primarily, instead of their wider political

agendas. When asked what they would tell the legislature about covenant marriage, one said that she would be ignored because "I [wouldn't) know how to do it without talking about patriarchy.... I'm so tired of being a cautious feminist." And another said that though she saw marriage reform as affecting women, men, and children each in their own significant ways, she knew that she would feel obliged to advocate for children primarily "because I think they seem to listen when you talk about children rather than when you talk about women." Thus, the feminist group's comparatively smaller focus on the costs of divorce and effects of covenant marriage on children may have been associated with their choice to reflect on women's and men's societal roles, rather than react to what they see as public pressure to define women as the primary nurturers of children in public and private life. Of course, if we are correct in this assumption, their strategic choice also may reflect a very classic divide between upwardly mobile, primarily White feminists who favor expanding individual civil liberties and feminists of color and working-class feminists who want a child-centered public debate (hooks, 1984).

Our key finding is that the low-income women showed an adept facility for bridging views from both the conservative and feminist camps and for illuminating their own insights into contemporary family trends, social problems, and recommendations for legal reform. Their debates and discussions reflected a willingness to assume all positions before rejecting any argument outright. As we listened to the discussions unfold, it was hard to avoid the conclusion that legislators pay altogether too much attention to activists from across the political spectrum and far too little attention to the muted but pragmatic, and often quite eloquent, voices of ordinary men and women who can ill-afford ideological excess or political correctness as they struggle with the challenges of day-to-day existence. Our covenant couples knew from the start that covenant marriage was a good thing; our feminists knew from the start that it was not. The women in public housing could only wonder.

Whether it is a good idea or not, many conservatives will continue to promote this nascent covenant marriage movement in the near future and lobby to pass covenant marriage in other states. They will also initiate further marriage-, divorce-, and parental-law reforms designed to strengthen two-parent, heterosexual married life. For their part, a number of feminists and feminist-influenced organizations will continue to insist that divorce is not the main problem and to agitate for greater equality in intimate relationships. Based on our results, we suggest that policy analysts devise ways to bring low-income and working-class constituencies more firmly into the debate about family values; otherwise, activists on both sides of the issue will continue talking past each other well into the next century.

The Family, Kinship, and the Community

Reading 5   The Female World of Cards and Holidays: Women, Families, and the Work of Kinship[1]

MICAELA di LEONARDO*

Why is it that the married women of America are supposed to write all the letters and send all the cards to their husbands' families? My old man is a much better writer than I am, yet he expects me to correspond with his whole family. If I asked him to correspond with mine, he would blow a gasket. [LETTER TO ANN LANDERS]

Women's place in man's life cycle has been that of nurturer, caretaker, and helpmate, the weaver of those networks of relationships on which she in turn relies. [CAROL GILLIGAN, In a Different Voice][2]

Feminist scholars in the past fifteen years have made great strides in formulating new under- standings of the relations among gender, kin- ship, and the larger economy. As a result of this pioneering research, women are newly visible and audible, no longer submerged within their families. We see households as loci of political struggle, inseparable parts of the larger society and economy, rather than as havens from the heartless world of industrial capitalism.[3] And historical and cultural variations in kinship and family forms have become clearer with the maturation of feminist historical and social- scientific scholarship.

Two theoretical trends have been key to this reinterpretation of women's work and family domain. The first is the elevation to visibility of women's nonmarket activities—housework, child care, the servicing of men, and the care of the elderly—and the definition of all these activities as *labor*, to be enumerated alongside and counted

Many thanks to Cynthia Costello, Rayna Rapp, Roberta Spalter-Roth, John Willoughby, and Barbara Gelpi, Susan Johnson, and Sylvia Yanagisako of *Signs* for their help with this article. I wish in particular to acknowledge the influ- ence of Rayna Rapp's work on my ideas.

*di Leonardo, Micaela. 1987. "The Female World of Cards and Holidays: Women, Families, and the Work of Kinship."
Signs: Journal of Woman in Culture and Society (12:2):440–453. © 1987 by the University of Chicago. All rights reserved.

as part of overall social reproduction. The second theoretical trend is the nonpejorative focus on women's domestic or kin-centered networks. We now see them as the products of conscious strategy, as crucial to the functioning of kinship systems, as sources of women's autonomous power and possible primary sites of emotional fulfillment, and, at times, as the vehicles for actual survival and/or political resistance.[4]

Recently, however, a division has developed between feminist interpreters of the "labor" and the "network" perspectives on women's lives. Those who focus on women's work tend to envision women as sentient, goal-oriented actors, while those who concern themselves with women's ties to others tend to perceive women primarily in terms of nurturance, other-orientation—altruism. The most celebrated recent example of this division is the opposing testimony of historians Alice Kessler-Harris and Rosalind Rosenberg in the Equal Employment Opportunity Commission's sex discrimination case against Sears Roebuck and Company. Kessler-Harris argued that American women historically have actively sought higher-paying jobs and have been prevented from gaining them because of sex discrimination by employers. Rosenberg argued that American women in the nineteenth century created among themselves, through their domestic networks, a "women's culture" that emphasized the nurturance of children and others and the maintenance of family life and that discouraged women from competition over or heavy emotional investment in demanding, high-paid employment.[5]

I shall not here address this specific debate but, instead, shall consider its theoretical background and implications. I shall argue that we need to fuse, rather than to oppose, the domestic network and labor perspectives. In what follows, I introduce a new concept, the work of kinship, both to aid empirical feminist research on women,

work, and family and to help advance feminist theory in this arena. I believe that the boundary-crossing nature of the concept helps to confound the self-interest/altruism dichotomy, forcing us from an either-or stance to a position that includes both perspectives. I hope in this way to contribute to a more critical feminist vision of women's lives and the meaning of family in the industrial West.

In my recent field research among Italian-Americans in Northern California, I found myself considering the relations between women's kinship and economic lives. As an anthropologist, I was concerned with people's kin lives beyond conventional American nuclear family or household boundaries. To this end, I collected individual and family life histories, asking about all kin and close friends and their activities. I was also very interested in women's labor. As I sat with women and listened to their accounts of their past and present lives, I began to realize that they were involved in three types of work: housework and child care, work in the labor market, and the work of kinship.[6]

By kin work I refer to the conception, maintenance, and ritual celebration of cross-household kin ties, including visits, letters, telephone calls, presents, and cards to kin; the organization of holiday gatherings; the creation and maintenance of quasi-kin relations; decisions to neglect or to intensify particular ties; the mental work of reflection about all these activities; and the creation and communication of altering images of family and kin vis-à-vis the images of others, both folk and mass media. Kin work is a key element that has been missing in the synthesis of the "household labor" and "domestic network" perspectives. In our emphasis on individual women's responsibilities within households and on the job, we reflect the common picture of households as nuclear units, tied perhaps to the larger social and economic system, but not to *each other.* We miss the point of telephone and soft drink advertising, of women's magazines' holiday issues, of commentators' confused nostalgia for the mythical American extended family: it is kinship contact *across households,* as much as women's work within them, that fulfills our cultural expectation of satisfying family life.

Maintaining these contacts, this sense of family, takes time, intention, and skill. We tend to think of human social and kin networks as the epiphenomena of production and reproduction: the social traces created by our material lives. Or, in the neoclassical tradition, we see them as part of leisure activities, outside an economic purview except insofar as they involve consumption behavior. But the creation and maintenance of kin and quasi-kin networks in advanced industrial societies is *work;* and, moreover, it is largely women's work.

The kin-work lens brought into focus new perspectives on my informants' family lives. First, life histories revealed that often the very existence of kin contact and holiday celebration depended on the presence of an adult woman in the household. When couples divorced or mothers died, the work of kinship was left undone; when women entered into sanctioned sexual or marital relationships with men in these situations, they reconstituted the men's kinship networks and organized gatherings and holiday celebrations. Middle-aged businessman Al Bertini, for example, recalled the death of his mother in his early adolescence: "I think that's probably one of the biggest losses in losing a family—yeah, I remember as a child when my Mom was alive . . . the holidays were treated with enthusiasm and love . . . after she died the attempt was there but it just didn't materialize." Later in life, when Al Bertini and his wife separated, his own and his son Jim's participation in extended-family contact decreased rapidly. But

when Jim began a relationship with Jane Bateman, she and he moved in with Al, and Jim and Jane began to invite his kin over for holidays. Jane single-handedly planned and cooked the holiday feasts.

Kin work, then, is like housework and child care: men in the aggregate do not do it. It differs from these forms of labor in that it is harder for men to substitute hired labor to accomplish these tasks in the absence of kinswomen. Second, I found that women, as the workers in this arena, generally had much greater kin knowledge than did their husbands, often including more accurate and extensive knowledge of their husbands' families. This was true both of middle-aged and younger couples and surfaced as a phenomenon in my interviews in the form of humorous arguments and in wives' detailed additions to husbands' narratives. Nick Meraviglia, a middle-aged professional, discussed his Italian antecedents in the presence of his wife, Pina:

> *Nick:* My grandfather was a very outspoken man, and it was reported he took off for the hills when he found out that Mussolini was in power.
> *Pina:* And he was a very tall man; he used to have to bow his head to get inside doors.
> *Nick:* No, that was my uncle.
> *Pina:* Your grandfather too, I've heard your mother say.
> *Nick:* My mother has a sister and a brother.
> *Pina:* Two *sisters!*
> *Nick:* You're right!
> *Pina:* Maria and Angelina.

Women were also much more willing to discuss family feuds and crises and their own roles in them; men tended to repeat formulaic statements asserting family unity and respectability. (This was much less true for younger men.) Joe and Cetta Longhinotti's statements illustrate these tendencies. Joe responded to my question about kin relations: "We all get along. As a rule, relatives, you got nothing but trouble." Cetta, instead, discussed her relations with each of her grown children, their wives, her in-laws, and her own blood kin in detail. She did not hide the fact that relations were strained in several cases; she was eager to discuss the evolution of problems and to seek my opinions of her actions. Similarly, Pina Meraviglia told the following story of her fight with one of her brothers with hysterical laughter: "There was some biting and hair pulling and choking...it was terrible! I shouldn't even tell you...." Nick, meanwhile, was concerned about maintaining an image of family unity and respectability.

Also, men waxed fluent while women were quite inarticulate in discussing their past and present occupations. When asked about their work lives, Joe Longhinotti and Nick Meraviglia, union baker and professional, respectively, gave detailed narratives of their work careers. Cetta Longhinotti and Pina Meraviglia, clerical and former clerical, respectively, offered only short descriptions focusing on factors of ambience, such as the "lovely things" sold by Cetta's firm.

These patterns are not repeated in the younger generation, especially among younger women, such as Jane Bateman, who have managed to acquire training and jobs with some prospect of mobility. These younger women, though, have *added* a professional and detailed interest in their jobs to a felt responsibility for the work of kinship.[7]

Although men rarely took on any kin-work tasks, family histories and accounts of contemporary life revealed that kinswoman often negotiated among themselves, alternating hosting, food-preparation, and gift-buying responsibilities—or sometimes ceding entire task clusters to one woman. Taking on or ceding tasks was clearly related to acquiring or divesting oneself of power within kin networks, but women varied in their interpretation of the meaning of this power. Cetta Longhinotti, for example, relied on the "family Christmas dinner" as a symbol of her central kinship role and was involved in painful negotiations with her daughter-in-law over the issue: "Last year she insisted—this is touchy. She doesn't want to spend the holiday dinner together. So last year we went there. But I still had my dinner the next day...I made a big dinner on Christmas Day, regardless of who's coming—candles on the table, the whole routine. I decorate the house myself too...well, I just feel that the time will come when maybe I won't feel like cooking a big dinner—she should take advantage of the fact that I feel like doing it now." Pina Meraviglia, in contrast, was saddened by the centripetal force of the developmental cycle but was unworried about the power dynamics involved in her negotiations with daughters- and mother-in-law over holiday celebrations.

Kin work is not just a matter of power among women but also of the mediation of power represented by household units.[8] Women often choose to minimize status claims in their kin work and to include numbers of households under the rubric of family. Cetta Longhinotti's sister Anna, for example, is married to a professional man whose parents have considerable economic resources, while Joe and Cetta have low incomes and no other well-off kin. Cetta and Anna remain close, talk on the phone several times a week, and assist their adult children, divided by distance and economic status, in remaining united as cousins.

Finally, women perceived housework, child care, market labor, the care of the elderly, and the work of kinship as competing responsibilities. Kin work was a unique category, however, because it was unlabeled and because women felt they could either cede some tasks to kinswoman and/or could cut them back severely. Women variously cited the pressures of market labor, the needs of the elderly, and their own desires for freedom and job enrichment as reasons for cutting back Christmas card lists, organized holiday gatherings, multifamily dinners, letters, visits, and phone calls. They expressed guilt and defensiveness about this cutback process and, particularly, about their failures to keep families close through constant contact and about their failures to create perfect holiday celebrations. Cetta Longhinotti, during the period when she was visiting her elderly mother every weekend in addition to working a full-time job, said of her grown children, "I'd have the whole gang here once a month, but I've been so busy that I haven't done that for about six months." And Pina Meriviglia lamented her insufficient work on family Christmases, "I wish I had really made it traditional . . . like my sister-in-law has special stories."

Kin work, then, takes place in an arena characterized simultaneously by cooperation and competition, by guilt and gratification. Like housework and child care, it is women's work, with the same lack of clear-cut agreement concerning its proper components: How often should sheets be changed? When should children be toilet trained? Should an aunt send a niece a birthday present? Unlike housework and child care, however, kin work, taking place across the boundaries of normative households, is as yet unlabeled and has no retinue of experts prescribing its correct forms. Neither home economists nor child psychologists have much to say about nieces' birthday presents. Kin work is thus more easily cut back without social interference. On the other hand, the results of kin work—frequent kin contact and feelings of intimacy—are the subject of considerable cultural manipulation as

indicators of family happiness. Thus, women in general are subject to the guilt my informants expressed over cutting back kin-work activities.

Although many of my informants referred to the results of women's kin work—cross-household kin contacts and attendant ritual gatherings—as particularly Italian-American, I suggest that in fact this phenomenon is broadly characteristic of American kinship. We think of kin-work tasks such as the preparation of ritual feasts, responsibility for holiday card lists, and gift buying as extensions of women's domestic responsibilities for cooking, consumption, and nurturance. American men in general do not take on these tasks any more than they do housework and child care—and probably less, as these tasks have not yet been the subject of intense public debate. And my informants' gender breakdown in relative articulateness on kinship and workplace themes reflects the still prevalent occupational segregation—most women cannot find jobs that provide enough pay, status, or promotion possibilities to make them worth focusing on—as well as women's perceived power within kinship networks. The common recognition of that power is reflected in Selma Greenberg's book on nonsexist child rearing. Greenberg calls mothers "press agents" who sponsor relations between their own children and other relatives; she advises a mother whose relatives treat her disrespectfully to deny those kin access to her children.[9]

Kin work is a salient concept in other parts of the developed world as well. Larissa Adler Lomnitz and Marisol Pérez Lizaur have found that "centralizing women" are responsible for these tasks and for communicating "family ideology" among upper-class families in Mexico City. Matthews Hamabata, in his study of upper-class families in Japan, has found that women's kin work involves key financial transactions. Sylvia Junko Yanagisako discovered that, among rural Japanese migrants to the United States, the maintenance of kin networks was assigned to women as the migrants adopted the American ideology of the independent nuclear family household. Maila Stivens notes that urban Australian housewives' kin ties and kin ideology "transcend women's isolation in domestic units."[10]

This is not to say that cultural conceptions of appropriate kin work do not vary, even within the United States. Carol B. Stack documents institutionalized fictive kinship and concomitant reciprocity networks among impoverished black American women. Women in populations characterized by intense feelings of ethnic identity may feel bound to emphasize particular occasions—Saint Patrick's or Columbus Day—with organized family feasts. These constructs may be mediated by religious affiliation, as in the differing emphases on Friday or Sunday family dinners among Jews and Christians. Thus the personnel involved and the amount and kind of labor considered necessary for the satisfactory performance of particular kin-work tasks are likely to be culturally constructed.[11] But while the kin and quasi-kin universes and the ritual calendar may vary among women according to race or ethnicity, their general responsibility for maintaining kin links and ritual observances does not.

As kin work is not an ethnic or racial phenomenon, neither is it linked only to one social class. Some commentators on American family life still reflect the influence of work done in England in the 1950s and 1960s (by Elizabeth Bott and by Peter Willmott and Michael Young) in their assumption that working-class families are close and extended, while the middle class substitutes friends (or anomie) for family. Others reflect the prevalent family pessimism in their presumption that neither working- nor middle-class families have extended kin contact.[12] Insofar as kin contact depends on residential proxim-

ity, the larger economy's shifts will influence particular groups' experiences. Factory workers, close to kin or not, are likely to disperse when plants shut down or relocate. Small businesspeople or independent professionals may, however, remain resident in particular areas—and thus maintain proximity to kin—for generations, while professional employees of large firms relocate at their firms' behest. This pattern obtained among my informants.

In any event, cross-household kin contact can be and is effected at long distance through letters, cards, phone calls, and holiday and vacation visits. The form and functions of contact, however, vary according to economic resources. Stack and Brett Williams offer rich accounts of kin networks among poor blacks and migrant Chicano farmworkers functioning to provide emotional support, labor, commodity, and cash exchange—a funeral visit, help with laundry, the gift of a dress or piece of furniture.[13] Far different in degree are exchanges such as the loan of a vacation home, multifamily boating trip, or the provision of free professional services—examples from the kin networks of my wealthier informants. The point is that households, as labor- and income-pooling units, whatever their relative wealth, are somewhat porous in relation to others with those whose members they share kin or quasi-kin ties. We do not really know how class differences operate in this realm; it is possible that they do so largely in terms of ideology. It may be, as David Schneider and Raymond T. Smith suggest, that the affluent and the very poor are more open in recognizing necessary economic ties to kin than are those who identify themselves as middle class.[14]

Recognizing that kin work is gender rather than class based allows us to see women's kin networks among all groups, not just among working-class and impoverished women in industrialized societies. This recognition in turn clarifies our understanding of the privileges and limits of women's varying access to economic resources. Affluent women can "buy out" of housework, child care—and even some kin-work responsibilities. But they, like all women, are ultimately responsible, and subject to both guilt and blame, as the administrators of home, children, and kin network. Even the wealthiest women must negotiate the timing and venue of holidays and other family rituals with their kins-woman. It may be that kin work is the core women's work category in which all women cooperate, while women's perceptions of the appropriateness of cooperation for housework, child care, and the care of the elderly varies by race, class, region, and generation.

But kin work is not necessarily an appropriate category of labor, much less gendered labor, in all societies. In many small-scale societies, kinship is the major organizing principle of all social life, and all contacts are by definition kin contacts.[15] One cannot, therefore, speak of labor that does not involve kin. In the United States, kin work as a separable category of gendered labor perhaps arose historically in concert with the ideological and material constructs of the moral mother/cult of domesticity and the privatized family during the course of industrialization in the eighteenth and nineteenth centuries. These phenomena are connected to the increase in the ubiquity of productive occupations *for men* that are not organized through kinship. This includes the demise of the family farm with the capitalization of agriculture and rural-urban migration; the decline of family recruitment in factories as firms grew, ended child labor, and began to assert bureaucratized forms of control; the decline of artisanal labor and of small entrepreneurial enterprises as large firms took greater and greater shares of the commodity market; the decline of the family firm as corporations—and their managerial work forces—grew beyond the capacities of individual families to provision them; and, finally, the rise of civil service bureaucracies and public pressure against nepotism.[16]

As men increasingly worked alongside of non-kin, and as the ideology of separate spheres was increasingly accepted, perhaps the responsibility for kin maintenance, like that for child rearing, became gender-focused. Ryan points out that "built into the updated family economy ... was a new measure of voluntarism." This voluntarism, though, "perceived as the shift from patriarchal authority to domestic affection," also signaled the rise of women's moral responsibility for family life. Just as the "idea of fatherhood itself seemed almost to wither away" so did male involvement in the responsibility for kindred lapse.[17]

With postbellum economic growth and geographic movement women's new kin burden involved increasing amounts of time and labor. The ubiquity of lengthy visits and of frequent letter-writing among nineteenth-century women attests to this. And for visitors and for those who were residentially proximate, the continuing commonalities of women's domestic labor allowed for kinds of work sharing—nursing, childkeeping, cooking, cleaning—that men, with their increasingly differentiated and controlled activities, probably could not maintain. This is not to say that some kin-related male productive work did not continue; my own data, for instance, show kin involvement among small businessmen in the present. It is, instead, to suggest a general trend in material life and a cultural shift that influenced even those whose productive and kin lives remained commingled. Yanagisako has distinguished between the realms of domestic and public kinship in order to draw attention to anthropology's relatively "thin descriptions" of the domestic (female) domain. Using her typology, we might say that kin work as gendered labor comes into existence within the domestic domain with the relative erasure of the domain of public, male kinship.[18]

Whether or not this proposed historical model bears up under further research, the question remains, Why do women do kin work? However material factors may shape activities, they do not determine how individuals may perceive them. And in considering issues of motivation, of intention, of the cultural construction of kin work, we return to the altruism versus self-interest dichotomy in recent feminist theory. Consider the epigraphs to this article. Are women kin workers the nurturant weavers of the Gilligan quotation, or victims, like the fed-up woman who writes to complain to Ann Landers? That is, are we to see kin work as yet another example of "women's culture" that takes the care of others as its primary desideratum? Or are we to see kin work as another way in which men, the economy, and the state extract labor from women without a fair return? And how do women themselves see their kin work and its place in their lives?

As I have indicated above, I believe that it is the creation of the self-interest/altruism dichotomy that is itself the problem here. My women informants, like most American women, accepted their primary responsibility for housework and the care of dependent children. Despite two major waves of feminist activism in this century, the gendering of certain categories of unpaid labor is still largely unaltered. These work responsibilities clearly interfere with some women's labor force commitments at certain life-cycle stages; but, more important, women are simply discriminated against in the labor market and rarely are able to achieve wage and status parity with men of the same age, race, class, and educational background.[19]

Thus for my women informants, as for most American women, the domestic domain is not only an arena in which much unpaid labor

must be undertaken but also a realm in which one may attempt to gain human satisfactions—and power—not available in the labor market. Anthropologists Jane Collier and Louise Lamphere have written compellingly on the ways in which varying kinship and economic structures may shape women's competition or cooperation with one another in domestic domains.[20] Feminists considering Western women and families have looked at the issue of power primarily in terms of husband-wife relations or psychological relations between parents and children. If we adopt Collier and Lamphere's broader canvas, though, we see that kin work is not only women's labor from which men and children benefit but also labor that women undertake in order to create obligations in men and children and to gain power over one another. Thus Cetta Longhinotti's struggle with her daughter-in-law over the venue of Christmas dinner is not just about a competition over altruism, it is also about the creation of future obligations. And thus Cetta's and Anna's sponsorship of their children's friendship with each other is both an act of nurturance and a cooperative means of gaining power over those children.

Although this was not a clear-cut distinction, those of my informants who were more explicitly antifeminist tended to be most invested in kin work. Given the overwhelming historical shift toward greater autonomy for younger generations and the withering of children's financial and labor obligations to their parents, this investment was in most cases tragically doomed. Cetta Longhinotti, for example, had repaid her own mother's devotion with extensive home nursing during the mother's last years. Given Cetta's general failure to direct her adult children in work, marital choice, religious worship, or even frequency of visits, she is unlikely to receive such care from them when she is older.

The kin-work lens thus reveals the close relations between altruism and self-interest in women's actions. As economists Nancy Folbre and Heidi Hartmann point out, we have inherited a Western intellectual tradition that both dichotomizes the domestic and public domains and associates them on exclusive axes such that we find it difficult to see self-interest in the home and altruism in the workplace.[21] But why, in fact, have women fought for better jobs if not, in part, to support their children? These dichotomies are Procrustean beds that warp our understanding of women's lives both at home and at work. "Altruism" and "self-interest" are cultural constructions that are not necessarily mutually exclusive, and we forget this to our peril.

The concept of kin work helps to bring into focus a heretofore unacknowledged array of tasks that is culturally assigned to women in industrialized societies. At the same time, this concept, embodying notions of both love and work and crossing the boundaries of households, helps us to reflect on current feminist debates on women's work, family, and community. We newly see both the interrelations of these phenomena and women's roles in creating and maintaining those interrelations. Revealing the actual labor embodied in what we culturally conceive as love and considering the political uses of this labor helps to deconstruct the self-interest/altruism dichotomy and to connect more closely women's domestic and labor-force lives.

The true value of the concept, however, remains to be tested through further historical and contemporary research on gender, kinship, and labor. We need to assess the suggestion that gendered kin work emerges in concert with the capitalist development process; to probe the historical record for women's and men's varying and changing conceptions of it; and to research the current range of its cultural constructions and material realities. We know that household boundaries are more porous than we had thought—but they are undoubtedly differentially porous, and this is what we need to specify. We need, in particular, to assess the relations of changing labor processes, residential patterns, and the use of technology to changing kin work.

Altering the values attached to this particular set of women's tasks will be as difficult as are the housework, child-care, and occupational-segregation struggles. But just as feminist research in these latter areas is complementary and cumulative, so researching kin work should help us to piece together the home, work, and public-life landscape—to see the female world of cards and holidays as it is constructed and lived within the changing political economy. How female that world is to remain, and what it would look like if it were not sex-segregated, are questions we cannot yet answer.

Reading 6   Mexican American Women Grassroots Community Activists: "Mothers of East Los Angeles"

MARY PARDO*

The relatively few studies of Chicana political activism show a bias in the way political activism is conceptualized by social scientists, who often use a narrow definition confined to electoral politics.[1] Most feminist research uses an expanded definition that moves across the boundaries between public, electoral politics and private, family politics; but feminist research generally focuses on women mobilized around gender-specific issues.[2] For some feminists, adherence to "tradition" constitutes conservatism and submission to patriarchy. Both approaches exclude the contributions of working-class women, particularly those of Afro-American women and Latinas, thus failing to capture the full dynamic of social change.[3]

The following case study of Mexican American women activists in "Mothers of East Los Angeles" (MELA) contributes another dimension to the conception of grassroots politics. It illustrates how these Mexican American women transform "traditional" networks and resources based on family and culture into political assets to defend the quality of urban life. Far from unique, these patterns of activism are repeated in Latin America and elsewhere. Here as in other times and places, the women's activism arises out of seemingly "traditional" roles, addresses wider social and political issues, and capitalizes on informal associations sanctioned by the community.[4] Religion, commonly viewed as a conservative force, is intertwined with politics.[5] Often, women speak of their communities and their activism as extensions of their family and household responsibility. The central role of women in grassroots struggles around quality of life, in the Third World and in the United States, challenges conventional assumptions about the powerlessness of women and static definitions of culture and tradition.

In general, the women in MELA are long-time residents of East Los Angeles; some are bilingual and native born, others Mexican born and Spanish dominant. All the core activists are bilingual and have lived in the community over thirty years. All have been active in parish-sponsored groups and activities; some have had experience working in community-based groups arising from schools, neighborhood watch associations, and labor support groups. To gain an appreciation of the group and the core activists, I used ethnographic field methods. I interviewed

*Pardo, Mary. 1990. "Mexican American Women Grassroots Community Activists: 'Mothers of East Los Angeles.'" *Frontiers* 11 (1):1–7. FRONTIERS Editorial Collective. Reprinted by permission.

six women, using a life history approach focused on their first community activities, current activism, household and family responsibilities, and perceptions of community issues.[6] Also, from December 1987 through October 1989, I attended hearings on the two currently pending projects of contention—a proposed state prison and a toxic waste incinerator—and participated in community and organizational meetings and demonstrations. The following discussion briefly chronicles an intense and significant five-year segment of community history from which emerged MELA and the women's transformation of "traditional" resources and experiences into political assets for community mobilization.[7]

THE COMMUNITY CONTEXT: EAST LOS ANGELES RESISTING SIEGE

Political science theory often guides the political strategies used by local government to select the sites for undesirable projects. In 1984, the state of California commissioned a public relations firm to assess the political difficulties facing the construction of energy-producing waste incinerators. The report provided a "personality profile" of those residents most likely to organize effective opposition to projects:

> *middle and upper socioeconomic strata possess better resources to effectuate their opposition. Middle and higher socioeconomic strata neighborhoods should not fall within the one-mile and five-mile radii of the proposed site. Conversely, older people, people with a high school education or less are least likely to oppose a facility.*[8]

The state accordingly placed the plant in Commerce, a predominantly Mexican American,

low-income community. This pattern holds throughout the state and the country: three out of five Afro-Americans and Latinos live near toxic waste sites, and three of the five largest hazardous waste landfills are in communities with at least 80 percent minority populations.[9]

Similarly, in March 1985, when the state sought a site for the first state prison in Los Angeles County, Governor Deukmejian resolved to place the 1,700-inmate institution in East Los Angeles, within a mile of the long-established Boyle Heights neighborhood and within two miles of thirty-four schools. Furthermore, violating convention, the state bid on the expensive parcel of industrially zoned land without compiling an environmental impact report or providing a public community hearing. According to James Vigil, Jr., a field representative for Assemblywoman Gloria Molina, shortly after the state announced the site selection, Molina's office began informing the community and gauging residents' sentiments about it through direct mailings and calls to leaders of organizations and business groups.

In spring 1986, after much pressure from the 56th assembly district office and the community, the Department of Corrections agreed to hold a public information meeting, which was attended by over 700 Boyle Heights residents. From this moment on, Vigil observed, "the tables turned, the community mobilized, and the residents began calling the political representatives and requesting their presence at hearings and meetings."[10] By summer 1986, the community was well aware of the prison site proposal. Over two thousand people, carrying placards proclaiming "No Prison in ELA," marched from Resurrection Church in Boyle Heights to the 3rd Street bridge linking East Los Angeles with the rapidly expanding downtown Los Angeles.[11] This march marked the beginning of one of the largest grassroots coalitions to emerge from the Latino community in the last decade.

Prominent among the coalition's groups is "Mothers of East Los Angeles," a loosely knit group of over 400 Mexican American women.[12] MELA initially coalesced to oppose the state prison construction but has since organized opposition to several other projects detrimental to the quality of life in the central city.[13] Its second large target is a toxic waste incinerator proposed for Vernon, a small city adjacent to East Los Angeles. This incinerator would worsen the already debilitating air quality of the entire county and set a precedent dangerous for other communities throughout California.[14] When MELA took up the fight against the toxic waste incinerator it became more than a single-issue group and began working with environmental groups around the state.[15] As a result of the community struggle, AB58 (Roybal-Allard), which provides all Californians with the minimum protection of an environmental impact report before the construction of hazardous waste incinerators, was signed into law. But the law's effectiveness relies on a watchful community network. Since its emergence, "Mothers of East Los Angeles" has become centrally important to just such a network of grassroots activists including a select number of Catholic priests and two Mexican American political representatives. Furthermore, the group's very formation, and its continued spirit and activism, fly in the face of the conventional political science beliefs regarding political participation.

Predictions by the "experts" attribute the low formal political participation (i.e., voting) of Mexican American people in the U.S. to a set of cultural "retardants" including primary kinship systems, fatalism, religious traditionalism, traditional cultural values, and mother country attachments.[16] The core activists in MELA may appear to fit this description, as well as the state-commissioned profile of residents least likely to oppose toxic waste incinerator projects. All the women live in a low-income community. Furthermore, they identify themselves as active and committed participants in the Catholic Church; they claim an ethnic identity—Mexican American; their ages range from forty to sixty; and they have attained at most high school educations. However, these women fail to conform to the predicted political apathy. Instead, they have transformed social identity—ethnic identity, class identity, and gender identity—into an impetus as well as a basis for activism. And, in transforming their existing social networks into grassroots political networks, they have also transformed themselves.

TRANSFORMATION AS A DOMINANT THEME

From the life histories of the group's core activists and from my own field notes, I have selected excerpts that tell two representative stories. One is a narrative of the events that led to community mobilization in East Los Angeles. The other is a story of transformation, the process of creating new and better relationships that empower people to unite and achieve common goals.[17]

First, women have transformed organizing experiences and social networks arising from gender-related responsibilities into political resources.[18] When I asked the women about the first community, not necessarily "political," involvement they could recall, they discussed experiences that predated the formation of MELA. Juana Gutiérrez explained:

Well, it didn't start with the prison, you know. It started when my kids went to school. I started by joining the Parents Club and we worked on different problems here in the area. Like the people who come to the parks to sell drugs to the kids. I got the neighbors to have meetings. I would go knock at the doors, house to house. And I told them that we should stick together with the Neighborhood Watch for the community and for the kids.[19]

Erlinda Robles similarly recalled:

I wanted my kids to go to Catholic school and from the time my oldest one went there, I was there every day. I used to take my two little ones with me and I helped one way or another. I used to question things they did. And the other mothers would just watch me. Later, they would ask me, "Why do you do that? They are going to take it out on your kids." I'd say, "They better not." And before you knew it, we had a big group of mothers that were very involved.[20]

Part of a mother's "traditional" responsibility includes overseeing her child's progress in school, interacting with school staff, and supporting school activities. In these processes, women meet other mothers and begin developing a network of acquaintanceships and friendships based on mutual concern for the welfare of their children.

Although the women in MELA carried the greatest burden of participating in school activities, Erlinda Robles also spoke of strategies they used to draw men into the enterprise and into the networks:[21]

At the beginning, the priests used to say who the president of the mothers guild would be; they used to pick

'um. But, we wanted elections, so we got elections. Then we wanted the fathers to be involved, and the nuns suggested that a father should be president and a mother would be secretary or be involved there [at the school site].[22]

Of course, this comment piqued my curiosity, so I asked how the mothers agreed on the nuns' suggestion. The answer was simple and instructive:

At the time we thought it was a "natural" way to get the fathers involved because they weren't involved; it was just the mothers. Everybody [the women] agreed on them [the fathers] being president because they worked all day and they couldn't be involved in a lot of daily activities like food sales and whatever. During the week, a steering committee of mothers planned the group's activities. But now that I think about it, a woman could have done the job just as well![23]

So women got men into the group by giving them a position they could manage. The men may have held the title of "president," but they were not making day-to-day decisions about work, nor were they dictating the direction of the group. Erlinda Robles laughed as she recalled an occasion when the president insisted, against the wishes of the women, on scheduling a parents' group fundraiser—a breakfast—on Mother's Day. On that morning, only the president and his wife were present to prepare breakfast. This should alert researchers against measuring power and influence by looking solely at who holds titles.

Each of the cofounders had a history of working with groups arising out of the responsibilities usually assumed by "mothers"—the education of children and the safety of the surrounding community. From these groups, they gained valuable experiences and networks that facilitated the formation of "Mothers of East Los Angeles." Juana Gutiérrez explained how preexisting networks progressively expanded community support:

> You know nobody knew about the plan to build a prison in this community until Assemblywoman Gloria Molina told me. Martha Molina called me and said, "You know what is happening in your area? The governor wants to put a prison in Boyle Heights!" So, I called a Neighborhood Watch meeting at my house and we got fifteen people together. Then, Father John started informing his people at the Church and that is when the group of two to three hundred started showing up for every march on the bridge.[24]

MELA effectively linked up preexisting networks into a viable grassroots coalition.

Second, the process of activism also transformed previously "invisible" women, making them not only visible but the center of public attention. From a conventional perspective, political activism assumes a kind of gender neutrality. This means that anyone can participate, but men are the expected key actors. In accordance with this pattern, in winter 1986 an informal group of concerned businessmen in the community began lobbying and testifying against the prison at hearings in Sacramento. Working in conjunction with Assemblywoman Molina, they

made many trips to Sacramento at their own expense. Residents who did not have the income to travel were unable to join them. Finally, Molina, commonly recognized as a forceful advocate for Latinas and the community, asked Frank Villalobos, an urban planner in the group, why there were no women coming up to speak in Sacramento against the prison. As he phrased it, "I was getting some heat from her because no women were going up there."[25]

In response to this comment, Veronica Gutiérrez, a law student who lived in the community, agreed to accompany him on the next trip to Sacramento.[26] He also mentioned the comment to Father John Moretta at Resurrection Catholic Parish. Meanwhile, representatives of the business sector of the community and of the 56th assembly district office were continuing to compile arguments and supportive data against the East Los Angeles prison site. Frank Villalobos stated one of the pressing problems:

> We felt that the Senators whom we prepared all this for didn't even acknowledge that we existed. They kept calling it the "downtown" site, and they argued that there was no opposition in the community. So, I told Father Moretta, what we have to do is demonstrate that there is a link (proximity) between the Boyle Heights community and the prison.[27]

The next juncture illustrates how perceptions of gender-specific behavior set in motion a sequence of events that brought women into the political limelight. Father Moretta decided to ask all the women to meet after mass. He told them about the prison site and called for their support. When I asked him about his rationale for selecting the women, he replied:

I felt so strongly about the issue, and I knew in my heart what a terrible offense this was to the people. So, I was afraid that once we got into a demonstration situation we had to be very careful. I thought the women would be cooler and calmer than the men. The bottom line is that the men came anyway. The first times out the majority were women. Then they began to invite their husbands and their children, but originally it was just women.[28]

Father Moretta also named the group. Quite moved by a film, *The Official Story,* about the courageous Argentine women who demonstrated for the return of their children who disappeared during a repressive right-wing military dictatorship, he transformed the name "Las Madres de la Plaza de Mayo" into "Mothers of East Los Angeles."[29]

However, Aurora Castillo, one of the cofounders of the group, modified my emphasis on the predominance of women:

Of course the fathers work. We also have many, many grandmothers. And all this is with the support of the fathers. They make the placards and the posters; they do the security and carry the signs; and they come to the marches when they can.[30]

Although women played a key role in the mobilization, they emphasized the group's broad base of active supporters as well as the other organizations in the "Coalition Against the Prison." Their intent was to counter any notion that MELA was composed exclusively of women or mothers and to stress the "inclusiveness" of the group. All the women who assumed lead roles in the group had long histories of volunteer work in the Boyle Heights community; but formation of the group brought them out of the "private" margins and into "public" light.

Third, the women in "Mothers of East L.A." have transformed the definition of "mother" to include militant political opposition to state-proposed projects they see as adverse to the quality of life in the community. Explaining how she discovered the issue, Aurora Castillo said,

You know if one of your children's safety is jeopardized, the mother turns into a lioness. That's why Father John got the mothers. We have to have a well-organized, strong group of mothers to protect the community and oppose things that are detrimental to us. You know the governor is in the wrong and the mothers are in the right. After all, the mothers have to be right. Mothers are for the children's interest, not for self-interest; the governor is for his own political interest.[31]

The women also have expanded the boundaries of "motherhood" to include social and political community activism and redefined the word to include women who are not biological "mothers." At one meeting a young Latina expressed her solidarity with the group and, almost apologetically, qualified herself as a "resident," not a "mother," of East Los Angeles. Erlinda Robles replied:

When you are fighting for a better life for children and "doing" for them, isn't that what mothers do? So we're all mothers. You don't have to have children to be a "mother."[32]

At critical points, grassroots community activism requires attending many meetings, phone calling, and door-to-door communications—all very labor-intensive work. In order to keep harmony in the "domestic" sphere, the core activists must creatively integrate family members into their community activities. I asked Erlinda Robles how her husband felt about her activism, and she replied quite openly:

> My husband doesn't like getting involved, but he takes me because he knows I like it. Sometimes we would have two or three meetings a week. And my husband would say, "Why are you doing so much? It is really getting out of hand." But he is very supportive. Once he gets there, he enjoys it and he starts in arguing too! See, it's just that he is not used to it. He couldn't believe things happened the way that they do. He was in the Navy twenty years and they brainwashed him that none of the politicians could do wrong. So he has come a long way. Now he comes home and parks the car out front and asks me, "Well, where are we going tonight?"[33]

When women explain their activism, they link family and community as one entity. Juana Gutiérrez, a woman with extensive experience working on community and neighborhood issues, stated:

> Yo como madre de familia, y como residente del Este de Los Angeles, seguiré luchando sin descanso por que se nos respete. Y yo lo hago con bastante cariño hacia mi comunidad. Digo "mi comunidad," porque me siento parte de ella, quiero a mi raza como parte de mi familia, y si Dios me permite seguiré luchando contra todos los gobernadores que quieran abusar de nosotros. (As a mother and a resident of East L.A., I shall continue fighting tirelessly, so we will be respected. And I will do this with much affection for my community. I say "my community" because I am part of it. I love my "raza" [race] as part of my family; and if God allows, I will keep on fighting against all the governors that want to take advantage of us.)[34]

Like the other activists, she has expanded her responsibilities and legitimated militant opposition to abuse of the community by representatives of the state.

Working-class women activists seldom opt to separate themselves from men and their families. In this particular struggle for community quality of life, they are fighting for the family unit and thus are not competitive with men.[35] Of course, this fact does not preclude different alignments in other contexts and situations.[36]

Fourth, the story of MELA also shows the transformation of class and ethnic identity. Aurora Castillo told of an incident that illustrated her growing knowledge of the relationship of East Los Angeles to other communities and the basis necessary for coalition building:

> And do you know we have been approached by other groups? [She lowers her voice in emphasis.] You know that Pacific Palisades group asked for our backing. But what they did, they sent their powerful lobbyist that they pay thousands of dollars to

get our support against the drilling in Pacific Palisades. So what we did was tell them to send their grassroots people, not their lobbyist. We're suspicious. We don't want to talk to a high-salaried lobbyist; we are humble people. We did our own lobbying. In one week we went to Sacramento twice.[37]

The contrast between the often tedious and labor-intensive work of mobilizing people at the "grassroots" level and the paid work of a "high salaried lobbyist" represents a point of pride and integrity, not a deficiency or a source of shame. If the two groups were to construct a coalition, they must communicate on equal terms.

The women of MELA combine a willingness to assert opposition with a critical assessment of their own weaknesses. At one community meeting, for example, representatives of several oil companies attempted to gain support for placement of an oil pipeline through the center of East Los Angeles. The exchange between the women in the audience and the oil representative was heated, as women alternated asking questions about the chosen route for the pipeline:

"Is it going through Cielito Lindo [Reagan's ranch]?" The oil representative answered, "No." Another woman stood up and asked, "Why not place it along the coastline?" Without thinking of the implications, the representative responded, "Oh, no! If it burst, it would endanger the marine life." The woman retorted, "You value the marine life more than human beings?" His face reddened with anger and the hearing disintegrated into angry chanting.[38]

The proposal was quickly defeated. But Aurora Castillo acknowledged that it was not solely their opposition that brought about the defeat:

We won because the westside was opposed to it, so we united with them. You know there are a lot of attorneys who live there and they also questioned the representative. Believe me, no way is justice blind.... We just don't want all this garbage thrown at us because we are low-income and Mexican American. We are lucky now that we have good representatives, which we didn't have before.[39]

Throughout their life histories, the women refer to the disruptive effects of land use decisions made in the 1950s. As longtime residents, all but one share the experience of losing a home and relocating to make way for a freeway. Juana Gutiérrez refers to the community response at that time:

Una de las cosas que me caen muy mal es la injusticia y en nuestra comunidad hemos visto mucho de eso. Sobre todo antes, porque creo que nuestra gente estaba mas dormida, nos atrevíamos menos. En los cincuentas hicieron los freeways y así, sin más, nos dieron la noticia de que nos teníamos que mudar. Y eso pasó dos veces. La gente se conformaba porque lo ordeno el gobierno. Recuerdo que yo me enojaba y quería que los demás me secundaran, pero nadia quería hacer nada. (One of the things that really upsets me is the injustice that we see so much in our community. Above everything else, I believe that our people were less aware; we were less challenging. In the 1950s—they made the freeways and just like that they gave us a notice that we had to move. That happened twice. The people accepted it because the government ordered it. I remember that I was angry and wanted the others to back me but nobody else wanted to do anything.)[40]

The freeways that cut through communities and disrupted neighborhoods are now a concrete reminder of shared injustice, of the vulnerability of the community in the 1950s. The community's social and political history thus informs perceptions of its current predicament; however, today's activists emphasize not the powerlessness of the community but the change in status and progression toward political empowerment.

Fifth, the core activists typically tell stories illustrating personal change and a new sense of entitlement to speak for the community. They have transformed the unspoken sentiments of individuals into a collective community voice. Lucy Ramos related her initial apprehensions:

I was afraid to get involved. I didn't know what was going to come out of this and I hesitated at first. Right after we started, Father John came up to me and told me, "I want you to be a spokesperson." I said, "Oh no, I don't know what I am going to say." I was nervous. I am surprised I didn't have a nervous breakdown then. Every time we used to get in front of the TV cameras and even interviews like this, I used to sit there and I could feel myself shaking. But as time went on, I started getting used to it.

And this is what I have noticed with a lot of them. They were afraid to speak up and say anything. Now, with this prison issue, a lot of them have come out and come forward and given their opinions. Everybody used to be real "quietlike."[41]

She also related a situation that brought all her fears to a climax, which she confronted and resolved as follows:

When I first started working with the coalition, Channel 13 called me up and said they wanted to interview me and I said OK. Then I started getting nervous. So I called Father John and told him, "You better get over here right away." He said, "Don't worry, don't worry, you can handle it by yourself." Then Channel 13 called me back and said they were going to interview another person, someone I had never heard of, and asked if it was OK if he came to my house. And I said OK again. Then I began thinking, what if this guy is for the prison? What am I going to do? And I was so nervous and I thought, I know what I am going to do!

Since the meeting was taking place in her home, she reasoned that she was entitled to order any troublemakers out of her domain:

If this man tells me anything, I am just going to chase him out of my house. That is what I am going to do! All these thoughts were going through my head. Then Channel 13 walk into my house followed by six men I had never met. And I thought,

Oh, my God, what did I get myself into? I kept saying to myself, if they get smart with me I am throwing them ALL out.[42]

At this point her tone expressed a sense of resolve. In fact, the situation turned out to be neither confrontational nor threatening, as the "other men" were also members of the coalition. This woman confronted an anxiety-laden situation by relying on her sense of control within her home and family—a quite "traditional" source of authority for women—and transforming that control into the courage to express a political position before a potential audience all over one of the largest metropolitan areas in the nation.

People living in Third World countries as well as in minority communities in the United States face an increasingly degraded environment.[43] Recognizing the threat to the well-being of their families, residents have mobilized at the neighborhood level to fight for "quality of life" issues. The common notion that environmental well-being is of concern solely to white middle-class and upper-class residents ignores the specific way working-class neighborhoods suffer from the fallout of the city "growth machine" geared for profit.[44]

In Los Angeles, the culmination of postwar urban renewal policies, the growing Pacific Rim trade surplus and investment, and low-wage international labor migration from Third World countries are creating potentially volatile conditions. Literally palatial financial buildings swallow up the space previously occupied by modest, low-cost housing. Increasing density and development not matched by investment in social programs, services, and infrastructure erode the quality of life, beginning in the core of the city.[45] Latinos, the majority of whom live close to the center of the city, must confront the distilled social consequences of development

focused solely on profit. The Mexican American community in East Los Angeles, much like other minority working-class communities, has been a repository for prisons instead of new schools, hazardous industries instead of safe work sites, and one of the largest concentrations of freeway interchanges in the country, which transports much wealth past the community. And the concerns of residents in East Los Angeles may provide lessons for other minority as well as middle-class communities. Increasing environmental pollution resulting from inadequate waste disposal plans and an out-of-control "need" for penal institutions to contain the casualties created by the growing bipolar distribution of wages may not be limited to the Southwest.[46] These conditions set the stage for new conflicts and new opportunities, to reform old relationships into coalitions that can challenge state agendas and create new community visions.[47]

Mexican American women living east of downtown Los Angeles exemplify the tendency of women to enter into environmental struggles in defense of their community. Women have a rich historical legacy of community activism, partly reconstructed over the last two decades in social histories of women who contested other "quality of life issues," from the price of bread to "Demon Rum" (often representing domestic violence).[48]

But something new is also happening. The issues "traditionally" addressed by women—health, housing, sanitation, and the urban environment—have moved to center stage as capitalist urbanization progresses. Environmental issues now fuel the fires of many political campaigns and drive citizens beyond the rather restricted, perfunctory political act of voting. Instances of political mobilization at the grassroots level, where women often play a central role, allow us to "see" abstract concepts like participatory democracy and social change as dynamic processes.

The existence and activities of "Mothers of East Los Angeles" attest to the dynamic nature of participatory democracy, as well as to the dynamic nature of our gender, class, and ethnic identity. The story of MELA reveals, on the one hand, how individuals and groups can transform a seemingly "traditional" role such as "mother." On the other hand, it illustrates how such a role may also be a social agent drawing members of the community into the "political" arena. Studying women's contributions as well as men's will shed greater light on the networks dynamic of grassroots movements.[49]

The work "Mothers of East Los Angeles" do to mobilize the community demonstrates that people's political involvement cannot be predicted by their cultural characteristics. These women have defied stereotypes of apathy and used ethnic, gender, and class identity as an impetus, a strength, a vehicle for political activism. They have expanded their—and our—understanding of the complexities of a political system, and they have reaffirmed the possibility of "doing something."

They also generously share the lessons they have learned. One of the women in "Mothers of East Los Angeles" told me, as I hesitated to set up an interview with another woman I hadn't yet met in person,

You know, nothing ventured nothing lost. You should have seen how timid we were the first time we went to a public hearing. Now, forget it, I walk right up and make myself heard and that's what you have to do.[50]

Reading 7   Muscogee Women's Identity Development

BARBARA B. KAWULICH*

This ethnographic study involved extensive fieldwork with the Muscogee (Creek) tribe of central Oklahoma. Sixteen Creek women participated in the study, answering in-depth questions about their work choices, influences, and motivators, and about how they perceived the dual effects of ethnicity and gender on their work choices and their success as workers. Data collected through participant observations, interviews, and document analysis indicated a strong sense of Creek identity for these women that was influenced by their extended families, pride, Muscogee (Creek) tradition and culture, a shared heritage and language, and by others' perceptions of them as Indian women.

INTRODUCTION

The original ethnographic study from which this manuscript is derived explored Muscogee (Creek) women's perceptions of work. Little is known about Native American women, particularly today's Muscogee (Creek) women. This study provided a voice for and contributed to our understanding of a little known group of American female minorities. Josselson (1987) suggested that little has been written about women, and that few have studied women phenomenologically or have looked at their self-definition, allowing them to give their stories. This has been particularly true until recently for women of color. For this reason, this study incorporated qualitative methods that encouraged in-depth

elaboration by Creek women about their own perspectives.

THEORETICAL UNDERPINNINGS

Three theories provided a foundation for the original study: culture theory, identity theory, and expectancy theory of motivation. The expectancy theory of motivation was seen as important to the original study because of the importance of the interaction of expected outcomes, performance, and rewards. Culture theory was deemed to be of particular interest to the original study, because life and work values are instilled as a result of cultural influence. Identity

*An abbreviated version was presented at the Couch/Stone Symposium of the Society for the Study of Symbolic Interaction, Dolphin Beach, Florida (January 2000).

theory was also an integral part, as identities developed within the context of culture. Only the latter two theories are considered pertinent to the discussion of identity development in this paper.

Culture Theory

Culture theory has typically provided anthropologists and historians with the basis for knowledge through their ethnographies. More recently, however, sociologists, psychologists, and educators have found culture studies to be relevant to their work with individuals and groups alike. Culture is defined as

> "a learned, socially transmitted set of behavioral standards. It is held, expressed, and shared by individuals through their personal values, norms, activities, attitudes, cognitive processes, interpretation of symbols, feelings, ideas, reactions, and morals" (Morris, Davis, and Allen, 1994, p. 70).

An understanding of culture was found to be an important foundation for meaning, because one's identity develops within the culture in which one is socialized.

Green (1995) noted an upsurge of ethnic consciousness being experienced globally. He highlighted the external and internal components of identity, that is, the group or cultural and the individual foci. When people share the same culture, they share the same cultural identity. Culture provides the framework for the development of one's individual identities.

Identity Theory

Identity has been defined in various ways. For example, Erikson defined identity as a psychosocial mechanism for adapting to change in the sociocultural environment (as cited in Fitzger-

ald, 1974). Jacobson-Widding (1983) defined identity as the expression of what Erikson described as self-sameness and a sharing of some "essential characteristics with others" (p. 14). Cultural identity has been defined by King (1974) as:

> The self-identification made by the creators and inheritors of a given culture history,...the human means of achieving an existential identity that is global in terms of experiential definition and total in the sense of awareness (p. 106).

Erikson's model of identity emphasized three elements:

1. one's behavior is ordered by one's values, beliefs, and principles, as well as one's expectations and those of others;
2. this self-sameness is constant over time, so that past and future are perceived in terms of today's self; and
3. identity exists within a framework of community of important others, where relationships and roles found therein support and legitimize one's identity development (Patterson, Sochting, and Marcia, 1992).

Josselson (1987) suggested that one of the most important jobs women face, as related to their development, is that of identity formation. Identity forms the basis for her sense of self and how her life is structured; identity, as described by Josselson (1987), involves the choices she makes, her priorities, and the principles that guide her decision making. She also suggested that identity is the means for organizing and understanding experience and for sharing meaning with others; at its core is one's system of ethics, what one chooses to place value upon or to disparage. Termed as such, identity forms the basis for one's judgment of herself with respect to her values and those that are meaningful to others with whom she identifies as cultural members. This process of identity formation varies by class, gender, age, and race (Deegan, 1987).

Identity development is mediated at each stage of socialization through actual interactive experiences with others (Lynn, 1992). As is the case with men, identity formation for women starts before adolescence, with late adolescence acting as a fine tuning instrument for resolving identity confusion tasks (Patterson et al., 1992). The identity that emerges acts as a dedication to a system of values and way of life related to important others (Patterson et al., 1992).

Regarding Native American identity, Deloria (1992) indicated that, because the old ways no longer exist, today's Native American young people must derive their principles of action and understanding from the traditional and adjust them to modern situations. Deloria suggested that "it seeks to transform the old ways of behaving into standards of action with definable limits set by the conception of Indian identity itself (p. 47). LaFramboise, Heyle, and Ozer (1990) explored the changing roles of women in Native American cultures. They noted that women used traditional American Indian coping mechanisms that reflect a sense of homeland and duty to her people and that differ by age, tribe, and environmental setting, to offset the geographic and cultural isolation they may feel when immersed in the dominant culture. The problems they experienced included breaking down social and psychological barriers about going to college; once in school, they reported problems associated with biculturality and the related pressures of conflicting expectations. Their response to their biculturality has been seen as taking a road toward retraditionalization, extending the traditional caretaker and cultural transmitter roles to include other activities related to American

Indian survival (LaFramboise et al., 1990). Green (1983) and Medicine (1983) noted that, while nonIndian feminists may emphasize such themes as independence and androgyny, American Indian women often view the work they do in terms of how it helps the family, the nation, and Mother Earth. LaFramboise et al. (1990) also observed that these women see preservation and restoration of their native cultures as being as important to them as are their personal professional goals; their perceptions are grounded in a solid sense of identity.

Very few studies were found that included Muscogee people in their sample. One culture study specified the inclusion of a Muscogee (Creek) female in its case study sample. Hill, Vaughn, and Harrison (1995) found that these women from matrilineal tribes were guided in their personal and professional lives by their ethnic identities that had developed within their tribal cultures.

HISTORICAL BACKGROUND

The 16th and 17th centuries saw explorers from Spain, Portugal, France, Sweden, Russia, the Netherlands, and Great Britain founding new colonies and trading posts. The native people were viewed as uncivilized, but were also seen as potential guides and trading partners. Early ethnographic literature indicated that the Creeks were the largest of the Muskogean-speaking groups of the southeast. Their original lands covered much of Alabama, Georgia, and upper Florida. They were a loose confederation of individual, independent chiefdoms comprised of 60 to 70 towns (Paredes, 1987). The Muscogee (Creek) people were (and are) matrilineal, which means that the children belong to the clan of their mothers. The father and his clan had no legal say in the raising of the children (Nunez, 1987). Social control and political leadership were related to their complex mix of phratries, matriclans, and moieties (Paredes, 1987). The matriclans are groupings of tribal members into clans through the maternal line. Clans were used for blood feud responsibilities, punishing clan members, and holding collective ceremonies, like Green Corn. Phratries are groupings of clans into two groups, Red or war towns and White or peace towns. These two groupings were exogamous, (Sattler, 1995). Moieties are the two divisions of unilateral tribes, in this case, Upper and Lower Creeks, both of which were endogamous. Moieties were used for marriage regulation, intratown ball games, channeling of suspicions and sorcery, and possibly intratown politics (Urban, 1994). The clans associated with the white moiety included the Wind, Skunk, Beaver, Bear, Wolf, and Bird clans. Those of the red moiety included the Fox, Panther, Wildcat, Potato, Alligator, Raccoon, Toad, and Deer clans (Swanton, 1987). Clan designations still exist today in Creek culture.

European contact began with Creeks in 1540 when Hernando de Soto invaded Creek lands. In the 1700s, Lower Creeks allowed Oglethorpe to establish a colony in Georgia to increase trade opportunities. This began a 100-year period of land acquisition from Creeks and other southeastern tribes by European settlers. Skirmishes and battles were fought to obtain land from the native people that would then be made available to European settlers. Hoping to stem some of the white movement into native lands, some tribes signed treaties. Some of the earliest tribes to sign these treaties were the Cherokee, Choctaw, Chickasaw, and Muscogee (Creek) people. These people coexisted with their European neighbors for many years, but the land grabbing continued. One exception to this peaceful coexistence was the Red Stick War between the White and the Creek band of Red Stick warriors. Though the southern tribes made

numerous treaties with the government(s), this cooperation failed to stop the land expansion process. This expansion continued into the 1800s, when churches began to send missionaries to Indian country to teach the Indians about Christianity and farming techniques. Several of the southern tribes had experienced some degree of acculturation, but the settlers did not see the process as occurring fast enough.

Before he left the Presidency in 1825, James Monroe established an Indian removal policy. Many white people in the northeast did not agree with this policy, among them Monroe's successor to the Presidency, John Quincy Adams. Forced removal attempts began in 1825. Conservative Lower Creeks stayed in the east, and, during the next three years, resettled in Alabama (Champagne, 1992). The McIntosh faction of about 1,300 Creeks moved to the west in 1828. By 1830, some 2,000 to 3,000 Creeks had moved to what is known now as Oklahoma. When Andrew Jackson succeeded Adams, he enacted in 1830, the Indian Removal Act, which legislated the use of force, if the Indians refused to move (Dinnerstein, Nichols, & Reimers, 1990). The removal of the Muscogee (Creek), Cherokee, and other southern tribes to Oklahoma, called the "Trail of Tears," was rife with intolerable conditions: unseaworthy boats, condemned meat, spoiled foods, inadequate clothing, disease, and poor weather conditions (Foreman, 1972). More than 20,000 American Indians made the 1,200 mile trip to Indian country under military guard; Debo (1942) put the number of Creeks removed at over 10,000 Creeks. Between 3,500 and 7,000 people were buried along the way (O'Brien, 1989).

The Muscogee (Creek) people brought their sacred fires with them. They brought their clan and tribal town names. They brought things that were special to them, like plates, silver gorgets, and sacred objects, along with their meager belongings. The Muscogee people regrouped in Oklahoma along the Canadian and Arkansas Rivers. More than one fourth of the population died within the first year as a result of starvation, malnutrition, abysmal living conditions, increased factionalism and harassment by indigenous tribes of that area (O'Brien, 1989). They reestablished their roots in this new Indian Country, building schools for their children, erecting churches for those who had adapted to Christianity, and finding new ceremonial grounds for traditional worshipers.

At the end of the Civil War, Muscogee people agreed to abolish slavery in their tribe and accepted freedmen, former Black slaves, as members of the tribe with full privileges (O'Brien, 1989). As of 1866, 44 tribal towns and three freedmen towns were recorded in Creek Territory. The next year Creek Nation united its factions into one constitution and code of laws and named Ocmulgee its capital. The Creek Council House building stands today as a museum in Ocmulgee, Oklahoma. Each town was allowed to send one council representative, based on population of the town, to the House of Warriors (Champagne, 1992). The mekko (also spelled mico, micco, miko), or principal chief, acted as president of the tribal council. The war-chief led the tribal warriors. These two positions were held to be sources of dignity and power for these men, (Bartram, 1987).

In 1887 the Dawes Severalty Act provided for the division of Indian lands, such that each family was to receive 160 acres to be held in trust by the U.S. government. An agreement with the Muscogee Nation two years later allowed homesteading in Indian Territory but assigned to the Creek Nation jurisdiction over civil and minor criminal cases involving U.S. citizens and others. By 1890 almost half of the 17,912 population of the Muscogee Nation were squatters and other non-Muscogee citizens. The Creek people demanded a complete census before Dawes commission allotments occurred. The census conducted in 1900 showed 18,761 citizens: 6,858 full blood Creeks; 5,094 mixed blood Creeks; and 6,809 freedmen. Oklahoma was admitted to the Union as the 47th state in 1907. Hagan (1961) suggested that, during the early part of this century, tribal identity became more pan-Indian, borrowing from other tribes' customs. One advantage is noted as resulting from the Indian boarding schools, that of encouraging intertribal communication in the common language of English, thereby contributing to a pan-Indian movement (Hagan, 1961).

The government oscillated back and forth in its stance about land allotment (Hagan, 1961). President Roosevelt signed the Wheeler-Howard Act, also known as the Indian Reorganization Act, in 1934; this gave tribes the choice to reorganize or not. This act expanded educational options, encouraged agricultural and industrial projects, condoned traditional religious and secular ceremonies and customs. Unfortunately, some of these traditions were lost during the previous years of enforced acculturation. The result encouraged tribal borrowing to blend with those customs that endured. This further encouraged a pan-Indian movement, providing a more unified identity for Indian people (Deloria, 1992). However, the rural isolation of central Oklahoma has enabled the Muscogee people to preserve many aspects of the culture that their ancestors brought with them.

The Muscogee people combined their executive and judicial bodies into one tribal council in 1937, as a result of the Oklahoma Indian Welfare Act (the Thomas Rogers bill). In 1970 a U.S. law was passed that allowed for election of their own tribal offices. And three years later, Principal Chief Claude Cox and committee drafted a new constitution with three independent branches: the executive branch, consisting of the Principal and Second Chiefs; the legislative branch, consisting of the Speaker, Second Speaker, the district representatives from the eight districts; and the judicial branch, consisting of the Supreme and District Courts.

Today, Creek Nation is involved in various industries, including bingo parlors, smoke shops, a truck stop, farming and agricultural ventures, and a sand and gravel contract. They have a tribal newspaper, *Muscogee Nation News.* The language persists, though many of the young to middle age members do not speak more than a few words of the Muskoke language; a growing number of this same age group speak with ease in either English or the native tongue. Their ceremonies, such as Green Corn, and their dances, including stomp dances, social dances, the women's ribbon dance, the men's feather dance, have also persisted.

METHODOLOGY

This study relied upon a purposefully selected sample of 16 Muscogee (Creek) women, age 35 to 84. The aim was to include a variety of women who had worked in various arenas representing the world of work to include work in the public (nontribal) and tribal arenas, work in the home, work in the community for pay or gratis, and representing a variety of occupational groups (such as medicine, education, politics, arts). Data was collected from repeated in-depth interviews with the women, from document analysis at the tribal center and tribal libraries, as well as a variety of governmental sources, and from numerous participant observations in various settings, including Creek homes, tribal center, tribal senior citizen centers, a job fair, Creek festival, ceremonial grounds, churches, schools, stomp dances, bingo halls, smoke shops, community centers, intertribal meetings, council meetings, and more. Triangulation was effected through use of one method used to substantiate data received through other methods. For example, participant observations acted to corroborate information obtained using ethnographic interviewing techniques. Informal field notes and journal entries also enabled me to substantiate information obtained through other sources. Lincoln and Guba's (1985) criteria of credibility, transferability, dependability, and confirmability were used to establish trustworthiness of the data. Methods used to establish this trustworthiness included prolonged engagement, persistent observation, triangulation, peer debriefing, member checks, audit trails, and negative case analysis.

Coding and data analysis were based on Strauss and Corbin's (1990) scheme of open, axial, and selective coding. My initial coding efforts took place in the field, in a cheap motel room with Post-it notes and color crayons, where I spent my "down time." I would return to my motel room at various times to record field notes and listen to taped interviews and code transcriptions, when I was not out data-gathering. The resulting coding scheme included three categories: Work, What it means to be a Creek woman (a portion of which is the focus of this paper), and Creek culture. There were 32 subcategories also. After all data had been coded, NUD-IST qualitative software was used solely as a data management tool. Miles and Huberman's (1994) data analysis techniques provided additional guidance in data analysis.

FINDINGS OF THE STUDY

To these Creek women, identity meant belonging, "knowing who you are and where you come from." As one woman put it, "this is part of you, this land, these people." They expressed their identities as being constructed through the influences of extended family, their pride in being

Creek, through a shared heritage, language, and customs, and by nonIndian people's perceptions of them. They identified first with their immediate families, then their clan, their tribal town, then with other Creek people, then with other indigenous people, and last to the mainstream culture.

Kleinfeld and Kruse (1982) pointed out that many government documents and gender studies failed to acknowledge the separate ethnic identity of Native American women. My study showed that Muscogee (Creek) women identified themselves as Muscogee (Creek), then as Native American, not White. Greenman (1996) noted that, by assuming that the ideas of people in the mainstream culture apply to all workers, cultural influences that affect identity development are not considered. As has been found in previous literature about American Indians, the women I interviewed shared several differences in values and work attitudes that conflict with the mainstream culture. As a result of these differences, two of the women stated that they did not want to work with nonIndians, that is, those not of their ethnic group. The following statement expresses what many of these women shared:

> "Well, since I'm a minority, I think that people look down on you and think that, some white people think that, if you're Indian, you don't know anything, can't learn anything.... I don't have anybody to stand up for me but myself."

One woman explained some of the differences in the Creek and mainstream cultures like this.

> "You don't just go up like I would at a, let's say, a reception. I mingle; that's part of my job. I go, and there's a group over here, maybe all male. I go up and I mingle. Maybe I know someone in that group or introduce myself. Among Indian people you don't do that. A man has his territory. Women have theirs. You don't cross those boundaries."

Another expressed it this way.

> If I weren't Creek,...I would lose my family, because I don't think white women have...closeness as in extended family as Indian people do.... White women don't have the culture that I have. Don't have something to fall back on. To know who you are and where you come from. To know that this is part of you, this land, these people. They're all a part of you. I'd lose all of that. I would lose my identity. You know, I am Creek. I don't have a choice. I don't have a choice if I'm going to be Indian or not Indian.... This is what I am.

Another woman explained her identity as an Indian like this.

> There's a connection to your tribe. It gives you a good feeling inside. It's nothing outside, I guess, you can see. It gives you your identity. Maybe it makes it more real when you realize being away from it, see, for so many years.

These women shared various experiences that explained some of the differences in the values and beliefs of Creek women and women of the prevalent culture. They felt that when they worked with other Indians, they experienced a sense of belonging that they did not feel with others. Several women shared stories about their work experiences that illustrated cultural discontinuity. One woman shared this story.

> I got hired in a Chinese café.... I couldn't understand them. They couldn't understand me. Went in there, first time I ever had a waitress job, being as a waitress.... And the first thing, these two couples came to the table, sat there with one another and talking, I guess. I went to them and tried to be polite and everything. They wanted a menu. I thought, What? Menu? It must be a dish. I thought, maybe Chinese. I went up there and told them (the Chinese owner/cook) they wanted to order a menu. Well, "right there," you know, he had it on the shelf. I thought, well, he was pointing, he was just pointing. He didn't tell what it was like, if it was something to eat or drink or nothing.... I looked, and it was a little black book sitting up there. I thought, well, is this what he's talking about? I hated to ask him again. He was kind of grouchy old Chinese. I said, "Menu." He turned around and came back around the door and "right there," slam it down. I thought, "oh, must have certain recipes." I took it to them and I gave it to them. Well, I guess that's menu, but all that time I thought they were talking about something to eat.... That was my new job and my new initiation.

Besides their ethnic identification with the Muscogee tribe, these women expressed the desire to work with indigenous people or Creek people, in particular. "To help the tribe," "to give something back to the people" were given as rea-

sons for choosing work, typically later in life. At the beginning of their careers, these women took whatever jobs were available to meet their survival needs. As these needs were met, they were able to seek better work, that is, work that was closer to home or that enabled them to work with children or with Indians, or to find other motivating work. Three fourths of the 16 women in this study moved away from the Oklahoma area and ultimately moved back home, with the exception of one, who felt strongly that she had experienced prejudice growing up there. Oklahoma Creek country was considered by all of these women to be their home land (because that is where the family/tribe is), their family home was considered home, and Georgia was considered to be the old home land. Even with these distinctions, these women also identified themselves with their clan and tribal town.

The descriptions the women shared about what being a Creek woman meant to them were centered around traditional and modern ways. Some descriptions of what they considered to be a modern Muscogee woman related to their failure to adhere to traditional ways in the home and spiritually. Their responses confirmed the use of the term traditional as reflecting one who worshiped in the traditional way of the Muscogee (Creek) people, rather than Christian. They also used the term traditional to mean adherence to Creek customs or traditional ways of interacting. The typical response was that traditional women adhered to the rules of the past for women's actions. Those rules implied that the woman's place is in the home, taking care of the family and its survival and maintenance, while the man brought home the paycheck. Being a traditional woman also meant that a Creek woman adhered to the rules related to ceremonial grounds worship. Their idea of a modern woman was one who does not follow the rules. Some of their comments about being traditional or modern follow.

But there are rules we have, when I say traditional, we still practice that. We also were raised up in the Indian church. There were rules to follow then. You didn't take communion if you were on your period. You didn't. Men sat on one side, women on the other. Now that was the old church.... So there were rules to follow. And the traditional side are those people who follow those rules. We don't question, well, who made these rules? Where did they come from? Did you just make them up? I don't want to do this. You don't. You don't question.... So I say I'm a traditional, because I still do those things. I don't use it just as a title. I practice it.... People don't believe those ways anymore. The way we bury our dead. We practice the ways that we were taught. The way we cook. The way that we live our individual lives. That's what makes you traditional. It's from your heart. It's not just skin color only. It's not showing my card. I don't have to prove to anyone that I'm Indian, that I must go to Creek. I know.

Another woman described the difference in modern and traditional like this.

Can you be both? I would have to say both.... a little poem...starts off, I am Indian, I am white.... it's a life-long fight. Because Indian and White, he has to live a double role. But yet, he has a single soul. And that's kind of how I feel about the tradition and modern. It's kind of like I'm traditional and also modern.... And they might say, your thoughts, your really deep down thoughts, it's

traditional, you're traditional. And sometimes, I think that. And then other times, I think what traditional is, what I think it is, and I'm modern.

Their explanations about being traditional typically involved adhering to such rules as were followed in the past by Creek women. These rules included not cooking or serving food to their families when they were on their period. They included adhering to the taboos related to ceremonial grounds worship, such as not eating corn prior to Green Corn. These rules also involved the separation of the sexes in interactions. Their explanation for what a modern Creek woman is related to Christian worship and to interacting with men, typically at work and in public places. The women who referred to themselves as modern women typically had been involved in work in the dominant culture, where they were expected to interact with both males and females and where there was less gender segregation. One woman who identified herself as traditional had worked in the dominant culture and shared her experience like this.

It depends on where I am. At work, I'm probably a modern. I know I'm a modern, but I don't forget my traditional values when I'm at work. [What are those values?] Most of all, I guess, just loving everybody. You know, not having hard feelings against anyone. You just, that's just the way it is. That's just the way it is. And even if somebody has hurt you or anything, you still go on. You don't hold grudges. That, to me, that's the traditional way. You walk in love wherever you go.

Another woman shared the guilt she felt for pursuing her education and for working outside the home, rather than staying home with her children as expected by tradition.

> *To me, the traditional is kind of like my dad told me. The woman is going to be staying in the home and caring for her family, children, and so forth. And won't be working out, so she doesn't necessarily need an education. It's not that important, good for them to learn, you know, but it's the home making things. So my mother is a wonderful homemaker.... Her housekeeping and her sewing and, you know, she's just wonderful. But that's, to me, that's the kind of traditional thinking about education, not that the woman doesn't learn or that she can't learn. But she would take second place, you know, in the learning.... I don't totally agree with that, and yet, there is some traditional in me, because, sometimes I've felt guilty, felt a little guilt in going on with my education and then working all 27 years in education.*

Another woman expressed it this way.

> *I really felt strongly about my culture, I'd been raised that way. I'd been raised as a traditional person. And in order for our culture to survive, you were going to have to have more educated people. I learned to balance my worlds. I did sacrifice some things.*

As the women in this study were growing up, they performed work that they typically described as men's work, such as heavy farm work, as well as work that they considered to be women's work. For the most part, they chose work outside the home that has typically been traditionally female dominated. Much of this work was an extension of their homemaking duties. These women had similar work choices to women of other ethnic groups and of the mainstream culture. Prior to World War II, they worked primarily in housekeeping and other domestic labors, or in work that extended their homemaking skills into the public arena, or in manufacturing plants, such as in sewing or canning factories. During the war, the women participated in traditionally male dominated work, such as in aircraft manufacturing. After the war, many of them returned to the home, and men took over their jobs. As with other ethnic groups, these women continued to work out in public, for the most part, as required by their circumstances. This was especially true when they were single mothers or as the need for two incomes in the family became necessary to survival. There were few opportunities for Creek women to receive recognition for their efforts. Having their family and their elders be proud of them was important to these women. Work out in the public arena was one way that they can "make a name for" themselves. Several of the women shared their accomplishments, their awards, their diplomas, and other artifacts indicative of their having been recognized for their work. They thrived on making contact with other people, as they are a communal people. Educational success provided a means for recognition for them. Success in school and in sports was recognized frequently in the tribal newspaper. Another way that females of the Muscogee and other Indian nations could achieve recognition for their efforts and can feel pride and respect from others is through the tribal princess pageants. Winners of these pageants receive scholarship money, recognition of tribal members, contact and exposure to mainstream culture as representative for the tribe, and the opportunity to acquire poise and public speaking skills. I was pleased to see that the emphasis was less on beauty than on talent, knowledge of Creek customs, and ability to represent the tribe with pride.

Bataille and Sands (1984) shared Vine Deloria, Sr.'s view of indigenous women as a whole. A male American Indian author, Deloria characterized American Indian women as being modest in dress and in "demeanor and attitude" (p. 18), as feeling responsible for maintaining the tribal traditions and values, and as being willing to defer their own personal goals until later in life. This description was applicable to today's Muscogee (Creek) women as well.

CONCLUSIONS

These women were proud to be Muscogee (Creek). They were also proud to be Creek women. As one woman said,

> I'm very proud of my heritage.... I've always known who I was. I always knew, and at times when I was growing,...we were looked upon as very low, low, low class people. And, of course, you learn to work through that.... I've always been proud of being a Creek woman.... When I was growing up,...there was a lot of prejudice there. But I always hung onto those values that us children, we crossed over a bridge every single day. We walked out our front gate and crawled on a yellow school bus and walked into another world, where we had to function. But when we came back home, we went right back into our own world. And so we always were Creek. We always knew who we were.

Identity for them was influenced by the extended family, pride in being Creek, by Creek tradition and culture, by a shared Muscogee (Creek) heritage and language, and by others' perceptions of them. Their ethnicity attachment was to other Native Americans, not the Anglo ethnic group in which the government and others continue to place them. Their isolation has helped to preserve this feeling of belongingness for them. Like many other Native Americans, they encountered differences in their values and expectations, causing them to experience cultural discontinuity and the tension that goes with it.

The women interviewed had a strong identity with their tribe over any occupational subculture to which they may belong. Their ethnicity is American Indian, not White. Not only do many Native Americans identify themselves as ethnically different from the majority culture, but also, anytime the government acts, such acts are seen with skepticism. Muscogee (Creek) culture has affected their beliefs, their expectations, and those of others. As a result, it has also provided a framework for identity development for these Creek women.

Reading 8   Long Distance Community in the Network Society: Contact and Support Beyond Netville

KEITH N. HAMPTON*   BARRY WELLMAN

The authors examine the experience of the residents of Netville, a suburban neighborhood with access to some of the most advanced new communication technologies available, and how this technology affected the amount of contact and support exchanged with members of their distant social networks.[1] Focusing exclusively on friends and relatives external to the neighborhood of Netville, we analyze "community" as relations that provide a sense of belonging rather than as a group of people living near each other. Computer-mediated communication (CMC) is treated as one of several means of communication used in the maintenance of social networks. Contrary to expectations that the Internet encourages a "global village," those ties that previously were "just out of reach" geographically, experience the greatest increase in contact and support as a result of access to CMC.

COMMUNITIES AS SOCIAL NETWORKS: ON AND OFF THE INTERNET

We usually think of communities as idyllic neighborhoods, where neighbors visit each other's private homes, chat on street corners, and get together in local cafes and bars (Oldenburg 1999). This image is broadly shared, by the public, the media, politicians, and indeed, scholars, for whom a "community study" means going to a neighborhood and seeing what transpires there (Wellman and Leighton, 1979).

Yet if we emphasize the *social* aspect of community over the *spatial,* then most community ties have been non-local for many decades (Fischer, 1982, 1984; Wellman, 1999). The social definition of "community" emphasizes supportive, sociable, relations that provide a sense of belonging rather than a group of people living near to each other. Seen this way, communities usually have many ties that extend well beyond the neighborhood. This was so even before the Internet, when people had to get into their cars to see friends and relatives, or fly on airplanes, or try to find them by telephone (often paying expensive long-distance charges; Wellman and Tindall, 1993). For example, in the Toronto borough of East York, only 13 percent of residents' activities are with people living in the same neighborhood (Wellman, Carrington and Hall, 1988).

Community is best seen as a network—not as a local group. We are not members of a society which operates in "little-boxes," dealing only with fellow members of the few groups to which we belong: at home, in our neighborhood, workplaces, or in cyberspace. Each person has his/her own "personal community" of kinship, friendship, neighboring and workmate ties. Personal communities traverse a variety of social settings and are generally far-flung, sparsely-knit, cross-cutting, loosely-bounded, and fragmentary (Wellman, 1999). Social ties vary in intensity and are maintained through multiple communication media: direct in-person contact, telephone, postal mail, and more recently fax, e-mail, chats, and discussion groups.

This networking of community—and indeed, of society—began well before the advent of personal computers connected by the Internet (Wellman, 1997). But a computer network *is* a social network when it connects people and institutions. The growth of computer-mediated communication (CMC) introduces a new means of social contact with the potential to affect many aspects of personal communities. This paper examines the experience of the residents of Netville, a suburban neighborhood with access to some of the most advanced new communication technologies available, and how this technology affected contact and support stretching beyond Netville to the residents' personal communities.

THE DEBATE ABOUT COMMUNITY GETS WIRED

Unlike the almost universal earlier fear that technologies such as the automobile and television would harm community (Stein, 1960), the debate about the Internet comes in two flavors (Wellman & Gulia, 1999). Enthusiasts hail the Internet's potential for making connections without regard to race, creed, gender, or geography. As Phil Patton early proclaimed: "Computer-mediated communication...will do by way of electronic pathways what cement roads were unable to do, namely connect us rather than atomize us, put us at the controls of a 'vehicle' and yet not detach us from the rest of the world" (1986, p. 20).

By contrast, contemporary dystopians suggest that the lure of new communication technologies withdraws people from in-person contact and lures them away from their families and communities (Kraut, et al., 1998; Nie and Erbring, 2000; Nie, this issue). They worry that meaningful contact will wither without the full bandwidth provided by in-person, in-the-flesh contact. As Texas commentator Jim Hightower warned over the ABC radio network: "While all this razzle-dazzle connects us electronically, it disconnects us from each other, having us 'interfacing' more with computers and TV screens than looking in the face of our fellow human beings" (quoted in Fox, 1995, p. 12).

Yet, several scenarios are possible. Indeed, each scenario may happen to different people or to the same person at different times. In an "information society" where work, leisure, and social ties are all maintained from within the "smart home," people could reject the need for social relationships based on physical location.

They might find community online, or not at all, rather than on street corners or while visiting friends and relatives. New communication technologies may advance the home as a center for services that encourage a shift toward greater home-centeredness and privatization. At the same time the location of the technology inside the home facilitates access to local relationships, suggesting that domestic relations may flourish, possibly at the expense of more distant ties.

Our research has been guided by a desire to study community offline as well as online. We are interested in the totality of relationships in community ties and not just in behavior in one communication medium or locale. In this we differ from studies of "virtual community" that only look at relationships online (see some of the chapters in Smith and Kollock, 1999) and from traditional sociological studies of in-person, neighborhood-based communities. The former overemphasizes the prevalence of computer-only ties, while the latter ignores the importance of transportation and communication in connecting community members over a distance. Unlike many studies of CMC that observe undergraduates in laboratory experiments (reviewed in Sproull & Kiesler, 1991; Walther, Anderson & Park, 1994), we study people in real settings. We focus here on the effect of new communication technologies on the residents of the wired neighborhood of Netville.

THE SOCIAL AFFORDANCES OF THE INTERNET[2]

Pre-Internet advances in transportation and communication technology partially emancipated community from its spatial confines. The cost of mobility and of social contact have decreased with the advent of technologies such as the train, automobile, airplane, and telephone (Hawley, 1986). People decentralized their active social ties as the financial and temporal costs of transcending space decreased. CMC—in the form of e-mail, chat groups and instant messaging—introduces new means of communication with friends and relatives at a distance. The Internet has the capacity to foster global communities, in which ties might flourish without the constraints of spatial distance. On the Internet, neighbors across the street are no closer than best friends across the ocean. In practice, the shrinking of the map of the world is unlikely to go so far. Most ties probably function through the interplay of online and offline interactions. Hence, CMC should lessen, but not eliminate, the constraints of distance on maintaining personal communities.

With the telephone, the cost of contact increases with physical distance. By contrast, with CMC the cost of contact does not vary with distance but is based on a flat fee, along with access to a personal computer and the Internet. For most, the decision to purchase a home computer has been based on a desire to expand educational or work opportunities and not directly out of a need to maintain contact with distant network members (Ekos, 1998). As a result, the ability to use CMC as a form of contact is largely a by-product of a financial investment in other activities.

In addition to reducing the financial cost of social contact specific forms of CMC, such as e-mail, provide temporal freedom. Asynchronous e-mail means that both parties do not have to be present for contact to take place. Analogous to the traditional paper letter, e-mail can be composed without the immediate participation of the receiving party. Those with free, high-speed, always-on Internet access, such as what was available to the residents of Netville, are even better situated to experience increased social contact with network members.[3] They can send messages whenever the urge hits them, without waiting to boot up the computer, dial the Internet, or worry about interfering with telephone calls. They can quickly send and receive pictures, audio messages, and e-mail. As temporal flexibility becomes more important with complex, individualized daily lives (Wellman, 2001), CMC should improve the ability of contact to take place for local as well as distant network members.

It is time to move from speculation to evidence. This paper tests the hypotheses that:

- Living in a wired neighborhood with access to free, high-speed, always-on Internet access increases social contact with distant network members.
- Those ties located at the greatest distance will experience the greatest increase in contact as a result of Internet access.

Previous studies have demonstrated that CMC can be used for the exchange of non-instrumental support, such as companionship and emotional aid (Haythornthwaite & Wellman, 1998). In this way CMC is similar to the telephone in its ability to participate in the exchange of social support regardless of physical distance. However, instrumental aid—such as lending household items and providing child care—relies more on physical access and is more appropriately exchanged with physically-available network members (Wellman & Wortley, 1990). For ties in close proximity, the introduction of CMC may help facilitate the delivery of aid but is likely limited to supplementing existing means of communication. At best CMC will contribute to a modest increase in support exchanged with nearby ties.[4]

The most physically distant ties are also unlikely to experience a significant increase in the exchange of support as a result of CMC. Regardless of the means of communication, distance between network members makes it dif-ficult to provide many goods and services. Support that does not require in-person contact—such as financial aid, companionship, and emotional aid—are the only forms of support likely to benefit from CMC between distant network members.

CMC is likely to afford the greatest increase in support among mid-range ties, located somewhere between the most distant network members and those who live nearby. CMC, particularly e-mail, should facilitate coordination with mid-range ties, increase awareness of network members' social capital, and increase the amount and breadth of support exchanged. Network members within this mid-range can provide non-instrumental aid that does not rely on in-person contact. With some coordination and effort, they can also provide some instrumental aid. The reduced cost and temporal flexibility of e-mail reduces previous barriers to obtaining such support from mid-range network members. We would therefore expect the greatest increase in the exchange of overall support to occur with those who were previously "just out of reach." We hypothesize that:

- Living in a wired neighborhood with free, high-speed, always-on Internet access increases overall levels of support exchanged with network members. In particular, mid-range ties (50–500 km) will experience the greatest increase in the exchange of overall support.

STUDYING NETVILLE[5]

Netville[6]

The evolving nature of the Internet makes it a moving research target. Almost all research can only describe what has been the situation, rather than what is now or what will soon be. We have been blessed with a window into the future by having spent several years studying "Netville": a leading-edge "wired suburb" filled with Internet technology that is not yet publicly available. The widespread use of such technology in Netville makes it an excellent setting to investigate the effects of CMC on community.

Netville is a newly-built development of approximately 109 medium-priced detached homes in a rapidly growing, outer suburb of Toronto. Most homes have three or four bedrooms plus a study: 2,000 square feet on a 40 foot lot. In its appearance it is nearly identical to most other suburban developments in the Toronto area. Netville's distinguishing feature is that it is one of the few developments in North America where all of the homes were equipped from the start with a series of advanced communication technologies supplied across a broadband high-speed local network. Users could reliably expect network speeds of 10 Mbps, more than ten times faster than other commercially available "high-speed," "always on"[7] Internet systems (i.e., telephone DSL and cable modem services), and more than 300 times faster than dial-up telephone connections. For two years, the local network provided residents with high speed Internet access (including electronic mail and Web surfing), computer-desktop videophone, an online jukebox, entertainment applications, online health services, and local discussion forums. In exchange for free access to these advanced services, Netville residents agreed to be studied by the corporate and scholarly members of the "Magenta Consortium," the organization responsible for developing Netville's local network.[8] Approximately 60 percent of Netville homes participated in the high bandwidth trial and had access to the network for up to two years. The other 40 percent of households, for various organizational reasons internal to the Magenta Consortium, were never connected to the network despite assurances at the time residents purchased their homes that they would be.[9] Those households not connected to the local network provide a convenient, quasi-random comparison group for studying the effects of computer-mediated communication.

Wired and non-wired Netville residents were similar in terms of age, education and family status (Hampton, 2001b). Residents were largely lower-middle class, English-speaking and married. More than half of all couples had children living at home when they moved into the community, and as with many new suburbs, a baby boom happened soon after moving in. Most residents were white, but an appreciable number were racial and ethnic minorities. About half had completed a university degree. Residents worked at such jobs as technician, teacher, and police officer. Their median household income in 1997 was C $75,000 (US $50,000). Netville residents were as likely to have a television, a VCR, cable TV, a home computer and home Internet access as other Canadians of similar socioeconomic status (Hampton, 2001b). While the decision of some to purchase a home in Netville was motivated by the technology available, only 21 percent of home purchasers identified Netville's "information services" as one of the top three factors in their purchasing decision.

As technology developed and fashions changed, the telecommunications company responsible for Netville's local network decided that the hybrid fibre coaxial technology used in the development was not the future of residential Internet services. They terminated the field trial early in 1999 to the dismay of the residents (Hampton, 2002).

Research Design

Our research objectives led us to gather information about residents' community ties online and offline, globally and locally, including: relations within Netville (see Hampton, 2001b; Hampton, 2001a; Hampton & Wellman, 1999), personal networks extending well beyond Netville (the subject of this paper), civic involvement, and attitudes toward community, technology and society. We used several research methods, principally ethnographic fieldwork and a cross-sectional survey.

Ethnography: In April 1997, one of us, Keith Hampton, began participating in local activities. Hampton moved into Netville in October 1997 (living in a resident's basement apartment), staying until August 1999. Given the widespread public interest in Netville, residents were not surprised about his research activity and incorporated him into the neighborhood. Hampton worked from home, participated in online activities, attended all possible local meetings (formal and informal), walked the neighborhood chatting, and did ethnographic participant-observation. Like other residents, he relied on the high-speed network to maintain contact with social network members living outside of Netville. His daily experiences and observations provided detailed information about how residents used the available technology, their domestic and neighborhood relations, and how they used time and local space. Insights gained through observation and interactions were instrumental in developing the survey.

Survey: The survey was first administered to those moving into Netville in April 1998 and was expanded to include existing wired and non-wired residents in September 1998. The survey obtained information on geographic perception, personal and neighborhood networks, neighboring, community alienation, social trust, work, experience with technology, time-use, and basic demographics. We tried to learn the extent to which Netville residents' personal networks were abundant, strong, solidary, and local. Our attempt to collect very detailed information on

residents' closest social ties was met with mixed success as a result of Magenta's decision to end the technology trial and problems in our use of computer-assisted interviewing (see Hampton, 1999). As a result, while recognizing that different types of ties (friends, relatives, etc.) and ties of different strengths are likely to provide different types of aid and support, this analysis does not include an analysis of specific types of ties or forms of support. Instead we focus exclusively on changes in social contact and exchange of support with friends and relatives at various distances. Noticeably absent from this analysis is a full review of Netville residents neighborhood ties and which will be explored in a forthcoming article (see Hampton, 2001b).

Although this paper relies principally on survey data, it is also informed by ethnographic observation, monitoring an online community forum, and observing focus groups.

Measuring Social Contact and Support

We report here on *change* in contact and support with *non-local* friends and relatives living outside Netville.[10] We asked 18 questions about change in support and contact with network members living at the distances of 1) less than 50 kilometers (excluding neighborhood ties), 2) 50 to 500 km, and 3) greater than 500 km in comparison to one year before their move to Netville.

Participants were asked to indicate on a five-point scale from −2 (much less) to +2 (much more) how their overall levels of contact and support exchanged with friends and relatives had changed. The 18 ordinal variables were combined into eight scales that document:[11]

1. Change in social contact with all social ties regardless of distance
2. Change in support exchanged with all social ties regardless of distance

3. Change in social contact with ties outside Netville but within 50 km
4. Change in support exchanged with ties outside Netville but within 50 km
5. Change in social contact with mid-range (50–500 km) social ties
6. Change in social support exchanged with mid-range (50–500 km) social ties
7. Change in social contact with ties more than 500 km away
8. Change in support exchanged with ties more than 500 km away.

To test hypotheses of how living "wired" in Netville, i.e., with access to the local high-speed network, affects contact and support exchanged with social network members, the distribution and mean scores for wired and non-wired participants are compared for change in social contact and support 1) regardless of distance, and with network members living at 2) less than 50 km (which includes Toronto, but excludes immediate neighbors), 3) 50–500 km, and 4) more than 500 km.

Social contact and support scales are dependent variables in regressions that include the independent variables of wired status (connected or not connected to Netville's high-speed network) and control variables for gender, age, years of education and length of residence (the length of time participants had lived in Netville at the time they were interviewed). The rationales for inclusion of the control variables are:

1. *Gender:* Women may be more likely than men to experience a change in social contact or support as a result of their role in maintaining the majority of household ties.
2. *Age:* Age may contribute to network stability and reduce the likelihood of experiencing change in social contact or support.
3. *Education:* Education contributes to greater social and financial capital which may help

in the maintenance of social contact and support networks.

4. *Length of Residence:* Moving may create instability in communication with network members. Length of residence in Netville is included to control for the possibility that early movers may report a drop in social contact and support in comparison to those who have had time to settle into their new home.

SOCIAL CONTACT AND SOCIAL SUPPORT

Overall Changes

Contact: Compared to one year before moving to Netville, 41 percent of Netville residents report a drop in social contact with friends and relatives, 32 percent report no change, and 28 percent report an increase. Yet wired residents had significantly more contact than non-wired: 68 percent of wired residents reported that their overall level of social contact either increased or remained the same as compared with only 45 percent of non-wired residents (Figure 8.1). On average, non-wired residents report a drop in contact and wired residents report almost no change in social contact compared to a year before their move (Table 8.1). Holding other factors constant, the negative intercept coefficient in Table 8.2 indicates that Netville residents generally experienced a drop in contact as a result of their move. This is consistent with the observations of S. D. Clark (1966) and Herbert Gans (1967) who observed a similar loss of social contact among new suburban dwellers. Although moving to a new suburban neighborhood generally decreased the contact of Netville residents with friends and relatives, access to the high-speed network helped wired residents to maintain contact. Both personal attributes and high-speed access affect contact with social network

TABLE 8.1.   Comparison of wired and non-wired residents by mean change in contact with social ties at various distances (kilometers).[a]

	Overall		Less than 50 km		50–500 km		More than 500 km	
	Non Wired	Wired	Non Wired	Wired	Non Wired	Wired	Non Wired	Wired
Mean	−0.33*	0.03*	−0.28	−0.13	−0.43*	0.03*	−0.30*	0.19*
SD	0.51	0.38	0.73	0.58	0.61	0.56	0.73	0.46
Min	−1.50	−0.67	−2.00	−1.50	−1.50	1.00	−2.00	−0.50
Max	0.33	1.17	1.00	1.00	0.50	1.50	1.00	2.00

[a]Scale for mean score ranges from –2 "lot less" to +2 "lot more"; N = 34 Wired, 20 Non-Wired.

Difference between means is significant at [+]$p < .05$ *$p < .01$ **$p < .001$ (ANOVA).

TABLE 8.2.   Coefficients from the regression of change in social contact on wired status and other independent variables at various distances (kilometers) (N=54).

Control Variables	Overall	Less than 50 km>	50–500 km	More than 500 km
Wired[a]	0.25[+]	—	0.45*	0.40[+]
	(0.26)		(0.36)	(0.32)
Female[b]	—	—	—	—
Education	0.06[+]	0.10[+]	—	—
	(0.26)	(0.32)		
Age	0.02[+]	—	—	0.03[+]
	(0.25)	—	—	(0.30)
Residency	—	—	—	—
Intercept	−1.73*	−1.74*	−0.43*	−1.16*
R^2	0.26*	0.10[+]	0.13*	0.24**

Note: Numbers in parentheses are standardized coefficients (β). Only those variables that significantly improved on the explained variance (R^2) are included in the final model; [+]$p < .05$ *$p < .01$ **$p < .001$.

[a]Dummy variable for wired status, reference category is wired—access to the high-speed network.

[b]Dummy variable for gender, reference category is female.

members. Being wired, better educated, and older positively affect change in overall contact (Table 8.2). Being connected to the local network has the same effect on boosting social contact as four more years of education or nearly 13 years of increased age. Among younger residents with fewer years of formal education, wired status is particularly important in helping maintain contact at pre-move levels.

Support: Fully 79 percent of wired Netville residents report the same or more support after moving as compared to only 50 percent of non-wired residents (Figure 8.2). As with social contact, wired residents on average have maintained support near pre-move levels while non-wired residents report significantly less support (Table 8.3). Controlling for other factors, those who moved into Netville report an overall decrease in support exchanged with network members across all distances (Figure 8.2). Living in Netville and being connected to the local high-speed network reverses this trend. On average, non-wired residents report a moderate drop in support while wired residents have been able to maintain support slightly above pre-move levels. Indeed, being wired is the only variable that is significantly associated with changes in the exchange of support (Table 8.4).

TIES LIVING WITHIN 50 KILOMETERS

Contact: Netvillers neighbor extensively and intensively. Many local friendships and commu-

TABLE 8.3.   Comparison of wired and non-wired residents by mean change in support exchanged with social ties at various distances (kilometers).[a]

	Overall		Less than 50 km		50–500 km		More than 500 km	
	Non Wired	Wired	Non Wired	Wired	Non Wired	Wired	Non Wired	Wired
Mean	−0.24*	0.05*	0.03	0.10	−0.51**	0.04**	−0.24*	0.01**
SD	0.50	0.20	0.72	0.41	0.64	0.21	0.52	0.19
Min	−1.50	−0.50	−1.50	−1.00	−2.00	−0.50	−1.50	−0.50
Max	0.33	0.58	1.00	1.00	0.25	0.75	0.50	1.00

[a]Scale for mean score ranges from –2 "lot less" to +2 "lot more"; N=34 Wired, 20 Non-Wired.

Difference between means is significant at +p < .05 *p < .01 **p < .001 (ANOVA).

TABLE 8.4.   Coefficients from the regression of change in support exchanged on wired status and other independent variables at various distances (kilometers) (N=54).

Control Variables	Overall	Less than 50 km	50–500 km	More than 500 km
Wired[a]	0.29*	—	0.55**	0.25*
	(0.39)			(0.33)
Female[b]	—	—	—	—
Education	—	—	—	—
Age	—	—	—	—
Residency	—	—	—	—
Intercept	−0.24*	—	−0.51**	−0.24*
R^2	0.15*	—	0.29**	0.11*

Note: Numbers in parentheses are standardized coefficients. Only those variables that significantly improved on the explained variance (R^2) are included in the final model; +p < .05 *p < .01 **p < .001.

[a]Dummy variable for wired status, reference category is wired—access to the high-speed network.

[b]Dummy variable for gender, reference category is female.

nity activities have developed. Although this is a usual characteristic of moving into a new suburban development (Gans, 1967), wired Netville residents neighbor much more than those who are offline. Wired Netville residents on average know the names of 25 neighbors as compared to eight for the non-wired, they visit in each other's homes 50 percent more often, and the neighbors they know are spread more widely throughout Netville (Hampton, 2001b).[12]

If being wired fosters neighboring, how does it affect contact and support with friends and relatives who live nearby, but not within Netville itself? We have hypothesized that as distance to ties increases access to CMC will facilitate increased contact. At this distance, 65 percent of wired and 55 percent of non-wired residents report either no change or a small increase in contact with nearby ties (Figure 8.3). On average, wired and non-wired residents both experienced a minor drop in contact with ties at this distance (Table 8.1). While non-wired residents average a slightly greater drop in contact, analysis of variance does not identify a statistically significant difference between the mean scores of wired and non-wired residents. Controlling for gender, age, education and length of residence fails to reveal an effect of wired status on contact with network members living within 50 km, but not within Netville (Table 8.2). Years of education is the only significant variable predicting contact. As in the previous analysis, the act of moving contributed to a loss of contact for all Netville residents. Those with 17 years of education have been able to maintain contact at pre-move levels, but all other residents experienced a drop in social contact with non-neighborhood ties living within 50 km compared to a year before their move.

In sum, being wired does not increase or decrease social contact with non-neighborhood network members living within 50 km. Much contact with these network members continues to use established means of communication, such as the telephone and in person meetings. Moving to Netville and accessing its high-speed local network does not appreciably change the amount of contact.

Support: Wired residents (82 percent) are more likely than non-wired (75 percent) to report either a small increase or no change in support from nearby network members (Figure 8.4). On average, non-wired residents report almost no change in social support while wired residents report a very slight increase compared to a year before their move (Table 8.3). The mean scores for wired and non-wired residents are not statistically different (Table 8.3), nor does any other variable predict to changes in support with nearby network members (Table 8.4). As hypothesized there is no effect of CMC on the exchange of support with non-neighborhood ties living within 50 km.

Mid-Range Ties (50–500 Kilometers Away)

Contact: When network members live 50 to 500 km away, they are at a distance where telephone and in-person contact become more costly and difficult, and where less costly CMC may be used more. Controlling for other factors, Netville residents had less contact with mid-range network members as a result of their move (negative intercept in Table 8.2). Unlike nearby ties, wired residents were able to maintain contact with mid-range ties while non-wired residents were not (Tables 8.1 and 8.2). Indeed, being wired is the only significant variable for change in contact with mid-range ties. The majority (62 percent) of wired residents report no change in contact, 18 percent report a decrease and 21 percent report an increase. By contrast, although 50 percent of non-wired residents report no change, fully 45 percent report some level of lost contact, and only 5 percent report increased contact (Figure 8.5).

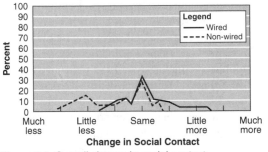

Figure 8.1. Overall change in social contact.

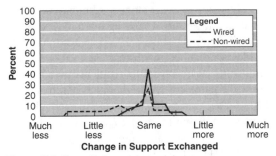

Figure 8.2. Overall change in social support.

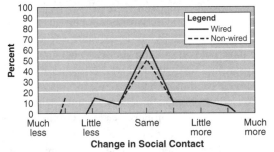

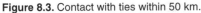

Figure 8.3. Contact with ties within 50 km.

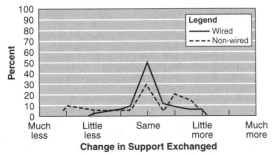

Figure 8.4. Support with ties within 50 km.

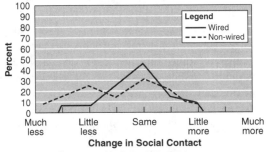

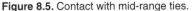

Figure 8.5. Contact with mid-range ties.

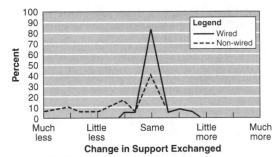

Figure 8.6. Support with mid-range ties.

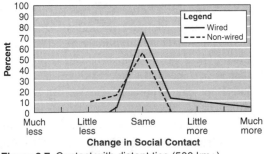

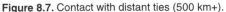

Figure 8.7. Contact with distant ties (500 km+).

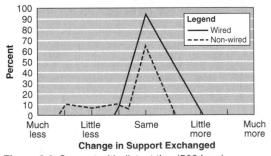

Figure 8.8. Support with distant ties (500 km+).

Support: Mid-range ties should experience the greatest increase in support as a result of being wired. They are far enough apart that CMC becomes especially useful for communication, but they are near enough to each other that the delivery of material aid (as well as emotional aid) can be accomplished without great strain. Mid-range support in Netville did not increase with being wired, but being wired has enabled residents to maintain pre-move levels of supportiveness with mid-range ties while residents who were not wired have exchanged significantly less support after moving (Tables 8.3 and 8.4). Fully 82 percent of wired residents report no change in support after moving, only 6 percent reported a decrease, and 12 percent an increase (Figure 8.6). By contrast, only 40 percent of the non-wired residents reported no change in support, the majority (55 percent) reported a decrease, and only 5 percent an increase. Moreover, being wired is the only variable significantly associated with changes in the level of support from mid-range ties (Table 8.4).[13] As with the previous analysis, there is evidence that moving to Netville introduced a barrier to the exchange of support with network members. However, when Netville residents became connected to the local high-speed network, they were able to overcome after-move barriers to the exchange of support with network members living 50 to 500 km away.

DISTANT TIES (MORE THAN 500 KILOMETERS AWAY)

Contact: Social contact by conventional means (i.e., telephone, in-person meetings) is increasingly expensive with network members who live more than 500 km away. To support the hypothesis that access to Netville's local network is most successful in increasing contact with the most distant social ties, wired residents should report an increase in contact relative to non-wired residents of greater magnitude than for their mid-range ties.

As expected, wired residents have been better able than the non-wired to maintain contact with network members living far away (Table 8.1, Figure 8.7). By contrast, non-wired residents have not been able to maintain pre-move levels of contact. This is the only measure of social contact where the wired have not only been able to maintain contact at pre-move levels but on average report an increase over pre-move levels. Being wired and being older both significantly affect contact at this distance (Table 8.2).[14] Those over the age of 38 and non-wired, and those over the age of 25 and wired have been able to maintain contact with distant network members at pre-move levels. Only one wired resident reports a decrease in social contact, while 74 percent report no change and 24 percent report an increase (Figure 8.7). By contrast, 35 percent of non-wired report a decrease in contact, 55 percent report no change, and only 10 percent an increase. The distribution of the social contact scale follows the trend of the previous two analyses: As distance to network members increases, so does the proportion of Netvillers reporting no change in social contact.

Support: By contrast to our expectation of increased *contact,* we did not expect that being wired would increase *support* exchanged with the most distant social ties. The lack of easy physical access makes distant network members ill-suited for exchanging tangible goods and services. Access to new methods of communication, provided through high-speed Internet access, may at best allow for a minor increase in the exchange of intangible, non-material support, such as emotional aid.

In practice, most wired and non-wired residents report no change after moving in the supportiveness of their most distant network members.

Yet there are significant differences between the wired and non-wired residents (Table 8.3). Once again, the Internet enables almost all wired residents (94 percent) to maintain support at pre-move levels (Figure 8.8). Only 3 percent have experienced an increase and 3 percent a decrease. By contrast, a significant minority (30 percent) of non-wired residents have experienced a drop in support with their most distant social ties, 65 percent of non-wired residents report no change, and only 5 percent an increase. Being wired is the only variable which affects changes in level of support with distant ties (Table 8.4).[15]

BEING WIRED FOSTERS CONTACT AND SUPPORT, NEAR AND FAR

Moving to Netville, a new suburban neighborhood, reduced contact and support with friends and relatives. The move to a new home and neighborhood is itself stressful, former neighbors are no longer at hand, and with the move to an outer suburb, distance may play a role in reducing contact and the exchange of support with network members (Gans, 1967; Clark, 1966). Yet Netville residents with access to a free, high-speed, always-on computer network have been more successful than the non-wired in maintaining contact and exchanging support with friends and relatives.

Relative to the non-wired, wired residents demonstrated increased contact as a result of CMC and were able to maintain contact at pre-move levels with network members living more than 50 km away. By contrast, non-wired Netville residents experienced a drop in contact with social ties at all distances in comparison to a year before their move.

As hypothesized, living in a wired neighborhood with access to free, high-speed, always-on Internet access increases social contact with distant network members. Comparing unstandardized regression coefficients at 50–500 km and 500+ km does not confirm the expectation that as distance increases, CMC facilitates greater contact (Table 8.2). Those who are wired experienced nearly the same change in social contact with ties beyond 500 km as they did with ties between 50–500 km. The slightly smaller regression coefficient for the effect of being wired on contact with ties 500+ km suggests a leveling off or even a slight drop in the effect of CMC on contact as distance increases. The slightly greater effect of being wired on contact with mid-range ties may relate to the types of support that are likely to be exchanged with ties at this distance. Frequent contact and the provision of tangible support reinforce each other (Homans, 1961; Wellman & Wortley, 1990; Wellman & Frank, 2001).

Netville residents had difficulty in maintaining pre-move levels of support with network members living more than 50 km away unless they were wired into the high-speed computer network. Wired residents maintained support at pre-move levels with ties at all distances, whereas non-wired residents had decreased support with ties more than 50 km away. Based on a comparison of unstandardized regression coefficients, being connected to Netville's high-speed network had nearly twice the effect on support with network members at the 50–500 km range as it did with those at more than 500 km (Table 8.4). This is consistent with the hypothesis that Netville's free, high-speed, always-on Internet access increased overall levels of support exchanged with network members, but that mid-range ties experienced the greatest increase in the exchange of support.

Although the move to a new suburb depressed contact and support, Netville's local computer network helped residents maintain contact and support at pre-move levels. The increased connectivity of a high-speed network should increase contact and support beyond pre-existing levels in an established neighborhood. It is not that the Internet is special. Rather, the Internet is another means of communication used along with existing media, especially in-person contact and the telephone. When distance makes in-person and telephone communication difficult, computer-mediated communication has the potential to fill the gap. Computer-mediated communication seems especially useful for increasing contact and support for those who previously had been just out of reach. The Internet fosters "glocalization": It increases local as well as global contact.

The blossoming of the Internet has affected the ways in which people connect with each other, eliminating the financial cost of long-distance communication, reducing the time cost of contacting far away people, and emphasizing communication by written text—e-mail—rather than by audio (phone) or audiovisual (in-person). Although some community ties function solely online, so-called "virtual communities" (Rheingold, 2000), in practice most people use whatever means are necessary to stay in contact with community members: in-person, by telephone, as well as the Internet (Wellman, Quan, Witte and Hampton, this issue). Contrary to dystopian predictions, new communication technologies do not disconnect people from communities. Computer-mediated communication reinforces existing communities, establishing contact and encouraging support where none may have existed before.

Part II

Gender Relations: Inequality, Sexuality, and Intimacy

Gender relations both within and outside of marriage and the family have been influenced by the ideology of patriarchal authority, which has been deeply entrenched in political, social, and economic institutions. Patriarchy has affected premarital, marital, and familial relationships and has been articulated in attitudes and behavior regarding sexuality, intimacy, power, and privilege.

However, the ideological revolutions regarding marriage and the family combined with the processes of industrialization and urbanization have produced a major reconceptualization of gender role relations within the last 200 years. Social scientists (Ariès, 1962; Shorter, 1975; Stone, 1977) have observed that prior to that period, the Western European and American nuclear family was not intimate and did not encourage domesticity or privacy. The inseparable and indistinguishable facets of social life were family and community. The notion of family privacy was practically unknown. Indeed, the very concept of the nuclear family did not emerge until the seventeenth century. The low valuation of the family in preindustrial Western society occurred because of the individual's almost total involvement with the community. The general situation was one in which most activities were public and one where people were rarely alone. The lack of privacy attributed to this overwhelming community sociability hindered the development of the family as we know it.

The family in this preindustrial period and extending into much later periods was patriarchal and authoritarian, and demanded deference. Husbands had virtually absolute power and control over wives and children. The relationship between husband and wife was not as intimate or private as it is today. In addition, the status and treatment of women varied with their involvement in economically productive work. When a woman contributed economically, she had more power and control over her own life. When she did not, her life was that of a domestically confined slave, servile and subservient to her master—her husband. The absolute power of the husband held true not only in economic terms but also in moral matters. Both women and children were relegated to subordinate legal positions that were based on the economic and political control of the husbands and fathers.

The rise of the national state, ideological changes that included emerging ideas about liberty and the importance of the individual, combined with the Industrial Revolution, all contributed to changes in the way marriage and the family were conceptualized. Traditional patriarchal relations were gradually replaced by romantic love, compassionate marriage, and an affectionate and permissive mode of child rearing. Edward Shorter (1975) labels the changes in the period after 1750 as the "Sentimental Revolution." The Sentimental Revolution ushered in a new emotional component to gender relations in three areas: courtship, the mother-child relationship, and the relationship of the family with the community.

The emergent emphasis on affection, friendship, and the romantic love ideology began to characterize courtship. As a result, marriage became more and more a matter of free choice rather than an arrangement determined by the parents on the basis of economic and social considerations. Attitudes toward children underwent a similar change, with new sentiments of affection and love emerging and neglect and indifference decreasing. An increase in the growth of maternal care and the development of a more loving attitude toward children by their mothers resulted. These shifting sentiments brought about a change in the relationship of the family to the community. Affection and caring tied the husband-wife relationship tighter and began to replace lineage, property, and economic considerations as the foundation of the marriage. Simultaneously, the couple's involvement with the community lessened.

In summary, the historical evidence illustrates two processes at work: the first is the couple's almost complete withdrawal from the community; the second is the corresponding strength of the ties of the couple with each other and with their children and close relatives. Taken together, these processes are often seen to have disturbed the grip of patriarchy on marriage and the family. The readings in this part of the book will investigate whether this has in fact occurred in the areas of dating and courtship (Chapter Three), sexuality, intimacy, and the family (Chapter Four), and in the interrelationship of gender roles, work, and the family (Chapter Five).

Most social historians believe that the modern American family emerged with the American Revolution and formed its major components by 1830. The four predominant characteristics of the American family are marriage based on affection and mutual respect, low fertility, child-centeredness, and what historian Carl Degler (1980) has called the "doctrine of the two spheres." This doctrine held that the primary role of the wife was child care and the maintenance of the household (the private sphere) while the husband's was work outside the home (the public sphere). Anchoring this doctrine was the belief that while the wife may be the moral superior in the relationship, legal and social power rests with the husband. The direct consequence is the subordination of women's roles to their husbands'. To deal with subordination, women carved out a source of power based on the emerging importance of mutual affection, love, and sexuality as integral components of modern marriage. As we shall see, a number of our readings will examine this development within an analysis of dating and courtship processes and in the expressions of sexuality.

An analysis of American courtship processes reflects historical changes that have shifted decision making from parental control to the couple themselves. This shift reflects the emerging nineteenth-century attitude that marriage should be based on personal happiness and the affection of the partners for each other. As marriage began to be equated with love and individualism, the growing acceptance of affection as the primary ground for marriage became an essential factor in the change in women's roles and a potential source of power and autonomy within the family. A woman could appeal to her husband's affection for her, and she, in turn, could manipulate that affection to increase her power or influence within marriage and the household.

Similarly, the expression of sexuality both within and outside of the courtship process took on a power component. The Victorian notion of the "passionlessness" woman can be seen as serving to improve women's status. Nancy Cott (1979) contends that the downplaying of sexuality could be used as a means of limiting male domination. The de-emphasis of feminine sexuality was replaced by an emphasis on women's moral and spiritual superiority over males and was used to enhance their status and widen their opportunities.

The doctrine of the two spheres that developed in the nineteenth century defined the essence of maleness as occupational involvement and the pursuit of worldly and material success. Women, on the other hand, were defined in terms of home—wife and mother—involvement and moral virtue. As a consequence, the idealization of masculine and feminine behavior affected courtship to the extent that romantic love took on greater importance as the criterion for marriage than ever before. Yet, ultimately, the doctrine of the two spheres continued to foster obstacles to friendship between the sexes, often resulting in a reliance on same sex friendships. Further, it severely handicapped the development of emotional bonds within courtship.

The study of dating and courtship patterns on college campuses in the United States has long fascinated sociologists. Perhaps the most famous analysis was conducted by Willard Waller (1937) in his study of what he called the "rating and dating complex," which he observed on the Pennsylvania State University campus in the 1930s. Waller described a mutually exploitative dating system in which male students sought sexual gratification while women sought to enhance their prestige by going out with the more desirable men and being taken to restaurants, theaters, amusements, etc. As a result, dating became a bargaining relationship with exploitative and antagonistic overtones. Waller further speculated that the gender-role antagonisms generated by the dating system were continued in courtship, love, and marriage, and led to undesirable emotional tensions throughout the couples' lives. He conceptualized the "principle of least interest" to describe how unequal emotional involvement could lead to the person with "least interest" exploiting the other throughout their relationship.

More than 60 years later, we see how a new technology, computers and the Internet, continues to transform dating patterns. Reading 9 provides an historical analytical update of dating patterns throughout the twentieth century. Lynn Schofield Clark's examination of the emerging practice of teenage dating on the Internet is developed out of a broader qualitative investigation on the role of media technologies on domestic households. The gains and risks of using the Internet for dating purposes, the impact on one's cyberspace identity, and the comparison of Internet dating to "real-life" relationships are investigated. Finally, the role of trust and intimacy in Internet relationships compared with "real-life" relationships comes under scrutiny. In her article, Clark's respondents were affluent Caucasians. She points out that teen dating experiences on the Internet are more common for this group than for other classes and races.

Our interest in the diversity of dating patterns leads to the next reading. The underlying assumptions of dating and courtship patterns on college campuses has significantly changed since Willard Waller's classic study of 1938. The authors of Reading 10, Alexandra Berkowitz and Irene Padavic report on significant differences in extramural patterns that exist between members of white and black sororities. White sororities encourage romantic pairings ("getting a man") while black sororities focus on careers and community service ("getting ahead"). The authors explain that the differences in orientations of these two groups lie in their different histories and current structural positions. For black sororities, historic images of strong, independent black women and the modern reality of black female marriage and poverty rates have shaped the sorority structure. White sororities, on the other hand, have emphasized finding a man as a source of support. The authors argue that this orientation is at odds both with a modern reality that dictates labor force participation for all women and with members' career aspirations.

Johanna Lessinger's discussion (Reading 11) is of arranged, semi-arranged, or love marriages among young people living in the United States whose parents are from India and who share the social and cultural of that society. Decisions regarding appropriate marital arrangements revolve around the issues of individualism and love versus tradition and family cultural continuity. The experiences of these young Indian-Americans echo those of their historical and contemporary immigrant and ethnic counterparts as they confront living in America.

Chapter Four, "Sexuality, Intimacy and the Family," opens with an exploration of how love is defined differently by women and men. Francesca M. Cancian explores the "feminization of love" in Reading 12. The feminized perspective defines love in terms of emotional expressiveness, verbal self-disclosure, and affection. Women are identified with this perspective. In contrast, the definition largely ignores love manifested by instrumental help or the sharing of physical activities that has been identified with masculine behavior. She argues that, by conceptualizing love in this manner, polarized gender-role relationships that contribute to social and economic inequality occur. Cancian calls for an androgynous perspective that rejects the underlying ideology of separate spheres and validates masculine as well as feminine styles of love.

The traditional nuclear family of mother, father, and children is often depicted and seen as the normative form of family life. As Susan E. Dalton and Denise D. Bielby point out in Reading 13, it seems to be both natural and biological and a taken-for-granted social institution. Yet, there are other well-functioning family life forms. In their discussion, Dalton and Bielby investigate mothers who live in lesbian-headed, two-parent families. These lesbian mothers examine institutionalized understandings of sex, gender, and sexual orientation in their construction of social arrangements such as parenting roles within the family. The women studied by the authors draw upon and transform institutionalized scripts, practices, and understandings of family roles and relations. By doing so, they organize their parenting based on the premise of mothering by two women and rewrite the traditional mother and father roles. Further, the authors argue, that as two-parent lesbian- or gay-headed families become more known and acceptable, social scripts regarding the appropriate sexual makeup of the two-parent family will begin to change as well.

Reading 14, "Islamic Family Ideals and Their Relevance to American Muslim Families," examines the relationship of gender roles to religious ideals and practices. Bahira Sherif believes that any discussion of Muslim families both in the United States and elsewhere must be grounded in an analysis of gender roles. A fundamental Islamic belief is that there is a distinct difference between males and females that is manifest in personalities, social roles, and functions. Male and female activities that occur outside of the family and in marriage and parent-child relationships can best be explained by this gender dichotomy. She further observes how differences in Muslim practices can be due to variations in culture, ethnicity and race, class, educational level, and place of residence. Her paper examines the American cultural influences on Islamic family ideals.

Chapter 5, "Gender Roles, Work, and the Family," contains three readings focusing on gender relationships in terms of the different allocations and divisions of labor that exist between outside work and the home. Arlie Russell Hochschild (1989) examined the contemporary dual-career family in her widely praised book, *The Second Shift*. Hochschild is concerned with how cultural definitions of "appropriate" domestic roles and labor-force roles affect marital dynamics. She observes that contemporary economic trends have altered women's lives much more than they have altered men's lives.

Women have found themselves in new circumstances: They are working full time in the paid labor force, yet, at the same time, they are seen as primarily involved in domestic work. As a result, women are experiencing a "culture lag" in the larger world and a "gender lag" in the home. There is a lag regarding both attitudes and behavior towards women's paid work and domestic work.

In her book, *The Time Bind*, Hochschild (1997) examines the ways in which women are also using work as an escape from domestic duties. Based on this research, Hochschild reports in Reading 15 that the demands of domestic work (shopping, cooking, cleaning, and childcare), especially in light of the fact that both women and men are employed outside the home, have led to a very curious development. Work for many is now becoming the site for refuge. No longer is one's home one's castle; the new "haven in a heartless world" is the work site. The real possibility of child neglect as a consequence of the removal of parents from the home is explored in Hochschild's provocative article.

In Reading 16, "Gender, Class, Family, and Migration: Puerto Rican Women in Chicago," Maura I. Toro-Morn provides another illustration of the interrelationship of migration patterns and gender relations within the family. Toro-Morn documents how women who joined their husbands in Chicago either participated in the paid economy or contributed with the reproductive work—the taking care of children, husbands, and families—that supported their husbands and families. She compares working-class to better-educated middle-class Puerto Rican women and examines how both had to confront dual responsibilities for the reproductive work that takes place in the home and the economically productive work that takes place outside the home.

The concluding reading (17) in this part of the book, "Baseball Wives, Gender and Work of Baseball," examines the private family life of baseball wives. Their baseball playing husbands are employed in a highly visible and public occupation. It's interesting that a sport such as baseball that affects so many lives in a broad societal way, is not studied in terms of the effects it has on people who are most personally involved with it. George Gmelch and Patricia Mary San Antonio utilize their anthropological training to examine how the structure and constraints of the occupation of professional baseball shapes the lives of the players' wives. The role of baseball wives is constrained by high geographical mobility, the husband's frequent absences, a lack of a viable social support network, and the precariousness of baseball careers. Baseball wives are expected to follow the traditional template of supportive wife and mother. However, the authors report that because of the nature of the baseball industry they become far more independent and resourceful than many American women, managing families and households on their own.

References

Ariès, Philippe. 1962. *Centuries of Childhood: A Social History of Family Life.* Translated by Robert Baldick. New York: Knopf.

Cott, Nancy. 1979. "Passionlessness: An Interpretation of Victorian Sexual Ideology, 1790–1850." Pp. 162–181 in *A Heritage of Her Own,* edited by Nancy F. Cott and Elizabeth H. Pleck. New York: Simon and Schuster.

Degler, Carl N. 1980. *At Odds: Women and the Family in America from the Revolution to the Present.* New York: Oxford University Press.

Hochschild, Arlie (with Anne Machung). 1989. *The Second Shift: Working Parents and the Revolution at Home.* New York: Viking.

Hochschild, Arlie Russell. 1997. *The Time Bind: When Work Becomes Home & Home Becomes Work.* New York: Metropolitan Books.

Shorter, Edward. 1975. *The Making of the Modern Family.* New York: Basic Books.

Stone, Lawrence. 1977. *The Family, Sex and Marriage in England 1500–1800.* Abridged edition. New York: Harper/Colophon Books.

Waller, Willard. 1937. "The Rating and Dating Complex." *American Sociological Review* 2:727–734.

3   Premarital and Mate Selection Relationships

Reading 9   Dating on the Net: Teens and the Rise of "Pure" Relationships

LYNN SCHOFIELD CLARK*

At the end of the 16th century, Marianne Dashwood, the fictional teenaged character in Jane Austen's novel *Sense and Sensibility,* committed an impropriety of great consequence to her own reputation: She wrote letters conveying her affection to John Willoughby, despite the fact that they were not engaged to be married (Austen, 1795/1989). Teenaged males and females, at least of the class and stature of which Austen wrote in the 18th century, did not interact except in suitably supervised situations or within the bounds of engagement to be married. Times certainly have changed.

Using qualitative interviews, participant observation, and teen-led focus groups, this chapter explores the emergent practice of teenage dating on the Internet. I consider these practices in the context of dating patterns throughout this century to develop an understanding of the possible cultural significance of the current practice. Net relationships provide many routes to emotional satisfaction among their participants, and Internet dating affords teen girls in particular the opportunity to experiment with and claim power within heterosexual relationships. Yet, are the resultant relationships more emancipatory than those found in the "real-life" experiences of teens as a result? Are new teen communities constituted as these seemingly egalitarian relationships are formed? And by extension, do these Net relationships foster change in the lived social relations of the teens' local context? I argue here that the practice of Internet dating shares many characteristics with the "pure" relationship, Anthony Giddens's (1991) term for those relationships, characteristic of modernity, which are engaged in primarily for the gratifications they offer through interpersonal intimacy. Internet dating provides an illustration of the "pure" relationship in its contemporary form. Yet Internet dating relationships among teens also challenge Giddens's analysis, suggesting that our cultural understandings of the nature of relationships, and how they are evaluated in relation to issues of trust, commitment, and longevity, may be changing in subtle and not fully emancipatory ways.

STUDYING TEENS AND THE INTERNET

This study on dating and the Internet emerged out of a broader qualitative study on the role of media technologies in the domestic context of the household.[1] Over the course of a year, I conducted a series of interviews and observations with 15 families and two focus groups, devoting between 4 and much more than 30 hours of conversation, observation, or both to each family. A total of 47 teens and 26 of their family members were included in the interviews, groups, and observations. An additional six families (14 teens) were interviewed by an associate researcher on the project, who has corroborated my findings.

From the families interviewed, three teenagers were selected for the further study of Internet use: Elizabeth, a 15-year-old white female from a lower-income single parent household; Jake, a 17-year-old white male from a middle-income blended (two-parent, second marriage) household; and Michael, a 15-year-old African American male from a lower income single parent household. These individuals were chosen because they represented "information-rich cases," in that I expected that they would yield findings that would contrast from expectations and from each other due to their differing social, economic, and political positions within the wider culture (Yin, 1994, pp. 45–46). As one example, Elizabeth, whose family is on a very limited income and is of course female, has been very active in on-line chat rooms, whereas Jake, the middle-class male in a well-educated family, has been the least active. Michael falls somewhere in between in chat room use, but he is noteworthy as an underprivileged youth who has developed competence in Web design through opportunities in a community center and through his own initiative. I also selected them for their ability to be thoughtful, articulate, and responsible, as I wanted to train them to serve as leaders of what I have called *peer-led discussion groups,*

focus groups that were led and participated in solely by teens. This format was adopted as a means to more closely observe how teenagers "really" talk about these issues when an adult is not present. The method follows the suggestion of qualitative methodology expert Elizabeth Bird (personal communication, 1995). In addition to training each of the teens to serve as a discussion group leader, I also worked with each of them to modify an interview guide I had constructed, making it appropriate and comfortable for each leader. Each of these teens recruited six friends of the same gender to participate in their discussion group, which the leader arranged, conducted, and tape recorded. Once the group had met, I transcribed the audiotapes and then met with the leaders once again to discuss the process and their responses to it. They listened to the tapes and checked to be sure that the statements were properly attributed. They also provided information about the group's dynamics, giving me insight into why some individuals may have answered (or declined to answer) as they did.[2]

Whereas my research primarily is based on these interviews and observations in "real life," I supplemented the knowledge gained through these methods by "lurking" in teen chat rooms. Elizabeth also allowed me to read many of the e-mail exchanges she had had with her on-line male friends.

Although many of the teens discussed using the Net for school-related research, the teens in my study primarily used the Net to communicate with other young people in the teen chat rooms of Microsoft Network, America Online, and the teen lobby of Yahoo! These "socially produced spaces" constitute a form of "synchronistic communication," in that the posts are ephemeral and immediate (Baym, 1995; Jones, 1995). They are seen by all those in the chat room at the same time, and answers to various queries posted to the chat room often overlap, creating a cacophony of conversation. Most of the teens with whom I spoke had experienced similar periods of intense experimentation in the chat rooms, sometimes devoting more than 4 hours a day to on-line chats for a period of several weeks or even months. In most cases, however, this period was followed by parent sanctioning, which either severely limited or discontinued the teen's chat room participation altogether. Despite the frequent warnings concerning the dangers facing teens on the Internet, parents were largely unaware of the content of the chat rooms; the limits were set based on what in some cases were alarmingly high bills from their service providers.[3]

Much like the adults on the Net discussed by Rheingold (1991) and others, teens seemed to be drawn to Internet chat rooms by the promise of fantasy and fun. As Kramarae (1995) noted in her critique of the overwhelmingly male population in cyberspace, the males far outnumbered the females in teen chat rooms as well. Yet there were also differences between the communications between teens and those I witnessed on the adult chat lines. Perhaps most obvious was the "age and sex check," the frequent request that resulted in the sharing of ages and genders among participants, often serving as a precursor for those of similar ages to break off into a separate chat room of only two persons, which the girls, at least, agreed constituted an "Internet 'date'" (the boys were less comfortable with the term "dating" to describe the interaction between males and females on the Net, as I will discuss more fully at a later point). As Elizabeth explained:

> What would usually happen is that we would meet for the first time in a chat room, and then if I decide I want to talk to them more personally, I would get a chat room for only like two or three people, so we wouldn't get people coming in and out all the time. And we'd talk for a little while, until one of us had to

> leave or something. We'd exchange e-mail addresses, and we'd like write every once in a while. And like, we could get together at a certain time. I'd say, "I'm gonna be on the 'Net' at this time, if you can meet me at this chat room at this time, then I'll see you there." And if they can't, then that's okay.

Sometimes these initial conversations between two teens would last for several hours. The topics of conversation mirrored those one might hear at a teen party. Internet dating, much like the practice's counterpart in "real life," exists within a specific environment that in many ways, not surprisingly, shares similarities with the other social contexts in which teens find themselves. Thus, we turn to a discussion of the environment of teen chat rooms within which (or out of which) Internet dating occurs, beginning with a review of the practice in its historical context.

Teenagers and Dating: A Brief History

Teenage "dating"—the casual romantic interactions between males and females (or, even more recently, between persons of the same gender)—is a relatively recent phenomenon. Historians argue that it emerged among middle-class teens in the 1920s during a time of gender role upheaval (Bailey, 1988). With the rise of both compulsory education and restrictive child labor laws during this era, teens of immigrant and farm families who once had been expected to work, as well as teens from more privileged classes, were now sent to school. Education was cemented into the American teen experience, affording increased public opportunities for young people to interact with one another under minimal supervision by their parents.

The rise of the "dance craze" in the 1920s also has been linked to the emergence of the practice of "dating" (Modell, 1989). Whereas some teens in the decade before had attended community dances that were sponsored by neighborhoods or other social clubs (and hence had fairly strict social restraints that limited the "tendency to overstep moral rules"), it was the opening of a dance "palace" in New York City in 1911 that ushered in new practices surrounding dancing and dating (Modell, 1989, p. 71). The large dance halls that subsequently sprang up in urban areas made dancing with relative strangers an accessible and intriguing new option for teens. The dance style of the period, as it moved away from formal steps and toward increased free expression and physical contact, encouraged the establishment of casual heterosexual relationships in a way not previously seen.

During the same era, film houses multiplied throughout urban as well as rural areas, and weekly attendance at motion pictures increased dramatically. The darkened theater and the heightened emotions film evoked offered further opportunities for physical closeness. Whereas films often were attended by groups of teens, they quickly became vehicles for the exploration of exclusive intergender relations as well (Blumer, 1933).

Modell (1989) credited middle-class girls of this era with actually initiating the practice of dating, as they had the most to gain from the establishment of the practice. He wrote, "Before dating, parents had tended to construe strictly girls' obligation to enter marriage untainted by even a hint of scandal, and they supervised courting accordingly, limiting both its occasion and the set of eligibles." As parents were more concerned with their daughters' reputations than their sons', "girls were far more constrained by parental oversight" (Modell, 1989, p. 95). Whereas dating in the early part of the century still required the male to take initiative, it shifted control over the girls' interactions—and by extension, her sexuality—from her parents to her peers. It thus served as a potent aspect of

youth rebellion against parents and their traditional ways. Whereas girls of this generation would not be considered sexually liberated by today's standards, dating enabled girls to play a more active role in constructing and maintaining heterosexual interaction through informal rules of conduct. Dating required teen boys to negotiate with teen girls and their peers directly, rather than through their families. To a significant extent, dating shifted the approval and sanctioning of romantic relationships from parents to peers.

Dating then, as now, consisted of going to movies, dances, or restaurants. As such, dating, and by extension romance, quickly came to be linked with leisure and consumption, as Illouz argued (Illouz, 1997). Moreover, as the rising consumerism of this era encouraged immediate gratification, young people began to think of self-denial for its own sake as old-fashioned, seeking in dancing and dating some fulfillment of the sexual tensions of adolescence (Fass, 1977). Whereas chaperoning and "calling" were steadily replaced among middle-class teens by the practice of dating, however, those teens of all races with less means were less likely to date. Part of this is due to the fact that these teens were usually encouraged to lighten the family's financial obligations either by seeking employment or marrying. By the middle of the century, however, in part due to the popular romanticized narratives of the practice in film, television, and magazines, "dating" became an integral part of the teen experience in the United States.

Since the cultural shifts and sexual revolutions of the 1960s, however, dating as a teenage institution has been in decline. Ironically, as Modell (1989) pointed out, dating, which originally caught on as a form of rebellion from establishment and traditional values, "had moved from a 'thrill'-based innovation half a century before to a somewhat fading bastion of essentially 'traditional' marriage values" by the

1960s (p. 303). Today teens use the term "dating" in a somewhat bemused way, often with self-conscious ironic reference to the 1950s version of the practice. Whereas they still go out on dates, these occasions are less fraught with specific expectations. They are less frequently planned in advance, for example, and there is also less compulsion to report on the experience to one's peers. "Dating" has become much more idiosyncratic, with less reference to the external peer group and more relation to the self-gratifications and pleasures of the individuals involved. This is part of a larger turn toward issues of self-reflexivity and identity as central aspects of relationships, as I will show.

Cyberdating Relationship as Emancipatory

Cyberdating's potential to limit emotional pain in relationships seems particularly appealing for teen girls. Indeed, the girls in my study were, on the whole, much more enthusiastic about the possibilities afforded to Net dating than the boys of the same age. "I'm not too popular with the guys," 15-year-old Elizabeth explained to me, noting that Net relationships held less potential for the pain of rejection. On the Internet, employing her excellent skills in verbal articulation and humor, she seemed to have no difficulty meeting and developing relationships with boys and was even "dating four guys at once." "Usually I act a lot more aggressive when I'm on the Internet," she stated. "I just express my feelings a lot more in the chat rooms and stuff, so if somebody talks about something that I don't like, then I'll say it. And I would, probably never do that in class, in school and everything." As Reid has written of the Net experience in general, "Users are able to express and experiment with aspects of their personality that social inhibition would generally encourage them to suppress" (Reid, 1991, cited in Baym, 1995, p. 143).

This suggests that girls may use the verbal skills they might otherwise suppress to parlay themselves into a stronger position in relationship to their male counterparts, thereby assuming more authority in the construction of the heterosexual relationship. This was illustrated in one of the peer-led discussion group's conversations about sexual behaviors on the Net:

Elizabeth: The only thing I didn't like about those guys [two "brothers" she was dating simultaneously] was that they liked sex just a little bit too much.
Vickie: Cybersex?
Lisa: Kinky?
Elizabeth: They liked sex, it was scary. They e-mailed me a message that like, had a lot to do with sex, and you know, we didn't—I didn't have my own screen name or e-mail address, so it was like, oh my God! [Either her mother or brother, who share her account, could have read it] So I like deleted it before I even read it. And when I was talking with them later, they're all, "did you get my message?" And I'm all, "uh, no. Yes, I did, but I didn't have a chance to read it. My brother tried to read it, so I deleted it before I could read it, I'm sorry." Yeah-right! [the girls all laugh]. But you know I never even told those guys I was getting off the Internet when I did. So I just kinda like, disappeared.
Betsi: How long do you think they were talking, thinking you were there?
Vickie: They're like, sitting there writing all these messages to you, and you're gone.

Elizabeth: Well, I got off the Internet, my mom canceled the thing [the AOL account], and I never told them that I was gonna cancel.

In this situation, unwanted sexual advances were not only rebuffed but resulted in Elizabeth's creation of a potentially embarrassing situation for the boys as they may have found themselves talking (or masturbating?) without an audience. Further, the boys were objectified as the story became a shared experience of female triumph among the girlfriends.

To further strengthen their position in the dating interaction, several teen girls reported that they adopt new physical personae, describing their looks in such a way as to appear more attractive to the males. This not only fulfills the function of avoiding potential pain and rejection but also neutralizes some of the power aspects of the heterosexist system in which beautiful girls are given more attention and more social opportunities (Brown & Gilligan, 1992). If everyone constructs their appearance in accord with the imagined "ideal," after all, no one can be judged more or less desirable based solely on appearances. Thus in effect, boys lose some of their power as one of the primary tools of the evaluation of desirability is removed from the equation. It would appear that in these relationships, it is no longer wholly a matter of the men as consumers and women as consumed, is has been argued in less interactive contexts (see, e.g., Kramarae, 1995). Girls feel empowered through the power of self-presentation.

Interestingly, both Michael and Jake state that they dislike it when girls lie about their looks in the chat rooms. As Jake said,

Jake: You can kinda like tell [if they're lying, because of] how they're putting it and all. Sometimes they get

too extreme with their lying. You're like, "whatever."
Interviewer: So that's kind of a turn-off, then, when you can tell that they're lying?
Jake: Yeah. "Bye." And then go back into the chat room.

Michael noted that looks are less important on the Net than they are in real life.

Interviewer: So what is the difference, do you think, between meeting someone in the chat room and dating somebody in person?
Michael: Well, when you're dating somebody and it seems like, you're more looking at them, but when you're like, chatting to them, you can't see them, but you can get that trust going with the person, and you can really get to know them before you see them. And if you know 'em before you see them, you'll like, even if they don't look physically attractive to you, you'll still like them because you know them and you have a lot in common.

When he learned that one of the girls with whom he was chatting had lied about her looks, Michael noted that he did not abandon the relationship because he had not entered it with romantic intent based on looks:

Michael: Okay, I ask them [girls he's met in chat rooms] to describe themselves, and some of them, they lie. Like one girl, she said she was 5'5," 130 some

*pounds, I forgot, and I went on
her Web page, and she was pretty
big. [laughs.] So I asked her why
she lied, she was like, "I was
scared you wouldn't like me." But
I talk to her still, though…*

*Interviewer: Have you ever, when
people have said what they
looked like, decided that you
didn't like them?*

*Michael: No. Mostly, when I go on
the Web, I'm looking for friends,
so it really doesn't matter what
they look like.*

Thus, even though boys may dislike the changing of looks, they are still able to find on-line relationships with girls satisfying. Instead of being under pressure by their peers to pair with the "right" girls whose looks approximate the ideal, the Internet allows for more egalitarian exchange freed from most of the restraint of peer approval. Indeed, several of the teens noted that what begins as somewhat romantic or titillating Internet exchanges often grows into positive, ongoing relationships with members of the opposite sex. This suggests some hope for the Net's ability to contribute to positive teen communities both in cyberspace and beyond. Also, because physical contact is (usually) impossible in a Net relationship, young people may find that they are able to communicate with one another free from the social and peer pressures toward expressed sexuality.

Yet, whereas this might suggest a depth of relationship is possible, my research actually affirmed that the opposite is much more common. This is not surprising, as the environment of teen chat rooms in many ways mirrors the social restraints teens experience in "real life." For example, let us return to the consideration of the fact that girls change their appearances to achieve

more social power. In this action, teen girls are not redefining standards of acceptability based on beauty but are using the Net to actively construct what they believe is a more socially acceptable version of themselves. Each of the teen discussion groups expressed agreement in the fact that "on the Internet, they [persons of the opposite sex] cannot see you." Whereas the lack of physical presence undoubtedly lowers inhibitions as Kiesler and colleagues argued, the fact that each group mentioned this when contrasting dating on the Internet to dating in "real life" demonstrates the importance of visual appearance in the currency of popularity and hence one's desirability as a "date" (Kiesler, Siegel, & McGuire, 1984). Not surprisingly, given the opportunities afforded on the Net, girls are very conscious of the on-line presentations of themselves. Elizabeth notes, for example, "Usually I describe myself skinnier or taller. Skinnier and taller, with longer hair, and a lighter color blond, usually." In this way, Elizabeth's employment of the technology is in keeping with social conventions concerning gender roles. She was not interested in meeting the boys with whom she conversed, as this might undermine her attractive and aggressive on-line persona. In fact, when one of the male friends suggested that they talk on the phone, she deliberately kept her phone line busy during the appointed time so that he would not be able to get through. She said that they did not "talk" again on-line after that, something she seemed to have no regrets about, even though she reported that the relationship had been fairly intimate before that time. She also noted that although she had never "met" anyone on-line from her own school, she had decided to terminate one relationship owing to the fact that the boy attended a neighboring school:

*We started comparing notes about
who we knew in each others' schools.*

But I didn't want to meet him, or someone from my own school, because then what if I knew who he was in person and he said something mean about me, I'd be like, hurt.

"Dates" with faceless and voiceless boys from faraway places held no such possible consequences. The fact that Elizabeth avoided rejection in "real" relationships and still sensed a need to censure her ideas when not on-line further demonstrates that the power afforded through self-construction on the Net does not translate into changed gender roles and expectations in the social world beyond cyberspace. Consistent with the findings of Rakow and Navarro in their study of the introduction of cellular phones, therefore, we must conclude that the possibility that new communication technologies might subvert social systems is limited (Rakow & Navarro, 1993; see also Rakow, 1988). Indeed, there is evidence of much more that is socially reproduced into the chat rooms from the environment of "real life."

BORDER PATROL: THE POLICING OF GENDER AND TABOO RELATIONSHIPS

The content of teen chat rooms on the whole appears to be much tamer than many of the adult that rooms.[4] Whereas adults are explicit about their desires, as Seabrook (1997) has illustrated, teens are much more reserved and, not surprisingly, less creative verbally. Much like the furtive illicit activities of the proverbial backseat, teens were reluctant to speak of their sexual experimentation, and what happened in the "private" two-person chat sessions was not up for discussion in the more public chat rooms.

Sex was an exciting but also heavily policed topic in the teen chat rooms. On several occasions in teen chat rooms, in fact, persons who issued explicit invitations for cybersex were sanctioned through prolonged "silences" (in which the on-screen dialogue was halted) followed by statements such as, "Whoa" or even "watch the language." There were also comments of mockery directed at the overzealous pursuer, such as the comment following an age and sex check: "ha ha RYAN, all 2 young 4 you!" On the whole, the teens seemed much less comfortable expressing their sexual desires and fantasies in the larger group of a teen chat room than the adults did in their counterpart rooms, although there were suggestive screen names adopted by the teens, such as "Tiger-lover," or the more explicit "Rydher69her."

Just as in "real life," teens in chat rooms seem to be more vocal than their adult counterparts in policing the boundaries of race and sex. In the following exchange, a racist remark was "policed" by calling on homophobic language, thus substituting gender for race in the goal of "policing" what is "normal":

> *Rydher69er: What the fuck was up with that racist remark earlier*
> *Rydher69er: That was gay ass shit!!!!!!*
> *Kandi1998: 17/f/cali*
> *UziKlown: gay, eh?*
> *UziKlown: Are you saying you like gay ass?*
> *Brocky8638: Right back where I started*
> *UziKlown: or just "gay ass shit"?*
> *Hhoneycutt: Nahh, I ain't racist*
> *UziKlown: Pretty messed up, I say*

This exchange illustrates another difference between adult and teen chat rooms: Teens are more overtly critical of homosexuality and use derogatory terms to police the boundaries of heterosexuality and to place themselves safely within its realm. In his analysis of the heterosexist culture of adolescent schooling, Friend (1993) has observed, "a systematic set of institutional and cultural arrangements exist that reward and privilege people for being or appearing to be heterosexual, and establish potential punishments or lack of privilege for being or appearing to be homosexual" (p. 210). Friend pointed to textbooks that assume a heterosexual norm and teachers reluctant to discuss homosexuality altogether as ways in which heterosexism is reinforced through silencing. Heterosexist ideas extended beyond the classroom to the adolescents' homes and are reinforced in the media through texts that assume the norm of heterosexuality. Being labeled a homosexual or lesbian by one's peers, regardless of the reason, then, has real material consequences: Loss of friendships, marginalization, and physical violence may result. Thus teens, both heterosexual and homosexual, have a great investment in maintaining a "straight" identity in the context of public schools and constantly seek to assert their heterosexuality. Teen chat rooms, along with other locations in which teen discussions occur, serve as platforms on which young people may assert their alignment with the dominant ideology of heterosexuality as a means of affirming that they are accepted and acceptable among their peers. One can therefore imagine the therapeutic and liberating potential of gay and lesbian teen chat rooms for young persons. I have not analyzed these chat rooms here because among the teens in my study, experiences in these locations were not discussed except in instances in which the speaker was asserting his or her own heterosexuality. For instance, mention of gay and lesbian chat rooms surfaced in the discussion groups when the peer leaders asked them, "which is the worst chat room to meet boys or girls?" In each group someone answered, "The gay [or lesbian] lounge," followed by raucous laughter.

In addition to overt sexual advances and the sanctioning of homosexuality, there were also at least three potential hazards of Internet communication that further illustrated the borders of acceptability in teen chat room communication. These involved gender confusion, mistaking a person in "real life" for an anonymous converser on the Net, and, for females, avoiding the potential adult male stalker. The first story came about when Elizabeth was asked, "Do you ever make friends with girls on-line?" She replied,

Yeah. A lot. Usually I'll post a BBS in some kind of folder, and it'll be like, "I'm new to the network. If you'd like to talk—." I'll like describe myself, what I like to do, and be like, "If you want to talk, then here's my address," and then I'll set up a time. And sometimes, most of the times, it was guys. 'Cause I think that's what a lot of people look for in relationships on the Internet. But sometimes I'd get a girl, and we'd talk about whatever. One time I was talking to this girl.... We both thought—I thought that she was a guy, and she thought that I was a guy. So we went in, and we started talking, and she goes, "Oh, I'm a model for Teen magazine." And I was like, "No-way!" And she said, "Yeah, I'm gonna be in next month's." And I looked at it, and there was a girl on the front cover, and I was like, "Wait a minute!" So it got me weirded out, and I got back on the Internet, and I said, "Are you a girl?" and she said, "Yeah, is there a problem with that?" and I said, "Well, I'm a girl, too." She goes, "Oh, my gosh! I thought you were a guy!" So sometimes you can get kind of confused if you don't specify who you are.

After this initial confusion, Elizabeth attempted to e-mail the girl again but noted that the "model" at first did not reply and then eventually explained that she did not have time to keep in touch with Elizabeth. The preferred method of communication on-line is apparently that of a heterosexual dyad, and while friendships between girls are permitted, the potential for misunderstood motives makes them more risky owing to the fears of homosexuality noted above. The mistaken identity problem also extends to on-line communication between two people who believe that they do not know one another, but actually do, as in these two stories offered during the girls' discussion group:

> Vickie: *My friend goes to school with this guy who she had had a crush on for like, years. Since 6th grade she's had a crush on this guy, and they've just been friends. One day she was on the Internet in a chat room, and she was sitting there talking and they were talking back, and all of a sudden—she has this thing about slinkies, and she gave her friend a slinky for good luck at his swim meet. And she's sitting there, they're talking, and he goes, "do you have a slinky?" She goes, "Matt?!" [uproarious laughter]*
> Elizabeth: *My cousin did that. He was talking on the Internet, it's like a small one, it's not all over the United States; it's just in Colorado or something, and she's talking to this guy. One thing led to another, and she asked if he likes*

> *"If They Were Giants." And he's like, "yeah," She goes, "Wow, my younger brother likes them, too." Turns out that she was talking to her younger brother on the Internet. She didn't even know! She's like, "Tristan?" [momentary silence]*
> Lisa: *How weird.*
> Allyson: *Weird.*
> Betsi: *That's odd.*

The Internet offers risks, therefore, that not only hold the potential of threatening one's cyber-space identity but of invading and confusing "real-life" relationships, as well. But perhaps the most fearsome example of how Internet relationships might disrupt real life were discussed in terms of an Internet stalker. This shadowy figure emerged when the leader asked, "What do your parents think about dating on the Internet? And if they don't know about it, what do you think they would think about it?"

> Allyson: *No! Absolutely no! They won't let me date at all. They're mean, evil people.*
> Betsi: *My parents think it's gross.*
> Lisa: *They wouldn't care, they'd think it was weird. They'd be like, "Okay, if you think so." But...*
> Elizabeth: *My mom didn't have a problem with it, because she knew that I couldn't do anything with this guy. Specially since most of the guys I met were like...*
> Allyson: *But you don't know...*
> Lisa: *Yeah, I don't think my parents would...*
> Betsi: *Well, I mean—are you crazy??*
> Allyson: *Some of them can be really gross perverts, and they can find*

*out where you live, and stuff,
which is really quite dangerous.*

*Elizabeth: Yeah. That's the only
thing my mom's paranoid about.
She's like, "don't give them your
phone number. Don't give them
your real name."*

*Vickie: And don't give them your
address.*

*Elizabeth: And don't tell them even
what state you live in. I always do
it anyway. They're like, "where do
you live?" I'm like, "Colorado."
Big deal. [sarcastically] It's a big
state, people, come on!*

*Lisa: "Where do you live? I live
in…"*

*Allyson: I'm sure they're gonna go
door-to-door and ask, "has anyone gone on the Internet with this
name? You don't have a computer? Okay, next house!" [up-
roarious laughter]*

Betsi: [laughing] I'm sure!

In this situation, the potential stalker is not discussed within the context of what has happened to
someone's friend (as was the case in the earlier
example of border patrol) or to one of the girls
themselves but in relation to what *could* happen.
Whereas parents are clearly not involved in the
teen chat rooms, their influence is felt in their
ability to convincingly warn their children of the
potential dangers of the practice of dating on the
Net. Yet, also in this instance, the teen chat room
is affirmed as a place for those of their own age,
as they discuss deflection of potential intruders
while simultaneously assuming greater expertise
over their environment than that displayed by
their parents.

The norm of interaction in teen chat rooms,
therefore, to extend the earlier argument, is of

heterosexual dyads between two persons of the
opposite sex and approximately the same age
who did not know one another in other contexts.
This of course echoes the norms of romantic
interaction occurring in the high school. Yet chat
room and follow-up e-mail experiences have
afforded teen participants an opportunity to
experiment with heterosexual relationships in
ways that are rather different from, and in certain
ways less risky than, those occurring in their junior high and high schools. Even with their limits
in terms of overturning gendered hierarchies,
therefore, these relationships suggest changes
that are occurring in the adolescent interactions
and expectations between males and females.

DATING AND THE "PURE RELATIONSHIP" IN A "RISK" SOCIETY

Much like the dance halls 70 years earlier, today's
cyberculture affords teenagers new opportunities
to experiment with gender relations, with results
potentially as far-reaching as those initiated during that time period. I would like to suggest that
the relationships on-line are characteristically
different along both physical and emotional
lines. The *physical* hazards of relationships, at
least in terms of consensual premarital sex, were
limited more than 30 years ago with the introduction of "the pill" and the consequent rise in
acceptability of other forms of birth control to
avoid pregnancy and sexually transmitted diseases. It is almost too obvious to state that the
Net introduces disembodied relations, thereby
limiting physical contact between most teens.
After all, even if they had wanted to meet their
Net romance in person, the challenges of distance and a lack of transportation or resources
limit this to a significant degree among teens.
Net relationships, therefore, operate in tandem
with or as verbal "practice" for the actual events

in "real life" rather than eliminating or restructuring the sexual mores that preceded them. Yet in the contemporary situation, "Internet dating" emerges as an alluring option for intimate hetero- and homosexual experimentation that holds the possibility of decreasing the potential *emotional* hazards of intimate relations.

Someone from an older generation might wonder why teens would feel that dating is an emotional minefield to be navigated carefully. After all, those older than teens might look back on the youthful dating scene as carefree. Yet dating, like other cultural institutions, must be considered in context. Borrowing the term from Ulrich Beck, Giddens referred to the current situation as a "risk society." (Beck, 1986, cited in Giddens, 1991). Giddens noted that this implies more than the increased exposure to new forms of danger:

> To accept risk as risk, an orientation which is more or less forced on us by the abstract systems of modernity, is to acknowledge that no aspects of our activities follow a predestined course, and all are open to contingent happenings.... Living in the "risk society" means living with a calculative attitude to the open possibilities of action, positive and negative, with which, as individuals and globally, we are confronted in a continuous way in our contemporary social existence. (p. 28)

As a part of their developmental process, therefore, teens must garner the skills necessary to envision various possible outcomes to their actions. Even as this has occurred, the decline of the authority of adult institutions throughout culture in general has left young people with more autonomy and hence more authority over their own behavior. Moreover, with the rise of part-time employment hours, young people themselves now have greater control over resources (financial and educational) that allow them to choose the timing of the events in their own life course to a greater extent than in previous generations. This combination of factors results in a strikingly different approach to the future than the concept of one's "fate," which teens of earlier generations had been taught to accept, even if implicitly. Perhaps in the past teens felt that society held a specific place for them and their task was simply to find out what that was by undergoing an "identity crisis" of some kind, as Erickson (1968) postulated. Instead, with the rise of a plethora of potential courses of action, teens learn that they will, throughout their lives, continually be called on to choose between "possible worlds." They have witnessed their parents and other adults in their lives changing their minds about mates, careers, and home locations, after all. Teens therefore have come to expect that while intimate relationships may offer fulfillment, such satisfaction may be ephemeral. Relationships are pursued as a part of a self-reflexive process in this context and may be understood in terms of what Giddens (1991) characterized as a "pure relationship":

> (Pure relationships] offer the opportunity for the development of trust based on voluntary commitments and an intensified intimacy. Where achieved and relatively secure, such trust is psychologically stabilizing, because of the strong connections between basic trust and the reliability of the caretaking figures. (p. 186)

The "pure" relationship, therefore, is not necessarily constrained by the structures of social or economic life, although of course, one's life *choices* are greatly conditioned by one's life *chances* (the latter referring to the Weberian phrase in which work is acknowledged as an economic, and hence social, determinant of the lifestyle options one has). The "pure" relationship, Giddens argued, is justified not in reference to one's kinship or other social ties but in reference to romantic love. Indeed, it is considered "pure" because it is no longer constituted within the social context of kin and community. Persons are no longer constrained in their selection of romantic partners by the social mores of their families or communities. Instead, relationships are sought out and maintained solely for the gratifications they provide to the persons involved. Therefore, these relationships of modernity, Giddens argued, are always organized in relation to the reflexive self who asks, "how is this relationship fulfilling to *me*?" With the lowering of sexual inhibitions through the social transformations of the last four decades, sex has come to be more closely aligned with contemporary concepts of intimacy and even identity and thus is a key aspect of the "pure" relationship. This is illustrated in Modell's (1989) argument:

> In the 1950s love had been defined in terms of meeting role expectations. Now it was "characterized by 'meeting the needs' of the other through interaction, commitment, affection, and non-possessiveness." Mutuality was no longer a theme of "coming together" in mystic sexual union but rather of each partner enhancing the other's happiness. Each couple represented a fresh negotiation of promising but uncertain potential that would endure while each partner gratified the openly pleasure-seeking self of the other. (p. 303)

Thus to some extent, by Giddens's definition at least, we would expect to find that sex among teens has been transformed from the externalized "thrill" of the 1950s "date" to something much more consensual, intimate, and important in the construction of self-identity. Selfhood, Giddens argued, emerges in relation to the negotiation of self-gratification in relationship.

Because the "pure" relationship is not anchored in anything beyond itself, Giddens argued, voluntary commitment plays a central role, and therefore the ability to trust the other becomes central to its continuance. Intimate communication that validates and develops the self, therefore, seems to be an integral goal of the "pure relationship" of which Giddens wrote. Conversely, therefore, I would argue that teens— much like adults—seek to avoid emotional risk because they see it as a potential threat to the self. Some of the teens and their parents with whom I spoke noticed this tendency among teens to avoid emotional investment. One parent contrasted this with her own generation's proclivity to seek "deep" relationships:

> *Mother: My kids, this generation, they're very surface. They don't get deep.*
> *Michael (15 years old): See, we're mellow.*
> *Mother: Back in the '60s, everybody got real deep. Even though they were into the free love and all that, they got into it real deeply. But this generation is more of, "don't make me go that far down into the situation."*
> *Interviewer (to the teens in the family): Do you think that's true?*
> *Paula (19 years old): I think that's true, and I think that's because of the way things are now. I feel that*

even with me, and a lot of my friends, there's so much violence, it's like, I don't know anybody that hasn't lost a good friend or brother or cousin or whatever to violence, so it's like, we don't try to get real deep in stuff. Everything's like, "whatever." If something happens it's like, "I don't care."

Michael: *And like, when a movie that comes out like that's all silliness, it kinda lets you escape from all the seriousness and stuff like that.*

Paula: *But even most serious movies, that are supposed to be real violent, my mom gets mad at us, 'cause she gets all sentimental about it, "oh, it's so terrible," and we're all like laughing at her. She always says we're morbid. And I'm like, well, you can't really get that into it, 'cause with the everyday thing, you'll just go crazy. You gotta kinda go with the flow.*

Interviewer: *So, is there something that gives you hope that things will be different sometime?*

Paula: *I don't know. [chuckles] Well.*

Michael: *Well, hope's just one day at a time.*

In this exchange, the older teen explains the motivation for the avoidance of emotional risk, or "depth" in relationships, in terms of violence and the potential for loss. In fact, there is so much loss in "the everyday thing" for her that she explains her own desensitization to media portrayals of violence as a part of her position of self-defense. In doing so, she demonstrates the way in which self-construction and self-preservation play an important role in determining per-

sonal relationships and in "reading" the cultural and mediated texts of relationships, as well. Thus dating as a social practice must be seen within this wider cultural reality in which risk to oneself, and the seeking of intimacy that validates the self, have become important aspects of teen discourse on relationships.

This would imply that the character of the relationships formed on-line may be quite different from those of the past owing to fundamental shifts in how individuals relate to one another along the axis of intimacy. Of course, there is the obvious difference of a lack of physical sexual intimacy as an aspect of the on-line form of the "pure" relationship. As noted earlier, one could imagine that such relationships might be more egalitarian as the restraints of power issues in sexual relations between males and females are bypassed. Teen chat room relationships therefore would be expected to favor intimacy that is achieved through conversation and self-revelation, which were important aspects of Giddens's (1991) "pure" relationship, as noted here:

The "pure" relationship depends on mutual trust between partners, which in turn is closely related to the achievement of intimacy.... To build up trust, an individual must be both trusting and trustworthy.... What matters in the building of trust in the pure relationship is that each person should know the other's personality, and be able to rely on regularly eliciting certain sorts of desired responses from the other. This is one reason (not the only one) why authenticity has such an important place in self-actualization. (p. 186)

Giddens suggested that trust and "authenticity," or truthful and open self-revelation, are central to self-gratifying relations.

In contrast, trust and "authenticity" are *not* central to teen chat room relationships; "fun" is. In fact, one important aspect of the "fun" is in working within the "mysterious" element, as Jake terms it, of not knowing the other person in the on-line relationship at all. As Jake noted, "It's pretty fun. 'Cause it's like, you don't really care, 'cause they don't know who you are, you don't know who they are. It doesn't matter, you're just talking about all this stuff." Michael concurred, as did Elizabeth, who noted,

> *You can be whoever you want to be, and the guys can be whatever they want to be. So it might not necessarily be an* honest *relationship, but it's fun. Because you don't get really serious, because, obviously you couldn't easily get involved with a guy on the Internet [when compared with one] you could actually talk to and see. So I think it's just for fun.*

These relationships, therefore, are constantly renegotiated between honesty and dishonesty, even as they evolve over time. Dishonesty, as Michael noted earlier, is not sufficient reason to discontinue the relationship. Is this solely because teens are less invested in these relationships? In part, of course, that is true. But I would also suggest that the type of relationship pursued by teens on the Net is perhaps best understood as an extension of the "pure" relationship, regardless of whether or not its content is perceived as primarily one of romance or of friendship by its participants. In fact, these teens suggest that even these distinctions are less important on the Net than they may be in other contexts. This is due to the fact that the function of the relationship has shifted even further toward the affirmation of self, its gratifications resting in its ability to provide opportunities for self-reflexivity and even self-consciously imagined (or constructed)

intimacy. The other person is important to this project but obviously to a much lesser extent than in the "pure" relationship described by Giddens. Whereas the on-line relations are connected to the lived experiences of the participants through the social contexts and mores in which the individuals are situated on a local level, there are even fewer possibilities for social constraints in these on-line relations. The peers of those who participate in Internet dating only know what their friends choose to reveal about these relations. The participants in the relations experience a satisfaction in relationships that have no reference to their peer group or social status and may be considered more individualistic as a result. Moreover, it is not a complete lack of commitment but a tenuous and ephemeral commitment that links the participants in the Internet date and provides satisfaction for its participants. In this context, it is perhaps not surprising that it does not matter whether or not the participant in the relationship is accessible in "real life," and why in some cases such connection is studiously avoided, as was illustrated in Elizabeth's avoidance of the male Net friend who wanted to speak with her on the telephone. The lack of accessibility fulfills a function in keeping such individualized expressions of intimacy and self-gratification from impinging on one's local, lived experience. In essence, the relationship has many of the benefits of the "pure" relationship but without the restraints of a commitment of time or emotional resources. In this sense it might be said to be a postmodern "pure" relationship: one comprised of self-reflexivity in which experimentation and self-construction are central. Unlike adult participants in chat rooms, teens are limited in their ability to parlay an emotional tie forged on the Net into something that would have material consequences in the local context. Thus, the relationships that emerge transcend time and space to deliver satisfaction through the medium of a disembodied, "surface" communication, allowing the teen to feel connected to others while allowing them to experience affirmation in an environment that does not risk their current social position.

CONCLUSION

What, then, might be the implications for a teen community on the Internet in this environment? I have argued that whereas teen dating relationships in chat rooms mirror the relationships of "real life" in their adherence to norms of heterosexism and sexism, we also see a difference in the role of trust and intimacy in these relations when compared with those of the past and in "real life." Internet dating, despite its possibilities for verbal intimacy and egalitarian relationships, is in actuality more frequently employed for fleeting, "fun" relationships that hold little consequence in the "real" lives of the teens who engage in them beyond self-gratification. Further, the emphasis on "fun" and inconsequentiality suggests that the norms of conduct for teens on-line may be localized to such an extent that teens feel no need to consider how their own participation might influence others. Because the focus in the Internet date is on individual gratification, teens experience no sense of obligation to the person with whom they are ephemerally committed; as Elizabeth noted, if a person fails to show up at the preappointed time, there are no consequences. Of course, this assumes that both parties agree to the lack of seriousness with which such relations are entered into. Denial of a more intimate connection is not out of maliciousness; those who believe that they are experiencing more than simply a "fun," ephemeral connection are assumed to be not "playing by the rules," as it were.

Teens participating in Internet dating also seem to feel no need to justify their actions among their "real-life" peers, as they might for other, more widely observable actions. In the Net environment, teens are unmoored from local peer groups in which so much of identity is constituted among this age group. Peers are only involved when the participant chooses to involve them, either by conversing about one's individual experiences on-line or, on frequent occasions, watching over one's shoulder as a friend converses with others on-line. Most frequently, however, teens on-line experience themselves as individuals removed, to some extent, from their local social context. As autonomous persons in interaction, teens are like the adult counterparts to Giddens's (1991) "pure" relationship in their search for connection yet are very different in that trust is not a factor in the relationships achieved, nor must they risk "authentic" self-revelation to achieve gratification.

It is also worth noting that much like the teen dating experiences of the midcentury, there is a noticeable absence of other classes and races beyond the Caucasian, middle-class norm of the Net. Participation in teen chat rooms is increasingly forbidden in school and community center contexts, and thus young people with limited means are less likely than their middle-class counterparts to have access to the technology.

This research, therefore, leaves us with several more questions regarding the future of the Internet as a possible site for community building, particularly among teens. If these postmodern "pure" relationships might be considered a youthful precursor to the more serious, "pure" relationships its participants will presumably enter on adulthood, one wonders: will authenticity in the lived environment appear less—or perhaps more—important as a characteristic of these meaningful relationships as a result? I think the fact that the "other" in the relationship is hardly considered, or is assumed to share one's level of commitment and self-gratification, is telling. Teens in chat rooms, after all, experience themselves as a gathering of unconnected individuals, seeking others (or usually one other) with whom to converse and thereby achieve gratification. Perhaps these individualistic relationships underscore the increased localization of caring, thus implying the increased lack of any communal sense of identity. Teen chat rooms become a space outside the stream of everyday life, a space for the development of the ideal "pure" relationship of the contemporary age:

one with imagined intimacy but no need for trust or commitment; thus one that is fulfilling and liberating, ultimately and primarily, to the self. In this sense, then, the self-gratification of dating on the Net can be seen as a natural outgrowth of current cultural conditions. The technology does not enable a wide-scale social change toward greater self-reflexivity but allows this already occurring practice to find a new avenue for its expression and development.

Reading 10   Getting a Man or Getting Ahead

A Comparison of White and Black Sororities

ALEXANDRA BERKOWITZ*   IRENE PADAVIC

In-depth interviews with thirteen white and thirteen black sorority members at two college campuses show that white sororities encourage romantic pairings ("getting a man") evidenced by their extensive social affairs and formal recognitions for women who achieve relationship milestones, while black sororities focus on careers and community service ("getting ahead") evidenced by their reliance on sorority alumnae for career networking and by their extensive involvement in community service. The authors argue that the key to understanding the variation lies in the different histories and current structural positions of the groups. For black sororities, historic images of strong, independent black women and the modern reality of black female marriage and poverty rates have shaped the sorority structure. White sororities have emphasized finding a man as a source of support, an orientation at odds both with a modern reality that dictates labor force participation for all women and with members' career aspirations.

Young women on the threshold of adulthood must pass through a maze of conflicting expectations about how a woman should organize her life. For white women, traditional societal expectations encourage her to devise a plan that relies on men for financial support, and thus, even at young ages, many concentrate significant amounts of energy in the pursuit of a man. The media, schools, parents, and peer groups all endorse this notion of female accomplishment (Cowie and Lees 1981; Handler 1995; Holland and Eisenhart 1990; Lees 1986; Martin and Hummer 1989; Sanday 1990). Yet, these young women receive a concurrent message about the importance of economic self-reliance in an era of rising rates of divorce and single-parent fam-

Authors' Note: Please address all correspondence to Alexandra Berkowitz, Department of Sociology, Indiana University, 747 Ballantine Hall, Bloomington, IN, 47405. We would like to thank William Corsaro, Lisa Handler, Betsy Lucal, Jim Orcutt, Mindy Stombler, and anonymous reviewers for their helpful comments.

ilies. More glamorous versions of this message emphasize the joys to be found in careers.

Young black women also receive the cultural injunction that feminine success entails marriage to a man, but such messages are tempered to a greater extent than they are for white women by admonitions for independence. As Collins (1991, 42) discovered when asking African American women students about lessons their mothers taught them about men, most answers stressed self-reliance and resourcefulness: "Go to school first and get a good education—don't get too serious too young"; "Make sure that you can take care of yourself before you settle down"; and "Want more for yourself than just a man." Higginbotham and Weber's (1992) quantitative analyses led them to similar conclusions. Whereas between 18 and 22 percent of white parents stressed marriage as a primary goal for their daughters in the sample, the corresponding figures for black parents were only between 4 and 6 percent. Even more tellingly, whereas between 56 and 70 percent of white parents stressed the need for an occupation to their daughters, 94 percent of black parents stressed this, leading the researchers to conclude that, "Unlike white women, Black women are typically socialized to view marriage separately from economic security, because it is not expected that marriage will ever remove them from the labor market" (Higginbotham and Weber 1992, 429; see also Ladner 1971, 131).

In this article, we examine one arena in which young women collectively try to make sense of these conflicting scripts[1] and shape their biographical trajectories: college sororities. We would be wrong to assume that young sorority women are simply passive recipients who internalize messages promoted by their communities. College life offers young people on the brink of adulthood their first extended brush with extrafamily life and the opportunity to develop alternative orientations to social scripts (Sanday 1990). Corsaro's (1997) and Corsaro

and Rosier's (1992) theory of interpretive reproduction, although concerned with children's sense-making processes, applies to sorority members as well: These young people collectively interpret, negotiate, and often refine and transform the information they receive from the adult world rather than passively internalize it. Sorority women's impetus for making such interpretations and refinements is to create sense out of the conflicting messages they receive. On one hand they are taught that finding a man is the key to organizing life, and on the other they are taught that having a career is the key. To interpret and respond to this conflicting information, they draw on historical frames of reference, which are based on their understandings of the past experiences of people they define as similar to them. Each sorority member actively contributes to the group's ideology according to her own historical frame of reference, and thus sorority culture is produced and reproduced.

Our interview data show that the results of this process of interpretive reproduction have led to sorority structures that vary dramatically by race: While white sororities are structured to largely ignore the career message and concentrate on the more traditional goal of pairing ("getting a man"), black sororities are organized to facilitate economic self-sufficiency ("getting ahead," in the words of these women) and to contribute to the betterment of the black community. We attribute these variations to the different historical and structural realities that have shaped black and white women's lives and the way these young women interpret and incorporate these orientations into their sororities.

It is not surprising that sorority experiences differ for black and white women. Whether scholars characterize the interaction of race and gender as "intersecting systems," "interlocking categories," or "multiple bases of oppression," they agree on the importance of examining how gender dynamics are affected by race and class in different contexts (Andersen and Collins

1992; Collins 1990; Dill 1979; hooks 1989; King 1988; West and Fenstermaker 1995, 9). King (1988) and hooks (1989) underscore the importance of understanding the social location of black women and point to their invisibility, as frequently the experience of black women is considered to be synonymous either with that of black men or white women. As Deborah King (1988) noted, "It is precisely those differences between blacks and women, between black men and black women, between black women and white women that are crucial to understanding the nature of black womanhood" (pp. 45–46). While many aspects of black women's and men's experience are similar, nevertheless, as bell hooks (1981) noted, "No other group in America has had their identity socialized out of existence as have black women. We are rarely recognized as a group separate and distinct from black men" (p. 7). Angela Davis (1981) noted another cleavage between the histories of black women and men: "If the most violent punishments of men consisted in floggings and mutilations, women were flogged and mutilated, as well as raped" (p. 7).

Nor does sharing a sex category ensure similarities between black and white women. While we do not want to ignore the structural impediments that patriarchy and capitalism impose on all women, it is crucial to acknowledge the different ways that these structures have played out in the lives of black and white women (Barrett and Phillips 1992). As West and Fenstermaker (1995) noted, "depending on how race, gender, and class are accomplished, what looks to be the same activity may have different meanings for those engaged in it" (p. 32). This article shows that sorority membership has different meanings for black and white members. In turn, these meanings stem from current marriage and labor force realities and from historical differences in the races' orientations to family, work, and community. These current and historical factors

appear in the sorority structures that these young women help to create as they respond to differing emphases on how a woman should organize her life.

BACKGROUND

Historically, black women did not have the option afforded middle-class white women of following the dictates of the dominant gender ideology that called for female passivity, domesticity, and reliance on men for their livelihood. As a result of racial discrimination, black men often could not provide the sole support for a household, thus leading to married black women's much higher rates of labor force participation compared to white women's (Amott and Matthaei 1991; Dill 1988). Due in part to the scarcity of good jobs at good wages for men, African American culture came to rely on an extended family system in which women provided material help to one another (Cherlin 1992; Stack 1974). This emphasis on familial ties with women has lessened the economic basis of the husband-wife bond that is so salient in the white culture (Cherlin 1992). These factors—men's marginality to the family's economy and women's high labor force participation—allowed the image of strong, self-sufficient black women to become a culturally available category for young black women to emulate today.

The history of work and family life is not the only heritage that valorizes strength in black women: Political examples can be found in the civil rights struggle. Indeed, women formed the backbone of the year-long Montgomery, Alabama bus system boycott, often opting to walk miles to their domestic and service jobs rather than take the bus (Barnett 1993; Jones 1985). According to Jones (1985), general grassroots support for the movement came from ordinary women, many of whom were "militant...in the community, outspoken, understanding and willing to catch hell, having already caught [their] share" (p. 280). Here, again, the notion of "strong, black womanhood" was a culturally available category for young women within the black community.

Modern structural conditions further encourage black women's greater reliance on paid work over marriage as a means of support. Black women are less likely than white women to marry, stay married, or remarry (Cherlin 1992). In fact, black women spend a total of 22 percent of their lives in marriage, compared to 43 percent for white women (Cherlin 1992). The chances of marriage for highly educated black women are even more slim: The ratio of single, black college-educated women to men is two to one (Strong and DeVault 1994). African American college women's own observations of family life, added to the media's popularization of these facts (along with those about black, female, single parenthood) probably further encourage self-sufficiency.

Turning to college women in particular, Holland and Eisenhart (1990) found that black college women anticipated being the most viable economic contributors to their future families and that they believed it was unwise to rely on men too much. While women of both races at the campuses they studied spent a great deal of time on thoughts of romantic relationships, the black women were less focused on finding a man. Holland and Eisenhart speculated that, like the white women, black women may have desired a male-centered life but were forced to adjust their aspirations to accommodate a reality that offered fewer marriageable men.

African American sororities were founded to provide an avenue for engaging in community service and general racial uplift (Davis 1982, 93; Giddings 1988). Their direct precursor was the black women's club movement, which flourished at the end of the eighteenth and beginning of the nineteenth centuries (Glover 1993, 8–9;

Lerner 1979). These clubs, which led to the founding of the first black sorority in 1908 (Davis 1982), sought to improve the lives of vulnerable members of the community by creating leaders to be involved in black community development. Giddings's (1988) history of Delta Sigma Theta described how the sorority's founders sought to provide a training ground for women leaders who could then influence the political and social issues of the day (see also Davis 1982; Lerner 1979; Shaw 1996).[2] Indeed, the sorority's first activity was participating in the women's suffrage march on the eve of President Wilson's inauguration in 1913. In the 1930s, the Deltas established traveling libraries in the South, where libraries were forbidden to blacks. In the 1960s, many chapters participated in freedom rides and sit-ins, where their involvement was so great that it inspired a new project: fund-raisers to obtain bail money for members. More recently, the sorority has helped create housing for elderly and handicapped African Americans. The community action orientation of this and other African American sororities (Davis 1982, 93) is congruent with the cultural image described above of black women as the strong, vocal center of the African American family and community. Finally, African American sororities have been instrumental in furthering members' careers (Glover 1993), an attribute that our interviews show is highly salient to current members.

Historically, the cultural dictates, desirable attributes, and structural conditions that white women faced have been very different. The cultural model that society has favored for them has promoted passivity, subservience, and domesticity—attributes that are a far cry from a model of strong womanhood. A white woman's worth traditionally has been tied very closely to having a man, and, until recently, middle-class white women have expected to rely on men, rather than the labor market, for financial support (Cancian

1989, 19). Economic dependency gave rise to the cultural correlate that women who could afford to do so should shape their lives based on intimate relationships (Blumstein and Schwartz 1989, 125).

In the first half of this century, cultural norms for young white women encouraged conformity, traditional gender behaviors, and strict sexual mores (Fass 1977; Horowitz 1987). These norms touted romance, love, and marriage as women's ultimate goals, with attractiveness and social skills offered as the keys to attaining them. The post-World War II period saw the institution of "going steady" develop along with the ritualization of other stages in romantic relationships, adding to the significance of relationships (Modell 1989). Many women students devalued intellectual pursuits as interfering with the more important goal of finding a husband (Modell 1989).

The second wave of the feminist movement in the 1970s allowed young women to experience greater educational opportunities and some freedom from oppressive gender expectations. These cultural trends were paired with changing economic and social conditions, such as a rising divorce rate and a stronger financial need for married women's income. As a result, more white women have entered the labor force, and fewer are relying on men for financial support. A new message that encouraged independence was now available to college women.

Despite these major changes in the social and economic world that young white women face, a preference for the gender relations of the 1950s seems to hold for some college women. Holland and Eisenhart (1990) claimed that for the white college women in their sample, "the business of being attractive and maintaining relationships with men was as salient to them as it was for their mothers and grandmothers."[3] The peer groups they analyzed valued neither academics nor female friendship bonds but instead concentrated on male-female romantic relationships. Most of the white women in their study considered other women to be peripheral; they turned to them to conduct the main activity of finding a man, and these friendships were at the mercy of the demands of boyfriends and romantic pursuits (Holland and Eisenhart 1990).

The tendency to concentrate on men is even more pronounced in white sororities, which encourage an ideology about gender arrangements that is based on the woman-homemaker, male-breadwinner cultural model described above. Predominantly white sororities were founded for many reasons: to guarantee an exclusive dating and mating pool (Fass 1977, 201), to provide supervised housing (Treichler 1985), and to offer access to campus political power (Horowitz 1987). Risman (1982) noted that ultimately, sorority life helped to socialize members to be male centered rather than career oriented. These organizations have maintained some 1950s ideals well past that decade, even though on graduation many sorority women will be working in the labor force and coping with career demands, underemployment, single parenting, and possibly poverty (Risman 1982). While it is unsurprising that in 1964 sorority members were found to have a greater "need" for heterosexual relationships than did "independents" (women unaffiliated with sororities) (Jackson and Winkler 1964, 380), it is surprising that in 1991 sorority women were still far more likely than independents to endorse male dominant-female-submissive attitudes (Kalof and Cargill 1991). Risman (1982) similarly found that sororities encouraged traditional orientations by teaching members that "their success depends not upon their personal achievement in school or sports, but upon their relationship to boys" (p. 240).

Despite their endorsement of traditional gender arrangements, modern sorority women (like college women more generally [Machung 1989]) are not planning lives that are exclusively family centered. Handler (1995) pointed out that larger structural changes are not lost on white sorority women and that sororities are changing with the times, for example by offering workshops on career networking. Moreover, sorority women tend to support positions associated with feminism, such as abortion rights and equal pay (Handler 1995). Clearly, white sorority women do not simply accept a traditional set of sorority ideals and incorporate them in an undiluted way into lives that will, for most, include labor force participation. Their task of reconciling these two competing orientations is more difficult. Nevertheless, we argue that, just as black sorority members' cultural legacy affects their current orientations to men and careers, white sorority members' cultural legacy of relying on men as a way of organizing life after graduation still affects theirs.

DATA AND METHOD

Data consist of twenty-six open-ended, in-depth interviews that the first author conducted with sorority members at two state universities (one predominantly black and one predominantly white) in the Southeast. Interviews were divided evenly between white and black sorority sisters. The white women represented eleven different national sororities (out of sixteen on campus), and the black women represented four (which comprises the total number of black sororities on both campuses).

We located interviewees through a "snowball" sampling method in which interviewees referred other interviewees. Interviews, which the first author conducted, tape recorded, and transcribed, lasted about an hour. Interviews took place in private at locations suggested by the interviewee, including university offices, dormitories, apartments, and sorority houses. Respondents signed a consent form at the beginning of the interview that ensured them of confidentiality.

Interviews centered on three broad areas; women's reasons for joining the sorority, the sororities' activities in regard to academic and social life, and women's career plans and the sorority's role in those plans. We analyzed the data in two ways. First, we figured percentages for questions that could be answered with a "yes" or "no" response. Second, the first author coded these and other data according to categories precipitated by the questions. Thus, examples of coding categories are "importance of boyfriend," "type of community service," and "best part of being in a sorority." Responses within categories were grouped and analyzed for similarities and differences between white and black sororities.

Members of all four black sororities on the two campuses were interviewed. (These four represent the four national sororities; we interviewed five members from one sorority, four from another, and two each from two more sororities). However, the large number of white sororities necessitated selecting a sample. To ensure representativeness, our sample consisted of four women from high-status sororities, five from medium-status, and four from low-status ones. The sorority-ranking scale is one that is understood by members of the Greek system (Risman 1982), who use the terms, *strong, moderate,* and *weak.*

The respondents were quite willing to be a part of the study and spoke openly about their experiences. The interviewer was able to relate easily to the respondents in part because of her own sorority membership, her similar age, and sex. Because the interviewer was white, her race could potentially have inhibited the responses of the black sorority members. We do not believe that this was the case: None of the black women she approached refused to be interviewed, she detected no signs of discomfort during interviews, and all of the black women willingly recommended other women for interviews.

Comparisons between the white and black sororities in this study are more complex than is perhaps immediately apparent. The issues that enhance this complexity include membership size, sorority location, and the presence of sorority houses. The white sororities had between 100 and 150 members, compared to between 10 and 45 members of the black sororities. In addition to their larger membership, the white sororities occupied residential houses, which did not exist for the black sororities on either campus. Finally, the white sororities were located on only one of the campuses identified in the study, while the black sororities are represented on both campuses. Due to the variation in responses that could result from such differences, we consider the implications of these issues in the analysis.

Because this study is confined to campuses in the southern United States, our results might have been different if other areas of the country had been included. Residents of the South tend to hold more conservative gender attitudes, although such attitudes have become far more liberal over time (Rice and Coates 1995). For whites, in particular, ideologies about "genteel ladies" (Rice and Coates 1995) still linger, and these notions may offer cultural support for more traditional orientations about gender among sorority members. How southern conservativeness might play out for black sorority members is somewhat unclear; Rice and Coates (1995) found southern black women to be less conservative than their male counterparts but more conservative than black women in other regions, and they speculate that the myth of the genteel lady may influence southern blacks as well as whites. If so, then our African American respondents may be more traditional than would be the case in sororities nationwide. Thus, we cannot make claims about the national representativeness of our study, but we note that while geographically limited ethnographic research cannot be considered definitive, it can add to our understanding by illustrating the processes by which sororities encourage romantic or career orientations.

RESULTS

Finding Men

While reporting percentages based on such small sample sizes ($n = 13$ for both black and white women) has the potential to be misleading, we find some differences dramatic enough to merit reporting. When we asked women, "How important is it to have a man in your life?" 54 percent of the white women (seven women) compared to only 15 percent of black women (two women) reported that it was very important. One white woman spoke for many interviewees:

> My roommates and I are constantly going on about why guys aren't calling us.... I feel weird if no guys call me during the week, whether it be a friend or a guy that I don't even like, but just to have a male call me. I need that.

Another spoke strongly of her need for her current boyfriend:

> It is the most stable thing that I have ever had in my life.... I don't seem to get along well with female friends; I don't know why. Having a boyfriend is something that I know is stable and I feel like I always have something and it is probably the only thing that keeps me sane.

These women's emphasis on relationships with men may reflect the ideology still current with many middle-class, white women in our society that, to some extent, women's worth rests on having a man.

Most black women in our sample did not share this orientation, perhaps because of the lack of eligible black men or because of the cultural proclivities laid out above. Fifty-four percent of the black sorority women (seven women) reported that men were not very important to them. For many, what was important was exploring other avenues for achievement, particularly being strong and independent. As one said,

> *A man falls after my religion, my sorority, and definitely after my school work. It is something that I would like to have but it isn't that important because I am all into this woman's lib thing and I feel that I can do things by myself.... So, if I have a man and he is bringing me down I would just rather be by myself.*

In fact, for some black women, the sorority provided an alternative to a dating relationship:

> *Having a boyfriend is not really that important. That is another reason why I joined the organization because I am not one of those types that always has a man on her arm every day. I knew that by joining the organization, regardless of whether I had a boyfriend or not, I could go to any city and have a bond with most of the sisters that I would contact and be a part of activities with.*

As these quotations illustrate, these women are not repudiating the idea of relationships with men; indeed, 15 percent (two women) claimed that having a man was very important. African American women may hold the same romantic goals as white women (Mullings 1997, 120). Elijah Anderson (1990) described black teenage girls' version of romantic love:

> *This dream involves having a boyfriend, a fiancé, a husband, and the fairy-tale prospect of living happily ever after with one's children in a nice house in a good neighborhood—essentially the dream of the middle-class American life-style, complete with nuclear family. (p. 115)*

Franklin (1992, 344) discussed the lessons taught by parents and noted that black girls are taught both to be self-sufficient and to get a man. Holland and Eisenhart (1990) found that college women of both races were obsessed with romance, emphasizing that notions of romantic fulfillment are probably not identical for white and black women, however. Mullings (1977) pointed out that "to the extent that the model is accepted as ideal, it must lead to the devalorization of African American women...because their life circumstances preclude the same sort of dependence" (p. 12). While we cannot shed light on the meaning that romance holds for them, we do argue that young black women do not look to sororities as the place to pursue that life goal.

We found sharp differences in the extent to which white and black sororities set up events to encourage male-female pairing. All white interviewees reported the existence of formal ceremonies for a sister who reaches a milestone in a romantic relationship. The most common milestone is being "laveliered," whereby a fraternity man gives the sorority woman a charm to wear as a necklace that signifies the strength of their romantic involvement. Increasingly serious milestones are "pinnings" (when a fraternity man gives his fraternity pin to a sorority woman), getting "promised" (when a woman receives a promise ring as a symbol of an impending engagement), and engagements. Sorority members announce these events at an emotionally charged ceremony known as "the candlelight." In this ritual, each woman keeps secret her laveliering or other new status until the night of the ceremony. The sorority members form a circle and pass around a candle while singing a special sorority song. The candle passes once for sisterhood, again for a lavaliere, a third time for a pin, then again for a promise ring and a final time for an engagement. A woman who has achieved a milestone blows out the candle at the appropriate time, announcing to the chapter the relationship event. Sorority women highly value and eagerly anticipate the ceremony. Clearly, candlelights are a formal, structured event wherein a woman can be publicly praised for her attainment of a man. One sister explained, "it is considered an honor in our sorority to [participate in] a candlelight ceremony. It is considered a very happy and lucky thing to have found a man." In contrast, she described academic achievement as far less important an honor in her sorority. In another sorority with an elaborate candlelight ceremony, the award to the woman with the highest grade point average was significantly less emotionally charged: She was awarded a bag of potato chips.

Indeed, women described the candlelight ceremony as a major highlight of sorority experience, something that many strove to obtain. One woman engineered her boyfriend's joining a fraternity for this express purpose:

The whole thing was that I wanted my boyfriend to join a fraternity so that I could be laveliered. I finally got to have a candlelight and it was the neatest thing. Everyone was so proud of me. I got thrown into the middle of the circle and jumped on and hugged. I had been waiting for a long time and everyone knew that, so when it finally came, it felt really good.

In contrast, the concept of laveliering does not even exist in the African American Greek system; other romantic milestones receive little commemoration. Only five of the African American sorority women reported any ceremonial acknowledgment of romantic relationships, and these ceremonies were only small add-ons to weddings, where the bride "gets chanted by the sorority with a special hymn." The African American interviewees said that romantic milestones mattered only insofar as they contributed to the happiness of a sister, and they saw no reason to have a ritual response to various romantic events.

The emphasis on a social life centering on interactions with men is further exemplified through the high number of date functions that the white sororities sponsored. All but one sponsored four or more a year, usually events like a formal, a semi-formal, a hay ride, a grab-a-guy (where women must find a date within a few hours for a party), and a crush (where each woman invites two men to a sorority party). While a date is not mandatory for crushes, they are mandatory for the other events. According to one member, "the idea is that you bring a date or you do not go."

Informal parties that do not require a date are held in conjunction with a fraternity and are usually at the fraternity house. All "socials" of this nature are open only to the participating Greek organizations. The atmosphere is bar-like: The music is loud and there is little to do but mingle and dance. This format emphasizes pairing with a man for the evening and perhaps for the night. To help facilitate this, women and men drink a great deal to "relax and interact better with each other." Because most sororities do not allow underage members to drink at fraternity houses, they usually stage a "pre-party" that allows all members to drink. According to one sorority member, "Everyone goes to the pre-party, gets drunk and then goes to the social. At the social, there is music and dancing. A lot of people hook up with a guy or at least try to."

These parties facilitate pairing partly because that is what sorority members want: About half reported that access to parties with fraternity men was their prime reason for joining, and many said that meeting men was the best part of their overall sorority experience. In the words of one woman, "It is necessary for us to have so many social events because it is the expectation of a lot of girls to come into a sorority for the social life. They want to meet guys." Another woman reported, "I wanted to see what it was like with the fraternities and all the socials. I knew a lot of people that went to them and I wanted to have that fun also."

Again in sharp contrast, the African American sororities did not actively encourage heterosexual unions. Two women reported that their sororities had no date functions at all, and the remaining eleven reported only one formal event or "ball" a year.[4] These balls are part of the sorority's "week," a time dedicated to several events centered on sorority unity, including step-dance shows and seminars. These events do not require dates. One woman explained, "No, you do not need a date [for the ball]; a lot of my sorors [sisters] have gone stag. You can come with your best girlfriend if you want to."

African American sororities' informal social functions (functions that do not require a date) are also quite different from their white counterparts'. The sororities, in conjunction with another sorority or a fraternity, sponsor parties held at a nightclub and open to the public. The goal is to raise funds for the sponsoring organizations. Sororities discourage or forbid drinking at these events because they believe that excessive drinking will impede the goal of fund-raising. Other informal gatherings—some with fraternities and some without—range from board-game tournaments to pot-luck dinners. One woman described her sorority's social events as follows: "Some are done in conjunction with a fraternity but most of them we do on our own. We do things like picnics, bowling or spades tournaments." Another described a typical social with a fraternity: "We might have a pizza party or something to get to know each

other better and have a closer relationship. It would be at someone's house and we would just chill out and have a good time."

This evidence implies that black sororities place less emphasis on coupling. Many of the activities, such as game tournaments, actually discourage breaking off into pairs and instead promote group dynamics. The wide variety of social activities that the sorority engages in gives the women a chance to interact and bond with women as well as men. We note, however, that the small size of the black organizations as compared to the white ones may account for some of the above differences. For example, the small size of black sororities may have necessitated nondate social gatherings such as bowling parties or card tournaments. If half the sisters of a small, twenty-person sorority do not have dates, a formal party requiring dates would be doomed, unlike in a one-hundred-member sorority. Similarly, black sororities' small size (along with the lack of black sorority houses on these campuses) may have been a factor in their hosting open parties at public clubs rather than events that were members-and-guests only. Thus, black sororities' small size may have exacerbated their tendency to downplay man hunting.

This section has shown that the white sororities had a stronger commitment to activities that facilitate romantic relationships. The high number of date functions creates a situation in which women are continuously searching for eligible dating partners. This puts pressure on women to find a steady partner to alleviate the anxiety of finding a different man for each event. The informal social functions do not require dates, but their format and high rate of alcohol use encourage coupling. The candlelight ritual offers women a status-oriented and tangible reason to strive for a romantic relationship. Sorority events for the African American women are usually more than ways to meet men, as exemplified by the fund-raising open parties and by the informal social functions that are more group oriented.

Engaging in Community Service

In keeping with their founding principles, African American sororities were much more community service oriented than their white counterparts. The black women described community service as a central and meaningful part of their sorority experience, while white women generally viewed it as a way to facilitate their social lives.

About half of the African American women cited community service as one of their main reasons for joining, while none of the white women reported it as a motivation. The African American women saw their sorority membership as a means to "give back to the community," a way of "uplifting" themselves and their black brothers and sisters:

> I joined because I saw the women as strong black women in the community and I saw their purpose as being a way to uplift the black community. I just wanted to help contribute to that because some of the characteristics that I saw in them, I saw in myself. I consider myself a strong black woman and I am always willing to help someone.

Moreover, all of the black women identified community service as the activity that took up most sorority time. This dedication to social improvement went beyond peripheral involvement in a high number of service projects. The women celebrated the idea that their sororities were originally founded to serve the community, and prior community service experience was a membership prerequisite: "If you do not have community service coming in…you are showing them that you are not a dedicated person."

All interviewees were able to give detailed descriptions of the local projects their sorority was involved in, ranging from tutoring children in underprivileged areas or serving dinner at the local homeless shelter to sponsoring blood drives and community clean-ups. In addition, the national chapters have designated community service projects that they require local chapters to be involved in: "We have a national project… which is geared towards unwed mothers. We go out to schools and have centers that teach prenatal care, help educate them as well as give them some career training." As these examples make clear, most projects centered on direct participation with the groups they seek to help—often in the black community—rather than on raising funds to send to a charity.

In contrast, the white sororities were far less focused on community service. Most had one philanthropic event a year, usually a fund-raiser. Fund-raisers were first and foremost social events, such as dance contests or sports tournaments, that brought many Greek organizations together. Sororities sent the money to a charity designated by the national chapter, a format that does not allow for direct involvement with the people receiving the money. Beyond this main yearly activity, some sororities conducted smaller fund-raisers and projects, but interviewees did not talk about community service with anything approaching the enthusiasm that was typical for the black interviewees nor was community service experience a prerequisite for membership. One sister described her group's involvement:

> We donate money to a pediatric ward. It is not a big part of the sorority life. It happens once a spring. It's a lip-sync contest…. The social part is big, but as far as helping the children, we basically send the money away. The purpose of the philanthropy is not a big part but the way to get the money is a big deal.

In sum, the black sororities were far more deeply involved in community service at the practical and ideological levels than were the white sororities.

Enhancing Careers

Sorority membership tends to be a life-long commitment for African American women; graduation signals a woman's transfer to the graduate alumnae chapter where participation is often more intensive. The African American women we interviewed said that their sorority affiliation was part of their identity and would remain with them throughout the course of their lives as "a source of help and support." In contrast, white women's sorority membership was limited to their college years; although opportunities to continue involvement after college graduation existed, no women planned to do so. Besides valuing the sister relationship in its own right, black women expected to realize a career payoff for their membership. White women had no such expectation. We examine these themes below.

Relationships with other women were the sine qua non of black sororities, and the organizations ensured continuity with programs that span the phases of the life course. Auxiliary groups of the sororities are made up of junior high and high school girls who participate in many of the collegiate chapters' activities and attend seminars that the graduate chapters host on study skills, etiquette, or on the sorority itself. Girls involved in auxiliary chapters usually seek to join the sorority when they reach college. One college woman said of her membership, "I was in the [adolescent group] for eight years so I knew that when I came to college what sorority I was going to pledge."

Graduating from college was by no means an end to sorority involvement; in fact, many anticipated that participation on the graduate level would be the most fruitful portion of their sorority experience. Graduate chapters sponsor the adolescent groups, are active in the collegiate chapter by donating funds for seminars, and sponsor their own community service projects and social functions.[5] Yet, it is the career connections that these groups offer that our African American interviewees felt to be the most significant part of sorority life after college. All thirteen anticipated that the sorority would be crucial in career networking:

> It will open doors.... The unwritten rule is that you are supposed to help that person [a sorority sister]. They are to come first. If she is a member, I should be able to get that position regardless of my credentials but my credentials should be up to standards before I come to her.

The idea of seeking strong, professional black women as role models and possible mentors was a recurrent theme for these college women, who spoke of ties with graduate chapters as a way to gain access to successful African Americans:

> When I came here [to college], I looked at the women who were already members and they were perfect. They had an aura about them and I wanted to be like them. The women in the graduate chapter are mostly professionals, a lot of teachers, administrative women. My pediatrician is a member.

White women's sorority involvement is almost exclusively at the collegiate level; white sororities do not sponsor adolescent auxiliary groups, and graduate chapters are inconsequential to career building. Because white members view sorority membership primarily as a means to a productive social life centering on men, few women planned to participate in alumnae chapters. Indeed, "too much" involvement indicates that a woman is still living in the past:

> After college, I would not mind going to rush a few times but I do not want

to be one of those ladies that is like the chapter advisor and is always hanging around the house like they are still in college.

Another concurred:

I think that it is important that when you are young that you do things to get them out of your system. I don't want to be thirty and feel like I have to go dancing and drinking at a bar with my girlfriends.

As for career connections, few white women believed that the sorority would benefit their careers. One woman described why she joined:

I don't think it will help me get ahead.... I think that the main thing that it will do for me is that I will be able to look back and say that at least I tried it and I did not miss out. I don't think I will have any contact with it when I graduate.

We do not mean to imply that white sorority women were not career oriented; they were. In describing their futures, the majority of both black and white women presented plans that included a husband, children, and a career for at least some period of their lives. Unlike the black women, however, the white women did not regard sorority membership as a means to that goal. It would help only remotely, by increasing a woman's chance of being selected for positions in high-status, Greek-dominated campus organizations that "look good on a resume."

Both white and African American sorority women claimed that sisterhood was an important reason for joining the sorority, but the meaning of sisterhood set the two groups apart. For the black women, sorority sisterhood entailed a lifelong commitment that they expected would remain salient to their identities even after their collegiate years. In contrast, the white women regarded sorority sisterhood as part of the college experience rather than part of their lifelong identity. Moreover, unlike their black counterparts, they did not expect a career payoff for membership. In sum, for both groups, sororities were the key group for facilitating important relationships that are difficult to forge alone. For white women, these relationships are with men; for black women, they are with other women and with black communities.

SUMMARY AND CONCLUSION

White sorority women in this sample regarded sorority membership as a way to lead a productive social life that they hoped would enable them to get a man. The structure of their sororities encouraged this pursuit of romantic relationships by sponsoring candle-lighting ceremonies, frequent formal date events, and informal functions whose bar-like ambiance and high rate of alcohol consumption facilitated coupling. Despite this emphasis, these women are not living in a time warp, and most had career aspirations: Ten of the thirteen mentioned careers as figuring in their future, although they acknowledged that sorority life will do little to further that goal. In contrast, African American women's sorority participation centered on community service and career advancement. Community service was the largest activity that the sororities engaged in and was a meaningful part of all phases of participation (adolescent, collegiate, and graduate). Interviewees described the role of sorority graduates in career networking as perhaps the most beneficial aspect of sorority life. Moreover, black sororities did not offer much institutional support for romantic relationships: They offered virtually nothing akin to candlelightings, sponsored few date functions, and centered informal social functions on group activities. Not surprisingly, most of the black women in this sample did not feel that having a romantic relationship was a necessity.

These different orientations affected women's sense of sisterhood and levels of commitment to the sorority. African American women's more intense involvement was fostered by opportunities to participate throughout the life course; in comparison, white women's orientation toward the sorority was much more phase oriented, limited to their college years, although their feelings toward it were strong during those years. The two types of sorority appear to be structured to facilitate different agendas: for white women, short-term participation geared to meeting men, and for black women, long-term participation geared to furthering both individual careers and the uplifting of the race through community projects.

We argue that the key to understanding the differences between the groups in their orientation to sorority life lies in their differing current structural positions and historical frames of reference. For the black sororities, historic images of strong, independent, black women and the modern statistical reality of black female marriage and poverty rates have shaped the sorority structure as well as the ideology and activities of their members. In the same way, the white sororities are responding to their cultural heritage, which has emphasized relying on a man for support and remaining within the domestic sphere. These differences influence the current structures of the sororities and the way that individual women interpret their own experiences.

Yet, white sorority women are in an odd position because this model no longer fits the modern social reality that prescribes labor force attachment for women (Risman 1982). The attempts of white sororities to put "new wine into old bottles"—to offer modern young women the man-centered solution to the question of how to organize a life—still seem to be successful: Sorority membership has been on the rise for the past two decades (Lord 1987). The conflict with sorority ideology that would seem to be inevitable as white sorority women become more independent and career oriented may have been averted by cosmetic changes such as sorority seminars on careers. We speculate, however, that white sorority women compartmentalize their career and their romantic goals and use sororities to further only the latter. This is not to say that the women themselves are not career oriented; it is to say that their sororities are not structured to offer ways to help them achieve that goal.

In sum, both sorority systems grew from different socio-historical roots. They stemmed from an earlier era and reflect those traditions today. We do not mean to glamorize the black sorority structure, because it has its own set of problems, especially in the area of hazing. Yet, it seems that the black sorority structure is more in tune with the probable labor force and family prospects of modern college women. Many features of black and white women's lives are converging. For the first time in history, the labor force participation of white women is equal to that of black women (Reskin and Padavic 1994), signifying the reality that most women—including white sorority alumnae—will be part of the workforce. White family patterns are also coming to more closely resemble African Americans' as white women are increasingly likely to be single parents (Saluter 1992). It seems that African American sororities' orientation toward career building is more in step with the reality of the modern college woman. The historical frame of reference that young black women bring to sorority life is more consistent with the demands of contemporary society. To ensure its survival, the white sorority structure will probably shift to accommodate the larger social changes that increasingly manifest themselves in individual members' lives.

We see these results as building on the insights of feminist scholars of race who caution against the tendency to assume white women's experiences can provide a template for understanding black women's. Often, the groups' experiences are just too different, as is the case for understanding the bases of their respective sorority systems and the meaning these organizations hold for members. According to Collins (1990, 23–25), black women's experiences provide them with a "unique angle of vision," grounded in their work and family experiences, that will manifest itself in their consciousness and in the organizations that they construct. In the same way, white women draw on different motifs in constructing their consciousness and organizations. By remaining open to racial differences in the ways that young women "negotiate femininity" (Davis and Fisher 1993, 7), we hope to add to the feminist project of understanding women's lives without collapsing the differences among them (see also Stombler and Padavic 1997). In this respect, we concur with postmodern feminist theory, which criticizes the notion that the structural impediments imposed by patriarchy operate similarly for women or that a feminist "privileged knower" holds a view of reality that can speak for all women (Barrett and Phillips 1992).

This study also furthers the project specified by West and Fenstermaker (1995, 13) of understanding the workings of race and gender in situated contexts. As they note, to capture what it actually means for a person to simultaneously experience these categories, research must focus on the particular mechanisms and situations that produce or mitigate inequality. In this study, we have identified mechanisms that perpetuate or mitigate the inequality that stems from women's dependence on men: Candle-lightings, formal date functions, and alcohol consumption encourage it; multigenerational membership, career networking, and an absence of date functions mitigate it. Drawing on Corsaro (1997), we note that sorority women have participated in the creation of these practices, and they have brought to that enterprise their understandings of the past experiences of their mothers, grandmothers, and other people of their own gender and race. Because of different historical frames of reference, black and white women create very different understandings. In showing how black and white sorority members collectively attempt to make sense of given scripts and arrive at interpretations and strategies for dealing with them, we have documented how these different understandings play out in one small setting. It is by adding such incremental pieces of the puzzle that we can hope to understand and perhaps improve women's lives.

Reading 11   Asian Indian Marriages—Arranged, Semi-Arranged or Based on Love?

JOHANNA LESSINGER*

The continued Indian immigrant preoccupation with female chastity is partly an effort to keep women subordinated and partly an effort to maintain an important cultural distinction between "us" and "the Americans." It is also closely connected with the system of arranged marriages. Such marriages, the norm in India, still prevail among Indian immigrants, complete with ostentatious receptions and large dowries provided by the bride's family. As Luthra (1989: 343) points out, the phrase "decent marriage" appearing in the matrimonial ads of immigrant newspapers signals a willingness to give or take dowry.

Arranged marriages are the subject of endless discussion among members of the second generation. Agarwal's sampling of prosperous California immigrants indicates that two thirds of the young people she spoke to rejected arranged marriages, at least in principle, and wanted to select their own mates. (1991:50). Not all manage to do so.

Raju, an aspiring writer, is somebody who has definitely rejected a marriage organized by his parents. Feeling the responsibilities of an only son he agreed some years ago to let his parents introduce him to one or two eligible girls. The dinner parties at which the introductions be-tween the two families took place were, according to Raju, "a farce, a nightmare. Everybody knew what this was for but everyone was pretending this was an ordinary party but silently thinking: 'Fall in love!' I sat there, she sat there, we were paralyzed and couldn't say a word to each other. I told my parents, 'Enough. Stop.'" Raju has since made his own choice, of a non-Indian artist; he and Ellen are not married but live together. His parents still hope this relationship is "just a phase" which Raju will outgrow and that he will eventually marry an Indian. "Well, they also hope I'll outgrow wanting to be a writer." Raju says. "Sorry. No."

Whatever their ideals, not all young people succeed in choosing their own mates. Many submit, if reluctantly, to having parents guide their choices or choose for them. For instance during the summer of Nalini's sophomore year in college, her parents told her that old friends had proposed a marriage between Nalini and their son. Nalini at first protested vigorously. When her parents asked why and suggested she loved somebody else, she insisted she did not. She simply resented the idea of being told whom to marry when. Her parents begged her to at least meet the young man, and promised not to push her if she disliked him. Nalini agreed reluctantly, and traveled with her parents to another state to meet the man, his parents and sister, and to inspect his apartment. Nalini decided that 26-year-old Dipak was handsome, shared her interest in classical Indian music, behaved politely to her parents and seemed kind. She also liked his sister, who lived near him. His apartment was large and modern. Dipak and his parents even promised that they would pay tuition so Nalini could transfer to a nearby college and finish her BA. The two were married at the end of the summer.

A certain number of young people actually view arranged marriages positively, in preference to the possible heartbreak and rejection involved in American-style dating. The Desais had fallen in love and gotten married as students in India. They migrated to the U.S. partly to escape the resulting family uproar and censure of this "love marriage." They were stunned when their own 22-year-old daughter asked their help in finding a husband. The young woman said she was too afraid of the American dating scene, involving premarital sex and potential rejection, to take responsibility for getting married. A year later their 24-year-old son asked for similar help in finding a bride.

Arranged marriage stems from a cultural concern with family unity and family cooperation. Indian society considers the background of a potential bride or groom to be just as important as individual personality when the two family circles join through marriage. Furthermore, since most Indians look on marriage as a lifelong commitment and consider divorce a shameful tragedy, it is practical to ask older people in the family to search out, and investigate, potential spouses and their families. Young people are believed to be too befuddled with romantic notions and sexual yearning to choose sensibly.

In a traditional arranged marriage, an all-points bulletin is broadcast through the network of family and friends when young people reach marriageable age, usually after finishing college or in the later years of graduate training. Newspaper advertisements or marriage brokers may be used to broaden the pool of candidates. Traditionally potential spouses were required to be of the same caste, from the same region of India, of the same general socio-economic status and to be moderately good-looking. Young men are still expected to have employment prospects and young women to have families willing to give good dowries. Within these constraints, the young couple's personal compatibility and common interests were considered, but family elders often put other considerations first.

Today marriage advertisements in U.S. immigrant newspapers like *India Abroad* give indications of how the arranged marriage institution is shifting and adapting in the American context. Phrases such as "no bars" in more and more ads show the declining importance of caste, language group or even religion in mate selection if people are otherwise compatible in terms of education and profession. Additionally, matrimonial notices are beginning to stress personality and interests—such as a sense of humor or an interest in physical fitness—alongside the inevitable height, weight, beauty and professional criteria. The greater attention to individual and personal qualities within the framework of arranged marriages seems to be an adaptive response to American life, which isolates married couples and demands that they be more interdependent, while denying them the support of the extended family.

Even the traditional arranged marriage is not devoid of love and romance. Indians assume that young couples of similar background and interests will gradually develop love and respect for each other after marriage, and that these feelings will be solidified by the responsibilities of parenthood and running a household. In India particularly, gender segregation means that husbands and wives do not necessarily have to become each others' closest friends; that role is taken on by other people of the same sex. In practice Indian arranged marriages, although different in emotional construction from American marriages, are neither cold nor loveless and no more unhappy or likely to fail than marriages elsewhere.

A further adaptation of the arranged marriage to modern life is the emergence of what is often called the "semi-arranged" marriage, both in India and in the U.S. For an urban upper middle class (but not for millions of less fortunate Indians) this is intended to retain parental control while accommodating the youthful yearning for romantic love which is fed by both Indian and American media. Many urban Indian professional families have in the last 15 years begun to introduce suitable, pre-screened young men and women who are then allowed a courtship period during which to decide whether they like each other well enough to marry. (See Narayan 1995 for an insider's account of such a match.) This differs from American-style dating in that parents and friends are still involved in the initial screening, the courtship is much shorter, little or no premarital sex is involved, and there is a pragmatic recognition by both parties that the aim of meeting is marriage. In the U.S. the friendship circles of immigrant adults often operate as informal marriage bureaus, bringing suitable young people into contact so that they choose each other with only minor parental manipulation. Of course even in India there have been, for several generations now, brave individuals who chose for themselves and made love marriages in the face of parental opposition and family ostracism. In the U.S. such marriages are more numerous, since they have support from the larger society and American culture. However they make many first generation parents uneasy and some try to arrange marriages when their children are young to cut off the possibility of a love marriage.

Immigration has added a complicating factor to the institution of arranged marriage. Indian parents in the U.S. have the option of seeking brides or grooms from India or from other parts of the Indian diaspora, as well as from the U.S. Marriages with the children of Indian immigrants in Canada or Britain are common. Certain Indian immigrants arrange to marry their children to people in India, largely to reenforce their own ties with family and friends there. It is no longer hard to locate potential spouses in India because of the wide-spread eagerness to migrate. For the parents of Indian-American women, there is a financial incentive in that grooms may accept the green card that comes with marriage to a legal resident or citizen in lieu of an expensive dowry of cash, jewelry or a house. Nevertheless there is great potential for exploitation in such arrangements. There are a number of tragic tales about "green card marriages" which collapsed after legal U.S. residence was established.

The question of marrying somebody from India versus marrying a fellow immigrant divides second generation men and young women. The women, with their American-bred sense of independence, tend to prefer young men raised, like themselves, in the U.S. They know that men from India will demand a kind of service and subservience they are not prepared to give. Many also complain that Indian men are shy, poorly dressed, awkward and unsure in American social situations. "They're totally uncool." (These complaints cut both ways. Young men in India believe immigrant women "have lost their culture" and make bad wives: too assertive toward men, unable to adjust to the demands of others, poor cooks and probably unchaste.)

For their part some young Indian-American men rather like the idea of having a "real Indian wife" who will be quiet, humble and certifiably "pure" and who will cater to them as their mothers did. An irate young Indian woman in New Jersey, thinking over those she knows, reports, "You have these lovely girls from India, really beautiful and educated, with PhDs, getting married off to real losers from here! Ugly guys or guys who haven't even finished high school!.... The parents do that because they couldn't find anyone here willing to marry those idiots. The girls do it for the green card. Their lives are ruined."

The one point on which Indian immigrants and their children generally agree is that it is important to marry and have children. Even young women headed for careers want a husband and one or two children as well. In general the second generation is almost as family-minded as the first. It is perhaps a tribute to Indian immigrant parents that so many young people want families of their own, even if the process of getting married is one of the most stressful in young Indian-American lives. Additionally, many of the second generation, having been strenuously taught to value Indian culture, also agree with their parents about the desirability of marrying a fellow Indian. Of course, some of the second generation have rejected traditional patterns by choosing to live with or marry Americans; others have opted for lesbian or gay relationships. Yet it is important to realize that these choices do not necessarily imply a rejection of Indian culture and Indian identity, but rather represent a recognition of a range of personal options American life offers. These are options the first generation rarely had.

4   Sexuality, Intimacy, and the Family

Reading 12   The Feminization of Love

FRANCESCA M. CANCIAN*

A feminized and incomplete perspective on love predominates in the United States. We identify love with emotional expression and talking about feelings, aspects of love that women prefer and in which women tend to be more skilled than men. At the same time we often ignore the instrumental and physical aspects of love that men prefer, such as providing help, sharing activities, and sex. This feminized perspective leads us to believe that women are much more capable of love than men and that the way to make relationships more loving is for men to become more like women.[1] This paper proposes an alternative, androgynous perspective on love, one based on the premise that love is both instrumental and expressive.[2] From this perspective, the way to make relationships more loving is for women and men to reject polarized gender roles and integrate "masculine" and "feminine" styles of love.

THE TWO PERSPECTIVES

"Love is active, doing something for your good even if it bothers me" says a fundamentalist Christian. "Love is sharing, the real sharing of feelings" says a divorced secretary who is in love

again. In ancient Greece, the ideal love was the adoration of a man for a beautiful young boy who was his lover. In the thirteenth century, the exemplar of love was the chaste devotion of a knight for another man's wife. In Puritan New England, love between husband and wife was the ideal, and in Victorian times, the asexual devotion of a mother for her child seemed the essence of love.[3] My purpose is to focus on one kind of love: long-term heterosexual love in the contemporary United States.

What is a useful definition of enduring love between a woman and a man? One guideline for a definition comes from the prototypes of enduring love—the relations between committed lovers, husband and wife, parent and child. These relationships combine care and assistance with physical and emotional closeness. Studies of attachment between infants and their mothers emphasize the importance of being protected and fed as well as touched and held. In marriage, according to most family sociologists, both practical help and affection are part of enduring love, or "the affection we feel for those with whom our lives are deeply intertwined."[4] Our own informal observations often point in the same direction: if we consider the relationships that are

*Cancian, Francesca M. 1986. "The Feminization of Love." *Signs: Journal of Women in Culture and Society* 11(4): 692–709.

the prototypes of enduring love, it seems that what we really mean by love is some combination of instrumental and expressive qualities.

Historical studies provide a second guideline for defining enduring love, specifically between a woman and a man.[5] In precapitalist America, such love was a complex whole that included work and feelings. Then it was split into feminine and masculine fragments by the separation of home and workplace. This historical analysis implies that affection, material help, and routine cooperation all are parts of enduring love.

Consistent with these guidelines, my working definition of enduring love between adults is a relationship wherein a small number of people are affectionate and emotionally committed to each other, define their collective well-being as a major goal, and feel obliged to provide care and practical assistance for each other. People who love each other also usually share physical contact; they communicate with each other frequently and cooperate in some routine tasks of daily life. My discussion is of enduring heterosexual love only; I will for the sake of simplicity refer to it as "love."

In contrast to this broad definition of love, the narrower, feminized definition dominates both contemporary scholarship and public opinion. Most scholars who study love, intimacy, or close friendship focus on qualities that are stereotypically feminine, such as talking about feelings.[6] For example, Abraham Maslow defines love as "a feeling of tenderness and affection with great enjoyment, happiness, satisfaction, elation and even ecstasy." Among healthy individuals, he says, "there is a growing intimacy and honesty and self-expression."[7] Zick Rubin's "Love Scale," designed to measure the degree of passionate love as opposed to liking, includes questions about confiding in each other, longing to be together, and sexual attraction as well as

caring for each other. Studies of friendship usually distinguish close friends from acquaintances on the basis of how much personal information is disclosed, and many recent studies of married couples and lovers emphasize communication and self-disclosure. A recent book on marital love by Lillian Rubin focuses on intimacy, which she defines as "reciprocal expression of feeling and thought, not out of fear or dependent need, but out of a wish to know another's inner life and to be able to share one's own."[8] She argues that intimacy is distinct from nurturance or caretaking and that men are usually unable to be intimate.

Among the general public, love is also defined primarily as expressing feelings and verbal disclosure, not as instrumental help. This is especially true among the more affluent; poorer people are more likely than they to see practical help and financial assistance as a sign of love.[9] In a study conducted in 1980, 130 adults from a wide range of social classes and ethnic backgrounds were interviewed about the qualities that make a good love relationship. The most frequent response referred to honest and open communication. Being caring and supportive and being tolerant and understanding were the other qualities most often mentioned.[10] Similar results were reported from Ann Swidler's study of an affluent suburb: the dominant conception of love stressed communicating feelings, working on the relationship, and self-development.[11] Finally, a contemporary dictionary defines love as "strong affection for another arising out of kinship or personal ties" and as attraction based on sexual desire, affection, and tenderness.[12]

These contemporary definitions of love clearly focus on qualities that are seen as feminine in our culture. A study of gender roles in 1968 found that warmth, expressiveness, and talkativeness were seen as appropriate for women and not for men. In 1978 the core features of gender stereotypes were unchanged although fewer qualities were seen as appropriate for only one sex. Expressing tender feelings, being gentle, and being aware of the feelings of others were still ideal qualities for women and not for men. The desirable qualities for men and not for women included being independent, unemotional, and interested in sex.[13] The only component perceived as masculine in popular definitions of love is interest in sex.

The two approaches to defining love—one broad, encompassing instrumental and affective qualities, one narrow, including only the affective qualities—inform the two different perspectives on love. According to the androgynous perspective, both gender roles contain elements of love. The feminine role does not include all of the major ways of loving; some aspects of love come from the masculine role, such as sex and providing material help, and some, such as cooperating in daily tasks, are associated with neither gender role. In contrast, the feminized perspective on love implies that all of the elements of love are included in the feminine role. The capacity to love is divided by gender. Women can love and men cannot.

SOME FEMINIST INTERPRETATIONS

Feminist scholars are divided on the question of love and gender. Supporters of the feminized perspective seem most influential at present. Nancy Chodorow's psychoanalytic theory has been especially influential in promoting a feminized perspective on love among social scientists studying close relationships. Chodorow's argument—in greatly simplified form—is that as infants, both boys and girls have strong identification and intimate attachments with their mothers. Since boys grow up to be men, they must repress this early identification, and in the

process they repress their capacity for intimacy. Girls retain their early identification since they will grow up to be women, and throughout their lives females see themselves as connected to others. As a result of this process, Chodorow argues, "girls come to define and experience themselves as continuous with others; . . . boys come to define themselves as more separate and distinct."[14] This theory implies that love is feminine—women are more open to love than men—and that this gender difference will remain as long as women are the primary caretakers of infants.

Scholars have used Chodorow's theory to develop the idea that love and attachment are fundamental parts of women's personalities but not of men's. Carol Gilligan's influential book on female personality development asserts that women define their identity "by a standard of responsibility and care." The predominant female image is "a network of connection, a web of relationships that is sustained by a process of communication." In contrast, males favor a "hierarchical ordering, with its imagery of winning and losing and the potential for violence which it contains." "Although the world of the self that men describe at times includes 'people' and 'deep attachments,' no particular person or relationship is mentioned. . . . Thus the male 'I' is defined in separation."[15]

A feminized conception of love can be supported by other theories as well. In past decades, for example, such a conception developed from Talcott Parsons's theory of the benefits to the nuclear family of women's specializing in expressive action and men's specializing in instrumental action. Among contemporary social scientists, the strongest support for the feminized perspective comes from such psychological theories as Chodorow's.[16]

On the other hand, feminist historians have developed an incisive critique of the feminized perspective on love. Mary Ryan and other social historians have analyzed how the separation of home and workplace in the nineteenth century polarized gender roles and feminized love.[17] Their argument, in simplified form, begins with the observation that in the colonial era the family household was the arena for economic production, affection, and social welfare. The integration of activities in the family produced a certain integration of expressive and instrumental traits in the personalities of men and women. Both women and men were expected to be hard working, modest, and loving toward their spouses and children, and the concept of love included instrumental cooperation as well as expression of feelings. In Ryan's words, "When early Americans spoke of love they were not withdrawing into a female byway of human experience. Domestic affection, like sex and economics, was not segregated into male and female spheres." There was a "reciprocal ideal of conjugal love" that "grew out of the day-to-day cooperation, sharing, and closeness of the diversified home economy."[18]

Economic production gradually moved out of the home and became separated from personal relationships as capitalism expanded. Husbands increasingly worked for wages in factories and shops while wives stayed at home to care for the family. This division of labor gave women more experience with close relationships and intensified women's economic dependence on men. As the daily activities of men and women grew further apart, a new worldview emerged that exaggerated the differences between the personal, loving, feminine sphere of the home and the impersonal, powerful, masculine sphere of the workplace. Work became identified with what men do for money while love became identified with women's activities at home. As a result, the conception of love shifted toward emphasizing tenderness, powerlessness, and the expression of emotion.[19]

This partial and feminized conception of love persisted into the twentieth century as the division of labor remained stable: the workplace remained impersonal and separated from the home, and married women continued to be excluded from paid employment. According to this historical explanation, one might expect a change in the conception of love since the 1940s, as growing numbers of wives took jobs. However, women's persistent responsibility for child care and housework, and their lower wages, might explain a continued feminized conception of love.[20]

Like the historical critiques, some psychological studies of gender also imply that our current conception of love is distorted and needs to be integrated with qualities associated with the masculine role. For example, Jean Baker Miller argues that women's ways of loving—their need to be attached to a man and to serve others—result from women's powerlessness, and that a better way of loving would integrate power with women's style of love.[21] The importance of combining activities and personality traits that have been split apart by gender is also a frequent theme in the human potential movement.[22] These historical and psychological works emphasize the flexibility of gender roles and the inadequacy of a concept of love that includes only the feminine half of human qualities. In contrast, theories like Chodorow's emphasize the rigidity of gender differences after childhood and define love in terms of feminine qualities. The two theoretical approaches are not as inconsistent as my simplified sketches may suggest, and many scholars combine them;[23] however, the two approaches have different implications for empirical research.

EVIDENCE ON WOMEN'S "SUPERIORITY" IN LOVE

A large number of studies show that women are more interested and more skilled in love than men. However, most of these studies use biased measures based on feminine styles of loving, such as verbal self-disclosure, emotional expression, and willingness to report that one has close relationships. When less biased measures are used, the differences between women and men are often small.

Women have a greater number of close relationships than men. At all stages of the life cycle, women see their relatives more often. Men and women report closer relations with their mothers than with their fathers and are generally closer to female kin. Thus an average Yale man in the 1970s talked about himself more with his mother than with his father and was more satisfied with his relationship with his mother. His most frequent grievance against his father was that his father gave too little of himself and was cold and uninvolved; his grievance against his mother was that she gave too much of herself and was alternately overprotective and punitive.[24]

Throughout their lives, women are more likely to have a confidant—a person to whom one discloses personal experiences and feelings. Girls prefer to be with one friend or a small group, while boys usually play competitive games in large groups. Men usually get together with friends to play sports or do some other activity, while women get together explicitly to talk and to be together.[25]

Men seemed isolated given their weak ties with their families and friends. Among blue-collar couples interviewed in 1950, 64 percent of the husbands had no confidants other than their spouses, compared to 24 percent of the wives.[26] The predominantly upper-middle-class men interviewed by Daniel Levinson in the 1970s were no less isolated. Levinson concludes that "close friendship with a man or a woman is rarely experienced by American men."[27] Apparently, most men have no loving relationships besides those with wife or lover; and given the

estrangement that often occurs in marriages, many men may have no loving relationship at all.

Several psychologists have suggested that there is a natural reversal of these roles in middle age, as men become more concerned with relationships and women turn toward independence and achievement; but there seems to be no evidence showing that men's relationships become more numerous or more intimate after middle age, and some evidence to the contrary.[28]

Women are also more skilled than men in talking about relationships. Whether working class or middle class, women value talking about feelings and relationships and disclose more than men about personal experiences. Men who deviate and talk a lot about their personal experiences are commonly defined as feminine and maladjusted.[29] Working-class wives prefer to talk about themselves, their close relationships with family and friends, and their homes, while their husbands prefer to talk about cars, sports, work, and politics. The same gender-specific preferences are expressed by college students.[30]

Men do talk more about one area of personal experience: their victories and achievements; but talking about success is associated with power, not intimacy. Women say more about their fears and disappointments, and it is disclosure of such weaknesses that usually is interpreted as a sign of intimacy.[31] Women are also more accepting of the expression of intense feelings, including love, sadness, and fear, and they are more skilled in interpreting other people's emotions.[32]

Finally, in their leisure time women are drawn to topics of love and human entanglements while men are drawn to competition among men. Women's preferences in television viewing run to daytime soap operas, or if they are more educated, the high-brow soap operas on educational channels, while most men like to watch competitive and often aggressive sports. Reading tastes show the same pattern. Women read novels and magazine articles about love, while men's magazines feature stories about men's adventures and encounters with death.[33]

However, this evidence on women's greater involvement and skill in love is not as strong as it appears. Part of the reason that men seem so much less loving than women is that their behavior is measured with a feminine ruler. Much of this research considers only the kinds of loving behavior that are associated with the feminine role and rarely compares women and men in terms of qualities associated with the masculine role. When less biased measures are used, the behavior of men and women is often quite similar. For example, in a careful study of kinship relations among young adults in a southern city, Bert Adams found that women were much more likely than men to say that their parents and relatives were very important to their lives (58 percent of women and 37 percent of men). In measures of actual contact with relatives, though, there were much smaller differences: 88 percent of women and 81 percent of men whose parents lived in the same city saw their parents weekly. Adams concluded that "differences between males and females in relations with parents are discernible primarily in the subjective sphere; contact frequencies are quite similar."[34]

The differences between the sexes can be small even when biased measures are used. For example, Marjorie Lowenthal and Clayton Haven reported the finding, later widely quoted, that elderly women were more likely than elderly men to have a friend with whom they could talk about their personal troubles—clearly a measure of a traditionally feminine behavior. The figures revealed that 81 percent of the married women and 74 percent of the married men had confidants—not a sizable difference.[35] On the other hand, whatever the measure, virtually all such studies find that women are more involved in close relationships than men, even if the difference is small.

In sum, women are only moderately superior to men in love: they have more close relationships and care more about them, and they seem to be more skilled at love, especially those aspects of love that involve expressing feelings and being vulnerable. This does not mean that men are separate and unconcerned with close relationships, however. When national surveys ask people what is most important in their lives, women tend to put family bonds first while men put family bonds first or second, along with work.[36] For both sexes, love is clearly very important.

EVIDENCE ON THE MASCULINE STYLE OF LOVE

Men tend to have a distinctive style of love that focuses on practical help, shared physical activities, spending time together, and sex.[37] The major elements of the masculine style of love emerged in Margaret Reedy's study of 102 married couples in the late 1970s. She showed individuals' statements describing aspects of love and asked them to rate how well the statements described their marriages. On the whole, husband and wife had similar views of their marriage, but several sex differences emerged. Practical help and spending time together were more important to men. The men were more likely to give high ratings to such statements as: "When she needs help I help her," and "She would rather spend her time with me than with anyone else." Men also described themselves more often as sexually attracted and endorsed such statements as: "I get physically excited and aroused just thinking about her." In addition, emotional security was less important to men than to women, and men were less likely to describe the relationship as secure, safe, and comforting.[38] Another study in the late 1970s showed a similar pattern among young, highly educated couples. The husbands gave greater emphasis to feeling responsible for the partner's well-being and putting the spouse's needs first, as well as to spending time together. The wives gave greater importance to emotional involvement and verbal self-disclosure but also were more concerned than the men about maintaining their separate activities and their independence.[39]

The difference between men and women in their views of the significance of practical help was demonstrated in a study in which seven couples recorded their interactions for several days. They noted how pleasant their relations were and counted how often the spouse did a helpful chore, such as cooking a good meal or repairing a faucet, and how often the spouse expressed acceptance or affection. The social scientists doing the study used a feminized definition of love. They labeled practical help as "instrumental behavior" and expressions of acceptance or affection as "affectionate behavior," thereby denying the affectionate aspect of practical help. The wives seemed to be using the same scheme; they thought their marital relations were pleasant that day if their husbands had directed a lot of affectionate behavior to them, regardless of their husbands' positive instrumental behavior. The husbands' enjoyment of their marital relations, on the other hand, depended on their wives' instrumental actions, not on their expressions of affection. The men actually saw instrumental actions as affection.[40] One husband who was told by the researchers to increase his affectionate behavior toward his wife decided to wash her car and was surprised when neither his wife nor the researchers accepted that as an "affectionate" act.

The masculine view of instrumental help as loving behavior is clearly expressed by a husband discussing his wife's complaints about his lack of communication: "What does she want? Proof? She's got it, hasn't she? Would I be knocking myself out to get things for her—like to keep up this house—if I didn't love her? Why does a man do things like that if not because he loves his wife and kids? I swear, I can't figure what she wants." His wife, who has a feminine orientation to love, says something very different: "It is not enough that he supports us and takes care of us. I appreciate that, but I want him to share things with me. I need for him to tell me his feelings."[41] Many working-class women agree with men that a man's job is something he does out of love for his family,[42] but middle-class women and social scientists rarely recognize men's practical help as a form of love. (Indeed, among upper-middle-class men whose jobs offer a great deal of intrinsic gratification, their belief that they are "doing it for the family" may seem somewhat self-serving.)

Other differences between men's and women's styles of love involve sex. Men seem to separate sex and love while women connect them,[43] but, paradoxically, sexual intercourse seems to be the most meaningful way of giving and receiving love for many men. A twenty-nine-year-old carpenter who had been married for three years said that, after sex, "I feel so close to her and the kids. We feel like a real family then. I don't talk to her very often, I guess, but somehow I feel we have really communicated after we have made love."[44]

Because sexual intimacy is the only recognized "masculine" way of expressing love, the recent trend toward viewing sex as a way for men and women to express mutual intimacy is an important challenge to the feminization of love. However, the connection between sexuality and love is undermined both by the "sexual revolution" definition of sex as a form of casual recreation and by the view of male sexuality as a weapon—as in rape—with which men dominate and punish women.[45]

Another paradoxical feature of men's style of love is that men have a more romantic attitude toward their partners than do women. In Reedy's study, men were more likely to select statements like "we are perfect for each other."[46] In a survey of college students, 65 percent of the men but only 24 percent of the women said that, even if a relationship had all of the other qualities they desired, they would not marry unless they were in love.[47] The common view of this phenomenon focuses on women. The view is that women marry for money and status and so see marriage as instrumentally, rather than emotionally, desirable. This of course is at odds with women's greater concern with self-disclosure and emotional intimacy and lesser concern with instrumental help. A better way to explain men's greater romanticism might be to focus on men. One such possible explanation is that men do not feel responsible for "working on" the emotional aspects of a relationship, and therefore see love as magically and perfectly present or absent. This is consistent with men's relative lack of concern with affective interaction and greater concern with instrumental help.

In sum, there is a masculine style of love. Except for romanticism, men's style fits the popularly conceived masculine role of being the powerful provider.[48] From the androgynous perspective, the practical help and physical activities included in this role are as much a part of love as the expression of feelings. The feminized perspective cannot account for this masculine style of love; nor can it explain why women and men are so close in the degrees to which they are loving.

NEGATIVE CONSEQUENCES OF THE FEMINIZATION OF LOVE

The division of gender roles in our society that contributes to the two separate styles of love is reinforced by the feminized perspective and leads to political and moral problems that would be mitigated with a more androgynous approach to love. The feminized perspective works against some of the key values and goals of feminists and humanists by contributing to the devaluation and exploitation of women.

It is especially striking how the differences between men's and women's styles of love reinforce men's power over women. Men's style involves giving women important resources, such as money and protection that men control and women believe they need, and ignoring the resources that women control and men need. Thus men's dependency on women remains covert and repressed, while women's dependency on men is overt and exaggerated; and it is overt dependency that creates power, according to social exchange theory.[49] The feminized perspective on love reinforces this power differential by leading to the belief that women need love more than do men, which is implied in the association of love with the feminine role. The effect of this belief is to intensify the asymmetrical dependency of women on men.[50] In fact, however, evidence on the high death rates of unmarried men suggests that men need love at least as much as do women.[51]

Sexual relations also can reinforce male dominance insofar as the man takes the initiative and intercourse is defined either as his "taking" pleasure or as his being skilled at "giving" pleasure, either way giving him control. The man's power advantage is further strengthened if the couple assumes that the man's sexual needs can be filled by any attractive woman while the woman's sexual needs can be filled only by the man she loves.[52]

On the other hand, women's preferred ways of loving seem incompatible with control. They involve admitting dependency and sharing or losing control, and being emotionally intense.

Further, the intimate talk about personal troubles that appeals to women requires of a couple a mutual vulnerability, a willingness to see oneself as weak and in need of support. It is true that a woman, like a man, can gain some power by providing her partner with services, such as understanding, sex, or cooking; but this power is largely unrecognized because the man's dependency on such services is not overt. The couple may even see these services as her duty or as her response to his requests (or demands).

The identification of love with expressing feelings also contributes to the lack of recognition of women's power by obscuring the instrumental active component of women's love just as it obscures the loving aspect of men's work. In a culture that glorifies instrumental achievement, this identification devalues both women and love.[53] In reality, a major way by which women are loving is in the clearly instrumental activities associated with caring for others, such as preparing meals, washing clothes, and providing care during illness; but because of our focus on the expressive side of love, this caring work of women is either ignored or redefined as expressing feelings. Thus, from the feminized perspective on love, child care is a subtle communication of attitudes, not work. A wife washing her husband's shirt is seen as expressing love, even though a husband washing his wife's car is seen as doing a job.

Gilligan, in her critique of theories of human development, shows the way in which devaluing love is linked to devaluing women. Basic to most psychological theories of development is the idea that a healthy person develops from a dependent child to an autonomous, independent adult. As Gilligan comments, "Development itself comes to be identified with separation, and attachments appear to be developmental impediments."[54] Thus women, who emphasize attachment, are judged to be developmentally retarded or insufficiently individuated.

The pervasiveness of this image was documented in a well-known study of mental health professionals who were asked to describe mental health, femininity, and masculinity. They associated both mental health and masculinity with independence, rationality, and dominance. Qualities concerning attachment, such as being tactful, gentle, or aware of the feelings of others, they associated with femininity but not with mental health.[55]

Another negative consequence of a feminized perspective on love is that it legitimates impersonal, exploitive relations in the workplace and the community. The ideology of separate spheres that developed in the nineteenth century contrasted the harsh, immoral marketplace with the warm and loving home and implied that this contrast is acceptable.[56] Defining love as expressive, feminine, and divorced from productive activity maintains this ideology. If personal relationships and love are reserved for women and the home, then it is acceptable for a manager to underpay workers or for a community to ignore a needy family. Such behavior is not unloving; it is businesslike or shows a respect for privacy. The ideology of separate spheres also implies that men are properly judged by their instrumental and economic achievements and that poor or unsuccessful men are failures who may deserve a hard life. Levinson presents a conception of masculine development itself as centering on achieving an occupational dream.[57]

Finally, the feminization of love intensifies the conflicts over intimacy between women and men in close relationships. One of the most common conflicts is that the woman wants more closeness and verbal contact while the man withdraws and wants less pressure.[58] Her need for more closeness is partly the result of the feminization of love, which encourages her to be more emotionally dependent on him. Because love is feminine, he in turn may feel controlled during intimate contact. Intimacy is her "turf," an area where she sets the rules and expectations. Talking about the relationship as she wants, may well feel to him like taking a test that she made up and that he will fail. He is likely to react by withdrawing, causing her to intensify her efforts to get closer. The feminization of love thus can lead to a vicious cycle of conflict where neither partner feels in control or gets what she or he wants.

CONCLUSION

The values of improving the status of women and humanizing the public sphere are shared by many of the scholars who support a feminized conception of love; and they, too, explain the conflicts in close relationships in terms of polarized gender roles. Nancy Chodorow, Lillian Rubin, and Carol Gilligan have addressed these issues in detail and with great insight. However, by arguing that women's identity is based on attachment while men's identity is based on separation, they reinforce the distinction between feminine expressiveness and masculine instrumentality, revive the ideology of separate spheres, and legitimate the popular idea that only women know the right way to love. They also suggest that there is no way to overcome the rigidity of gender roles other than by pursuing the goal of men and women becoming equally involved in infant care. In contrast, an androgynous perspective on love challenges the identification of women and love with being expressive, powerless, and nonproductive and the identification of men with being instrumental, powerful, and productive. It rejects the ideology of separate spheres and validates masculine as well as feminine styles of love. This viewpoint suggests that progress could be made by means of a variety of social changes, including men doing child care, relations at work becoming more personal and nurturant, and cultural conceptions of love and gender becoming more androgynous. Changes that equalize power within close relationships by equalizing the economic and emotional dependency between men and women may be especially important in moving toward androgynous love.

The validity of an androgynous definition of love cannot be "proven"; the view that informs the androgynous perspective is that both the feminine style of love (characterized by emotional closeness and verbal self-disclosure) and the masculine style of love (characterized by instrumental help and sex) represent necessary parts of a good love relationship. Who is more loving: a couple who confide most of their experiences to each other but rarely cooperate or give each other practical help, or a couple who help each other through many crises and cooperate in running a household but rarely discuss their personal experiences? Both relationships are limited. Most people would probably choose a combination: a relationship that integrates feminine and masculine styles of loving, an androgynous love.

Reading 13   "That's Our Kind of Constellation"

Lesbian Mothers Negotiate Institutionalized Understandings of Gender within the Family

SUSAN E. DALTON*   DENISE D. BIELBY

Building on more than two decades of feminist analysis of the family, this article takes a neoinstitutionalist approach to examine some of the ways that sex, gender, and sexual orientation intersect in lesbian-headed two-parent families, affecting how they construct their roles as mothers. Institutionalist theory tends to de-emphasize how actors deliberately construct social arrangements such as parenting roles within the family. The authors' analysis of interviews from 14 lesbian mothers remedies this deficiency by focusing both on how they draw upon and transform institutionalized scripts, practices, and understandings of family roles and relations. Their findings reveal how these mothers reinscribed gendered understandings while simultaneously challenging heteronormative ones in their efforts to construct and maintain socially viable two-parent families.

As feminists and others have observed for more than a decade, the monolithic notion of the traditional nuclear family is difficult to dispel because it seems to be natural and biological, the most timeless and unchanging of all social institutions. Although the family is a central, enduring, and taken-for-granted social institution, it is also one of the most variable, contested, debated, and analyzed by scholars, policy makers, special interest groups, and family members alike. Feminist scholars argue that the family is an ideological concept as much as it is a set of experiences and an institution and that even its boundedness as a private institution unto itself that can be

Authors' Note: This research was assisted by a Sexuality Research Fellowship from the Social Science Research Council, with funds provided by the Ford Foundation. An early version of this work was presented at the American Sociological Association annual meeting in San Francisco in 1998. We thank the editors of the special issue and anonymous reviewers for their helpful comments.

wholly separated from the public sphere needs reconsideration (Ferree 1990; Osmond 1987). Embodied in cultural assumptions and gendered relations are the practical, material, and ideological notions that construct family.

Child rearing occurs almost exclusively within social groups that are recognized as family arrangements. That these social arrangements are understood to constitute families speaks to caregiving for children as an experience powerfully linked to institutionalized scripts about family. When lesbians come out, one of the main consequences is the anticipated or actual loss or alteration of the "straight," "biological," or "blood" ties to their families of origin. This outcome contributes to popular beliefs that lesbians and gay men live without families (Burch 1997). However, anthropological studies of lesbian and gay men show how their chosen families are composed of a fluid structure of kinship ties based on social identity, friendship, and emotional commitment (Weston 1991). These families are not easily recognizable because they are not patterned on conventional biological and marital ties. As such, they are "unconventional" in the sense that there are no widely shared institutionalized understandings of chosen families as families. As Burch observes,

> *New kinship ties created within lesbian and gay culture have little social recognition. Relationships even between lovers usually lack legal standing, and [their] extended networks of "kin"—friends and ex-lovers who become a committed part of each other's lives, who are similar to the extended family in heterosexual terms— have none at all. (1997, 149)*

The absence of legal standing becomes especially problematic when a lesbian couple decides to bring a child into their lives. The legal invisibility of lesbian two-parent families stems from the historical development of family law. In the United States, the law generally recognizes three types of persons as legal parents: those who biologically reproduce a child, individuals who adopt the legal or biological child of their spouses, and men who are legally married to and living with women who reproduce a child.[1] Because two women are unable to biologically reproduce a child together, and because marriage in the United States is limited to male-female couples only, nonbiological mothers in lesbian-headed two-parent families remain legally unrelated to the children they co-parent unless they successfully complete a formal adoption proceeding.

For lesbian and gay couples, however, adoption is not an easy procedure. Indeed, all adoption statutes, except those pertaining to single-parent adoption, assume a legal marriage.[2] This has meant that lesbians who want to adopt their partners' legal and/or biological children have had to convince superior court judges to reinterpret adoption statutes in ways that are inclusive of the lesbian co-parent family. (For an explanation of the limited consent adoption process used by lesbian couples, see Dalton 1999; Patt 1987–88; Ricketts and Achtenberg 1990; Zuckerman 1986.)

Our research examines how lesbian mothers accomplish co-parenting arrangements. It is guided in part by feminist scholarship that emphasizes symbolic displays of gender in understanding family relations. Research on heterosexual households shows how gender defines normative expectations for those who comprise the domestic unit (Berk 1985; Brines 1993), and it illustrates the centrality of emotion work to the gendered social construction and enactment of the family (Erickson 1993; Luxton 1991). But in households where symbolic displays of partners' gender differences are less salient, how are roles divided and enacted, particularly in the traditionally pivotal context of parenting? Scholarship on heterosexual couples is not adequate for understanding co-parenting among lesbian couples, so we draw upon recent research on lesbian relationships to analyze how cultural assumptions about parenting in general and mothering in particular shape the enactment of parenting roles among lesbians (Benkov 1994).

Specifically, we examine how lesbian mothers rely on gender as a resource for actively reconstructing the institution of the family. The data for this study were collected from 14 in-depth interviews with lesbian mothers. These data allow us to study how these mothers use co-parenting arrangements to signify commitment to a relationship, redefine the legal and social entitlements of biological fathers, accomplish dual-mother identities, and negotiate public recognition. Examining how their interactional strategies and practices are accomplished and understood yields insight into how lesbian mothers effect change in institutional definitions of the family and alter gendered conceptualizations of the two-parent family.

Institutionalization and Family Formation

According to neoinstitutional theory, "Institutions do not merely reflect the preferences and power of the units constituting them; the institutions themselves shape those preferences" (DiMaggio and Powell 1991, 7). Through custom, law, or other social traditions, institutions, such as the family, exist prior to and outside of the desires of individual constituents. Institutionalization itself is seen as a process by which certain social relationships and actions gradually come to be taken for granted. Additionally, institutions are built on shared cognitions that define "what has meaning and what actions are possible" (9).

Institutional theory tends to de-emphasize actors' deliberate constructions of social arrangements to achieve desired outcomes. However, individuals do act purposively, demonstrating agency based on understandings, shared or otherwise, of their social contexts as the basis for action (Emirbayer and Mische 1998; Sewell 1992). Thus, individual agency within institutions like the family is manifested as choices and preferences made within specific cultural and historical contexts. Choices and preferences themselves are not universal and unchanging, although once social practices are institutionalized, they become self-sustaining. Thus, people choose actions because they offer socially constructed and practical routes for solving certain social and individual needs. A same-sex couple, for example, might participate in a commitment ceremony to demonstrate their dedication to a relationship that is not legally sanctioned by the state. By doing so, they are drawing upon and transforming institutionalized scripts about marriage and family.

Institutional analysis also draws attention to the ideological and symbolic significance of social arrangements within families as they relate to the organization and enactment of familial relationships themselves. Members' social scripts are guides to action. In families, personal attributions (such as assumptions about enacting the provider role), habit (such as division of labor in household tasks or in caretaking of kin), and practical action (such as who organizes family dinners or holiday events) are central to members' ongoing participation. For lesbian couples, guides to action may be proactively constructed and flexibly scripted, but they are by no means fully insulated from dominant institutional understandings of marital and parenting roles.

The Legal Construction of Parenthood

The social construction of the family is based on a biological model of reproduction in which there is one male/father and one female/mother. Within the family, gender—who is the mother and who is the father—is enmeshed with heteronormativity— that the family unit is organized around one man and one woman. The law, as an institution that grants formal legitimacy to social arrangements and practices, invokes the biological model of reproduction to define what it recognizes as the family; based on that model, the family has one mother and one father. In the eyes of the law, because the biological mother is readily identifiable as she who gave birth, all other women are excluded from making claims to natural mother status. Biological fathers, on the other hand, are often harder to identify, making it easier for judges to substitute one father, the biological father, with another, the social father.

In the law, lesbians who are nonbiological parents are disadvantaged relative to nonbiological fathers because of their gender. In custody hearings involving divorcing heterosexual couples where legal parental obligations are at issue, courts sometimes make presumptions of paternity based on judges' ability to imagine biological consanguinity to be true. Men who are married to women who give birth during the marriage are automatically presumed to be the biological fathers of those children. Until recently, the same presumption had never been applied to a nonbiological mother. That changed in 1998 when the courts for the first time granted a nonbiological mother parental status without a formal adoption proceeding. The case involved a married couple who contracted a surrogate mother to carry to term a fetus created from a donated egg and donated sperm. Legal parental status had to be defined on the surrogate's relinquishing of that status. The court relied on the legally recognized marriage of the couple to confer upon both the husband and the wife legal parental status even though neither was a biological parent.[3] However, in a subsequent case, the court refused to apply this precedent to the nonbiological parent in a lesbian couple because they could not be legal spouses[4]

(for a more detailed discussion, see Dalton 1999). Thus, legal barriers to parental standing of the lesbian nonbiological parent lead lesbian couples to other means for attaining parental status.

Challenging Heteronormativity While Reinscribing Gender

Although lesbian mothers may draw from gendered scripts to construct themselves as two-parent families, they do so in ways that fundamentally challenge implicit heteronormative assumptions. West and Fenstermaker argue that "gender…is a situated accomplishment of societal members, the local management of conduct in relation to normative conceptions of appropriate attitudes and activities for particular sex categories" (1995a, 21). When lesbian couples construct themselves as two-parent families, they directly challenge normative conceptions of the traditional model of the two-parent family as it is socially and legally constructed from a biological model of reproduction. By selectively combining predominant notions of a biological model of reproduction with those from a social model of reproduction, the lesbian mothers in our study purposively sought to modify the traditional, biologically based model. More specifically, most lesbian two-parent families consist of one biological parent and one social parent, a configuration that directly challenges traditional models of the family. As one of our mothers claimed, "That's our kind of constellation." Families like hers challenge gendered understandings as well as heteronormative conceptions of the family.

Nevertheless, being a parent is fundamentally a gendered concept. Mothers and fathers are not interchangeable, especially within the law. When viewed as individuals, lesbian mothers may be judged as performing gender appropriately. However, within the context of the two-parent family, they are seen as performing gender inappropriately, and they are frequently held accountable as gender nonconformists. Their responses to this, while occurring at the level of social interaction among individuals, have the potential to affect institutional understandings of the family (West and Fenstermaker 1995a, 1995b).

Lesbian two-parent families have achieved limited recognition and legitimacy within the legal arena, primarily through the development of the second-parent adoption process. However, even those mothers who successfully complete such adoptions continue to remain largely invisible in other areas of society. We examine how active efforts to escape this invisibility at an individual level challenge heteronormative assumptions that underlie traditional conceptions of the two-parent family. The results we present below suggest that lesbian mothers confront and challenge heteronormativity through a two-step process: First, they consciously and with considerable forethought employ shared cognitions to create and describe their own families. Second, they actively negotiate their family status with those around them, a process that challenges institutionalized scripts regarding the "proper" male/father, female/mother configuration of the family. These negotiations, when successful, eventually have a cumulative impact that has the potential to change widely held gendered notions of family. Nevertheless, gender-based attributions and understandings about biology and about provider and caregiving roles invariably interject gender as an element into lesbian families.

Research on Family Practices in Heterosexual, Lesbian, and Gay Households: The Gendering of Parent Roles

Research that compares decision making and power among heterosexual, lesbian, and gay couples begins to disentangle the effect of gendered institutions and, specifically, notions of masculinity upon family relations (Kurdek 1993). Burgeoning research on lesbian and gay partners shows how same-sex couples are affected by the normative ideologies of both gender and the family as they define household labor and related activities. Blumstein and Schwartz's pioneering 1983 study of the domestic practices of same-sex and heterosexual couples found that household responsibilities, including emotion work, are more equally shared among lesbian and gays, regardless of employment status. However, compared to lesbians, gays tend to have a more traditional division of labor in the household, meaning the breadwinner/primary-caretaker arrangement (McWhirter and Mattison 1984; Peplau and Cochran 1990).

Recent research also shows that deliberate efforts to avoid patriarchally based gender inequality in lesbian households can make a difference in the instrumental and affective division of labor in lesbian co-parenting practices. However, achieving such equity requires a conscious and deliberate effort to counter social scripts that otherwise prescribe role relationships. In a study of lesbian co-parents, Sullivan (1996) found that in many couples, partners allocated their paid work and family responsibilities so that neither parent assumed an unequal share of the labor and so that neither partner was economically dependent on the other. Specifically, Sullivan found that when partners explicitly and self-consciously commit to equitable parenting, neither parent assumed a disproportionate share of household tasks. However, when lesbian couples decided to adhere to a traditional breadwinner/primary-caregiver arrangement, the stay-at-home partner was rendered economically vulnerable by forgoing ties to paid employment. In particular, this arrangement resulted in a noticeable decline in the stay-at-home partner's capacity to influence family decisions and negotiate for her needs associated with child care and other domestic practices. The intrusion of economic dependency reaffirms, once again, the importance of gender and income for power and other aspects of family relations.

Empirical research documents how the division of labor in heterosexual households is negotiated around symbols of masculinity and femininity (see Brines 1993; Goffman 1977). These negotiations are contingent not only on the degree to which spouses hold themselves and each other accountable to cultural definitions of gender but also on how they are held accountable by others (see also Blumstein and Schwartz 1983; Bolak 1997; Pyke and Coltrane 1996; Thompson 1993; West and Zimnerman 1987). Blumstein and Schwartz (1983) find that the relationship between earnings capacity and power was greatest among gay couples and lowest among lesbians, suggesting that culturally defined notions of masculinity shape power dynamics.

Finally, an important factor contributing to both asymmetry in co-parenting roles and emerging institutional understandings of lesbian and gay families is the biological relationship between the child and each of its parents. For example, lesbian couples negotiate parental roles within a larger societal context where the biological parent is considered the "real" parent (McCandlish 1992). Thus, a nonbiological parent who attempts to negotiate a mothering role does so in a context where her co-parent has undeniable claim to that role via her biological connection to the child.

From an institutionalist perspective, the research summarized above suggests that as lesbian couples enact their family roles, they do so in a context of strongly prescribed heteronormative expectations and gendered scripts. At the same time, whether because of lack of social support from intergenerational familial ties (Slater 1995) or because of ideological commit-

ment to more equitable familial roles (Sullivan 1996), lesbian couples are also reconstructing cultural understandings of family and parenting. They must do so because gender difference—the traditional basis for dividing labor—is not a taken-for-granted part of their "constellation" and therefore is unavailable to them. Research on parenting by lesbians and gays provides an important comparative context for studying the intersection of gender ideology and practice (Patterson 1995). Our research contributes to this line of scholarship by examining how lesbians who face resistance to their co-mother status attempt to negotiate recognition by simultaneously accommodating many of the gendered expectations of motherhood while attempting to redefine those used to mark them as deviant.

METHOD

The data for this article come from 14 in-depth interviews with lesbian mothers in California. These interviews were collected as part of a larger research project on the experiences of lesbian and gay parents who were seeking second-parent adoptions or who were biological or nonbiological parents in lesbian or gay co-parenting partnerships.[5] The lesbian mothers obtained their parental status in one of three ways: (1) They gave birth to children, some in the context of heterosexual marriages, but most in the context of lesbian relationships; (2) they adopted children, usually but not always their partners' children; or (3) they entered into parenting agreements with their partners in which the couple together sought a donation of sperm, used it to impregnate one member of the couple, and then proceeded to co-parent the resulting child. Of these three methods for attaining parental status, only the first two are recognized under California law. Courts in the state of California have repeatedly refused to recognize the parenting contracts of lesbian couples, leaving the nonbiological mother in these relationships without legal protection should her parental status be challenged.

The respondents are a self-selected group of lesbian mothers who initially heard about the study in one of three ways. The largest group, six women, received information about the study via e-mail, either while participating in a popular lesbian mothers e-mail list or reading the general news list for the University of California Lesbian, Gay, Bisexual, Transsexual, Transgender Association. Many of the remaining respondents heard about the study via word of mouth. Some received word from friends who had read the e-mail solicitations, others from friends who had previously participated in the study, and a few from lawyers who were interviewed for the study and who then passed the first author's name on to their clients. One respondent answered a small advertisement run in the newsletter for the National Center for Lesbian Rights, and one was an acquaintance of the first author.

The interviews lasted between one and four hours, and they followed one of three basic formats that varied depending on the respondent's individual route to motherhood. All the interviewees, however, began with a recounting of how the mothers met their partners; if, when, and how they established themselves as families; and their experiences with conception, birth, and child rearing. This was followed by discussion about how and why they entered the California legal system and their experiences therein. All of the interviews were audiotaped and transcribed, and the data were coded using a basic qualitative data management program.

The data for the analysis reported here are drawn from the family formation, conception, birth, and child-rearing sections of these interviews. This information was solicited using broad, open-ended questions such as, "Can you tell me the story of how your relationship with your co-parent began?" "At what point did you reach the decision to have children?" "How did you decide who would actually carry the child?" and "How do you and your partner manage the day-to-day work of caring for your child(ren)?"

On the whole, the respondents were very willing, even eager, to share their stories. The interviews were all carried out by the first author, who, like the respondents, is in the process of completing a second-parent adoption of her young son. The respondents all knew of the interviewer's status as both a lesbian and mother, and the interviews often began with an informal swapping of family information involving such things as the number, ages, and developmental stages of their respective children and recent funny stories involving the children. Several respondents made note of the fact that the shared status of both lesbian and mother was important to their willingness to share their stories and their feelings that what they said would be understood.

These mothers resided in seven distinct locations in California, including large cities and small communities, with the highest concentration (seven) residing in the San Francisco Bay Area. All the mothers have advanced degrees, and all, with the exception of two who were completing advanced degrees, worked outside the home. The household income for these families varied in range from $21,000 to $40,000 (one couple), $41,000 to $60,000 (two couples), $61,000 to $80,000 (two couples), and $81,000 to $100,000 (three couples). While household incomes were not reported for all couples, social worker reports from the larger sample indicate that most lesbian mothers seeking second-parent adoptions, which, at nine women, was the most frequently represented category in this study, have household incomes above the norm for two-parent families in California. The median household income for lesbian mothers obtaining second-parent adoptions averages between $60,000 to $80,000 per year.

The respondents varied in age from 31 to 48 years. When asked about their race/ethnicity, four categorized themselves as white, one as white/Native American, three as Jewish, and one as Filipino (five did not report their race/ethnicity). These women's children (defined here as children born or adopted into the lesbian relationship focused on in this study), of which there are 18, ranged in age from 7 weeks to 9 years. In addition, three of the respondents reported helping raise children from their partners' previous relationships, and these children, of which there are three, ranged in age from 9 to 19 years. Finally, all the women reported themselves to be out to their parents, siblings, and social communities. Indeed, several respondents commented on the impossibility of having children and remaining in the closet. Only one respondent reported being in her first lesbian relationship, and only two respondents reported remaining closeted at work.

Overall, the sample is skewed in the direction of white, middle- and upper-middle-class, well-educated, slightly older (when compared to the average age of heterosexual women parenting children younger than 10), professional women. This corresponds with reports from social workers, lawyers, and judges regarding the segment of the lesbian and gay community most likely to turn to the courts for assistance with child custody matters. The skewed nature of the sample with regard to race, class, age, and education is due, in large part, to the fact that most women in the sample, 9 of 14, entered the legal system by petitioning for a second-parent adoption. Due to the developmental history of this particular type of adoption, it remains both expensive, averaging between $4,000 to $6,000 per adoption, and relatively unfamiliar to many lesbians (Dalton 1999). As one lawyer reported, if you asked "10 lesbians whether or not they thought they could [get a second-parent adoption], at least half of them will tell you 'no.'" She continued, "Ask 20 lawyers and 5 of them would say you couldn't."

Indeed, in an attempt to avoid a right-wing backlash that could effectively eliminate access to the procedure altogether, many lawyers have shied away from widely publicizing the availability of second-parent adoptions, resulting in an information distribution method that resembles snowball sampling; that is, lawyers and mothers who have used the procedure pass the information on to friends and colleagues. This particular method of distributing legal information, coupled with the restrictive cost of the procedure, has worked to limit access to second-parent adoptions to those women who are both well connected and financially able to afford it. Lesbians who are young, poor, and/or women of color are less likely to know the procedure exists, and even if they have heard of it, they are less likely to be able to afford it. Because this sample is small and consists primarily of white, middle-class, well-educated, slightly older lesbians, the generalizability of findings is limited to lesbian women in similar socioeconomic circumstances. Nonetheless, the analysis is informative and addresses an important missing link between the realms of institutionalized norms and face-to-face interaction.

FINDINGS

Creating Family: Parenthood as a Commitment Process

For many lesbian couples, the decision to become parents figures centrally in each partner's commitment to the relationship. For several women in our study, the experience of a stable and singular involvement included initial conversations early on in the relationship about having a child: "I made it clear from the beginning, she's 11 years older than me, that if we were going to be together I really wanted to have a baby. It was like I said that on our first date" (Lisa). For many of our respondents, retrospective accounts of their approach to parenthood convey a sense of the importance of the decision to the seriousness of their relationship. As one explained,

And then I met my partner and in spite of myself we became involved and I told her from the get go that this [becoming a parent] was something that I wanted to do and that I had intent, that I was intending on doing one way or another and in fact when we first got together I had said to her you know you don't have to do this, you don't have to be involved. And she was pretty light about it. It wasn't a reality but she said she always wanted children too; it wasn't a negative thing for her at all. (Stacey)

As Lisa elaborated,

I've been with my partner for almost seven years. And when I got involved with her she had a 12-year-old son who's now almost 19. So I was helping to raise him.... So it was sort of...we know that we were going to have a kid, another one, and it took a while. She made me wait longer than I wanted to wait to get pregnant but eventually I did and we had [our son] a little more than three years ago.... Once we decided to have a child, it was very committed.

Among the lesbians in our study, the desire to have children was not something that was contradicted by their sexual identity. Instead, the decision to co-parent was understood to be one that drew upon their identity as women, affirm-

ing their growing commitment to their relationships. One mother explained,

For me, it was just something growing up that I had the urge to have children and somehow being a lesbian never seemed to be a contradiction to that, it was just something I wanted. I have younger siblings and I, you know, helped take care of them and such and it was just something I grew up expecting to do. OK, you know, so for me it was just something I wanted to do. I mean, it was just one of those things that, you know, society sort of tells you; you grow up and you have children, and I bought into that. (Mary)

Another mother elaborated,

I always wanted another child and she always wanted a child or children and so we were really kind of just waiting until we felt that we were stable enough. There was some stresses and strains in our relationship that made us, you know, unsure, could we really, you know, make it together, and on the other hand her biological clock was ticking and so, you know, when we felt like well we hadn't worked out everything, but you know we kind of felt like probably we could. Then rather than sort of waiting until we were in an ideal place we said this is good enough and let's get started.... But certainly having a child together was obvious to both of us is the most serious commitment you can make. (Mariel)

Consistent with Burch (1997, 152) who argues that the decision to become a mother is not necessarily a reworking of a gendered sense of self, the women in our study, at least in retrospect, did not view the decision to parent or mother as something that had to be reconciled with their identity as lesbians. Instead, to most, it represented both a natural evolution in their relationships and a signal of their commitment to a family relationship. In short, in the absence of taken-for-granted understandings of familial and parenting roles, lesbians more or less self-consciously make choices about the ways their commitments to parenting are simultaneously commitments to their relationships (Weston 1991). Moreover, consistent with the findings of others, such choices do not necessarily require negotiating new notions of gender identity (Burch 1997). Indeed, the biological and nonbiological mothers in this study saw both their mothering and their partners' mothering as completely gender appropriate; none referred to either themselves or their partners as anything other than a mother, and their mother identity appeared to make up a central component of their gender identity.

For lesbian women, the role of parenthood in generating commitment to a relationship differs from what research shows regarding women in heterosexual relationships. For heterosexual women, the decision to marry typically signifies a commitment to family, and that commitment is not strengthened further when children are born (Bielby and Bielby 1989). In contrast, state-sanctioned marriage, which serves as a public declaration of commitment to family formation and procreation for heterosexual women, is not an option for lesbians. Additionally, as will be discussed below, publicly announcing a lesbian or gay wedding often entails confronting the resistance of others to what they identify as either gender or sexual nonconformity within the institution of family, something many lesbian cou-

ples are unwilling or unable to do during the early stages of a relationship. While institutional scripts about becoming a family through marriage often exclude lesbian couples, scripts about becoming a parent remain readily available to lesbians contemplating parenthood. Thus, the decision to co-parent frequently replaces marriage as the signifier that a familial relationship exists between two women. As one mother said, "I think that before I got pregnant we knew we were serious, but once I got pregnant it's like everything changed" (Stacey).

What to Do about Daddy? Finding a Place for the Biological Father in Lesbian-Headed Two-Parent Families

Many lesbian couples, seeking to create two-parent families that structurally resemble most two-parent families around them, often seek a donation of sperm that is used to impregnate, via artificial insemination, one member of the couple. This practice raises the issue of what role the biological father plays in both the child's life and the family constellation. Those considering artificial insemination face three choices. First, should they rely on an anonymous donor or a known donor? Second, if the donor is known, should his identity be made known to the child, and if so, when? Third, if the donor is known, should he have any parenting or other social tie to the child, and what limits should be placed on his involvement?

Relying on an anonymous donor circumscribes the contribution of the male and in effect eliminates the social role of father from the family equation. Some women gave practical reasons for this choice.

> [I wanted] to make it, you know, as impossible as possible for anyone to lay claim, you know, anyone other than my partner, to lay claim to the

child. My partner and me. We'd just heard too many horror stories about supposed, you know, friends changing their minds. And it doesn't matter what they agree to in writing, the courts just universally consider paternity to be just so overwhelming. (Samantha)

At the time that (older daughter) was conceived there was no legal protections for the nonbiological parent so we just didn't want to get into a situation where we had a child and then somebody could come along and contest, you know, our rights to be parents together. (Olivia)

It was not only interference from the donor himself that these women feared. If anything were to happen to the biological mother, both the donor and his relatives would have grounds to seek guardianship of the child, something the nonbiological mother—a legal stranger to the child—is unlikely to be able to prevent.[6] As one mother explained, it is not just the known donor, "but the known donor's grandparents, parents, siblings, anybody could challenge you know their right and win because of the biological bond. And that freaked us out" (Linda). By using an unknown donor, these mothers attempted to secure their right to be a two-parent family. More specifically, having an unknown donor eliminated the possibility that the biological father could displace the nonbiological mother within the family by claiming that he was the child's legal parent. It also protected the nonbiological mother from his kin whom upon the death of the biological mother could claim that they, and not she, were in fact the child's legal next of kin.

These mothers' decision to remove the nonbiological father from their children's lives did not mean that they were either insensitive to or unaware of the importance the culture places on male role models for children. As Mary recounted,

We worry about (daughter) not having experience with males. We wanted her to know the difference… just being comfortable interacting with the whole world and not a select gender I think was important to us. We also have lots of straight friends so she gets daddy time.

As Stacey explained,

It's pretty important [to have a male role model in their son's life]. Not now, I mean I'm not worried about you know until, for another good five, six years I'm not worried about it. But by the time he's about six or seven I hope by then that we will have found somebody.

The rationale for choosing a known donor is quite different. A mother who had considered an anonymous donor for related reasons ultimately decided to go with a "yes donor"[7] so that her son could learn the identity of his biological father at his 18th birthday. She said,

I guess for me, I have a very close relationship with my father and he's very important to me, and I think that's what influenced me the most, and that I, I feel like you should know where you come from and that that is sort of a basic need that people experience. You know he's not going to have a male role model in the house like other kids do. And I felt that was enough and that I wanted

him to know where he came from....
But for me, I really had a high value
on (younger son) being able to look
this guy in the face and talk to him
and know where he came from and
know his roots. It felt really impor-
tant to me. (Lisa)

Articulating a similar logic, another mother pre-ferred a known donor[8] because "legacy is impor-tant and secrets are bad" (Michelle).

For some lesbian co-parents, placing spe-cific limits on a known donor's involvement with the child is very important. One couple de-scribed the difficulty in managing selective in-volvement of the donor as follows:

We were not looking for another par-
ent, we were looking for somebody
the kids could know, and that's a
hard thing to ask somebody, I think,
to be...I think to ask somebody to
be an anonymous donor is fairly easy
and to ask them to be an involved
parent, but so the in-between, we
want you to be a known person but
not involved is, I think, takes a fairly
special person to be able to have that
sort of a role. (Lauren)

Another lesbian mother's comments illustrate the complexity of differentiating between involvement and fatherhood:

I wanted someone who was already
a father and who was sort of emo-
tionally mature enough to know
what he was agreeing to.... So he's
(son's) biological dad or donor. We
don't really call him a dad. (Lisa)

Although many of these mothers clearly wanted their children's biological fathers to be

involved in their children's lives, they all strug-gled with how to maintain themselves as les-bian-headed two-parent families in the face of normative cognitive prescriptions about the two-parent family. Although some solved this prob-lem by simply eliminating the biological father from the picture altogether, replacing him with male role models who had no legal or social claim to father status, others attempted a com-promise in which the biological father remained present but was redefined from father to sperm donor and, in some cases, to uncle or close fam-ily friend. Men who agreed to play this role often relinquished both their social and legal claim to co-parent status, making it possible for the non-biological mother to fill that role.

Although known donors did not play a paren-tal role in these children's lives, many remained in close contact with the couple after the child's birth, often creating bridges between the lesbian mothers' families and their own legal families. When asked if her donor's extended family knew about her children, Lauren responded,

They do now, they didn't originally.
Our kids have met his family. It was
odd. It felt very peculiar meeting
these people who I know my kids
had a connection with that I really
didn't have a connection with. And I
was glad I did it and would like to do
it periodically to let my kids just meet
with them. I mean they were very
nice and warm and it was probably
very awkward for them too and they
were, considering how particularly
awkward it could have been, it was a
very comfortable meeting.[9]

Mariel noted that their donor has since mar-ried and started a family of his own and that both his wife and their children "know all about it."

And Lisa, who specifically wanted a donor who was willing to be involved in her child's life related that "he [the donor] lives about an hour away and (their son) has a close relationship to him." In addition, this donor has a son who is 10 years older than the lesbian couple's son. When asked if the older boy knew about their son, Lisa responded,

He adores (our son).... He loves him. And I don't, that probably won't last so long since they're so many years apart. But for right now this boy is quite interested in (our son) also. Probably in a few years when he gets to be an adolescent he won't be so interested in a little kid tagging after him. For right now they have a really strong relationship.

These mothers appear to reconstruct a gendered notion of parenting by labeling themselves and their partners as mothers and by labeling men as fathers, regardless of the extent of a man's involvement in either procreation or parenting. In addition, these mothers invoke a biological model of reproduction in which parental roles are clearly gendered. In this way, these mothers appear to be reconstructing gendered notions of the parent while interrupting heteronormative constructions of the family.

Lesbian-Headed Families and the Development of Dual-Mother Identities

The enactment of gender, both symbolically and practically, defines the extent to which women and men are considered to be fulfilling their sex- and gender-linked rights, responsibilities, duties, and obligations within the family. In heterosexual couples, this is usually conflated with biological sex. Lesbian parents also confront symbolic and practical definitions of parenthood that can be strongly, if not invariably, shaped by biological ties. For individual mothers, the experience of biologically parenting a child may be a powerful source of identification and bonding between a mother and child. At an institutional level, this biological connection is often regarded as the sole determinant of motherhood. Several of the biological mothers in our sample spoke directly about the experience of biology, that is, of having carried a child in utero, and of breast-feeding, and how that shaped and enhanced the maternal relationship for them as biological mothers compared to their partners' role as nonbiological mothers. As one mother noted,

It's kind of weird.... I'm connected to both of them, but there's a kind of more of a, there's a different type of connection with (nonbiological daughter) than I have with (biological daughter). It's kind of like (biological daughter), I mean not that I feel like, you know, totally enmeshed with her or anything, but I kind of feel her in my body, you know? It's kind of like I know how her body feels in a different way than (nonbiological daughter's) and the only thing I can figure is that it's because of the biology. You know, it's like I know the shape of her head, I know how her body moves and stuff like that. (Olivia)

When one partner is the biological parent, does the biological tie invariably shape parental roles and the division of labor in parenting? It is clear from our interviews that self-conscious effort was required to establish equity in roles and responsibilities between the mothers when one was a biological parent. This effort was undertaken by both parties who shared a strong commitment to establishing the nonbiological parent as a mother in her own right. Many of the parents, both biological and nonbiological, recounted ways in which they consciously sought to resist and overcome cultural imperatives based on biological ties. One emphasized the significance of the decision to avoid a differentiation between mothering and provider roles:

And the other thing is I think that in our relation, well, my partner is totally committed to us being equal mothers…. One of the reasons we wanted to have a baby while we were both in school is so that we could do equal time in terms of child care so we could both be at home and one of us wouldn't be the breadwinner and the other one the mom. (Michelle)

The sharing of caregiving tasks for a newborn was emphasized repeatedly by our respondents. As one noted,

I would get up in the middle of the night and get (daughter) and bring her to (partner) for breast-feeding and then take her back. And did almost all the laundry and that kind of thing. The feeding, when she left the bottle, when she went to food, I was very, very involved. (Charlotte)

Similarly, another nonbiological mother recounted, "But I figured just during the first year anyway my main job was to keep my partner sane and going by doing as much as I possibly could to share the burdens and the sleeplessness" (Samantha). The equal sharing of parenting of older children was also emphasized by some of our respondents. One mother, explaining the difference between her family and the typical two-parent heterosexual family, said,

We're much more equal. Our children really have relationships with both of us. They see us equal amounts of time. We both take them to dance lessons and the playground and the swimming lessons and the gymnastic lessons and the shopping and, you know, the dry cleaning, and the, you know, we, we are equal parents…. It's not unusual for them to do any activity with [just] either parent. (Linda)

Finally, nonbiological parents developed specific techniques for primary bonding with newborns. A nonbiological mother of two described how complementary skills allowed each parent to establish those bonds with their children:

Well, for starters I had this very special kind of rock that (partner) never acquired so it actually was a problem when [our two daughters] didn't want to nurse. She couldn't really put them down to sleep or soothe them because she, it was an easy out, she could always stick a breast in their mouth…. And then just now that the kids are getting older, our personalities aren't real alike [and so] we do different things with them. We're different people and it works differently for each of the kids. (Lauren)

Thus, in reconfiguring the traditional two-parent family to include two active mothers, these women consciously sought ways to overcome the strong biologically based cultural prescriptions of parental and household roles. Mothering an infant in our culture means doing certain types of labor that include feeding, changing, rocking the baby, and laundry. If the nonbiological mother is going to socially construct herself as a primary parent, a mother, she must partake in this labor.

The construction of a two-parent family consisting of women, both of whom seek to perform parenting in gender appropriate ways— that is, they strive to be good mothers—means that the traditionally single role of mother is divided between the women, with both actively and consciously sharing the same parental tasks. At the same time, these women, with one exception, apportioned the provider role. Some shared that responsibility contemporaneously, while others made explicit decisions to take turns in being the primary wage earner. While heterosexual couples often share the provider role as well, as Risman (1998) and others have observed, in the vast majority of role-sharing heterosexual couples, the mothers retain primary responsibility for the children while the fathers remain the primary breadwinners. If the family needs one parent to leave the labor force, even for a short period of time, it is almost always the mother who does so. Indeed, this tradition among couples in Western societies may well explain why all but one of the nonbiological lesbian mothers in our study reduced paid work to care for their children. If normatively accepted understandings of motherhood in the United States include the belief that good mothers put their children's needs above their commitment to the labor force, and nonbiological lesbian mothers are using the same scripts to socially construct themselves as mothers, it makes sense that they would share this burden with their partners. As Linda, the biological mother of one daughter and the nonbiological mother of another, explained,

I work currently 40 to 50 hours a week and (partner) probably works

15 to 20 so right now she's doing more of the cooking, cleaning, laundry detail. The kind of daily maintenance, and then on the weekend everybody pitches in and you do half of whatever's left. And that, you know, changes depending who's working more. When I was home dissertating and pregnant I did all of that and (partner) worked, was the worker bee, and worked 40 to 50 hours a week.

The desire to share child care, and thus the mothering role, equally led some mothers to develop complex child care arrangements. As Stacey explained,

Mondays and Thursdays he goes to child care all day and when I had a job,... as of yesterday I'm unemployed, but when I had a job we both worked all day Mondays and Thursdays. Then Tuesdays he goes to day care only in the mornings and he's with my partner in the afternoon. Wednesdays he's with me in the mornings and he goes to day care in the afternoon. And theoretically on Fridays we were both home with him as we were for the weekends but it ended up being that most Fridays she was with him because I had to work.

Interactional Conflicts: Negotiating Nonconformity

While these lesbian mothers appear to adhere fairly closely to traditional gendered conceptualizations of motherhood, the fact that they form both their intimate and co-parenting relationships with other women challenges normative conceptions regarding heteronormative configurations of the family. Indeed, all the mothers in this study offered detailed accounts in which others attempted to hold them accountable for this perceived nonconformity. In those accounts, the reactions of others ranged from confusion and general discomfort to outright rejection of the mothers' claims that they, together with their partners and children, formed viable two-parent families.

All of our respondents described incidents where they experienced skepticism or surprise from others regarding their dual-mothering arrangements. Often this took the form of comments about the nonbiological mother's relationship to the child. One respondent, a nonbiological mother, described the response from members of her son's massage class when her partner came to class and nursed the baby:

> And then the next day when they saw him nursing on her, people like came up to us afterward and were like "I just can't believe you're not his biological mom; you're just so close." And I was like, "You know if I had adopted this baby and I was his adopted mother, no one would question that we were connected." But it was like, "Oh, because there's another mom therefore we can't be connected." It was just so interesting to kind of see people's attachment to there only being one mother. (Michelle)

A second mother described how she would become invisible as a mother whenever the family was in a new social situation. When they enrolled their son in school, for example, she explained, "At least initially, they would view my partner as the mother and me as sort of some-

body else. Other people were not perceiving us as equal parents whereas we felt we were equal parents" (Mary).

Even individuals who are fully aware of each woman's relationship to the child sometimes refuse to acknowledge their dual-mothering arrangement. For example, one attorney representing the child's biological father in an adoption case involving a lesbian couple insisted on referring to them as "the mommy figure" and "the daddy figure" as opposed to "mommy one" and "mommy two" (Peggy).

Interestingly, it is not just outsiders but sometimes the mothers themselves who perpetuate normative prescriptions regarding the "proper" gender makeup of the family. In this case, a biological mother speaks of her partner's experience of invisibility and her own participation in that experience.

> When I was pregnant people would just talk to me and ignore her or when he was a newborn they'd be asking how I was doing and not too many people checked in with her [partner]. And she [partner] just kept saying a lot, "I really understand how dads feel, I really understand," or why dads just sometimes recede. Because not only the spouse is maybe being really protective in wanting to be in charge of everything, like I, we had a lot of fights about me, you know. I'd pack the diaper bag, I'd remind her, you know, I was treating her more like a babysitter than that she could make her own decisions and do things her way. And we had to work that out pretty early on that I wanted to control her interactions with him. And then, you know, the rest of the world didn't really see her

as, didn't acknowledge her [as his mother]. (Lisa)

Some women responded directly with counternormative attributions about their children's parentage. As one woman explained, she and her partner would "just persistently correct people and say no, we are both his parents, there is no father" (Mary). Sometimes the children themselves actively participated in this process. As another mother explained, "Our son just very matter of factly just says 'I don't have a father' if somebody says something that you know would indicate thinking that he does" (Samantha). And this strategy appeared to pay off in the long run. As Samantha related,

Our kids are in a fairly large day care place and we were the first lesbian moms and we've introduced several others since our arrival five years ago and so now it's just like nobody blinks an eye when the next family shows up. Which is nice and it also just reinforces it in all of the other kids' minds as well.

While these mothers often rely on their powers of persuasion in social situations to convince others that they are legitimate two-parent families and should be treated accordingly, most remain acutely aware that their sexual nonconformity makes them continually vulnerable to others' attempts to negate their familial claims. Unlike two-parent heterosexual-headed families who routinely enjoy both wide-spread social acceptance and a broad range of legal protections,[10] lesbian-headed two-parent families are denied access to most of the privileges and benefits afforded heterosexual parents. Indeed, the only legal means available for protecting lesbian-headed two-parent families is the second-parent

adoption, a legal procedure that is not yet available in all counties in California. This specialized adoption creates a legal relationship between both parents and the child simultaneously. It does nothing, however, to legalize the relationship between the adults and thus cannot be used to pressure others, such as employers or insurance providers, to recognize that familial relationship. Additionally, second-parent adoptions can only be initiated after the birth of a child, and they routinely take between 10 and 12 months to complete. Thus, even for adults who have access to second-parent adoptions, there remains a significant amount of time in which the relationship between the nonbiological mother and the child is legally unprotected. This lag time may be crucial if it is the nonbiological mother who has access to important resources such as health insurance (for a detailed discussion regarding second-parent adoptions, see Dalton 1999). These drawbacks in the second-parent adoption system leave many lesbian mothers scrambling for ways to legally protect their families. As one mother explained,

Around the birth of our son we tried to get everything in order. We have wills where we name each other. We have power of attorney and also other things like, you know, life insurance, and, you know, our finances are intermingled and things of that nature that doesn't involve the legal system. (Mary)

Another lesbian mother spoke of the importance of making use of every available institutional mechanism for protecting her family:

Actually, when I was pregnant, we read the legal guide for gay and lesbian folks, whatever that's called, and we did everything they told us to do. We had living wills, we had parenting agreements, we had financial agreements, we did everything they said to do that you could possibly do to protect yourself because second-parent adoption I don't think actually was an option when we started trying to get pregnant. So we did financial and parenting contracts where we specified what we were committed to in this relationship and in our child-rearing roles. (Linda)

Despite the popularity of legal texts that provide sample parenting contracts for lesbian and gay parents, the California courts have repeatedly determined all parenting agreements made outside the legal institution of marriage to be invalid (see *West v. Superior Court*).[11] This means that despite their best efforts, lesbian mothers who choose to form two-parent families must do so without many of the important legal protections our society commonly grants heterosexual-headed two-parent families.[12] This might explain, at least in part, why many of our respondents, as well as a growing number of lesbian and gay couples across the nation, have begun to plan and carry out public wedding ceremonies, ceremonies that often lead to active confrontation over the lesbian mothers' rights to claim the label of family for themselves.

The Lesbian Wedding: Taking the Proactive Position

Six of the 14 lesbians in our study had either recently married or were planning to marry in the near future. For respondents who chose to participate in a public marriage ceremony, the likelihood of confronting individuals who would reject their attempts to redefine institutionalized understandings of "appropriate" sexual configu-

rations within the family was extremely high. Even lesbians who had been out to their friends and family members for a considerable period of time were likely to encounter resistance. As one respondent reported regarding her mother's reactions to their plans to have a public marriage ceremony,

She just thought it was totally wrong that we were doing that. Like I think if we had had like a commitment ceremony, or, you know like not called it a wedding. [But] it's really important to us that we call it a wedding and it's a wedding, and...we're not going to like call it something else... that really bothered her. (Michelle)

This respondent's mother reacted this way even though she had known about her daughter's lesbianism for at least 12 years.

As another respondent explained, having a wedding ceremony means coming out in a very public way, an act that often exposes one's entire family to scrutiny based on the perceived sexual transgressions of the lesbian or gay individual. This mother recounted,

My mom's very protected you know. She really, you know, she's much more defined by what people think and so the whole thing of us having a wedding was she liked the idea because I think she liked the idea of us always being together, you know, on some level. But the other side of the coin was that she didn't want me to invite my godfather or invite people from the Filipino community and I just kind of left that to her. You know I kind of felt like okay those are your friends. If you want to be closeted with your friends that's, you know, that's fine. It's like but just don't, you know...don't expect me to be closeted in front of them. (Peggy)

The resistance these mothers experienced to their attempts to redefine institutionalized understandings of the family did not come from family members alone. Michelle recounted that when she attempted to place their wedding announcement in her local religious community's newspaper she was told that "because legally it's not a wedding" the newspaper would not announce it as such. Instead of simply dropping the matter and thus allowing the newspaper to control the institutionalized definition of family in a way that excluded her family, this mother fought back by designing an announcement that described her wedding plans in great detail. While the announcement clearly described a traditional wedding, including the temple in which the ceremony would be held, the name of the rabbi who would officiate, and where the happy couple would honeymoon after the ceremony, she succeeded in convincing the paper to run it by arguing that because she never actually used the term *wedding* in the text she did not violate the newspaper's policy.

When asked why a public wedding was so important, especially given the strong resistance she encountered, Michelle explained,

I mean...beforehand we thought, "Oh this will be really fun," but in retrospect it was just this incredible signifier for everybody in our lives—I mean our professors, our colleagues, our friends, our families—that we're a couple and we want everybody to help us stay together. And I think that, I'd been in this long-term relationship before I met (partner) and I

felt that, I was with someone for seven years, and I felt that our entire relationship our communities were trying to break us up. I mean our family, our biological families and our sort of heterosexual communities. And I never felt that there was this incredible support to keep us together.

As another mother explained,

We were both raised Catholic and we both really wanted to have our family and our community in this very public acknowledgment of our relationship and we felt like, you know, that was really important groundwork for spending the rest of your life together and raising a family together.... I mean in our ideology it's kind of like that whole, you know, networking of your family. We had sponsors and, you know, we're going to have godparents and all that. (Peggy)

When asked if things had changed for her following the wedding, Michelle replied, "Since the wedding...everybody who I know asks about her [the partner]. [It's] a given that she's been invited to every [office] event with me."

The lesbian wedding is perhaps the most deliberately self-conscious strategy available to lesbian mothers for simultaneously challenging heteronormativity and gaining public recognition for their family arrangements. Denied legal recognition, the public wedding ceremony (as opposed to a "commitment ceremony") is a collective affirmation by the couple, their friends, and kin that their union is sanctioned by the most revered symbolic representation of marriage. Cherlin has written about remarriage as an incomplete institution in which "customs and conventions of family life are deficient when applied to remarriages after divorce" (1978, 648). Lesbian mothers find themselves in a similar predicament but with a more exclusionary response from legal institutions. As a result, they engage in a variety of strategies. On one hand, through second-parent adoptions, they seek strong, formal legitimacy for their familial arrangements. On the other hand, the wedding ceremony is a kind of quasi-legal strategy to garner support from their social networks and public recognition of their family arrangements. While the motivation for a lesbian wedding is partially strategic, its symbolic and ritualistic aspects—the ceremony, public announcement, photos, and gifts—also contribute to the institutionalization of their version of the family.[13]

CONCLUSION

Our study of lesbian co-parents demonstrates some of the ways in which sex, gender, and sexual orientation intersect as lesbians socially construct their roles as parents. We examined how lesbian couples simultaneously draw upon and resist dominant cultural practices, scripts, and assumptions about the institution of the family in order to organize parenting based on the premise of mothering by two women. In doing so, the women we studied were often able to transcend biologically based notions of motherhood and fatherhood.

We found that lesbian couples rewrite both the mother and the father roles in interesting ways. Like many heterosexual mothers, the mothers of these families expanded the notion of mother to encompass the provider role. At the same time, however, the mother role is disconnected from biology such that both the birth mother and her partner may lay claim to the role. While the mother role may still contain a biolog-ical component, this loses importance relative to its social aspect.

The father role, on the other hand, is significantly modified and sometimes eliminated altogether. While men who donate sperm are not necessarily labeled fathers, men who are not biologically related to the children may be given the honorary title "daddy." Either way, fathers remain outside the family constellation. If, as we suggest in the introduction, parenting is fundamentally gendered, to destabilize this model requires replacing the biological model of reproduction with a social model of reproduction. For this to be accomplished, the definition of mother and father must be unhinged from biology. The mothers in our study have begun this process by arguing that the legal definition of mother should not be limited to those women who biologically reproduce children but should be broadened to include other individuals who actively participate in the social reproduction of a child. This opens the door to redefining the concept of mother; in principle, anyone who actively participates in the act of social reproduction could be deemed a mother as well.

At the same time, the women in our study appear to reinscribe gender when they insist on labeling women who reproduce—either biologically or socially—as mothers, and men who reproduce—again, either biologically or socially—as fathers. Their adoption of the label of mother for women and of father for men serves to strengthen the association between biological reproduction and parenthood in that those individuals who are theoretically capable of giving birth to a child become mothers, while those who cannot, that is, men, are labeled fathers. The only way to fully degender the concept of parent and deheterosexualize the concept of family is through the development of a gender-neutral concept of parent, one that focuses on parenting behaviors rather than on biological reproduction.[14]

Finally, these mothers are redefining at the social and institutional level what it means to be a two-parent family by challenging heteronormative conceptions of the family. At the same time, however, they are, in large part, reinscribing gendered notions of what it means to be a mother at the individual level. At that level, these mothers actively negotiated space for the nonbiological mother as mother within their families, transforming their families from single-biological-mother families to ones organized and enacted as co-mother families. These mothers, through their day-to-day interactions with individuals outside their immediate families, negotiate changes in institutionalized scripts regarding gendered relations within the family by insisting on a recognition and acceptance of their co-mother family constellations as legitimate by outside others.

Although this analysis examines only a few locations in which this type of negotiation process regularly occurs, that is, in extended families, schools, and religious communities, the possibilities are endless. Indeed, anywhere lesbian- or gay-headed families successfully obtain recognition and legitimation (e.g., family memberships at the YMCA, domestic partnership registries from city councils, family health insurance benefits from employers, family membership privileges at the local zoo), institutional scripts regarding sexual configurations of the two-parent family are subjected to challenge. And this is, no doubt, why so many of the changes enacted by our respondents inspire vigorous opposition from those expressing a desire to "save" the traditional family.

While the mothers in this study appear particularly adroit at convincing others to accept their family constellations as legitimate two-parent families, this ability is no doubt greatly enhanced by a variety of social advantages including high educational attainment and high socioeconomic status. These social advantages allowed the mothers to control many of the situations in which these negotiations occurred. For instance, mothers who were able to afford private schooling for their children tended to shop around until they found schools whose administrators express a willingness to accept lesbian and gay families. By employing the strategy of confronting teachers who might oppose their insistence on open recognition of their two-mother family status within the classroom, the efforts of these mothers to transcend institutionalized understandings of the family became considerably easier when they knew that their position would be supported by the school's administration. Likewise, mothers who are economically advantaged are much more likely than others to be able to obtain legal supports such as second-parent adoption. These legal supports allow mothers to threaten legal action anytime anyone, such as an employer or insurance company, resists the family's definition of itself as a legitimate two-parent family. Additionally, as many of these mothers demonstrated, the development of reasoning and verbal skills that commonly accompany high educational achievement allowed them to debate their opponent's reasoning, undermining their ability to resist the mother's attempts to redefine institutional scripts regarding the two-parent family.

Finally, our findings contribute to institutional theory by examining the kinds of individual-level interactions and agency that may bring about change within institutions. While no one individual-level interaction leads to change in social scripts that serve as guides to action, repeated interactions in which individuals or groups of individuals are first exposed to and then come to accept new understandings, in this case of the two-parent family, slowly lead to change at the structural level (see also Zucker 1991). As our research shows, as ever more individuals come to know and accept as legitimate two-parent lesbian- or gay-headed families, social scripts regarding the appropriate sexual makeup of the two-parent family begin to change in ways that are inclusive of these families as well.

Our findings suggest that the social organization of lesbian-headed families continues to be affected by institutional factors, as well as institutional systems, such as the law. Some of the factors affecting those families include the fact that lesbians and gays are excluded from the institution of marriage and all the legal benefits that come with it. This lack of institutional recognition forces lesbian and gay two-parent families into the position of having to continually negotiate their family status. Our results illustrate the far more complex paths lesbian couples follow as they commit themselves to their families and draw upon those commitments as resources from which to construct relationships. In contrast to the formation of conventional heterosexually committed relationships, lesbian and gay couples must evolve outside the support of various legal institutions and social rituals that signal, legitimate, and approve the existence of a committed couple. Lacking those social supports, for lesbian co-parents the decision to parent is by necessity a more deliberative and less socially scripted process. Their practical actions in coming to terms with the realities of parenting under such circumstances contribute to new cultural understandings of parenting.

Reading 14   Islamic Family Ideals and Their Relevance to American Muslim Families

BAHIRA SHERIF*

This chapter examines the definition of Islamic family ideals and their relevance to contemporary Muslim communities in the United States. The focus is on gender relations, marriage, and the parent-child relationship. Although certain ideals provide the ideological basis for all Islamic families, their realization differs in practice, due to variation in culture, ethnicity and race, class, educational level, and place of residence. Nevertheless, shared religious convictions bind Muslims all over the world into one community, and this shared set of beliefs includes values and ideals related to the Islamic family.

A significant phenomenon over the past decade has been the rapid rise of an Islamic consciousness in the United States, which can be attributed to two major factors. Recent immigration from conservative Islamic countries has made second- and third-generation Muslims more aware of their Islamic identity. In addition, certain groups see a rapid decline in moral values in the West and advocate Islam as the "right path" to guide individual lives. This increasing Islamization is characteristic of both immigrant and African American communities. Estimates of the number of Muslims in this country currently range from 3 to 6 million, and it is widely acknowledged that Islam is the fastest growing religion in the United States (Stone, 1991, p. 25; *World Almanac,* 1998, p. 651). Nevertheless, there is an astonishing lack of scholarship on American Muslims and on their family life, in particular. The issue is complicated by the fact that their origins are diverse, including the Middle East, Africa, Southeast Asia, and the United States itself, in the case of African Americans who either follow the Nation of Islam or identify themselves as Sunni Muslims. Recent events, popularized by the media, indicate that many people in the United States tend to fear adherents of the Muslim faith. In several regions of the country, children have been taken from Muslim couples because of court decisions that it is more beneficial for them to grow up in Christian homes. Much of the fear and prejudice can be attributed to misconceptions and lack of knowledge about Islam and associated values and traditions, particularly with regard to the family. Issues such as polygamy, the subjugation of women, early arranged marriages of females, and veiling dominate popular conceptions of Islamic life. This work seeks to clarify aspects of

*Sherif, Bahira. "Islamic Family Ideals and Their Relevance to American Muslim Families." Pp. 203–212 in Harriette Pipes McAdoo (ed.), *Family Ethnicity: Strength in Diversity.* Second Edition. Copyright 1999 by Sage Publications, Inc. Reprinted by permission of Sage Publications, Inc.

Islamic family ideals and how they relate to Muslims living in the United States.

THE GENDER ISSUE

Central to any discussion of Muslim families is gender roles. A fundamental Islamic belief is the distinct difference between male and female in terms of their personalities, social roles, and functions. Practices such as veiling and distinct male and female activities, both within and outside the family, reinforce this gender dichotomy.[1] Contemporary constructions of what it means to be a Muslim male or female are shaped not only by Islamic traditions but also by Western images, indigenous forms of feminism, and new Islamicist views on women. Gender ideology is an actively negotiated aspect of most Muslims' daily lives.

In part, the increasing Islamization of Muslims in the United States can be attributed to the perception of lax gender relations (the casual intermixing of the sexes, premarital sex, and pornography) and the declining value of the institution of marriage (Haddad & Smith, 1996, p. 21). Fundamentalist discourses, imported from abroad, lend legitimacy and cultural authenticity to inflexible positions on the appropriate role of men and women in society. Much of this discourse is based on the "dangerous" nature of women and the evils of unbridled sexuality. Thus, gender relations are to be controlled and restricted, particularly in what is perceived as an environment that encourages moral decay and immorality. Legitimacy for this argument is derived by citing central texts of the religion.

References to women and their appropriate behavior are scattered throughout the *Qur'an* and the *hadiths* (the sayings of the prophet), and their meanings and interpretation have been a source of controversy since the earliest days of Islam. Various passages in the *Qur'an* focus on women's unique nature, women's place in society, and their role within the general congregation of believers. As Fernea and Bezirgan (1977, p. 13) emphasize, even though the *Qur'an* is the central source of Islamic belief, there is considerable controversy about the meaning of each of these passages and their implications for the status of women. Sacred writings, or theological arguments about their relevance, are often used as empirical data for sociological explanations of a gender hierarchy in which women are subordinate to men (Marcus, 1992; Mernissi, 1987). Contemporary scholarship has shown that, rather than determining attitudes about women, parts of the *Qur'an* are only used at certain times to legitimate particular acts or sets of conditions that concern women. This selective use is part of the way in which gender hierarchy and sexuality are negotiated and enforced. It does not explain gender roles; instead, it is part of a constant process of gender role negotiation.

Underlying all Islamic ideological formulations is the belief that women must remain "in their place" in order for political and social harmony to prevail. If women do not adhere to this moral order, then society runs the risk of degenerating into *fitna* (temptation or, more important, rebellion, social dissension, or disorder). A saying of Muhammad is that there is "no fitna more harmful to men than women." Women are so potentially powerful that they are required to submit to their husbands, segregate themselves from men to whom they are not immediately related, and restrain themselves, lest the pattern of gender relations at the core of a properly ordered society be overturned. To maintain this pattern, the institution of marriage is perceived as central to the ordering of society.

MARRIAGE

According to the *Qur'an,* all Muslim men and women are expected to marry, and marriage is governed by a complex set of legal and social rules. The founding of a Muslim family is based on the concept of a contractual exchange that legally commences with a marriage contract and its consummation. In all schools of Islamic law, marriage is seen as a contract, the main function of which is to make sexual relations between a man and a woman licit. The essential requirements for a valid Muslim marriage are consent of the woman, consent of her legal guardian, two legal witnesses, and payment of dowery, or *mahr.* Through the signing of the contract, women are to receive the mahr, a suitable home, maintenance (food, clothes, and gifts), and a partial inheritance from the husband. They are not legally required to share in the costs and expenditures of their spouse or their male relatives. They are not expected or required to work outside the home. In return for his financial investment, the husband acquires authority as the head of the family as well as access to the sexual and reproductive abilities of the wife.

Beyond its legal components, marriage is also regarded as a religious obligation and is invested with many ethical injunctions. Any sexual contact outside marriage is considered fornication and is subject to severe punishment. Furthermore, Islam condemns and discourages celibacy. In this manner, marriage acquires a religious dimension because it preserves morals and allows the satisfaction of sexual desires within the limits set by God. Muslim jurists have gone so far as to elevate marriage to the level of a religious duty. The *Qur'an* supports this notion: "And marry such of you as are solitary and the pious of your slaves and maid servants" (24:32), which is commonly interpreted as advocating marriage to "complete the religion." A hadith, often quoted, particularly among men, states that "the prayer of a married man is equal to seventy prayers of a single man." Thus, all individuals are encouraged to marry, and societal traditions, such as the importance of family reputation, discourage being single. For both men and women,

marriage is the only acceptable alternative to living with parents. Both natal and conjugal families play a crucial role in the lives of Muslims.

Once an Islamic marriage becomes valid through the signing of the marital contract, it is the duty of the husband to provide for his wife under three conditions: She also signs this contract, she puts herself under her husband's authority and allows him free access to her, and she obeys him for the duration of the marriage. According to the *Qur'an,*

> *Men are in charge of women, because Allah hath made the one of them to excel the other, and because they spend of their property [for support of women]. So good women are the obedient, guarding in secret that which Allah hath guarded. As for those from whom ye fear rebellion, admonish them and banish them to beds apart, and scourge them. Lo! Allah is ever High Exalted, Great. (4:34)*

The man has authority over the woman in the family setting and has the obligation to provide her with material support. Particularly for American Muslims, this strict hierarchy is not always followed, as it is common for women to work and contribute to the family income. Such economic involvement does not support the Islamic model of distinct marital spheres. Instead, among many American Muslims, a more egalitarian model of shared economic responsibilities and household obligations is becoming the norm.

The significance of the Islamic ideals of marriage inherent in the *Qur'an* and the *shari'a* (legal interpretations) is that they provide a primary frame of reference for legitimizing the actions of individuals. These ideals validate certain power relations within the family. But an ideology is not unchanging. It is forged, negotiated, and reexpressed in connection with other social, economic, and historical factors.

MOTHERHOOD

Among Muslims, the importance of marriage and family elevates the role of mother. Mothers are idolized and respected, both on an intimate, personal level and in the community. They are portrayed as caring, nurturing, loving, and self-sacrificing. Their lives center around children, and they gain their most important identity through this role. The duties within the home, especially caring for and educating the children, are considered a woman's most important responsibilities, and these are also highly appreciated tasks in the societal context. Women are seen as the center of the family, and this is considered their natural, God-given role. Families are supposed to be arranged around the concept that men and women simply have different natures, talents, and inherent tendencies. Among Muslims, this strong consensus about the natural roles for men and women permeates all discussions of gender (Macleod, 1991, p. 41). Both genders believe that each has a different temperament and that each, consequently, has a different role to play in life. Innate differences between the sexes are not perceived as a dichotomy of superior and inferior but as complementary. Men and women are biologically different and have different strengths, weaknesses, and paths in life. These are considered to be natural qualities, not socially constructed concepts. Women are at the center of the family as wives and mothers; men are providers, husbands, and fathers. Having children and being a "good" parent is perceived by women and men alike as being their most significant role in life.

THE TIE THAT BINDS: THE ROLE OF CHILDREN

Children play an important part in every aspect of Islamic thought on family.[2] The *Qur'an* and

many significant Islamic texts indicate the primary importance of children and their well-being. This emphasis can be attributed to several factors. Children strengthen the marital tie, continue the family line by carrying their father's name, provide for their parents in old age, and are partial inheritors of their parents' estate. They are an integral part of the family unit.

The *Qur'an* and the *sunna* (practices) are extremely concerned with motherhood, fatherhood, and the protection of children from the moment of conception until the age of maturity. Islam stresses the rights and obligations of both parents and children. The legal aspects of Islam deal with the socioeconomic conditions of children both within the family and in the event of divorce or death of the parents (Schacht, 1964, p. 168). An examination of some of these ideals gives further insight into the structuring of Islamic families.

According to religious law, the parent-child relationship parallels the rights and obligations established through marriage, notwithstanding specific social content. The shari'a has developed specialized topics that reflect the highly protective attitude of the *Qur'an* toward minors and aged parents. Specifically, the primary legal relationship centers on adequate maintenance of dependent children and needy parents. The economic and social welfare of children is a major parental responsibility enforceable under Islamic law (Fluehr-Lobban, 1987, p. 184). It is the legal responsibility of children to take care of their aged parents both financially and socially.

Islamic law states that every Muslim infant is entitled to *hadana,* which loosely translates into the fulfillment of the physical and emotional needs of a child.[3] Besides care and protection, this includes socialization and education. The child is entitled to love, attention, and devotion to all its needs because it is unable to take care of itself.

In comparison to Western standards, children are incorporated into the adult sphere very early in their development. Due to extensive visiting within families, children constantly interact with adults, and they are expected almost immediately to display certain gender-specific behaviors. Even the very young are constantly reminded that some actions are more appropriate for boys or for girls. In particular, parents stress the development of masculinity in baby boys right from birth. It is quite common for a man to scold his wife if he feels she is "feminizing" the boy toddler, and men will discourage their wives from teaching baby boys "girlish" things. Boys are encouraged to play with "male" toys and are not to try on girls' clothes, hair ornaments, or jewelry. Girls learn from a very young age to behave in certain ways around boys and men, and they are always encouraged to be shy and modest in dress. Almost from infancy, children are made aware that they belong to either a male or female sphere and therefore must observe certain behaviors and practices.

From birth onward, children also learn other important social behaviors. They are taught to be conscious of their religion, proud of their extended family, and thankful for the food they eat. These behaviors are enforced by the parents, as well as visiting grandparents, aunts, uncles, and cousins. One often sees young children, in particular little boys, going through the motions as adults pray in the home. Prayer in young children is not considered necessary, but older people often remark that this is a sign of real piety in the child.

Children are instructed to greatly value their relatives. Most extended families are involved in an intricate pattern of visits, ranging from once a day to at least twice a week. Often, on days when relatives do not see one another, everyone speaks for hours on the phone. Children learn very early that family and community are very important components in their lives.

Children are also taught not to question the authority of either parent. This socialization is constantly reinforced with reference to the *Qur'an* and its emphasis on respect for one's parents. Even in relatively nonreligious families, strong social pressures constantly reinforce conformity and discourage rebelliousness of any sort, at least in public. Children are not allowed to raise their voices when speaking with parents or to argue back when told to do something. A young child quickly learns that it is shameful to disregard parental directives. Conformity to parental authority extends to all spheres of life, such as the choice of a major in college and, at times, the choice of a spouse. Decisions that most Americans consider individual choices are, for Muslims, the result of extensive group discussions and negotiations. The individual may make the final decision but only after a great deal of familial input. This does not mean there are no disagreements within families or that children always submit completely to parental authority. Nevertheless, there is very strong social pressure for children not to deviate openly from acceptable forms of behavior.

IMMIGRANT MUSLIM COMMUNITIES

While there are many variations among Islamic communities, families, and generations, one finds similar patterns in most immigrant Muslim families (Barakat, 1985, p. 37). Fear of the foreign culture, a strong sense of family, and adherence to Islamic tradition leads them to focus on their local community and isolate themselves from the mainstream culture. Parents tend to be very concerned about how best to transmit their Islamic heritage to their children, and they will often enforce rules more strictly than they would in their home country.

Immigrant Muslim families with unmarried daughters face a unique set of problems. According to the *Qur'an,* Muslim women must marry a Muslim, but the reverse is not true. Traditional norms restrict daughters from participating in such American practices as dating and living away at college. The pool of suitable potential spouses may, thus, be limited (Hermansen, 1991, p. 198). In small communities, any disgrace becomes magnified and likely will further shrink the pool. In an effort to preserve their Muslim identity and their daughters' marriageability, parents attempt to restrict their daughters' movements, which often leads to conflict. Sons tend to be given more freedom and are able to integrate more easily into the mainstream culture, but that also may create family tensions. When the children acquire values incompatible with parental beliefs, parents are faced with the need to accommodate conflicting points of view, and frequently there are no models within their community to help them resolve the issue.

AFRICAN AMERICAN MUSLIM COMMUNITIES

Even though immigrant Muslims and African American Muslims share the same faith and familial ideals, there is little if any interaction between these communities throughout the United States (Kolars, 1994, p. 477). Language skills, historical factors, racial issues, and vastly different cultural traditions form major barriers between these groups. Furthermore, unlike the immigrants, many African Americans are converts, and every aspect of their life is altered to fit their new religion. They usually adopt Muslim names, styles of dress (particularly among women, veiling), and consciousness. The new identity may take precedence over their former ethnic/racial identity. In contrast, many Muslim immigrants maintain their ethnic identity while trying to assimilate into American culture. Nonetheless, the teachings of Islam, particularly with regard to family life, are a common bond between the two groups (Hermansen, 1991, p. 198).

In an effort to follow Islamic ideals, both groups tend to adhere strictly to the defined roles for men and women and for children and parents.

THE IMPORTANCE OF FAMILY TO MUSLIM SOCIAL RELATIONS

As indicated above, the family is the basic unit of social organization among all Muslims, whether immigrants or African Americans. The family, not the individual, is the foundation of social, religious, and economic activities, the dominant social institution through which people and groups inherit their religious, class, and cultural identity (Barakat, 1985, p. 28). All members work together to secure a livelihood and to uphold and improve family standing in the community. The extended family provides security and emotional support in times of individual stress. In exchange, members are expected to place the group's survival above their personal desires, especially at the time of marriage, and to preserve family reputation by behaving properly and "maintaining the family honor" (Fernea, 1985, p. 153). The success or failure of an individual becomes that of the family as a whole: Each is held responsible for the acts of every other member.

Among non-Muslims, the family socializes and readies the individual for life outside the family. In contrast, Muslims are socialized to remain part of the group, and they are expected to sacrifice personal needs for the greater good of the family (Macleod, 1991, pp. 37–41). Personal status is defined by group membership, not individual achievement. Particularly for women, relations with family members are the strongest links in their lives. In general, women's primary ties and ultimate sources of economic security lie in their relationship to their father, brothers, and sons. Family provides a sense of place, a congenial setting, and a social network for financial and personal support. Western life, with its emphasis on individual needs and pursuits, seems lonely and self-centered to many Muslims. For them, the structure and ideology of family provides a crucial network of resources and sense of identity.

CONCLUSION

The significance of the ideals of family inherent in Islamic law does not lie in the extent to which they reflect actual practice but in the frame of reference they provide for legitimizing individual actions. These ideals validate certain power relations within the family but are not unchanging. They are forged, negotiated, and reexpressed in connection with other social, economic, and historical factors.

The rapid increase of Islam in the United States calls for more serious and extensive scholarly examination of American Muslims. This focus must be coupled with recognition of a growing diversity of family life within and across Muslim communities. Human service professionals and educators need information about the cultural traditions and values of their Muslim clients, students, neighbors, and colleagues. There is also a clear need for an extended dialogue to help dispel some of the negative stereotypes of Muslims in the United States. An understanding of the ideals, traditions, and values associated with Muslim family life can shed light on a religious tradition that draws its appeal, in part, from an emphasis on practice as well as belief.

5 | Gender Roles, Work, and the Family

Reading 15   There's No Place Like Work

ARLIE RUSSELL HOCHSCHILD*

It's 7:40 a.m. when Cassie Bell, 4, arrives at the Spotted Deer Child-Care Center, her hair half-combed, a blanket in one hand, a fudge bar in the other. "I'm late," her mother, Gwen, a sturdy young woman whose short-cropped hair frames a pleasant face, explains to the child-care worker in charge. "Cassie wanted the fudge bar so bad, I gave it to her," she adds apologetically.

"*Pleeese,* can't you take me with you?" Cassie pleads.

"You know I can't take you to work," Gwen replies in a tone that suggests that she has been expecting this request. Cassie's shoulders droop. But she has struck a hard bargain—the morning fudge bar—aware of her mother's anxiety about the long day that lies ahead at the center. As Gwen explains later, she continually feels that she owes Cassie more time than she gives her—she has a "time debt."

Arriving at her office just before 8, Gwen finds on her desk a cup of coffee in her personal mug, milk no sugar (exactly as she likes it), prepared by a co-worker who managed to get in ahead of her. As the assistant to the head of public relations at a company I will call Amerco, Gwen has to handle responses to any reports that may appear about the company in the press—a challenging job, but one that gives her satisfaction. As she prepares for her first meeting of the day, she misses her daughter, but she also feels relief; there's a lot to get done at Amerco.

Gwen used to work a straight eight-hour day. But over the last three years, her workday has gradually stretched to eight and a half or nine hours, not counting the E-mail messages and faxes she answers from home. She complains about her hours to her co-workers and listens to their complaints—but she loves her job. Gwen picks up Cassie at 5:45 and gives her a long, affectionate hug.

At home, Gwen's husband, John, a computer programmer, plays with their daughter

Over three years, I interviewed 130 respondents for a book. They spoke freely and allowed me to follow them through "typical" days, on the understanding that I would protect their anonymity. I have changed the names of the company and of those I interviewed, and altered certain identifying details. Their words appear here as they were spoken. —A. R. H.

while Gwen prepares dinner. To protect the dinner "hour"—8:00–8:30—Gwen checks that the phone machine is on, hears the phone ring during dinner but resists the urge to answer. After Cassie's bath, Gwen and Cassie have "quality time," or "Q.T.," as John affectionately calls it. Half an hour later, at 9:30, Gwen tucks Cassie into bed.

There are, in a sense, two Bell households: the rushed family they actually are and the relaxed family they imagine they might be if only they had time. Gwen and John complain that they are in a time bind. What they say they want seems so modest—time to throw a ball, to read to Cassie, to witness the small dramas of her development, not to speak of having a little fun and romance themselves. Yet even these modest wishes seem strangely out of reach. Before going to bed, Gwen has to E-mail messages to her colleagues in preparation for the next day's meeting; John goes to bed early, exhausted—he's out the door by 7 every morning.

Nationwide, many working parents are in the same boat. More mothers of small children than ever now work outside the home. In 1993, 56 percent of women with children between 6 and 17 worked outside the home full time year round; 43 percent of women with children 6 and under did the same. Meanwhile, fathers of small children are not cutting back hours of work to help out at home. If anything, they have increased their hours at work. According to a 1993 national survey conducted by the Families and Work Institute in New York, American men average 48.8 hours of work a week, and women 41.7 hours, including overtime and commuting. All in all, more women are on the economic train, and for many—men and women alike—that train is going faster.

But Amerco has "family friendly" policies. If your division head and supervisor agree, you can work part time, share a job with another worker, work some hours at home, take parental leave or use "flex time." But hardly anyone uses these policies. In seven years, only two Amerco fathers have taken formal parental leave. Fewer than 1 percent have taken advantage of the opportunity to work part time. Of all such policies, only flex time—which rearranges but does not shorten work time—has had a significant number of takers (perhaps a third of working parents at Amerco).

Forgoing family-friendly policies is not exclusive to Amerco workers. A 1991 study of 188 companies conducted by the Families and Work Institute found that while a majority offered part-time shifts, fewer than 5 percent of employees made use of them. Thirty-five percent offered "flex place"—work from home—and fewer than 3 percent of their employees took advantage of it. And an earlier Bureau of Labor Statistics survey asked workers whether they preferred a shorter workweek, a longer one or their present schedule. About 62 percent preferred their present schedule; 28 percent would have preferred longer hours. Fewer than 10 percent said they wanted a cut in hours.

Still, I found it hard to believe that people didn't protest their long hours at work. So I contacted Bright Horizons, a company that runs 136 company-based child-care centers associated with corporations, hospitals and Federal agencies in 25 states. Bright Horizons allowed me to add questions to a questionnaire they sent out to 3,000 parents whose children attended the centers. The respondents, mainly middle-class parents in their early 30's, largely confirmed the picture I'd found at Amerco. A third of fathers and a fifth of mothers described themselves as "workaholic," and 1 out of 3 said their partners were.

To be sure, some parents have tried to shorten their hours. Twenty-one percent of the nation's women voluntarily work part time, as do 7 percent of men. A number of others make under-the-table arrangements that don't show up on surveys. But while working parents say they need more time at home, the main story of their lives does not center on a struggle to get it. Why? Given the hours parents are working these days, why aren't they taking advantage of an opportunity to reduce their time at work?

The most widely held explanation is that working parents cannot afford to work shorter hours. Certainly this is true for many. But if money is the whole explanation, why would it be that at places like Amerco, the best-paid employees—upper-level managers and professionals—were the least interested in part-time work or job sharing, while clerical workers who earned less were more interested?

Similarly, if money were the answer, we would expect poorer new mothers to return to work more quickly after giving birth than rich mothers. But among working women nationwide, well-to-do new mothers are not much more likely to stay home after 13 weeks with a new baby than low-income new mothers. When asked what they look for in a job, only a third of respondents in a recent study said salary came first. Money is important, but by itself, money does not explain why many people don't want to cut back hours at work.

A second explanation goes that workers don't dare ask for time off because they are afraid it would make them vulnerable to layoffs. With recent downsizings at many large corporations, and with well-paying, secure jobs being replaced by lower-paying, insecure ones, it occurred to me that perhaps employees are "working scared." But when I asked Amerco employees whether they worked long hours for fear of getting on a layoff list, virtually everyone said no. Even among a particularly vulnerable group—factory workers who were laid off in the downturn of the early 1980's and were later rehired—most did

not cite fear for their jobs as the only, or main, reason they worked overtime. For unionized workers, layoffs are assigned by seniority, and for nonunionized workers, layoffs are usually related to the profitability of the division a person works in, not to an individual work schedule.

Were workers uninformed about the company's family friendly policies? No. Some even mentioned that they were proud to work for a company that offered such enlightened policies. Were rigid middle managers standing in the way of workers using these policies? Sometimes. But when I compared Amerco employees who worked for flexible managers with those who worked for rigid managers, I found that the flexible managers reported only a few more applicants than the rigid ones. The evidence, however counterintuitive, pointed to a paradox: workers at the company I studied weren't protesting the time bind. They were accommodating to it.

Why? I did not anticipate the conclusion I found myself coming to: namely, that work has become a form of "home" and home has become "work." The worlds of home and work have not begun to blur, as the conventional wisdom goes, but to reverse places. We are used to thinking that home is where most people feel the most appreciated, the most truly "themselves," the most secure, the most relaxed. We are used to thinking that work is where most people feel like "just a number" or "a cog in a machine." It is where they have to be "on," have to "act," where they are least secure and most harried.

But new management techniques so pervasive in corporate life have helped transform the workplace into a more appreciative, personal sort of social world. Meanwhile, at home the divorce rate has risen, and the emotional demands have become more baffling and complex. In addition to teething, tantrums and the normal developments of growing children, the needs of elderly parents are creating more tasks for the modern family—as are the blending, unblending, reblending of new stepparents, stepchildren, exes and former in-laws.

This idea began to dawn on me during one of my first interviews with an Amerco worker. Linda Avery, a friendly, 38-year-old mother, is a shift supervisor at an Amerco plant. When I meet her in the factory's coffee-break room over a couple of Cokes, she is wearing blue jeans and a pink jersey, her hair pulled back in a long, blond ponytail. Linda's husband, Bill, is a technician in the same plant. By working different shifts, they manage to share the care of their 2-year-old son and Linda's 16-year-old daughter from a previous marriage. "Bill works the 7 a.m. to 3 p.m. shift while I watch the baby," she explains. "Then I work the 3 p.m. to 11 p.m. shift and he watches the baby. My daughter works at Walgreen's after school."

Linda is working overtime, and so I begin by asking whether Amerco required the overtime, or whether she volunteered for it. "Oh, I put in for it," she replies. I ask her whether, if finances and company policy permitted, she'd be interested in cutting back on the overtime. She takes off her safety glasses, rubs her face and, without answering my question, explains: "I get home, and the minute I turn the key, my daughter is right there. Granted, she needs somebody to talk to about her day.... The baby is still up. He should have been in bed two hours ago, and that upsets me. The dishes are piled in the sink. My daughter comes right up to the door and complains about anything her stepfather said or did, and she wants to talk about her job. My husband is in the other room hollering to my daughter, 'Tracy, I don't ever get any time to talk to your mother, because you're always monopolizing her time before I even get a chance!' They all come at me at once."

Linda's description of the urgency of demands and the unarbitrated quarrels that await her homecoming contrast with her account of arriving at her job as a shift supervisor: "I usually come to work early, just to get away from the house. When I arrive, people are there waiting. We sit, we talk, we joke. I let them know what's going on, who has to be where, what changes I've made for the shift that day. We sit and chitchat for 5 or 10 minutes. There's laughing, joking, fun.

For Linda, home has come to feel like work and work has come to feel a bit like home. Indeed, she feels she can get relief from the "work" of being at home only by going to the "home" of work. Why has her life at home come to seem like this? Linda explains it this way: "My husband's a great help watching our baby. But as far as doing housework or even taking the baby when I'm at home, no. He figures he works five days a week; he's not going to come home and clean. But he doesn't stop to think that I work seven days a week. Why should I have to come home and do the housework without help from anybody else? My husband and I have been through this over and over again. Even if he would just pick up from the kitchen table and stack the dishes for me, that would make a big difference. He does nothing. On his weekends off, he goes fishing. If I want any time off, I have to get a sitter. He'll help out if I'm not here, but the minute I am, all the work at home is mine."

With a light laugh, she continues: "So I take a lot of overtime. The more I get out of the house, the better I am. It's a terrible thing to say, but that's the way I feel."

When Bill feels the need for time off, to relax, to have fun, to feel free, he climbs in his truck and takes his free time without his family. Largely in response, Linda grabs what she also calls "free time"—at work. Neither Linda nor Bill Avery wants more time together at home, not as things are arranged now.

How do Linda and Bill Avery fit into the broader picture of American family and work life? Current research suggests that however hectic their lives, women who do paid work feel less depressed, think better of themselves and are more satisfied than women who stay at home. One study reported that women who work outside the home feel more valued at home than housewives do. Meanwhile, work is where many women feel like "good mothers." As Linda reflects: "I'm a good mom at home, but I'm a better mom at work. At home, I get into fights with Tracy. I want her to apply to a junior college, but she's not interested. At work, I think I'm better at seeing the other person's point of view."

Many workers feel more confident they could "get the job done" at work than at home. One study found that only 59 percent of workers feel their "performance" in the family is "good or unusually good," while 86 percent rank their performance on the job this way.

Forces at work and at home are simultaneously reinforcing this "reversal." The lure of work has been enhanced in recent years by the rise of company cultural engineering—in particular, the shift from Frederick Taylor's principles of scientific management to the Total Quality principles originally set out by W. Edwards Deming. Under the influence of a Taylorist world view, the manager's job was to coerce the worker's mind and body, not to appeal to the worker's heart. The Taylorized worker was de-skilled, replaceable and cheap, and as a consequence felt bored, demeaned and unappreciated.

Using modern participative management techniques, many companies now train workers to make their own work decisions, and then set before their newly "empowered" employees moral as well as financial incentives. At Amerco, the Total Quality worker is invited to feel recognized for job accomplishments. Amerco regularly strengthens the familylike ties of co-workers by holding "recognition ceremonies" honoring particular workers or self-managed production teams.

Amerco employees speak of "belonging to the Amerco family," and proudly wear their "Total Quality" pins or "High Performance Team" T-shirts, symbols of their loyalty to the company and of its loyalty to them.

The company occasionally decorates a section of the factory and serves refreshments. The production teams, too, have regular get-togethers. In a New Age recasting of an old business slogan—"The Customer Is Always Right"—Amerco proposes that its workers "Value the Internal Customer." This means: Be as polite and considerate to co-workers inside the company as you would be to customers outside it. How many recognition ceremonies for competent performance are being offered at home? Who is valuing the internal customer there?

Amerco also tries to take on the role of a helpful relative with regard to employee problems at work and at home. The education-and-training division offers employees free courses (on company time) in "Dealing With Anger," "How to Give and Accept Criticism," "How to Cope With Difficult People."

At home, of course, people seldom receive anything like this much help on issues basic to family life. There, no courses are being offered on "Dealing With Your Child's Disappointment in You" or "How to Treat Your Spouse Like an Internal Customer."

If Total Quality calls for "re-skilling" the worker in an "enriched" job environment, technological developments have long been de-skilling parents at home. Over the centuries, store-bought goods have replaced homespun cloth, homemade soap and homebaked foods. Day care for children, retirement homes for the elderly, even psychotherapy are, in a way, commercial substitutes for jobs that a mother once did at home. Even family-generated entertainment has, to some extent, been replaced by television, video games and the VCR. I sometimes watched

Amerco families sitting together after their dinners, mute but cozy, watching sitcoms in which television mothers, fathers and children related in an animated way to one another while the viewing family engaged in relational loafing.

The one "skill" still required of family members is the hardest one of all—the emotional work of forging, deepening or repairing family relationships. It takes time to develop this skill, and even then things can go awry. Family ties are complicated. People get hurt. Yet as broken homes become more common—and as the sense of belonging to a geographical community grows less and less secure in an age of mobility—the corporate world has created a sense of "neighborhood," of "feminine culture," of family at work. Life at work can be insecure; the company can fire workers. But workers aren't so secure at home, either. Many employees have been working for Amerco for 20 years but are on their second or third marriages or relationships. The shifting balance between these two "divorce rates" may be the most powerful reason why tired parents flee a world of unresolved quarrels and unwashed laundry for the orderliness, harmony and managed cheer of work. People are getting their "pink slips" at home.

Amerco workers have not only turned their offices into "home" and their homes into workplaces; many have also begun to "Taylorize" time at home, where families are succumbing to a cult of efficiency previously associated mainly with the office and factory. Meanwhile, work time, with its ever longer hours, has become more hospitable to sociability—periods of talking with friends on E-mail, patching up quarrels, gossiping. Within the long workday of many Amerco employees are great hidden pockets of inefficiency while, in the far smaller number of waking weekday hours at home, they are, despite themselves, forced to act increasingly time-conscious and efficient.

The Averys respond to their time bind at home by trying to value and protect "quality time." A concept unknown to their parents and grandparents, "quality time" has become a powerful symbol of the struggle against the growing pressures at home. It reflects the extent to which modern parents feel the flow of time to be running against them. The premise behind "quality time" is that the time we devote to relationships can somehow be separated from ordinary time. Relationships go on during quantity time, of course, but then we are only passively, not actively, wholeheartedly, specializing in our emotional ties. We aren't "on." Quality time at home becomes like an office appointment. You don't want to be caught "goofing off around the water cooler" when you are "at work."

Quality time holds out the hope that scheduling intense periods of togetherness can compensate for an overall loss of time in such a way that a relationship will suffer no loss of quality. But this is just another way of transferring the cult of efficiency from office to home. We must now get our relationships in good repair in less time. Instead of nine hours a day with a child, we declare ourselves capable of getting "the same result" with one intensely focused hour.

Parents now more commonly speak of time as if it is a threatened form of personal capital they have no choice but to manage and invest. What's new here is the spread into the home of a financial manager's attitude toward time. Working parents at Amerco owe what they think of as time debts at home. This is because they are, in a sense, inadvertently "Taylorizing" the house—speeding up the pace of home life as Taylor once tried to "scientifically" speed up the pace of factory life.

Advertisers of products aimed at women have recognized that this new reality provides an opportunity to sell products, and have turned the very pressure that threatens to explode the home into a positive attribute. Take, for example, an ad promoting Instant Quaker Oatmeal: it shows a smiling mother ready for the office in her square-shouldered suit, hugging her happy son. A caption reads: "Nicky is a very picky eater. With Instant Quaker Oatmeal, I can give him a terrific hot breakfast in just 90 seconds. And I don't have to spend any time coaxing him to eat it!" Here, the modern mother seems to have absorbed the lessons of Frederick Taylor as she presses for efficiency at home because she is in a hurry to get to work.

Part of modern parenthood seems to include coping with the resistance of real children who are not so eager to get their cereal so fast. Some parents try desperately not to appease their children with special gifts or smooth-talking promises about the future. But when time is scarce, even the best parents find themselves passing a system-wide familial speed-up along to the most vulnerable workers on the line. Parents are then obliged to try to control the damage done by a reversal of worlds. They monitor mealtime, homework time, bedtime, trying to cut out "wasted" time.

In response, children often protest the pace, the deadlines, the grand irrationality of "efficient" family life. Children dawdle. They refuse to leave places when it's time to leave. They insist on leaving places when it's not time to leave. Surely, this is part of the usual stop-and-go of childhood itself, but perhaps, too, it is the plea of children for more family time, and more control over what time there is. This only adds to the feeling that life at home has become hard work.

Instead of trying to arrange shorter or more flexible work schedules, Amerco parents often avoid confronting the reality of the time bind. Some minimize their ideas about how much care a child, a partner or they themselves "really need." They make do with less time, less attention, less

understanding and less support at home than they once imagined possible. They *emotionally downsize* life. In essence, they deny the needs of family members, and they themselves become emotional ascetics. If they once "needed" time with each other, they are now increasingly "fine" without it.

Another way that working parents try to evade the time bind is to buy themselves out of it—an approach that puts women in particular at the heart of a contradiction. Like men, women absorb the work-family speed-up far more than they resist it; but unlike men, they still shoulder most of the workload at home. And women still represent in people's minds the heart and soul of family life. They're the ones—especially women of the urban middle and upper-middle classes—who feel most acutely the need to save time, who are the most tempted by the new "time saving" goods and services—and who wind up feeling the most guilty about it. For example, Playgroup Connections, a Washington-area business started by a former executive recruiter, matches playmates to one another. One mother hired the service to find her child a French-speaking playmate.

In several cities, children home alone can call a number for "Grandma, Please!" and reach an adult who has the time to talk with them, sing to them or help them with their homework. An ad for Kindercare Learning Centers, a for-profit child-care chain, pitches its appeal this way: "You want your child to be active, tolerant, smart, loved, emotionally stable, self-aware, artistic and get a two-hour nap. Anything else?" It goes on to note that Kindercare accepts children 6 weeks to 12 years old and provides a number to call for the Kindercare nearest you. Another typical service organizes children's birthday parties, making out invitations ("sure hope you can come") and providing party favors, entertainment, a decorated cake and balloons. Creative Memories is a service that puts ancestral photos into family albums for you.

An overwhelming majority of the working mothers I spoke with recoiled from the idea of buying themselves out of parental duties. A bought birthday party was "too impersonal," a 90-second breakfast "too fast." Yet a surprising amount of lunchtime conversation between female friends at Amerco was devoted to expressing complex, conflicting feelings about the lure of trading time for one service or another. The temptation to order flash-frozen dinners or to call a local number for a homework helper did not come up because such services had not yet appeared at Spotted Deer Child-Care Center. But many women dwelled on the question of how to decide where a mother's job began and ended, especially with regard to baby sitters and television. One mother said to another in the breakroom of an Amerco plant: "Damon doesn't settle down until 10 at night, so he hates me to wake him up in the morning and I hate to do it. He's cranky. He pulls the covers up. I put on cartoons. That way, I can dress him and he doesn't object. I don't like to use TV that way. It's like a drug. But I do it."

The other mother countered. "Well, Todd is up before we are, so that's not a problem. It's after dinner, when I feel like watching a little television, that I feel guilty, because he gets too much TV at the sitter's."

As task after task falls into the realm of time-saving goods and services, questions arise about the moral meanings attached to doing or not doing such tasks. Is it being a good mother to bake a child's birthday cake (alone or together with one's partner)? Or can we gratefully save time by ordering it, and be good mothers by planning the party? Can we save more time by hiring a planning service, and be good mothers simply by watching our children have a good time? "Wouldn't that be nice!" one Amerco mother exclaimed. As the idea of the "good mother" retreats before the pressures of work and the expansion of motherly services, mothers are in fact continually reinventing themselves.

The final way working parents tried to evade the time bind was to develop what I call "potential selves." The potential selves that I discovered in my Amerco interviews were fantasy creations of time-poor parents who dreamed of living as time millionaires.

One man, a gifted 55-year-old engineer in research and development at Amerco, told how he had dreamed of taking his daughters on a camping trip in the Sierra Mountains: "I bought all the gear three years ago when they were 5 and 7, the tent, the sleeping bags, the air mattresses, the backpacks, the ponchos. I got a map of the area. I even got the freeze-dried food. Since then the kids and I have talked about it a lot, and gone over what we're going to do. They've been on me to do it for a long time. I feel bad about it. I keep putting it off, but we'll do it, I just don't know when."

Banished to garages and attics of many Amerco workers were expensive electric saws, cameras, skis and musical instruments, all bought with wages it took time to earn. These items were to their owners what Cassie's fudge bar was to her—a substitute for time, a talisman, a reminder of the potential self.

Obviously, not everyone, not even a majority of Americans, is making a home out of work and a workplace out of home. But in the working world, it is a growing reality, and one we need to face. Increasing numbers of women are discovering a great male secret—that work can be an escape from the pressures of home, pressures that the changing nature of work itself are only intensifying. Neither men nor women are going to take up "family friendly" policies, whether corporate or governmental, as long as the current realities of work and home remain as they are. For a substantial number of time-bound parents, the stripped-down home and the neighborhood devoid of community are simply losing out to the pull of the workplace.

There are several broader, historical causes of this reversal of realms. The last 30 years have witnessed the rapid rise of women in the workplace. At the same time, job mobility has taken families farther from relatives who might lend a hand, and made it harder to make close friends of neighbors who could help out. Moreover, as women have acquired more education and have joined men at work, they have absorbed the views of an older, male-oriented work world, its views of a "real career," far more than men have taken up their share of the work at home. One reason women have changed more than men is that the world of "male" work seems more honorable and valuable than the "female" world of home and children.

So where do we go from here? There is surely no going back to the mythical 1950's family that confined women to the home. Most women don't wish to return to a full-time role at home—and couldn't afford it even if they did. But equally troubling is a workaholic culture that strands both men and women outside the home.

For a while now, scholars on work-family issues have pointed to Sweden, Norway and Denmark as better models of work-family balance. Today, for example, almost all Swedish fa-

thers take two paid weeks off from work at the birth of their children, and about half of fathers and most mothers take additional "parental leave" during the child's first or second year. Research shows that men who take family leave when their children are very young are more likely to be involved with their children as they grow older. When I mentioned this Swedish record of paternity leave to a focus group of American male managers, one of them replied, "Right, we've already heard about Sweden." To this executive, paternity leave was a good idea not for the U.S. today, but for some "potential society" in another place and time.

Meanwhile, children are paying the price. In her book "When the Bough Breaks: The Cost of Neglecting Our Children," the economist Sylvia Hewlett claims that "compared with the previous generation, young people today are more likely to "underperform at school; commit suicide; need psychiatric help; suffer a severe eating disorder; bear a child out of wedlock; take drugs, be the victim of a violent crime." But we needn't dwell on sledgehammer problems like heroin or suicide to realize that children like those at Spotted Deer need more of our time. If other advanced nations with two-job families can give children the time they need, why can't we?

Reading 16   Gender, Class, Family, and Migration:

Puerto Rican Women in Chicago

MAURA I. TORO-MORN*

Using in-depth interviews with women in the Puerto Rican community of Chicago, this article explores how migration emerged as a strategy for families across class backgrounds and how gender relations within the family mediate the migration of married working-class and middle-class Puerto Rican women. The women who followed their husbands to Chicago participated in another form of labor migration, since some wives joined their husbands in the paid economy and those who did not contributed with the reproductive work that supported their husbands and families. This article also explores how Puerto Rican women confront the basic duality of reproductive and productive work.

Recently, there has been a surge of scholarly interest about immigrant women (Diner 1983; Ewen 1983; Glenn 1986; Hondagncu-Sotelo 1992; Lamphere 1987; Simon and Brettell 1986; Weinberg 1988). Although women have always participated in population movements (Tyree and Donato 1986), suddenly newspaper reports are calling women the "new immigrants." Initial attempts at making immigrant women visible owe much to the efforts of feminist researchers of the 1960s and 1970s (Morokvasic 1983). The first wave of research on immigrant women helped to fill in the gaps by calling attention to the presence of women in migratory movements and by providing the much needed descriptive detail on the employment status and family situations of particular groups, but, according to Morokvasic (1983), this early research did not break with the traditional individualist approach so pervasive in immigration research. It continued to analyze women as if their decisions to migrate were determined by their individual

I am indebted to Judith Wittner, Loyola University of Chicago, for her invaluable assistance and suggestions during the early stages of this work and to *las mujeres del barrio* for sharing their experiences with me. I would also like to thank Margaret Andersen and the anonymous reviewers for their comments and suggestions.

motives and desires; consequently, important questions were left unanswered: How do we account for women's migration and should the migration of women be treated in the same conceptual framework as male migrants or do they require separate analysis? Recently, a new wave of research has begun to correct some of the problems unresolved by the earlier research. Scholars have begun to move beyond the additive approach to articulate how gender affects and shapes the migration process (Hondagneu-Sotelo 1992; Kibria 1990). This new research shows that immigrant women's relationship to market and nonmarket conditions is unique. The place of immigrant women in the labor market is shaped by class and their statuses as immigrants and racial/ethnic minorities; this intersection creates a particular and distinct experience (Glenn 1986).

Much empirical research has been done linking the entrance of women into labor migrations because of the emergence of export-led manufacturing zones in the Caribbean, Mexico, and Asia (Fernandez-Kelly 1983; Sassen-Koob 1984). In addition, studies have examined the incorporation of immigrant women into the labor force (Garcia-Castro 1985; Prieto 1986) and the consequent labor market outcomes in terms of occupational distribution and income differences from native populations (Boyd 1986; Simon and DeLey 1986; Sullivan 1984; Tienda, Jensen, and Bach 1984). Still, much empirical work remains to be done to explain how these processes differ by race and ethnicity.

This article examines how working-class and better-educated middle-class Puerto Rican women enter the migration process, how gender relations shape their move, and how women adapt to their new homes in the United States. Specifically, I focus on the experiences of married working-class and middle-class women. My interviews suggest that while both groups mi-

grated to the United States as part of what sociologists have called a "family stage migration," there are important differences between them that challenge our understanding of women's migration. In the first part of this article, I explore how working-class and middle-class Puerto Rican women moved to the United States. I pay particular attention to the language women used to describe this process. While middle-class women talked about their migration as motivated by professional goals, working-class Puerto Rican women talked about how they came to take care of their children, husbands, and families. When confronted with these answers, I found that the experiences of married working-class women did not fit the traditional explanations found in the migration literature. Here, I draw on the feminist construct of productive and reproductive work, to argue that our current definition of "labor migration" is too narrow. Not all labor migrations need to relate to productive activities (i.e., the entrance of immigrant women in the labor market). One very important aspect of labor migrations should include the work of women who migrate and do not necessarily join the labor force, but stay and do the reproductive work that supports families and immigrant communities. Within this category, there are women who migrate as wives, as grandmothers, or as relatives, and whose major responsibility is to help with the reproductive tasks—be they housework or child care—of their own families and/or their extended families.

The second part of this article explores how, once in the United States, both working-class and middle-class Puerto Rican women had to confront the duality of being responsible for the reproductive work that takes place at home and the productive work outside the home. The interviews indicate that both working-class and middle-class Puerto Rican women tried to provide as much continuity in the process of forming and re-creating family life. Again, important class differences emerged when comparing married working-class and middle-class migrants. interviews suggest that working-class husbands may have accommodated to their wives temporary employment, but that did not change the traditional division of labor within the household. Instead, working-class women had to develop strategies to accommodate their roles as working wives. Middle-class women developed strategies both as family members and as individuals in the process of adjusting to life in Chicago. The strategies they devised, however, reflected their class position. When juggling family and work responsibilities, educated and professional women gave career goals equal standing alongside family obligations.

METHODOLOGY

From March 1989 to July 1990, I interviewed women in the Puerto Rican community of Chicago, which covers the areas of West Town, Humboldt Park, and Logan Square. I participated in community activities and attended cultural events. These activities allowed me to meet the women of the community and, through informal snowball sampling techniques, to select interviewees. The interviews took place in the homes of the informants and lasted between one to three hours. Interviews were conducted in Spanish. The interview questions were organized around a series of themes, ranging from their migration history to family, work, and community experiences.

The sample of married women consisted of 17 informants. Eleven were mostly working class, with little education, who came to Chicago in the early 1950s and 1960s. Generally, at the time of migration, they were married—or were soon to be married—and most had children. The six professional and educated women in the

sample had all migrated in the late 1960s and had over 14 years of education at the time of their move. Most educated informants described themselves as predominantly middle class and from urban backgrounds in Puerto Rico. At the time of the interview, two informants had earned doctorate degrees. Ten respondents were in their sixties; seven were in their forties and fifties. Different respondents will be identified by pseudonyms.

Being Puerto Rican and bilingual, I was able to establish rapport with informants. Most of the older migrant women spoke little English, and conducting the interviews in Spanish facilitated the exchange. By the same token, being fluent in English allowed women to use the language with which they felt most comfortable. Sometimes the interview started in Spanish and ended in English. On other occasions, women switched back and forth.

GENDER, CLASS, AND MIGRATION

The most significant movement of Puerto Ricans to the United States took place at the end of World War II (Dietz 1986; Falcon 1990; History Task Force 1979; Pantojas-Garcia 1990). In the late 1940s, the impact of U.S. investment and modernization of the economy transformed Puerto Rico from a predominantly agricultural to an industrial economy. Operation Bootstrap, as the development model became popularly known in Puerto Rico, attracted labor intensive light manufacturing industries such as textiles and apparel to Puerto Rico by offering tax incentives, cheap labor, and easy access to U.S. markets (Dietz 1986; Pantojas-Garcias 1990). These changes in Puerto Rico's economy had profound consequences for Puerto Rican families. The development model was unable to create enough jobs, and working-class Puerto Ricans began to leave the island, heading for familiar places like New York City and new places like Chicago. News about jobs spread quickly throughout the island, as informal networks of family members, friends, and relatives told people of opportunities and helped families migrate.

My interviews suggest that working-class women and their families used migration as a strategy for dealing with economic problems. Married working-class women, in particular, talked about migration as a family project. For them, migration took place in stages. Husbands moved first, secured employment and housing arrangements, and then sent for the rest of the family. Even single men frequently left their future brides in Puerto Rico, returning to the island to get married as their employment and economic resources permitted. Some women came as brides-to-be, as they joined their future husbands in Chicago. For example, Rosie's mother came to Indiana in order to join her husband working in the steel mills. He had been recruited earlier, along with other workers in Puerto Rico. Once at the mills in Indiana, these men often found better jobs and moved on. They went back to Puerto Rico, got married, and returned to Indiana. Others arranged for the future brides to join them in Chicago. Alicia's explanation indicates how these decisions took place within the family context.

My husband and I were neighbors in San Lorenzo. Before he left to come to Chicago, he had demonstrated an interest in me. Initially, I did not accept him, because I did not want to get married so young. We started corresponding and I agreed to the relationship.... In one letter, he asked me to marry him and come to live with him in Chicago. I told him that he needed to ask my father's permission.... He wrote to my father but my father did not agree...it took some convincing by my cousins who were coming to Chicago so that he would let me come and get married. My cousin took it upon himself to be responsible for me and that's how I came. Within two weeks of getting here, we got married.

Alicia's experience suggests that even within the constraints of a patriarchal society, single women were active in negotiating their moves to Chicago.

Married working-class women left the island to be with their husbands and families, even though some reported to have been working before leaving. Lucy and Luz were working in apparel factories in Puerto Rico when their unemployed husbands decided to move. Economic opportunities seemed better for their husbands in the United States and they both quit their jobs to move. For others, like Teresa and Agnes, both husband and wife were looking for work, when news about job opportunities came via relatives visiting the island. Similarly, Agnes also came with her husband in the 1970s after a cousin who was visiting from Chicago convinced them that there were better job opportunities for both of them.

Working-class women also talked about the struggles over the decision to move. Fear of the unknown bothered Lucy. In addition, with a baby in her arms and pregnant with a second child, Lucy did not have anyone to help her in Chicago, but accompanied by her sister and her youngest child, Lucy followed her husband. Shortly after her migration, Lucy's mother and her sister-in-law arrived to care for the children while Lucy worked. Asuncion's husband could not find work in Puerto Rico either, so he migrated to Chicago with his relatives. Asuncion took a vacation from work and came to visit. Her family

> started talking about how they were recruiting case workers in the welfare office that could speak Spanish. They all had connections there and could very easily help me get a job. In fact, I went just to try it.

Asuncion gave in to the pressure and started working while still holding her job in Puerto Rico:

> I worked for six months, but I had so many problems, I wanted to go back. Life here [in Chicago] is really different when compared to the Island's. I was really confused. I cried a lot. I had left my children behind and I missed them a lot.

In fact, Asuncion went back to Puerto Rico because she missed her daughters; she was uncertain about what would happen to her marriage. She remembered how she felt when her husband took her to the airport:

> I really did not know whether I was going to see him again. He wanted to stay here and start a new life. I really did not care about what would happen to us and our relationship; I thought about my daughters. I owe it to my mother that my marriage was saved. After I returned to Puerto Rico, she sat me down and told me that my place was to be with my husband. That he was a good man and that my place was next to him. That I had to think about my children growing up without a father, so I returned again.

As Asuncion's case illustrates, she struggled between her husband's needs in Chicago and those of her children on the Island. Ultimately, moving to Chicago meant maintaining the family and saving her marriage.

Victoria's story is somewhat similar. She was living in her hometown of Ponce when she fell in love with the son of a family visiting from Chicago. She became pregnant and, in keeping with Puerto Rican culture, she was forced to marry him. Without consulting with Victoria, the young man's parents sent him a ticket so that he could return to Illinois. Once in Chicago, he expected she would follow.

> I did not want to come....One day he sent me a ticket for me and my baby girl. I sent it back because I did not want to come. But he send it back again. So I had to come....I had no idea where I was going, I had lived all my life in Ponce and had never left Ponce. I was so scared.... In 1966, she followed her husband to Chicago against her will.

The emotional and cultural shock was very strong:

> I cried my eyes out. In Puerto Rico, you are always outside and carefree. Here, we lived in small apartments, we could not go outside. We could not open the windows. We did not know the language.

When her second child was to be born, Victoria was so intimidated with the city that she asked her mother to send a plane ticket so that she might give birth in Puerto Rico. Within less than a year, she had returned to Puerto Rico. Eventually her husband joined her also, but he was not happy. Soon he began to disappear and neglect his responsibilities as a father. In one of his escapades, he went back to Chicago. Once again, he sent for her. This time, however, Victoria began to analyze the situation in different ways.

> *In Puerto Rico, I did not have any money to pay rent, electricity, and other bills or even feed my babies. I recognized it was a difficult situation, but I thought to myself that if I stayed I had less opportunities to do something with my life. So, I thought that if I returned and brought my other brother with me they could help me and eventually even my mother could come and I could get myself a job. I had noticed that there were factories close to where we lived and my sister-in-law had offered to help as well. My brother who had moved with me the first time had gotten married and brought his wife with him.*

Victoria had changed; as a married woman who followed her husband to Chicago, she began to develop her own agenda and use migration as a way for its realization.

Of the women who followed their husbands to Chicago, only two (Luz and Rita) complained that their husbands failed to fulfill their end of the bargain, forcing them to use migration as a way to assert their claims as wives. Lucy's husband had just returned from the military when he began talking about migrating to Chicago. Initially he went to Indiana where some relatives helped him find a job. When he was laid off, he learned through other friends that there were job opportunities in Illinois. He then moved to Chicago, promising to send for the family once he secured employment. But, according to Luz, he had been working for quite a while and had not

sent for her and the children. Also, he was not sending any money to support the family. Instead, her husband kept putting off sending for her, and she was forced to confront him. Finally, Lucy left Arecibo in 1951 to join her husband and save her marriage. Rita was also forced to confront her husband by letter, reminding him of his promise to bring the rest of the family to Chicago. Even though it was over 20 years ago, Rita stated with emotion that she

> *had to write him a letter. Because it had been over a year and he didn't send for me. I had three babies and I was alone. When he left, he said that he was going to send for me shortly and it had been a year and I was still waiting.*

He replied that he did not want her to come, because living in Chicago was hard and she and the children would not be able to get used to the weather. She replied, "either you send the ticket or send me the divorce papers." Apparently, this was a typical problem for Puerto Rican women when their husbands preceded them in migration. Juarbe (1988) reported that Puerto Rican women migrants in New York experienced similar problems. Juarbe's (1988) informant, Anastacia, stated that after her husband had migrated, he did not want her to come. He had been living and working for over three months. He wrote occasionally but did not send any money. Apparently, she had some money saved and was able to buy the ticket without his knowledge. Anastacia wrote him a letter announcing her arrival.

Middle-Class Migrants

The migration of educated and professional middle-class Puerto Ricans to Chicago remains an unanswered empirical question. Sanchez-

Korrol's (1986) study of migration to New York City hints at the possibility that middle-class Puerto Ricans had been involved in the migration process; furthermore, surveys by the Planning Office in Puerto Rico between 1957 and 1962 found higher literacy levels and English proficiency among migrants than among the population as a whole (Rodriguez 1989). Pantojas-Garcia (1990) comes closest to analyzing the changing political economy in Puerto Rico and its impact on middle-class and educated workers. He points out that skilled and professional workers have increasingly joined semiskilled and unskilled workers in the migration process. As Pedraza (1991) points out, despite the growing importance of the "brain drain" as a type of migration, from a gender perspective, it remains the least understood.

In contrast to working-class migrants, moving was a joint family project for married middle-class women. In addition, the language this group used to describe the move differs from that of the working-class married woman. Middle-class women came with their husbands and had an agenda of their own. Aurea met her husband while attending the University of Puerto Rico. Initially, the couple moved from San Juan to Boston to enable her husband to take a university position. In 1971, a new job opportunity brought them to Chicago. In fact, Aurea talked about moving as a mutual arrangement between her and her husband. She saw the move to Chicago as an opportunity to join community and political struggles. Shortly after arriving in the city, they bought a house—something that took years for working-class families to accomplish.

Brunilda had just completed her bachelor's degree and was working as a field researcher for the University of Puerto Rico when she was asked to work with a group of American scholars who came to Puerto Rico to conduct research in the 1970s. The researchers were very pleased with her work and offered her a position if she would relocate to Chicago. They promised they would help her to make the transition. She had just been married when the job offer came, and she felt that was a big problem:

My husband did not want to come, he said that he did not know English. He just did not want to come. I told him that there were no doubts in my mind as to what that job meant for me. It was a great opportunity, and I was not going to let it go. If he did not want to come, then I guess that was it, I knew I was coming with him or without him.

In this case the roles changed. It was the husband who was asked to follow his wife; initially he resisted, but the job meant so much to Brunilda that she was willing to sacrifice her marriage. Brunilda, therefore, moved within a professional rather than a family network. In addition, she did not live close to other Puerto Ricans in Chicago because the research team found her a place to stay closer to the university. After completing her work with the university researchers, Brunilda started graduate studies at a local university. She went to school full time for a year and in 1971 started working as a community organizer in the south side of Chicago.

Vilma moved from San Juan to Wisconsin to go to graduate school. While in Madison, she met her future husband and they moved in together. They had completed their degrees when he was offered a job in Chicago. In 1986, they both relocated to Chicago. Vilma described her move

as very traditional in terms that I had just finished my masters and was looking for a job when my "compañero" (living in boyfriend) got a job offer in Chicago. I followed him to Chicago, but I came not only for him, but also knowing that in Madison there was no professional future for me.

Comparing the migration of married working-class and middle-class Puerto Rican women offers some insights into how gender and class shapes the migration process. As my interviews suggest, both working-class and middle-class Puerto Rican women found themselves migrating as part of a family migration. Married working-class women came to support their husbands and be with their families. In other words, their roles as mothers and wives compelled them to migrate. The narratives suggest that some women struggled over the decision to move. In contrast, educated married middle-class women were less encumbered by such relations of authority. They shared in the decision making and were less dependent on other family members to make the move. As Vilma's and Brunilda's stories indicate, these middle-class migrants clearly had professional agendas of their own. How does each confront the problem of balancing family and work responsibilities?

GENDER, FAMILY, AND WORK

In Puerto Rican culture, there is a gender-specific division of labor consisting of men's work (*trabajo de hombre*) as the providers and women's work (*trabajo de mujer*) as the caretakers of the home and children. Underlying this gender division of labor is a patriarchal ideology, machismo, emphasizing men's sexual freedom, virility, and aggressiveness, and women's sexual repression and submission (Acosta-Belen 1986). Machismo represents the male ideal and plays an important role in maintaining sexual restrictions and the subordination of women. This ideology rationalizes a double standard where a woman can be seen as *una mujer buena o una mujer de la casa* (a good woman or a good homemaker) or as *una mujer mala o una mujer de la calle* (a bad woman or a woman of the streets). A man has to show that *él lleva los pantalones en la casa* (he is the one who wears the pants in the family) and that he is free to *echar una canita al aire* (literally meaning, blow a gray hair to the wind; culturally, it means to have an affair).

The counterpart of machismo is *marianismo* in which the Virgin Mary is seen as the role model for women (Sanchez-Ayendez 1986, 628). Within this context, a woman's sexual purity and virginity is a cultural imperative. Motherhood, in Puerto Rican culture, lies at the center of such ideology. A woman is viewed in light of her relationship to her children and, as Carmen, one of my informants, put it, in her ability "dar buenos ejemplos" (to provide a good role model).

Among working-class Puerto Ricans, gender roles are very rigid (Safa 1984). Although industrialization and the entrance of women in the labor force completely contradicts this ideal of *la mujer es de la casa* (women belong to the home), in Puerto Rico the domestic role of working class remains intact. Working mothers are primarily responsible for the care of the home and the children.

In Chicago, in keeping with this ideology surrounding family values, some working-class husbands resisted their wives working. The men would take a double shift so that wives could stay home, take care of the children, and do housework. Carmen stayed home to care for her children and was very proud of her accomplishments as a mother, but economic necessity obliged other husbands to conform to women's work outside the home. Like Lucy said, "I did not come here to work, but I had to." Alicia elaborates, "in those days one paycheck was like nothing. We put together both paychecks and there were times that he had very little next to nothing left. By that time there were other relatives living with us and there were lots of mouths to feed."

The same network of family and friends that helped in the process of migration helped working wives find employment in Chicago factories. Josefa, Lucy, Luz, Rita, and Teresa all reported working in factories. Chicago's political economy in the 1950s allowed these women to find factory jobs with relative ease; however, most working-class married women viewed employment as a temporary necessity. The way women talked about their work experiences reflected this attitude. Josefa and her husband worked not only to meet the family needs but also to take care of the medical expenses of their child. When her daughter started going to school, she stopped working. Alicia worked in a factory prior to getting pregnant; after having the baby, she stopped working. When the family wanted to buy a house, Alicia went back to work for two years. After her second child, she stopped working altogether. Brunilda started working in a factory immediately upon arriving from Puerto Rico, but when she became pregnant, she stopped. Lucy was the only married respondent who stayed in the factory for a prolonged period of time. Eventually, she stopped working when she got sick.

Although most working-class married women gave in to their husbands' wishes for them to stay home, Rita illustrates how a woman resisted those traditional roles and even sought to change them. Rita's husband did not want her to work. According to Rita:

After I got to Chicago, my husband didn't want me to work. But I wanted to work. I wanted to work because you can meet people, learn new things, and one can also leave the house for a while. I saw all the

women in the family, his sisters and cousins, working and earning some money, and I wanted to work too. They used to tell me that I should be working. But I had four children, and who was going to take care of them?

Rita succumbed to the pressure and started working secretly for about three months. When asked how she managed to work without her husband knowing about it, Rita replied that

since he left to work very early, I found someone to take care of my smallest child, and the others went to school. My work hours were from 9:00 to 3:30, so by the time my husband got home, I had everything done. I had the house clean, the children were cleaned and had eaten, and I was all put together. My husband did not like when I was not put together.

Rita eventually told her husband about her work escapades because she did not like doing things *a la escondida* (in hiding); however, her husband's traditionalism prevailed, and Rita was forced to give up working. To relent was a blow, because the money she had earned had gone to clothe the children and to purchase a sewing machine. Note the tone of pride:

With the money I earned I was able to buy my sewing machine and I felt so proud of myself that I was able to buy it with my own money. We saved a lot of money afterwards. I sew for the family; I felt so proud.

Although she gave in to her husband's traditionalism, Rita found a source of pride and accomplishment even within the confines of the house. She may have stopped working, but her contributions to the household continued as she was able to sew her children's clothing and other items for the house and the family.

Others reported that they stopped working for wages, but continued to contribute to the family's income by working in their husbands' neighborhood stores. They used the word "helped," but, in reality, they actually ran the stores while their husbands worked elsewhere.

Puerto Rican men may have accommodated to the wife's employment, but the traditional division of labor within the family did not change. Lucy best articulated the working woman's problem:

It was very hard work because I had to take care of the house, the children, and the store. Since my husband never learned how to drive, I had to learn to drive. I had to go to the warehouse, do the bookkeeping, everything. In the store, I used to do everything. My husband helped, but I was practically in charge of everything.

Puerto Rican working mothers, regardless of whether they worked outside the home or with their husbands in the family business, were still responsible for the care of the children and housework. Child care first became a problem at the time of migration since families could not afford to travel all at once. A strategy women used to deal with this problem was to leave the children in Puerto Rico in the care of grandparents. This arrangement was a widespread practice in the Island for many years.

Once the family was in Chicago, women developed short-term arrangements to deal with the daily problems of child care. Shift work represented one strategy that couples used to allow these women to stay home with the children. The husband could work the day shift, and the wife worked at night. Haydee's father worked the day shift in a factory, while her mother worked the evening shift as a cook in a hotel. Josefa worked the night shift in a candy store; her husband worked the day shift. I asked Josefa if they ever switched, where he worked nights and she worked days. She replied that working at night allowed her to take care of her daughter during the day.

When children were school age, both husband and wife might be able to work during the day. For wives, however, there was always the added responsibility of returning home to care for the children and do the household chores. Here, girls were introduced to the household responsibilities very early and were left to care for younger brothers and sisters. When Claudia reached nine years, she acquired household responsibilities. She was given keys to the apartment, and after school she was expected to clean the kitchen, pick up around the house, and start dinner. This was also a way mothers trained their daughters in the traditional gender roles.

Given the ease of migration, other working-class women brought over relatives with them to help care for the children, suggesting that women can get involved in the migration process to do the reproductive work, allowing other women to do work outside the home. Lucy and Daniela brought their mothers, and Teresa brought a younger sister to Chicago to help take care of the children. Teresa's sister stayed home and took care of her children until she met a fellow and got married. That was when Teresa then turned to a woman in her building who took care of them for a small fee. Teresa gave her $12.00 weekly for the two girls and provided their food.

Sanchez-Korrol (1983, 98) found the same kind of informal child care practices in the early "colonias" in New York City in which "childcare tasks previously undertaken by relatives defaulted to friends and acquaintances outside the kinship network who provided the services in exchange for a prearranged fee." This grassroots system served both employed women and women who had to stay at home. The arrangement usually consisted of bringing the child, food, and additional clothing to the "mother-substitute" and collecting the child after work. This system provided a practical way to increase family earnings and was an extralegal system with advantages not found in established child care institutions. These informal child care arrangements allowed children to be cared for in a familiar environment, where there was mutual trust, agreement between the adults involved, and flexibility. Children were cared for in a family setting where the language, customs, and Puerto Rican traditions were reinforced.

When Teresa stopped working, she became a child care provider for the women in her building. Now, she no longer cares for other people's children, but instead cares for her own grandchildren. Teresa's history represents an example of the cycle of care that women provided. Such a cycle may begin when a woman places her children with a neighbor while she works. Then she may care for other neighbor's children while they work and, finally, care for her own children's children.

Middle-Class Migrants

Middle-class women placed their career goals equally alongside their family responsibilities. Rosa talked about how she had managed to work full time in Puerto Rico and go to school to acquire an associate's degree because her extended family helped take care of the children and the household chores. In Chicago, since they did not have their extended family, they had to adjust differently. Shortly after arriving in the city,

Rosa, had given birth to her youngest child, who opted to stay home with her children until they were of school age. Rosa recognized that she wanted to be with her children, but she also wanted to stay active.

> *When I arrived, I saw a lot of possibilities, but I chose to stay home with my baby because I wanted to be with my children. When the baby was three years old, I started thinking what can I do to keep myself busy? In Puerto Rico, I had always worked, and I was not used to be a full-time mom. I was very independent. I was very active. So I started helping the church. I started just because I wanted to get out of the house.*

Eventually it became a full-time job. Then, when she started working full time, her husband took on more household responsibilities:

> *Here he has learned all kinds of domestic chores. At times I get home from work and he has everything ready, I don't have to do a thing in the house. Other times, we decide to go out for dinner.*

Brunilda could not have made it without her husband, who helped her take care of the children as she pursued both her educational goals and, later, her political activism:

> *My husband was very understanding of my goals and political interest. We shared many of the household responsibilities.... I have to admit that I spent a lot of time outside of the house during my children's childhood; for that I am a little bit sorry.*

Later on she elaborated on her struggles and how she resolved them:

> When you are a professional, you face what Americans call "conflicting priorities." It's like I want to be everywhere at the same time. For me, community work has always interested me, whereas being a housewife has always been secondary. I feel more gratification in my role as a professional.

At the time of the interview, Brunilda worked as a professor in a local university. Aurea too placed her community activism (which was her professional orientation) alongside her family responsibilities:

> For me, both are part of the same process. I define my family network beyond the nuclear family, or better yet, beyond the traditional American concept of the nuclear family. My family is part of my social activism.

I asked whether this brought about any conflicts. She replied:

> Without doubt, my husband is part of this sexist society and obviously expects privileges that this society accords men, but we have worked and negotiated these roles quite successfully; moreover, we both made a political pact. It worked rather well because he shares the same vision of the world and social change as I do.

CONCLUSION

Evidence from this research has only begun to show how, in the context of changing political economy, migration emerged as a strategy for families across class backgrounds. Initially, migration was a strategy working-class families used to deal with shrinking economic opportunities for the men in the family, but eventually middle-class better-educated men and women joined working-class Puerto Ricans in the migration process.

The political economy that rendered working-class husbands unemployable forced women to migrate to Chicago as part of a family strategy. Gender relations within the family were a major factor shaping the migration of married working class women to Chicago. Some married women went willingly, thinking that the move would improve their families' financial situation. Others resisted, but ultimately their roles as mothers and wives compelled them to follow their husbands to Chicago.

Whether working class or middle class Puerto Rican women, like other immigrant women, confronted a basic duality in family and work. Families provided economic and emotional support. They see the family as the only area where people are free to be themselves, and where people come for affection and love, but the family is also an institution that has historically oppressed women (Glenn 1986). When individuals and families confront economic deprivation, legal discrimination, and other threats to their survival, conflict within the context of the family is muted by the pressure of the family to unite against assaults from the outside. The focus on the family as a site of resistance often underestimates how certain family arrangements can be oppressive to women. Often misunderstood by scholars is the reproductive work of women on behalf of the family and the benefits such work brings to the men (Glenn 1987, 192).

Working-class women saw themselves in keeping with Puerto Rican culture as primarily *mujeres de la casa*, but many found themselves working, albeit temporarily, given the family's economic situation. Here, families accommodated to the wives' temporary employment, but in ways that did not challenge the traditional patriarchal structure in the family. Wives were still responsible for cooking, cleaning, and child care. Given this situation, working-class married women developed strategies to accommodate their roles as working wives.

The area of child care best reflects the resourcefulness of working-class Puerto Rican women migrants in developing accommodating strategies. Some women left their children behind in Puerto Rico, others brought relatives from Puerto Rico to help them. Still others turned to older daughters as helpers. Some became involved in a cycle of child care similar to the one developed by Puerto Rican women migrants in New York City.

Married working-class Puerto Rican women adapted to life in Chicago in ways that did not disturb traditional family arrangements. They also developed strategies to resist some arrangements. Some sought to change their husbands' view about work outside the home and created networks to help accomplish their goals. Others stopped working for wages, but continued con-

tributing as mothers, giving them influence and power within the family. In addition, some women remained active in income-generating activities, such as working in the family business. When husbands neglected their responsibilities as fathers, women took charge of the household, providing for their children and family.

Although middle-class women felt differently about work and family obligations, they also struggled over their roles as mothers and wives. They rejected traditional ideologies about women's roles and saw no conflict in doing both. Some husbands supported them, but when husbands resisted, they also negotiated the work and family responsibilities. Their class position afforded them options, such as staying home until they were ready to return to work, hiring help, postponing having children, and organizing their schedule around their children's schooling. This study has only begun to explore a very small slice of the Puerto Rican experience in Chicago, namely that of married working-class and middle-class women. Much empirical work needs to be done to fully understand how gender shapes the migration process for other groups of Puerto Rican women in different family arrangements and across class backgrounds.

Reading 17   Baseball Wives

Gender and the Work of Baseball

GEORGE GMELCH*   PATRICIA MARY SAN ANTONIO

This article focuses on how the structure and constraints of the occupation of professional baseball shapes the lives of the players' wives. The major constraints on the role of baseball wives include high geographical mobility, the husband's frequent absence, lack of a social support network, and the precariousness of baseball careers. Baseball wives are expected to fulfill a traditional role of support for their husbands and families. Baseball wives play a backstage supporting role but in so doing become far more independent and resourceful than many American women, managing families and households on their own.

Most of the writing on baseball has been written by men, for men, and about men (for example, Bosco 1989; Fireovid and Weingardner 1991; Golenbock 1991; Gooden and Woodley 1985; Jordan 1975; Ripken and Brian 1997). Most accounts of ballplayers' lives focus on their achievements on the field, with comparatively little attention given to life at home or to their wives and families.[1] The typical fan's image of players' wives—which comes primarily from televised glimpses of them in the stands—is that they are pretty, wear stylish clothes, and lead a life of privilege. "When people discover that I am married to a ballplayer they are usually im-

pressed," said Heather Gajkowski, wife of Seattle Mariner Steve Gajkowski.

> *They think it's glamorous and they ask a lot of questions about the life. Even when you tell them how hard it can be, how much the players are away from home or how little money you make in the minor leagues, they don't seem to get it.*

So, what is it like to be the partner of a man whose work is as all encompassing as professional baseball? This article looks at how the structure and

Authors' Note: We would like to thank Jean Ardell, Lynn Lovullo, Heather Gajkowski, Sharon Gmelch, and Bill Kirwin for their helpful comments on an earlier draft.

constraints of pro ball shape the lives of the players' wives. First, it examines the major constraints on the women, including high geographical mobility, the husband's frequent absence, lack of a social support network, and the precariousness of baseball careers. It then turns to what is expected of the wives and how their role impinges on their self-identity and career choices.

METHOD

The data for this study were collected over a six-year period between 1993 and 1999 as part of a larger research project on the culture and life cycle of professional baseball players. Formal, tape-recorded interviews were conducted with twenty-five wives from all levels of pro ball. In the sample, twelve women were married to men playing in the minor leagues, about half at the Class A level and the other half divided between Double A and Triple A farm clubs. Eight wives were married to major leaguers, and five were married to former players who were now coaching or managing (two in the major leagues and three in the minor leagues). The wives ranged in age from twenty to forty-three; half were younger than age thirty. Twenty-two were white, two were Hispanic, and one was African American. The sampling was opportunistic in that the names of prospective interviewees were gathered from players and front-office officials.[2] Often, they were merely asked which wives were likely to be present at the ballpark that night and if an interview could be arranged with one of them. It is likely that the more outgoing and articulate wives were often the first to be recommended. However, about half the women interviewed were simply individuals that we chanced upon in the stadium or near the family lounge (major league clubs provide a lounge for the players' wives and children). The responses to requests for an interview were excellent: only one wife declined. In addition, two interviews were conducted with the adult children of baseball families about their experiences growing up in a baseball household and their perceptions of the roles of their mothers.

An open-ended interview guide of a dozen items was used to get the interviews under way. Several of the opening "grand tour" questions were the following: "How is your life, being married to a ballplayer, different from the lives of the women you grew up with who aren't married to ballplayers?" "What have you found difficult about being a baseball wife?" "For you, what have been the benefits of being in professional baseball?" The interviews, which usually lasted from one hour to ninety minutes, were done at the ballpark and usually before the game. They were usually conducted in a secluded and quiet part of the stands and sometimes in or near the family lounge. All were done with the husbands absent to minimize the men's influence over what their wives might say. Some follow-up interviews were conducted over the telephone.

Overall, the women were cooperative and open; many were eager to talk about what the baseball life had meant for them. Big league wives in particular felt their lives had been overly glamorized by the press and that the public had little understanding of the liabilities that go with their position. But the most outspoken were often the wives of players who were still in the minor leagues. They were less concerned about the confidentiality of their remarks than were major league wives who had experience with the press. Many of the wives clearly enjoyed being interviewed, perhaps because it resembled the outside attention normally reserved for their player husbands.

MOBILITY

Mobility is the feature of pro ball that exerts the greatest influence on the wives and families of ballplayers. In the minor leagues, the men play in a different town almost every season. If they make it to the major leagues, trades and free agency make them almost as transient there. Because ballplayers rarely play in their hometowns, their wives and children must move every year, not once but several times. In March, some wives follow their husbands to Florida or Arizona for spring training; six weeks later, when spring camp breaks, they relocate to the city of the husband's team; and finally, when the season ends in September, they return to their hometown.[3] If their husbands play winter ball, they may move yet again, usually to the Caribbean or Latin America.

Every trade, promotion, or demotion during the season means an additional move. One baseball wife who had spent ten years in the minor leagues calculated that she had moved twenty-three times and lived in every region of the United States. "We could probably stop in any state in the country and know someone from baseball," she said. Jan Butterfield, wife of Arizona Diamondbacks coach Brian Butterfield, moved a dozen times in her first four years as a baseball wife.

When a husband is traded or moved within the organization, he gets a plane ticket and a ride to the airport. The player's wife is left with the burden of moving—disconnecting the utilities, closing the bank account, removing the kids from school or camp, and then reestablishing the household in a new locality. It is she who packs the household possessions, loads the U-haul, and transports the kids to the new town. In the words of Mary Jane Davis, who has been a baseball wife for thirteen years while her husband, Doug, first played for the Angels and Rangers and now manages in the Mets organization,

Moving is probably the toughest part, especially when you have little ones. When we didn't have any children, I made like, "Okay, this is a vacation. Let's go here and let's go there." But when you have children,

it's different. They're moving all over, making new friends and then they have to leave them. It gets a little tough on them. I used to be very structured, keeping a schedule book and all, but I've thrown that out the window because there is no way I can be like that anymore. You just go with the flow. There were times that Doug got called up to the majors. He'd have to leave the next morning at six, and here I was stuck with the apartment, the car, the kids, and the dogs. You're excited for him moving up but you are the one who has to pack everything up and drive down. I've lived or traveled in South America, Canada, and pretty much all of the United States. But you live out of a suitcase, and wherever you end up is usually not where your family is.... That's tough on the kids. They want to see Grandma.

Some wives do enjoy the travel, especially in the early years before they have children. As Mary Jane Davis said, "You get to see a lot of the world.... There are only a few states we haven't been in or lived in, and a lot of people can't even say that at the age of fifty or sixty." Yet, however exotic and exciting the travel may be at first, the appeal wears off for most wives. Moreover, the call to move usually comes without warning. Sharon Hargrove wrote about the frustration of a wife she knew who had just paid sixty-seven dollars for a phone jack, had cable television hooked up, opened a bank account and ordered checks when, after a mere ten days in town, her husband was reassigned (Hargrove and Costa 1989, 48). This instability—reassignments and trades being the main culprits—causes many baseball families to postpone buying homes and possessions. After nine years of marriage, Nancy Marshall said the only furniture she owned was a set of bunk beds, a television, and a rocking chair (Bouton and Marshall 1983, 85).

ABSENT HUSBANDS, BASEBALL WIDOWS

Because every team plays half of its games on the road, husbands are away often during the season. Inevitably, baseball wives spend a great deal of time alone; from April through September they are without husbands about half the time. Several of the women we interviewed jokingly referred to themselves not as baseball wives but as baseball widows. While on the road, the men are among teammates and companions; their wives are home alone. Most wives have no local friendships to depend on, nor do they typically belong to any groups in town. They are friendly with fellow baseball wives, but these relationships are seldom long-standing or deep, again due to their husbands' mobility. Even major league wives who have enjoyed a long tenure in one locality often do not have many local friends. "There are so many people out there who want to be around you just because of who you are, who your husband is, that you have to be wary," one Baltimore Oriole wife explained. Not surprisingly, wives frequently find themselves eating out or seeing a movie alone. Many of the young wives interviewed admitted to being lonely when their husbands were away. Chrissy Estrella, age twenty, had never been apart from her parents and siblings before marrying a ballplayer and moving from Port St. Lucie, Florida, to Pittsfield, Massachusetts, for her husband's first season. Other than the manager's wife, she was the only baseball spouse in town:

When he is on the road there is no-body, nobody to hang out with.

That's the hardest thing. I call my family [in Florida] and I cry to them, you know. When he was on the road this last trip I found myself sleeping all the time just to pass up the time. I think I gained five pounds because I didn't do my normal stuff. I don't know the gyms in this area like I do in Florida. I finally found a job [as a clerk in a Polo outlet store] because I was so bored and lonely.

Toward the end of the season, two members of the Pittsfield Mets Booster club tried to help out by telephoning Chrissy when the team was on the road and occasionally inviting her out. Talking to their husbands on the phone, of course, reduces the loneliness, but in the low minors many couples cannot afford the expense of frequent long-distance phone calls. Indeed, some couples run up huge phone bills before they realize it. Many wives listen to their husbands' road games on the radio primarily to make them feel closer to them and lessen the loneliness.

Young wives, who may be only a few years out of high school, are not just lonely but feel vulnerable and insecure being on their own. "Before the guys leave for a road trip you hear some of the wives talk in the stands about how scared they are to stay by themselves," said a veteran wife of ten seasons. "Some get nervous and will keep the lights on; some of them have alarm systems. Of course, there are others who aren't bothered one bit." Some wives mentioned times when they felt especially defenseless. Fran Kalafatis watched her husband and teammates board the team bus for a road trip in the Southern League as a hurricane approached, leaving her and the children in the parking lot to deal with the approaching storm. As the bus pulled away, the players yelled out warnings and instructions to their wives. In her memoir, Sharon Hargrove recounts two wives who were left alone in Kinston, North Carolina, to cope with a tornado watch. Having come from regions unaccustomed to severe weather, the women were clueless about what to do (Hargrove and Costa 1989). Several wives lamented about being alone while pregnant and not having their husbands at the hospital when they gave birth.

Even when the team is at home, husbands are not around the house much. Ballplayers may spend late mornings at home, but they typically leave for the ballpark by early afternoon, and by the time the game has ended and they have showered and changed, it is after eleven o'clock. Even then, many players like to go out to eat and unwind from the game before going home. In short, a player's schedule does not mesh well with the needs of a family. Children are in school when he is home in the mornings, and they are asleep by the time he arrives home at night. School summer vacations fall in the middle of the season, when the father is most occupied in the baseball world. Nor do the men have weekends free like most other workers. In fact, major leaguers have only about three days off per month (minor leaguers even less), which are often spent traveling. Even when they are home, the physical grind of the baseball schedule leaves husbands with little energy for family life. Referring to the groupies who pursue ballplayers, Waleska Williams, wife of Yankee centerfielder Bernie Williams, said,

> If the young women that have these fantasies about being with ballplayers really knew what it is like being married to one, they might not be so eager. They don't know that you don't have him around for half of every year, and that there are times you wish he were in some other profession so he would be home every night.

LEARNING INDEPENDENCE

The husband's absence means that his wife cares for the children by herself—supervising homework, preparing meals, setting standards, enforcing discipline—acting as both father and mother for much of the baseball year. Amused by the irony, Waleska Williams described how in the absence of her husband, it was she who taught their six-year-old son how to play baseball. "It's really like being a single parent," said another wife. Lynn Rigney Schott, the daughter of former player and manager Bill Rigney, recalled her mother's experiences:

> As I look back on what it must have been like for her, I realize it wasn't easy. She struggled with a lot of stuff. Even things like teaching her kids to drive.... They want dad not mom to do it. My mother had to do that with all three of us. My dad should have been the one teaching us to drive. It's a small thing, but it created a lot of tension and stress for her. When we'd get in trouble at school, the things that teenagers do.... I came home a couple of times in really deep water because I had told her a song and dance and she'd end up calling my dad in Detroit or somewhere because it's two in the morning and Lynn isn't home yet and she's worried sick. That's pretty crummy. It was hard for her to shoulder all that herself. And we weren't bad—just normal teenage stuff. It was real hard for her. If my Dad had been at home no way would I have stayed out till two in the morning.

What wives object to most is being left alone during holidays, birthdays, pregnancies, and special events in their children's lives, such as a toddler taking her first steps. "I want a normal life. I want to have cookouts with my kids in the summer and camping trips, do the things that normal people do," said one disgruntled wife. In the words of a mother of three,

> My husband has been gone on every one of my kids' first birthdays. My daughter played T-ball for the first time this summer and he missed that. It's funny, people think that because your husband is a coach that your kid is going to be a talent, but the truth is they aren't ever there to help the kids.

Lynn Rigney Schott remembers that the only real family vacation that she ever had as a child was the year her father was fired as the manager of the California Angels. For a few months, he was free to travel with his family.

With husbands away so much and the operation of the household and its decisions left to her, it is not surprising that the baseball life requires a wife to be independent. "There are things I never dreamed I would deal with that I have become comfortable with," said Jan Butterfield. Some of the things women learn to do for themselves are often reserved for men in more conventional households, such as repairing the car, fixing the plumbing, or disciplining the children. Explained Birmingham Barons manager Tony Franklin, "It takes a very independent woman to get by in baseball. It takes a woman that does not depend on you to make her life worthwhile. When you are not there, she can't be afraid to do things for herself." Former player and coach and now baseball analyst Tom House (1989) thinks that baseball wives grow up faster than their husbands do because they have to stay at home to "anchor" the relationship and deal with the real world while

their husbands are off living in a fantasy world. Some older wives said they now enjoy the independence their lifestyle fosters. Fran Kalafatis found that the time her husband was away encouraged her to develop new interests, which she now values. Danielle Gagnon Torrez (1983) finally came to view the time when her husband was gone as a "mini-vacation."

THE SUPPORTING ROLE

Clearly, the baseball wife's primary role is to support her husband and his career. Baseball careers are not only demanding; they are usually short—an average of just four years in the major leagues. Competition from other players, trades, injuries, and prolonged slumps can end a career at any time. Given this uncertainty, husbands and wives want to do everything to maximize his chances of success. To this end, husbands want to be able to focus on baseball, which means that wives are expected to shield husbands from distractions. So, wives arrange household and children's schedules to suit their husbands, and they screen phone calls and field requests for tickets. Mary Jane Davis tries to get her son involved in new activities to keep him occupied and prevent him from complaining and becoming unhappy, "and that helps him, which helps me, which helps my husband. It's like a chain reaction." "His job is baseball, mine is the home and the kids; I take over all household authority during the season," said Jan Butterfield. "I am both the mother and the father until September," explained Megan Donovan.

Most wives said they were expected not to trouble their husbands with domestic problems, except for crises, while the men were at the ballpark. While most wives of businessmen, doctors, and university professors have no qualms about calling their husbands at the office, it is nearly unthinkable for baseball wives to call their husbands at the clubhouse. The ballpark is sacrosanct. Beverly Crute (1981), who wrote her doctoral dissertation on the wives of professional athletes, quotes one baseball wife: "You just don't call at the ballpark unless they're [the children] on their deathbed or something. I mean, there are girls that have babies while their husbands are at the ballpark, and they don't call them" (p. 82). The enormous financial rewards for those who make it to the major leagues, and the brevity of the average career, justify in the minds of most wives the sacrifice required. Not surprisingly, most wives are deeply concerned with their husbands' performance, both for his sake and because it affects their joint fortune. "I'm very nervous when he pitches," said Heather Gajkowski,

> I can't sit still, I pace the stands or stand on the ramp just out of view so I barely see him. I am especially nervous if he isn't doing well. When he is on the road and I am listening to the game on the radio, I turn the volume down when he isn't pitching well.

When we asked one player how his wife felt about the burdens of being a baseball wife, he replied,

> Fine. That's what really attracted me to her, because I knew that she was going to stick by me one hundred percent. She knows I love the game and she's pretty much in it for me. That's what's great [about our relationship].

A wife supports her husband not just by listening to him talk about his performance and attending his home games but sometimes even participating in his superstitions. Wade Boggs's wife prepared chicken dishes for him every day for years. Megan Donovan reported that her husband insisted that she wash her hair each day he was to pitch. In her memoir, Danielle Torrez (1983) reported that one "rule" she learned as a baseball wife was

> to support your husband's superstitions, whether you believe in them or not. I joined the player's wives who ate ice cream in the sixth inning or tacos in the fifth, or who attended games in a pink sweater, a tan scarf, or a floppy hat. (p. 225)

THE UPSIDE

Baseball life is not completely burdensome, of course. Many wives say they feel fortunate to be able to go to the games and watch their husbands at work and that ballgames are usually enjoyable affairs. By providing free tickets, child care, family lounges, and special sections in the stands for wives and children, the teams encourage family attendance. Being at the games can strengthen a wife's identification with her husband's career. As Jan Butterfield said, "You become more involved and you can talk about it more with him because you are experiencing the moment with him. It creates a bond that might not exist otherwise." At the ballpark, wives also learn a lot about the business of baseball, which enables them to better handle the decisions made by the club about their husbands' careers. Being at the ballpark also exposes the wife to the fairly unique situation of seeing people cheer or jeer her husband's performance. The wives of teachers, dentists, or stockbrokers never experience anything remotely like it.[4]

LOOKING GOOD

Baseball wives and girlfriends are expected to look attractive, and most are. "Yes, the wives are usually very striking; you see one and you're like, 'Wow. She must belong to one of the players,'" said one public relations director. "They wear no numbers; they are not on any roster. But you can tell they are player's wives," writes baseball observer Jean Ardell, about wives at spring training games in Arizona.

> It isn't just the jewelry: the golden earrings, rings, and bracelets; a Rolex watch so dazzling with diamonds that you cannot see the time. Nor is it what you might call their daytime evening clothes: backless, strapless, silky numbers that set off their tans and two-carat diamonds. These women are as well kept and sleek as cats. They also possess a feline watchfulness, beyond that of even the most die-hard fan.... It is an unlikely sorority. Day after day, the women sit together, their only common interest being their baseball-playing husbands. (Ardell 1994, 365)

In the words of a San Francisco Giants official,

> When you see them all sitting together, it's like a fashion show. They don't come out to the ballpark like other folks, just to have a good time. They are here to watch their husbands play, but they also know they are being looked at and that they have to put their best foot forward. Their appearance is very important to them and to their husbands.

Such comments reveal another aspect of the role of the baseball wife—she is viewed in large measure as a player's property, part of the assets he brings to the game. When team public rela-

tions directors were asked about interviewing wives, they invariably said that the husbands should be asked for permission first. After doing so, I would then approach a wife, saying that we had spoken with her husband and that he said it would be all right to do an interview. Usually, that was good enough for the wife to consent.

At no time is looking good more important than during playoff or World Series games, when television cameras pan the wives' section and zoom in at different moments. Danielle Gagnon found the attention she received during the World Series, when her husband Mike Torrez was on the mound, to be a poignant reminder of the degree to which wives are seen as window dressing. She complained that press photos always showed her and the other wives with "glossy lipstick, white pompons, and continual smiles" (Torrez 1983, 7).

A wife's looks and behavior, some wives claimed, can even affect her husband's baseball career. "You're part of the package, and if you don't look the part, well, some are going to notice," said Sherry Fox. Fran Kalafatis remembers being told by veteran wives how a baseball wife was to act:

> It was the older wives that taught the new recruits that you were to dress up for the games and you were to look good. We wore pantyhose in Montgomery, Alabama when it was 99 degrees. It was insane when you look back on it. But you thought it might just make the difference between your husband being called up [to the big leagues] or not if you were presentable. These were the unwritten, unsaid thoughts among the wives.

To capitalize on the fans' fascination with baseball wives—on the wives' public relations value—some major league teams organize public appearances for the wives and involve them in charity work. Baltimore Oriole wives, for example, sponsor a yearly canned-food drive for local food banks. Canned goods are collected at the stadium during which the Oriole wives, each wearing an outsized jersey with her husband's name and number, staff the collection areas throughout the stadium. The charity drive reflects well on the wives and on the team. Fans, of course, are attracted to the promotion by the opportunity to see the wives up close.

STATUS AND IDENTITY

Baseball wives enjoy a measure of status by virtue of being married to professional ballplayers. When they are with their husbands in public, they also receive attention. Television cameras focus on them at games, they are asked to participate in community and charity events, and they may meet celebrities outside baseball. But their identities are always tied to their husbands. This holds true for the wives of many professional athletes (McKenzie 1999; Powers 1990; Thompson 1999). Marilyn Monroe aside, the baseball wife's identity is submerged under that of her husband. He is seen as the breadwinner, and if he is in the major leagues, he probably earns more in a year than she will in a lifetime. He is in the limelight; he is in demand. As Danielle Gagnon Torrez came to understand, her role outside the home was as an accessory (Torrez 1983). To the public, baseball wives are not known by their own names; rather, they are always Mrs. Roger Clemens, Mrs. Bernie Williams, and so forth. One wife, who is a high school teacher, resented that during the baseball season she simply became an extension of her husband. Others spoke of the irritation they felt when people would approach them in public and direct all their conversation and eye contact at their husbands, sometimes

never even acknowledging their presence. We came across an ironic illustration of this on the dust jacket of Sharon Hargrove's memoir *Safe at Home* (Hargrove and Costa 1989). Despite having written the book, in which she discusses the identities of baseball wives as ancillary to their husbands, the biographical blurb about the author on the dust jacket reads, "Sharon Hargrove is the wife of Mike Hargrove, formerly a big league baseball player and presently a minor league manager." Nothing else is said about the author, other than her having four children.

Mobility is partially to blame for the wives' dependent identity in that transience makes it next to impossible for women to pursue their own careers. Even those who have the credentials or degrees have difficulty finding work. "No one wants to hire you if you are only going to be in town for five months," said one wife with a social-work degree. Several wives talked of being unable to seriously plan careers of their own as long as their husbands were in baseball. The few wives that we met who had careers were schoolteachers. They stayed behind when their husbands went to spring training and for the early part of the season and then joined them during the long school summer vacation. Otherwise, most wives with career ambitions just had to put them on hold until their husbands retired from baseball. As Jessica Stockam put it, "We will start our life when he gets out of baseball." She meant that she could not begin a normal life until her husband's career was over and they could settle permanently in one place. She did not want him to leave baseball, and she was not unhappy being a baseball wife; she simply recognized that for all its benefits, there were certain things baseball did not allow. Above all, it does not offer the kind of stable life most American women expect.

Elinor Nauen, editor of an anthology of women writers on baseball, described the players' wives she came to know in the Eastern League: "Even the ones who had gone to college and weren't stupid had very much accepted that the important life in the family was his." Danielle Gagnon Torrez, who had to scale back her modeling career when she married Montreal Expos pitcher Mike Torrez, noted that it was unusual to meet a baseball wife who saw the need to have her own achievements apart from her husband's (Torrez 1983). One wife compared her marriage to a wheel in which her husband was the hub while she was merely one spoke, with the other spokes being his career, his education, and his other interests. Nancy Marshall writes to fellow wife Bobbie Bouton in their book *Home Games*,

> One of the things I think you and I did wrong from day one was to act like puppy dogs at our husbands' feet. They had all the success, all the glory, and the notoriety. It was only natural that we fell into the trap of idolizing them much as their fans do. (Bouton and Marshall 1983, 170)

It would be wrong, however, to claim that all wives feel this way. Marshall is looking back on her dozen years of marriage to a ballplayer. The discontent that she describes builds over time and is uncharacteristic of younger wives. Most of the wives that we got to know accepted their subservient role as temporary but necessary, and although they complained about the loneliness and the burdens they shouldered, few were eager to exchange it for a "normal" life.

Another dimension of the wife's dependency is that her status among the other baseball wives is influenced by her husband's status. In the major leagues, there is usually a loose pecking order among the wives in which their individual standing is swayed by their husband's salary, performance, and standing on the team. The wives of star players bask in the glow of their husbands' reflected fame, while wives of lesser players, no matter how talented the women themselves may be, enjoy less prestige. As one major league wife explained,

> Somebody who has been in the big leagues for a while might talk about stuff that is way over your head—you know, "Oh, I went to Bloomingdales today and I bought all this stuff and it's being delivered. Well it's very hard for someone who has just come up from Triple A to relate to spending that much money on shopping. But a lot, too, depends on the person's personality. It's not just money. Nolan Ryan's wife was the nicest person I ever met and she would talk to you even if you'd only been in the big leagues for two days.

Children confound the pecking order a bit in that wives caring for young children are often drawn to other wives with young kids, overriding other considerations. Team hierarchy also influences relationships in that the spouses of players and the spouses of coaches do not mingle much, even when they are of similar age. They may sit together at the ballpark but rarely do they fraternize on the outside, just as in the business world the wives of management do not socialize with the wives of workers. The anomaly in baseball is that the workers and their wives are usually much wealthier than the managers and their wives.

DEALING WITH UNCERTAINTY

Baseball wives probably contend with more uncertainty than do most American women. In addition to having to move without notice, an injury to her husband can suddenly end his career and their livelihood at any time. The vagaries of baseball performance in which bad times or slumps inevitably follow good times can make the baseball life an emotional roller coaster, and all of it is beyond the wife's control. About the uncertainty big league wives face, Tom House (1989) observed,

> One day you're the toast of the town, the next day you're invisible. That's the reality of it. It's an incredibly insecure existence, made tolerable by the false sense of security created by the success and fame. When those start to fade—or, even worse, when they're suddenly yanked away—both husband and wife go down together. (p. 59)

It is not much better for the wives and families of managers and coaches. Most are on annual contracts and have little job security. When ownership or general managers change, the new regime usually cleans house and brings in its own people. "It's always in the back of your head," said Mary Jane Davis, the wife of a Class A manager:

> It takes just one person to buy out the team or come in and take over and they'll want all their men to manage and coach. Hopefully another organization will pick you up, but you never know. You try not to look too far into the future with baseball because it's a crazy situation, you never know what is going to happen.

CONCERNS OVER GROUPIES

Wives may also worry about their husbands' faithfulness, especially while they are on the road.

Perhaps in all occupations where men travel and are away from home a good deal, there are concerns about infidelity. But many wives say the concerns are greater in baseball, where there is temptation in every town from groupies who pursue ballplayers. Cyndy Garvey, wife of former Dodger first baseman Steve Garvey, described her discovery of her husband's "little black book":

> I leafed through it. On the back page was a listing of National League cities. New York. Chicago. Cincinnati. St. Louis. And next to each city there was a woman's name and phone number. Some of the names had stars next to them. It was horrible. Too horrible. Too much of a bad cliche to be true. (Garvey 1989, 132)

While many players do not indulge in such relationships, groupies are successful often enough to make some wives uneasy about what their husbands do while away from home. One major league spouse reported this about wives sitting in the stands together:

> You can tell those who have close relationships with their husbands and aren't worrying from those who are paranoid, who aren't sure and are listening to his answering machine, going through his briefcase, and being nosy. Sometimes you just wonder if your own husband has the moral fiber to turn down the easy sex and good times.

Bouton and Marshall (1983) devoted an entire section to the groupie problem in their joint memoir. They describe three stages in the evolution of the baseball wife's concern about her husband's fidelity. In the first or "true believer" stage, the wife fully trusts her husband

and thinks that he is always faithful. Then, in the "knock on the head" stage, the evidence and suspicions of infidelity incrementally mount until finally, in the "realism" stage, the wife becomes fully aware that her husband sometimes sleeps with other women on the road. She is disillusioned but also realizes—perhaps rationalizes—that it really doesn't reflect on her, that the players' infidelities are really "entertainment" for the men while they are away.

Not all wives are so philosophical. Discovery of infidelity does sometimes lead to the breakup of the marriage, although probably much less often in baseball than in other professions. Beverly Crute (1981) found that some wives coped by excusing their husbands' behavior with "boys will be boys" or "what he does on the road is his business, what he does at home is my concern" (p. 124). Pete Rose's wife, Karolyn, declared to some of her husband's teammates, "I know Pete gets fucked on the road all the time: I say as long as he doesn't do it at home, I don't care" (House 1989, 59). Karolyn eventually tired of his extramarital escapades, however, and divorced him. Many players, of course, do not sleep around, although their wives may still wonder. Some players talked about making an effort to allay their wives' concerns. As one Oakland A's player put it,

> We go on a ten-day road trip and there are groupies out there looking for ballplayers in every city. My wife knows that. There's got to be a lot of trust in the marriage.... I call home every night and do things that try to make her [wife] at ease. Baseball wives should get a lot of respect for what they have to go through.

Overall, the wives have little choice but to accept the insecurity, although some said they tried to keep their husbands happy at home in the belief that a contented husband is less tempted to fool around.

BASEBALL WIVES AND THE GENDER ORDER

Recent writing on sports, and baseball in particular, has explored the role of sports in creating and maintaining gender hierarchy, which includes the notion of "hegemonic masculinity" (Burstyn 1999, Disch and Kane 2000, Trujillo 2000). Hegemonic masculinity refers to a culturally idealized set of masculine characteristics, such as aggression and competitiveness, and views the male body as privileged, celebrated, and connected to familial patriarchy, including male dominance over women and children (Trujillo 2000, 15). Media coverage of sports and the public consumption of this media, by glorifying the occupation of the male professional athlete, reinforces male privilege, gender differences, and the gendered division of labor (Burstyn 1999, Davis 1997, Trujillo 2000).

Many sports maintain male privilege largely through taboos on female participation. In baseball, women are consigned to auxiliary roles as wives and fans (Disch and Kane 2000) or, more disreputably, as groupies (Gmelch and San Antonio 1998; Voigt 1978). This female audience exaggerates and emphasizes the power of the male athlete (Disch and Kane 2000). Karlene Ferrante (1994), for example, writes that "baseball embodies a nostalgia for a pure and perfect experience of individual, masculine achievement, and that the sacredness of that ideal is protected against the mundane by the taboo against women [participants]" (p. 238).

These characteristics of baseball—male privilege and the relegation of women to auxiliary roles—would suggest that baseball wives have low status. But this is not the case, as we have seen throughout this article. Instead, the all-consuming nature of the men's work in baseball mitigates against the low status of wives. In her discussion of athletes' wives, Crute (1981), borrowing from Coser's (1974) work on "greedy institutions," refers to the encompassing nature of many professional sports, which demand their members' time, labor, and loyalty. Baseball players and coaches are a perfect example of this. So, in baseball families, it is the wives who during the baseball season rule the family and run the household, including single-handedly moving the family to new locations. While baseball culture idealizes masculinity and male dominance, it also idealizes images of home and family (Ferrante 1994; Trujillo 2000). Players and coaches need wives to have "homes." Wives provide companionship, stability, and emotional support off the field—all positive goods in the baseball world.

We think that male absence and the reliance of players on their wives to maintain the home lessen the male dominance fostered by baseball. There are many examples in the anthropological literature of patriarchal systems in which women have power in the domestic sphere because their men are away or otherwise occupied outside the home (e.g., Abu-Lughod 1993; Menon 1996; Rogers 1975, 1991; Sanday 1981; Sirman 1995). Men may have authority and receive deference from women, but women control important resources and make important decisions (Rogers 1975). Women's work may often be invisible, but it is no less important than men's work (Moore 1988).

CONCLUSION

Clearly, there are both significant rewards and costs to being the wife of a professional ballplayer. Baseball wives are fortunate to have the prestige and financial security if their husbands reach the major leagues, but they must also deal with isolation, heavy responsibility in daily life

and parenting, and the postponement of their own career plans. It is no wonder that some people refer to the baseball wife as "the fifth base," an anchor point outside of the field but bound to the game itself.

In conversations with players, we found that many seemed insensitive to or downplayed the considerable burdens their wives shouldered. Nor did we detect much of an effort by the players to lighten their wives' responsibilities, but that may be due to our reliance on interview data. Observation of daily life in baseball households might lead to a different conclusion. Yet, there is much that argues that players may really be somewhat indifferent. The ready availability of attractive women is clearly a factor. Groupies offering themselves to ballplayers may well increase the player's sense of self-importance (and sense of his attractiveness to women), which perhaps lessens his empathy for a spouse or girlfriend. Also, sociologist Gary Fine (1987) reported in his study of Little Leaguers, *With the Boys,* that from an early age the athletes come to see male dominance as the natural order of things. As youths, Fine says, athletes define their masculinity in terms of attributes that females lack, notably competitiveness and aggression, and they learn to avoid displaying feminine qualities, such as emotional expressiveness, nurturance, and compassion (Fine 1987). The latter are the very qualities that would make ballplayers more understanding and compassionate spouses.

Many baseball wives have no idea of what they are getting into when their courtships with ballplayers begin, whether they start in school or when the players are already in pro ball. In one respect, these baseball wives represent a traditional gender role, sacrificing for their husbands' careers, but in another sense, precisely because of this sacrifice, they become far more independent and resourceful than many American women, managing families and households on their own.

Part III

Generational Relationships

Part II of this reader was largely devoted to examining the marriage and family dynamics of gender relationships. We now shift our attention to readings that study relationships between family members of different ages.

All human societies are differentiated on the basis of age and sex. Throughout history, the social roles of men and women have been separate, as have the roles of children, adults, and the aged. The family is composed of members of various ages who are differentially related. Most sociological accounts of the family have emphasized how age differentiation of family members enhances their solidarity. The interdependence of family members has been seen to foster emotional attachments, structural solidarity, and family cohesion. Yet, inherent in this differential age structure is the potential for conflict and tension.

Differential age structures have always been linked to status discrepancies in power, privilege, and prestige. Just as a power dimension is often articulated in gender relationships, families can be viewed in terms of hierarchical social structures in which older generations or older siblings hold positions of power, authority, and prestige over their younger counterparts. There are various degrees of family stratification by age. But the universal tendency is for the elders to exercise control over younger family members.

The readings contained in the two chapters that make up this part of the book will examine how families define sets of people according to age. These age categories influence family members' relations to one another. Distinguishing family members by age also has implications for the conceptualization of persons placed in particular age groups. The conceptualizations of childhood and adolescence, adulthood, and the aged reflect conceptualizations of the family, and they should be seen in terms of cultural diversity and social-historical context.

Philippe Ariès in his classic study, *Centuries of Childhood: A Social History of the Family* (1962), put forth the striking theme that Western ideas about childhood and family life have changed and developed from the Middle Ages to modern times. Ariès sought to document how in medieval life the child was integrated into the community. It was not until the development of bourgeois capitalist society that the segregation of children occurred. He argued that, in the earlier period, children were treated as small adults. As soon as they were capable of being without their mothers, children interacted in the adult world, sharing the same world of work and play. By the age of seven or eight, they were treated as if they had the same mental capacities for understanding and feeling as their adult counterparts.

The lack of awareness of the particular nature of childhood and the full participation of children in adult life is associated with the nature of the family and the community. Ariès depicted the medieval community as intense; no one was left alone because the high density of social life made isolation virtually impossible. This sociability practically nullified the reality and the conceptualization of the private home and the private family. The distinct sense of privacy so characteristic of modern-day families was absent.

Ariès saw the transition to the modern conceptualization of the child beginning to emerge during the seventeenth century. Economic changes led to a revival of interest in education. This, in turn, introduced the idea that a period of special preparation was necessary before individuals could assume their place as adults. Children began to be treated differently, they were expected to behave differently, and their nature was viewed as being different. Children were now coddled, and a greater interest and concern for their moral welfare and development became common.

Ariès emphasized that this emerging concept of childhood developed and was given expression in the emergence of the bourgeois family. He argued that, from a relatively insignificant institution during the Middle Ages, there developed a growing belief in the virtue of the intimate and private nuclear family. The rise of the private family and the growth of the sentimental bonds among its members consequently came about at the expense of the public community.

The continued inward development of the family and its creation of a private sphere of life removed from the outside world was intertwined with the increased importance given to children. The outside community came to be viewed with suspicion and indifference. Proceeding into the industrial era, the family began to withdraw its nonproductive members, women and children, from involvement with the surrounding community. The increased division of labor of family members and the consequent isolation of women and children within the home resulted.

Here again, the broad historical survey of Western patterns of parenthood and child-rearing needs to be modified through an examination of the experiences of racial ethnic families in the United States. In Chapter Six, "Patterns of Parenthood, Childhood, and Adolescence," Patricia Hill Collins (Reading 19) does just that. Collins observes that motherhood must be seen both in its historical context and in the context of the interlocking structures of race, class, and gender. Collins argues that the feminist perspective has often failed to recognize the diversity of patterns of motherhood. It takes the experience of white, middle-class women as universal. This has led to two fundamental assumptions on motherhood that are erroneous. The first is the belief that work and family have always been separate spheres.

The second relates to women's identity conceptualizations as seeing themselves in search of personal autonomy. Let's briefly summarize Collins's line of thought here.

The "separate spheres" doctrine relegated women to household work characterized by childbearing, child rearing, and domestic labor, or "reproductive work." This model was based on patriarchal authority in which men's economic activities allowed them to control the family. Women, while having few legal rights, were protected under the umbrella of patriarchy in their designated roles as wives, mothers, and daughters. This model was essentially the pattern prevalent among white middle-class women. Collins observes that the circumstances of racial ethnic women were quite different.

Similarly, women of color were concerned with working for the physical survival of themselves, their children, and their community. Motherhood was not centered on the search for personal autonomy (as with their white middle-class counterparts) but with helping to teach their children how to construct their individual and collective racial identity to help them survive in an often hostile cultural climate. Collins's social-historical analysis of Native American, African American, Hispanic, and Asian American patterns of motherhood demonstrates the necessity for the recontextualization of motherhood from multiple perspectives. This is what she means by the title of her essay "Shifting the Center."

Elaine Bell Kaplan (Reading 20) examines the relationship between Black teenage mothers and their mothers. She reports in her study of twenty-two teenage mothers that they felt that their mothers did not support them emotionally. Their mothers, in turn, concurred in this belief. They felt that their daughters' early motherhood reflected badly on them and threatened their held moral values. In this essay we are shown, once again, how relational problems must be seen through linking socioeconomic conditions with gender, race, and class inequalities.

Valerie Mannis (Reading 18) further extends our understanding of parenthood as a social and cultural as well as a biological phenomena by studying women who have chosen to become single mothers. These women have educated backgrounds and are financially independent. They have support networks that are composed of family, friends, employers, clergy, physicians, and in some cases a foreign adoption agency. Their experience reflects the demographic changes in the family that allows them to make their nontraditional choice possible.

Just as societal conditions have allowed for the emergence of new forms of motherhood, they have also shaped the articulation of the role of fatherhood. Ralph LaRossa and his colleagues (Reading 21) examine the changing culture of parenthood in the last 60 years of the twentieth century. Their data source, is quite innovative. They conducted a content analysis of Father's Day and Mother's Day comic strips from 1940 to 1999. They reported that the culture of fatherhood has fluctuated over that time span. During this time period there were periods when "incompetent" fathers were depicted, in other periods fathers were mocked, and in still other periods fathers were seen as nurturant and supportive toward children. The authors investigated what were the crucial factors during these different time periods that accounted for the differential depiction of fatherhood.

Chapter Seven, "The Family and the Elderly," is concerned with the nature of generational relationships between the elderly and the family. Earlier, we commented that the universal tendency has been for elders to exercise control over younger family members. Indeed in more traditional societies that are less susceptible to social change, the elderly have been seen as the repositories of strategic knowledge and religious custom, controlling the ownership of property, and having major influence over kinship and extended family rights and obligations. But, with the movement toward modernization, individualism, and the private family there has been a significant decline in the influence, power, and prestige that the elderly have in the family. The elderly have relatively little importance in an industrial society that emphasizes individual welfare, social and economic progress and change, and that is opposed to the ideology of family continuity and tradition.

Karen Pyke (Reading 23) picks up on this theme through her examination of the ways that children of Korean and Vietnamese immigrants describe growing up in their families and their plans for filial care. The care that they plan for their parents when they get older is based on a perceived favorable societal view on the close family ties associated with Asian immigrants. This runs somewhat counter to their own experiences of Asian parents as being overly strict, emotionally distant and deficient as compared to the image of the "Normal American Family." Yet, the positive descriptions of their families generated by American culture helps shape the desires, disappointments, and subjective realties of children of immigrant minorities.

The significant decline in the mortality rate, especially in the last decades of the twentieth century, has fundamentally changed the character of the relationship between elders and their mature children, grandchildren, and great-grandchildren. This decline has given contemporary grandparenthood (the children of the elders) new meaning associated with the rise of the four-generation family. This demographic change has greatly increased the potential for family interaction across more than two generations.

The relationships between members of these different generations can be quite problematic. Some of the difficulty stems from the fact that the great-grandparent generation is composed of old people whom society views as residuals and somewhat useless. Our society has deprived old people both of responsibility and of function. By so doing, it has provided the basis for the roleless position of the elderly.

Often the one place that old people can find refuge and have a role is within the family. Yet that role is not clearly defined, and often the great-grandparent generation is found to strain the emotional as well as economic resources of their children in the family. Particularly caught in the middle is this grandparent generation. Known in the popular literature as the "sandwich generation," they are sandwiched between their children and their parents, both of whom need care. They often are asked to assist their children as they enter early adulthood and married and family life, while at the same time they are expected to care for their aged parents. People in this sandwich generation are experiencing stresses associated with their own stage in life and the family life cycle. Many are contemplating their own aging as they face retirement and perhaps their own financial and health problems. This generation has the brunt of generational responsibility thrust on it.

Women within the sandwich generation are the ones who often take on a disproportionate share of the time and emotional involvement with their elderly parents. For many of them, the "mommy track" is being replaced by the "daughter track." The shift is from balancing work, career, and child rearing to balancing work, career, and elder-caring. Indeed, these women are often working mothers and caretakers. They provide both for their parents and for their children while often holding down a full-time job.

However, what happens to the elderly when their adult children cannot take care of them and when they no longer can take care of themselves? This is the concern of Reading 22. The editor of this anthology, Mark Hutter, reports on a family situation when this occurs. His analysis goes beyond the examination of the relationship of adult children and their parents to an examination of the web of relationships that emerge when a paid health care worker—the "intimate stranger"—enters the picture.

REFERENCES

Ariès, Philippe. 1962. *Centuries of Childhood: A Social History of the Family.* New York: Knopf.

6 | Patterns of Parenthood, Childhood, and Adolescence

Reading 18   Single Mothers by Choice

VALERIE S. MANNIS*

This study used in-depth qualitative interviews with ten women who chose to become single mothers to describe multiple individual and social contextual factors that women felt made their nontraditional choice possible. A grounded theory analysis revealed that for this sample of educated, financially autonomous women, single motherhood was chosen with support from family, friends, employers, clergy, physicians, and sometimes the foreign adoption industry. These results give a new face and voice to the single mother, expanding our understanding of postmodern families.

Single-mother households constitute a significant part of the contemporary American family profile. In 1970, homes maintained by a mother with children under 18 made up 12% of the U.S. total. Single-mother homes rose to 19% in 1980, to 24% in 1990, and to 26% in 1995. Nonmarital births have increased in all age groups from 15 to over 35 years of age. In 1970, 10.7% of all births were to unmarried women; by 1993, this had grown to 31%. By 1994, 37.8% of all births were to unmarried women; of these, 20.6% were births to unmarried women between the ages of 30 and 44 years (U.S. Bureau of Census, 1996).

This demographic change in the American family has been met with different responses.

Some scholars take a pessimistic view seeing the family in decline, the father vanishing from the lives of children, the loss of traditional values, and a breakdown of the social order (Blankenthorn, 1995; Popenoe, 1993). Others hold a postmodern view suggesting families are not declining but changing, with new family configurations emerging to cope with new work and social patterns (Stacey, 1993, 1996). Some emphasize that women's choices are influenced by economic forces (Gerson, 1985) and by men's changing attitudes and commitment to family life (Gerson, 1993, 1997).

Researchers do not agree on the reasons for widespread, nonmarital births. Many believe

*Mannis, Valerie S. "Single Mothers by Choice." *Family Relations, 1999, 48,* pp. 121–128. Copyright 1999 by the National Council on Family Relations, 3989 Central Ave. NE, Suite 550, Minneapolis, MN 55421. Reprinted by permission.

that mother-only families result from a breakdown of a stable family or death of the father. In academia, the bias that single-mother families are a misfortune rather than a choice remains (Miller, 1992). This concentration on the negative does not sufficiently incorporate an understanding of the variance in this population group. A notable exception to this approach is Burns and Scott's (1994) study describing and explaining the increase in single mothering worldwide. This was not, however, an ethnographic study that would allow us to hear from single mothers in their own voice.

Though divided in interpretation of the trends, little disagreement has been voiced that change is occurring (Stacey, 1993; Glenn, 1993; Cowan, 1993; Popenoe, 1993). Single mothers in the United States and worldwide represent an ever-growing proportion of the adult population (U.S. Bureau of Census, 1996), and the proportion of mothers who are single is growing across all socioeconomic groups (Thompson & Gongla, 1983).

While there is slow but growing acceptance of single mothers in the popular press (e.g., Leslie, 1994; Ludtke, 1997) and some self-help efforts have surfaced to even encourage this family form (Mattes, 1994; Saffron, 1994), most scholarly research and public policy continues to focus on negative aspects of single mothering. Concern is justifiable considering the disproportionate levels of poverty found in mother-headed families, their social consequences, and their intersection with race, class, and gender inequities (Foster, Jones, & Hoffman, 1998; Garfinkel & McLanahan, 1986; McLanahan & Booth, 1989; McLanahan & Sandefur, 1994; Polokow, 1993).

Taking a lifecourse approach enriched by a feminist perspective, this study focused on a subgroup of single mothers that has not received much scholarly attention: financially independent, adult women who are single mothers by choice. Using in-depth, qualitative interviews and grounded theory analysis, this study sought to elucidate the process whereby some women make this still unconventional choice and the factors that were perceived to be supportive and problematic in making such decisions.

In order to isolate agency, this project was deliberately narrowed to women who had the financial autonomy to consider mothering alone without the help of a partner and the education and maturity to seek lone mothering through a variety of means, including adoption and artificial insemination. Rejecting a focus on the youth, race, poverty, and negative social context of single mothers as well as the assumption that these women have few avenues of choice, a challenge in this project was to recognize, as agency, the very acts of women that dominant discourse might label deviancy or carelessness or morally questionable. This snapshot explores the capacity for autonomous action that these particular women had at this particular time in their lives.

CONCEPTUAL FRAMEWORK

The lifecourse perspective suggests a dynamic and interdisciplinary approach to the study of the family. It moves "…beyond a static view of development to a focus on process itself. The cumulative nature of experience is revealed; the past bears upon the present, and together, they stake a claim on the future" (Allen & Pickett, 1987, p. 518). According to this perspective individuals exert agency by selecting, ignoring, and modifying socializing influences. This perspective suggests that development arises out of many contextual influences: biological, psychological, social, historical, and evolutionary factors (Featherman, 1983).

Single mothering by choice may be one concrete instance of women's demonstration of agency in development. Demographics and social institutions change over time; the individual adapts and her developmental outcomes are shaped by these changes. Changes in adoption laws, expansion of medical technologies, and greater cultural acceptance of diversity of family forms are but a few examples of an evolving environment that might facilitate a woman's family choices. The lifecourse perspective envisions adults who are self-directed within an ever-changing environment (Bengsten & Allen, 1993).

As the stories of the mothers in this study unfold, the impact of their individual past on their choices emerges. Their choices may be influenced by their relationship with their own mothers and fathers or their experience in their family of origin. Life-course theory moves from a focus on normative stages to a focus on individual and family variations (Allen, 1989). The research reported here reveals a broader and more accepting view of this family form than is found in most of the existing literature with only recent notable exceptions (Hertz & Ferguson, 1997; Ludtke, 1997; Stacey; 1990).

Most social institutions operate as if the traditional heterosexual, married, two-parent family is the only family form. This places burdens and stigma on nontraditional families. The dominant view supports the traditional family as ideal and the norm against which other families are compared. Other family structures are viewed as deficit models (Rice, 1994).

Feminism views contemporary women as generally oppressed, excluded, exploited, and devalued by society, although individual women may thrive within the current social framework. Feminists critique dominant intellectual traditions and, in doing so, challenge the status quo. As noted previously, research has largely tended to emphasize negative aspects of the single-mother phenomenon. By contrast, this research adopted feminist assumptions that include the normality and value of women's varied experience and a focus on the female standpoint in that experience. Feminists generally deny a universal or single ideal of the family. Most importantly feminists

provide new ways of seeing and suggest ways to rethink our assumptions, "...especially about issues of gender, power, and the very nature and boundaries of 'family'." (Osmond & Thorne, 1993, p. 591).

From a feminist perspective, denying the validity of and ignoring the existence of an alternative family form, like that of single mothers by choice, marginalizes women's agency. It does so by refusing to acknowledge that a choice to parent could be made without centralizing a sexual relationship (Fineman, 1995). This study rejected this "normative" family form and considered a single-mother family form variant legitimate, to be understood in its own terms, and not in deficit contrast to any other family form.

PREVIOUS RESEARCH

The limited research on single mothers by choice (Linn, 1991; Pakitzegi, 1990; Potter & Knaub, 1988) includes a small number of studies that seek a better understanding of women who choose to mother alone and who do so for positive reasons (Anderson & Stewart, 1994; Hertz & Ferguson, 1997; Linn, 1991; McCartney, 1985; Miller, 1992; Pakitzegi, 1990; Potter & Knaub, 1988). Often these are women who have financial power, education, social and family support, and a strong, long-standing desire to mother. They build their own families without husbands or significant others and without a plan or expectation that they will ever have a co-parent.

Earlier studies do not confront the issue of choice directly but instead consider related issues. Studies examine artificial insemination and the single woman (McCartney, 1985; McGuire & Alexander, 1995). Studies deal with coping strategies, the relationship with the child and biological father, and difficulties with society and implications for social support (Anderson & Stewart, 1994; McKaughan, 1987; Merritt & Steiner, 1984; Renovise, 1985). More recent studies address single-mother adoption and special needs adoption of children who are older, medically disabled, or bi-racial. Women are responsible for an increase in single parent adoptions, and special needs adoptions play a role in this increase, as does international adoption, which has increased 62% worldwide in the past decade (Groze, 1991; Kane, 1993).

Ward (1983) interviewed two groups who had made nontraditional childbearing choices: women who had elected to have a child as a single mother and married women who elected to remain child-free. She found the women perceived themselves as special and had received the message as youngsters that unconventional choices were acceptable. These respondents were reared in traditional homes with dominant fathers and passive, caretaking mothers. They saw their mothers as victims and decided early in life to take more personal control over their lives.

Kornfein's (1985) longitudinal study compared "intact" families with elective, single-mother families. Using a deficit perspective, Kornfein explored how single-mother families "cope" with "fatherlessness" and emphasized the negative, social contexts in which the mother's choice was made (e.g., "the marriage squeeze" created by fewer eligible men, poor marriages in the mothers' families of origin, hurtful relationships with their own fathers, Lesbian circumstances). Kornfein documents women's agency as expressed within women's life constraints, but theorizes in a dominant discourse. This problematizes single motherhood and so fails to account for and truly consider these acts as personal choices.

Only a few researchers have begun with the assumption that women can and do make the choice to mother alone. Hertz and Ferguson (1997) report on creative kinship strategies and self sufficiency among women who chose to be mothers as unmarried women. They focus on ways that single mothers manage their families and increase their "mother-time" using friends, family, and community resources.

METHODS

Qualitative Research and Grounded Theory

In-depth, open-ended interviews were used to generate the story of a critical time of parenting choice in a woman's life. The story, the manner in which she told it, and its relation to the stories of other mothers and to the larger society were then examined. Analysis of the data was done with an awareness of the socially constructed nature of the research, the impact of the researcher on the work (Bertaux, 1981), and with an emphasis on the diversity and complexity of the lives described.

Postmodern scholarship recognizes multiple sites from which to know the world (Lather, 1991). This study sought to understand from the point of view of the mothers; it sought to construct knowledge by reflecting on their unique experiences; it abandoned an either/or mode of thinking, considering that while a person's life story and actions may hold contradictions that does not eliminate an expression of choice and autonomy that enriches life.

Participants

Potential participants were recruited through a combination of networking and active solicitation. A screening instrument was used to limit the sample to: (a) women who began raising their child without a live-in partner or a plan or expectation she would have a co-parent; (b) women who continued to live without a sexual partner in the household; (c) women who began mothering at age 21 or older; (d) women who were financially independent at conception, never received public assistance, and remained financially independent; and (e) women who made the choice to be a single mother within the last five years.

Ten mothers who first chose to become single mothers in their late 30s and early 40s were selected to participate in the study. All participants were White. All but one of the participants had college degrees. Incomes reflected participants' education with five earning over $50,000 annually, and one mother earning under $25,000 annually. Nine participants came from large families; one had a single sibling. Participants came from small, mid-sized, and large communities; two grew up on farms.

Five participants had been married and divorced before going forward with the pregnancy or adoption; five had never married. Two had abortions in the past. Seven participants had children age 5 years; three participants had children ages 9, 10, and 12 years. Six participants had their child by natural childbirth; four adopted children. Five children were White, four children were Chinese, and one child was bi-racial.

Procedure

Participants were interviewed once for one to three hours, each choosing the interview setting. Six interviews took place in the participant's home, three in the interviewer's office, and one in the participant's office. The interview schedule, consisting of open-ended questions and probes, covered: (a) The decision-making process, including reactions of friends and family; (b) the resources and supports available to the participant as she was making her decision; (c) the woman's memory of her own experience of being parented by mother and father; (d) a description of models or events that may have influenced her decision; (e) her attitude toward men; and (f) her attitude toward the experience. At the close of each interview the participant completed a brief personal history data sheet.

Interviews were taped and an interpretive summary of each was written within twenty-four hours which included documenting the interviewer's personal impressions (Briggs, 1992), the tone and mood of the meeting, and any other reflections (Richardson, 1994). Verbatim transcription of tapes were created including stuttering, uhs, and ums (Atkinson, 1992) and thus providing three "texts" to analyze (Wolcott, 1994).

Coding Transcriptions and Conditional Matrix

Transcriptions were coded and analyzed using grounded theory (Strauss & Corbin, 1990; Rubin & Rubin, 1995) and the development of a Coding Key (Farnesworth & Allen, 1996). Initially, transcripts were open coded. Open coding is a line-by-line analysis in which word and sentence fragments are selected and noted. Each interview produced a large list of codes which were then sifted into the four main categories that emerged: (a) Themes; (b) Concepts; (c) Events; and (d) Stages.

Working with fragments, words, and conceptual ideas eventually led to the creation of larger categories that began to cluster around some theme or category. This created the axial coding categories. "Axial coding puts those data back together in new ways by *making connections between a category and its subcategories.*" (Strauss & Corbin, 1990, p. 97). It was at the point of developing axial codes that comparisons were made within each person's transcript, within each category, and across all transcripts (Rubin & Rubin, 1995).

By drawing upon the axial coding categories, a conditional matrix was constructed (Strauss & Corbin, 1990) to illustrate the myriad influences on these women who wanted to be mothers without the plan or expectation that they would have a co-parent. Creating this matrix was guided by lifecourse and feminist theories which suggest the importance of the larger context on human behavior and development.

The conditional matrix was a useful tool to provide an overview of a large body of data, and an effective means of developing initial generalizations from the data. Working with this rough schematic of influences, selective coding was used to determine which core categories or central phenomena to focus on and how to relate them to other categories (Strauss & Corbin, 1990). Selective coding produced 11 major codes and 31 subcodes.

Each interview was coded before going on to the next interview. By the eighth interview, response patterns were clear. The final two interviews were used as confirmation and to focus sharply on the themes, concepts, and processes that had emerged in earlier interviews. Saturation of knowledge was achieved with ten interviews (Bertaux, 1981; Farnesworth & Allen, 1996).

RESULTS AND DISCUSSION

Textual Analysis

Four categories of textual analysis were identified: Themes, Concepts, Events, and Stages.

Five major Themes emerged in the textual analysis. The *desire to nurture* was an overarching theme. The theme of *social support* included family, friends, and workplace considerations. The theme of the mother's *attitude or mind set* considered whether she had a "can do" attitude with a sense of empowerment or an "it's tough" attitude with worries about the child's development and the time pressures. It was not unusual to find complex and even contradictory attitudes. The *love experience* theme concerned the unconditional exchange of love the mothers expressed with the child, and the *racial self-consciousness* theme sometimes accompanied interracial mothering and adoption.

Four major Concepts, defined as abstract ideas generalized from particular instances, were shared by the participants. *Financial au-* *tonomy* was an integrating concept. It tied many concepts together and created the particular type of experience related by the participant (Rubin & Rubin, 1995). The sense of the woman's *time running out* included both biological and sociological clocks. The biological clock was the awareness that soon the participant would no longer be capable of conception or birth without increasing risk. The sociological clock was the awareness that people in her life noticed that she may never have children and that these people could interfere with her efforts to become a mother or may disapprove of her. Textual analysis manifested two major concepts that clustered around contextual influences: *family of origin influence* and *cultural influence.* A constellation of influences clustered around cultural influence and included the impact of community stereotyping of single mothers, the participant's sense of what womanhood means, and the positive or negative global/media/community reactions.

Events, the third category of textual analysis, included *abortion, change in relationships* (e.g., breaking up with a boyfriend), and *pregnancy.* Finally, the fourth category, Stages, encompassed patterns that could be described as a series of positions or stations. These included the *decision-making process,* the *pregnancy* itself, and the *adoption experience.*

Findings

The social contextual influences on women's decisions to mother alone were wide ranging—from her most personal experience in her home of origin to international political forces that provided transnational opportunities for her to adopt a child. In between, changing social mores, expanding reproductive technologies, and even the influence of the media upon her understanding of her options all played a role in shaping her choices.

What made agency possible for this single mother? The lifecourse perspective suggests that it is important to consider the intersection of individual biography and history when attempting to understand human development and behavior (Featherman, 1983). The women of this study became mothers between the ages of 37 and 45 with five of them 37 when their child was born or adopted. They came of age in the 1970s, a time of great social change for women. In some ways, the personal choices of this cohort facilitated major changes in society launched in the 1970s. The feminist movement of the 1970s with its drive for equal rights and full feminist expression created an atmosphere encouraging women to see themselves as agents in their own destiny who were capable of assessing their own needs, putting demands on government and social institutions, and effecting change. Pamela had a complex and intellectualized response to the impact of social changes and cultural influences on her decision to adopt a child alone.

I think the social changes...of the last couple of decades...and the history that led up to them, made it possible for me to do it. I mean I have the job, I have the income, and even though I don't know any other single mothers who've done this...I knew of them — but I don't know them per-sonally so they don't have a personal influence on me. But just knowing that they're out there in a sense makes it feasible. So I think those changes have made it feasible — but in a sense they've also made it nec-essary because in an earlier age I would have married one of my early boyfriends and had children when neither of us would have had fertility problems because we would have been young...So it's kind of a mixed ...thing. I mean it's made it possible but it's also part of how I ended up

single and...affluent in sort of late middle age. So, [sigh]...which is better?...I don't know...(Pamela)

Two behaviors significant in effecting social change (Gerson, 1985) are relevant here: work-force involvement and fertility decisions. Most of these women showed a significant attachment to the workforce and delayed fertility years beyond earlier cohorts. Nine were college edu-cated with eight having advanced degrees. They were, however, not invulnerable. Serious, pro-longed illness or loss of a job could thrust most of them into acute financial straits.

...I find the responsibility daunting ...she has only me in a sense to pro-tect her and to make sure she gets taken care of and that's a lot of re-sponsibility for one person. And I get very tired of having to make sure that there's something to eat for dinner every night! (Pamela)

All participants had experienced mature rela-tionships with men in the past, but none felt mar-riage was likely for them at the time they made their decision to become single mothers. All were sexually active, benefitting from a variety of birth control devices. These women reflected the wide-spread acceptance of sexual expression outside of marriage that has been part of the social fabric for over twenty years. Two women had had abor-tions. All identified themselves as Christian, with only one saying she was not active in church. They grew up in diverse settings ranging from rural communities to large urban areas. All but one of these women came from large families who were supportive of their status of unmarried motherhood, but also traditional in their alle-giance to the importance and primacy of family.

What lifecourse influences bear on her de-cision? The lifecourse perspective encourages consideration of cumulative life histories and of individual and family variations across the life span. These participants were influenced by changing and emerging social institutions and patterns, such as expanded workplace opportunities, fluid or serial intimate relationship patterns, and feminist ideas. However, they also retained significant memories of nurturance in their own past which usually included more traditional families of origin. They wanted to repeat their early family experience with a child of their own.

The *desire to nurture* was the overarching theme found in this study. Across all interviews and across all categories, the desire to nurture is heard plainly; it is never absent. Mothers expressed their desire to nurture over and over again in a variety of ways. "I always wanted to be a mother" was repeated time and time again. They described falling in love with the child and the satisfaction that comes with unconditional exchange of love. Several spoke of the joys of pregnancy and birthing and also of the unique companionship of a family of two.

I always wanted to be a parent and, and I, um, I always assumed I would get married and have lots of children but um, I dated men who never wanted to make a commitment of any kind and when I was let's see, I was thirty-nine years old and I read an article in "Ladies Home Journal" about all the abandoned children in China and that China lets single women adopt and it just seemed like the right decision and I read the article on a Sunday afternoon and by Tuesday had contacted a social worker and started the process immediately. My first appointment was December of 1994 and by May of '95, five months later, I was on an air-

plane going to China, so it all went very quickly. (Cara)

In her decision to mother alone, Cara was influenced by the media attention to children in China. She was also influenced by authority figures closer to home.

My pastor who's married and has two adopted children from Paraguay and whenever I played with her children and she said, "You have to adopt a baby." And I said, "No, you have to have two parents." I said, "Single women can't adopt babies and I said I just can't handle it what would I do?" [And when was this that you said that?] Long before I ever read that article...And then I was just reading the article I just, instantly decided I guess, that I, that I could do it. (Cara)

The women spoke of social support for their long-standing desire to mother. Some were encouraged by family and friends to have a child when no partner was forthcoming. Some used books and periodicals for ideas and practical advice; some referred to film and television examples as shorthand means to describe their actions; some were encouraged by physicians. Some received more support than they expected. Mandy adopted a child and was surprised at her friends' reaction.

I guess going in I thought I was going to be pretty much on my own. I didn't know it was going to be such a popular decision for me. My friends were extremely supportive and excited. They were just tremendous, always calling, asking where I'm in the process, did I need any-

thing, um, did, do I need character references, etc. (Mandy)

Kenna decided to go forward with an unplanned pregnancy after doing a formal cost/benefit analysis. A professional in a demanding field, she needed to consider how she would handle the responsibility. Like others in the study, she didn't want to involve the father so he wasn't part of her decision-making. Instead she talked with friends and a therapist.

My friends' reactions were all pretty supportive and not shocked or that kind of thing. I remember at one point talking with one friend about you know this is what I'd do if this happens and if that happens and she said, "What if you had to go into the hospital for two weeks?" And I thought through all the supports I had in place and so, that can't happen, I just can't have it, I can't allow that to happen. And in fact I have, have been fortunate with the health [mumbled], knock on wood. (Kenna)

What was her context, her standpoint? What were her alternatives? Most of the women examined all avenues to becoming mothers. Some tried, for years, to adopt or attempted pregnancy through artificial insemination by donor. Tonia conceived a child with someone she knew who was not living in the area and was not involved in parenting. She knew she would be parenting alone. She says she is not simply rationalizing an unexpected pregnancy. She thought about becoming a mother alone for years.

I had tried to adopt for a while, too. I mean this wasn't...ya know: getting pregnant wasn't my first option. I'd tried. I thought about foster care

and then I thought no, I don't want to be just a kind of a sometime mom. I tried to adopt and because I was single and White, it was almost impossible to find, to get me a child ...I couldn't afford a fifteen or twenty thousand dollar foreign adoption. I started looking at adoption when I was probably thirty, thirty-one. I spent about four or five years. I spent at least two years and maybe three years in eligibility for adoption. I spent a year just going through all the training and getting ready to adopt. Spent a couple of years working in foster care—learning about the system and considering foster care...I mean I would love to have more children. (Tonia)

Artificial insemination by donor (AID) is an option several mothers considered. It is a route with its own complexities. It is expensive and uncertain. Sperm banks sometimes refuse to work with single mothers. One mother was concerned about health factors.

That [AID] also played into my decision to adopt after I talked to my doctor about the artificial route and what expense I could be getting myself into trying and not knowing if I could even have one. She said you could go through all the fertility tests but those aren't cheap either...a lot of women are more comfortable with the clinics that hardly charge, you know, a couple hundred dollars for artificial insemination. But I just wasn't comfortable with that. I wanted screening...I didn't realize until I started reading more about it how loose the regulations are in a lot of the sperm banks…the government is behind on imposing certain screening that a lot of clinics opt to take…I have to honestly say that I didn't spend a lot of time researching artificial insemination because the first one I looked into or the first information I gathered raised the whole issue of how safe it was and I thought for that I'll go home and find somebody who's walking out of the bar at bar time [laughs]. You know, I mean that's about as comfortable as it felt…[Dawn's doctor was willing to assist her with an artificial insemination.] I had talked to my gynecologist, and there was a place in Virginia where he went [a sperm bank]. And he had no problem with it. He says he knew at the University they were pretty strict, but he had no problem with a single woman doing that. He knew my situation and he's just very honest and says he felt that was fine. He would do the insemination. (Dawn)

Ultimately, Dawn decided not to use artificial insemination and instead adopted two children from China. Here she explains how she developed misgivings about AID. Though her daughters will have no father, she says, they will have a better life than they would have had as orphans in China.

It was harder mentally. I mean I talked to a lotta people, and my friends really supported it, and they said, "why can't you do it?" ya know. I said, it was, it was just emotionally hard. I don't know anything about the father. And when the child asks, "What was my Dad like?" All I

could tell 'em was on this little strip of paper…And they did a lotta testing, so it was pretty, it's supposed to be pretty safe. But I, I think maybe part of it was that I grew up with the concept you had a father and mother. And when they're abandoned [as in China], you're not consciously making that choice to say you're not gonna have a father. We know you're not gonna have a father, but I'll take you and give you a better life than they could [in the orphanage in China]. (Dawn)

"It's tough. It's not a cakewalk" All mothers spoke with insight about their contradictory experiences and feelings. At the same time they reported loving their children and said they had no regrets, they were often graphic in describing how difficult it was to parent alone. While they welcomed not having the hassle of a spouse and often said they felt they were better off than divorced women because they never expected to have any help, they showed the strains of being the only parent as their child matured. Amidst the most glowing descriptions of happiness with their children, these women are often quick to say, "it's tough." They didn't interpret this duality as a contradiction; it is simply the way things are for them.

It's not a cake walk. I'm not—I don't want to give the impression that we—It can be tough…. There are a lot of down sides to being a single mom. But I think the plus sides far outweigh them…I try to focus on the good, because you can't…if you're going to focus on the bad you're going to get overwhelmed real easy. So I guess, for me it's natural to start with the positive and then interject the negative, with a touch of positive to it. Because you can't dwell on it or you are going to question why you did it in the first place. And if you're not set up with a good support system, you've got to really reconsider your decision to do it. (Dawn)

I think the reason I agreed to do the interview—the need to talk about it—because I don't think people understand how difficult it is… physically it's, it's you know my days start at five o'clock in the morning and you know like last night I worked until eleven o'clock. So, it's working, it's uh, you know then doing all the…[Here in describing how difficult it was to do everything required of her, the mother was so overcome with tears she could not go on for some minutes. Then she continues with these comments.]…my family's been very supportive but I don't think they realize what they have and how much easier it is for them. My days are very long, you know, I have to do all the stuff it takes two of them to do. You know, cooking, cleaning, laundry, keeping the house up. And it, I mean, it gets really tough, emotionally I'm on a roller-coaster. I, I feel guilty when I'm at work, I feel guilty when I'm at home, I feel guilty that he doesn't have a father…(Ellie)

The "it's tough" is incredibly consistent and strong throughout the interviews with these educated, well-employed, financially stable, and socially well-supported women. One can only imagine how much more "tough" it must be for women with less advantages and fewer options.

CONCLUSIONS

Through the use of in-depth interviews with participants who do not conform to popular stereotypes of the single mother, the results of this study reveal that some women actively choose single motherhood with help from family, friends, and community. Though not enough institutional support is available, many who know the mother help her. Through the powerful voices of the mothers themselves, a clear picture of the duality of joy in the mothering experience and difficulties of parenting alone is achieved.

These single mothers, who were generally well-educated and well-employed, provide an opportunity to hear in women's own voices how they chose and how they planned their pregnancies and adoptions. The stories they tell of their movement toward motherhood is an agentic odyssey that includes multiple influences of their needs and capacities as well as support in their social contexts. Their actions emerge as planned, purposeful movement toward motherhood influenced by their earlier life experiences. When they are confronted with stereotypes and negative social attitudes about single mothers, these women rely upon their maturity, financial security, and family and community support to either distance themselves from the stereotypes or ignore the negative social discourse surrounding them.

The small sample analyzed by this study limits generalization of the results beyond these ten mothers. It will relate only to mothers in similar situations with similar options. Nevertheless, the use of qualitative research techniques have provided revealing portraits of women exercising significant acts of agency in their own lives. The diverse ways the choice to mother alone occurred even among this small sample of women highlights multiple contextual influences on their choices. In a society dominated by powerful institutions that continue to speak of a traditional family consisting of a married man and woman with a male as dominant breadwinner, it is informative to hear and integrate into our understanding of postmodern family life the stories of women who are consciously constructing their own new families and who are supported in this by those who love them.

This study exposes an area of research that needs exploring. In order to isolate and witness the agency involved in choosing to become a single mother, the project was deliberately narrowed to women with a capacity for autonomous action; with the financial, family, and social support to make certain choices; and with the options that higher education offers. The obvious subsequent question would be whether women of other social conditions may also be making similar choices with similar planning and deliberation. Do poor women also make the deliberate choice to mother despite the fact that they do not have a partner and do not expect to have one? Do they also make that choice out of a deep felt desire to mother? Are they also encouraged by family and extended social networks?

The proportion of mothers who are single grows across all socioeconomic groups and increases worldwide. Obviously, not all options are available to women who are poor or less financially secure. They cannot afford to fly to another continent to adopt a child, but they may choose other formal and informal adoption arrangements closer to home. AID treatment and mail order sperm banks are costly and uncertain, but the exchange of sperm for parenting, on an informal basis, is not unusual. Researchers have begun to document the planning, negotiation, and formal and informal agreements which may be involved (Mattes, 1994; Saffron, 1994). Additional research will be useful in exploring issues of female agency as regards parenting in all social groups.

Katherine Allen's noteworthy study of single women (Allen, 1989) demonstrated that single women from the 1910 birth cohort had intense family lives and family commitment although they did not include having a child. Viewed forty years later in terms of the life-course perspective, single women in this study, born between 1937 and 1947, continue to negotiate complex family units. Today the choice of having a child is available to them. This study demonstrates how some of them make that choice.

IMPLICATIONS

One goal of this study was to positively influence the self-perceptions of women and, ultimately, the perceptions of the general public. While these results may not generalize to teenage mothers or mothers dealing with poverty (two social conditions that comprise a significant percentage of today's single mothers), exploding the negative myth that the single mother is young and poor and that she became a mother because of carelessness, poor judgment, or the desire for a government stipend may serve to improve the public's perception of single mothers and hence the support network available. Documenting significant acts of female choice in a society that ignores or marginalizes them is important for family life educators, family counselors, and other family practitioners. Three implications for practitioners follow:

First, respect for the varieties of families, including subvarieties of single-parent families, is critical in this era of the changing family. Professionals who work with families and scholars who seek to understand and write about them need to be aware of possible hidden bias in purported scientific objectivity (Cowan, 1993).

Second, women make the choice to mother alone and their choices are often facilitated by changes in society. Economic power and sexual liberalization have expanded women's options.

Social forces from international adoption to new reproductive technologies affected the women of this study. Further research is needed to consider whether the actions of these women may unmask a legitimization of illegitimacy in the culture.

Finally, it is as significant to elicit social constructions of agency as it is to elicit those of victimhood in relation to single parenting in helping to understand how these families function and how they can be served.

Scholars and practitioners can contribute to transforming the public dialogue and social welfare practices related to single mothers to better reflect the variance in this family group. Active rejection of a blaming, pejorative, scape-goating of single mothers and insistence that the discourse and the social institutions flowing from that discourse be supportive of all family arrangements will facilitate that transformation. We acknowledge the diversity of single mothers. Whether affluent or needful, young or mature, having achieved single motherhood through a variety of means, e.g., divorce, widowhood, and even choice, we can grant them the presumption that positive forces (e.g., desire to nurture, love of family life, encouraging social support network) drove them toward mothering.

While the experience of these ten women tells a collective story of a narrow social category, it is a category that has been marginalized and even silenced. A collective story can create an individual response in others who recognize their own story and feel less alone (Richardson, 1995).

> [The] collective story overcomes some of the isolation and alienation of contemporary life. It provides a sociological community, the linking of separate individuals into a shared consciousness. Once linked, the possibility for social action on behalf of the collective is present and therewith the possibility of social transformation. (Richardson, 1995, p. 214).

Reading 19   Shifting the Center: Race, Class, and Feminist Theorizing About Motherhood

PATRICIA HILL COLLINS*

I dread to see my children grow, I know not their fate. Where the white boy has every opportunity and protection, mine will have few opportunities and no protection. It does not matter how good or wise my children may be, they are colored.

—an anonymous African-American mother
in 1904, reported in Lerner, 1972 p. 158.

For Native American, African-American, Hispanic, and Asian-American women, motherhood cannot be analyzed in isolation from its context. Motherhood occurs in specific historical situations framed by interlocking structures of race, class, and gender, where the sons and daughters of white mothers have "every opportunity and protection," and the "colored" daughters and sons of racial ethnic mothers "know not their fate." Racial domination and economic exploitation profoundly shape the mothering context, not only for the ethnic women in the United States, but for all women.[1]

Despite the significance of race and class, feminist theorizing routinely minimizes their importance. In this sense, feminist theorizing about motherhood has not been immune to the decon-

textualization of Western social thought overall.[2] While many dimensions of motherhood's context are ignored, the exclusion of race and/or class from feminist theorizing generally (Spelman 1988), and from feminist theorizing about motherhood specifically, merit special attention.[3]

Much feminist theorizing about motherhood assumes that male domination in the political economy and the household is the driving force in family life, and that understanding the struggle for individual autonomy in the face of such domination is central to understanding motherhood (Esenstein 1983).[4] Several guiding principles frame such analyses. First, such theories posit a dichotomous split between the public sphere of economic and political discourse and the private sphere of family and household responsibilities. This juxtaposition of a public, political economy to a private, noneconomic and apolitical domestic household allows work and family to be seen as separate institutions. Second, reserving the public sphere for men as a "male" domain leaves the private domestic sphere as a "female" domain. Gender roles become tied to the dichotomous constructions of these two basic societal institutions—men work and women take care of families. Third, the public/private dichotomy separating the family/household from the paid labor market shapes sex-segregated gender roles within the private sphere of the family. The archetypal white, middle-class nuclear family divides family life into two oppositional spheres—the "male" sphere of economic providing and the "female" sphere of affective nurturing, mainly mothering. This normative family household ideally consists of a working father who earns enough to allow his spouse and dependent children to withdraw from the paid labor force. Due in large part to their superior earning power, men as workers and fathers exert power over women in the labor market and in families. Finally, the struggle for individual autonomy in the face of a controlling oppressive, "public" society, or the father as patriarch, comprises the main human enterprise.[5] Successful adult males achieve this autonomy. Women, children, and less successful males, namely those who are working-class or from racial ethnic groups, are seen as dependent persons, as less autonomous, and therefore as fitting objects for elite male domination. Within the nuclear family, this struggle for autonomy takes the form of increasing opposition to the mother, the individual responsible for socializing children by these guiding principles (Chodorow 1978; Flax 1978).

Placing the experiences of women of color in the center of feminist theorizing about motherhood demonstrates how emphasizing the issue of father as patriarch in a decontextualized nuclear family distorts the experiences of women in alternative family structures with quite differ-

ent political economies. While male domination certainly has been an important theme for racial ethnic women in the United States, gender inequality has long worked in tandem with racial domination and economic exploitation. Since work and family have rarely functioned as dichotomous spheres for women of color, examining racial ethnic women's experiences reveals how these two spheres actually are interwoven (Glenn 1985; Dill 1988; Collins 1990).

For women of color, the subjective experience of mothering/motherhood is inextricably linked to the sociocultural concern of racial ethnic communities—one does not exist without the other. Whether because of the labor exploitation of African-American women under slavery and its ensuing tenant farm system, the political conquest of Native American women during European acquisition of land, or exclusionary immigration policies applied to Asian-Americans and Hispanics, women of color have performed motherwork that challenges social constructions of work and family as separate spheres, of male and female gender roles as similarly dichotomized, and of the search for autonomy as the guiding human quest. "Women's reproductive labor—that is, feeding, clothing, and psychologically supporting the male wage earner and nurturing and socializing the next generation—is seen as work on behalf of the family as a whole, rather than as work benefiting men in particular," observes Asian-American sociologist Evelyn Nakano Glenn (1986, p. 192). The locus of conflict lies outside the household, as women and their families engage in collective effort to create and maintain family life in the face of forces that undermine family integrity. But this "reproductive labor" or "motherwork" goes beyond ensuring the survival of one's own biological children or those of one's family. This type of motherwork recognizes that individual survival, empowerment, and identity require group survival empowerment, and identity.

In describing her relationship with her "Grandmother," Marilou Awiakta, a Native American poet and feminist theorist, captures the essence of motherwork.

Putting my arms around the Grand-mother, I lay my head on her shoul-der. Through touch we exchange sorrow, despair that anything really changes.

Awiakta senses the power of the Grandmother and of the motherwork that mothers and grand-mothers do.

"But from the presence of her arms I also feel the stern, beautiful power that flows from all the Grandmoth-ers, as it flows from our mountains themselves. It says, "Dry your tears. Get up. Do for yourselves or do with-out. Work for the day to come." *(1988, p. 127)*

Awiakta's passage places women and moth-erwork squarely in the center of what are typi-cally seen as disjunctures, the place between human and nature, between private and public, between oppression and liberation. I use the term "motherwork" to soften the existing di-chotomies in feminist theorizing about mother-hood that posit rigid distinctions between private and public, family and work, the individ-ual and the collective, identity as individual au-tonomy and identity growing from the collective self-determination of one's group. Racial ethnic women's mothering and work experiences occur at the boundaries demarking these dualities. "Work for the day to come," is motherwork, whether it is on behalf of one's own biological children, or for the children of one's own racial ethnic community, or to preserve the earth for those children who are yet unborn. The space

that this motherwork occupies promises to shift our thinking about motherhood itself.

SHIFTING THE CENTER: WOMEN OF COLOR AND MOTHERWORK

What themes might emerge if issues of race and class generally, and understanding of racial eth-nic women's motherwork specifically, became central to feminist theorizing about motherhood? Centering feminist theorizing on the concerns of white, middle-class women leads to two prob-lematic assumptions. The first is that a relative degree of economic security exists for mothers and their children. The second is that all women enjoy the racial privilege that allows them to see themselves primarily as individuals in search of personal autonomy, instead of members of racial ethnic groups struggling for power. It is these assumptions that allow feminist theorists to concentrate on themes such as the connections among mothering, aggression, and death, the effects of maternal isolation on mother-child rela-tionships within nuclear family households, maternal sexuality, relationships among family members, all-powerful mothers as conduits for gender oppression, and the possibilities of an idealized motherhood freed from patriarchy (Chodorow and Contratto 1982; Eisenstein 1983).

While these issues merit investigation, cen-tering feminist theorizing about motherhood in the ideas and experiences of African-American, Native American, Hispanic, and Asian-American women might yield markedly different themes (Andersen 1988; Brown 1989). This stance is to be distinguished from one that merely adds racial ethnic women's experiences to preexisting femi-nist theories, without considering how these expe-riences challenge those theories (Spelman 1988). Involving much more than simply the consulting of existing social science sources, the placing of ideas and experiences of women of color in the center of analysis requires invoking a different epistemology. We must distinguish between what has been said about subordinated groups in the dominant discourse, and what such groups might say about themselves if given the opportunity. Personal narratives, autobiographical statements, poetry, fiction, and other personalized statements have all been used by women of color to express self-defined standpoints on mothering and motherhood. Such knowledge reflects the authentic standpoint of subordinated groups. Therefore, placing these sources in the center and supplementing them with statistics, historical material, and other knowledge produced to justify the interests of ruling elites should create new themes and angles of vision (Smith 1990).[6]

Specifying the contours of racial ethnic women's motherwork promises to point the way toward richer feminist theorizing about motherhood. Themes of survival, power, and identity form the bedrock and reveal how racial ethnic women in the United States encounter and fashion motherwork. That is to understand the importance of working for the physical survival of children and community, the dialectical nature of power and powerlessness in structuring mothering patterns, and the significance of self-definition in constructing individual and collective racial identity is to grasp the three core themes characterizing the experiences of Native American, African-American, Hispanic and Asian-American women. It is also to suggest how feminist theorizing about motherhood might be shifted if different voices became central in feminist discourse.

MOTHERWORK AND PHYSICAL SURVIVAL

When we are not physically starving we have the luxury to realize psychic and emotional starvation. (Cherrie Moraga 1979, p. 29.)

Physical survival is assumed for children who are white and middle-class. The choice to thus examine their psychic and emotional well-being and that of their mothers appears rational. The children of women of color, many of whom are "physically starving," have no such choices however. Racial ethnic children's lives have long been held in low regard: African-American children face an infant mortality rate twice that for white infants; and approximately one-third of Hispanic children and one-half of African-American children who survive infancy live in poverty. In addition racial ethnic children often live in harsh urban environments where drugs, crime, industrial pollutants, and violence threaten their survival. Children in rural environments often fare no better. Winona LaDuke, for example, reports that Native Americans on reservations often must use contaminated water. And on the Pine Ridge Sioux Reservation in 1979, thirty-eight percent of all pregnancies resulted in miscarriages before the fifth month, or in excessive hemorrhaging. Approximately sixty-five percent of all children born suffered breathing problems caused by underdeveloped lungs and jaundice (1988, p. 63).

Struggles to foster the survival of Native American, Hispanic, Asian-American, and African-American families and communities by ensuring the survival of children comprise a fundamental dimension of racial ethnic women's motherwork. African-American women's fiction contains numerous stories of mothers fighting for the physical survival both of their own biological children and of those of the larger Black community.[7] "Don't care how much death it is in the land, I got to make preparations for my baby to live!" proclaims Mariah Upshur, the African-American heroine of Sara Wright's 1986 novel *This Child's Gonna Live* (p. 143). Like Mariah Upshur, the harsh climates which confront racial ethnic children require that their mothers "make preparations for their babies to live" as a central feature of their motherwork.

Yet, like all deep cultural themes, the theme of motherwork for physical survival contains contradictory elements. On the one hand, racial ethnic women's motherwork for individual and community survival has been essential. Without women's motherwork, communities would not survive, and by definition, women of color themselves would not survive. On the other hand, this work often extracts a high cost for large numbers of women. There is loss of individual autonomy and there is submersion of individual growth for the benefit of the group. While this dimension of motherwork remains essential, the question of women doing more than their fair share of such work for individual and community development merits open debate.

The histories of family-based labor have been shaped by racial ethnic women's motherwork for survival and the types of mothering relationships that ensued. African-American, Asian-American, Native American and Hispanic women have all worked and contributed to family economic well-being (Glenn 1985; Dill 1988). Much of their experiences with motherwork, in fact, stem from the work they performed as children. The commodification of children of color, starting with the enslavement of African children who were legally "owned" as property, to the subsequent treatment of children as units of labor in agricultural work, family businesses, and industry, has been a major theme shaping motherhood for women of color. Beginning in slavery and continuing into the post-World War II period, Black children were put to work at young ages in the fields of Southern agriculture. Sara Brooks began full-time work in the fields at the age of eleven, and remembers, "we never was lazy cause we used to really work. We used to work like men. Oh, fight sometime, fuss sometime, but worked on" (Collins 1990, p. 54).

Black and Hispanic children in contemporary migrant farm families make similar contributions to their family's economy. "I musta been almost eight when I started following the crops," remembers Jessie de la Cruz, a Mexican-American mother with six grown children. "Every winter, up north. I was on the end of the row of prunes, taking care of my younger brother and sister. They would help me fill up the cans and put 'em in a box while the rest of the family was picking the whole row" (de la Cruz 1980, p. 168). Asian-American children spend long hours working in family businesses, child labor practices that have earned Asian Americans the dubious distinction of being "model minorities." More recently, the family-based labor of undocumented racial ethnic immigrants, often mother-child units doing piecework for the garment industry, recalls the sweatshop conditions confronting turn-of-the-century European immigrants.

A certain degree of maternal isolation from members of the dominant group characterizes the preceding mother-child units. For women of color working along with their children, such isolation is more appropriately seen as reflecting a placement in racially and class stratified labor systems than as a result of a patriarchal system. The unit may be isolated, but the work performed by the mother-child unit closely ties the mothering experiences to wider political and economic issues. Children, too, learn to see their work and that of their mother's not as isolated from wider society, but as essential to their family's survival. Moreover, in the case of family agricultural labor or family businesses, women and children work alongside men, often performing the same work. If isolation occurs, the family, not the mother-child unit, is the focus of such isolation.

Children working in close proximity to their mothers receive distinctive types of mothering. Asian-American children working in urban family businesses, for example, report long days filled almost exclusively with work and school. In contrast, the sons and daughters of African-American sharecroppers and migrant farm children of all backgrounds have less access to educational opportunities. "I think the longest time I went to school was two months in one place," remembers Jessie de la Cruz. "I attended, I think, about forty-five schools. When my parents or my brothers didn't find work, we wouldn't attend school because we weren't sure of staying there. So I missed a lot of school (de la Cruz 1980, p. 167–8)." It was only in the 1950s in fact, that Southern school districts stopped the practice of closing segregated Black schools during certain times of the year so that Black children could work.

Work that separated women of color from their children also framed the mothering relationship. Until the 1960s, large numbers of African-American, Hispanic, and Asian-American women worked in domestic service. Even though women worked long hours to ensure their children's physical survival, that same work ironically denied mothers access to their children. Different institutional arrangements emerged in these mothers' respective communities, to resolve the tension between maternal separation due to employment and the needs of dependent children. The extended family structure in African-American communities endured as a flexible institution that mitigated some of the effects of maternal separation. Grandmothers are highly revered in Black communities, often because grandmothers function as primary caretakers of their daughters' and daughters-in-law' children (Collins 1990). In contrast, exclusionary immigration policies that mitigated against intergenerational family units in the United States led Chinese-American and Japanese-American families to make other arrangements (Dill 1988).

Some mothers are clearly defeated by the demands for incessant labor they must perform to ensure their children's survival. The magnitude of their motherwork overwhelms them. But others, even while appearing to be defeated, manage to pass on the meaning of motherwork for survival to their children. African-American

feminist June Jordan remembers her perceptions of her mother's work:

> As a child I noticed the sadness of my mother as she sat alone in the kitchen at night.... Her woman's work never won permanent victories of any kind. It never enlarged the universe of her imagination or her power to influence what happened beyond the front door of our house. Her women's work never tickled her to laugh or shout or dance. (Jordan 1985, p. 105)

But Jordan also sees her mother's work as being essential to individual and community survival.

> She did raise me to respect her way of offering love and to believe that hard work is often the irreducible factor for survival, not something to avoid. Her woman's work produced a reliable home base where I could pursue the privileges of books and music. Her woman's work invented the potential for a completely new kind of work for us, the next generation of Black women: huge, reward ing hard work demanded by the huge, different ambitions that her perfect confidence in us engendered. (Jordan 1985, p. 105)

MOTHERWORK AND POWER

Jessie de la Cruz, a Mexican-American migrant farm worker, experienced firsthand the struggle for empowerment facing racial ethnic women whose daily motherwork centers on issues of survival.

> How can I write down how I felt when I was a little child and my grandmother used to cry with us

'cause she didn't have enough food to give us? Because my brother was going barefooted and he was cryin' because he wasn't used to going without shoes? How can I describe that? I can't describe when my little girl died because I didn't have money for a doctor. And never had any teaching on caring for sick babies. Living out in labor camps. How can I describe that? (Jessie de la Cruz 1980, p. 177)

A dialectical relationship exists between efforts of racial orders to mold the institution of motherhood to serve the interests of elites, in this case, racial elites, and efforts on the part of subordinated groups to retain power over motherhood so that it serves the legitimate needs of their communities (Collins 1990). African-American, Asian-American, Hispanic, and Native American women have long been preoccupied with patterns of maternal power and powerlessness because their mothering experiences have been profoundly affected by this dialectical process. But instead of emphasizing maternal power in dialectical with father as patriarch (Chodorow 1978; Rich 1996), or with male dominance in general (Ferguson 1989), women of color are concerned with their power and powerlessness within an array of social institutions that frame their lives.

Racial ethnic women's struggles for maternal empowerment have resolved around three main themes. First is the struggle for control over their own bodies in order to preserve choice over whether to become mothers at all. The ambiguous politics of caring for unplanned children has long shaped African-American women's motherwork. For example, the widespread institutionalized rape of Black women by white men, both during slavery and in the segregated South, created countless biracial children who had to be absorbed into African-American families and communities (Davis 1981). The range of skin colors and hair textures in contemporary African-American communities bears mute testament to the powerlessness of African-American women in controlling this dimension of motherhood.

For many women of color, choosing to become a mother challenges institutional policies that encourage white, middle-class women to reproduce, and discourage and even penalize low-income racial ethnic women from doing so (Davis 1981). Rita Silk-Nauni, an incarcerated Native American woman, writes of the difficulties she encountered in trying to have additional children. She loved her son so much that she only left him to go to work. "I tried having more after him and couldn't," she laments.

"I went to a specialist and he thought I had been fixed when I had my son. He said I would have to have surgery in order to give birth again. The surgery was so expensive but I thought I could make a way even if I had to work 24 hours a day. Now that I'm here, I know I'll never have that chance." (Brant 1988, p. 94).

Like Silk-Nauni, Puerto Rican and African-American women have long had to struggle with issues of sterilization abuse (Davis 1981). More recent efforts to manipulate the fertility of women dependent on public assistance speaks to the continued salience of this issue.

A second dimension of racial ethnic women's struggles for maternal empowerment concerns the process of keeping the children that are wanted, whether they were planned for or not. For mothers like Jessie de la Cruz whose "little girl died" because she "didn't have money for a doctor," maternal separation from one's children becomes a much more salient issue than maternal isolation with one's children within an allegedly private nuclear family. Physical and/or psychological separation of mothers and children, designed to disempower individuals, forms the basis of a systematic effort to disempower racial ethnic communities.

For both Native American and African-American mothers, situations of conquest introduced this dimension of the struggle for maternal empowerment. In her fictional account of a Native American mother's loss of her children in 1890, Brant explores the pain of maternal separation.

> *It has been two days since they came and took the children away. My body is greatly chilled. All our blankets have been used to bring me warmth. The women keep the fire blazing. The men sit. They talk among themselves. We are frightened by this sudden child-stealing. We signed papers, the agent said. This gave them rights to take our babies. It is good for them, the agent said. It will make them civilized (1988, p. 101).*

A legacy of conquest has meant that Native American mothers on "reservations" confront intrusive government institutions such as the Bureau of Indian Affairs in deciding the fate of their children. For example, the long-standing policy of removing Native American children from their homes and housing them in reservation boarding schools can be seen as efforts to disempower Native American mothers. For African-American women, slavery was a situation where owners controlled numerous dimensions of their children's lives. Black children could be sold at will, whipped, or even killed, all without any recourse by their mothers. In such a situation, getting to keep one's children and raise them accordingly fosters empowerment.

A third dimension of racial ethnic women's struggles for empowerment concerns the perva-

sive efforts by the dominant group to control the children's minds. In her short story, "A Long Memory," Beth Brant juxtaposes the loss felt by a Native American mother in 1890 whose son and daughter had been forcibly removed by white officials, to the loss that she felt in 1978 upon losing her daughter in a custody hearing. "Why do they want our babies?" queries the turn-of-the-century mother. "They want our power. They take our children to remove the inside of them. Our power" (Brant 1988, p. 105). This mother recognizes that the future of the Native American way of life lies in retaining the power to define that worldview through the education of children. By forbidding children to speak their native languages, and in other ways encourage children to assimilate into Anglo culture, external agencies challenge the power of mothers to raise their children as they see fit.

Schools controlled by the dominant group comprise one important location where this dimension of the struggle for maternal empowerment occurs. In contrast to white, middle-class children, whose educational experiences affirm their mothers' middle class values, culture, and authority, the educational experiences of African-American, Hispanic, Asian-American and Native American children typically denigrate their mothers' perspective. For example, the struggles over bilingual education in Hispanic communities are about much more than retaining Spanish as a second language. Speaking the language of one's childhood is a way of retaining the entire culture and honoring the mother teaching that culture (Morago 1979; Anzaldua 1987).

Jenny Yamoto describes the stress of continuing to negotiate with schools regarding her Black-Japanese sons.

> *I've noticed that depending on which parent, Black mom or Asian dad, goes to school open house, my oldest son's behavior is interpreted as disruptive*

and irreverent, or assertive and clever.... I resent their behavior being defined and even expected on the basis of racial biases their teachers may struggle with or hold.... I don't have the time or energy to constantly change and challenge their teacher's and friends' misperceptions. I only go after them when the children really seem to be seriously threatened. (Yamoto 1988, p. 24).

In confronting each of these three dimensions of their struggles for empowerment, racial ethnic women are not powerless in the face of racial and class oppression. Being grounded in a strong, dynamic, indigenous culture can be central in these women's social constructions of motherhood. Depending on their access to traditional culture, they invoke alternative sources of power.[8]

"Equality, per se, may have a different meaning for Indian women and Indian people," suggests Kate Shanley. "That difference begins with personal and tribal sovereignty—the right to be legally recognized as people empowered to determine our own destinies" (1988, p. 214). Personal sovereignty involves the struggle to promote the survival of a social structure whose organizational principles represent notions of family and motherhood different from those of the mainstream. "The nuclear family has little relevance to Indian women," observes Shanley. "In fact, in many ways, mainstream feminists now are striving to redefine family and community in a way that Indian women have long known" (p. 214).

African-American mothers can draw upon an Afrocentric tradition where motherhood of varying types, whether bloodmother, othermother, or community othermother, can be invoked as a symbol of power. Many Black women receive respect and recognition within their local communities for innovative and practical approaches not only to mothering their own "blood" children, but also to being othermothers to the children in their extended family networks, and those in the community overall. Black women's involvement in fostering Black community development forms the basis of this community-based power. In local African-American communities, community othermothers can become identified as powerful figures through their work in furthering the community's well-being (Collins 1990).

Despite policies of dominant institutions that place racial ethnic mothers in positions where they appear less powerful to their children, mothers and children empower themselves by understanding each other's position and relying on each other's strengths. In many cases, children, especially daughters, bond with their mothers instead of railing against them as symbols of patriarchal power. Cherrie Moraga describes the impact that her mother had on her. Because she was repeatedly removed from school in order to work, by prevailing standards Moraga's mother would be considered largely illiterate. But she was also a fine storyteller, and found ways to empower herself within dominant institutions. "I would go with my mother to fill out job applications for her, or write checks for her at the supermarket," Moraga recounts.

We would have the scenario worked out ahead of time. My mother would sign the check before we'd get to the store. Then, as we'd approach the checkstand, she would say—within earshot of the cashier—"oh, honey, you go 'head and make out the check,'" as if she couldn't be bothered with such an insignificant detail. (1979, p. 28)

Like Cherrie Moraga and her mother, racial ethnic women's motherwork involves collaborating to empower mothers and children within structures that oppress.

MOTHERWORK AND IDENTITY

Please help me find out who I am. My mother was Indian, but we were taken from her and put in foster homes. They were white and didn't want to tell us about our mother. I have a name and maybe a place of birth. Do you think you can help me? (Brant 1988, p. 9)

Like this excerpt from a letter to the editor, the theme of lost racial ethnic identity and the struggle to maintain a sense of self and community many of the stories, poetry and narratives in Beth Brant's volume, *A Gathering of Spirit*. Carol Lee Sanchez offers another view of the impact of the loss of self "Radicals look at reservation Indians and get very upset about their poverty conditions," observes Sanchez.

But poverty to us is not the same thing as poverty is to you. Our poverty is that we can't be who we are. We can't hunt or fish or grow our food because our basic resources and the right to use them in traditional ways are denied us. (Brant 1988, p. 165)

Racial ethnic women's motherwork reflects the tensions inherent in trying to foster a meaningful racial identity in children within a society that denigrates people of color. The racial privilege enjoyed by white, middle-class women makes unnecessary this complicated dimension of the mothering tradition of women of color. While white children can be prepared to fight racial oppression, their survival does not depend on gaining these skills. Their racial identity is validated by their schools, the media, and other social institutions. White children are socialized into their rightful place in systems of racial privilege. Racial ethnic women have no such guarantees for their children; their children must first be taught to survive in systems that oppress them. Moreover, this survival must not come at the expense of self-esteem. Thus, a dialectical relationship exists between systems of racial oppression designed to strip subordinated groups of a sense of personal identity and a sense of collective peoplehood, and the cultures of resistance extant in various racial ethnic groups that resist the oppression. For women of color, motherwork for identity occurs at this critical juncture (Collins 1990).

"Through our mothers, the culture gave us mixed messages," observes Mexican American poet Gloria Anzaldua. "Which was it to be—strong, or submissive, rebellious or conforming?" (1987, p. 18). Thus women of color's motherwork requires reconciling contradictory needs concerning identity. Preparing children to cope with and survive within systems of racial oppression is extremely difficult because the pressures for children of racial ethnic groups to assimilate are pervasive. In order to compel women of color to participate in their children's assimilation, dominant institutions promulgate ideologies that belittle people of color. Negative controlling images infuse the worlds of male and female children of color (Tajima 1989; Collins 1990; Green 1990). Native American girls are encouraged to see themselves as "Pocahontases" or "squaws"; Asian-American girls as "geisha girls" or "Suzy Wongs"; Hispanic girls as "Madonnas" or "hot-blooded whores"; and African-American girls as "mammies", "matriarchs" and "prostitutes." Girls of all groups are told that their lives cannot be complete without a male partner, and that their educational and career aspirations must always be subordinated to their family obligations.

This push toward assimilation is part of a larger effort to a second dimension of the mothering tradition involves equipping children with skills to confront this contradiction and to challenge systems of racial oppression. Girls who become women believing that they are only capable of being maids and prostitutes cannot contribute to racial ethnic women's motherwork.

Mothers make varying choices in negotiating the complicated relationship of preparing children to fit into, yet resist, systems of racial domination. Some mothers remain powerless in the face of external forces that foster their children's assimilation and subsequent alienation from their families and communities. Through fiction, Native American author Beth Brant again explores the grief felt by a mother whose children had been taken away to live among whites. A letter arrives giving news of her missing children.

This letter is from two strangers with the names Martha and Daniel. They say they are learning civilized ways. Daniel works in the fields, growing food for the school. Martha is being taught to sew aprons. She will be going to live with the schoolmasters wife. She will be a live-in girl. What is live-in girl? I shake my head. The words sound the same to me. I am afraid of Martha and Daniel. These strangers who know my name. (Brant 1988, pp. 102–103)

Other mothers become unwitting conduits of the dominant ideology. Gloria Anzalduce (1987, p. 16) asks:

How many time have I heard mothers and mothers-in-law tell their sons to beat their wives for not obeying them, for being hociconas *(big mouths), for*

being callajeras *(going to visit and gossip with neighbors), for expecting their husbands to help with the rearing of children and the housework, for wanting to be something other than housewives?*

Some mothers encourage their children to fit in, for reasons of survival. "My mother, nursed in the folds of a town that once christened its black babies Lee, after Robert E., and Jackson, after Stonewall, raised me on a dangerous generation's old belief," remembers African-American author Marita Golden.

Because of my dark brown complexion, she warned me against wearing browns or yellow and reds...and every summer I was admonished not to play in the sun "cause you gonna have to get a light husband anyway, for the sake of your children." (Golden 1983, p. 24)

To Cherrie Moraga's mother,

On a basic economic level, being Chicana meant being "less." It was through my mother's desire to protect her children from poverty and illiteracy that we became "anglocized"; the more effectively we could pass in the white world, the better guaranteed our future. (1979, p. 28).

Despite their mothers' good intentions, the costs to children taught to submit to racist and sexist ideologies can be high. Raven, a Native American woman, looks back on her childhood:

I've been raised in white man's world and was forbade more or less to converse with Indian people. As my

*mother wanted me to be educated
and live a good life, free from poverty. I lived a life of loneliness. Today
I am desperate to know my people.
(Brant 1988, p. 221)*

To avoid poverty, Raven's mother did what she
thought best, but ultimately, Raven experienced
the poverty of not being able to be who she was.

Still other mothers transmit sophisticated
skills to their children, enabling them to appear
to be submissive while at the same time to be
able to challenge inequality. Willi Coleman's
mother used a Saturday-night hair-combing ritual to impart a Black women's standpoint to her
daughters:

*Except for special occasions mama
came home from work early on Sat-
urdays. She spent six days a week
mopping, waxing and dusting other
women's houses and keeping out of
reach of other women's husbands.
Saturday nights were reserved for
"taking care of them girls'" hair and
the telling of stories. Some of which
included a recitation of what she had
endured and how she had tri-
umphed over "folks that were lower
than dirt" and "no-good snakes in
the grass." She combed, patted,
twisted and talked, saying things
which would have embarrassed or
shamed her at other times. (Coleman
1987, p. 34)*

Historian Elsa Barkley Brown captures this delicate balance that racial ethnic mothers negotiate. Brown points out that her mother's behavior
demonstrated the "need to teach me to live my
life one way and, at the same time, to provide all
the tools I would need to live it quite differently"
(1989, p. 929).

For women of color, the struggle to maintain an independent racial identity has taken
many forms: All reveal varying solutions to the
dialectical relationship between institutions that
would deny their children their humanity and institutions that would affirm their children's right
to exist as self-defined people. Like Willi Coleman's mother, African-American women draw
upon a long-standing Afrocentric feminist
worldview, emphasizing the importance of self-
definition, self-reliance, and the necessity of demanding respect from others (Terborg-Penn
1986; Collins 1990).

Racial ethnic cultures, themselves, do not
always help to support women's self-definition.
Poet and essayist Gloria Anzaldua, for example,
challenges many of the ideas in Hispanic cultures concerning women. "Though I'll defend
my race and culture when they are attacked by
non*mexicanos*,... I abhor some of my culture's
ways, how it cripples its women, *como burras,*
our strengths used against us" (1987, p. 21). Anzaldua offers a trenchant analysis of the ways in
which the Spanish conquest of Native Americans fragmented women's identity and produced
three symbolic "mothers." *La Virgen de Guadalupe*, perhaps the single most potent religious,
political and cultural image of the Chicano people, represents the virgin mother who cares for
and nurtures an oppressed people. *La Chingada
(Malinche)* represents the raped mother, all but
abandoned. A combination of the other two, *La
Llorona* symbolizes the mother who seeks her
lost children. "Ambiguity surrounds the symbols
of these three 'Our Mothers,'" claims Anzaldua.

*In part, the true identity of all three
has been subverted—Guadalupe, to
make us docile and enduring, la
Chingada, to make us ashamed of
our Indian side, and la Llorona to
make us a long-suffering people.
1987, p. 31)*

For Anzaldua, the Spanish conquest, which brought racism and economic subordination to Indian people, and created a new mixed-race Hispanic people, simultaneously devalued women:

No, I do not buy all the myths of the tribe into which I was born. I can understand why the more tinged with Anglo blood, the more adamantly my colored and colorless sisters glorify their colored culture's values—to offset the extreme devaluation of it by the white culture. It's a legitimate reaction. But I will not glorify those aspects of my culture which have injured me and which have injured me in the name of Protecting me. (Anzaldua 1987, p. 22)

Hispanic mothers face the complicated task of shepherding their children through the racism extant in dominant society, and the reactions to that racism framing cultural beliefs internal to Hispanic communities.

Many Asian-American mothers stress conformity and fitting in as a way to challenge the system. "Our parents are painted as hard workers who were socially uncomfortable and had difficulty expressing even the smallest opinion," observes Japanese-American Kesaya Noda, in her autobiographical essay "Growing Up Asian in America" (1989, p. 246). Noda questioned this seeming capitulation on the part of her parents: "'Why did you go into those camps,' I raged at my parents, frightened by my own inner silence and timidity. 'Why didn't you do anything to resist?'" But Noda later discovers a compelling explanation as to why Asian-Americans are so often portrayed as conformist:

I had not been able to imagine before what it must have felt like to be an American—to know absolutely that

one is an American—and yet to have almost everyone else deny it. Not only deny it, but challenge that identity with machine guns and troops of white American soldiers. In those circumstances it was difficult to say, "I'm a Japanese-American." "American" had to do. (1989, p. 247)

Native American women can draw upon a tradition of motherhood and woman's power inherent in Native American cultures (Allen 1986; Awiakta 1988). In such philosophies, "water, land, and life are basic to the natural order," claims Winona LaDuke.

All else has been created by the use and misuse of technology. It is only natural that in our respective struggles for survival, the native peoples are waging a way to protect the land, the water, and life, while the consumer culture strives to protect its technological lifeblood. (1988, p. 65)

Marilou Awiakta offers a powerful summary of the symbolic meaning of motherhood in Native American cultures. "I feel the Grandmother's power. She sings of harmony, not dominance," offers Awiakta. "And her song rises from a culture that repeats the wise balance of nature: the gender capable of bearing life is not separated from the power to sustain it" (1988, p. 126). A culture that sees the connectedness between the earth and human survival, and sees motherhood as symbolic of the earth itself, holds motherhood as an institution in high regard.

CONCLUDING REMARKS

Survival, power and identity shape motherhood for all women. But these themes remain muted when the mothering experiences of women of color are marginalized in feminist theorizing. Feminist theorizing about motherhood reflects a lack of attention to the connection between ideas and the contexts in which they emerge. While such decontexualization aims to generate universal "theories" of human behavior, in actuality, it routinely distorts, and omits huge categories of human experience.

Placing racial ethnic women's motherwork in the center of analysis recontexualized motherhood. While the significance of race and class in shaping the context in which motherhood occurs remains virtually invisible when white, middle-class women's mothering experiences assume prominence, the effects of race and class on motherhood stand out in stark relief when women of color are accorded theoretical primacy. Highlighting racial ethnic mothers' struggles concerning their children's right to exist focuses attention on the importance of survival. Exploring the dialectical nature of racial ethnic women's empowerment in structures of racial domination and economic exploitation demonstrates the need to broaden the definition of maternal power. Emphasizing how the quest for self-definition is mediated by membership in different racial and social class groups reveals how the issues of identity are crucial to all motherwork.

Existing feminist theories of motherhood have emerged in specific intellectual and political contexts. By assuming that social theory will be applicable regardless of social context, feminist scholars fail to realize that they themselves are rooted in specific locations, and that the specific contexts in which they are located provide the thought-models of how they interpret the world. While subsequent theories appear to be universal and objective, they actually are partial perspectives reflecting the white, middle-class context in which their creators live. Large segments of experience, specifically those of women who are not white and middle-class, have been excluded (Spelman 1988).

Feminist theories of motherhood are thus valid as partial perspectives, but cannot be seen as *theories* of motherhood generalizable to all women. The resulting patterns of partiality inherent in existing theories, such as, for example, the emphasis placed on all-powerful mothers as conduits for gender oppression, reflect feminist theorists' positions in structures of power. These theorists are themselves participants in a system of privilege that awards them for not seeing race and class privilege as being important.

Theorizing about motherhood will not be helped by supplanting one group's theory with that of another, for example, by claiming that women of color's experiences are more valid than those of white, middle-class women. Varying placement in systems of privilege, whether race, class, sexuality, or age, generates divergent experiences with motherhood; therefore, examination of motherhood and mother-as-subject from multiple perspectives should uncover rich textures of difference. Shifting the center to accommodate this diversity promises to recontexualize motherhood and point us toward feminist theorizing that embraces difference as an essential part of commonality.

Reading 20   Black Teenage Mothers and Their Mothers: The Impact of Adolescent Childbearing on Daughters' Relations With Mothers

ELAINE BELL KAPLAN*

The popular view assumes that Black families condone teenage motherhood. This study argues that this assumption is incorrect, finding instead that teenage motherhood can produce long-term conflict both in family relations and structure. The 22 teenage mothers interviewed for this qualitative study believed that their mothers did not support them emotionally. Interviews with nine adult mothers[1] of the teenagers substantiated this belief: Their daughters' early motherhood threatened their deeply held moral values as well as their reputations in the community. This study concludes that sociologists need to address these relational problems through linking these mothers' socioeconomic conditions with gender, class, and race inequalities.

> Well, my momma said to me, "You shouldn't have gotten pregnant. You ain't married. You don't have no job. You ain't this and you ain't that" (16-year-old Susan).

> Susan should give the baby up to foster care, to someone who can take care of it (37-year-old Janet).

As these quotes suggest, relations between teenage mothers and their mothers can be complex and disturbing: Teenage motherhood serves as a source of conflict for everyone involved. Social scientists who study teenage motherhood have engaged in an on-going theoretical and, many times, politicized debate about these mother-daughter relationships. Embedded in some theoretical posi-

A version of this paper was presented at the 1994 annual meeting of the American Psychological Association. A special thanks to Gwyneth Kerr Erwin. Eun Mee Kim, Mike Messner, Pierrette Hondagneu-Sotelo, Barrie Thorne, and the anonymous reviewers for *Social Problems* for their comments on an earlier draft. The material in this study was taken from a larger study, "'Not Our Kind of Girl' Black Teenage Motherhood: Realities Hiding Behind the Myths" (forthcoming).

tions is a culture-of-poverty notion that Black, female-headed families produce more of their kind: that is, teenage girls with few values—a slap in the face of the central ideas of America's "family values" (Moynihan 1965). In this theory it is the rule of the father (and not the mother) that establishes the family's mainstream values and behavior.

Wilson (1987) responds to this position by arguing that economic restructuring during the 1960s created havoc for Black families—high unemployment rates for Black men, which in turn led to high divorce rates or fewer marriages. These changes produced a population of Black mothers who live in depleted and hostile inner-city neighborhoods. In such neighborhoods, Black mothers watch their sons seek shelter in gang involvement while their daughters seek significance in motherhood. While Wilson (1987) shows how family life is changed by economic conditions and how people's sense of their lives is mitigated by their structural conditions, his theory does not pay sufficient attention to the way gender ideology contributes to family dynamics, nor does he directly tackle the thorny question: Do teenage mothers and their mothers share values that are antithetical to mainstream values?

I argue that these political debates have limited our view of Black teenage mothers. Rather, they have produced stereotypical portrayals of Black teenage mothers and their mothers, obscuring both the way in which Black women's norms and values are actually shaped by mainstream ideology and the complex nature of their obligations as mothers, especially when their adolescent daughters become young mothers.

So far, the research focusing specifically on relations between mothers and daughters suggests that it is common for mothers and daughters to struggle over issues of independence and identity during the daughters' adolescent years (Rich 1990; Fischer 1986; Gilligan 1990). However, most of these studies primarily focus on white middle-class daughter-mother relationships; therefore they limit the ability to theorize about how Black teenage mothers and their mothers might respond to a crisis such as teenage motherhood.

There are studies that focus on the relationships of Black daughters and mothers (George and Dickerson 1995; Mayfield 1994; Rogers and Lee 1992; Apfel and Steiz 1991; Collins 1987; Burton and Bengston 1985; Ladner and Gourdine 1984; Furstenberg 1980). But these studies do not sufficiently discuss the conflict between teenage mothers and their mothers. Some find that "baby getting" and "baby keeping" are cultural survival strategies (Stack 1974) that do not have a long-term negative effect on the mother (Geronimus 1990). Ladner and Gourdine (1984) studied Black mothers and daughters' relationships to find that adult mothers do not condone their daughters' pregnancies. While this study shows that adult mothers feel themselves swept up in a "tide of circumstances with few options available to them" (p. 23), it does not sufficiently articulate the underlying mothering obligation, nor its subsequent conflicts. These studies do not link gender, race, and class in their analyses.

Collins (1990), who explores the institution of motherhood from the standpoint of Black mothers, argues that Black motherhood as an institution is both dynamic and dialectical. Collins argues that an ongoing tension exists between the dominant society's efforts to mold the institution of Black motherhood to benefit systems of race, gender, and class oppression and efforts by Black women to define and value their motherhood experiences (also see Brewer 1995).

My study explores gender, racial, and economic oppressions by examining how Black teenage mothers and their daughters cope with teenage motherhood. Gender ideology in U.S. society has been crucial to the notion that motherhood is the primary task for women of all racial and class backgrounds. In the literature on women's obligations as mothers, Russo (1976) argues that, in U.S. society's view, it is the women, but not the men, who are charged with caring for others. Further, being a good mother carries the responsibility of providing moral training to their children, supporting their children regardless of one's own needs, and spending all one's time and energy on children, even getting them out of difficult life experiences (Russo 1976). Russo's (1976) theory of motherhood directly connects the family structure to patriarchy—fathers provide the economic leadership and authority, while mothers are responsible for the reproduction of children's mainstream values and behavior. Especially during a child's early and teenage years, a mother's role in reproducing these values in children is considered to be crucial.

Similarly, racism and economic inequality are key factors in creating high numbers of Black mothers raising teenage daughters who are also mothers and in limiting the financial and emotional support they receive from others (see Bell Kaplan forthcoming; Wilson 1987). The key to understanding the dynamics between the teen and adult mothers lies in the gender, race, and class inequities wherein poor, Black women are positioned at the bottom of the labor market. These inequalities are present in systems of discrimination wherein Black women, but not Black men, are punished, or expect to be punished, for stepping outside the traditionally assigned middle-class norms and values regarding teenage parenthood.

This study offers a sample of 22 teen mothers and 9 adult mothers of the teen mothers, using their perceptions of experiences to elucidate the complexities, contradictions, and conflicts arising within family relationships as the result of teenage pregnancy. The families in this study do not reveal a deviant culture. Nor are they the super-strong women who can cope without

needing support (Myers 1980). Indeed, these teen mothers thought that motherhood would provide them with some kind of control over their lives. By contrast, the adult mothers thought their daughters' motherhood would further erode the little control adult mothers already had over their family life. The pivotal question is: What happens to family relationships when adolescent girls and their families have to deal with the pressures created by teenage motherhood?

I suggest the conflict between daughters and mothers can be traumatic for both if the daughters, as 15- or 16-year-old mothers, find themselves abandoned by the school system, their fathers, and the babies' fathers and feel that their mothers are their only source of support. What happens to these relationships when the mothers of teenage mothers themselves feel vulnerable, especially if they are young, single, have limited resources, and are in need of support themselves? These relationships may be further complicated if the adult mothers believe that their daughter's pregnancy is a reflection of lower-class behavior. These adult mothers may feel that they are also affected because the daughters' pregnancy is not their fault, but they will be perceived by others to be responsible for their daughters' situation. The adult mothers distance themselves from their daughters' behavior and align themselves with conventional expectations about teen mothers by linking themselves to traditional culture in unique ways (see Stokes and Hewitt 1976). In this study, when the daughters became pregnant, both daughters and mothers were angry and resentful of the other. That anger and resentment was debilitating and had long-term consequences on the mothers' relationships with their mothers.

SAMPLE AND METHODOLOGY

The interviews involved in this study are taken from a larger three-year study on Black teenage mothers who lived in Oakland and Richmond, California, between 1986 and 1989. This paper focuses on interviews with 22 teen mothers who lived in single-parent/mother only households. I also interviewed nine adult single-parent mothers of teenage mothers.

I met 12 of these teen mothers and 9 of their mothers through volunteer consulting work at a nonprofit teen parenting service agency in Oakland. The rest were drawn from a snowball sample in which the teen mothers provided me with names of other teen mothers. I gave the teen mothers written and verbal information on the research and asked their permission to interview their mothers. All mother were interviewed for two to two-and-one-half hours, usually in their homes. (See Tables 20.1 and 20.2 for the demographic characteristics of the teen and adult mothers' samples.)

To gain the trust of the women in this study, I tried to create a nonhierarchical interview setting and a casual interview atmosphere. Also, being of the same race and gender, having my little boy accompany me on some visits, sharing

TABLE 20.1   Teenage Mothers' Demographic Characteristics

Name	Age	Age at Birth	Educational Background	Source of Income	Family Origin	Age of Mom at First Birth
Dana	21	15	D	AFDC	F	16
DeLesha	17	15	D	Emp.	2p.	20
Denise	25	18	HSG.	Emp.	F	15
De Vonya	17	15	11 grd.	AFDC	F	16
Diane	20	17	S.C.	AFDC	F	22
Evie	43	17	C.Deg.	Disab.	2p.	23
Georgia	16	15	11 grd.	AFDC	F	15
Irene	21	18	D	Unemp.	F	16
Jackie	17	15	11 grd.	AFDC	F	15
Jasmine	17	16	10 grd.	Pt. Emp.	F	17
Joanne	25	14	D	Emp.	F	21
Junie	15	14	9 grd.	Mom	F	24
LaShana	17	15	D	AFDC	F	22
Lenora	20	15	D	Emp.	2p.	16
Lois	27	15	D	AFDC	2p.	15
Margaret	35	15	S.Col.	Emp.	F	22
Mamie	16	15	D	AFDC	2p.	20
Melanie	17	15	11 grd.	AFDC	2p.	20
Terry	20	16	D	AFDC	F	16
Tracy	16	16	10 grd.	AFDC	F	16
Shana	17	16	D	AFDC	F	15
Susan	16	15	D	Mom	F	21

Key:
Education Level: D = high school dropout. HSG = high school graduate. C. Deg. = college degree. S. Col. = Some College. Income Source.: Disab. = Workers' Compensation Insurance. Family Origin Type: F = Female Headed Household. 2p. = Two parent household.

TABLE 20.2   Adult Mothers of Teenage Mothers' Demographic Characteristics

Name (Daughter)	Age	Marital status	Educational Back-ground	Source of Income	Annual** Income
Middle-Class Status Sliders					
Marie (Evie)	66	M	C.Deg.	Retired	$45,000
Alma (Diane)	42	W	C.Deg.	Emp.	32,000
Selma (Joanne)	46	M	C.Deg.	Emp.	25,000
Salina (Jackie)	32	S	HSG.	Emp.	23,000
Working-Class and Poor High Aspirers					
Martha (Margaret)	57	S	D.	Emp.	$13,000
Janet (Susan)	37	S	S.C.	Emp.	11,000
Jessie (Marnie)	36	S	D	AFDC	8,000
Mary (De Vonya)	54	S	D	Disab.	7,000
Ruth (Junie)	39	S	D	AFDC	6,500

Key:
Education Level: D = high school dropout. HSG = high school graduate. C. Deg. = college degree. S. Col. = Some College. Income Source.: Disab. = Workers' Compensation Insurance. Family Origin Type: F = Female Headed Household. 2p. = Two parent household. Marital Status: M = married. S = Single. W = widower. **Approximation of income.

with them my own similar family and class background, may have helped me establish rapport with the mothers (see Reinharz 1992).

Using Goffman's (1963) stigma analysis as a frame of reference, I suggest that discredited people will often act to cover whatever stigma they believe discredits them so that they can appear like others. With this in mind, I asked the teen and adult mothers about their attitudes and reactions to teenage motherhood. I wanted to know how they reorganized and redefined themselves within a context of difficult economic circumstances. Along with asking the teen mothers such questions as, "Who was the 'most' and 'least' supportive before, during, and after your pregnancy?" I asked adult mothers, "How did you respond to the news of your daughter's pregnancy?" and "Did your relationship with your daughter change after her pregnancy?" The

interviews aptly illustrate both entrenched and emerging patterns in these daughter-mother relationships.

BLACK TEENAGE MOTHERS AND THEIR MOTHERS

All of the teen and adult mothers lived in economically depressed inner-city areas of Oakland and Richmond in the midst of a visible drug and gang culture. Several of the teen mothers lived in neighborhoods where, "over 40 percent of the families were headed by single mothers and virtually all the single mothers received AFDC" (Oakland City Council Report 1988). Sixteen of the twenty-two teen mothers and their babies were living with their mothers. Two of these teen mothers were ineligible for welfare assistance because their mothers' annual income exceeded the family eligibility limits. The rest were receiving welfare assistance and living on their own.

Susan serves as an example of the teen mothers who were living with their mothers. Susan, a 16-year-old mother who dropped out of the ninth grade when she learned she was pregnant, lived with her mother and two sisters in a cramped two bedroom apartment in East Oakland. Her baby's father was serving a two-year term in a youth camp facility. Susan's father, who left the family when she was very young and moved to Oklahoma, refused to pay child support and seldom visited his children. To make matters worse, Susan said, her mother's nurses' aide income of $11,000 disqualified Susan for welfare assistance.

According to Susan, her mother, Janet, was resentful and constantly complaining to Susan about the additional money it cost her to support her family since the baby's birth. Janet said she was indeed shocked when she learned that her daughter was pregnant. She thought that Susan (the first person in her family to become a teenage mother) was too young and had a too "irresponsible nature" to be a good mother. These problems exacerbated the hostility between the mother and daughter, and their arguments escalated until they fell over tables and chairs trying to hit each other.

Twelve teen mothers qualified for welfare assistance. The rest were employed. Many thought they could resolve their problems by moving out of their mothers' homes. However, only a few of the older teenage mothers were able to establish stable households. Younger teen mothers had to count on friends to lend them sleeping space; sometimes, it was on the floor. Generally, the teen mothers couldn't stay longer than a week before they would have to look for new arrangements (see Elliott and Krivo 1991). For example, 16-year-old De Vonya, the youngest of six siblings, recalled moving into her friend's home after an argument with her mother when she told her she was pregnant. De Vonya did find her own apartment in a housing complex, a hangout for drug dealers. Within two weeks of moving in, faced with mounting expenses she couldn't afford, De Vonya moved out, leaving no forwarding address or telephone number.

De Vonya's mother, Mary, a single mother who depended on monthly Social Security checks, had trouble coping with De Vonya since the baby's birth. Mary said she wanted her daughter to do something with her life other than follow in her footsteps by being a teenage welfare mother. Mary was angry, hurt, and resentful that her youngest child, De Vonya, would repeat a family cycle of teenage pregnancy that began when her own mother gave birth to Mary at age sixteen. De Vonya's father, who stopped speaking to her for several months after he learned she was pregnant, refused to offer her much in the way of support. De Vonya's reaction was: "Sometimes he gets on my nerves." Losing his support was extremely difficult for De Vonya, especially since her baby's father also broke off their relationship shortly after she became pregnant.

Most of the teen and adult mothers had poor educational skills, while some were educated and employed. But even those who were employed felt afraid that they could lose it all "in the wink of an eye," said 32-year-old Salina, mother of 16-year-old Jackie. As a result, they didn't see much of a future for themselves. When I asked the teen mothers (and adult mothers who had been teen mothers) why they became mothers so young, most responded like 16-year-old De Vonya: "Maybe I'll feel loved by having my own child." Being a mother was something she could do to feel good about herself, perhaps feeling she could be a mother even if she didn't have other options. All of the teen mothers agreed that they were only beginning to comprehend the impact of teenage motherhood on all aspects of their lives.

THE ISSUE OF GENDER: MOTHERS' OBLIGATIONS

First, teenage mothers reported that being teenage mothers placed great stress on their relations with their mothers, who strongly believed that their daughters had failed to adhere to the gendered norms about girls' sexual behavior. Second, these teen mothers were also adolescents, a period during which girls are often experiencing anxiety and confusion as they strive for maturity and are striving to develop trust and make connections with others.

Third, further complicating the challenges felt by these teen mothers is that, like all children, they felt their mothers were obligated to care for them, regardless of the mothers' own problems. The teen and adult mothers' comments in this study underscore a crucial element of the norm concerning the mothering obligation: Mothers should be able to exert control over their daughters' sexual behavior. The teen mothers also reveal the daughters' expectations that their mothers be good mothers, offering unconditional love, understanding, and forgiveness. If mothers withdraw support, they are failing. These teen mothers idealized the concept of "a good mother" and became angry when their mothers didn't conform. These adult mothers are caught in an impossible dilemma. If a mother offers support, chances are others will pass on the stigma of her daughter's deviant status to her (see Goffman 1963): The family has "slipped" in its community standing. It was common, the adult mothers said, to hear neighbors say, "These girls have no guidance" in judging their mothers' maternal abilities.

Compounding these challenges were problems caused by the break-up of important relationships: the babies' fathers disappearing from their lives, "so-called" friends gossiping about them, as one teen mother put it—abandonments that caused the teen mothers to turn to their mothers for increased emotional and financial support, only to find both unavailable. At the same time, they were having to learn how to be mothers.

Fourth, the adult mothers, many of whom were barely making enough money to support their existing families, reported that teenage motherhood ran counter to their values about marriage and motherhood. The adult mothers, overwhelmed by their new situations, negatively evaluated their daughters' actions, fearing they would be held responsible for their grandchildren's welfare. Not only did the adult mothers not appreciate their daughters' pregnancies, they took adversarial positions, often failing to be supportive of their daughters. They also felt at risk both economically and morally.

The adult mothers developed impression management strategies that distanced them from their daughters' actions. These strategies are juxtaposed against the daughters' impression management strategies that linked them to their babies and motherhood. These critical feelings led to new tensions between mothers and daughters, or exacerbated old ones.

Negotiating the Status Transition

Mothers and daughters often mark transitions in their relationships by struggling to negotiate new ways of dealing with the changes in their status (Fischer 1986). In this regard, the teen mothers demonstrate how a disproportionate amount of negotiation occurs between daughters who are moving from non-mother to mother status and mothers who are moving on to being grandmothers—all of which is occurring at an inappropriate time in their lives.

These struggles emerge in the teen mothers' responses to the first research question, "Who was most or least supportive of you before, during, and after your pregnancy?" Before pregnancy, most of the teens had fights with their mothers over time allocated to television viewing, cleaning their rooms, and doing their homework—all typical family issues. Once pregnancy was established, 6 of the 22 teens had mothers who continued being supportive of them. Sixteen-year-old Georgia typified these mothers when she said her mother (who had also been a teen mother) helped her by sharing her own experiences. Another teen mother, Terry, gave her mother credit for being emotionally supportive of her and for giving her helpful information about her own pregnancy. Her mother often told Terry how happy she was when Terry was born.

For 16 teen mothers, the family fights took on a new edge when pregnancy occurred. Only a third of these teenagers expected their mothers not to react negatively to the news of their pregnancies. Many anticipated a fight. Several said they were "scared" and feared their mothers' reactions when they were told the news, so they tried to hide their pregnancies from their mothers as long as possible. Seventeen-year-old Jasmine's story demonstrates this untenable strategy: "I didn't show until I was six months. I kept it in. Then I got sick. So my mother took me to the hospital for an examination and they told her."

The most compelling stories come from teen mothers responding to my question: "Who was the least supportive of you?" Sixteen teen mothers said that they left or were leaving their mothers' homes because of ongoing fights with their mothers. Seventeen-year-old De Vonya said:

> She asked me whether I was going to keep it and who's the father and where were I going to stay. I told her, "Yeah, I'm going to stay." And she said "How do you know that I want you here? I've already raised my kids."

De Vonya's expectations illustrate the norms and roles associated with the mothering obligation: Mothers should always be available and supportive of their children and never waver in that support regardless of their own problems. De Vonya expected her mother to mother her again and to continue previous levels of support, despite the extra demands an additional child would make on her mother. Her mother, who had her own set of problems, worried that the responsibility for her grandchild would fall on her shoulders. Why was she worried? I suggest two reasons: First, she was the only parent available to care for her grandchild; second, she knew that her daughter expected her to offer all of her resources to help her grandchild.

Sixteen teen mothers associated the news of their pregnancies with a decline in their mothers' support. To Diane, from a middle-class family, her mother's feelings about status superceded her love for her daughter: "She looks down on people on AFDC, it's the same thing with teenage mothers." When Diane told her mother she had been pregnant for a month, her mother said she had to have an abortion right away, or she couldn't live in her house anymore. Diane was surprised by this strong reaction; until then, she and her mother had been fairly close. She moved out that night, stayed at a motel for a few days, and applied for emergency welfare aid. "This is not the life I had in mind," the young mother said.

Most teen mothers with unsupportive mothers said their mothers assailed their characters: "My mother called me a bitch and a whore." Their mothers' epithets apparently continued throughout the pregnancies, as illustrated by 15-year-old Junie, whose revelations about her mother's reactions are especially poignant:

> When I was pregnant, she used to call me, "You're a whore, you're a tramp." I remember she was talking

*to a friend and calling me a whore
and a tramp to her friends. I ran to
my room and started crying. I left.
When I got back, she said, "You big
fat blimp, you don't need to be having this baby. You're too young."*

Junie, like most teen mothers, was confused
by her mother's negative labeling of her. These
teen mothers, knowing other sexually active
girls who were not pregnant, saw themselves as
no different from those other girls. For the first
time, many of the teenage mothers had to deal
with a powerful negative label, one that was imbedded in the minds of others about Black girls
who become mothers.

The Anti-Abortion Stand as an Affirmation of Motherhood

All but one of the adult mothers demanded that
their daughters have abortions. While adult
mothers demanded abortions, and an abortion
could have resolved the issue of impending
motherhood, the teens chose not to. A typical
response by both sets of mothers came to light
during these interviews. Junie said her mother
called everyone in the family, including the
teen's long-absent father, to garner support for
her daughter having an abortion. In lieu of abortion, her mother wanted her to marry the baby's
father. Junie said she wouldn't marry a man who
refused to acknowledge his baby's existence.

Even mothers who themselves had been
teen mothers wanted their daughters to have
abortions. For example, Terry, whose mother
was supportive of her, said she planned on having an abortion because her mother demanded it.
Her plans fell through when the baby's father left
town without giving her the agreed-upon half of
the abortion fee. "Anyway," she justified her decision, "I'm glad I didn't. I wouldn't know what
to do if I didn't have my baby."

When asked why they refused to have abortions, the teen mothers responded in "us against
them" terms. Seventeen-year-old Melanie said
with moral conviction: "My mother didn't get rid
of me." Margaret, whose baby's father moved to
a southern state shortly after she became pregnant, remembered thinking at the time, "I'm going to have my baby. It's going to be rough but
we'll make it."

At issue in this teen mother's statements
about abortion and motherhood, is what C. Wright
Mills (1956:5) would call, "Matters that transcend
those local environments of the individuals and
the range of [their] inner life." Melanie (like the
others), did not consider herself particularly religious. But the moral convictions revealed in her
comments may reflect the general religiosity of
the Black community. Along with these moral beliefs, Melanie's and Margaret's comments also reveal that motherhood provided a coping strategy:
a way to gain control over their lives and a way of
fulfilling both social expectation and personal desire. Ironically, these teen mothers, who according
to the popular view, do not have mainstream family values, were choosing a traditional model of
women—motherhood. It didn't matter if their
mothers approved or disapproved of their pregnancies, these teen mothers, who lived in depressed neighborhoods where there were few
successful role models for girls, were driven by
the desire to fit into the norms of the larger society.

LINKING GENDER AND RACE: THE LIMITED SUPPORT OF EXTENDED FAMILY

At one time, Black mothers could rely on their
extended families as a resource when faced with
a crisis (Stack 1974). Today, many of these
Black families are too poor to help other family
members (Staples 1994). De Vonya's interview
provides a powerful example of a large Black

family with little to offer in way of support to the teenage mother. Of De Vonya's five siblings, one brother was in jail, the other brother had disappeared years ago, and her three sisters were all single parents on welfare. Her aunts and uncles worked at odd jobs or were unavailable to offer any support. Other mothers had similar stories, confirming that the extended Black family system has declined in recent years (Staples 1994).

I asked the teen mothers who else offered them support during and after they became pregnant. Fathers and other kin were virtually nonexistent in the teen mothers' assessments. Most teen mothers either did not know their fathers or know much about them. Two teen mothers said their fathers were "somewhat supportive." Twenty said that they counted primarily on one or two women friends for financial support. Only two of the teen mothers and adult mothers said they could rely on what Stack (1974) refers to as a mutual exchange system. Twenty-seven-year-old Lois, who became a mother at fifteen, lived with her grandmother and sister and considered her immediate family and a few women friends her family support system. But, the help she received from them was not consistent, since they had their own money problems. For two teen mothers, it was a matter of pride. As 16-year-old Tracy explained, "I was just too embarrassed to ask anyone [for help]."

Despite the lack of family support, these interviews illuminate the teens' expectations that nothing in the relationship with family, especially adult mother, should change—the norms and values associated with the way women mother would require that their mothers follow through with the needed support. The daughters perceived their mothers' refusals to be repudiations of this obligation rather than statements of economic powerlessness. The teens' ideas legitimize the wider society's view that mothering is women's essential nature.

Conforming to Cultural Norms

Before we discuss further specific aspects of the interviews with the adult mothers, we should consider why adult mothers in this study reacted so strongly to their daughters' pregnancies. Most adult mothers were deeply disappointed with their daughters; they all expected that their daughters would graduate from high school and go on to college. According to Furstenberg (1980), the mother who nurtures a teen girl in her early years could be the same person who, acting from her own needs, punishes the child she sees as immoral especially when feeling challenged by someone whom she considers under her authority.

In this study, the mothers were reacting to the breaking of at least three strongly held gender expectations or norms about childbearing and sexuality. The mothers' negative labeling of their daughters reveals their adherence to the first of these norms: Young girls should not have babies before reaching adult status, and certainly not before marriage. In a study of Black mothers who have teenage daughters, Burton and Bengtson (1985:34) find that, "The off-time accession to the lineage role creates," for many young mothers, conflicts in their view of themselves and in their families' systems of cohesion and social support.

For example, when 16-year-old Susan's baby was born, the tension between daughter and mother became unbearable, often dissolving into swinging matches. During one of my visits with Susan's mother, Janet—an attractive woman with two younger children who said she didn't think of herself as a grandmother—she threatened to put her daughter into a foster home. Susan fought back by warning her mother that she neglected her own children. Janet believed her daughter to be a lazy mother whose baby should be taken away from her because, "She stays out late, leaves the baby with me all the time, doesn't do any work around the house, and sleeps late every day." Both mothers' comments reflect the increasing frustrations intrinsic in any relationship that has to adjust to sudden changes.

The second social norm aggravating the conflict between daughters and mothers is the cultural taboo against age inappropriate sexual behavior. Most of the adult mothers, including those who were themselves teen mothers, found it difficult to acknowledge that their 14- or 15-year-old daughters were sexually active. After the daughters' admissions, the mothers had to deal with the stigma (see Goffman 1963) and deviancy associated with Black teenage mothers:

> I know she was only 14 when she got pregnant and some of my church friends couldn't stop blaming me for what happened to my daughter. Like I can follow her around everywhere to stop her from getting pregnant.

Forty-three-year-old Evie recalled her mother's reaction 25 years ago as if it just happened. With a trace of bitterness, she remembered:

> The bigger I got during my pregnancy, the more my mother hated me. By the time I reached my seventh month she'd look at me, and close the door to my bedroom. So I finally left.

This vignette also illustrates the longevity of conflict between nine former teen mothers and their mothers. Evie's mother Marie said:

> I wanted her to really be something, to go on and finish school, and I wanted to send her to Europe, to just be something other than a mother.

Despite Evie returning to school to earn a college degree in social work, her mother continued to imply she has failed: "My mother insinuates I could have done so much more, but I've ruined my chances for a good marriage and career." Evie believed her mother was concerned only about damage to her own reputation. Evie cried softly as she recalled old memories, "My mother hated me for it. I was just alone."

The third norm surfacing in these interviews is that "successful" mothering obligates one to pass on society's social values to children. Therefore, when a teen becomes pregnant, her mother's (but not her father's) abilities to socialize the daughter gain in significance. Mothers fear their daughters' failure may be linked to them: If the adult mother has been a teen mother herself her daughter's failure will be perceived as her own ongoing moral failure; if she is middle-class, others will think she doesn't properly control her daughter. By criticizing the daughter, the mother affirms her place in the world of convention: "Why am I being blamed? It's her fault," said one mother, distancing herself from the stigma of her daughter's sexual behavior.

The daughters' interviews bore out their mothers' concerns that friends were gossiping about them. Joanne, a 30-year-old former teen mother, provides an example. At the time of her teen pregnancy, she became estranged from her mother when church members threatened her mother's status in the community. Joanne's mother, Selma, carried herself as a model of moral virtues and taught her daughter to do the same. Joanne shared her mother's moral beliefs until she became pregnant, "I wanted to be married and to not have a baby at an early age."

Joanne describes how her mother's set of moral values affected her ability to grapple with Joanne's pregnancy. Her mother saw her family disgraced by ugly talk about her daughter:

My mother thought she had failed. She, as well as me, was being talked about. That was the first sign in my family that all was not well.

Her mother grew increasingly concerned with the gossip, "My mother could not overcome her moral sense, and this had a tremendous impact on our relationship." Selma says Joanne's pregnancy was an indication that, "I didn't have control over her; she was irresponsible and didn't have control over herself."

ADULT MOTHERS: VARIATIONS BY CLASS

In considering the logic of the culture of poverty's perspective of the Black matriarchal family structure and the circumstances of the teens' adult mothers, what become significant are the meanings these adult mothers gave to their daughters' situations in concert with the daughters' perceptions of their mothers. The daughters' expectation that their mothers be available and approachable at all times (see Fischer 1986), collided with the mothers' expectation that their daughters would follow the traditional path to motherhood, by marrying first. Exacerbating the conflict was that the adult mothers were young themselves and still raising other children.

Adding weight to these meanings was the influence of the adult mothers' economic status: Three of the nine adult mothers had incomes of $6,500 to $8,000 a year, two working-class mothers earned yearly incomes of $11,000 to $13,000; four of the mothers were middle-class professionals with yearly incomes of $23,000 to $45,000. Neither class variation nor the mothers' status as former teen mothers illustrated marked differences in the problems they had with their teenage daughters. But, as we shall see, class

variations and status did impact the meaning the adult mothers made of their daughters' pregnancies, affecting the way they justified their coping strategies. Further, as we shall see, the adult mothers in this study shared certain common characteristics.

Before describing the adult mothers' perceptions of their daughters, I want to make an analytical contrast between sliders and aspirers. Both concepts refer to the aspirations people have regarding their dreams, abilities, and sense of place within the economic structure (see MacLeod 1987). Class sliders wanted to preserve their-hard-won middle-class status for themselves (and their daughters). Class aspirers wanted their daughters to pull them up the class ladder by attaining a higher class status than they themselves had achieved.

MIDDLE-CLASS STATUS "SLIDERS"

Four of the mothers were employed in middle-class professions: Two were school teachers, one was employed in a supervisory civil service occupation, and another worked as an insurance agent. Three were the first in their families to earn college degrees. I refer to this group as "class sliders." All of these mothers expressed concerns that their daughters' pregnancies would change their middle-class image for the worse; they linked teenage pregnancy to lower-class behavior, so they tried to distance themselves from their daughters. On the practical level, as the sole financial providers for their families, they had to be concerned about financially supporting another child, a burden that could spell downward economic mobility for them.

Alma, an elementary school teacher, said that teenage mothers have "ghettoized mentalities." Only low-class teenage girls, living in poor families where teenage pregnancy is a way of life, become pregnant. In line with this reasoning, when her daughter Diane became the first teenage welfare mother in her family, Alma felt that Diane gave the family a "ghetto" image, thereby creating distance between the mother and daughter.

Evie's mother, a retired high school teacher, thought of her daughter's pregnancy as a "stigma." Evie's mother's inability to "forgive" Evie 25 years later demonstrates the long-term affect teenage motherhood can have on these mother-daughter relationships.

Another adult mother, Martha, a Deaconess in the church and moral authority in the family, demanded her 15-year-old pregnant daughter, Margaret, confess her "sin" to the church congregation, asking for forgiveness. Margaret did so but moved out of her mother's home. When Margaret, now 35 and a re-entry pre-law student, told her mother she had just registered for college, her mother didn't believe her, she doubted her daughter could do anything well.

WORKING-CLASS AND POOR ADULT MOTHER "CLASS ASPIRERS"

Unlike the middle-class mothers, four of the five "class aspirer" mothers had been teenage mothers, two were still raising small children and on disability, welfare, or employed in low-wage service occupations. Notions of upward mobility echoed throughout these mothers' interviews, stressing their wish that their daughters lead the good life, climb the class ladder, and help the family do so as well. Sadly, the adult mothers tried to put their views across by putting themselves down: They felt that the only way to handle their experiences was to serve as negative role models for their daughters, as Ruth told me, of "what not to do." A 36-year-old mother of four, Ruth was disappointed with 15-year-old Junie: "She wanted to go to college. Now she be like me."

Ruth was afraid of being stigmatized as a "bad mother" who passed on "low moral standards" to her daughter. Often, this fear drove adult mothers like Ruth to act harshly toward their daughters. When 54-year-old Mary learned that De Vonya was pregnant, she refused to help her. Her own life had been "pure drudgery:" her daughter's pregnancy made it all the worse: "I wanted her to go to college, because this is what she keeps talking about."

Thirty-six-year-old Jessie, whose mother was fifteen when she was born, wanted her teenage daughter, Marnie, also pregnant at fifteen to "go to school and be a doctor or something." When her daughter became pregnant, she was "so hurt I can't describe it." Marnie, who expected compassion, was confused by her mother's lack of support, "After all, it happened to her. Instead of helping me she called me a bunch of names and still does."

Many of the daughters of "class aspirers" thought their mothers were punishing them. According to 17-year-old Shana, "She didn't really want me to have the baby, and she was given' me a hard time." Sixteen-year-old Marnie had a similar story:

> [My mother] told me, "You do everything. No company, no telephone. The rest of the [children] can go out." She was punishing me for having my baby.

Was Marnie's mother punishing her daughter or merely assigning her daughter household tasks as many parents do? Each adult mother made different meanings of these experiences. Marnie's mother was afraid she would have to raise her grandchild, something she wasn't financially or emotionally prepared to do. The same was true for Mary, De Vonya's mother:

This is my daughter's responsibility.
This is her mistake. It's not mine. It's
not like I'm trying to punish her. But
her baby days are over.

Mary saw her daughter's new motherhood as a signal of adult status (see Apfel and Seitz 1991). But whatever Mary's intentions, De Vonya, like Marnie, saw the housework assignments as a punishing strategy, creating friction between daughter and mother: "I can't stand her attitude and she can't stand mine," De Vonya declared. Shortly after the baby was born, De Vonya moved out of her mother's home. When 14-year-old Junie became pregnant, her mother, Ruthie, didn't know how to handle the news: "So I called her a bunch of names. I made her stay in her room for weeks at a time—I was so angry." As Stokes and Hewitt (1976:842) argue, when people confront a situation that seems "culturally inappropriate" they "organize their conduct, individually and jointly to get it back on track." One way the adult mothers could reorganize their lives was to develop impression management strategies that allowed them to cope with their daughters' "appalling" situation.

IMPRESSION MANAGEMENT STRATEGIES

The adult mothers' interviews reveal the use of several impression management strategies in an effort to defend themselves against their daughters' "soiled identity" as Goffman (1963:65) would say, keeping the spotlight off themselves. According to Goffman's discussion of stigmatized people:

The issue is not that of managing tension generated during social contacts, but rather that of managing information about their failing: "To

display or not to display; to tell or not to tell; to let on or not to let on; to lie or not to lie; and in each case, to whom, how, when, and where to disclose discrediting information about the self (1963:63).

A number of adult mothers used a "covering" strategy (Goffman 1963) as a way to distance themselves from the stigma associated with their daughters: adding a few years to their ages or to that of their daughters. Even now, one mother pretends that her 25-year-old daughter is older than her actual age. Evie, the daughter, said of her mother: "She didn't tell anybody she had a grandchild until he was three years old."

Another strategy most of the adult mothers used, I call "redirecting the gaze." Feeling the need to criticize a daughter during the interview, Alma, like other adult mothers, said she tried to raise her daughter well: "What can you do when she wants to hang out all day with those characters from the school? She's just like them." For this adult mother (as with most class sliders and aspirers), labeling her daughter worked as an impression management strategy. It allowed her to place, measure, and compare the obvious sign of her daughter's sexual behavior with other teenage girls' sexual and non-sexual involvements in explaining her daughter's pregnancy and to remove any issue of her responsibilities as a mother, detaching herself from her daughter's stigma.

In attempting to get their lives "back on track," the daughters developed their own impression management strategies. Most tried to shift the perception of themselves as problem daughters to that of good mothers. Tracy, a 16-year-old mother using this strategy, said she was a "regular old lady" who devoted all of her time to her baby, implying that the baby's birth gave her maturity and, in turn, made her a good mother. These young women also tended to deny they were having problems with their own lives. What they said about their home life, relations with their fathers and babies' fathers, along with my own observations of their living arrangements, tell another story. For example, Tracy, who was attending school, was inclined to say that everything was going well, despite having to study at the same time she was having to care for her child. She was failing in school. Another way to see the teen mothers' denial strategies is to understand that these are adolescent girls, and as such, they tend to want to fit in with others and appear as if they are in control of their situation.

SUMMARY AND DISCUSSION

Consequences for Teen Mothers and Their Mothers

These interviews suggest the importance of understanding women's interactions with each other, along with how they confront a threatening situation, noting when these problems are structured by gender, race, and class. Affluent white middle-class mothers may find themselves encountering fewer severely critical events like their teenage daughter's motherhood. When they do, they usually have the children's fathers in the home who provide adequate financial resources (Fischer 1986). In this study, both teen and adult mothers made note of absent adult fathers and babies' fathers (see Wilson 1987). Mary, De Vonya's mother, compared her life with that of her husband's:

> My husband, he leaves. Where would I find the money to leave? Where would I go? How would I live? And what would people say about me if I left like he did?

Mary's words convey a sense of being trapped by her daughter's (and her other children's) difficulties, touching on the real problems within these daughter-mother relations. Neither teen nor adult mother has others who can provide them with the resources they need to deal with serious problems such as teenage motherhood. Even Alma, with a middle-class professional job, had to handle all of her daughter's problems alone. The absence of the fathers, or other supportive people, meant that these mother-daughter relationships became riddled with unresolvable dependency needs.

Health Problems

The friction and anger voiced by both teen and adult mothers must be understood on a deeper level than the typical struggle between mothers and daughters that ends when the daughters grow up. The lack of adequate support has serious consequences for adult mothers like Alma, Janet, and Mary. Studies of low income Black families (Allen and Britt 1984; Ladner and Gourdine 1984) find that they experience low levels of social support and high levels of acute stress. In this study, examples of such stress emerged as teen and adult mothers talked about their health problems. They experienced a disproportionate amount of anxiety and depression as indicated by a number of accidents, heart attacks (Evie had two), hypertension (six adult mothers), and back problems (two adult mothers). Many adult and teen mothers were involved in car accidents (five each), job-related injuries (seven adult mothers), and physical abuse (three teens/four adult mothers).

The adult mothers recognized the problems their daughters would bring to their already depleted lives. As Collins (1987) notes in her study of Black mothers, the mothering tasks can be so overwhelming for women who have so little that often they can't offer even motherly affection.

The daughters in this study, angry and confused adolescents, looked at their mothers without understanding the socioeconomic problems forcing their mothers to take such a strong stance.

CONCLUSION: DEBUNKING THE MORAL VALUE ARGUMENT

While this study is small and is limited to a particular region of the country, the findings do suggest that teenage motherhood stings as it stigmatizes both teenage and adult mothers, causing problems for them. To say that these adult mothers have deviant values they pass on to their daughters, thereby failing as mothers, ignores the obvious: Their capacity to be good mothers was tested by the severity of the problems they faced as Black mothers. But to suggest that Black mothers are superhuman—a common tendency in the literature—and can go it alone, is to suggest also that gender inequality, racism, and money problems do not affect them.

This study adds complexity to the structural perspective, providing rich evidence that Black mothers are not the "other," as the literature suggests. Rather, they are women with complex perceptions and problems. This research supports other findings (Bell Kaplan, forthcoming; Fischer 1986; Ladner and Gourdine 1984) that daughters and mothers may reevaluate each other as daughters move into early motherhood. They tend to confront and negatively sanction each other when they have to deal with such realities. Therefore, this study refutes the current idea (McGroy, 1994) that, "Illegitimacy has pretty much lost its sting in certain ghetto neighborhoods" (McGrory 1994:25), and, "We need to stigmatize it again" (p. 25).

We need to develop a more sophisticated understanding of the way in which gender relations and socioeconomic conditions transform daughter-mother relationships and the way society's beliefs about moral values influence the perception of these relationships.

The issue of moral values is an extremely important one for these mothers, since the image of deviant mothers raising deviant daughters incites politicians to call for the end of welfare and other social policies. In the current political climate, welfare opponents argue that taxpayers should not support social policies for "immoral" Black mothers and their "immoral" teenage daughters. This study proposes that just such a need—the creation of family policies to assist teenage mothers and their adult mothers—is vital to the well-being of these mothers (and, ultimately, society), as evidenced by the number of health problems they report and by my findings that socioeconomic strains only multiply these problems.

These findings are also important because they indicate the need to place the causes of these family problems (and the causes of teenage pregnancies in the first place), within their historical, social, and economic context (Hardy and Zabin 1991; Ladner and Gourdine 1984). We need to understand that mothering as an ideology can and does exist apart from the practice of mothering. The Black mothers in this study adhered to the same ideology as white mothers in that they feel responsible for raising children, for the way children turn out, and for the values children espouse. Since these Black women, as compared to white women, are often raising teenage daughters alone, such mothering can become a daunting task.

Relational problems between daughters and mothers will persist, even increase, if politicians and social welfare agencies do not adequately address these mothers' social and economic problems. The adult mothers' needs are undercut by the stereotyped perceptions of them as failed mothers or as super-strong women who can cope with all kinds of hardship—a conservative ideology that assumes Black women have such unfailing personal character that they need little support from people in power. These mothers' economic realities, buttressed by wrongheaded sociological stereotypes, reinforce hostile conservative views and harmful political agendas.

As the teen mother interviews show, the real tragedy is that these teenagers have to expend energy on activities other than complex adolescent developmental issues. When adolescence is skipped, as it is for teenage mothers, girls may not learn how to develop their confidence and independence: to do as adolescents learn to do, move away from mothers, and then move back again as adults. Instead, much like sexually abused girls (see Musick 1987), they have problems making the leap across the developmental gap and become involved in defining themselves only in relation to the trauma inherent in being teenage mothers.

Older women's interviews, like Evie's for example, show that even women who find some measure of success in their adult lives find their success undermined by having been teenage mothers, especially when they have no way of understanding that experience other than from the moral perspective. The problem becomes more egregious when adult mothers are not able to offer them the kind of emotional and financial support they need to feel safe and secure as they handle teenage motherhood at the same time they must deal with adolescent issues.

FUTURE PROBLEMS

Several candid teen mothers revealed another relationship problem. Terry, a 19-year-old mother with a three-year-old son, said she liked babies until they reached the age of two, when they became problems. When I asked 16-year-old De Vonya if she had any advice for other teenage girls, she yelled into the microphone, "Don't have no babies!" These teen mothers' reactions are more realistic than the "regular old lady" comment made earlier by 16-year-old Tracy. The dilemma for these mothers is that at this age and stage of adolescent development, a teen mother may not be able to push aside her own need to be mothered in order to adequately mother her child. Yet at the time these teenage daughters need "to become daughters again" (Fischer 1986), adult mothers can't afford to keep mothering their teenage daughters, economically, socially, or emotionally.

Negative messages about teenage and adult mothers' moral character also threaten the positive development of the teenage mothers' children, who need both mothers and grandmothers, since men are absent from their lives. Without financial resources and family policies providing support, without rebuilding the extended-family social support system, we may expect increased alienation within these families. The tragic consequence may be the further erosion of the already fragile social fabric of Black mother-headed families. As this study demonstrates, we can develop a complex and beneficial sociological framework if a comprehensive understanding incorporating a gender, race, and class perspective is used to find solutions to the problems experienced by young mothers, helping us discover preventative alternatives to teenage pregnancy.

Reading 21   The Changing Culture of Fatherhood in Comic-Strip Families: A Six-Decade Analysis

RALPH LAROSSA*   CHARLES JARET
MALATI GADGIL   G. ROBERT WYNN

A content analysis of 490 Father's Day and Mother's Day comic strips published from 1940 to 1999 indicates that the culture of fatherhood has fluctuated since World War II. "Incompetent" fathers appeared frequently in the late 1940s, early 1950s, and late 1960s but were rarer in the late 1950s, early and late 1970s, early 1980s, and early 1990s. Fathers who were mocked were especially common in the early and late 1960s and early 1980s but were less common in the late 1940s, early and late 1950s, and early and late 1970s. Fathers who were nurturant and supportive toward children were most evident in the late 1940s, early 1950s, and early and late 1990s, with the longitudinal pattern resembling a U-shaped curve. Differences between fathers and mothers also oscillated from one decade to the next.

How do popular portrayals of fathers in the 1970s, 1980s, and 1990s compare with popular portrayals of fathers in the 1940s, 1950s, and 1960s? Have the portrayals improved? Have they gotten worse? Is there any variation at all?

The issue here is not whether the conduct of fatherhood has shifted, but whether the culture of fatherhood has changed (LaRossa, 1988). When it comes to conduct, studies have shown

that with the increase in the number of dual-earner families, more fathers are spending large blocks of "quality time" with their children, although men still lag behind women in this regard (Pleck, 1997). On the other hand, because of the long-term escalation in divorce, many nonresident fathers have only minimal contact with their daughters and sons. The behavioral picture of the contemporary male parent thus can be said to

Authors' Note: We want to thank Linda Verrill for her research assistance during the early stages of the project and Maxine Atkinson, Elisabeth Burgess, Maureen Mulligan LaRossa, and Wendy Simonds for their helpful suggestions on earlier drafts of the article.

have both a good side and a bad side (Fursten-berg, 1988).

What about the culture of fatherhood (i.e., the norms, values, beliefs, and expressive symbols pertaining to fatherhood)? How much change can be discerned here? Scholars may be better equipped today to answer this question than they were 15 years ago, but a careful examination of the four studies that have directly tested "the changing-culture-of-fatherhood hypothesis" (Day & Mackey, 1986; LaRossa, Gordon, Wilson, Bairan, & Jaret, 1991; Atkinson & Blackwelder, 1993; Coltrane & Allan, 1994) indicates that much still remains unknown.

In the first effort to systematically tackle the question, Day and Mackey (1986) compared single-panel family cartoons published in the *Saturday Evening Post* between 1922 and 1968 with similar kinds of cartoons published between 1971 and 1978 to see whether "the role image of the American father" in popular culture had been transformed. They found that up to the late 1960s, fathers were significantly more likely than were mothers to be characterized as incompetent (e.g., as "awkward," "unhandy," or "gawky"), but in the 1970s, the incidence of incompetence for men and women was statistically similar. Because of the convergence in how cartoons portrayed fathers and mothers during the second period in contrast to the disparity of their portrayals in the first, Day and Mackey concluded that the 1970s marked a paradigmatic shift in the culture of fatherhood. As they saw it, the percentage of mothers in the labor force, the decline in birth rates, and the fervent advocacy of gender equality in the 1970s (brought on by the feminist movement) had prompted the traditionally minded *Saturday Evening Post* cartoonists to reduce their satirical attacks on fathers. A new, improved version of fatherhood had come on the scene.

Social scientists have long recognized that humor can reveal patterns of stratification (e.g.,

see Mulkay, 1988; Wilson, 1979), hence the premise that the incompetence level of cartoon characters could be used as a barometer of social trends does have validity. Nonetheless, were Day and Mackey (1986) correct about the 1970s? Had the image of the American father basically been consistent until then?

In a follow-up study, LaRossa et al. (1991) examined the same kinds of *Saturday Evening Post* cartoons that Day and Mackey (1986) had, but focused more closely on the years 1924, 1928, 1932, 1936, 1940, and 1944, when historical conditions were analogous to those in the 1970s (i.e., the labor force participation rate of mothers had increased, birth rates had alternated, and the first wave of the 20th century women's movement was reverberating). LaRossa et al. discovered that whereas fathers were significantly more likely than were mothers to be depicted as incompetent in the 1920s, the disparity with respect to incompetence had disappeared in the 1930s and especially the early 1940s. If gender parity in cartoon humor is a sign of "role image" change, as Day and Mackey suggested, then it would seem that the 1970s were not the first time fathers were taken seriously. The paradigmatic shift that Day and Mackey had assumed was peculiar to the 1970s also may have occurred in the 1930s and 1940s. Synthesizing the findings from the two studies, LaRossa et al. inferred that a fluctuating pattern was a more accurate model of how the culture of fatherhood had changed over the course of the 20th century.

Next, in another study that relied on print media but not on cartoons, Atkinson and Blackwelder (1993) examined popular magazine articles published in the middle years of every decade from the early 1900s to the 1980s to see what had happened to "fathering role definitions" in the interim. Calculating the ratio of articles accentuating "nurturant fathering" to articles accentuating "providing fathering," they found that in the 1920s and 1930s, the emphasis on "providing fathering" was predominant, but that from the 1940s through the 1980s "nurturant fathering" was the more common theme. They also noted that for the latter part of the 20th century, the ratios moved up and down, reporting scores of 2.5, 1.3, 1.4, 3.3, and 2.8 for the 1940s, 1950s, 1960s, 1970s, and 1980s, respectively (i.e., fathers were 2.5 times more likely in the 1940s to be defined as "nurturing," and so on.). These figures suggest that traditional gender roles were more likely to be endorsed in the 1950s and 1960s and that the concept of the "New Father" (i.e., the more involved father) was strongest in the 1970s. The pattern would appear to support both Day and Mackey's (1986) claim that the 1970s were a high water mark for nurturant fathering and LaRossa and colleagues' (1991) contention that the culture of fatherhood had fluctuated. Left unanswered, however, was why there would be a lower ratio in the 1980s than there was in the 1970s. Interesting, too, was the similarity between the 1950s and 1960s. Did the feminist movement of the 1960s have no immediate effect on definitions of fatherhood?

In the most recent study, based on electronic rather than print media, Coltrane and Allan (1994) compared representations of fatherhood and motherhood in television advertising in the 1980s with representations in the 1950s. Characters appearing in "classic" and award-winning commercials were judged on a variety of criteria, including whether they were parents or paid workers and whether they were nurturant and supportive when performing the parental role. On the first measure, Coltrane and Allan found that in the 1950s, men were six times more likely to be shown as workers than as parents, whereas women were twice as likely to be shown as parents than as workers. In the 1980s, the portrayal of men had changed only slightly, whereas the portrayal of women had become more similar to

that of the men; three decades later, men were almost four times as likely, and women were twice as likely, to be shown as workers than as parents. The convergence in the portrayal of men and women as workers indicated that some change had occurred, but Coltrane and Allan pointed out that gender differences continued to be visible in that "men were still more likely to be pictured in occupational roles than were women" (p. 51).

Coltrane and Allan's (1994) study revealed little change on the issue of whether men and women were depicted as nurturant and supportive. In the 1950s, 75% of the fathers and 89% of the mothers displayed nurturant and supportive behaviors; in the 1980s, 71% of the fathers and 78% of the mothers displayed nurturant and supportive behaviors. In other words, most of the advertisements tended to present fathers and mothers as "warm and fuzzy," but there was no greater tendency to do so in the 1980s, which is unexpected if one were looking for evidence of an increase in the concept of the "New Father." Coltrane and Allan concluded that previous research had probably overestimated the extent of change: "Our findings must be considered tentative because of sampling limitations [e.g., only four men and nine women were pictured as parents in the 1950s], but we challenge the common perception that the popular culture of fathering was transformed in fundamental ways during the 1980s" (p. 61).

Taking the studies together, what can be said about the culture of fatherhood in late-20th-century America? First, it appears the researchers agree that change has occurred but disagree on the magnitude of change. Whereas Day and Mackey (1986) described a "paradigmatic" shift in the "role image of the American father," and Atkinson and Blackwelder (1993) referred to the amount of change in "the popular conceptualization of parenthood" as "remarkable" and "important," Coltrane and Allan (1994) were of the opinion that the change in "fatherhood imagery" was minimal at best and largely overstated. Second, there is an absence of consensus among the researchers on the timing and duration of change. Day and Mackey and Atkinson and Blackwelder offered evidence that the 1970s were critical years in the cultural history of fatherhood, but if Coltrane and Allan were correct, the moment must have been short lived. The downturn that Atkinson and Blackwelder reported for the 1980s also would suggest a dampening effect. Third, there is a lack of clarity on the shape of change. Is there a fluctuating pattern, as LaRossa et al. (1991) and Atkinson and Blackwelder believe? If so, how do we make sense of Coltrane and Allan's findings, which imply that the 1950s and 1980s were similar?

OBJECTIVE

The goal of this article is try to answer the above questions and, in so doing, reduce some of the confusion that now exists. Drawing on a six-decade content analysis of 490 comic strips published on Father's Day and Mother's Day, we endeavor to determine whether and how the culture of fatherhood has changed since World War II.

Why comic strips? More than 100 million people read comic strips every day (Wood, 1987, p. 186), and, as with television sitcoms, they occupy a central place in American society. A study of comic strips thus has the potential to tap into a nation's collective consciousness. Also, because comics have been around for more than a century (Inge, 1979, 1990), they lend themselves to the investigation of long-term cultural trends (Harrison, 1981; Kasen, 1979, 1980). Given how often they revolve around domestic situations, they have proven an especially valuable index of family ideologies and gender stereotypes (e.g., see Brabant, 1976; Brabant & Mooney, 1986, 1997).

Interestingly enough, despite the role that political cartoons have played in exposing the foibles of the powerful, comic strips often perpetuate rather than challenge gender stereotypes (Chavez, 1985; Mooney & Brabant, 1987, 1990). Choosing comic strips for our database thus made it more likely that we would not find any historical differences. With comic strips as our criterion, the changing-culture-of-fatherhood hypothesis faced a stiffer challenge.

As for deciding to examine comic strips published on Father's Day and Mother's Day, this carried with it several advantages. First, we felt that chronological comparisons would be more meaningful if we focused on comics published on the same day from one year to the next. Second, Father's Day and Mother's Day are public rites or ceremonies that cryptically symbolize the social value of fatherhood and motherhood in America. Third, content analyzing comic strips on Father's Day and Mother's Day allowed each holiday to serve as a point of reference for the other.

One may ask the question, what connection do comic strips have to public attitudes and behaviors? One answer is they have no connection at all. That is, some may say that comic strips are too oblique and too divorced from everyday life to have any relationship to what is "really going on." But then why are they funny? Humor essentially entails a paradoxical juxtaposition of two realities, conventional and unconventional (Macionis, 1989). Thus, it could be argued that a father making a mess of the kitchen while preparing a Mother's Day breakfast was a recurring theme in the comics we studied because of both its familiarity and its absurdity (the gift, sincerely offered, backfires). The fact that, in contrast, there was not a single comic that had a mother mismanaging a Father's Day breakfast— and that if there were, it probably would seem odd (unless it were ingeniously crafted)—says something about how fathers and mothers are portrayed in American culture and about how they think and act. The many published studies that have shown empirically how comic strips reflect gender, race, and class divisions, among other realities, also make a strong case for taking them seriously in social science.

To say that there is a connection between comic strips and everyday life is not to say that the connection is simple. Internalizing culture, of which comic strips are a part, is not akin to downloading software on a computer. Rather, the socialization process is more selective and more interactive. Culture basically operates as a framing device—channeling, not determining, attitudes and behaviors (W. Griswold, 1994; Zerubavel, 1991, 1997). Culture, therefore, is "more a 'tool kit' or repertoire" from which people choose assorted "pieces" to construct "strategies of action" (Swidler, 1986, p. 277). One could say that comic strips are part of a society's cultural supermarket. A strip's presence "on the shelves" makes its stories and vocabularies (e.g., "Good grief!" from *Peanuts*) available for selection and incorporation into the amalgam of norms, values, beliefs, and expressive symbols that influence people's perceptions and behaviors.

METHOD

Comics and Characters

We carefully reviewed the humorous comics (i.e., the funnies as opposed to the dramatic serials) published in the *Atlanta Journal and Constitution* on Father's Day and Mother's Day from 1940 to 1999 and marked for coding those comics that (a) explicitly mentioned or implicitly alluded to Father's Day or Mother's Day or (b) had fatherhood, motherhood, or parenthood as a theme. We limited the study to humorous comics because when we first scanned the comic-strip pages, it appeared to us that humorous comics were more likely to present the kinds of stories that would reveal attitudes toward fatherhood and motherhood. When we completed the review, 216 Father's Day and 274 Mother's Day comics were found to fall into one category or the other. These 490 comics were then individually photocopied, making them black and white,

and randomly numbered so as to disguise their publication dates.

In our analysis, we focused on the designated Father's Day or Mother's Day parents; if the comic did not explicitly mention or implicitly allude to one of the holidays, we focused on the parents who were the most central (if identifiable). The focus also could be a grandparent or stepparent or, in a few cases, a father or mother figure. Fathers and mothers could be humans, animals (e.g., ants), or even machines (e.g., robots). Among the 490 comics, there were 357 fathers and 389 mothers who were singled out for "observation."

Because the comics analyzed in this study included every comic in the *Atlanta Journal and Constitution* published on Father's Day and Mother's Day that mentioned or alluded to the holiday or that focused on fatherhood, motherhood, or parenthood, we had the entire population of relevant comics, rather than only a sample of them. Our comparisons, of the Father's Day and Mother's Day comics thus do not require significance tests because the percentages derived are not subject to sampling error.

Although we relied on a single newspaper, the fact that Sunday comics are syndicated meant that many of the comics appeared in hundreds, if not thousands, of newspapers nationwide. The recognizability and range of the comics also are indicative of a set that is more representative than idiosyncratic. Some of the comics selected were: *B.C., Blondie, Bloom County, Cathy, Dennis the Menace, The Family Circus, For Better or Worse, Garfield, Gasoline Alley, Hagar the Horrible, Hi and Lois, Little Orphan Annie, Peanuts, Pogo, The Wizard of Id,* and *Ziggy,* (among others). The oldest syndicated comic in the grouping was *Gasoline Alley,* first published in 1919. The second oldest was *Blondie,* first published in 1930 (Goulart, 1995, pp. 96, 125; Kinnaird, 1963, pp. 92–93).

Men penned the majority of comics under investigation, reflecting the patriarchal culture of the newspaper industry. Women drew some of the newer comics, however (e.g., *Cathy, For Better or Worse,* and *Stone Soup*), suggesting movement toward gender equality, albeit slight. Also, until recently, all the comic-strip characters appear to be White. Only in the 1990s, with the addition of comics such as *Curtis, Jumpstart,* and *The Boondocks,* have we seen more frequent representations of people of color. In total, 5.1% of the 490 comics in our sample feature an African American parental figure. Finally, we had hoped to determine whether socioeconomic status might be a factor but soon discovered that almost all the comic-strip families were middle class (based on the quality of the furnishings inside the home, among other indicators). The typical Sunday comic strip thus resembles the typical popular magazine article or television show in at least one respect: Each tends to offer a homogenized portrait of social life.

Coding

What messages, relevant to the culture of fatherhood, can be found in a comic strip? First of all, it is important to recognize that there are no messages "in" a comic. Rather, there are various meanings that the reader may give to the pictures and words on the page. To the cartoonist, a particular comic may symbolize one thing. To the publisher, it may symbolize something else. Among the audience, multiple readings may exist. As with any text (whether it be a painting, a poem, or a historical or legal document), a comic can be subject to a variety of interpretations (Mukerji and Schudson, 1991).

We take the issue of multiple messages in texts seriously. Nonetheless, we also believe that, with care, it is possible for someone immersed in a culture to reliably and validly ascertain (i.e., code) the mutually understood and shared definitions of a comedic situation that are held by many, if not most, of the inhabitants of that culture. Indeed, we would contend that the

ability to accomplish this feat is what makes a successful cartoonist.

With an awareness of the challenges involved, coding was a multistep process. First, MG and GRW would independently code the comics. Then, the four of us would meet to discuss the comics and reconcile any discrepancies that had emerged in the first round. These group sessions provided a forum where we would toss back and forth how best to approach some of the more subtle comics.

Although RL and CJ were aware of the goals of the project from the beginning, MG and GRW were deliberately not told what the study was about while they were coding, and they were asked not to read any of the previously published literature on the subject. Because of the nuances in comic-strip humor and the complexity of the codes employed, coding took longer than was originally planned. Contemplating how to "speed things up," we considered bringing in another coder to serve as a tiebreaker. After a while, however, we came to realize that our team approach and in-depth familiarity with the comics greatly enhanced the reliability and validity of the coding process. Our different disciplinary ties and diversity in gender, age, and national and regional background also contributed positively to the content analysis. (Note: The set of comics published in 1999 were a late addition to our sample and were coded by RL and CJ. The rules that had become institutionalized in the group sessions were applied to the 1999 set.)

Measures

Attention Given to Father's Day and Mother's Day. How much attention was given to Father's Day and Mother's Day from 1940 to 1999? To address this question, we counted for each year the number of comic strips that explicitly mentioned or implicitly alluded to Father's Day or Mother's Day. More often than not, if Father's Day were mentioned or alluded to at all, it was in a comic published on Father's Day; and more often than not, if Mother's Day were mentioned or alluded to at all, it was in a comic published on Mother's Day. But there were instances where an acknowledgment of Father's Day would appear on Mother's Day, or an acknowledgment of Mother's Day would appear on Father's Day. (Sometimes a single comic would give attention to both, for example.) We also included these crossovers in our counts.

Incompetence. To measure the level of incompetence exhibited by the fathers and mothers in the strips, we built upon the coding scheme that LaRossa et al. (1991) used. In that study, coders were asked: "Is the father in this family (whether he is pictured in the cartoon or not) being depicted as incompetent?" Each cartoon was given one of the following codes: 0 *Not applicable* (Father is not in the cartoon, and no reference is made to him or about him); 1 *Not incompetent* (Father is in cartoon or is referenced in the cartoon, but he is not depicted as incompetent); or 2 *Incompetent* (Father is in cartoon or is referenced in the cartoon, and he is depicted as incompetent). The question was then repeated so that it applied to the mother. To be "incompetent," the father or mother would have to behave in a way that could be classified as ignorant, inadequate, incapable, ineffectual, inefficient, inept, stupid, unable, unfit, or weak (first-order synonyms for incompetence in the Wordperfect thesaurus).

In this study, coders reviewed 27 activities that fathers and mothers could enact and made the following judgment: "Is the Father's Day (FD) Father/Grandfather or the male spouse of the Mother's Day (MD) Mother/Grandmother in this comic (whether he is pictured in the comic or not) enacting any of the following activities; if so, is he depicted as incompetent in the activity?" Each cartoon was given one of the following codes: 0 *Not applicable* (FD/MD father is not in comic and no reference is made to him or about him); 1 *Activity not enacted* (FD/MD father is in comic or

referenced in comic, but is not involved in the activity); 2 *Incompetent* (FD/MD father is in comic or is referenced in comic, and he is depicted as incompetent on this particular issue); or 3 *Activity enacted competently or enacted in such a way that competence or incompetence is not an issue* (FD/MD father is in comic or referenced in comic, is involved in the activity, and is competent in his performance, or the question of competence or incompetence is not relevant on this particular activity). The question was then repeated so that it would apply to the mother. The synonyms for "incompetence" used in the LaRossa et al. (1991) study also were used in this study. The list of activities included not only child-care activities (e.g., verbally or physically expresses affection toward children), but also marital activities (e.g., engages in negative emotional interaction with spouse), household activities (e.g., does traditionally feminine household chores), employment-related activities (e.g., performs paid work), gender-socializing activities (e.g., shows a child what it means to "be a man"), and activities related to Father's Day or Mother's Day (e.g., gives or is about to give Father's Day or Mother's Day gift).

Mocked. Recognizing that it is possible for a parent to be made, to look foolish even though he or she is not acting foolishly, we decided to ask more globally, and without focusing on any specific activities: "Does this comic make a deliberate point to mock anyone in particular or in general?" Children and others were sometimes mocked in the comics, but for this analysis, we will report only the numbers for fathers and mothers.

Nurturant and Supportive Parenting Behaviors I. Coltrane and Allan (1994) operationalized nurturant and supportive parenting behaviors as verbally or physically expressing affection toward a child, serving or caring for a child, verbally encouraging a child, or comforting a child or inquiring about the child's feelings and thoughts. To compare what Coltrane and Allan found when they looked at television ads with what we might find when we looked at comic strips, we included their four examples of nurturant and supportive behaviors in our list of 27 activities.

Nurturant and Supportive Parenting Behaviors II. While pretesting our coding instrument, we discovered that comic-strip fathers and mothers also could be nurturant and supportive by praising a child for a completed task or activity or for a job well done, listening to a child's problem, or purposefully teaching a child. We thus added these three nurturant and supportive behaviors to Coltrane and Allan's (1994) four nurturant and supportive behaviors to construct a seven-item composite measure, Nurturant and Supportive Parenting Behaviors II. For this measure, as well as the previous measure, verbally encouraging a child meant explicitly "during a task or activity," so as to distinguish it from praising a child "for a completed task or activity."

RESULTS

Attention Given to Father's Day and Mother's Day

Table 21.1 reports the number of comics by half decade that explicitly mentioned or implicitly alluded to Father's Day or Mother's Day. (We opted for half-decade cutting points because of significant intradecade variations uncovered in our analysis.) Several trends are revealed, the most important of which are: (a) the shift from the 1940–1944 period when there were no comics that acknowledged Father's Day or Mother's Day to the 1945 and after period when there were many that did, (b) the general rise over time in the number of comics that acknowledged the holidays, (c) the greater attention given to Mother's Day compared with Father's Day overall (for every 10 acknowledgments of Mother's Day, there were about 8 acknowledgments of Father's Day), and (d) the much greater attention given to Mother's Day compared with Father's Day from 1995 to 1999 (the difference in the late 1990s accounts for almost half of the difference in the totals).

Incompetence

Table 21.2 reports how the fathers and mothers in the entire sample were portrayed (i.e., among the 357 fathers and 389 mothers pictured or referenced in the 490 comics that explicitly mentioned or implicitly alluded to Father's Day or Mother's Day, or had fatherhood, motherhood, or parenthood as a theme).

The first-row totals indicate that over all the years, 10.9% of the fathers and 5.7% of the mothers in the comics were depicted as incompetent. These percentages are fairly small and mean that the parents in the Father's Day and Mother's Day comics were much more often than not depicted as capable, efficient, and so forth, or they were shown performing activities in which competence or incompetence was not an issue. Given the higher scores for father and mother incompetence in studies of single-panel

TABLE 21.1 Number of Comics that Explicitly Mentioned or Implicitly Alluded to Father's Day or Mother's Day, 1940–1999

	40–44	45–49	50–54	55–59	60–64	65–69	70–74	75–79	80–84	85–89	90–94	95–99	Totals
Father's Day	0	6	5	8	14	9	14	17	20	28	37	35	193
Mother's Day	0	8	7	8	15	16	19	19	22	35	40	56	245
Difference	0	−2	−2	0	−1	−7	−5	−2	−2	−7	−3	−21	−52

TABLE 21.2 Percentage of Fathers and Mothers Depicted as Incompetent, Mocked, or Shown to Be Nurturant and Supportive Parents in Comics Explicitly Mentioning or Implicitly Alluding to Father's Day or Mother's Day, or Having Fatherhood, Motherhood, or Parenthood as a Theme, 1940–1999

	40–44	45–49	50–54	55–59	60–64	65–69	70–74	75–79	80–84	85–89	90–94	95–99	Totals
Incompetent													
Fathers	—	21.4	33.3	0.0	14.3	21.1	8.3	8.0	3.6	14.9	5.4	12.3	10.9
Mothers	—	28.6	0.0	7.1	5.0	4.5	6.7	0.0	3.0	4.0	9.2	3.2	5.7
Difference	—	-7.2	33.0	-7.1	9.3	16.6	1.6	8.0	0.6	10.9	-3.8	9.1	5.2
Mocked													
Fathers	—	14.3	11.1	13.3	33.3	31.6	12.5	12.0	25.0	19.1	18.9	19.8	18.8
Mothers	—	21.4	0.0	7.1	5.0	4.5	0.0	0.0	3.0	4.0	10.5	8.4	6.0
Difference	—	-7.1	11.1	6.2	28.3	27.1	12.5	12.0	22.0	15.1	8.4	11.4	12.8
Nurturant and Supportive Parenting Behaviors I													
Fathers	—	35.7	33.3	6.7	19.0	15.8	12.5	12.0	14.3	17.0	23.0	38.3	23.0
Mothers	—	28.6	20.0	42.9	20.0	18.2	16.7	44.0	12.1	36.0	39.5	36.8	31.6
Difference	—	7.1	13.3	-36.2	-1.0	-2.4	-4.2	-32.0	2.2	-19.0	-16.5	1.5	-8.6
Nurturant and Supportive Parenting Behaviors II													
Fathers	—	42.9	55.6	20.0	28.6	31.6	20.8	16.0	28.6	36.2	36.5	53.1	36.4
Mothers	—	42.9	50.0	64.3	30.0	22.7	23.3	48.0	21.2	48.0	48.7	51.6	42.9
Difference	—	0.0	5.6	-44.3	-1.4	8.9	-2.5	-32.0	7.4	-11.8	-12.2	1.5	-6.5
ns													
Fathers Pic/Ref	—	14	9	15	21	19	24	25	28	47	74	81	357
Mothers Pic/Ref	—	14	10	14	20	22	30	25	33	50	76	95	389
Difference	—	0	-1	1	1	-3	-6	0	-5	-3	-2	-14	-32

Saturday Evening Post cartoons (Day & Mackey, 1986; LaRossa et al., 1991), we surmise that the cartoonists were less inclined to portray parents as incompetent on holidays intended to honor them.

The reluctance to disparage parents on Father's Day and Mother's Day makes the difference between fathers and mothers in the comics all the more relevant. Over time, the tendency to depict mothers as incompetent generally remained at a stable low, whereas the tendency to depict fathers as incompetent fluctuated. Note the large gender difference in the early 1950s and late 1960s and the near convergence in the early 1970s and early 1980s, all due largely to changes in how the fathers were portrayed. The fact that mothers were depicted as more incompetent than were fathers in the late 1940s, late 1950s, and early 1990s is also interesting.

Fathers and mothers also diverged in the kinds of activities that, when performed, had higher rates of incompetence. For fathers, these activities included showing a child what it means to "be a man," doing feminine household chores, nonphysically disciplining a child, and playing sports. For mothers, these activities included physically or nonphysically disciplining a child, giving a Father's Day gift, and comforting a child.

Mocked

The second-row totals in Table 21.2 indicate that 18.8% of the fathers and 6.0% of the mothers were mocked. These totals corroborate the cartoonists' tendency not to make fun of parents on Father's Day and Mother's Day, but they also demonstrate, from another vantage point, that if any parent were to be targeted on the holidays, it was likely the father and that the propensity to disparage men fluctuated. Note the large gender difference in the 1960s and 1980s, compared to the 1950s, 1970s, and 1990s. Note, too, that mothers were mocked more than fathers were in the late 1940s.

Nurturant and Supportive Parenting Behaviors I

The third row in Table 21.2 reports the results for our first measure of nurturant and supportive parenting behaviors. Overall, 23.0% of the fathers and 31.6% of the mothers were shown verbally or physically expressing affection toward a child, serving or caring for a child, verbally encouraging a child, or comforting a child or inquiring about the child's feelings and thoughts. The half-decade percentages for the fathers exhibited a U-shaped pattern, whereas the percentages for the mothers spiked in the late 1950s and late 1970s.

Nurturant and Supportive Parenting Behaviors II

The fourth row in Table 21.2 reports the results for our second measure of nurturant and supportive parenting behaviors. When we added to the activities listed above the additional activities of praising a child for a completed task, activity, or a job well done; listening to a child's problem; and purposefully teaching a child, the percentages increased across the board: 36.4% of the fathers and 42.9% of the mothers were shown to be nurturant and supportive. The longitudinal pattern of the first measure was repeated, however. The percentages for the fathers looked more-or-less U-shaped, and the percentages for the mothers spiked in the late 1950s and late 1970s. Significant is the fact that this parenting measure showed fathers increasing in nurturance and support beginning in the 1980s and continuing through the 1990s.

DISCUSSION

Has the culture of fatherhood changed over the past six decades? Viewed through the prism of Father's Day and Mother's Day comic strips, it would appear that it has, but not in a linear or simple way.

Changes in Attention Given to Father's Day and Mother's Day

When we looked at the amount of attention given to Father's Day and Mother's Day, we found that Father's Day was generally acknowledged less frequently. In this respect, the comics parallel other indicators of "popularity": regardless of how the holidays are compared (by number of phone calls made, cards sent, meals eaten out, or cartoonists' recognition) Father's Day comes up short (see Ward, 1993).

When we looked at the amount of attention given to Father's Day and Mother's Day over time, we found the amount of attention generally going up. This increase, we learned, was not because the number of comics published in a given year had risen but because family-oriented comics had come to dominate the comic-strip page. Publishers may have decided that readers prefer these kinds of comics to the more serious strips (e.g., *Brenda Starr* or *Mary Worth*) or adventure strips (*Tarzan* or *Steve Canyon*).

We did wonder whether the amount of attention given to Father's Day would increase in the 1970s, given that 1972 marks the year President Richard Nixon signed Father's Day into law. (Previously, Father's Day was on the calendar, and presidential proclamations acknowledging the holiday were a matter of routine, but it was not until 1972 that Father's Day was made "legal." Mother's Day was certified a federal holiday in 1914.) The data do show that the amount of attention given to Father's Day started to climb in the 1970s, but we would be hard pressed to say that the upward movement had anything to do with the government's actions. We do know that none of the comics parodied the signing.

The large difference in the amount of attention given to Father's Day, compared with Mother's Day, in the late 1990s is puzzling, given the higher level of nurturant and supportive parenting behaviors exhibited by fathers in this period. The reason for the gap is that the number of comics that explicitly mentioned or implicitly alluded to Father's Day leveled off (from 37 to 35), whereas the number of comics that explicitly mentioned or implicitly alluded to Mother's Day continued to rise (from 40 to 56). Something else happened as well, something that is not apparent from the tables. Even though the number of comics acknowledging both Father's Day and Mother's Day was fairly high in the 1990s, the comic strips referring to these parental holidays actually constituted a smaller share of the family-oriented comics overall. That is, the proportion of comics that did not acknowledge Father's Day or Mother's Day but did have fatherhood, motherhood, or parenthood as a theme mushroomed, from only a minute fraction in the years before to nearly 25% overall in the 1990s. Also, the proportions differed for Father's Day and Mother's Day and for the first and second half of the decade. For Father's Day, the proportions were 22% in the early 1990s and 34% in the late 1990s. For Mother's Day, the proportions were 25% in the early 1990s and 19% in the late 1990s. In other words, cartoonists were more likely in the 1990s than they were in decades before to craft stories about parenthood without mentioning or alluding to either holiday, and they were more likely in the late 1990s than they were just a few years before to craft stories about fatherhood without mentioning or alluding to Father's Day.

One possible explanation is that cartoonists in the 1990s were more adept at communicating their viewpoints without framing the comic as a holiday message. Another possibility is that the fragility of family ties in the 1990s made the acknowledgment of both Father's Day and Mother's Day problematic. Because it could be awkward for children and others who are separated or estranged from their fathers or mothers to be reminded of Father's Day and Mother's Day, some cartoonists may have tried to display sensitivity by not bringing attention to the holidays. Still a third possibility, not exclusive of the others, is that cartoonists in the late 1990s had difficulty reconciling the concept of the "New Father" with its opposite, the nonresident "Absentee Dad," a manifestation of both the good and bad sides of male parenthood in the late 20th century (Furstenberg, 1988). Some attitudinal shift, whatever the cause, does seem to be at work because the changes in the scores cannot be attributed to changes in the composition of comic-strip families. There was, for example, no increase in single-mother characters.

Changes in the Portrayal of Fathers and Mothers

Regardless of whether the comics are about Father's Day, Mother's Day, or family life in general, one thing is clear. In recent years, there have been many more comic-strip characters who are parents and thus many more opportunities for readers to view fictitious fathers and mothers engaged in child-care activities. This expansion is important. If, hypothetically speaking, the number of fathers in a set of comics were to increase significantly from one decade to the next, while the percentage of nurturant and supportive fathering behaviors were to remain the same, there would still be more nurturant, supportive fathers in the comics for readers to observe. This, in turn, could affect the social reality of fatherhood because observing more male comic-strip characters acting fatherly could lead people to assume that the same kind of activity was occurring among their neighbors and friends. (These assumptions need not be correct. What people believe fathers do and what fathers actually do is the difference between the culture and conduct of fatherhood; LaRossa, 1988.)

Similarly, Coltrane and Allan (1994) made the point that "[t]he salience of a few men cuddling babies...[can] create the impression that things have changed dramatically," even if

"quantitative findings indicate that viewers continue to be bombarded with even more images of men as heroes, lovers, and loners" (p. 55). Coltrane and Allan reported that although the percentage of fathers in television ads who were nurturant and supportive did not increase between the 1950s and 1980s, the percentage of parents who were fathers did: in the 1950s, men accounted for 31% of all parents pictured in ads, but in the 1980s, they accounted for 71% of all parents pictured in ads. The 1980s profile could have inflated viewers' estimates of the prevalence of the "New Father," despite the fact that the more standard comparison (percentage of nurturant, supportive fathers then and now) suggested no change.

When we looked at how often fathers and mothers in the comics were portrayed as incompetent, we found that incompetence was not a usual theme, indicating a reluctance on the part of cartoonists to lampoon parents on Father's Day and Mother's Day. The few cases there were, however, were not randomly distributed across the decades. Consider the small difference between the portrayal of fathers and mothers in the 1970s. Day and Mackey (1986) found that fathers were no more likely than were mothers to be depicted as incompetent in the 1970s. We found this, too, but we also found additional support for the proposition that the portrayal of fathers has wavered over time. If we place chronologically the results from LaRossa and colleagues' (1991) study of the early 20th century alongside the results of this study of the late 20th century, we can see that the relative gender parity in the 1930s and early, 1940s (compared with the 1920s) reported in the first study, coupled with the relative gender parity in the 1970s (compared with the 1960s) reported in the current study, makes for a fluctuating pattern in the culture of fatherhood.

A picture of fluctuation also emerged when we looked at how frequently comic strips mocked fathers and mothers. With the single-item mocking question, which is more sensitive than is the incompetence measure to satirical nuance, the shift upward from the 1940s–1950s to the 1960s and the shift downward from the 1960s to the 1970s are unmistakable. With this variable, it also appears that the fluctuating pattern continued after the 1970s. Fathers were more likely to be mocked in the 1980s and 1990s than they were in the 1970s. Both Day and Mackey (1986) and Atkinson and Blackwelder (1993) offered evidence to suggest that the 1970s were a time when fatherhood was more likely to be culturally validated. If the extent to which fathers are mocked is a guide, our results reinforce their rendition of this decade.

With regard to nurturance and support, Coltrane and Allan (1994) found continuity when they examined the nurturant, supportive behaviors of fathers and mothers in television advertising in the 1950s and 1980s. Using their operational definition of nurturant, supportive behavior, we also found some degree of continuity when we aggregated the two decades and compared them. We do not infer from this, however, that no transformation in fatherhood imagery has occurred. For one thing, the continuity between the 1950s and 1980s on this particular measure belies the discontinuity between other decades on the same measure. Second, the half-decade analysis indicates that the fathers' up-down pattern for the early and late 1950s was not the same as the fathers' relatively stable pattern for the early and late 1980s. Third, a modified version of the Coltrane and Allan measure, what we called Nurturant and Supportive Parenting Behaviors II because of the addition of three child rearing activities, yielded results that showed sharper differences between the 1950s and 1980s, especially when we employed a half-decade analysis.

Critical, too, was the dramatic increase in paternal nurturance and support beginning in the 1980s and continuing through the 1990s. Although the gender disparities did not vanish—for the most part, mothers were depicted as more nurturant and supportive than were fathers—the concept of the "New Father" did seem to gain ground, even though it did so, ironically, at the same time that the attention given to Father's Day was becoming more ambiguous.

Equally interesting was the high level of maternal nurturance and support in the late 1980s and early and late 1990s. The cartoonists may have tried to acknowledge the concept of the "New Father," but they did not do so at the expense of motherhood. Indeed, if anything, they seemed to pay homage to both fatherhood and motherhood at the end of the millennium. Keep in mind, however, that the families in the comics were mainly White, middle class, and nuclear in structure. Single fathers and mothers, among others, were largely absent and not praised.

Knowing that we would also be making comparisons with the 1950s, as well as with the late 1940s, and because we were familiar with how scholars and popular writers have characterized the post-World War II era (sometimes called the Cold War or Baby Boom era), we fully expected that the comics published in these years would offer unequivocal displays of paternal buffoonery and maternal domesticity. However, our results turned out to be more complex. First, we found differences between the late 1940s and early and late 1950s. In the immediate postwar period, fathers were less likely than were mothers to be depicted as incompetent (by one character) and less likely to be mocked (by one character), but they were also more likely, or as likely, to be nurturant and supportive (depending on whether Nurturing and Supportive Parenting Behaviors I or II is used). We suspect men's relatively positive portrayals in the late 1940s, were a continuation of the development of the concept of the "New Father" that accelerated in the 1920s and 1930s and that was at full throttle in the early 1940s, helped by a war accentuating men's role as the defenders of the nation (LaRossa, 1997). Women's less positive portrayals were another matter. In the 1940s, childrearing experts were disparaging mothers for being overprotective and for stifling independence. Philip Wylie, in *Generation of Vipers* (1942), coined the term "momism" to denote "the [smother] mother problem" (p. 196). Edward A. Strecker, in *Their Mothers' Sons* (1946), charged that women had turned millions of men into "sissies" unfit for combat. Cartoonists may have been swayed by the negative propaganda.

Then, there were the contrasts between the 1950s and 1960s. Although fathers during the 1950s were more likely to be mocked than were mothers of the day, the disparity between fathers and mothers in the 1950s was actually smaller than it was in the 1960s. The changes in the level of nurturant and supportive behaviors, considered in conjunction with the changes in the extent to which fathers were mocked, highlights the significance of this decade in the cultural history of fatherhood. As it turns out, the 1960s were a time when fathers were as likely as mothers to be depicted as nurturant and supportive, but they were also more likely to be mocked. When we look at the change in percentages, we see that the convergence in nurturant and supportive parenting behaviors was not because the fathers in the comics increased their "warm and fuzzy" quotient between the 1950s and 1960s, but because the mothers decreased theirs. Nonetheless, it was the fathers, not the mothers, whom the cartoonists ostensibly targeted in the 1960s.

In this regard, the parallels between the 1920s and the 1960s are striking. In the 1920s, there was much talk not only about the "New Father," who was supposed to become more involved with his children, but also about the "New Woman," who was perceived as having less to do with hers; simultaneously, there were more jokes manifestly at men's expense (LaRossa et al., 1991). However, things are not always what they seem. In a society in which motherhood is the more sacred and fatherhood is the more profane and in which attitudes toward fathers and mothers are so intertwined, satire manifestly aimed at one quarry can be implicitly aimed at another. Hence, the real targets of the almost exclusively male cartoonists in the 1920s—and the 1960s—may not have been men or fathers per se, but the "battle of sexes," that, to some pundits, epitomized the two decades.

In general, our study supports the conclusions of Atkinson and Blackwelder (1993) and LaRossa et al. (1991) more than it supports the conclusions of Coltrane and Allan (1994) and Day and Mackey (1986): Fluctuation is the mode. Apart from the different data sets employed, the conflict in views may come down to the fact that Coltrane and Allan and Day and Mackey used a binary historical approach, examining only two points in time (the 1950s vs. the 1980s in the first case, 1922–1968 vs. 1971–1978 in the second), whereas Atkinson and Blackwelder, LaRossa et al., and the current study used a multiple-points-in-time approach. Two waves of data may be said to provide some information about social change and, strictly speaking, "constitute a longitudinal study," but such designs have serious methodological limitations (Rogosa, 1995). Multiwave studies are more sensitive to the complexities of cultural history.

Why the fluctuation? There are so many contradictory economic and political factors that have contributed to the ebb and flow of fatherhood in the late 20th century, it would be difficult to imagine events moving in a straight line (see Coltrane, 1996; R. Griswold, 1993). The changes that we uncovered, however, were not entirely the result of materialist conditions. Ours is a study of comic strips, of authored texts. Comics and other cultural objects are created by people and do not appear out of the blue (W. Griswold, 1994). Thus, another question to ask is, was there anything about comic strips as a genre or about the comic-strip artists that might explain the fluctuation? One thing we discovered is that two comic strips dating back to the 1950s—*Dennis the Menace* and *The Family Circle*—wavered hardly at all from one decade to the next. The consistency of these strips prompted us to reflect on the fact that comic strips are similar to soap operas in which stories are dictated by the characters' personalities and the fictitious families' routines. Even minor modifications can alter the flow of a successful comic and mean audience disapproval and cancellation.

If, indeed, some principle of inertia and caution prevents long-running strips from altering their narratives in response to structural trends, then the historical changes that we report would have to be a partial function of different comics with different authors entering and leaving the comic-strip section of the newspaper. The changes in the 1990s, for one, may have mirrored the changing gender and age composition of the cartoonists themselves. As more women and more artists from different age cohorts broke into the comic-strip trade, the tableaus of fatherhood and motherhood in the comics were literally and figuratively redrawn and "updated."

The lesson to derive from this is that studies of the culture of fatherhood must focus more on how the various norms, values, beliefs, and ex-pressive symbols pertaining to fatherhood are manufactured. It is not just a question of "what" is produced about fatherhood, but also a question of "who" produces it (LaRossa, 1997). What would we have learned had we interviewed the cartoonists about their work? What were the cartoonists contemplating when, pen in hand, they sat at their drawing tables preparing the comics that would be published on Father's Day and Mother's Day? Studies of the culture of fatherhood also must focus more on how the various norms, values, beliefs, and expressive symbols pertaining to fatherhood are read and interpreted. Virtually every day, the populace is bombarded with "information" about fathers, some of it comedic. How much is known about what goes on in people's minds when they see this material? (Two excellent examples of cultural studies, although not of fatherhood, that took at these issues are Radway, 1984, and Simonds, 1992.)

Ultimately, researchers must not lose sight of the relationship between the "objectivation" of fatherhood and the "externalization-internalization" of fatherhood (Berger & Luckmann, 1966). Whereas the former refers to a cultural product, the latter refers to a process through which that product is constructed and incorporated into people's consciousness on an ongoing basis. Fully comprehending the first will require detailed studies of the second.

Chapter

7

The Family and the Elderly

Reading 22   Intimate Strangers: The Elderly and
Home-Care Worker Relationships

MARK HUTTER*

Ours is an aging society. Demographic trends reveal that there will be a sharp rise in the elderly population in the foreseeable future. In 1900, around 3 million people in the United States were over the age of 65. They represented 4 percent of the population. In 1980 there were 25.5 million people over 65 years old. This was a 28 percent increase since 1970. Ten years later, in 1990, 31.7 million people representing 12.7 percent of the population was in this age group. This group is expected to increase to nearly a quarter of the population by the year 2050. The median age, at which half the population is younger and half is older, rose in the decade that ended in 1990 from 30 years to 32.7 years. The factors accounting for this rise were that the proportion of people age 65 or over is increasing while the proportion of people under the age of 15 is decreasing (Thorson, 1995). These statistics indicate a sharply rising median age over the next three decades and have major implications for the elderly, for families, and for society.

The age of grandparents covers much of the human life span—from the early 30s to the 100s. Obviously, there will be a great variation in generational relationships depending on the re-spective ages. Much of the research is on the three-generation family that covers the period when the senior generation is from 50 to 70 years of age, the middle generation 30 to 50, and the youngest generation from birth to teenage years. However, four-generation families are becoming more common.

Cherlin and Furstenberg (1986) observe that the revolution in the health conditions of the elderly, combined with their economic independence, enable them to pursue independent lives and live apart from the family. The title of their book, *The New American Grandparent,* and its subtitle, *A Place in the Family, A Life Apart,* characterizes the role of the grandparent generation during this stage of the life cycle when they are still relatively healthy. But, what happens when the oldest generation becomes older and moves into their 70s, 80s, 90s, and beyond? Often this proves to be a very difficult period in the lives of family members in all three generations, and problems can be exacerbated when the grandchildren become parents.

Some of the difficulty stems from the fact that the elder generation is composed of old people whom society views as residuals and somewhat useless. Irving Rosow (1976) has astutely

*A version of this paper was presented at the Couch/Stone Society for the Study of Symbolic Interaction Symposium, February 20–22, 1998, Houston, Texas.

observed that our society has deprived old people both of responsibility and of function; by so doing, it has provided the basis for the roleless position of the elderly. In Rosow's terms, the lives of the elderly are "socially unstructured" (1976:466); that is, these people in their 70s, 80s, and 90s have no role models and no role prescriptions that they can use to fashion their own present-day roles.

For adult children, and especially women, changing role expectations both in career and familial involvements complicate matters. These people are known in the popular literature as the "sandwich generation" because they are sandwiched between their own children who need care and their older parents who also need care. These people experience stress associated with their own stage in the family life cycle (Thorson, 1995). Many are contemplating their own aging as they face retirement and perhaps their own financial and health problems. This generation has the brunt of generational responsibility thrust on it. They often are asked to assist their own children as they enter early adulthood and married and family life, while at the same time they are expected to care for their aged parents. Ethel Shanas (1980) quotes a woman who speaks for this generation: "I've raised my family. I want to spend time with my husband or my wife. I want to enjoy my grandchildren. I never expected that when I was a grandparent, I'd have to look after my parents" (1980:14).

It is not accidental that the above quote is by a woman. Women within that sandwich generation are the ones who often take on a disproportionate share of the time and emotional involvement with their elderly parents. In 1988, a U.S. House of Representatives report observed that the average woman will spend even more years (18 years) taking care of elderly parents than they did (17 years) raising their children. Commenting on this fact, *Newsweek* (1990) observes that the "mommy track" is being replaced by a "daughter track." The shift is from balancing work, career, and child rearing to balancing work, career, and elder-caring. Indeed, often these women are working mothers and caregivers. They provide both for their parents and for their children while holding down full-time jobs.

Elaine Brody of the Philadelphia Geriatric Center has found that among her clientele, working wives are taking on the same responsibilities as nonemployed women. "They don't give up caring for their parent. They don't slack off on responsibility to their jobs or their husbands. They take it out of their own hides" (Brody quoted in Gelman et al., 1985:68). The gender role and family literature often talks about the "double burden" or "dual roles" of women. For these women, we can now see a "triple burden." And yet, as Brody laments, there is little attention paid to the problems of these women by the government, industry, or the women's movement.

The research on adult children taking care of their parents is growing. Much of that research reports that it is a daughter who is usually the family member who takes on the responsibility of caring for aging parents and other elderly kin (Brody, 1990). Elaine M. Brody and her associates (1992) have investigated the effects of women's marital status on their parent care experience. They found that the stress of caregiving was lessened for women who had husbands, had more socio-emotional and instrumental support, and were financially well-off and thus experienced less financial strain from caregiving. Brody and her coauthors found that the changing lifestyles of women—higher divorce rates and higher rates of not ever marrying—increase the difficulties of the parent care years. A never-married daughter expresses the concerns and anxieties of these women without extensive kin involvements but who have taken on the major responsibility of parental care: "It's an awesome responsibility. It's scary to think what would happen if anything happens to me" (Brody et al., 1992:65).

Sandra J. Litvin (1992), a colleague of Brody's, is concerned with elderly care receivers' status transitions, that include the loss of good health and declining social activities with friends and family members. She is also concerned with the effect that these status transitions have on the caregivers. Such a status transition can cause considerable fear and anxiety over the future for both the care receiver and the caregiver. This relationship itself is susceptible to breakdown.

Litvin observed that the caregiver experienced role conflict when the care receiver had a lack of social participation with family and friends. Many of these caregivers perceived their care receivers as being in better health and participating more in social activities than did the care receivers. Litvin explains, "If caregivers can rationalize that their infirm elderly kin are independent and have adequate social interaction with family and friends, then the burden is temporarily lifted from their shoulders" (Litvin, 1992). For the caregiver knows that if their elderly kin participate less with others, then they will focus more of their expectations on increased emotional and instrumental support on the caregiver.

Litvin observes that as the aging population continues to grow, and where a major part of this growth is among the very old (those in their 80s and 90s and beyond), it becomes essential to understand the changing nature of intergenerational relationships when status transitions occur. Litvin calls for the need for more studies to examine variations in the caregiving/care receiving experience by race, gender, and social class.

In this paper I am concerned with the relationships that develop when an "intimate stranger"—a home-care worker—comes to provide care for an elderly person who, for whatever reasons, cannot maintain their own everyday independence and family members and friends cannot aid them to do so. My particular focus is on the relationships surrounding one elderly individual—a close relation.

THE HOME-CARE WORKER

While at least two-thirds of home care for the elderly is still provided by relatives and other non-paid caregivers, that figure is growing smaller (Conover, 1997). It is the growing dilemma of our age. In an increasingly mobile society, grown children seldom live a short commuting distance from their parents. Of the estimated 25 million Americans who serve as caregivers to an elder, more than a quarter are doing it long distance. And that number is expected to grow as more baby boomers take on the heartwrenching task of mothering and fathering their parents. Further, as the baby boomers in turn age, an even larger number of their children will find themselves in the same position in the years ahead. In 1980 there were 25.6 million Americans over the age of 65. By the year 2030 it is estimated that that population will more than double to around 70 million people.

Many elders are managing their own lives. Those that are more affluent live in retirement communities and senior citizen homes. Others live in their own homes. An estimated 75 percent of the old remain in independent living situations. Another 18 percent live with an adult child. A relatively small number live in isolation. About 80 percent of older people see a close relative every week, according to Dr. Franklin Williams, director of the National Institute on Aging (Gelman et al., 1985).

The support and helping patterns between adult children and aged parents are most likely to occur when the elder generation is still relatively healthy and economically independent. Unfortunately, it is in circumstances when the elders become dependent (whether because of illness or financial matters) that adult children find themselves in a most difficult situation. This would especially be the case when there is a potential for conflict between adult children's career, spousal, and parental commitments and their concerns and commitments to their aged parents. As the elder generation ages, they increasingly find that they cannot meet their own everyday needs, and often their adult children cannot provide the necessary aid.

As they move into the new "age frontier," the elderly are confronted with a dazzling array of services from home health aides to community-living facilities (*Newsweek,* 1997). Instead of nursing homes, seniors are increasingly choosing either assisted-living facilities or continuing-care retirement communities (CCRCs). The former, which charge anywhere from several hundred to several thousand dollars a month, offer residents meals, housekeeping services, and help with basic tasks such as dressing and bathing. CCRCs offer a wider range of living choices, enabling tenants to move from apartments to nursing facilities within the same complex. They cost more as well. For a one-bedroom apartment, entry fees alone run as high as $87,000, with monthly rents of $1,000 and up (*Newsweek,* 1997).

Despite these options, many seniors—even those confined to wheelchairs—prefer to stay in their own homes. As a result, home health care services are booming. The home health care industry has grown phenomenally since the early 1980s. The number of certified home-care agencies has nearly doubled since 1989. This boom reflects a response to the cost of assisted-living facilities and CCRCs as well as the desire to spend their final years at home. The home provides a familiar setting and the situational context where the person is best able to exercise self-determination and maintain ties and relationships with friends and neighbors.

The rise of the American home health care industry began in the early 1980s as a response

to the increasing number of people over the age of 65 and to the cost of nursing-home care. *The New York Times Magazine* (Conover, 1997) reports that 7 million people now receive some form of paid home care. Medicare and Medicaid began to provide funding in 1967 and 1971, respectively. For those over 65 needing skilled recuperative care after an acute illness, Medicare will pay up to 4 hours a day, 7 days a week for 40 days or so. For the poor, Medicaid pays for ongoing home care for those with chronic maladies. When the cost for such care reaches 90 percent of the cost of a nursing home, the patient is usually sent to such a facility.

In the coming years, the home-care field is expected to be one of the fastest-growing industries. The Bureau of Labor Statistics predicts a 119 percent increase in jobs for home-care aides from 1994 to 2005 (cited in Conover, 1997). Today, there are over 1,000 geriatric-care-management businesses; in the New York City metropolitan area alone there are three dozen. These firms oversee all aspects of the care of an aging person including scheduling of doctor appointments and providing accounting help for monthly bills. These agencies—and others that are not as comprehensive in their management facilities—often arrange for health care aides to take care of the everyday needs of elderly people. They may work for a few hours a day, or they may provide 24-hour around-the-clock help 7 days a week.

As Conover observes (1997), the quality and experience of these aides varies widely; many have little or no formal training. They are not there to provide the care that only a registered nurse can provide. Rather, they are people who provide companionship along with light housekeeping that includes grocery shopping, cooking, and cleaning for those elderly that need little else. For those elderly who require help in bathing, dressing, and the taking of medicine, a licensed home health aide with at least 75 hours of training is required.

Conover, in his *New York Times Magazine* cover story on the "new nanny," reports:

> *You see it on the sidewalks and in the parks and lobbies of neighborhoods throughout cities like New York: elderly people, often white, assisted or simply accompanied by younger women, usually black or Hispanic. As our parents and grandparents live longer, and spend fewer and fewer of their final years with us, a caring woman from the Caribbean—her face, her voice, her touch—will very likely be the last human contact many of them will have. (1997:127)*

AN INTIMATE STRANGER RELATIONSHIP CASE STUDY

A close relation, Ben N., died January 2, 1998, 6 months to the day after he was diagnosed with pancreatic cancer. At the time of diagnosis, his physician informed his two daughters that he had between 3 to 6 months to live. While his death was predictable, events in the unfolding time period would prove problematic. The focus of this case study is on the last 2 months of his life and the relationships that developed—not so much between Ben and his home-care worker, Georgette, but rather between Georgette and Ben's companion of 5 years, Mary; between Georgette and Ben's two daughters, Phyllis and Judith; and between Mary and the two sisters.

Ben was 87 when he died. He was married for 52 years. His wife, Freida, died in 1992. Shortly thereafter he began an intimate relationship with Mary, a woman 15 years his junior. Mary was a widow whose only child died in early adulthood. She had no immediate relatives

that she interacted with on an everyday basis. During the 5 years that they were companions, they kept separate apartments in a cooperative apartment house complex in Brooklyn. Blessed with good health, Ben continued the pattern of autonomy from his children and their families that characterized his retirement years with Freida. He saw them periodically, and they kept in touch weekly by telephone. He and Mary spent much of their time together relatively uninvolved with other family members, friends, or neighbors.

Ben's grandparenthood role follows Cherlin and Furstenburg's observation that many grandparents prefer to have "a place in the family, [and] a life apart." This characterized Ben's relationship with his children and grandchildren both during the period when Freida was alive and after he was with Mary.

In turn, Ben's daughters also had their own separate involvements. Phyllis lives in the Philadelphia metropolitan area, 100 miles away from her father. She is employed full-time as a special education teacher. Her sister Judith lives in Suffolk County, Long Island, New York, and she and her self-employed husband own a second home in Florida to which they commute on a regular basis. Both daughters have adult children who are on their own but remain in constant contact either through daily phone chats or frequent visits.

Following the schema developed by Herbert Gans (1962), both sisters' conjugal families fall into the "adult directed" category characteristic of the upper-middle class. Predominantly college educated, this family type is interested in and participates in the activities of the larger world. Its activities are not confined to the local community. Extended kinship ties and the home are given low priority. Frequently, the wife pursues a career prior to having children and is either working or has aspirations to work as the children are growing. Domestic household activities are alleviated to some extent through the employment of service help or the sharing of activities by both spouses. Children serve as a common focal point of interest and concern. These upper-middle-class couples are concerned with the intellectual and social development of their children. They are highly motivated to provide direction in the lives of their children, so that family life is child centered as well as adult directed.

In contrast, Ben and Freida's family pattern through most of their marriage can be characterized, utilizing Gans's schema, as "adult centered." Here the husband and wife live gender-segregated roles. They have separate family roles and engage in little of the companionship typically found in the middle class. The husband is predominantly the wage earner and the enforcer of child discipline. The wife's activities are confined to household tasks and child rearing. Children are expected to follow adult rules and are required to act "grown up"; they are disciplined when they act childish. Family life is centered around the desires and interests of the adults and does not cater to the demands of the children. This was Ben and Freida's parental pattern. Gans also observes that husbands and wives are frequently involved with extended kin and with neighbors and friends, albeit different ones for each. In Ben and Freida's case this did not hold true; they were minimally involved with such others.

This "adult centered" pattern continued throughout their marriage. Soon after Freida's death, Ben developed a companionship relationship with Mary that essentially took on the same pattern. Ben's independence from his family continued until his complaint of abdominal pain was diagnosed as pancreatic cancer on July 1997. Ben, although not told of the full implications of his illness, was now confronted with the realization that he would need medical care in the short term (chemotherapy), and that he would need full-time care in the not-to-distant future. He also knew that Mary would be unable to provide that help. Further, he knew that his daughters' own concerns and involvements would prevent them from providing full-time care.

The daughters realized that they were faced with a dilemma common in our geographically mobile society. They would have to become increasingly more involved in the day-to-day life of their father to ensure his well-being, yet they did not live in easy commuting distance from him. Further, their own personal and professional commitments would have to temper that involvement.

It was in July that Ben underwent a 10-week chemotherapy treatment. Judith and her husband took him and Mary to the treatment center each week. The chemotherapy weakened him, but it had the positive effect of minimizing pain. He was beginning the process of slow physical decline and was getting progressively more tired and weak. Yet, his desire for independence and to be on his own strongly motivated his behavior. He continued to drive, albeit on shorter trips. Rather than walk to the neighborhood diner, he drove; he also drove to the doctor. And on a day that he felt particularly strong, he and Mary took a 1-day bus excursion to the casinos in Atlantic City.

But the signs were clear. When he fell going to the bathroom one night and had difficulty getting up, he realized that he would need everyday help. In the fourth month into his terminal illness, it was decided among Ben, Judith, and Phyllis that Mary should not and could not take care of him as he started slipping into a steady health decline. A home-care aide would help provide the round-the-clock personal care that Ben required. The aide would also be able to take on light housekeeping duties such as grocery shopping and cooking. It was in early October that a home health care agency was contacted.

After the hiring of two unsatisfactory aides, Georgette was hired. Like many other aides,

Georgette was from Jamaica, in the Caribbean. Health care is one of the few careers traditionally open to women in Jamaica—a fact that dovetails nicely with Americans' growing needs (Conover, 1997). Extended family relationships are strong for many people of the Caribbean, and the integration of elderly people into the nuclear family is common. Such involvements and experience make it relatively easy to transfer that caring relationship to strangers. One Jamaican woman home-care giver asserts:

In the countryside, we always take care of old people ourselves, Lorna says. And frankly, she feels, it is superior to the American system. When you do it yourself, "You give them more love, you understand much more about them. You make them more happy." That happiness is important, she says, because "you have some old people who just give up on their life." (Conover, 1997:127)

However, many such women often find themselves in a sense victimized by the global economy. The pressing needs of the elderly in the United States provides them with economic opportunities to move to this country and fill a gap in the health care of the elderly. But paradoxically, at the same time that they provide service to the elderly, they often find themselves forced to leave their own parents and children. That was the case for Georgette. Her 7-year-old son, Robert, was cared for by her mother in Jamaica. Much of the money she earned was earmarked for her family back home. If financially feasible, between jobs she tried to return to Jamaica to see her family. In the meantime she lived with the elders and, when she did have time off she had space in her aunt's apartment.

For Ben, Georgette proved to be an ideal employee. She was young, attractive, and more importantly, had a warm personality and was quick to smile and laugh. Arlie Hochschild talks of "emotion work," and this was an essential feature of Georgette's work. She took care of the home—cleaned, grocery shopped, and did some cooking. Most importantly, she allayed Ben's increasing fear of dependency.

Intimacy became an integral part of their relationship. The literature on the dying observes that because an aide tends to spend the most time with the dying patient, the relationship may become intimate (Marrone, 1996). Similarly, Tracy X. Karner (1998), in a study of home-care workers with elderly care recipients, found that a sphere of intimacy often develops between the care recipient and the caregiver that takes the form of a familial relationship. She observes that the home-care worker may be "adopted" as "fictive kin." Fictive kin is defined as individuals who are not related by blood but by choice. These adopted family members accept the affection, obligations, and duties of actual kin.

The two sisters fully appreciated how important Georgette's supportive and expressive role behavior was for both Ben and for themselves. She could provide the everyday care and attentiveness that the sisters were unable to provide. During the 2-month period that Georgette lived with Ben, the sisters felt comforted by the fact that Ben was not alone. This stranger was providing an emotional haven that helped Ben cope with his increasingly debilitating illness. During the numerous times that they called each day, Georgette would answer the phone and give the current progress report on Ben's behavior: what and how much he ate, if he went outside for a brief stroll, if he slept through the night, etc. Judith would visit one day during the week, and Phyllis would come on a weekend day to check on things and to spend time with her father.

Mary, however, had a different relationship with both Georgette and the sisters after Georgette's arrival. Mary realized the need for such an aide; she was not capable, emotionally or physically, of providing the 24-hour care that Ben increasingly required. At the same time, she did not relish another woman entering Ben's everyday life. From the outset, Mary responded antagonistically to Georgette's work efforts. She constantly complained to the two sisters as well as to Ben of her belief that Georgette was not performing her duties in a satisfactory manner. She felt that the aide was not looking after Ben in a way the she would have and that the aide did not devote sufficient attention to him. It was the very intimate nature of the relationship between Georgette and Ben that Mary found most upsetting and threatening. Jealousy—for no other word seems appropriate—governed Mary's perception of Georgette. That Ben was developing a beneficial attachment to Georgette was interpreted by Mary as a threat to her relationship with Ben and his daughters.

At the end of November, around Thanksgiving, Ben had to go into the hospital for a medical procedure to relieve some of his discomfort. Georgette spent the full day with Ben. Mary visited for a few hours each day. When either sister went to the hospital to visit, Mary would express her dissatisfaction with Georgette. Both were more concerned with their father's health and mental outlook than they were with Mary's insistence that Georgette was doing things wrong. They had to admonish Mary on separate occasions to control her dislike for Georgette because it was only upsetting them and their father. The relationship between Mary and the sisters was becoming more and more strained.

Ben returned home a week later, and the home-care pattern continued. Georgette continued to fulfill her role, and Mary took every opportunity to demean it. At times, Mary threatened not to visit, but she continued to see Ben. On New Year's Eve, Ben had to go into the hospital for another medical procedure. He died on January 2. Mary saw him that morning and left. Georgette spent the day with him. Phyllis and her husband and their daughter visited him in the afternoon. He got up to go to the bathroom, collapsed, and died.

After Ben's death, Judith telephoned Mary. Mary's response was a hysterical diatribe against Georgette—that through Georgette's negligence Ben died much sooner than he should have. Rather than expressing her grief at his death, she castigated Judith and, in turn, Phyllis, for (as she perceived it) their inattentiveness toward Ben during the last months of his life.

Lyn Lofland (1992), citing the literature on loneliness, observes that there is considerable social isolation of men and women following the death of their spouses or the breakdown of their marriages. She quotes Helena Lopata, who relates this phenomena to widows:

Many wives enjoy company parties, golf, couple-companionate dinners, and such events, and will not engage in them after the husband dies or have them no longer available since it was his presence which formed the connecting link in the first place. (Lopata, 1969, p. 253 [emphasis added] cited in Lofland, 1992:165)

Similarly, in the case of a companion, this social isolation is even more likely to occur. The relationship of a companion with the children of her partner is quite tenuous. Indeed, the relationship that existed between Mary and Ben's daughters can at best be defined as courteous, and by no means did an emotional bond develop. Mary was invited as a matter of course to all family gatherings, including Judith's eldest son's wedding. One would suspect that Mary feared that with the death of Ben her relationship with the daughters would also die. Through her actions, a self-fulfilling prophecy occurred.

At the funeral, Mary refused to go to the cemetery with the family. Georgette was also at the funeral, and she expressed her regrets. The sisters subsequently wrote a letter of recommendation and personally thanked her for the comfort that she provided for their father. They have not spoken to or been in contact with Mary since the funeral.

CONCLUSION

Of crucial concern in the years ahead is the increasing number of people over the age of 65 and the increasing number who will live beyond 85. The prospects, then, are of an aging population taking care of a very old population, with all the consequent emotional and financial strains. Given these demographic trends, the problems of the elderly and the sandwich generation will multiply in ways that we are only just beginning to comprehend.

Shanas (1980) cautions that we still know relatively little about the quality of the living arrangements of the elderly. "In much the same way, we do not know whether the visits between older parents and their children and relatives are brief or lengthy, friendly and warm, or acrimonious and hostile" (Shanas, 1980:13). We know that they do occur and that there is social exchange, but "[t]he nature of such an exchange may just be, as people say, 'a visit,' or it may involve actual help and services between the generations" (1980:13).

This observation can be extended to the elderly–home-care aide relationship. The study by Karner (1998) observes that the reconstruction of the care recipient and home-care worker relationship from a professional and task-oriented relationship to a fictive kin relationship has positive consequences for both recipient and the caregiver.

Defining the relationship in this manner allows the elder to feel more comfortable in accepting and expecting care from an individual outside of the family. For the home-care worker, much of their job (such as performing basic household tasks like cleaning, shopping, and meal preparation, and personal care like bathing and grooming) is often routine and tedious. Defining the relationship "as one of fictive kin with all the attendant responsibilities and obligations of blood relations…" allows "the homecare worker a means to negotiate the devaluation and lack of status of her employment" (Karner, 1998:80).

Conover (1997), however, cautions that while there are many case studies of positive relationships that have developed between the home health care aide and the elderly, there are many case studies that report on negative relationships. These include abusive relationships with both the elderly abusing the aide and the aide abusing the elderly. There are reports of wholesale theft. More systematic research needs to be done on this relationship.

Further, what little research there is on the relationship between the elderly and the health care worker there are virtually no studies on the relationship between the health care worker and the elderly's family members, companions, and friends. In one of the few studies done, Davis (1992) reports that when home-care worker services are delivered in conjunction with family caregiving, the relationship may result in "interpersonal triangles" involving the elderly, the worker, and family members. The impact of these relationships on the well-being of the elderly has not been studied.

The government has done little to regulate and examine this relationship of intimate strangers in any systematic detail. The case study relationships reported here were positive for Ben and Georgette and for Georgette and the two sisters and quite negative for Mary in her dealings with

Georgette and the two sisters. Other relationships may have strikingly different outcomes.

There is an obligation for cooperation between the government and the family to care for the elderly. Home health care, nursing care and nursing homes will become even more significant in the future as more elderly people find that they do not or cannot live with their families. The cost for such care, as well as the increased share of the national budget needed to be devoted to health care for the elderly, must be confronted now. Further, and most important, the quality of that care must be secured; yet, we find little systematic governmental attention to this future problem.

Shanas is optimistic that the four-generation family and the emerging kinship ties will continue to demonstrate the amazing resiliency that they have through the centuries. "They may be different for old people in the future from what they are now, but they will continue to provide safe harbor for their members however long they may live" (Shanas, 1980:14). Gelman, in his 1985 *Newsweek* article concludes

> *If a society can be judged by the way it treats its elderly, then we are not without honor—so far. But as we all grow older, that honor will demand an ever higher price. (Gelman et al., 1985:68)*

Reading 23 "The Normal American Family" as an Interpretive Structure of Family Life Among Grown Children of Korean and Vietnamese Immigrants

KAREN PYKE*

This article examines the ways that children of Korean and Vietnamese immigrants describe growing up in their families and their plans for filial care. Based on an analysis of 73 in-depth interviews, this study finds that respondents repeatedly invoked a monolithic image of the "Normal American Family" as an interpretive framework in giving meaning to their own family life. The Family served as a contrast structure in respondents' accounts of parents—and Asian parents in general—as overly strict, emotionally distant, and deficient. However, when discussing plans for filial care, respondents relied on favorable images of the close family ties associated with Asian immigrants, such as those depicted in "model minority" stereotypes. In so doing they generated positive descriptions of their families, particularly in contrast to mainstream American families. The findings suggest that narrow and ethnocentric images of the Family promulgated throughout mainstream culture compose an ideological template that can shape the desires, disappointments, and subjective realities of children of immigrant minorities.

The use of monolithic images of the "Normal American Family" as a stick against which all families are measured is pervasive in the family wars currently raging in political and scholarly discourses (Holstein & Gubrium, 1995). The hotly contested nature of these images—consisting almost exclusively of White middle-class heterosexuals—attests to their importance as re-

Author's Note: I am grateful to Katherine Allen, Susan Blank, Francesca Cancian, Tran Dang, Yen Le Espiritu, Joe Feagin, Jaber Gubrium, Nazli Kibria, Pyong Gap Min, Karen Seccombe, Darin Weinberg, Min Zhou, and the reviewers for their suggestions. I also thank Van-Dzung Nguyen and Mumtaz Mohammedi for their research assistance, the Department of Sociology at University of California-Irvine for its support of this research, and the many students who eagerly participated as research assistants or respondents.

sources in national debates. Many scholars express concern that hegemonic images of the Normal American Family are ethnocentric and that they denigrate the styles and beliefs of racial-ethnic, immigrant, gay-lesbian, and single-parent families while encouraging negative self-images among those who do not come from the ideal family type (Bernades, 1993; Dilworth-Anderson, Burton, & Turner, 1993; Smith, 1993; Stacey, 1998; Zinn, 1994). Yet we still know little about how the Family ideology shapes the consciousness and expectations of those growing up in the margins of the mainstream. This study examines the accounts that grown children of Korean and Vietnamese immigrants provide of their family life and filial obligations. The findings suggest that public images of the Normal American Family constitute an ideological template that shapes respondents' familial perspectives and desires as new racial–ethnic Americans.

FAMILY IDEOLOGY AS AN INTERPRETIVE STRUCTURE

Images of the Normal American Family (also referred to as the Family) are pervasive in the dominant culture—part of a "'large-scale' public rhetoric" (Holstein & Miller, 1993, p. 152). They are found in the discourse of politicians, social commentators, and moral leaders; in the talk of everyday interactions; and in movies, television shows, and books. Smith (1993, p. 63) describes these ubiquitous images as an "ideological code" that subtly "inserts an implicit evaluation into accounts of ways of living together." Such images serve as instruments of control, prescribing how families ought to look and behave (Bernades, 1985). Most scholarly concern centers on how this ideology glorifies and presents as normative that family headed by a breadwinning husband with a wife who, even if she works for pay, is devoted primarily to the care of the home and children. The concern is

that families of diverse structural forms, most notably divorced and female-headed families, are comparatively viewed as deficient and dysfunctional (Fineman, 1995; Kurz, 1995; Stacey, 1998). Scholars concerned about the impact of such images point to those who blame family structures that deviate from this norm for many of society's problems and who suggest policies that ignore or punish families that don't fit the construct (e.g., Blankenhorn, 1995; Popenoe, 1993, 1996).

In addition to prescribing the structure of families, the Family ideal contains notions about the appropriate values, norms, and beliefs that guide the way family members relate to one another. The cultural values of "other" families, such as racial-ethnic families, are largely excluded. For example, prevailing family images emphasize sensitivity, open honest communication, flexibility, and forgiveness (Greeley, 1987). Such traits are less important in many cultures that stress duty, responsibility, obedience, and a commitment to the family collective that supersedes self-interests (Chung, 1992; Freeman, 1989). In further contrast to the traditional family systems of many cultures, contemporary American family ideals stress democratic rather than authoritarian relations, individual autonomy, psychological well-being, and emotional expressiveness (Bellah, Madsen, Sullivan, Swidler, & Tipton, 1985; Bernades, 1985; Cancian, 1987; Coontz, 1992; Skolnick, 1991). Family affection, intimacy, and sentimentality have grown in importance in the United States over time (Coontz, 1992), as evident in new ideals of fatherhood that stress emotional involvement (Coltrane, 1996).

These mainstream family values are evident in the therapeutic ethic, guiding the ways that those who seek professional advice are counseled and creating particular therapeutic barriers in treating immigrant Asian Americans (Bellah et al., 1985; Cancian, 1987; Tsui and Schultz,

1985). Family values are also widely disseminated and glorified in the popular culture, as in television shows like *Ozzie and Harriet, Leave It To Beaver, The Brady Bunch, Family Ties,* and *The Cosby Show,* many of which are rerun on local stations and cable networks (Coontz, 1992). Parents in these middle-class, mostly White, television families are emotionally nurturing and supportive, understanding, and forgiving (Shaver, 1982; Skill, 1994). Indeed, such shows tend to focus on the successful resolution of relatively minor family problems, which the characters accomplish through open communication and the expression of loving concern. Children in the United States grow up vicariously experiencing life in these television families, including children of immigrants who rely on television to learn about American culture. With 98% of all U.S. households having at least one television set, Rumbaut (1997, p. 949) views TV as an immense "assimilative" force for today's children of immigrants. Yet, he continues, it remains to be studied how their world views are shaped by such "cultural propaganda." The images seen on television serve as powerful symbols of the "normal" family or the "good" parent—and they often eclipse our appreciation of diverse family types (Brown & Bryant, 1990; Greenberg, Hines, Buerkel-Rothfuss, & Atkin, 1980). As the authors of one study on media images note, "The seductively realistic portrayals of family life in the media may be the basis for our most common and pervasive conceptions and beliefs about what is natural and what is right" (Gerbner, Gross, Morgan, & Signorielli, 1980, p. 3). Family scholars have rarely displayed analytic concern about the emphasis on emotional expressiveness and affective sentimentality that pervades much of the Family ideology, probably because the majority—who as middle-class, well-educated Whites live in the heartland of such values—do not regard them as problematic. As a result, this Western value orientation can seep imperceptibly into the interpretive framework of family research (Bernades, 1993; Dilworth-Anderson et al., 1993; Fineman, 1995; Smith, 1993; Thorne & Yalom, 1992).

The theoretical literature on the social construction of experience is an orienting framework for this study (Berger & Luckmann, 1966; Holstein & Gubrium, 1995). According to this view, cultural ideologies and symbols are integral components of the way individuals subjectively experience their lives and construct reality. The images we carry in our heads of how family life is supposed to be frame our interpretation of our own domestic relations. This is evident in the different ways that Korean and Korean American children perceived their parents' childrearing behavior in a series of studies. In Korea, children were found to associate parental strictness with warmth and concern and its absence as a sign of neglect (Rohner & Pettengill, 1985). These children were drawing on Korean family ideology, which emphasizes strong parental control and parental responsibility for children's failings. In this interpretive framework, parental strictness is a positive characteristic of family life and signifies love and concern. Children of Korean immigrants living in the United States, on the other hand, viewed their parents' strictness in negative terms and associated it with a lack of warmth—as did American children in general (Pettengill & Rohner, 1985). Korean American children drew on American family ideology, with its emphasis on independence and autonomy, and this cast a negative shadow on their parents' strict practices.

Although pervasive images of the Normal American Family subtly construct Asian family patterns of interaction as "deviant," countervailing images of Asians as a "model minority" are also widely disseminated. News stories and scholarly accounts that profile the tremendous academic success among some immigrant Asian children or describe the upward economic mobility observed among segments of the Asian immigrant population credit the cultural traditions of collectivist family values, hard work, and a strong emphasis on education. Such images exaggerate the success of Asian immigrants and mask intraethnic diversity (Caplan, Choy, & Whitmore, 1991; Kibria, 1993; Min, 1995; Zhou & Bankston, 1998). Meanwhile, conservative leaders use model minority images as evidence of the need to return to more traditional family structures and values, and they blame the cultural deficiency of other racial minority groups for their lack of similar success, particularly African Americans and Latinos (Kibria, 1993; Min, 1995; Zhou & Bankston, 1998). The model minority construct thus diverts attention from racism and poverty while reaffirming the Family ideology. In the analysis of the accounts that children of immigrants provided of their family life, references to such cultural images and values emerged repeatedly as a mechanism by which respondents gave meaning to their own family lives.

KOREAN AND VIETNAMESE IMMIGRANT FAMILIES

This study focuses on children of Vietnamese and Korean immigrants because both groups constitute relatively new ethnic groups in the United States. Few Vietnamese and Koreans immigrated to the United States before 1965. However, from 1981 to 1990, Korea and Vietnam were two of the top five countries from which immigrants arrived (*Statistical Yearbook*, 1995, table 2, pp. 29–30). Thus adaptation to the United States is a relatively new process for large groups of Koreans and Vietnamese, one that is unassisted by earlier generations of coethnic immigrants. The children of these immigrants, located at the crossroads of two cultural worlds, offer a good opportunity to examine the familial perspectives and desires of new racial–ethnic Americans.

Most in-depth study of children of immigrants examines only one ethnic group, which makes it difficult to know which aspects of adaptation are shared with other ethnic groups and which are distinct. Studying only one Asian ethnic group also contributes to a tendency to overgeneralize the findings to all Asian ethnic groups. Thus this study was designed to compare two Asian ethnicities so that ethnic differences and similarities could be noted. The author selected Koreans and Vietnamese because, in addition to being new American ethnic groups, their economic status and pathways to immigration differ. Whereas Koreans have immigrated voluntarily, in search of better economic opportunities and educations for their children, most Vietnamese arrived as political refugees or to rejoin family members, some doing so after spending time in Vietnam's prisons or "re-education camps" (Gold, 1993; Hurh, 1998; Kibria, 1993; Min, 1998). Vietnamese immigrants have been, overall, less educated and from more rural and poorer backgrounds than Korean immigrants. Only 12% of first-generation Vietnamese heads of household have a college degree, compared with 45% for Koreans (Oropesa & Landale, 1995). Family socioeconomic status is important to the study of adaptation because it affects the kinds of neighborhoods where immigrant children grow up and attend school (Zhou, 1997). However, equally important are the cultural practices that organize family relationships, including parental values and childrearing practices, and the expectations that parents have of their children. It is here that ethnic differences among Koreans and Vietnamese appear more subtle.

Due to the relatively short history of massive Asian immigration, Asian American family research has been fragmented and limited. As Uba (1994) points out, most of the research has been descriptive rather than explanatory, has focused on Chinese Americans and Japanese Americans, and has given little attention to between-group differences. Thus the empirical picture of Korean and Vietnamese family systems is incomplete. What we do know is that the philosophical values of Chinese Confucianism have influenced the traditional family systems of Korea and Vietnam. These values emphasize solidarity, hierarchal relations, and filial piety (Kibria, 1993; Hurh, 1998; Min, 1998; Sue & Morishima, 1982). Confucianism provides a firm set of rules about how family members are supposed to behave toward one another (Cha, 1994; Chung, 1992; Kim & Choi, 1994; Min, 1998; Zhou & Bankston, 1998). Priority is placed on family interests over individual desires and needs in order to maintain stability and harmony. Status distinctions guide the way in which members are to interact with one another. Younger members are expected to display respect, deference, and obedience to elders (including to older siblings, especially brothers), and wives are expected to show the same to their husbands and parents-in-law. Children—including adult offspring—are forbidden from expressing dissenting opinions or confronting parents, which is viewed as disrespectful (Chung, 1992; Kibria, 1993; Min, 1998; Pettengill & Rohner, 1985). Emotional expressiveness, including displays of affection, is discouraged, while self-control is emphasized (Hurh, 1998; Uba, 1994). Family ties and roles are central from birth until death, with a strong emphasis on family devotion. In general, parents are expected to rely on their children's support in later life. Confucianism assigns the care and financial support of aging parents to the eldest son and his wife, who are expected to live under the same roof as the parents. Korean and Vietnamese cultures also derive from Confucianism a respect

for the well educated, and education is considered the primary means for social mobility. This undergirds the great importance that many Asian parents place on their children's education (Min, 1998; Zhou & Bankston, 1998). The economic hardships of many immigrant parents strengthen their emphasis on the education of their children, whom they expect to forge success in the United States (Kibria, 1993; Min, 1998).

There are, of course, ethnic differences between Korean and Vietnamese families, as well as differences in the degree to which they conform to traditional family practices. Although the comparative research is scant, Confucianism appears to have a stronger influence on the traditional family system in Korea than in Vietnam. For example, in Vietnamese families there is a greater tendency for siblings to pool resources in providing filial care rather than relying on the elder son alone, which might be related to their poorer economic circumstances. Additionally, Vietnamese women are permitted stronger kinship ties to their family of origin upon marriage than are Korean women, who are expected to live with their in-laws if they marry an elder son (Hurh, 1998; Kibria, 1993).

Although more research is needed that closely examines Asian ethnic differences in family practices, the existing literature reveals patterns of similarities among the family systems of Koreans and Vietnamese that differentiate them from American family patterns. The role prescriptions, family obligations, hierarchal relations, lack of emotional expressiveness, and collectivist values associated with the traditional family systems of Korea and Vietnam contrast sharply with the emphasis on individualism, self-sufficiency, egalitarianism, expressiveness, and self-development in mainstream U.S. culture (Bellah et al., 1985; Cancian, 1987; Chung, 1992; Hurh, 1998; Kim & Choi, 1994; Min, 1998; Pyke & Bengtson, 1996; Tran, 1988; Uba,

1994). Immigrant children tend to quickly adopt American values and standards, creating generational schisms and challenges to parental control and authority. That parent-child conflict and cultural gaps exist in many Asian immigrant families is well documented (Gold, 1993; Freeman, 1989; Kibria, 1993; Min, 1998; Rumbaut, 1994; Zhou & Bankston, 1998; Wolfe, 1997). However, no study to date has closely examined the cultural mechanisms at play in this process. This study begins that task.

METHOD

The data are from an interview study of the family and social experiences of grown children of Korean and Vietnamese immigrants. Respondents were either located at a California university where 47% of all undergraduates are of Asian descent (Maharaj, 1997) or were referred by students from that university. In-depth interviews were conducted with 73 respondents consisting of 34 Korean Americans (24 women, 10 men) and 39 Vietnamese Americans (23 women, 16 men). Both parents of each respondent were Korean or Vietnamese, except for one respondent, whose parents were both Sino-Vietnamese. Respondents ranged in age from 18–26 and averaged 21 years. Only one respondent was married, and none had children.

Respondents were either born in the United States (second generation) or immigrated prior to the age of 15 (1.5 generation), except for one Vietnamese American woman who immigrated at 17. The foreign born accounted for 77% of the sample, and immigrated at an average age of 5 years. The remaining 23% were born in the United States. Most respondents in this sample spent their entire adolescence in the United States, and a majority lived in the United States for most, if not all, of their childhood. Eight percent of the Vietnamese American respondents

TABLE 23.1   Sample Characteristics

Ethnicity	n	Average Age (years)	Foreign Born (%)	Average Age at Immigration (years)
Korean American women	24	21	62	5
Korean American men	10	21	60	7
Vietnamese American women	23	21	96	5
Vietnamese American men	16	22	81	5
Total for sample	73	21	77	5

were born in the United States, compared to 38 percent of Korean American respondents (see Table 23.1 for gender and ethnic differences). All study participants were college graduates or students and all resided in California, where one-third of U.S. legal immigrants arrive and 45% of the nation's immigrant student population lives (Zhou, 1997). Thus the sample over-represents those who are academically successful. Because the respondents have endured sustained exposure to assimilation pressures from the educational system, higher levels of assimilation were expected in this sample than in the larger immigrant population. As a result, these respondents were perhaps more likely to invoke American cultural ideals in describing their family life than a more representative sample that included the less educated and those who immigrated at older ages.

The author gathered the 73 individual interviews analyzed here in the preliminary phase of data collection for a larger on-going project sponsored by the National Science Foundation (#SBR-9810725). The larger study includes a sample of

184 who participated in individual and focus group interviews. Only the initial phase of data collection was designed to prompt respondents' extensive descriptions of family life. The purpose of the larger study is to compare the dynamic complexities and structural contexts of adaptation and ethnic identity among children of immigrants, with special attention to their subjective experiences in mediating different cultural worlds. Because ethnic identity development differs for males and females (Espiritu, 1997; Waters, 1996), I also stratified the sample by gender.

As previously discussed, I stratified the sample by ethnicity, as well, in order to compare the effects of structural and cultural factors on adaptation processes. Despite Korean and Vietnamese distinctions in socioeconomic status, pathways to immigration, and cultural practices, I did not observe ethnic differences relevant to the central focus of this analysis. Although this is surprising, ethnic differences in the specific areas of family life that I was investigating are probably relatively subtle, particularly from the viewpoint of American children of Asian immigrant parents. More specifically, because respondents relied on American family ideology in giving meaning to their domestic relations, their focus was on how immigrant family life differs from the American ideal rather than from other Asian ethnic groups. This can blur ethnic distinctions and serve as a basis for shared personal experiences across ethnic groups. In fact, the rise of an Asian American ethnic identity among Asian-origin individuals is believed to result, in part, from the shared experiences of growing up American in an Asian home (Kibria, 1997).

Gender differences observed in these data focused on the nature of respondents' criticisms of parents, with females complaining that parents grant more freedom and respect to sons. Males also complained of strict parents, but, when asked, acknowledged receiving more respect and freedom than sisters. These observed differences are not central to this analysis and are presented elsewhere (Pyke & Johnson, 1999).

A five-page interview guide with open-ended questions and follow-up probes concerning the familial and social experiences of respondents directed the intensive interview process. All respondents were asked what being a child of immigrants was like, how they think immigration affected their family, what their parents were like when the respondent was growing up, what communication was like with their parents, what their parents' marriage was like, how close they feel to their parents, whether they ever felt embarrassed by their parents, whether they ever deceived their parents, what kinds of things their parents would do to get them to obey, whether they have ever disappointed their parents in any way, how they would change their parents if they could change anything about them they wanted, what kinds of assistance they plan to provide for their parents, and how they feel about providing assistance. The author conducted about one-third of the interviews, and several trained student assistants conducted the remainder. The student assistants took a qualitative methods course with the author, in which they learned interviewing skills and conducted practice interviews. They also received extensive training and practice with the interview guide prior to collecting project data. Most trained student interviewers were children of Asian immigrants near in age to the respondents. They were therefore able to establish rapport with respondents, and they typically received candid responses, as revealed by respondents' frequent use of colloquialisms and profanity in interviews. Interviews were conducted in 1996 and 1997 and lasted between 1½ and 3 hours. They were tape-recorded and transcribed for analysis.

This research began with the general goal of learning about the subjective family experiences of children of Asian immigrants. I used a grounded research approach that emphasized an inductive method of generating explanation from the data (Glaser & Strauss, 1967; Strauss & Corbin, 1990). Except for the general assumption that respondents are active agents in the construction of their family experiences, I imposed no apriori assumptions, hypotheses, or specific theoretical frames on the research process. This allowed unanticipated data to emerge. Interviews focusing on family dynamics were conducted until a point of saturation was reached, as indicated by the recurring nature of the data and the emergence of clear trends (Ambert, Adler, Adler, & Detzner, 1995; Glaser & Strauss, 1967).

The overwhelming majority of respondents provided negative descriptions of their parents and upbringing in at least one domain, such as discipline, emotional closeness, or communication; only a small minority provided wholly positive accounts. Despite such intergenerational strain or distance, most respondents were strongly committed to caring for their parents in later life. In order to more closely examine the interview data, and thus to uncover deeper layers of understanding to these prominent patterns, two research assistants coded data into topical categories that corresponded with the questions asked. These coded segments were extracted for ease in theoretical sorting. I then analyzed the data, moving back and forth between emerging theoretical categories of the extracted data and the full interviews in order to check the validity of the findings. Because I am a native-born White American and wanted both to guard against the introduction of personal bias in the analysis and to acquire greater awareness of ethnic meanings, I shared my interpretive understandings of the data with Asian American students and student assistants. I then incorporated their insights into the analysis.

During the analysis, I noted recurring references in one form or another to notions about so-called normal families. Respondents used such references for one purpose only—as a point of contrast to life in their families. Three categorical expressions of this theme emerged in the data: (a) comparisons with television families; (b) comparisons with families of non-Asian friends; and (c) contrasts with specific family behavior or characteristics described as normal or American. I did not anticipate the importance of such family imagery when I devised the interview guide; thus I never asked respondents about family life on TV or among friends, or what they regarded as a normal or ideal family. Rather this theme emerged unexpectedly in the interviews. The unprompted and recurring nature of these references indicates their importance as resources in respondents' construction of their family experiences. In the following discussion, I present a sample of the qualitative data, in the form of quotes, to illustrate the observed patterns (Ambert et al., 1995). Respondents chose the pseudonyms used here.

RESULTS

I examine two ways in which respondents commonly used the typification of American family life as a contrast structure against which behavior in immigrant Asian families was juxtaposed and interpreted (Gubrium & Holstein, 1997). When describing relations with their parents, most respondents provided negative accounts of at least one aspect of their relationship, and they criticized their parents for lacking American values that emphasize psychological well-being and expressive love. Recurring references to a narrow Americanized notion of what families ought to look like were woven throughout many such accounts. However, when respondents described the kinds of filial care they planned to provide for their parents, the respondents switched to an interpretive lens that values ethnic family solidarity.

In this context, respondents' references to notions of the Normal American Family became a negative point of comparison that cast their own immigrant families, and Asian families in general, in positive terms.

Viewing Parental Relations Through an Americanized Lens

Respondents were asked to fantasize about how they would change their parents if they could change anything about them that they wanted to change. The three areas of desired change that respondents mentioned most often reveal their adoption of many mainstream American values. They wished for parents who: (a) were less strict and gave them more freedom; (b) were more liberal, more open-minded, more Americanized, and less traditional; (c) were emotionally closer, more communicative, more expressive, and more affectionate. These three areas are interrelated. For example, being more Americanized and less traditional translates into being more lenient and expressive. A small minority of respondents presented a striking contrast to the dominant pattern by describing, in terms both positive and grateful, parents who had liberal attitudes or Americanized values and parenting styles.

The communication most respondents described with parents focused on day-to-day practical concerns, such as whether the child had eaten, and about performance in school and college, a major area of concern among parents. Conversations were often limited to parental directives or lectures. For the most part, respondents were critical of the emotional distance and heavy emphasis on obedience that marked their relations with their parents. Chang-Hee, an 18-year-old who immigrated from Korea at 8, provided a typical case. When asked about communication, she disparaged her parents for not talking more openly, which she attributed to their being Asian. Respondents typically linked parental styles with race and not with other factors such as age or personality. Like many other respondents, Chang-Hee constructed an account not only of her family relations, but also of Asian families in general.

> To tell you the truth, in Asian families you don't have conversations. You just are told to do something and you do it.... You never talk about problems, even in the home. You just kind of forget about it and you kind of go on like nothing happened. Problems never really get solved. That's why I think people in my generation, I consider myself 1.5 generation, we have such a hard time because I like to verbalize my emotions.... [My parents] never allowed themselves to verbalize their emotions. They've been repressed so much [that] they expect the same out of me, which is the hardest thing to do because I have so many different things to say and I'm just not allowed.

Some respondents volunteered that their parents never asked them about their well-being, even when their distress was apparent. Chang-Hee observed, "If I'm sad, [my mom] doesn't want to hear it. She doesn't want to know why.... She's never asked me, 'So what do you feel?'" This lack of expressed interest in children's emotional well-being, along with the mundane level of communication, was especially upsetting to respondents because, interpreted through the lens of American family ideology, it defined their parents as emotionally uncaring and distant.

Several respondents longed for closer, more caring relationships with their parents that included expressive displays of affection. Thanh, a married 22-year-old college student who left Vietnam when she was 6, said, "I'd probably make them more loving and understanding, showing a bit more affection.... A lot of times I just want to go up and hug my parents, but no, you don't do that sort of thing."

Research indicates that the desire for greater intimacy is more common among women than men (Cancian, 1987). Thus it was surprising that many male respondents also expressed strong desires for more caring and close talk—especially from their fathers, who were often described as harsh and judgmental. Ralph, 20, a Korean American man born in the United States, said:

> My dad, he's not open. He is not the emotional type. So he talks...and I would listen and do it. It's a one-way conversation, rather than asking for my opinions.... I would think it'd be nicer if he was...much more compassionate, caring, because it seems like he doesn't care.

Similarly, Dat, a 22-year-old biology major who left Vietnam when he was 5, said:

> I would fantasize about sitting down with my dad and shooting the breeze. Talk about anything and he would smile and he would say, "Okay, that's fine, Dat." Instead of, you know, judge you and tell me I'm a loser....

A definition of love that emphasizes emotional expression and close talk predominates in U.S. culture (Cancian, 1986). Instrumental aspects of love, like practical help, are ignored or devalued in this definition. In Korean and Vietnamese cultures, on the other hand, the predominant definitions of love emphasize instrumental help and support. The great divide between immigrant parents who emphasize instrumental forms of love and children who crave open displays of affection was evident in the following conversation, which occurred between Dat and his father when Dat was 7 or 8 years old. Dat recalled, "I tried saying 'I love you' one time and he looked at me and said, 'Are you American now? You think this is *The Brady Bunch*? You don't love me. You love me when you can support me.'" These different cultural definitions of love contributed to respondents' constructions of immigrant parents as unloving and cold.

The Family as a Contrast Structure in the Negative Accounts of Family Life

Many of the images of normal family life that respondents brought to their descriptions came in the form of references to television families or the families of non–Asian American friends. Although these monolithic images do not reflect the reality of American family life, they nevertheless provided the basis by which respondents learned how to be American, and they served as the interpretive frame of their own family experiences. By contrasting behavior in their immigrant families with mainstream images of normalcy, the respondents interpreted Asian family life as lacking or deficient. Dat referred to images of normal family life in America, as revealed on television and among friends, as the basis for his desire for more affection and closeness with his father:

> Sometimes when I had problems in school, all I wanted was my dad to listen to me, of all people. I guess that's the American way and I was raised American.... That's what I see on TV and in my friends' family. And I expected him to be that way too. But it didn't happen.... I would like to talk to him or, you know, say "I

love you," and he would look at me and say, "Okay." That's my ultimate goal, to say, "I love you." It's real hard. Sometimes when I'm in a good mood, the way I show him love is to put my hands over his shoulders and squeeze it a little bit. That would already irritate him a little.... You could tell. He's like, "What the fuck's he doing?" But I do it because I want to show him love somehow. Affection. I'm an affectionate person.

Similarly, Hoa, a 23-year-old Vietnamese American man who immigrated at age 2, referred to television in describing his own family: "We aren't as close as I would like...We aren't as close as the dream family, you know, what you see on TV. Kind of like.... *Leave It To Beaver.* You know, stuff I grew up on."

Paul, a 21-year-old Korean American born in the United States, also criticizes his father, and Asian fathers in general, in relation to the fathers of friends and those on television:

I think there is somewhat of a culture clash between myself and my parents. They are very set on rules—at least my father is. He is very strict and demanding and very much falls into that typical Asian father standard. I don't like that too much and I think it is because...as a child, I was always watching television and watching other friends' fathers. All the relationships seemed so much different from me and my father's relationship.... I guess it's pretty cheesy but I can remember watching The Brady Bunch *reruns and thinking Mike Brady would be a wonderful dad to have. He was always so sup-*

portive. He always knew when something was wrong with one of his boys. Whenever one of his sons had a problem, they would have no problem telling their dad anything and the dad would always be nice and give them advice and stuff. Basically I used what I saw on television as a picture of what a typical family should be like in the United States. I only wished that my family could be like that. And friends too—I used to see how my friends in school would be in Little League Baseball and their dad would be like their coaches or go to their games to cheer their sons on and give them support. I could not picture my father to be like that kind of man that I saw on TV, or like my friends' fathers.

Respondents did not refer to non–Asian American friends who had distant, conflict-ridden family relationships. Yet many respondents likely did have contact with such individuals. It appears as though respondents see only in ways permitted by the Family ideology. That is, as Bemades argued, "the image or idol of 'The Family' rather than the reality of people's lives is taken as the object of attention" (1985, p. 288). Looking at "American" families through this ideological lens determines which families are "seen." Those that do not fit the cultural imagery are not seen or are viewed as atypical. "Atypical" families are not referenced in these accounts, even though, in actuality, they are probably closer to the empirical reality of American family life. Friends whose families do comply, on the other hand, loom large as symbols that verify the existence of the Family ideal.

In comparison to this ideal, even parents who had adopted more American parenting practices fell short. For example, the parents of Mike, 22, who had immigrated to the United States from Vietnam as an infant, were less strict than the parents of most respondents. Nevertheless, Mike said:

My parents were really easy. They let me hang out with my friends, they had no problem with me sleeping over or other people sleeping over. So having friends in high school wasn't hard at all, and going out wasn't a problem at all. It was just, you know, you go over to your friend's house and he just talks to his parents about everything. So I got a little bit jealous. You know, I wished I could talk to my parents about stuff like that but I couldn't.

Sometimes respondents simply made assumptive references to normal or American families, against which they critically juxtaposed Asian immigrant families. Being American meant that one was a member of the Normal American Family and enjoyed family relations that were warm, close, and harmonious. Being Asian, on the other hand, meant living outside such normality. Thuy, a 20-year-old Vietnamese American woman who had immigrated when 13, said:

If I could, I would have a more emotional relationship with my parents. I know they love me, but they never tell me they love me. They also are not very affectionate. This is how I've always grown up. It wasn't really until we came to the United States that I really noticed what a lack of love my parents show. American kids are so lucky. They don't know what it's like

to not really feel that you can show emotion with your own parents.

Similarly, Cora, 20, a Korean American woman born in the United States, remarked:

I would probably want [my parents] to be more open, more understanding so I could be more open with them, 'cause there's a lot of things that I can't share with them because they're not as open-minded as American parents.... 'Cause I have friends and stuff. They talk to their parents about everything, you know?

When asked how he was raised, Josh, 21, a Vietnamese American man who immigrated when 2, responded by calling up a construction of the "good" American Family and the "deficient" Asian Family. He said, "I'm sure that for all *Asian* people, if they think back to [their] childhood, they'll remember a time they got hit. *American* people, they don't get hit."

Respondents repeatedly constructed American families as loving, harmonious, egalitarian, and normal. Using this ideal as their measuring stick, Asian families were constructed as distant, overly strict, uncaring, and not normal. In fact, respondents sometimes used the word "normal" in place of "American." For example, Hoa, who previously contrasted his family with the one depicted in *Leave It To Beaver,* said, "I love my dad but we never got to play catch. He didn't teach me how to play football. All the stuff a *normal* dad does for their kids. We missed out on that." Thomas, 20, a Korean American who arrived in the United States at age 8, said, "I always felt like maybe we are not so normal. Like in the real America, like Brady Bunch normal.... I always felt like...there was something irregular about me." Similarly, after describing a childhood where she spoke very little to her parents, Van, 24, who immigrated to the United States from Vietnam at 10, began crying and noted, "I guess I didn't have a *normal* childhood." To be a normal parent is to be an American parent. Asian immigrant parents are by this definition deficient. Such constructions ignore diversity within family types, and they selectively bypass the social problems, such as child abuse, that plague many non-Asian American families. It is interesting, for example, that respondents did not refer to the high divorce rate of non–Asian Americans (Sweet & Bumpass, 1987) to construct positive images of family stability among Asian Americans. This may be because, applying an Americanized definition of love, many respondents described their parents' marriage as unloving and some thought their parents ought to divorce.

Respondents relied on the Family not only as an interpretive framework, but also as a contrast structure by which to differentiate Asian and American families. This juxtaposition of American and Asian ignores that most of the respondents and the coethnics they describe are Americans. "American" is used to refer to non–Asian Americans, particularly Whites. The words "White" and "Caucasian" were sometimes used interchangeably with "American." Indeed, the Normal American Family *is* White. This Eurocentric imagery excludes from view other racial minority families such as African Americans and Latino Americans. It is therefore not surprising that racial–ethnic families were not referenced as American in these interviews. In fact, respondents appeared to use the term "American" as a code word denoting not only cultural differences but also racial differences. For example, Paul, who was born in the United States, noted, "I look Korean but I think I associate myself more with the *American race*." The oppositional constructions of Asian and American families as monolithic and without internal

variation imply that these family types are racialized. That is, the differences are constructed as not only cultural but also racially essential and therefore immutable (Omi & Winant, 1994). By defining American as White, respondents revealed the deep-seated notion that, as Asian Americans, they can never truly be American. Such notions dominate in mainstream depictions of Asian Americans as perpetual foreigners. For example, in a speech about foreign donations, Ross Perot read the names of several Asian American political donors and commented, "So far we haven't found an American name" (Nakao, 1996). When respondents centered Whites as a point of reference in these accounts, they reaffirmed the marginalized position of racial–ethnic minorities in the Family ideology and in U.S. culture writ large.

These data illustrate how Eurocentric images of normal family relationships promulgated in the larger society served as an ideological template in the negative accounts that respondents provided of their immigrant parents. However, as described next, when respondents discussed their plans for filial care, they presented positive accounts of their immigrant families.

Maintaining Ethnic Values of Filial Obligation

Respondents were not consistent in their individual constructions of Asian and American families as revealed in their interviews. When discussing future plans for filial care, most respondents positively evaluated their family's collectivist commitment to care. Such an interpretation is supported by model minority stereotypes in mainstream U.S. culture that attribute the success enjoyed by some Asian immigrants to their strong family values and collectivist practices (Kibria, 1993; Zhou & Bankston, 1998).

The majority of respondents valued and planned to maintain their ethnic tradition of filial care. For example, Josh, who criticized his parents (and Asian parents in general) for using physical forms of punishment, nonetheless plans to care for his parents in their old age. He said, "I'm the oldest son, and in Vietnamese culture the oldest son cares for the parents. That is one of the things that I carry from my culture. I would not put my parents in a [nursing] home. That's terrible." In contrast to White Americans who condition their level of filial commitment on intergenerational compatibility (Pyke, 1999), respondents displayed a strong desire to fulfill their filial obligation and—especially among daughters—were often undeterred by distant and even conflict-ridden relations with parents. For example, after describing a strained relationship with her parents, Kimberly, 20, who came to this country from Vietnam when 7, added, "I would still take care of them whether I could talk to them or not. It doesn't matter as long as I could take care of them." Similarly, in Wolf's study of 22 grown children of Filipino immigrants, respondents who complained of tension and emotional distance with parents nonetheless experienced family ties and responsibilities as a central component of their daily lives and identities (1997).

Most respondents expected to begin financially supporting their parents prior to their elderly years, with parents in their 50s often regarded as old. A few respondents had already begun to help out their parents financially. Many planned on living with parents. Others spoke of living near their parents, often as neighbors, rather than in the same house, as a means of maintaining some autonomy. The tradition of assigning responsibility for the care of parents to the eldest son was not automatically anticipated for many of these families, especially those from Vietnam. Respondents most often indicated that responsibility would be pooled among siblings or would fall exclusively to the daughters. Several said that parents preferred such arrangements, because they felt closer to daughters. Although the tendency for daughters to assume responsibility for aging parents is similar to the pattern of caregiving common in mainstream American families (Pyke & Bengston, 1996), several respondents noted that such patterns are also emerging among relatives in their ethnic homeland.

The Importance of Collectivism as an Expression of Love

Respondents typically attributed their future caregiving to reciprocation for parental care in the past and a cultural emphasis on filial respect and support. Yet the enthusiasm and strong commitment that pervades their accounts suggests that they are motivated by more than obligation. For example, Vinh, 26, a graduate student who immigrated from Vietnam at age 5, said about his parents:

> They are my life. They will never be alone. I will always be with them. When I was growing [up] as a child, my parents were always with me. And I believe…when you grow up, you should be with them; meaning, I will take care of them, in my house, everything. Your parents didn't abandon you when you were a kid. They did not abandon you when you [were] pooping in your diaper. Then when they do, I will not abandon them…. Whatever it takes to make them comfortable, I will provide it. There is no limit.

Unable to express love via open displays of affection and close talk, filial assistance becomes a very important way for adult children to symbolically demonstrate their affection for their parents and to reaffirm family bonds. Blossom, 21, who immigrated to the United States from Korea when 6, described the symbolic value of the financial assistance her father expects. She said, "Money is not really important, but it's more about our heart that [my dad] looks at. Through money, my dad will know how we feel and how we appreciate him." Remember that Dat's father told him, "You love me when you can support me." Because instrumental assistance is the primary venue for expressing love and affection in these immigrant families, adult children often placed no limits on what they were willing to do. For example, John, 20, who immigrated from Vietnam when 3, remarked "I'm willing to do anything (for my parents), that's how much I care."

Parental financial independence was not always welcomed by those children who gave great weight to their role of parental caregivers. For example, it was very important to Sean, 19, an only child, to care for his Sino-Vietnamese parents. Sean, who planned to become a doctor, commuted from his home to a local university. He said, "I want my parents to stay with me. I want to support them.... I'll always have room for my parents.... When I get my first paycheck, I want to support them financially." As reflected in the following exchange with the interviewer, Sean viewed his parents' retirement plan with some hurt.

> Sean: They have their own retirement plan, and they keep track of it themselves, so they're all prepared for me to be the disobedient son and run away.
> Interviewer: Is that how you feel?
> Sean: Yes I do.... Or if I don't succeed in life, they'll be taken care of by themselves.
> Interviewer: So is that how you see their retirement plan, as a kind of symbol that they're...?

> Sean: They're ready for me to mess up.

The emotional centrality of family ties is also apparent in Sean's description of his hurt when his father—who worries that the time Sean spends away from home studying or at his job is pulling him away from the family—occasionally tests his son's commitment by suggesting that he leave the family home and "fly away." With tear-filled eyes, Sean explained:

> It hurts me because I've never had that idea to fly away.... I don't want to go and that's what hurts me so bad. I mean, I could cry over things like that. And this is a 19-year-old kid that's crying in front of you. How seldom do you get that?

The Family as a Contrast Structure in the Positive Accounts of Filial Obligation

Many respondents distinguished their ethnic collectivist tradition of filial obligation from practices in mainstream American families, which they described as abandoning elderly parents in retirement or nursing homes. The belief that the elderly are abandoned by their families is widespread in U.S. society and very much a part of everyday discourse. Media accounts of nursing home atrocities bolster such views. Yet most eldercare in this country is not provided in formal caregiving settings but by family members (Abel, 1991). Nonetheless, respondents used this tenacious myth as a point of contrast in constructing Asian American families as more instrumentally caring. For example, Thuy, who previously described wanting a "more emotional relationship" with her parents, like "American kids" have, explained:

> With the American culture, it's...not much frowned upon to put your par-

ents in a home when they grow old. In our culture, it is a definite no-no. To do anything like that would be disrespectful.... If they need help, my brother and I will take care of them, just like my mom is taking care of her parents right now.

Similarly, Hien, 21, a Vietnamese American woman who arrived in this country as an infant, noted, "I know a lot of non–Asians have their parents go to the nursing homes...but I personally prefer to find a way of trying to keep them at home."

Mike, who wished he could talk to his parents the way his friends do to theirs, plans to care for his Americanized parents even though they have told him they do not want him to. He was not alone in remaining more committed to filial care than his parents required him to be. He said:

They tell me to just succeed for yourself and take care of your own family. But [referring to filial care] that's just how the Vietnamese culture is. Here in America, once your parents are old, you put them in a retirement home. But not in my family. When the parents get old you take care of them. It doesn't matter if they can't walk, if they can't function anymore. You still take care of them.

When discussing relationships with their parents, respondents used the Family as the ideological raw material out of which they negatively constructed their parents as unloving and distant. However, when the topic changed to filial care, respondents switched to an ethnic definition of love that emphasizes instrumental support and that casts a positive and loving light on their families. As Katie, 21, a Korean American woman born in the United States, observed:

When you say that you are close to your parents here in America, I think most people would take that as you are affectionate with your parents, you hang out with them, you can talk to them about anything.... more of a friendship thing. But Korean families are not like that.... They do not get close to their children like that. They are not friends with them. The kids of Korea do not open up with their parents. Their parents are really their parents.... But still, no matter what, they are very close, Here in America...Caucasians don't take care of their parents like we do. They just put them in an old people's home and that's it. It's like they say, "You are too old for me. I don't need you anymore and I'm just going to put you here 'cause it's convenient for me and you'd be in the way anyway...." And in that way, Americans are not close to their parents. So it really depends on how you define the word "close"—the answer changes. [Note that the words "Caucasian" and "American" are used synonymously here, as previously discussed.]

In describing their plans for parental care, respondents turned their previous construction of Asian and American families on its head. In this context the Family was constructed as deficient and uncaring, while the families of respondents—and Asian families in general—were described as more instrumentally caring and closer. Respondents' view of American families as uncaring should not be interpreted as a departure from mainstream family ideology. There has been much concern in the public discourse that today's families lack a commitment to the care of their elders and children (e.g., Popenoe, 1993; see Coontz, 1992, pp. 189–191). Indeed, the pervasive criticism that "individualism has gone haywire" in mainstream families—bolstered by references to the solidarity of model minority families—provides ideological support for ethnic traditions of filial care. That is, children of immigrants do not face ideological pressure from the dominant society to alter such practices; rather, they are given an interpretive template by which to view such practices as evidence of love and care in their families. In fact, U.S. legislative attempts to withdraw social services from legal immigrants without citizenship, with the expectation that family sponsors will provide such support, structurally mandate collectivist systems of caregiving in immigrant families (Huber & Espenshade, 1997). In other words, the dominant society ideologically endorses and, in some ways, structurally requires ethnic immigrant practices of filial care. Filial obligation thus serves as a site where children of Korean and Vietnamese immigrants can maintain their ethnic identity and family ties without countervailing pressure from the mainstream.

DISCUSSION

Interweaving respondents' accounts with an analysis of the interpretive structure from which those accounts are constructed suggests that the Family ideology subtly yet powerfully influences the children of immigrants, infiltrating their subjective understandings of and desires for family life. Respondents relied on American family images in two ways. When discussing their relations with parents and their upbringing, respondents used the Family ideology as a standard of normal families and good parents, leading them to view their immigrant parents as unloving, deficient, and not normal. However, when respondents discussed filial care, a complete reversal occurred. Respon-

dents referred to negative images of rampant individualism among mainstream American families, specifically in regard to eldercare, to bolster their positive portrayals of the instrumental care and filial piety associated with their ethnic families. Thus the Family ideology was called upon in contradictory ways in these accounts—in the denigration of traditional ethnic parenting practices and in the glorification of ethnic practices of filial obligation.

Findings from this study illustrate how a narrow, ethnocentric family ideology that is widely promulgated throughout the larger culture and quickly internalized by children of immigrants creates an interpretive framework that derogates many of the ethnic practices of immigrant families. As others have argued, the cultural imposition of dominant group values in this form of "controlling images" can lead minorities to internalize negative self-images (Espiritu, 1997). That is, racial–ethnic immigrants can adopt a sense of inferiority and a desire to conform with those values and expectations that are glorified in the main-stream society as normal. Indeed, many respondents explicitly expressed a desire to have families that were like White or so-called American families, and they criticized their own family dynamics for being different. Rather than resist and challenge the ethnocentric family imagery of the mainstream, respondents' accounts reaffirmed the Normal American Family and the centrality of White native-born Americans in this imagery. This research thus reveals a subtle yet powerful mechanism of internalized oppression by which the racial–ethnic power dynamics in the larger society are reproduced. This is a particularly important finding in that racial–ethnic families will soon constitute a majority in several states, causing scholars to ponder the challenge of such a demographic transformation of the cultural and political hegemony of White native-born Americans (Maharidge, 1996). This study describes an ideological mechanism that could undermine challenges to that hegemony.

This research also uncovered an uncontested site of ethnic pride among the second-generation respondents who drew on mainstream images of elder neglect in their positive interpretation of ethnic filial commitment. As previously discussed, the belief that mainstream American families abandon their elders is tenacious and widespread in the dominant society, despite its empirical inaccuracy. This negative myth has been widely used in popular discourse as an example of the breakdown of American family commitment, and it sometimes serves as a rallying cry for stronger "family values." Such cries are often accompanied by references to the family solidarity and filial piety celebrated in the model minority stereotype. Thus the mainstream glorification of ethnic filial obligation, as contrasted with negative images of abandoned White American elders, provided respondents with a positive template for giving meaning to ethnic practices of filial care. The mainstream endorsement of filial obligation marks it as a locale where respondents can maintain family ties and simultaneously produce a positive self-identity in both cultural worlds. This might explain why some respondents were steadfastly committed to filial care despite parental requests to the contrary.

It remains to be seen, however, whether these young adults will be able to carry out their plans of filial obligation. It is likely that many will confront barriers in the form of demanding jobs, childrearing obligations, geographic moves, unsupportive spouses, competing demands from elderly in-laws, and financial difficulties. Furthermore, parents' access to alternative sources of support such as Social Security and retirement funds could diminish the need for their children's assistance. Some research already finds that elderly Korean immigrants prefer to

five on their own and are moving out of the homes of their immigrant children despite the protests of children, who see it as a public accusation that they did not care for their parents (Hurh, 1998). Although this research examined first-generation immigrant adults and their aging parents, it suggests a rapid breakdown in traditional patterns of coresidential filial care that will likely be reiterated in the next generation. Future research is needed to examine these dynamics among second-generation immigrants, to look at how they will cope with inabilities to fulfill ethnic and model minority expectations of filial obligation, and to assess the impact of any such inabilities on their ethnic identity.

This study makes a unique contribution to the small and largely descriptive literature on Asian immigrant families. Rather than simply reiterating as descriptive data the accounts of family life offered by respondents, I examined the ideological underpinnings of those accounts. In so doing, I uncovered a subtle process by which White hegemonic images of the Family infiltrate the ways that children of immigrants think about their own family lives. Although scholars have often assumed that the prescriptive and moralistic characteristics of the Family are hurtful to those whose families do not comply, the findings presented here provide an empirical description of how such ideology negatively biases the family accounts of children of immigrants. It must be noted, however, that because the sample in the study was demographically predisposed to higher levels of assimilation, the respondents are probably more likely than a less assimilated sample to view their families through an Americanized lens. This suggests the need for further study of how variations in acculturation levels affect the accounts that children of immigrants provide of their family lives.

A broader sample of families that do not conform with images of the Normal American

Family also needs to be investigated. This sample should include native-born racial minorities and children of single parents, as well as immigrants. Studying a broader sample will allow greater understanding of whether narrow cultural notions of a normal family life influence the subjective experience of diverse groups of children growing up in the margins of the mainstream. It is particularly important, as family scholars begin to respond to the burgeoning numbers of ethnically and structurally diverse family forms, that researchers generate culturally sensitive interpretive frameworks that do not automatically and unconsciously perpetuate existing notions that certain family types and practices are inferior. The effort to develop such frameworks requires researchers to examine not only the values and assumptions they bring to their analyses (Dilworth-Anderson et al., 1993), but also the values and assumptions that respondents bring to their accounts. To summarize, this study suggests the need for family researchers to analytically bracket as problematic the ideological structures that shape the empirical accounts of family life we rely upon in our research.

Part IV

Families in Crisis and Change

In this part of the reader, we examine two problematic aspects of marriage and family life. The ensuing selections will illustrate how patriarchy has been a major contributor to marital and familial tensions and problems. Patriarchal ideology supported by economic, social, political, and religious institutions often enables men to exert the upper hand in many aspects of marital and family relationships. Similarly, the domination of older family members over younger ones has often been the consequence of age stratification processes operating in family systems. In Chapter Eight, "Family Stress, Crisis, and Violence," the first two deal with the ultimate abuse of marital and familial patterns of stratification and power—family violence.

Intimate violence, whether it takes the form of wife battering or child abuse, can be seen as an irrational outgrowth of the excesses of patriarchal authority. The legitimation of male prerogatives, privilege, authority, and power can be abused, and in the case of wife battering, it is. This results in the severe mistreatment of women. Contemporary American society has just recently discovered the prevalence of marital abuse, which has been hidden from history because the belief that "normal" marriages are happy and well adjusted and that violence is an aberration has led to the underestimation of such abuse. This misunderstanding has further led to the treatment of marital abuse erroneously as a psychologically determined pathology and not as a social phenomenon.

Similarly, child abuse can be seen as a negative consequence of the conceptualization of children and adolescents as essentially inferior and subordinate human beings. Structural characteristics of the private nuclear family also play important contributory roles. Governmental policies and the underlying assumptions of the helping professions, too, often work against the best interests of children.

Sarah Goodrum, Debra Umberson, and Kristin L. Anderson are three sociologists who work out of the symbolic interaction perspective of social psychology. That perspective is often concerned with how individuals continually adapt to situations and how these adaptations affect self concepts. Goodrum, Umberson, and Anderson (Reading 24) observe that there have been numerous studies on the experiences of battered women, who find themselves living through episodic outbursts of violence from their mates. The consequences of that victimization on their sense of identity, and why so often they stay in abusive relationships, is the focus of that research. They report, however, that relatively few studies have examined battery from the perpetrator's perspective. They find that male batterers minimize others' negative views of themselves and they dissociate themselves from their partner's physical and emotional injuries. The authors conclude that an understanding of the batterer's perception of himself and others in domestic violence is important to understanding the causes of domestic violence and can prove beneficial to developing programs that can effectively stop male violence against women.

In the next reading (25), Murray A. Straus discusses the ten myths that are seen to perpetuate corporal punishment. This reading comes from Straus's larger study, *Beating the Devil Out of Them* (1994). Straus is concerned with spanking and its widespread prevalence. He demonstrates how taken-for-granted notions, religious admonitions, child-rearing advice books, and legal statutes all permit and often encourage the use of corporal punishment in response to a child's misbehavior. As a consequence, a "conspiracy of silence" has prevailed whose effect has prevented the investigation of potentially harmful effects of corporal punishment on children. Straus observes that in recent years there has been a cultural debate that centers on questioning such beliefs as: spanking works better, spanking is needed as a last resort, spanking is harmless, and if you don't spank, your child will be spoiled or run wild. Straus calls these "myths that perpetuate corporal punishment." In five European countries—Finland, Sweden, Norway, Denmark, and Austria—legislation has been passed that has outlawed physical punishment of children, including spanking. In the United States, Straus sees the beginning of a social trend that seeks to redefine expected parental behavior into reprehensible behavior.

The concluding reading (26) in this chapter examines the effects of homelessness on family relationships. The homeless family became a visible phenomena on the American scene in the 1980s. Government figures on the number of homeless range from 350,000 to 2,000,000. Advocates of the homeless put the figure much higher, into the double digits—10 to 20 million. The variation in these estimates is attributable to the difficulty in getting accurate assessments of people who are highly transient and often unwilling to be counted. Who are these homeless people? The evidence that has been collected indicates that they vary greatly from the "old" homeless who populated the nation's Skid Rows of the 1950s and 1960s who were almost all white males with an average age of around fifty years. The new homeless are characterized by extreme poverty and little family support. They are much younger—around thirty years of age—25 percent are women, and proportionately, African Americans and Hispanics constitute an increasing number of them (Rossi, 1994).

The primary reason for the upsurge in homelessness is related to the structural changes occurring in the economy as it moves from a manufacturing base with large numbers of low-skill manual jobs to a service base requiring higher educational attainment and greater occupational skills (Rossi, 1994). The deteriorating value of AFDC payments and the crisis in affordable housing are contributing factors. The most significant change in the demographic composition of the new homeless was the appearance of homeless families. These families are identified as being single-parent, mostly young mothers in their twenties, with very young children. How these economic changes have impacted on families is given a human dimension in the excerpt (Reading 26) from Steven Vanderstaay's (1992) *Street Lives: An Oral History of Homeless Americans.* "Karla" is the oral history of a woman with two children; Mark and Linda Armstrong are the parents of teenage children.

The final chapter of the book, Chapter Nine, "Divorce, Remarriage, and the Future of the Family," contains six readings. Divorce is a major form of marital dissolution. It represents an ultimate manifestation of marital and familial instability. Divorce has been viewed by some as an indicator of the breakdown of the American family and as a reflection of societal decline. Conversely, others see it as the outcome of a positive individual act, ultimately beneficial to all family members and, as such, a sign of societal strength.

Karla B. Hackstaff presents an examination of marriage in what she calls a "culture of divorce." In this reading (27), Hackstaff discusses the meanings on the importance of individualism, commitment, and marriages from *both* female and male perspectives in a larger context that discusses the emerging gendered patterns of marriage. Divorce culture is ultimately seen to have the potential of moving marriage into new and egalitarian directions.

The effects of divorce on children and adolescents has long been a concern of sociologists. These effects have become an even more urgent matter in light of the continued high divorce rate in the United States and the fact that an increasing number of children are affected. In 1960, the number of children involved in divorce was 500,000; 30 years later it had more than doubled. Nearly half of all children under the age of 18 experienced divorce in the last decade of the twentieth century. Joyce A. Arditti (Reading 28) examines the qualitative aspects of divorced mother-child relationships and the strengths in these resultant divorced families. She examines the implications of mothers' divorced families and of mothers' reliance on their children for emotional support and their affects on adolescent development. New patterns of generational relationships are seen to be emerging.

Terry Arendell, in an examination of divorce research, observes that while attention has been paid predominantly to mothers and children, fathers have been relatively neglected. In her ethnographic monograph, *Fathers and Divorce* (1995), she examines a group of divorced fathers and their views and behavior on a wide range of topics from noncustodial parenting to relationships with their former spouses to fathers' rights. Arendell refers to the views of these fathers as a "masculinist discourse of divorce." In an earlier article, "The Social Self as Gendered: A Masculinist Discourse of Divorce" (Reading 29), Arendell developed this perspective.

She observes that to understand this shared discourse, we must see it in terms of the larger context of gender arrangements and identities. That is, to understand how men perceive, recognize, and act toward divorce and divorce relationships, we must put this masculinist discourse in the larger context of men's views of gender, marriage, parenthood, and the family.

Emma Jean Lawson and Aaron Thompson (Reading 30) focus on the impact of divorce on fatherhood identities among Black men. These identities were shaped by family and community models. In this reading, the authors examine the role of fatherhood for noncustodial parents, explore the barriers that prevent closer ties with their children, and the psychological stress felt by them. The relationship that they have with stepchildren is also examined.

The study of remarriage has increasingly become an interest of sociologists who study the family. There is a myth surrounding remarriage that says the second marriage is more successful than the first—that "love is better the second time around." According to popular opinion, this is so because remarried individuals are now older, wiser, and more mature. Also, it is assumed that divorced persons who remarry will work harder to ensure a more successful second marriage. Yet Andrew Cherlin (1978), in a much-cited article, reported that the divorce rate for remarried parents was higher than for persons married for the first time. According to this researcher, insufficient institutional supports and guidelines to ensure optimal success of these marriages account for the high rate of divorce among remarried people with children. Cherlin observed that family members of such remarriages faced unique problems that do not exist in first-marriage families. He believes that the origins of these problems lie in the complex structure of remarried families and the normative inadequacies to define these familial roles and relationships. Cherlin's seminal article pointed out the necessity for a more systematic investigation of remarriage. In Reading 31, Mary Ann Mason and her colleagues did just that by examining remarriage through a study of laws that affect it.

In Reading 31, the authors observe that in most states, stepparents have little or no legal decision-making authority. Further, stepchildren do not receive legal recognition, nor are they covered under a legal safety net in event of death and divorce. Concomitantly, stepparents have no legal rights to visitation or custody. The authors feel that the lack of legal recognition does not reflect contemporary situations. Stepfamily functioning is investigated in the hope that it will aid in the creation of new policy orientations toward stepfamilies.

The concluding reading (32) of this anthology addresses new directions in family law that are reflections of changes in American families. Mary Ann Mason continues her examination of family legal matters. Here, with other colleagues, they review changes in family law over the last 30 years. These include legal changes in the areas of marriage, divorce, child custody, remarriage and stepfamilies, unwed fathers, third-party visitation, nontraditional partnerships, assisted reproduction, and adoption. The role that the social sciences have had in the reformulation of family law is investigated and has used to develop their speculations about future changes in family law and the role that the social sciences will play in legal reforms.

References

Arendell, Terry. 1995. *Fathers and Divorce.* Berkeley: University of California Press.
Cherlin, Andrew. 1978. "Remarriage as an Incomplete Institution." *American Journal of Sociology* 84(3):634–650.
Hackstaff, Karla B. 1999. *Marriage in a Culture of Divorce,* 1999. Philadelphia: Temple University Press.

Rossi, Peter H. 1994. "Troubling Families: Family Homelessness in America." *American Behavioral Scientist* 37 (January) 3:342–395.

Straus, Murray A. 1994. *Beating the Devil Out of Them: Corporal Punishment in American Families.* New York: Lexington Books.

Vanderstaay, Steven. 1992. *Street Lives: An Oral History of Homeless Americans.* Philadelphia, PA: New Society Publishers.

8 Family Stress, Crisis, and Violence

Reading 24   The Batterer's View of the Self and Others in Domestic Violence

SARAH GOODRUM*   DEBRA UMBERSON
KRISTIN L. ANDERSON

Researchers estimate that 3–4 million women are abused by intimate partners each year, and the United States Surgeon General reports physical abuse as the leading cause of injury to women in the U.S. Although numerous studies have examined survivors' perceptions of domestic violence, few have examined battery from the perpetrator's perspective. We use a symbolic interactionist perspective to examine in-depth interviews with thirty-three male batterers and a demographically matched comparison group of twenty-five non-violent male subjects. Our findings indicate that batterers minimize others' negative views of themselves, and they dissociate themselves from their partners' physical and emotional injuries. The comparison subjects, on the other hand, consider others' negative views of themselves, and they describe a deeper understanding of their intimate others' problems. We argue that an understanding of the batterers perception of himself and others in domestic violence will help counselors develop techniques to stop male violence against women.

For more than twenty years, survey data, police reports, and emergency room records have pointed to the seriousness of male violence against women in the United States (see Gelles 1980; Stark and Flitcraft 1996; Straus 1978). Each year women in the U.S. sustain more than half a million acts of violence at the hands of intimate partners (Zawitz 1994). Although a large research literature has examined the accounts of abuse offered by survivors of male violence, we know little about the batterer's perception of himself and others in domestic violence.[1] The batterer's perspective is important to theoretical work on the etiology of domestic violence and to

Sociological Inquiry, Vol. 71, No. 2, Spring 2001, 221–40 © 2001 by the University of Texas Press, P.O. Box 7819, Austin, TX 78713-7819

develop programs that can effectively stop male violence against women (Carden 1994; Stets 1988).

The limitations of current batterer research result, in part, from data collection strategies. First, survey research on domestic violence tends to address rates of domestic violence in American households (Straus, Gelles, and Steinmetz 1980) and the effect of sanctions on abusive men (see Hirschel, Hutchison, and Dean 1992; Pate and Hamilton 1992; Sherman, Schmidt, Smith, and Rogan 1992). This research provides very important information about the scope of the problem and the sanctions for it, but it does not provide the detail and depth for understanding the dynamics and complexities of problems like domestic violence. Very few surveys allow batterers to describe their domestic violence experiences in their own words. The Conflict Tactics Scale (CTS) has been the main tool for collecting information about rates of domestic violence (Straus 1979); however, Yllo (1993, p. 53) argues that the CTS neglects the "meanings, contexts or consequences of individual acts" of violence. Qualitative methods, such as in-depth interviewing, provide the opportunity to explore the rich details and contexts of this problem (Carden 1994). A second limitation of previous research is that few studies compare batterers to nonviolent subjects. Without a standard of comparison, it remains difficult to identify and understand the dynamics of this problem. We address both of these limitations through analysis of in-depth interviews conducted with a sample of domestically violent men and a demographically matched comparison group of nonviolent men.

THEORETICAL FRAMEWORK

We use symbolic interactionism as a framework for organizing and interpreting our analysis of in-depth interviews. The symbolic interactionist perspective delineates the construction of the self and its interaction with others within social and cultural contexts; it also describes how individuals plan and reason their action and inaction with both themselves and others in society (Athens 1994; Athens 1995; Blumer 1969; Mead 1934). A large research literature examines the ways in which survivors of domestic violence define their situations (Dobash and Dobash 1984; Kirkwood 1993; Martin 1976, Walker 1984), but less attention has been paid to perpetrators' constructions of the violence within their relationships. Most research on battery has been conducted from feminist, psychological and social structural perspectives. These perspectives have provided valuable insight to the problem of domestic violence, such as the feminist perspective's critical view of taken for granted assumptions about domestic violence research and practice, the psychological perspective's identification of characteristics associated with abusive behavior, and the social structuralist perspective's explication of the cultural and organizational constraints influencing this problem. The symbolic interactionist perspective, on the other hand, acknowledges the free will of the actor and the interpersonal and social forces shaping and constraining that action.

Understanding the perpetrator's construction of himself and his female partner is essential to a theoretical and practical understanding of the dynamics of battery. The decision to use domestic violence is an active one on the part of the perpetrator. Batterers plan violent actions through an interactive process that is influenced by their constructions of the self and others. Our findings delineate the methods batterers use to build a nonviolent self perspective and how that perspective shapes their subsequent interactions. Respondents' in-depth interview answers reveal the complexity and contradictions in the seemingly logical steps people, in this case batterers, take to resolve conflicts between their and others' views of the self. The application of this perspective to domestic violence also serves to broaden our understanding of abstract symbolic interactionist concepts.

Athens (1992, 1994, 1995, 1997), Lempert (1994), Denzin (1984), Scully (1990), and Forte, Franks, Forte, and Rigsby (1996) use symbolic interactionism and in-depth interviews to describe the ways in which violent offenders' constructions of reality influence their decisions to perpetrate violent acts, as well as the ways in which victims interpret acts of violence against them. Athens (1994) expands on Mead, Blumer, Dewey, James, and Cooley's conceptions of the self by positing that soliloquizing allows the individual to construct a self-portrait. The self emerges in the context of social relationships, and these contexts influence the ways that the individual comes to see himself or herself and others. The soliloquizing self can reflect on the self and take the role of the "other" (Athens 1994). The individual (1) considers how significant others think and feel about him or her and (2) decides how to think about others' thoughts and feelings about himself or herself. Athens notes that conflicts and contradictions emerge in the self when there are discrepancies among significant others' viewpoints. The more discrepancies, the more contradictory the individual's self-portrait will be. Similarly, Lempert (1994) reports that battered women struggle to explain their partners' violence because it is shocking and difficult to reconcile. Female survivors of domestic violence often dissociate the self from the other to cope with and escape from the reality of the violence in their intimate relationships. Athens (1997) further explains that violent offenders use their current self-view, life experience and evaluation of the situation in their decision to act violently. An offender's self-image always relates to his or her interpretation of the situation, and that image

directly influences how one decides to act for oneself and toward others.

The symbolic interactionist framework recognizes that one's self-image and definition of the situation occur in interaction with, not in isolation from, others in society. In the case of domestic violence, Denzin (1984) notes that the batterer unwittingly alienates his partner through his physical violence; his partner's subsequent remoteness threatens his confidence in the relationship; and, in turn, he again employs violence to restore his control. We have yet to understand, however, how the batterer's self-image shapes his definition of the situation and subsequent social interaction. Scully (1990) uses the rapist's perceptions of both himself and women (the other) to explore the rapist's viewpoint and to argue that rapists execute our culture's interest in the subordination of women. Some of the men studied by Scully rejected the notion that their crime could or should be conceptualized as rape. Scully's (1990) deniers had a very limited definition of rape, no understanding of the female's viewpoint, and no perception of the female's view of sexual violence. Powerful people and groups have little need or incentive to take the role of the other (Franks 1986; Scully 1990). Men, historically the dominant gender in our culture, have less need to take the role of the other, and convicted rapists act on this dominance to a horrific extreme. Following an extensive review of the literature on batterer typologies, Holtzworth-Munroe and Stuart (1994) hypothesize that batterers' levels of empathy (a form of role-taking) are inversely related to their levels of violence. Forte et al. (1996) find that abused women develop keen role-taking abilities to anticipate, prevent, and minimize their partners' physical violence. Drawing on insights from the symbolic interaction literature, we explore ways in which men's construction of the self and others facilitate or constrain their violent behavior.

DATA COLLECTION AND ANALYSIS

In 1995 and 1996, we conducted a case-comparison study of domestic violence. We interviewed 58 men, 33 with a recent history of domestic violence (batterer or case group) and 25 with no history of domestic violence (comparison group). The comparison subjects were recruited and screened to demographically match the case subjects. The case-comparison design provides the opportunity to contrast a case group on a specific issue of interest (e.g., domestic violence) with a comparison group not demonstrating the issue of interest (Schlesselman 1982). This method is helpful in research concerning uncommon forms of behavior because the investigator can target a small group of perpetrators without screening a large population (Goodman, Mercy, Layole, and Thacker 1988; Loftin and McDowall 1988).

The present study analyzes the in-depth portions of project interviews to focus on the batterer's view of himself and others in domestic violence. We recruited men with a history of domestic violence from a local family violence counseling center (Center). The Center offers a six-week psychoeducational program for men who batter, and it sees approximately 500 to 700 men per year for this purpose. Consistent with similar batterer counseling programs, 85 to 90% of the men participating in the Center program were court-ordered to attend (see also Pence and Paymar 1993). The court-mandated clients were referred by the municipal court, the county probation office, the county court, and the county attorney through a protective order. The remaining participants joined the program voluntarily or at the suggestion of another person (e.g., attorney or therapist). To reduce the possibility that the group meetings would influence the respondents' views of themselves, their violence, and their partners, we recruited respondents pri-

marily through orientation sessions. We recruited 27 case subjects from the Center.

To recruit demographically matched comparison subjects, we posted 58 project flyers in the zip code areas (e.g., laundromats and restaurants) of the case subjects recruited from the Center. We also posted flyers at several community colleges, trade and technical schools, and a telecommunications reservation center. When potential comparison subjects responded to the posted notices, they were screened for age, income, occupation, education, zip code, and marital status to match the case group. We matched case and comparison subjects on these characteristics to make the two groups comparable in the areas that may influence one's view of the self and others. The matched comparison group design attempts to minimize but does not eliminate differences between the case and comparison group subjects. The high rates of violence reported among the comparison group subjects suggests that our efforts to recruit comparison subjects similar to our case subjects was successful. We recruited 33 comparison subjects from the community.

Of the 33 men recruited to be comparison subjects, 36% ($n = 12$) reported perpetrating at least one act of domestic violence against their partner in the past year. The project coordinators reviewed the Conflict Tactics Scale (CTS) and in-depth portions of the interviews to assess the reported violence of these 12 comparison subjects. Six of these men reported committing one or more severe acts of violence against their partners, numerous "minor" acts of violence against their partners, and/or a prior arrest for domestic violence; these 6 men were reassigned to the case group. Four of the 12 men reported very minor acts of violence (e.g., pushing, shoving); these 4 men remained in the comparison group. The remaining 2 men were dropped from the study because of discrepancies in their reports of violence.

Research indicates that batterers tend to underreport their violence (Walker 1979), so it is possible, but very unlikely, that an unidentified batterer remains in our comparison group. It is unlikely for three main reasons. First, interview subjects had multiple opportunities to reveal their violent tendencies during the 60-to-90 minute interviews. Second, as noted above, there were high rates of violence reported among the comparison group subjects. Third, two investigators reviewed all respondents' CTS and in-depth responses for mention of violent behavior. Our final sample includes 33 case subjects and 25 comparison subjects.

To compare our sample to the Center population, we gathered information on age, income, marital status, race and referral from men participating in the Center program from July to December 1994. This comparison allows us to consider the possibility that the batterers volunteering to participate in a study of domestic violence were different from the Center's population of batterers. In fact, we find that the volunteer sample is comprised of men who have, on average, a higher socioeconomic status than the population of batterers in the Center program. The volunteer sample had a higher income than the Center sample's mean income of $14,123. The Center sample contained fewer men who were cohabiting, divorced/separated, African American and European American. The study sample also contained a larger number of self-referred, as opposed to court-mandated, Center participants. If these differences were to result in biased data, it would presumably be in the direction of accepting greater culpability, exhibiting greater insight into their own behavior, and expressing greater empathy toward their partners. This sort of sampling bias would then work against finding support for our key research questions. That we find support for our research questions even with this more educated and higher-income study sample suggests that the underlying processes involving feelings of culpability, personal insight and empathy are quite strong.

The mean age of the 33 case subjects in the study sample was 31.7 years old. The median household income was $40,000 to $59,999. Of the case subjects; 46% were white, 27.4% were Hispanic, 21.2% were African American, and 6% identified themselves as Other. The majority of the batterers were married (45.5%) or cohabiting (36.4%), and 15.1% of the batterers were separated, while 3% were divorced. The average age of the 25 comparison subjects was 32.1 years old. The median household income for the comparison group was $30,000 to $39,999. Sixty-eight percent of the comparison subjects were white, 20% were Hispanic, and 12% identified themselves as Other. The marital status of the comparison subjects was 60% married, 28% cohabiting, 12% separated.

In-depth interviews allow researchers to obtain detailed information about individuals' definitions of the situation in their own words; this method is particularly helpful when applying a symbolic interactionist framework and exploring the dynamics of domestic violence. The interviews were conducted by three white middle-class women. In mock interviews with a project investigator, all three interviewers practiced both asking the interview questions and expressing neutrality. In the interviews, respondents were asked to talk in their own words about their partner, couple arguments and family role expectations. The first series of in-depth questions were: (1) "How did you meet your wife/partner?" (2) "What attracted you to her in the first place?" (3) "What do you think attracted her to you?" (4) "What would you change about her if you could?" and (5) "What do you think she would change about you?" The second series of in-depth questions asked respondents to describe the "worst" and "most recent" arguments with their female partner. The final series of in-depth questions, which were not used in this analysis, asked respondents about their behavior expectations for their partner and children, including (1) "What does it mean to you to be a good father? A good mother? A good child?" and (2) "Does your own partner (and child) fit your view of a good mother (child)? Why or why not?"

We used Strauss's (1987) guidelines for qualitative data analysis to code the in-depth interviews. Each transcript was read several times and coded into thematic categories that were pulled from the literature, interviews and analysis. We used 24 codes to analyze the interviews. The codes included Expresses Empathy for Partner, Expresses Lack of Empathy for Partner, Male Felt Sad, Female Felt Sad [according to the respondent], Male Felt Bad, Female Felt Bad [according to the respondent], Doesn't Blame Self. Whenever a quote reflected a particular code, the quote and the corresponding case or comparison subject number was copied to a data file organized by codes. If a quote reflected more than one code, it was listed under all relevant codes with a note listing the cross-listed codes. Here, we present the quotes that most clearly illustrate the recurrent themes, and we note cases where there were exceptions to the general theme. We present the results of the analysis in three parts: the self, the intimate other and important others.

RESULTS

Seeing the Self

Mead (1934, p. 135) says the self "is something which has development; it is not initially there, at birth, but arises in the process of social experience and activity, that is, develops in the given individual as a result of his [or her] relations to that process as a whole and to other individuals within that process." The self is reflexive (Athens 1994; Mead 1934). It functions as an object when an individual considers another person's description of himself, and it functions as the subject when the individual considers one's own view of himself.

The Batterer's View of Self. Many batterers expressed frustration when their partners described them as abusive or violent. They did not feel those terms adequately described them, because, they explained, their violence toward their partners did not reflect their "true" selves. Symbolic interactionists call this reaction a fragmentation (Athens 1995; Baker 1996) or dissociation (Athens 1994; Mead 1934) of the self. Freud (1923) calls it a defense mechanism. Dissociation results from a difficult social experience that is not easily incorporated into personal life, and it often destroys previous assumptions (Athens 1995). As mentioned earlier, when a significant other sees one differently from how one sees oneself, conflict arises in the self. Conflicting views of the self can create dissociations, or situations that cause emotional upheaval for the self (Athens 1994; Athens 1995; Baker 1996; Mead 1934), and this discord can cause a unified self to split into two or more selves (Athens 1994; Athens 1995; Baker 1996).

Batterers expressed their dissatisfaction with the terms "batterer" and "abusive" through denial and blame. First, batterers expressed their discomfort through denial. The batterer was not a "batterer" because he had either only abused one woman in his life or he had never really beaten her. The following explanation comes from a man who reported slapping his ex-wife three times and forcing sex on her twice in the year before the interview.

> *I'd say the worst time [we had an argument that became physical] was one night at our house she attempted to pack my stuff and get me to leave. And, it was a lot of top-of-the-lungs yellin' and screamin' and blah, blah, blah. Understand our fights were never to where I'd...beat her up. I'd*

just hit her. I think one night, we went on and on for about two to three hours, ya' know. On and off, slappin' her and this, that and the other... she...liked to label me the typical abuser. I just don't think that's the right answer. Like I said,...I've never hit another woman in my life beside the one that I'm with. (Case Subject #8, 26 years old)

I reached out and popped her on the jaw. It was just a reflex deal. But after it happened...I was like, "Man, that felt really good, you know, finally." [Laughs] But other than that and this one night a couple of months back, I'm not in the habit of doing that. (Case Subject #12, 40 years old)

The "this is not me" reaction to one's violence makes sense under the symbolic interactionist view of the self (see also Freud 1923), and it is characteristic of the dysphoric/borderline type of batterer to be discussed in more detail in the discussion section (Holtzworth-Munroe and Stuart 1994). These reactions allow the individual to uphold a positive self-view in the face of evidence to the contrary (Freud 1923; Mead 1934). If a person can both interpret another's view (as the object) and one's own view (as the subject), then that person can use self-interaction to accept or dismiss the other's viewpoint (see Athens 1994).

There were some exceptions to the denial theme. In these cases, the batterers admitted to being inappropriately violent with their partners, and then either expressed guilt for their violence or said that they had an anger control problem. The implications for these guilt and anger explanations are discussed in more detail later.

Blame represents the second theme in the "this is not me" response to the batterer label. Batterers frequently blamed their partners for

their violent outbursts (Gondolf 1985; Walker 1979); this reaction is characteristic of the generally violent/antisocial type of batterer (Holtzworth-Munroe and Stuart 1994).

She just has a knack for bringin' out the worst in me, and [short pause] as I said, I felt bad after every time afterwards. Then again, I guess I had some sort of consolation in the fact that she may have called my mom a fat bitch, you know...I mean, I tried to take some sort of consolation out of what I did. And not place total blame on myself. (Case Subject #8, 26 years old)

There were some exceptions. Not all batterers blamed their partners for their violence, and several admitted that they needed help learning how to stop their violence. In general, batterers used denial and blame to dismiss others' indications that they were violent people. The comparison subjects, on the other hand, were more willing to consider their partners' critical views of themselves as well as the reasons for those views.

The Comparison Subject's View of the Self. The comparison subjects in this study described a greater depth of consideration for and understanding of their partners' negative views of themselves. These findings provide substantial insight into how violent and nonviolent men see or decline to see themselves through the eyes of others. First, unlike the case subjects, the comparison subjects were more willing to consider and accept their partners' critical views of themselves. This theme of consideration is illustrated by a comparison subject who described how he felt when he realized that he had not noticed how his hectic work and school schedules were affecting his wife. His lack of awareness for her needs upset him, and it made him realize that his life was "out of hand."

*[After the argument I felt] depressed
…like, you know, I knew what I was
doing [working long hours and not
spending time with my wife and
child], but wasn't aware…it was having that big of an impact on her. And
I guess I [was] kind of self-critical, like,
"this is really out of hand, because
you obviously don't have enough
time to realize what's going on in your
wife's head or heart." (Comparison
Subject #47, 27 years old)*

This comparison subject used his partner's concerns to think about his behavior and re-evaluate
his priorities.

The comparison subjects also discussed
their consideration for how one of their personality traits could upset their partner. When they
did so, they often mentioned their partners' emotional state or relationship history, and they indicated that they understood her viewpoint.

*Sometime she thinks I'm insensitive.
Obviously, it goes along with her
sensitivity…she says that I'm very flir-
tatious, my ways, my demeanor is flir-
tatious, and I've talked to people and
I guess I can recognize the problem
but to me I think it's almost harmless
flirting, but I guess I would probably
have a problem with it too. (Comparison Subject #49, 28 years old)*

This respondent recognized that his partner had
a different view of himself than he did, and he
indicates that it was both his partner's feelings
and his behavior that created tension in their
relationship.

Understanding was the second major theme
in the comparison subjects' discussions of themselves. Many men in the comparison group described their partners' childhood and relationship

history to explain their partners' perceptions of
them. We will later see that the comparison group
subjects also had a greater awareness of the ways
their partners' life experiences influenced her current attitudes and behaviors.

*If she could change [anything about
me]…she'd change that I'd be more
understanding about stuff…I think,
she thinks [I think] the world revolves
around me, that whatever I say
should go, which I don't but I guess
to a point, I kind of grew up where,
what I want to happen should happen. (Comparison Subject #62, 22
years old)*

While he did not completely agree with her view
of him, he was willing to consider the possibility
that he could be more understanding and that his
background had not encouraged such behavior.
There were some outliers to the understanding
theme among comparison subjects. Three comparison subjects expressed no or limited understanding for their partners' feelings.

Overall, the comparison subjects used a
wider frame of reference to make sense of their
partners' negative views of themselves. Symbolic interactionists explain that the view of the
self emerges, not in isolation from, but in participation and interaction with one or more others
(Mead 1934). Thus, the following two sections
will focus on the men's perceptions of intimate
and important others, and how those perceptions
shape their own view of the self and the people
in their world.

RELATING TO THE INTIMATE OTHER

The individual can plan his behavior in anticipation of others' reactions to him and his behavior
by "taking the role of the other" (Mead 1934).

The individual actor uses his life experience and knowledge of others to plan his course of action and to take the role of the other though a series of self-interactions. Mead writes (1934, p. 254):

> *The immediate effect of such role-taking lies in the comparison which the individual is able to exercise over his own response. The comparison of the action of the individual...can take place in the...individual himself if he can take the role of the other.*

Self-interaction precedes all thoughtful, but not routine, human action. Blumer (1969) adds that the process of self-interaction provides individuals with an array of behavior options, and these options exist on a continuum ranging from abandonment to magnification. Blumer (1969) would find problems with a batterer's claim that his violence was beyond his control (see Gondolf 1985), because it is the individual's decision to act violently or nonviolently toward others.

The batterer's view of the other. Batterers demonstrated their role-taking abilities in response to in-depth questions about their partners' physical injuries and emotional pain following an episode of violence. Similar to batterers' denial and blame strategies for dissociating their violent and their true selves, batterers minimized their partners' physical and emotional injuries. They also described their partners' attempts to influence their behavior as annoying.

First, batterers used avoidance to minimize the reality of their partners' physical injuries. Some batterers did not see their partners' injuries because of their arrest and/or jailing for domestic violence, but others simply did not return home for a few days in hopes that the problem would disappear. The following man did not return home after the particularly violent episode that he describes here in which his live-in girl-

friend was hospitalized because he had severely choked, punched, and kicked her.

> *[The incident] was terrible. It was like I spent a solid hour picking her up and throwing her back down on the bed as hard as I could. Well, what I was told was that, her...larynx had been crushed, the retina on her eye, something with one of her eyes had got messed up, and there was internal bleeding, busted ribs. But as far as actually seeing something, I never saw. The worst thing I saw was some black and blue marks on her wrist where I know that I was actually grabbing her. Other than that though, I never saw any, you know, any marks anywhere. (Case Subject #12, 40 years old)*

This avoidance is probably characteristic of the family-only batterer, who is generally only violent with family members, not with people outside of his family (Holtzworth-Munroe and Stuart 1994). This type of batterer is moderately violent and does not usually perpetrate psychological or sexual abuse against family members.

The second theme in this section concerns the batterer's view of the other's emotions. This theme demonstrates batterers' ability to take the role of the other through empathy. To varying degrees, the case subjects took the emotional role of the other when they described their partners' emotional pain following an abusive incident. Although there was some overlap (i.e., some men expressed limited empathy in one incident and deep empathy in another), we break the men's expressions of empathy into three general categories: no empathy, limited empathy, and empathy.

First, nine of the thirty-three case subjects did not see the connection between their physical abuse and their partners' emotional distress (see also Denzin 1984). One man indicated that his partner's only memory of his violence was in her physical injury. Once those physical wounds healed, he explained, she would be okay.

> *If it had not been for her black eye, she coulda got over this faster. But every time she had to look in the mirror, and see the black eye. And that's the only thing. (Case Subject #8, 26 years old)*

This respondent neglects the possibility that his partner could also have sustained emotional injuries from his abuse. This response reflects a limited ability to role-take his partner's emotional state, which is characteristic of the generally violent/antisocial type of batterer (Holtzworth-Munroe and Stuart 1994). Of the three types of batterers Holtzworth-Munroe and Stuart (1994) identify, the generally violent/antisocial batterer expresses the least empathy and is the most likely to be psychopathological.

Second, ten case subjects expressed limited empathy for their partners' emotional state following an episode of violence through a series of one-word descriptions, like sad, betrayed, and scared. Limited empathy is characteristic of the dysphoric/borderline batterer, who expresses intermediate levels of empathy and has some psychological distress and schizoidal personality characteristics. In the below excerpt, the batterer explains how both he and his partner felt after they pushed each other, she tried to kick him, and he pushed her to the ground.

> *I felt bad in a way, but in another way, I had to give her a reason or a thought of me—that I wasn't going to accept her brother's decisions. I just wanted hers. And to me, I guess that helped a little bit because I had to express myself to her. She felt bad*

> *because she thought I was going to leave her. And she felt sad and she was crying and all that. And, to me, she felt like she was lonely. (Case Subject #14, 26 year old)*

This batterer explains that, although he felt bad about it, he needed to use violence to get his message across. He expresses an unwillingness to accept her information, but a willingness to acknowledge her feelings. This simultaneous ability and inability to take the role of the other may be better understood when we consider the aspects of the other with whom this batterer is role-taking. He role-takes her emotions, not her viewpoint. The difference is that emotional role-taking is less likely to challenge one's position in an argument (and perhaps a relationship) than viewpoint role-taking is. Batterers, more than nonviolent men, feel threatened by challenges to their authority and views, and they often react to such threats with violence. Emotional role-taking also may be self-interested, because feeling bad for his victim helps the batterer to argue that he's not such a bad person (Scully 1990).

The limited empathy ($n = 10$) and empathy ($n = 8$) batterers' abilities to see the others' pain indicates that some batterers can take the role of the other in domestic violence. Holtzworth-Munroe and Stuart (1994, p. 488) would argue that the batterers expressing high levels of empathy are probably the family-only type of batterer, because this group is "most likely to feel remorse" and "the most empathetic toward their wives." One would expect that the more violent the batterer, the less understanding he would be of his partner's feelings (see Holtzworth-Munroe and Stuart 1994). Our comparison of the batterers' in-depth interview responses and the Conflict Tactics Scale scores, however, suggests that there is no relationship between the amount of violence a batterer perpetrates against his partner and the degree to which he expresses empathy for her emotional and physical pain. Some of the most violent men in this study expressed deep sadness for the partner.

The final theme in the analysis of the batterers' discussions of the intimate other involves the men's descriptions of their partners' attempts to influence them. Batterers indicated that their partners used annoying games and ineffective techniques to control their behavior. This finding describes how these beliefs play out in batterers' thoughts about and behavior towards their intimate partner. This finding illuminates previous researchers' characterization of batterers as believing women should obey, not influence, their husbands (see Gondolf 1985; Walker 1979). This finding becomes clearer when we discuss comparison subjects' responses to women's influence in relationships below.

> *And I really think she had me thrown in jail to keep me under control, knowing that I'm going to have to deal with lawyers and now I'm at her mercy. (Case Subject #13, 38 years old)*

Batterers minimized their partners' physical and emotional injuries and characterized their partners as interfering to emotionally distance themselves from both their violence and their intimate others.

The comparison subject's view of the other. We find significant differences in how violent and nonviolent men view intimate others. The most interesting differences appear in the comparison subjects' discussions of their partners' personal well-being, relationship history, and influence over them. First, when we asked comparison subjects what they would change about their partner, twelve of the twenty-five said they wanted to improve her feelings about herself. While the batterer group often expressed an interest in changing their partners' behavior and their relationships with their families, the

comparison subjects wanted to change things to better their partners' lives.

> *[I would change] the things that she worries about—things that she can't, that she doesn't have any control over. (Comparison Subject #40, 36 years old)*

> *I would change her insecurity. She's very insecure about herself, about everything she does…So, maybe she needs to get a little more confidence in herself. (Comparison Subject #49, 28 years old)*

The comparison group subjects also expressed understanding and appreciation for their partners' childhood and relationship history. Several comparison subjects described their partners' childhood neglect to explain the factors influencing their current relationship difficulties.

> *[Her] mom was so busy and dad was so non-caring that anytime as a child she would do things seeking nurturing, the responses from her parents, it wasn't ever given. Never. Never. She'd get a hug, "Go to your room, mom's busy, go to your room, dad's busy." When you grown up like that, I mean truly, sometimes you start to think, well, she kind of came to the conclusion when she was younger that, "I'm not supposed to have love or get love." (Comparison Subject #41, 30 years old)*

Unlike the batterers, the comparison subjects used a much wider range of information to understand their partners' feelings and to take the role of their intimate other. There were a few exceptions to this rule in the batterer group. Three batterers said their partners had been abused in previous relationships with their fathers, boyfriends or both; these batterers explained that these previous experiences with abusive men left their partners feeling particularly betrayed by their current partners' violence.

The final theme emerging from comparison subjects' descriptions of the "other" concerns influence and control. Different from batterers' views that their partners' attempts to control them were annoying, several comparison subjects viewed their partners' influence as positive.

> I don't want to change anything [about her]. Because if I changed her attitude, then it would mess me up. Because then I could just run do whatever I wanted to do, right?... She's told me, she keeps me out of trouble. (Comparison Subject #56, 37 years old)

The comparison subjects did not express feelings of threat or challenge, like the case subjects did, when their partners attempted to influence their behavior (see quotes from Case Subjects #13 and #14 in the previous section).

RELATING TO IMPORTANT OTHERS

Individuals actively, rather than passively, consider the reactions of others and society, and plan their behavior accordingly. These considerations reflect the personal and social control that individuals both experience and express in both self and social interaction. Six of the thirty-three batterers expressed an appreciation and understanding for their children and the police's reactions to their violence, but they did not express the same type of understanding for their partners' reactions to their violence. They seemed to have an easier time taking the role of important others that were not their partners or their partners' supporters.

The batterers view of important others. Six batterers described outside interference from their children and police as regretful but also necessary, particularly during a violent episode. These important others often seemed to act as the batterer's conscience, because they alerted the batterer to his violence and helped to interrupt it. Batterers expressed sadness when their children witnessed their violence toward their partners and their children's mothers.

> That's why I would say it, it was the worst [physically violent argument we ever had] because the kids were there.... She was scared. The children were scared, and I had just, I had lost control you know. (Case Subject #1, 25 years old)

In most cases, when batterers realized that their children had seen their violence, they stopped immediately. Similar to children, police involvement in domestic violence seemed to offer an important perspective for batterers. While these men regretted law enforcement's involvement in their relationships, several of them recognized the need for police action during a particular incident. Law enforcement seemed to represent a more legitimate critic to the batterer.

> So, she called the police. I am glad she called the police because something really awful could have happened. (Case Subject #2, 37 years old)

The interference of the woman's family or friends, on the other hand, presented a problem for several batterers. Batterers often considered these outsiders to be a challenge to their authority and their sense of order in the relationship. This reaction illustrates the insecurity that many batterers seem to feel in their relationships, and it captures the literature's characterization of batterers' interest in maintaining their roles of authority in intimate relationships (Gondolf 1985; Walker 1979).

> We had an argument because she was paying attention to her brothers. I used to tell her, "We're going to do this, and this way." And she used to say, "Okay." And then later during the day, she used to come and say, "My brothers say this way, this way. I think it's better the way my brothers said it." And I used to get mad. (Case Subject #14, 26 years old)

> I want her to be more independent from her family.... Well, she blamed [my abuse of her] all on herself, saying that you know, "I'm too close to my...parents. I'm bringing them into our relationship." And, she took the blame for all of it, saying that she wouldn't do that any more. (Case Subject #24, 23 years old)

The comparison subject's view of important others. The issue of outside interference in intimate relationships did not come up as frequently or in the same manner in interviews with comparison subjects as it did in interviews with case subjects. A few comparison subjects believed that their friends' comments about their wives or girlfriends had stirred up problems for them. Even in these cases, however, comparison subjects described the comments as embarrassing and thought-provoking, not as threatening like the case subjects did. One man explained that his friends' continuous inquiries about his girlfriend's relationship with her ex-boyfriend led him to feel that he should not be comfortable with her talking to her ex-boyfriend.

> It's not that, I mean, I don't want to look bad; it's just that when some-

> body persistently asks you a question ...sometimes, I just feel uncomfortable [that she is spending time with her ex-boyfriend]. (Comparison Subject #53, 20 years old)

Like the intimate other, important others—like children, friends, and police—can present other views of one's self. In the case of infidelity, several comparison subjects indicated that they regretted their parents' or in-laws' involvement in their relationship problems. The following case subject had an affair with another woman during his engagement. When his fiance asked him to leave their home, he moved in with his parents. His mother's knowledge of his affair created additional problems for him.

> I felt really bad [when my partner found out I cheated on her]. I felt, maybe embarrassed, because my mom knew about it, and she's a woman, and you know, the way a woman may look at it and a man may look at it two different ways.... But I felt disrespecting of myself, you know, the way my mother looked at me, when my wife looked at me, and it still to this day it bothers me. (Comparison Subject #50, 25 years old)

DISCUSSION

Social contexts and social interactions shape the way that we think about ourselves and others. The individual learns about how others perceive him, and he decides how to think about those perceptions of himself. Conflicts arise in the self when there are discrepancies among the individual's and others' views of the self. While the creation of multiple selves is a normal product of social life, it can become pathological, or a dissociation, when one is unaware of one or more selves (Mead

1934). "Dissociation appears passive but is, in fact, active resistance affirming a measure of autonomy in the maintenance of the self" (Lempert 1995, p. 433), and it is a way to block any movement toward dramatic self-change (see Athens 1995; Baker 1996; Mead 1934).

Batterers used strategies of denial and blame to dissociate their violent selves from their "true" selves (Mead 1934). Batterers denied that they could be a "batterer" because they had either abused only one woman or slightly abused only a few women. Scully (1990) finds similarly narrow definitions of sexual violence among convicted rapists. The denying group of rapists in her study defined rape to exclude the behavior for which they were arrested, charged and convicted. In our study, the denier group of batterers took the most extreme measures to dissociate, and this extreme dissociation suggests a psychological pathology (see Mead 1934). Interestingly, the batterers using denial to minimize their violent behavior did not provide alternative terms to describe their violence. Perhaps this happened because we do not have a term for men who only abuse one woman. According to the legal system and battered women's centers, abuse is abuse, no matter how rare or minor.

Comparison subjects managed negative feedback about themselves differently than the case subjects did. Instead of finding ways to deny criticisms, the comparison subjects used their knowledge of themselves, their partners', and their relationship history to evaluate their partners' criticisms. Unlike the case subjects, the comparison subjects used such criticisms to begin dramatic self-change by altering their assumptions about themselves (fragmentation stage) and considering the new insights about themselves (provisional stage) (Athens 1995, p. 574–76). This self-understanding emerged in the context of social interaction with others. Thus, others play an important role in how people view themselves.

Taking the role of the other demonstrates a process of cooperative and controlled activity (Mead 1934). Our findings suggest that an individual's ability to understand another's view—positive or negative—of the self is associated with his ability to understand that other.

Batterers demonstrated a range of role-taking abilities in their discussions of three issues: their partners' physical injuries, emotional pain, and influence in the relationship. Although these men had carried out the physical violence that seemingly caused their partners' injuries, they used avoidance strategies to distance themselves from the reality of their violence. This distance helped them to avoid taking the role of the other in terms of the victims' physical wounds. Scully (1990) found similar deficiencies in convicted rapists' abilities to take the role of the other (i.e., their victims). Convicted rapists did not understand the woman's perspective in general and of sexual violence in particular (Scully 1990). She argues that people in power are not pressed to understand the "other," because their place of power in society allows them to set the terms of their interactions with others (Franks 1986; Scully 1990).

Batterers expressed different degrees of empathy for their partners' emotional pain. Despite previous researchers' assumptions (Holtzworth-Munroe and Stuart 1994), the case subjects' levels of expressed empathy did not vary inversely with their levels of violence. Some of the most violent men in this study described the sadness and fear their partners' felt after an abusive incident with a surprising depth of understanding. There are two possible explanations for this apparent contradiction. First, this discrepancy may be indicative of the borderline and schizoidal personality traits of the dysphoric/borderline type of batterer (see Holtzworth-Munroe and Stuart 1994). This type of batterer perpetrates moderate to severe violence against his partner and expresses an intermediate level of empathy. Second, previous research indicates that there are self-interested reasons for such expressions of empathy. Scully (1990) argues that this type of remorse is simply a means to separating the bad self from the good self. This dissociation, via guilt or empathy, allowed convicted rapists, like it did these batterers, to argue that they were overall good guys (Scully 1990). Batterers also said that their partners made unreasonable and unnecessary efforts to control their behavior. The comparison subjects, on the other hand, talked about their partners' personal happiness, relationship history and positive influence. These men indicated that their partners' influence made them a better person.

These findings suggest that teaching batterers to take the role of the other may not be the answer to stopping all male violence against women. It may be that the effect of taking the role of the victim differs for different types of batterers. Future research should examine the role-taking abilities of the different types of batterers delineated by Holtzworth-Munroe and Stuart (1994).

Batterers expressed more tolerance for important others' (such as their children or the police) views of themselves, than they did for their intimate others' views. From the batterer's perspective, children and police officers may serve as unbiased third parties in couple disputes. Whereas a woman's relatives and friends originate from the woman's side, thus they tend to serve as her supporter and a subsequent threat to the batterer. Law enforcement's involvement in a domestic violence dispute may reflect society's general disapproval for violence against women, and it may be a type of social control for the batterer. Ironically, none of the batterers in this study accepted similar types of disapproval from their intimate partners. This dynamic may explain why batterers dismissed their partners'

(and her supporters') views of themselves, but considered their children's or the police's views of themselves. Perhaps the woman's relatives and friends shift the balance of power in the relationship toward the woman and away from the batterer. These parties may represent less of a threat to the batterers' place in their intimate relationship, and they, in many cases, can exercise power over the male batterer that his female partner cannot.

CONCLUSION

Batterers' perceptions remain under-studied in research on domestically violent men. This study provides insight into the batterer's viewpoint, and it compares and contrasts batterers' and comparison subjects' perspectives in intimate relationships, specifically in reference to the self and others. We find that batterers deny both responsibility for and the wrongness of their behavior (see also Ptacek 1988). We also identify the strategies batterers use to minimize their violence, including denial and blame. In the context of preserving the "self," these strategies allow the batterer to dissociate himself from the "batterer" label, and these dismissals allow the batterer to stall self-change (see Athens 1995). These perceptions, as well as the comparison of violent versus nonviolent men's responses, indicate that batterers take elaborate measures to construct a nonviolent self-image in the context of their intimate relationships. It is not clear, however, how batterers might construct their violent versus nonviolent self-image in other contexts, such as with friends or coworkers. This type of construction deserves further study.

The batterers in this study held both the idea of their violent selves and the evidence of their violent selves at a distance. While the men admitted to administering the abuse, several of them said they never actually saw their partners' physical injuries. The ability to avoid seeing the consequences of one's violence is instrumental in constructing and maintaining a nonviolent self-view. These constructions created contradictions in their social lives that inhibited their ability to relate to or take the role of the intimate other. Batterers also described their intimate others' annoying attempts to influence them. This finding indicates that the batterer's perceptions of the woman's role shades his interpretation of her behavior as well as his decision to act violently toward her. In comparison to the case group, the comparison group described a deeper understanding for their intimate others' physical and emotional pain. The comparison group used that understanding to take the role of the other in their intimate relationships.

Although batterers described their partners' annoying attempts to influence their behavior, they described their children or the police's attempts to influence their abuse as sometimes helpful and necessary. During a violent outburst, the presence of their children or the police raised the batterer's consciousness about the inappropriateness of violence, and gave him a different view of himself. A few comparison subjects reported very minor negative encounters with outsiders becoming involved in their relationships, but they described these encounters as thought-provoking, not threatening.

Our findings suggest that batterer counseling programs could take steps to help batterers acknowledge the inappropriate nature of their violence toward their intimate partners; batterers also need to learn to incorporate their recognition of the violent selves into their global self-views before they can begin dramatic self-change (see Athens 1995). Our finding that the majority of batterers express no or limited understanding for their partners (see also Scully 1990), but not their children or the police remains important. This area needs further exploration. Furthermore, we hypothesize that the batterer's ability to take the role of the other may differ by his personal power in a particular relationship; possible sources of power may be one's gender, employment status or legal authority. Sherman et al. (1992) find that in some cities and for employed batterers, arrest and jail time decreased the likelihood of recidivism. Our findings suggest that batterers have more respect for the police's reaction to their violence than for their intimate partners' reaction to their violence. It seems that, for now, batterer counseling programs can attempt to tap into batterers' abilities to take the role of some others as a means to modeling how to take the role of their intimate others.

Reading 25 Ten Myths That Perpetuate Corporal Punishment

MURRAY A. STRAUS*

Hitting children is legal in every state of the United States and that 84 percent of a survey of Americans agreed that it is sometimes necessary to give a child a good hard spanking. Almost all parents of toddlers act on these beliefs. Study after study shows that almost 100 percent of parents with toddlers hit their children. There are many reasons for the strong support of spanking. Most of them are myths.

MYTH 1: SPANKING WORKS BETTER

There has been a huge amount of research on the effectiveness of corporal punishment of animals, but remarkably little on the effectiveness of spanking children. That may be because almost no one, including psychologists, feels a need to study it because it is assumed that spanking is effective. In fact, what little research there is on the effectiveness of corporal punishment of children agrees with the research on animals. Studies of both animals and children show that punishment is *not* more effective than other methods of teaching and controlling behavior. Some studies show it is less effective.

Ellen Cohn and I asked 270 students at two New England colleges to tell us about the year they experienced the most corporal punishment.

Their average age that year was eight, and they recalled having been hit an average of six times that year.[1] We also asked them about the percent of the time they thought that the corporal punishment was effective. It averaged a little more than half of the times (53 percent). Of course, 53 percent also means that corporal punishment was *not* perceived as effective about half the time it was used.

LaVoie (1974) compared the use of a loud noise (in place of corporal punishment) with withdrawal of affection and verbal explanation in a study of first- and second-grade children. He wanted to find out which was more effective in getting the children to stop touching certain prohibited toys. Although the loud noise was more effective initially, there was no difference over a longer period of time. Just explaining was as effective as the other methods.

A problem with LaVoie's study is that it used a loud noise rather than actual corporal punishment. That problem does not apply to an experiment by Day and Roberts (1983). They studied three-year-old children who had been given "time out" (sitting in a corner). Half of the mothers were assigned to use spanking as the mode of correction if their child did not comply and left the corner. The other half put their non-complying child behind a low plywood barrier and physically enforced the child staying there. Keeping the child

---

*Straus, Murray A. 1994. "Ten Myths That Perpetuate Corporal Punishment." Chapter 10 in *Beating the Devil Out of Them: Corporal Punishment in American Families*. New York, NY: Lexington Books. Reprinted by permission of the author.

behind the barrier was just as effective as the spanking in correcting the misbehavior that led to the time out.

A study by Larzelere (1994) also found that a combination of *non*-corporal punishment and reasoning was as effective as corporal punishment and reasoning in correcting disobedience.

Crozier and Katz (1979), Patterson (1982), and Webster-Stratton et al. (1988, 1990) all studied children with serious conduct problems. Part of the treatment used in all three experiments was to get parents to stop spanking. In all three, the behavior of the children improved after spanking ended. Of course, many other things in addition to no spanking were part of the intervention. But, as you will see, parents who on their own accord do not spank also do many other things to manage their children's behavior. It is these other things, such as setting clear standards for what is expected, providing lots of love and affection, explaining things to the child, and recognizing and rewarding good behavior, that account for why children of non-spanking parents tend to be easy to manage and well-behaved. What about parents who do these things and also spank? Their children also tend to be well-behaved, but it is illogical to attribute that to spanking since the same or better results are achieved without spanking, and also without adverse side effects.

Such experiments are extremely important, but more experiments are needed to really understand what is going on when parents spank. Still, what Day and Roberts found can be observed in almost any household. Let's look at two examples.

In a typical American family there are many instances when a parent might say, "Mary! You did that again! I'm going to have to send you to your room again." This is just one example of a nonspanking method that did *not* work.

The second example is similar: A parent might say, "Mary! You did that again! I'm going to have to spank you again." This is an example of spanking that did *not* work.

The difference between these two examples is that when spanking does not work, parents tend to forget the incident because it contradicts the almost-universal American belief that spanking is something that works when all else fails. On the other hand, they tend to remember when a *non*-spanking method did not work. The reality is that nothing works all the time with a toddler. Parents think that spanking is a magic charm that will cure the child's misbehavior. It is not. There is no magic charm. It takes many interactions and many repetitions to bring up children. Some things work better with some children than with others.

Parents who favor spanking can turn this around and ask, If spanking doesn't work any better, isn't that the same as saying that it works just as well? So what's wrong with a quick slap on the wrist or bottom? There are at least three things that are wrong:

- Spanking becomes less and less effective over time and when children get bigger, it becomes difficult or impossible.
- For some children, the lessons learned through spanking include the idea that they only need to be good if Mommy or Daddy is watching or will know about it.
- As the preceding chapters show, there are a number of very harmful side effects, such as a greater chance that the child will grow up to be depressed or violent. Parents don't perceive these side effects because they usually show up only in the long run.

MYTH 2: SPANKING IS NEEDED AS A LAST RESORT

Even parents and social scientists who are opposed to spanking tend to think that it may be needed when all else falls. There is no scientific evidence supporting this belief, however. It is a myth that grows out of our cultural and psychological commitment to corporal punishment. You can prove this to yourself by a simple exercise with two other people. Each of the three should, in turn, think of the most extreme situation where spanking is necessary. The other two should try to think of alternatives. Experience has shown that it is very difficult to come up with a situation for which the alternatives are not as good as spanking. In fact, they are usually better.

Take the example of a child running out into the street. Almost everyone thinks that spanking is appropriate then because of the extreme danger. Although spanking in that situation may help *parents* relieve their own tension and anxiety, it is not necessary or appropriate for teaching the child. It is not necessary because spanking does not work better than other methods, and it is not appropriate because of the harmful side effects of spanking. The only physical force needed is to pick up the child and get him or her out of danger, and, while hugging the child, explain the danger.

Ironically, if spanking is to be done at all, the "last resort" may be the worst. The problem is that parents are usually very angry by that time and act impulsively. Because of their anger, if the child rebels and calls the parent a name or kicks the parent, the episode can escalate into physical abuse. Indeed, most episodes of physical abuse started as physical punishment and got out of hand (Kadushin and Martin, 1981). Of course, the reverse is not true, that is, most instances of spanking do not escalate into abuse. Still, the danger of abuse is there, and so is the risk of psychological harm.

The second problem with spanking as a last resort is that, in addition to teaching that hitting is the way to correct wrongs, hitting a child impulsively teaches another incorrect lesson—that being extremely angry justifies hitting.

MYTH 3: SPANKING IS HARMLESS

When someone says, I was spanked and I'm OK, he or she is arguing that spanking does no harm. This is contrary to almost all the available re-search. One reason the harmful effects are ignored is because many of us (including those of us who are social scientists) are reluctant to admit that their own parents did something wrong and even more reluctant to admit that we have been doing something wrong with our own children. But the most important reason may be that it is difficult to see the harm. Most of the harmful effects do not become visible right away, often not for years. In addition, only a relatively small percentage of spanked children experience obviously harmful effects.

The delayed reaction and the small proportion seriously hurt are the same reasons the harmful effects of smoking were not perceived for so long. In the case of smoking, the research shows that a third of very heavy smokers die of lung cancer or some other smoking-induced disease. That, of course, means that two-thirds of heavy smokers do *not* die of these diseases (Mattson et al., 1987). So most heavy smokers can say, I've smoked more than a pack a day for 30 years and I'm OK. Similarly, most people who were spanked can say, My parents spanked me, and I'm not a wife beater or depressed.

Another argument in defense of spanking is that it is not harmful if the parents are loving and explain why they are spanking. The research does show that the harmful effects of spanking are reduced if it is done by loving parents who explain their actions. However, a study by Larzelere (1986) shows that although the harmful effects are reduced, they are not eliminated. The harmful side effects include an increased risk of delinquency as a child and crime as an adult, wife beating, depression, masochistic sex, and lowered earnings.

In addition to having harmful psychological effects on children, hitting children also makes life more difficult for parents. Hitting a child to stop misbehavior may be the easy way in the short run, but in the slightly longer run, it makes the job of being a parent more difficult. This is because spanking reduces the ability of parents to influence their children, especially in adolescence when they are too big to control by physical force. Children are more likely to do what the parents want if there is a strong bond of affection with the parent. In short, being able to influence a child depends in considerable part on the bond between parent and child (Hirschl, 1969). An experiment by Redd, Morris, and Martin (1975) shows that children tend to avoid caretaking adults who use punishment. In the natural setting, of course, there are many things that tie children to their parents. I suggest that each spanking chips away at the bond between parent and child.

Part of the process by which corporal punishment eats away at the parent-child bond is shown in the study of 270 students mentioned earlier. We asked the students for their reactions to "the first time you can remember being hit by one of your parents" and the most recent instance. We used a check list of 33 items, one of which was "hated him or her." That item was checked by 42 percent for both the first and the most recent instance of corporal punishment they could remember. The large percentage who hated their parents for hitting them is important because it is evidence that corporal punishment does chip away at the bond between child and parent.

Contrary to the "spoiled child" myth, children of non-spanking parents are likely to be easier to manage and better behaved than the children of parents who spank. This is partly because they tend to control their own behavior on the basis of what their own conscience tells them is right and wrong rather than to avoid being hit (see Figure 25.1).[2] This is ironic because almost everyone thinks that spanking "when necessary" makes for better behavior.

MYTH 4: ONE OR TWO TIMES WON'T CAUSE ANY DAMAGE

The evidence indicates that the greatest risk of harmful effects occurs when spanking is very fre-

quent. However, that does not necessarily mean that spanking just once or twice is harmless. Unfortunately, the connection between spanking once or twice and psychological damage has not been addressed by most of the available research. This is because the studies seem to be based on this myth. They generally cluster children into "low" and "high" groups in terms of the frequency they were hit. This prevents the "once or twice is harmless" myth from being tested scientifically because the low group may include parents who spank once a year or as often as once a month. The few studies that did classify children according to the number of times they were hit by their parents show that even one or two instances of corporal punishment are associated with a slightly higher probability of later physically abusing your own child, slightly more depressive symptoms, and a greater probability of violence and other crime later in life. The increase in these

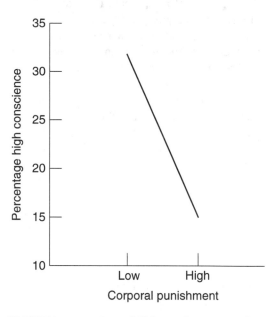

FIGURE 25.1   Few children of parents who use a lot of corporal punishment have a well-developed conscience.

harmful side effects when parents use only moderate corporal punishment (hit only occasionally) may be small, but why run even that small risk when the evidence shows that corporal punishment is no more effective than other forms of discipline in the short run, and less effective in the long run.

MYTH 5: PARENTS CAN'T STOP WITHOUT TRAINING

Although everyone can use additional skills in child management, there is no evidence that it takes some extraordinary training to be able to stop spanking. The most basic step in eliminating corporal punishment is for parent educators, psychologists, and pediatricians to make a simple and unambiguous statement that hitting a child is wrong and that a child *never*, ever, under any circumstances except literal physical self-defense, should be hit.

That idea has been rejected almost without exception everytime I suggest it to parent educators or social scientists. They believe it would turn off parents and it could even be harmful because parents don't know what else to do. I think that belief is an unconscious defense of corporal punishment. I say that because I have never heard a parent educator say that before we can tell parents to never *verbally* attack a child, parents need training in alternatives. Some do need training, but everyone agrees that parents who use *psychological* pain as a method of discipline, such as insulting or demeaning the child, should stop immediately. But when it comes to causing *physical* pain by spanking, all but a small minority of parent educators say that before parents are told to stop spanking, they need to learn alternative modes of discipline. I believe they should come right out, as they do for verbal attacks, and say without qualification that a child should *never* be hit.

This is not to say that parent education programs are unnecessary, just that they should not be a precondition for ending corporal punishment. Most parents can benefit from parent education programs such as The Nurturing Program (Bavolek, 1983 to 1992), STEP (Dinkmeyer and McKay, 1989), Parent Effectiveness Training (Gordon, 1975), Effective Black Parenting (Alvy and Marigna, 1987), and Los Ninos Bien Educado Program (Tannatt and Alvy, 1989). However, even without such programs, most parents already use a wide range of non-spanking methods, such as explaining, reasoning, and rewarding. The problem is that they also spank. Given the fact that parents already know and use many methods of reaching and controlling, the solution is amazingly simple. In most cases, parents only need the patience to keep on doing what they were doing to correct misbehavior. Just leave out the spanking! Rather than arguing that parents need to learn certain skills *before* they can stop using corporal punishment, I believe that parents are more likely to use and cultivate those skills if they decide or are required to stop spanking.

This can be illustrated by looking at one situation that almost everyone thinks calls for spanking: when a toddler runs out into the street. A typical parent will scream in terror, rush out and grab the child, and run to safety, telling the child, No! No! and explaining the danger—all of this accompanied by one or more slaps to the legs or behind.

The same sequence is as effective or more effective *without the spanking*. The spanking is not needed because even tiny children can sense the terror in the parent and understand, No! No! Newborn infants can tell the difference between when a mother is relaxed and when she is tense (Stern, 1977). Nevertheless, the fact that a child understands that something is wrong does not guarantee never again running into the street; just as spanking does not guarantee the child will not run into the street again.

If the child runs out again, nonspanking parents should use one of the same strategies as spanking parents—repetition. Just as spanking parents will spank as many times as necessary until the child learns, parents who don't spank should continue to monitor the child, hold the child's hand, and take whatever other means are needed to protect the child until the lesson is learned. Unfortunately, when non-spanking methods do not work, some parents quickly turn to spanking because they lose patience and believe it is more effective. But spanking parents seldom question its effectiveness, they just keep on spanking.

Of course, when the child misbehaves again, most spanking parents do more than just repeat the spanking or spank harder. They usually also do things such as explain the danger to the child before letting the child go out again or warn the child that if it happens again, he or she will have to stay in the house for the afternoon, and so on. The irony is that when the child finally does learn, the parent attributes the success to the spanking, not the explanation.

MYTH 6: IF YOU DON'T SPANK, YOUR CHILDREN WILL BE SPOILED OR RUN WILD

It is true that some non-spanked children run wild. But when that happens it is not because the parent didn't spank. It is because some parents think the alternative to spanking is to ignore a child's misbehavior or to replace spanking with verbal attacks such as, Only a dummy like you can't learn to keep your toys where I won't trip over them. The best alternative is to take firm action to correct the misbehavior without hitting. Firmly condemning what the child has done and explaining why it is wrong are usually enough. When they are not, there are a host of other things to do, such as requiring a time out or depriving the child of a privilege, neither of which involves hitting the child.

Suppose the child hits another child. Parents need to express outrage at this or the child may think it is acceptable behavior. The expression of outrage and a clear statement explaining why the child should never hit another person, except in self defense, will do the trick in most cases. That does not mean one such warning will do the trick, any more than a single spanking will do the trick. It takes most children a while to learn such things, whatever methods the parents use.

The importance of how parents go about teaching children is clear from a classic study of American parenting—*Patterns of Child Rearing* by Sears, Maccoby, and Levin (1957). This study found two actions by parents that are linked to a high level of aggression by the child: permissiveness of the child's aggression, namely ignoring it when the child hits them or another child, and spanking to correct misbehavior. The most aggressive children in Figure 25.2 are those at the upper right. They are children of parents who permitted aggression by the child and who also hit them for a variety of misbehavior. The least aggressive children are at the lower left. They are children of parents who clearly condemned acts of aggression and who, by not spanking, acted in a way that demonstrated the principle that hitting is wrong.

There are other reasons why, on the average, the children of parents who do not spank are better behaved than children of parents who spank:

- Non-spanking parents pay more attention to their children's behavior, both good and bad, than parents who spank. Consequently, they are more likely to reward good behavior and less likely to ignore misbehavior.
- Their children have fewer opportunities to get into trouble because they are more likely to child-proof the home. For older children, they have clear rules about where they can go and who they can be with.

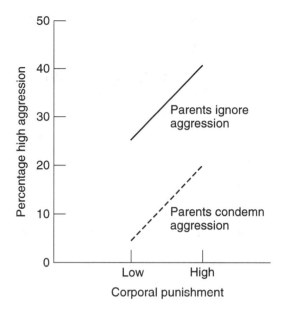

FIGURE 25.2 Children of parents who use a lot of corporal punishment tend to be aggressive, especially if the parents ignore their aggression.

- Non-spanking parents tend to do more explaining and reasoning. This teaches the child how to use these essential tools to monitor his or her own behavior, whereas children who are spanked get less training in thinking things through.
- Non-spanking parents treat the child in ways that tend to bond the child to them and avoid acts that weaken the bond. They tend to use more rewards for good behavior, greater warmth and affection, and fewer verbal assaults on the child (see Myth 9). By not spanking, they avoid anger and resentment over spanking. When there is a strong bond, children identify with the parent and want to avoid doing things the parent says are wrong. The child develops a

conscience and lets that direct his or her behavior. That is exactly what Sears et al. found (see Figure 25.1).

MYTH 7: PARENTS SPANK RARELY OR ONLY FOR SERIOUS PROBLEMS

Contrary to this myth, parents who spank tend to use this method of discipline for almost any misbehavior. Many do not even give the child a warning. They spank before trying other things. Some advocates of spanking even recommend this. At any supermarket or other public place, you can see examples of a child doing something wrong, such as taking a can of food off the shelf. The parent then slaps the child's hand and puts back the can, sometimes without saying a word to the child. John Rosemond, the author of *Parent Power* (1981), says, "For me, spanking is a first resort. I seldom spank, but when I decide…I do it, and that's the end of it."

The high frequency of spanking also shows up among the parents described in this study. The typical parent of a toddler told us of about 15 instances in which he or she had hit the child during the previous 12 months. That is surely a minimum estimate because spanking a child is generally such a routine and unremarkable event that most instances are forgotten. Other studies, such as Newson and Newson (1963), report much more chronic hitting of children. My tabulations for mothers of three- to five-year-old children in the National Longitudinal Study of Youth found that almost two-thirds hit their children during the week of the interview, and they did it more than three times in just that one week. As high as that figure may seem, I think that daily spanking is not at all uncommon. It has not been documented because the parents who do it usually don't realize how often they are hitting their children.

MYTH 8: BY THE TIME A CHILD IS A TEENAGER, PARENTS HAVE STOPPED

Parents of children in their early teens are also heavy users of corporal punishment, although at that age it is more likely to be a slap on the face than on the behind. More than half of the parents of 13- to 14-year-old children in our two national surveys hit their children in the previous 12 months. The percentage drops each year as children get older, but even at age 17, one out of five parents is still hitting. To make matters worse, these are minimum estimates.

Of the parents of teenagers who told us about using corporal Punishment, 84 percent did it more than once in the previous 12 months. For boys, the average was seven times and for girls, five times. These are minimum figures because we interviewed the mother in half the families and the father in the other half. The number of times would be greater if we had information on what the parent who was not interviewed did.

MYTH 9: IF PARENTS DON'T SPANK, THEY WILL VERBALLY ABUSE THEIR CHILD

The scientific evidence is exactly the opposite. Among the nationally representative samples of parents in this book, those who did the least spanking also engaged in the least verbal aggression.

It must be pointed out that non-spanking parents are an exceptional minority. They are defying the cultural prescription that says a good parent should spank if necessary. The depth of their involvement with their children probably results from the same underlying characteristics that led them to reject spanking. There is a danger that if more ordinary parents are told to never spank, they might replace spanking by ignoring misbehavior or by verbal attacks. Consequently, a campaign to end spanking must also stress the importance of avoiding verbal attacks as well as physical attacks, and also the importance of paying attention to misbehavior.

MYTH 10: IT IS UNREALISTIC TO EXPECT PARENTS TO NEVER SPANK

It is no more unrealistic to expect parents to never hit a child than to expect that husbands should never hit their wives, or that no one should go through a stop sign, or that a supervisor should never hit an employee. Despite the legal prohibition, some husbands hit their wives, just as some drivers go through stop signs, and a supervisor occasionally may hit an employee.

If we were to prohibit spanking, as is the law in Sweden (Deley, 1988; and Haeuser, 1990), there still would be parents who would continue to spank. But that is not a reason to avoid passing such a law here. Some people kill even though murder has been a crime since the dawn of history. Some husbands continue to hit their wives even though it has been more than a century since the courts stopped recognizing the common law right of a husband to "physically chastise an errant wife" (Calvert, 1974).

A law prohibiting spanking is unrealistic only because spanking is such an accepted part of American culture. That also was true of smoking. Yet in less than a generation we have made tremendous progress toward eliminating smoking. We can make similar progress toward eliminating spanking by showing parents that spanking is dangerous, that their children will be easier to bring up if they do not spank, and by clearly saying that a child should *never*, under any circumstances, be spanked.

WHY DO THESE MYTHS PERSIST?

Some of the myths we just presented are grounded in society's beliefs that spanking is effective and relatively harmless. Let's turn to some of the reasons these two types of myths persist.

The Myth of Effectiveness

There are a number of reasons why almost everyone overestimates the effectiveness of spanking, but a central reason is what has been called "selective inattention." This occurs when people do not remember the times when spanking fails because it contradicts what they believe to be true, namely, that spanking works. On the other hand if someone knows that the parents do *not* spank, it is assumed that the child must be spoiled or wild. So there is a tendency to overlook the good behavior of the child and to attribute the inevitable instances of misbehavior to the lack of spanking. This provides the evidence that parents who don't spank "when necessary" have spoiled children. These all-too-human errors in information processing create the perception that spanking is much more effective than it really is. This error may be the main reason for the persistence of the effectiveness myth. The reality is that although all children misbehave, the behavior of children who are not spanked, although far from perfect, is on the average better than the behavior of children whose parents spank.

The idea of selective inattention raises the question of why the "necessity" of spanking is such a deeply held belief. Why do most Americans have a vested interest in defending spanking? The following are some of the possible reasons:

- Almost all have been spanked as children, so it is part of their normal life experience.
- Even if someone is suffering from one of the harmful side effects, such as depression, he or she may not realize that having been spanked may be one of the reasons why. He or she continues to believe that spanking is harmless.
- Almost all parents slap or spank toddlers. So, if a parent accepts the idea that spanking is wrong, it implies that he or she is a bad parent, at least in this respect. That is difficult to admit.
- Almost everyone has been hit by his or her parents. So, to say corporal punishment is wrong is to condemn your own parents. Few people are comfortable doing that.
- These beliefs and attitudes have been crystallized as part of American culture and the American view of what a good parent owes a child. There is abundant evidence that people tend to misperceive things that are contrary to basic tenets of their culture and beliefs (Higgins and Bargh, 1987).
- Most spanking occurs when parents are frustrated and angry. In that context parents tend to get emotional release and satisfaction from spanking, which is confused with effectiveness in changing the child's behavior.

There is almost always a kernel of truth behind myths and stereotypes. The belief in the usefulness of spanking is no exception. The truth is that some parents who do not spank also do not attempt to correct misbehavior. As explained earlier, children of these extremely permissive or neglectful parents do tend to be out of control. However, such parents are a minority of nonspanking parents. Their children tend to be difficult to deal with or sometimes even to be around. These few and unrepresentative cases get burned into memory.

The Myth of Harmlessness

Probably the most important reasons for the myth of harmlessness are because the harmful effects do not become visible right away, often not for years, and because only a relatively small percentage of spanked children experience obviously harmful effects.

It is now widely accepted that smoking causes lung cancer, but that fact was hotly disputed only a generation ago. The research on spanking children associates it with delinquency, wife beating, depression, and other problems later in life. But just as the research on smoking a generation ago, the evidence is not conclusive. Those favoring spanking can dismiss it, just as those favoring smoking dismissed the early inconclusive evidence.

When there is more conclusive evidence on the harmful effects of spanking, it may be harder to get people to give up spanking than it was for them to give up smoking. Spanking may be more firmly entrenched because almost everyone was spanked or is a spanker, but not everyone was a smoker.

Another reason spanking will be hard to eliminate is because the chance of falling victim to one of the harmful effects of spanking is much lower than the risk of experiencing the harmful effects of smoking. For example, spanked children are about four times more likely to be highly aggressive and about twice as likely to hit their spouses later in life. These are large risks, but the effects of smoking are much larger. A high rate of smoking tends to increase the chances of lung cancer by 34 times, even though two-thirds of very heavy smokers do not die of a smoking-related disease (Mattson et al., 1987).

Spanking is associated with a two-to-four-times greater rate of harmful behavior, whereas smoking increases the lung cancer rate by 34 times. Therefore, it can be argued that smoking is a much more serious problem. On the other hand, it also can be argued that spanking is the more serious problem of the two because almost all parents spank, and spanking puts entire generations at risk of harm. There is no need to decide if spanking is worse than smoking. Both are harmful, both need to be eliminated, and both can be eliminated. In the case of spanking, even though it may increase the probability of harm "only" two to four times, it is an unnecessary risk because children are more likely to be well-behaved if parents do not spank.

Reading 26   Karla and the Armstrongs: Two Oral Histories of Homeless American Families

STEVEN VANDERSTAAY*

KARLA—ST. LOUIS, MISSOURI

*"We'll start with what happened,"
Karla begins. Young, bright, a mother
of two children, she is part of a
growing phenomenon: single-parent
mothers on assistance who cannot
afford a place to live.*

*Cities handle such families differ-
ently. New York City houses many
women like Karla in so-called welfare
hotels, while other cities place them in
barracks-style emergency shelters or
housing projects. Karla could find
nowhere to go.*

*Karla is an African American in
her twenties. We met at a Salvation
Army shelter for homeless families.*

I was working up until the time I had my
second baby. I lived with my mom but we
weren't getting along. She took care of the first
child but the second, that was too much. Then
she felt that once I had the children ... well, her
words were, "Two grown ladies can never manage in the same house." So I got on AFDC and
went to stay with my littlest girl's aunt.

Well, three weeks ago now, her landlord
called and said the building didn't pass inspec-
tion. See, the building was infested with bugs
and mice.

I didn't have any money saved 'cause I was
spending all the AFDC and food stamps on us. I
do have qualifications for a lot of jobs, but
they're all $3.35. And it's not worth getting a job
where you have no medical or dental insurance,
not if you have kids. It's not worth giving up
welfare. I would work at $3.35 if they let me
keep Medicaid and the food stamps, but they
don't. They'll cut you off.

But AFDC's not enough to live on either. I
started looking for another place but all the
apartments I could afford were just like the one
we were living in. It wasn't worth leaving one
condemnation to go to another.

Then my daughter's aunt, she moved in with
her sister. There was no way I could afford an
apartment on my own, not and eat too—and like I
said, they were all as bad as the first place. So me
and the kids—I have a 3-year-old and a 9-month-
old—we just stayed in the building. They boarded
it up but we got in through the back window.

There was this older lady that lived next
door. We were friends and if she could have

*Vanderstaay, Steven. 1992. "'Karla' & 'The Armstrongs, Mark and Linda.'" Pp. 170–176 in *Street Lives: An Oral His-
tory of Homeless Americans*. Philadelphia, PA: New Society Publishers, 4527 Springfield Ave., Phila., PA. Reprinted
with permission.

helped me she would have. But she already had her four grown kids, plus their kids, livin' with her in a two-bedroom apartment. There's a lot of that these days.

She gave us blankets, though, and I wrapped us up in them. We'd stay outside all day, do something—go to the library or I'd take 'em to the museum. Something. Nights we'd go back into the apartment, light candles, and sleep.

Then it rained real bad. And it was cold. The electrical was off, the gas was off, we were going by candlelight. Mice and rats came out really bad. I woke up one morning and there was a mouse on my 9-month-old's head . . . we couldn't stay in there.

So we went outside, walked around all day. Night came and we slept in a car I found. We were wet and both my kids caught a cold real bad. I took 'em to the emergency room and we slept at the hospital.

The next night we were in this laundromat . . . it was so awful. I was crying, the kids were still sick. And my oldest, Robert, he asked a lot of questions. "Momma, why did we sleep in the car? Why are we outside? It's raining, Momma, I'm cold. I don't feel good."

I couldn't explain. And we had been out for the last three days, never being able to rest. He hadn't eaten anything that night 'cause I didn't have any more money.

Then the man at the laundromat, he gave me $4 to get Robert something to eat. And I stole my baby a can of milk.

THE ARMSTRONGS, MARK AND LINDA— SEATTLE, WASHINGTON

The Armstrongs lived in Bellevue, a young, largely affluent city east of Seattle, until a medical emergency and the sudden loss of Mark's job forced the family to seek emergency housing.

Since Bellevue has little emergency housing, the Armstrongs were advised to seek shelter in nearby Seattle. Eventually, the family was moved to a large public housing project in the city's Central District. Each morning they awake at 5:00 for the long bus ride back to Bellevue for work and school.

Mark and Linda both work, as do their teenage children. Speaking to them, I am struck that they are the quintessential American family: hardworking, supportive, patriotic, loving. And now homeless. The Armstrongs' difficulties—underemployment, housing, grocery bills, health costs, insurance problems—mirror those of other homeless families driven from affluent communities.

They are African Americans in their early thirties.

Mark:

I designed and built conveyor belts, and was good at it. I was making over $15 an hour. And I can go back there right now and get you a letter of recommendation from the company and let you read what they wrote about me. That in itself tells you what kind of worker I am.

The company went out of business. Bang! Didn't even know it was coming. I was between jobs three or four months. I could have found work right away if I wanted to make minimum wage, but I got pretty high standards for myself. I don't even want to make what I'm making now. We could barely afford rent then, how can we now? But when you got kids to feed and bills to pay, you have to do the best you can.

But minimum wage—that's insulting. I don't knock it for high school students. They're getting training, learning about working, making their pocket money. That's fine. But you take a person . . . I got six kids. $3.35, $4 an hour, I spend more than that wage in a day's time on a grocery bill. I mean you can accept some setbacks, but you can't tell a person, "I don't care if you've been making $15 something an hour, the minimum is what you've got to make now." If I hand you this letter, give you my resumé, my military record, show you the kind of worker I am, talk about my family, how can you degrade me by offering me the minimum wage?

Then we had trouble with the house we were renting. And, well, the biggest part of it was hospital bills. My son had to have emergency surgery. Since the company was going out of business it let the insurance lapse, so I got stuck with the bill. Spent every penny we had saved and there's still fourteen hundred dollars on it. You would think by being medical that it wouldn't affect the credit, but it does.

Now I'm working with Safeway's warehouse. I work in the milk plant. Swing shift. Sometimes I'm off at 12:30, 1:00 at night, and then turn right around and go back at 8:30 the next morning. Yeah, it's hard sometimes. I'm not making half of what I used to. I'm a helper—I used to have people working for me. I'd worked my way up through the ranks. But like I was saying, you adjust, you do what you have to do. I'm the kind of person, I get with a company I want to stay, be a part of it. I like to get along with people and work, get my hands dirty. See something accomplished. I'm low man on the totem pole but I'll stay and work my way up.

The warehouse, it's refrigerated on one end and kind of hot on the other. They make their own milk cartons out of plastic so you have to deal with heat and cold. You have to know how to dress 'cause you're dealing with both extremes.

Linda:

I've been a custodian, nurse's aid; now I work at K-Mart. I still have to bus back to the East side [Bellevue] every day. It's okay but I'm looking for something else. You know, it's $4 an hour, and there's no benefits, no discounts at the store, nothing like that.

And I'm in school now, too. I'm going for business training, probably computers or administration. When school starts I'll either bring the little ones there with me or have one of the older ones bring them home.

Working full-time and going to school. Six kids, seventeen on down to twelve. Three in high school, three in grade school. Two of them work at Jack in the Box. They've been working the same shift but my oldest, he's on the football team, so he might be working at a different time than my daughter. And then there's the church, and those football games. Yes we're busy! Just an all-American family. One that's hit a string of bad luck, that's all.

The hardest thing is getting up early enough to bus back over there. As soon as school gets started that's really going to be a problem. It might be a couple of hours, both ways. And if they find out our kids are living here they'll want them in school in Seattle. But they like the schools there and I like them. They're better. And that's where we've lived, that's where we work.

But we get by. The kids, they cook, they clean, they wash and iron their own clothes. And the older ones, they all work. We're so proud of them. Oh, we have the same problems everybody else has, with teenagers and so forth. But we get through 'em. Just thank God they're not on drugs. That's the biggest problem here.

Mark:

When we had to move and lost the house, when I lost my job, we told the kids the truth, the flat out truth. With no misconception; none whatsoever. Kids are not dumb. If you lie to kids, why should they be honest with you? They know exactly what we're going through and they know why.

Same thing when we moved here—six kids, three rooms, writing all over the walls, the drugs and crime. We tried to avoid the move but we didn't have any choice. They knew exactly where we were moving to, as best as I could explain it. We told them we didn't want to come, but if it came down to it we were coming. And we did.

Now my worst fear...there's so much drugs in this area. And people think every apartment in the projects is a drug house. They knock on the doors, knock on the windows—they stop me out there and ask where it is. It's here, so close to us all the times. And all the shooting and fighting...you can look out the window any given night and see the police stopping people and searching everyone.

If I can't look out my door and see my kids, I send for 'em. And I'm afraid when I can't see 'em. 'Cause when they get to shootin' and fightin' and carryin'-on a bullet don't got no names on it. Sometimes when I come in from work, three, four o'clock in the morning, I wonder just when they're going to get me. But my worst fear, my worst fear is the kids.

Linda:

Over in Bellevue they think if you can't afford it then you shouldn't be there. You know, who cares if you work there.

The first house that we had, we were the first blacks in the neighborhood. When I moved over there I said, "Where the black people?" [laughs, then moves her head from side to side as if searching]...no black people? Then the neighbors, they got to looking, came out, they were surprised, too. "Oooh, we got black people over here now" [laughs]. The kids were the only black kids around.

Mark:

People don't want to rent to a family. And you know the kind of rent they're asking over there in Bellevue, that's not easy to come up with. And

you need first, last month's rent, security.... And then people automatically assess, they stereotype you. Maybe sometimes it's 'cause we're black—I'm not saying this is true, I'm saying that sometimes I *felt* that the reason we didn't get a place was because we were black. But most of the time it's the family. People would rather you have pets than kids these days.

One guy, he had six bedrooms in this house. But he didn't want a family. Why would you have six bedrooms if you didn't want to rent to a family? May not be legal, but they do that all the time.

Now there is some validity in what they say about children tearing up things. But the child is only as bad as you let him be. You're the parent, he's going to do exactly what you let him do and get away with. If my kids tear something up I'll pay for it. But me, I tell my kids that if I have to replace something they've destroyed, then one of their sisters or brothers isn't going to get something they need. And when they do something they answer to me.

I'm not bitter...I mean I'm somewhat so. I'm not angry bitter. It's just that I don't like dragging my kids from one place to the next, and I don't think we've been treated right. We had to take places sight-unseen, just to get 'em. We paid $950 a month, and during the wintertime $300, $400 a month for electric and gas bills. Then bought food, kept my kids in clothes. How you supposed to save to get ahead with all that?

And the house, when we moved in the landlords said they'd do this and that, fix this and that. Said we would have an option to buy it. We said, "Okay, and we'll do these things." We had an agreement.

We never got that chance to buy, and they never fixed those things. But we kept paying that $950 a month. They had a barrel over us: we needed some place to go. And they made a small fortune those years. A month after we moved out we went by: all those things they wouldn't do were done.

Before that the guy decided to sell his house, just like that, and we had to move. It was December, wintertime. For a while we were staying with her mother in a two-bedroom. Nine people. We had to be somewhere so we took that second place before we had even seen it.

Everybody has to have a place to live. And people will do what they have to do to survive. A lot of things that you see going on around here are for survival [he sweeps his hand, indicating the housing projects]. I'm not taking up for them, there's a lot of things happening here that I oppose. But where there's a will there's a way, you know.

9 | Divorce, Remarriage, and the Future of the Family

Reading 27   Divorce Culture

A Quest for Relational Equality in Marriage

KARLA B. HACKSTAFF*

When people marry they do not simply tie a knot, but weave a complex of relationships according to pre-existing patterns. In U.S. history, the institution of marriage has been like a loom through which several threads of social relations have been woven. Marriage has been a monogamous, lifelong commitment that has regulated gender, sexuality, and the physical and social reproduction of the generations. This Western marital pattern is being redesigned. We are still responding to the tapestry of old, but the various threads are being disaggregated and rewoven. Our society is deeply divided regarding the value and meaning of these new and partially woven designs.

Over the past decade, family scholars have debated whether we should be optimistic or pessimistic about marital and family life (Glenn 1987, 349).[1] Optimistic theorists have argued that families are not falling apart, but simply changing and adapting to new socioeconomic conditions (Riley 1991; Scanzoni 1987; Skolnick 1991).

They stress the value of embracing family diversity and removing structural obstacles for the well-being of all families. Optimists emphasize the oppression that has attended women's sacrifices in marriage and point to the potential for greater self-determination and happier relationships today (Cancian 1987; Coontz 1992, 1997; Riessman 1990; Skolnick 1991; Stacey 1990, 1996). These theorists are concerned about threads that have regulated gender and sexuality and have subordinated women in marriage.

Pessimistic theorists have argued that the institution of marriage is a cause for concern—that divorce rates signify an unraveling of social bonds (Bellah et al. 1985; Glenn 1987; Lasch 1979; Popenoe 1988; Popenoe, Elshtain, and Blankenhorn 1996; Spanier 1989; Whitehead 1997a). Above all, pessimists argue that divorce suggests an increasingly tenuous thread of commitment and a growing "individualism" among today's adults, particularly since marital dissolution by divorce, rather than death, entails individual choice. In this view, marriage represents the singular commitment that sustains intergenerational family relationships, especially parenthood. Indeed, several recent books urge a return to lifelong marriage for the sake of children (Blankenhorn 1995a, 1995b; Popenoe, Elshtain, and Blankenhorn 1996; Whitehead 1997a).

Pessimists fear that with the advent of divorce culture we have forsaken nurturance, commitment, and responsibility. Because these are the very virtues that have traditionally been valorized in women, these divorce debates are always implicitly, if not explicitly, about gender. As one optimistic scholar has argued, "when commentators lament the collapse of traditional family commitments and values, they almost invariably mean the uniquely female duties associated with the doctrine of separate spheres for men and women" (Coontz 1992, 40). Critics of divorce do not always or necessarily reject gender equality in marriage, but they do tend to set it apart. Many scholars assume that the thread of gender ideology can be easily disentangled from the thread of commitment.

The middle-class '50s and '70s couples in this study, in combination with those in other studies, enhance our knowledge of the newly constructed meanings of marriage. Among the '70s spouses, I found a reproduction of divorce culture among the married, a growth in a marital work ethic, and fluid, even contradictory, beliefs regarding marital and gender ideologies. These findings validate the concerns of both optimists and pessimists.

Pessimists may be dismayed by the sense of contingency in the talk of married couples and may be confirmed in their belief that commitments are unraveling. On the other hand, optimists may feel validated in their views that spouses do not take divorce lightly; rather, "working" on marriages is the prevailing belief among spouses—though wives are still trying to equalize this work. A full-blown marital work ethic has

arisen, because of divorce anxiety and marital instability, yet it has also arisen because of instabilities in beliefs about gender. Spouses must be reflexive about the nature of marriage since the authority of marriage culture and male dominance have lost their hegemony hold. The fluid beliefs among '70s spouses suggest that spouses do not wholly embrace either marriage or divorce culture. This may disturb pessimists more—at least those who would like to see marriage culture regain the hegemony of generations past.

At this point in time, marriage does not seem to be forever for almost half of all marriages. Is this a result of culture and the decline of values such as commitment, or are there other factors contributing to marital contingency today? Could divorce culture be transitional—a means to the goals of equality and new tapestries of commitment, rather than an end in itself? While the individualism of divorce culture has brought new problems, we should neither overlook the structural sources of these troubles nor forget the costs of marriage culture, particularly to women.

THE COSTS OF MARRIAGE CULTURE

Women's greater participation in the labor force, increased activity in the political sphere, and greater initiation of divorces suggest that women like Mia Turner and Roxanne Kason-Morris are claiming their rights and appropriating a model of individualism. However, my research suggests that women's increasing "individualism" needs to be understood in context. Because we proceed from a history of male-dominated marriages, individualism does not *mean* the same thing for women as for men.

Historically, we know that as heads of the household, even when not primary breadwinners, most husbands have had greater authority, and therefore greater freedom to be independent, than wives. Economic and legal structures have not only firmly anchored a white man's family authority in the public sphere, but have recognized and applauded his individualism. His autonomy, integrity, rights, and self-expression were never constrained to the same degree as those of wives, though he carried heavy financial responsibilities. Not all men have been able to accomplish or benefit from the provider role—working-class men and men of color have often been thwarted by economic and racial injustice. However, for those able to realize the ideal of the male provider role, these responsibilities have optimized men's freedoms and prerogatives.

Wives who are more individualistic are often trying to counter the legacy of male dominance in marriage. At face value, "contingent marriage" dilutes commitment by making it conditional. Marital commitment and contingency stand in an uneasy relation to one another. The unconditional commitment requires flexibility and a long-range view of reciprocity and rewards over time; it permits conflict, serendipity, and unforeseen developments without threatening the commitment; it builds trust that only a sustained history can provide. Yet, "marriage as forever" can also obscure the latent terms of commitment that have prevailed under conditions of male dominance. Paradoxically, a sense of contingency can enable wives to elicit values such as commitment, responsibility, caretaking, and equality. In short, it provides a powerful lever to set the terms of marriage.[2]

Of course, both men and women can use the lever of contingency in heterosexual marriage. Indeed, a male-dominated divorce culture may be a greater threat to the values of responsibility, caretaking, and equality than a male-dominated marriage culture. Yet, as I have suggested, securing power through individualism is not a new means for men within divorce culture. Thus, this lever is more important for women, who have had less economic and political power in the

marital relationship. In fact, contingent marriage may be crucial for redefining marriage in an egalitarian direction. Most women are hungry not for power but for "the absence of domination" (M. Johnson 1988, 261). Yet, how can wives challenge domination without engaging the power of individualism?

A belief in equality is more widespread today—the '70s spouses did not generally embrace male dominance as their '50s counterparts did, but rather voiced support for gender equality.[3] Yet, ongoing conflicts over gender equality are apparent in husbands' and wives' "hidden agendas." When there is evidence of rights equality—such as a wives' participation in the labor force—husbands tend to assume that equality has been achieved; they are unaware of ongoing inequalities, such as marital work, and their enduring privileges to set the terms of marriage. Rights equality has more often been a masculinist discourse in U.S. law and culture (Arendell 1995; Coltrane and Hickman 1992; Weitzman 1985).

Many wives also embrace rights equality, yet women's conventional responsibilities for caretaking, child rearing, kin work, and marital work continue to incline women toward a vision of equality that focuses upon relational responsibilities, expressiveness, equity, and interdependence. Relational equality has been more often feminized in U.S. society (Cancian 1987; Riessman 1990). It is not that women are "essentially" relational, but rather that they have been expected and positioned to accomplish relationality. While some women are undoubtedly more individualistic today, as critics of divorce culture argue (Hewlett and West 1998, 200; Whitehead 1997a, 172, 181), more women increasingly want to share the marital and family labors that optimists have documented. Women are frustrated by men's lack of participation in marital work—and the emotion work, kin work, and housework that such reflexive assessment encompasses (Blaisure and Allen 1995; Cancian 1987; DeVault 1987; di Leonardo 1987; Goldscheider and Waite 1991; Hochschild 1983; Hochschild with Maching 1989; Oliker 1989; Thompson and Walker 1989; Thompson 1991).

These gendered marital visions, are also apparent in the retrospective accounts of the divorced. Among divorced women and men, Riessman (1990, 164–65, 184) found that "freedom" encapsulated the positive meaning of divorce, but this gateway to freedom did not necessarily hold the same meaning. Women reported a freedom from subordination and the freedom for self-development—reflecting limits to equality in marriage; men reported freedom from obligations demanded by wives and a freedom from wives' scrutiny—reflecting some dissatisfaction with marital labors. Also, while former wives described their "transformations in identity" as learning to balance relatedness with self-reliance, former husbands discovered the value of "talk" and becoming more relational (199). This latter change by some husbands is ironic for former wives if, as I have argued, relational inequality contributes to marital instability and contingency.

In their suburban divorced sample, Kitson and Holmes (1992) found that ex-husbands and ex-wives similarly ranked a "lack of communication or understanding" as the top marital complaint (though wives ranked this higher) and similarly ranked "joint conflict over roles" as a key complaint.[4] Most interesting, however, was a notable gender difference on the marital complaint "not sure what happened"; for ex-husbands it ranked third, for ex-wives it ranked 28th (123). This suggests that men were less attuned to what the marriage lacked—a prerequisite for doing marital work.

Some '70s husbands—such as Robert Leonetti, Gordon Walker, and Paul Nakato—do marital work. Yet, more often than not, wives initiate and try to redistribute the actual "marital work" of communicating, caring, fulfilling needs, adjusting, and planning for marital well-being. To advocate shared marital work is to degender the rights and responsibilities conventionally attached to marital practices, to challenge male authority, and to disrupt power relations. Recent research that aims to predict marital happiness and divorce, as well as to improve the efficacy of marital therapy, reveals that a husband's refusal to accept influence from his wife is a key factor for predicting divorce (Gottman et al. 1998, 14,19).

The above research suggests that marital work and the relational equality that it entails may be as important as rights equality for wives in a culture of divorce. The cultural irony is that even though wives may want a relational marriage, they may need to draw upon individualism to secure it. If secured, that is, if husbands keep up with wives' changes, wives may change the power dynamics of their marriage. Yet, ultimately what many wives want is not freedom from commitment, but freedom within an egalitarian and relational marriage. However, if relationality is unsecured, these wives may choose the gateway of divorce.

It is worth recalling that it was primarily the wives and not the husbands who thought about divorce among '50s couples ensconced in marriage culture. What does this reveal about the gendered costs of marriage culture? Writing about marriage and the nuclear family, Stacey (1996, 69) noted: "It seems a poignant commentary on the benefits to women of that family system that, even in a period when women retain primary responsibility for maintaining children and other kin, when most women continue to earn significantly less than men with equivalent cultural capital, and when women and their children suffer substantial economic decline after divorce, that in spite of all this, so many regard divorce as the lesser of evils." In light of women's postdivorce commitments to children, to charge such mothers with an egoistic or self-centered individualism reveals a refusal to recognize the costs of marriage culture to women.

Are there no costs for men in marriage culture? While research continues to find that marriage is better for men than women in terms of overall health and mortality rates (Hu and Goldman 1990), men are adjusting to new gender ideologies and practices too. Historically, the ability to provide and the ability to head a household have rooted men's identities. Working women and growing beliefs in equality are increasingly uprooting these means to manhood, as distinct from womanhood. As Furstenberg (1988, 239) has observed: "Men looking at marriage today may sense that it offers them a less good deal than it once did. This is the inevitable result of reducing male privileges, female deference to men, and a range of services that were customarily provided as part of the conjugal bargain. The loss of these privileges has persuaded some men to opt out of family life altogether." Paul Nakato's observation that some '70s men would rather be "right" than "married"—echoes Goode (1992, 124) on the sociology of superordinates: "Men view even small losses of deference, advantages, or opportunities as large threats and losses." Craig Kason-Morris felt increasingly underappreciated for all his work; yet his solution was to devote more energy to breadwinning, risking the relational needs of his marriage.

If we ignore the emotional costs of marriage culture and its connection to gender inequality, we will fail to see that divorce culture is a transitional phenomenon. We will also advance the costs of divorce culture—the impoverished single mothers, estranged fathers, and affected children—of concern to pessimists and optimists alike.

THE COSTS OF DIVORCE CULTURE

The gendered patterns of divorce follow from those of marriage. Just as women usually do the primary parenting during a marriage, they generally obtain custody of children after divorce. Fathers are overwhelmingly noncustodial parents—only 14 percent of custodial parents are fathers (Sugarman 1998, 15). Just as fathers help support children during marriage, they are expected to contribute to child support upon divorce. Yet, many noncustodial fathers have become estranged from their children and delinquent on child support. Single, custodial mothers must often raise children on one slim paycheck. More widespread divorce seems to have increased women's and children's impoverishment, undermined fathers' economic and emotional commitment to children, and deprived children of the emotional and economic goods that two parents can provide.

Pessimists acknowledge structural impediments to marital commitments—the decline of the male wage and the need for two wage earners in a postindustrial economy. Yet, they see the decline in cultural and family values, such as commitment, as the more pivotal factor fostering these new social problems. On the other hand, optimists regularly argue that our failure to respond to the new global and postindustrial economy—the low priority given to families by corporate and government entities—is more basic to these problems, and that these new conditions demand solutions that do not discriminate on the basis of marital status. Although structural solutions are central, optimists are also concerned with cultural and family values—though the values of equality or justice are of greater concern than commitment.

Optimists and pessimists alike are concerned about the economic costs of divorce for mothers and their children. About a third of female-headed households are in poverty—six times the rate of married-couple households (U.S. Bureau of the Census 1995, P60-187). A re-evaluation of one study's claims about the economic consequences of divorce a year after divorce, finds that women's standard of living declines by 27 percent and men's increases by 10 percent (Peterson 1996, 534).[5]

A key solution to poverty for many pessimistic family scholars is reinforcing marriage and the nuclear family structure (Blankenhorn 1995b; Hewlett and West 1998; Popenoe et al. 1996; Whitehead 1997a). Marriage has functioned to redistribute economic resources in the past.[6] Also, today more than ever, two earners are necessary to secure a middle-class standard of living. However, to imply that unmarried motherhood or divorce are the *cause* of poverty among women and children, and marriage the only solution, is to use family structure to solve problems generated by the social structure. Such an approach overlooks the enduring gender inequality in economic structures. Also, marriage does not necessarily reverse poverty, particularly for working-class women and women of color. For instance, Brewer (1988, 344) noted that "an emphasis on female-headed households misses an essential truth about black women's poverty: black women are also poor in households with male heads." Higher wages in female-dominated jobs may be a more effective solution than marriage. This would not only help married, nuclear family households, but all families and households.

Similarly, marriage culture will not solve the larger economic problem of declining wages for working- and middle-class men brought by a postindustrial, service, and global economy.[7] Indeed, we could transform divorce culture by repairing wage declines for those most disadvantaged by this postindustrial economy—including many working-class men, especially men of color. This could remove sources of conflict and resentment within and across family groups. Yet, to address structural sources of inequality would only mitigate, and not reverse, divorce culture unless we attend to cultural beliefs about gender as well.

Pessimists advocate marriage culture in part because it would seem to solve so many problems of divorce culture at once, most especially divorced men's failure to provide and care for their children. Of all policies, child support has received the most attention by legislators and media over the last two decades. Only about half of custodial mothers with child support orders receive the full amount (Arendell 1995, 39). In 1991 the "average monthly child support paid by divorced fathers contributing economic support" was only $302 (for an estimated 1.5 children), and "child support payments amounted to only about 16% of the incomes of divorced mothers and their children" (Arendell 1997, 162). As a result of the Family Support Act of 1988, the mechanisms for securing child support from fathers have become more rigorous (Furstenberg and Cherlin 1991, 109); there are established formulas for calculating child support payments and, since 1994, all new child support payments are withheld from the paychecks of absent parents (mostly fathers). Yet, as Hewlett and West (1998, 180) observe, in spite of all the policies and prison terms, "the number of deadbeat dads has declined only slightly since 1978."[8]

We need new ways to address fathers' "failure to provide"—clearly, some fathers partly withdraw from marriage and children because they cannot be "good providers."[9] Yet, to focus on the provider role is to limit fatherhood to a model that evolved during the industrial era and is at odds with a postindustrial economy. One could say that this approach merely exchanges a "fragmented" fatherhood for its predecessor: a "shrinking" fatherhood (Blankenhorn 1995a).[10]

Indeed, to focus on providing alone will only sustain men's detachment from parenting. "Studies do show that fathers who visit more regularly pay more in child support" (Furstenberg and Cherlin 1991, 274). Whether these payments are due to visiting or greater commitment, attention to the relational aspects of fathering would seem crucial.

Both optimistic and pessimistic scholars are concerned about the lack of paternal participation in children's lives. Most research shows a substantial and unacceptable decline over time in father-child contact after a divorce (Furstenberg and Cherlin 1991). Data from the recent National Survey of Families and Households reveals that about 30 percent of children of divorce have not seen their fathers at all in the preceding year, and many more see their fathers irregularly and infrequently (Arendell 1995, 38). Speaking of unmarried as well as divorced fathers, Hewlett and West (1988, 168) report that "close to half of all fathers lose contact with their children."

Thus, all family scholars see a need to revitalize and redefine fatherhood. For example, a supporter of divorce culture, Arendell (1995, 251) protests: "Why should it be so difficult to be a nurturing, engaged father? Where are the institutional and ideological supports for parenting?" Arendell adds: "That caring fathers are subject to criticism and stigmatization points to a seriously flawed ideological system" (251). Also, advocates of marriage culture Hewlett and West (1998, 173) assert that "a withering of the father-child bond devastates children, stunts men, and seriously erodes our social capital." In spite of shared concerns, the means to a revitalized fatherhood are contested.

Just as critics of divorce culture suggest that marriage will alleviate the impoverishment of single mothers, they argue that fathers cannot be effective parents outside of the marriage structure (Blankenhorn 1995a; Hewlett and West

1998; Popenoe 1996; Wallerstein and Blakeslee 1989; Whitehead 1997a). For example, Hewlett and West (1998, 171–72) note that single males are more likely to die prematurely due to self-neglect, more likely to abuse drugs and alcohol, and are responsible for a disproportionate share of violence—including murder, robbery, and rape. They reason, like Durkheim, that marriage and children have a "civilizing" effect upon men.[11] In Blankenhorn's (1995a) view, both co-residence and a parental alliance with the mother are preconditions for effective fatherhood.

Undoubtedly, co-residence assists in the building of relationships—including, and especially, parent-child relationships. Yet, there is evidence to suggest it is not a precondition for effective fatherhood. In her study of divorced fathers, Arendell (1995) describes "innovative" divorced fathers (not all of whom had single custody) who were able to detach being a father from being a partner, separate anger at an ex-wife from their love for their children, focus on the children's needs rather than adult rights, and combine breadwinning with caretaking in ways that developed their nurturing and relational skills. While such fathers are too rare, fathers who parent effectively after divorce suggest that marriage or co-residence are not prerequisites—though alliances between parents do seem to be important whether outside or inside the marriage structure. Further, studies on nonresidential mothers show they are more active participants in their children's lives (Maccoby and Mnookin 1992, 212; Arendell 1997, 170). Finally, even if custody determinations were divided equally between women and men, co-residence would not always be an option for father and child. Suggesting marriage as the solution for divorce—and effective fathering—is empty advice for those compelled to divorce.[12]

Divorced fathers' flagging commitment seems to have exposed a tenuous responsibility for children in the first place. This may represent a "male flight from commitment" that started in the 1950s (Ehrenreich 1984); even so, this too should be understood as a legacy of separate spheres that identified masculinity with the provider role and devalued men's caretaking capacities (Bernard 1981; Coontz 1992). Since women still do the bulk of child rearing during a marriage, many divorced fathers have to learn how to be a primary parent after divorce (Arendell 1997, 163). As optimists and pessimists alike have observed, men appear to depend upon wives to mediate their relationship to their children (Arendell 1995, 33; Furstenberg and Cherlin 1991, 275; Wallerstein and Blakeslee 1989; Whitehead 1997b).[13] This may explain why marriage seems like the only solution for effective fathering for the pessimists.

Another route for expanding paternal participation—and overcoming the historical equivalence between breadwinning and masculinity[14] —would be to construct men as nurturers, caretakers, and responsible fathers. Arendell (1995, 251) calls for "a more vocal and widespread critique of the conventions of masculinity." A construction of masculinity that goes beyond putting all of men's eggs into one "breadwinner" basket (Bernard 1981) is long overdue. Perhaps marriage has an important "civilizing function" for men because of a flawed construction of masculinity in the first place; men have been deprived of the expectation or opportunity to advance their relationality—from boyhood to manhood.

Reinforcing marriage by compelling "divorce as a last resort" would obscure, not solve, this paternal disability. Rather than advocating marriage or reinforcing the provider role as pessimists do, many optimists argue that men need to combine providing with caretaking just as women have combined caretaking with providing. In the aggregate, women are changing faster than men. To keep up with wives' changes

means that husbands must be willing to recognize the legitimacy of a wife's relational concerns, embrace what has been largely a devalued sphere, and to share power with their wives.

If a redistribution of relational responsibilities were to take place in marriage, this might extend fathers' involvement with their children in the event of divorce. More important, this could prevent divorces based on relational inequalities in the first place.[15] Indeed, in my research, paternal participation is part of the "marital labor" that egalitarian wives wanted to share. Reconstructing masculinity (and therefore gender in marriage) might provide the stronger deterrent to divorce for which pessimists have been searching.

IS DIVORCE EVER A GATEWAY FOR CHILDREN?

Given children's attenuated relations with their fathers and the downward mobility most children share with their mothers, is divorce ever a gateway for children? Not only do two-thirds of divorces involve children (U.S. Bureau of the Census 1995, P60-187), but few people object to divorce by childless couples today. Because it is children that electrify the divorce debates, I only sampled married parents. Are children paying the price for adults' individualism and lapsed family values, as the critics of divorce culture would argue? Or, could they be paying the costs of marriage culture and the quest for equality—interpersonal and institutional—that I have described?

Divorce is rarely experienced as a "gateway" for children—even perhaps, when it should be. It is, however, a turning point that is distinct from the adult experience. There is a tendency in the debates about the effects of divorce upon children to project adult experiences and capacities onto children. One recent study found that parents' and children's experiences were generally "out of synch" (Stewart et al. 1997, cited in Arendell 1998, 227). Parents may overestimate their child's well-being. Kitson with Holmes (1992, 227) found that most parents attribute very low levels of distress to their children, even though we know that the early period is hard for children. Whether divorce is due to a spouse's adultery, violence, or self-centeredness, the decision is not the child's to make. Of course, children survive and thrive after the temporary crisis of parental divorce, just as they survive other crises. Yet, the assumption that children are resilient should be tempered with the view that the endurance of parental relationships (even if they divorce) matters to children. Neither "divorce as a last resort" nor "divorce as a gateway" capture the divorce turning point for children, because they both presume some choice in the matter.[16]

Many studies agree upon some costs borne by children after a parental divorce, yet the source, extent, and meaning of these costs are fiercely debated (Wallerstein and Kelly 1980; Wallerstein and Blakeslee 1989; Amato and Booth 1997; Maccoby and Mnookin 1992; Hetherington, Law, and O'Connor 1993; Furstenberg and Cherlin 1991; Whitehead 1997a). The conditions preceding, surrounding, and following divorce matter a great deal, including the quality of parent-child relationships, custodial arrangements, the quality of the ex-spousal and coparenting relationships, the economic and social supports available, and the child's own psychological strengths (Furstenberg and Cherlin 1991; Kelly 1988, 134). The age and gender of the child may matter—though gender effects have been questioned (Arendell 1997, 175; Wallerstein and Kelly 1980; Kelly 1988; Wallerstein and Blakeslee 1989). Remarriage and new stepfamily relations affect a child's adjustment over time; indeed, some research suggests remarriage may be more of an adjustment than divorce (Ahrons and Rodgers 1987, 257).

Drawing upon an analysis of 92 studies involving 13,000 children, Amato (1994, 145) reports consistent findings that children of divorce experience "lower academic achievement, more behavioral problems, poorer psychological adjustment, more negative self-concepts, more social difficulties, and more problematic relationships with both mothers and fathers. Also, children of divorce are reported to become pregnant outside of marriage, marry young, and divorce upon becoming adults (McLanahan and Bumpass 1988; Glenn and Kramer 1987).

Taken together, these findings would seem to be alarming. The pessimists are alarmed. Yet, we should not assume that divorce is the "cause" when divorce is correlated with undesirable effects among children. Research on the adverse effects of divorce for children consistently finds that other factors that accompany divorce may be more important than the divorce itself. For example, "income differences account for almost 50 percent of the disadvantage faced by children in single-parent households" (McLanahan and Sandefur 1994; Coontz 1997, 101). Changes of residence and schools help to explain the other 50 percent of disadvantage. Above all, prospective and longitudinal studies of families suggest that marital conflict is more crucial than divorce in explaining behavioral and emotional problems for those children who are troubled (Amato and Booth 1996, 1997; Block, Block, and Gjerde, 1986; Coontz 1997, 102). Longitudinal studies have discovered that children's problems are apparent over a decade before the parents' divorce. Thus, in some cases, divorce and a single-parent household is better for children than continued marital conflict (Amato, Loomis, and Booth 1995).

Furthermore, Amato's (1994) analysis of multiple studies also reveals that the effects of divorce are very weak and that differences between children of divorce and children in continuously intact families are quite small (Amato and Keith 1991; Amato 1994; Amato and Booth 1996, 1997). As the optimist Coontz (1997, 99) clarifies, this research does not suggest that children of divorced parents have *more problems,* rather that *more children* of divorced parents have problems than do children of married parents. Yet, children of divorce show greater variability in their adjustment (Amato 1994). This means that some children of divorce do better than children of married parents. Children from all kinds of families fare well and poorly. When we focus on the difference between family structures, we overlook the extensive overlap in children's well-being across family structures. Further, research increasingly suggests that the quality and consistency of family life, and not family structure, influences children's well-being (Arendell 1997, 187).

Most of the '70s couples I interviewed did not believe in staying together "for the sake of the children" if there was marital conflict. Parents sense that if their marriage is continuously in conflict, then this harms children too. Divorce is not a singular solution to conflict or violence since both can be exacerbated upon separation and divorce (Arendell and Kurz, 1999). Yet the gateway is crucial for such troubled marriages. Recall that the '50s Dominicks stayed together miserably for thirty years in spite of extramarital affairs, separation, and indications of violence— all for the sake of the children. These were justifiable conditions under the terms of marriage culture. One wonders to what degree the "sake of the children," among other deterrents, inhibited divorces that should have been when marriage culture reigned uncontested.[17]

Kurz's (1995, 52) random sample of divorced mothers revealed that 19 percent pursued divorce specifically because of violence; however, an astonishing 70 percent reported at least one incident of violence during the marriage or separation. Most research shows that violence remains a graver problem for wives than husbands—particularly in terms of injuries (Gelles and Straus 1988; Kurz 1989; Straton 1994). Also, research increasingly finds that witnessing

spouse abuse *is* child abuse—even when a child is not physically violated (Holden, Geffner, and Jouriles 1998). Thus, removing children from the perpetrator, however much he (or she) is loved, is arguably for the sake of the children.

Believers in "divorce as a gateway" may want to make parental happiness equivalent to children's happiness when it is not. Pessimists correctly stress that the child's experience of divorce is distinct from the parents' experience. Thus, scholars are increasingly advocating parenting education classes for divorcing parents (Arendell 1995; Wallerstein 1998). Yet, believers in "divorce as a last resort" also mistakenly presume that the maintenance of marriage and a nuclear family is equivalent to children's happiness. We should not ignore the injuries that have attended marriage culture—particularly a male-dominated marriage culture. When egalitarian spouses become parents there is often a shift toward "increased traditionality of family and work roles in families of the 1980s and 1990s," and this "tends to be associated with *more* individual and marital distress for parents" (Cowan and Cowan 1998, 184). This represents the pinch between egalitarian beliefs and the structural impediments to equality in practice. Further, to the degree that we idealize a male-dominated, nuclear family model we cannot fail to reproduce such constructions of inequality among children. While some children are paying a price for the quest for equality, children also pay a price when the thread of commitment is tangled with the thread of male dominance. Moreover, children do find happiness and another vision of equality in alternative family forms.

THE FUTURE OF DIVORCE CULTURE

From Durkheim (1961) to Giddens (1979, 1991), sociologists have regularly addressed transitional periods such as our own. Norms, ideals, and authorities that guided our marital practices in the past are inadequate to families' needs in today's socioeconomic context. Could divorce culture represent a new tapestry of ideals and norms for guiding today's family lives? Even as the practices of '70s spouses are shaped by novel conditions, spouses attempt to shape them in turn—drawing alternatively, selectively, and even haphazardly on available ideologies and practices. Although divorce culture seems to be replacing marriage culture, it should be seen as a transitional means for "people to make sense of the circumstances in which they find themselves" (Mullings 1986), providing alternative strategies for action when marriage culture falls short. Still, like the '70s spouses, many people are ambivalent about divorce culture. Moreover, marriage culture endures.

Because divorce culture is new and unsettling there is a tendency to inflate its power and prevalence. Marriage culture is widely embraced. "Marriage as forever" is a belief that is not only sustained by married couples, but also the divorced (Riessman 1990). The reintroduction of grounds in "covenant marriages" represents a political effort to value the old tapestry that sustained "divorce as a last resort." Finally, "marrying as a given" lives on. While rates of marriage and remarriage have decreased since the mid-1960s (U.S. Bureau of the Census, 1992, P23-180, 8)—suggesting that fewer people experience marriage as an imperative—the majority of people eventually marry. Also, the two-parent family continues to be the predominant family form—so concern with its decline can be overstated (Cowan and Cowan 1998, 189).

Marriage culture also lives on in the next generation's aspirations. The majority of young people say they value marriage and plan to marry (Landis-Kleine et al. 1995). A 1992 survey, showed that of all extremely important goals in life, the most valued by 78 percent of the high school respondents was "having a good marriage and family life" (Glenn 1996, 21). "Being able to find steady work" was ranked a close second by 77 percent of these students, and "being successful in my line of work" and "being able to give my children better opportunities than I've had" tied for third, at 66 percent.

Will the '90s spouses continue, reverse, or transcend the advance of divorce culture? How will they cope with the rise of divorce culture and its problems? Because a culture of divorce creates "divorce anxiety," premarital counseling would seem to be increasingly important. One valuable component of "covenant marriage" advanced by pessimists (in spite of critiques of therapeutic culture) has been to encourage religious or secular premarital counseling. Instituting therapy before marriage might prepare '90s spouses for the reflexive process and the marital work that characterizes marriage in an era of change, choice, and uncertainty.[18] Such counseling should not only attune spouses to one another's hopes, dreams, and desires, but should also provide information on the social conditions faced by married couples today. For example, the arrival of children is a vulnerable period of transition in marriage even when children are deeply desired (Cowan and Cowan 1998). Also, '90s spouses should know that aspirations for lifetime marriage, for thriving children, and a good job are not new; most people getting married share these hopes for themselves even as they harbor doubts about others. What thwarts their resolve and aspirations? Do they simply become individualistic?

This analysis of divorce culture has tried to situate the charges that a high divorce rate represents increased individualism in recent generations. On the one hand, like the pessimists, I agree that divorce culture is marked by individualism. Individualism clearly links and underlies the tenets of divorce culture: the choice to marry, to set conditions, and the chance to unmarry all speak to the primacy of the individual to redesign his or her life. However, my research complicates these claims. Individualism is not in a zero-sum relationship with commitment. It can be morally responsible rather than egoistic, it has not been absent for men in marriage culture, and it is not necessarily an end in itself. Divorce culture exposes how the terms of marital commitment reflect a legacy of male dominance. For married women, individualism can be a tool to resist old and enforce new terms of marital commitment— including nurturance, commitment, and relational responsibility shared by both spouses. When mothers use the power of individualism for relational ends—by working to provide, by removing children from violent households, or by refusing to be subordinated—individualism is neither an end in itself nor easily severed from committed responsibility. The meaning of pulling the individualistic lever of divorce culture cannot be stripped from interactional or institutional contexts. Thus, '90s spouses would also do well to take the insights of optimists into account. Our quest for equality is ongoing.

Finally, an overemphasis on the individualism of women or men diverts our attention from the ways our social structures obstruct this quest for equality. The variety of families today may not represent a failure of commitment as much as individuals' valiant struggles to sustain commitments in a society that withholds structural supports from workers and families. Indeed, until the 1993 Family and Medical Leave Act, the United States had no family policy at all.[19] Other scholars have suggested an array of family policies—from easing work and family conflicts to providing economic and social supports—for today's burdened families, which I will not repeat here (see Arendell 1995; Burggraf 1997; Hewlett and West 1998; Hochschild 1997; Mason, Skolnick, and Sugar-

man 1998). Yet, two things are clear—when we allow corporate and government policies to neglect the needs of working parents, we are undermining marriage culture, and when we ignore enduring gender inequalities we advance divorce culture.

While divorce culture is flawed, I see it as a means to propel marital and family relationships in an egalitarian direction. Both "optional marriage" and "divorce as a gateway" recognize commitments apart from marriage, expose the costs of marriage culture, and legitimate diverse family arrangements. Critics of divorce culture advocate a return to the singular design of the nuclear family structure; however, in many ways this sustains a white, middle-class ethnocentrism,[20] and a heterosexism[21] that has marked our family ideals. By challenging "marriage as a given" and "divorce as a last resort," divorce culture helps to destigmatize unmarried families.

As we reconstruct the terms of marriage culture with the tool of divorce culture, we risk sacrificing relationality for rights equality. Rights language is essential for justice, dignity, and self-determination. Yet, it is not an unmitigated good, and only the young, childless, wealthy, or powerful can indulge in a sense of independence and obscure interdependence by relying upon others to sustain the illusion. Only when the relational responsibilities, still constructed as "feminine," are practiced and valued by men, and by the society at large, will we be able to move beyond the individualism of divorce culture and beyond a notion of equality limited to individual rights and obscuring relational responsibilities. Whether divorce culture eventually supplants rather than contests marriage culture, or generates "family cultures" that transcend this contestation, will depend upon social structural change and the quest for relational equality in the next generation.

Reading 28 Rethinking Relationships Between Divorced Mothers and Their Children: Capitalizing on Family Strengths

JOYCE A. ARDITTI*

Based on interview data from 58 young adult children who experienced parental divorce, this study examines qualitative aspects of mother-child relationships and strengths in these relationships. Boundary issues and roles shifts between children and their divorced mothers are particularly emphasized. A content analysis revealed that often times, mothers were viewed as friends, especially by daughters, and their withdrawal from caregiving was generally welcomed. Implications of mothers' reliance on their children for emotional support are explored from the child's perspective. While such behavior has largely been pathologized in the clinical literature, this data suggests that mothers' leaning on children for emotional support and advice contributed to a sense of equality, closeness, and friend status. These qualities appeared to be valued by the participants in this study. Implications for family practitioners and scholars, as they relate to notions of boundary violation and adolescent development, are discussed from a family strengths perspective.

Emphasis in the area of mother-child relationships during and after divorce has tended to focus on the negative implications of mothers' eroding discipline, parenting stress, and role strain for children's adjustment (Capaldi & Patterson, 1991; Forehand, Thomas, Wierson, Brody, & Fauber, 1990; Hetherington, 1989). While the consensus is that divorce does not greatly *damage* children's relations with custodial mothers (Acock & Demo, 1994; Aquilino, 1994; Peterson & Zill, 1986) compared to children and mothers in two parent families, many scholars fail to address the transformational qualities divorce might bring to mother-child relationships. As with the fathers literature, little is known about qualitative aspects of the relationships divorced mothers have with their children, especially from children's perspectives.

*Arditti, Joyce A. "Rethinking Relationships Between Divorced Mothers and Their Children: Capitalizing on Family Strengths." *Family Relations, 1999, 48,* pp. 109–119. Copyright 1999 by the National Council on Family Relations, 3989 Central Ave. NE, Suite 550, Minneapolis, MN 55421. Reprinted by permission.

Guttman (1993) comments on the dearth of in-depth studies of single mother-child relationships. He observes that what we do know about children's relationships with their divorced mothers often involves comparisons between single mothers and married mothers, and is based on the belief that a marriage is necessary in order for a family system to be defined as "legitimate." Such stigma, according to Guttman, ignores the potential diversity of experience for family members and misrepresents the relationships in many single-mother households. Even in the most benign sense, positive findings are interpreted within a deficit framework, emphasizing success despite the hardships of divorce and stress of single parenting (Aquilino, 1994). It is a rare study that considers single mothers' strengths with regard to parenting and household management (see for example, Arditti & Madden-Derdich, 1995; Richards & Schmiege, 1993).

One of the central concerns about parenting after divorce involves the implications of shifting boundaries between parents and children resulting from the ending of the spousal system. Such a consideration is rooted in family systems theory whereby the characteristics of relationship subsystems (e.g. parent-child; spousal) shape the boundaries that separate them. Family therapists have particularly emphasized the problems that can be associated with boundary "violations" which might occur when the intergenerational boundaries between parents and children are weak or distressed (Fish, Belsky, & Youngblade, 1991). Examples of boundary violations include drawing children into marital disputes as well as shifts in power between parents and children (Minuchin, 1974). Satir (1967) emphasized the danger of elevating the child to a level of false equality with the parents, which in turn leaves the child's developmental needs unmet and leads to distrust in their later relationships. The critical feature of such alliances, according to many family systems theorists, is

that parents turn to their children for emotional sustenance and intimacy that is usually derived from the spousal relationship. Parents may share secrets with their children, and expect their children to listen to their problems, and provide empathy and affection. It is assumed that, in doing this, parents are unable to provide their children with the needed parental guidance and support (Jacobvitz & Bush, 1996).

Fish et al. (1991) point out that empirical investigation of boundary phenomena is limited—especially in non-clinical families—due to methodological challenges inherent in operationalizing such constructs and the value laden context of boundary issues. Yet these basic premises have shaped much of what is presumed to be desirable in terms of process between parents and children, and generally have been formulated based on studies of children and/or parents in distressed, two-parent families. It is unknown how patterns of family interaction, such as strong alliances between mothers and their children, would impact family interaction and child outcomes in single parent households.

Johnston (1993) applies this basic orientation in her study investigating family transitions and children's functioning. She emphasizes the negative outcomes of role confusion and blurred generational boundaries for children. For example, she states: "When the parental alliance breaks down and parents are less able to distinguish their own needs from those of their children, the children are often induced to assume inappropriate roles or attempt to fulfill spousal/parental functions." (p. 20). Johnston identifies several facets of "role disturbance" resulting from divorce, including alignments, role reversals, and role diffusion. Behavioral indicators of role reversal include when a child assumes the role of confidante, peer, or mentor to a distressed parent.

Finally, mother-child boundaries have systemic significance for children's capacity for self-differentiation (Kerr & Bowen, 1988). It is generally accepted by developmentalists that family processes that encourage and support the individuation and separateness of older children and adolescents are the most effective in generating competence (Hines, 1997). While individuation should occur in balance with *connection* to parents, much of the literature on children's adjustment to divorce presumes disturbances in parent-child connection. This literature highlights parental difficulty in either facilitating individuation, because of the potential for mothers "overdependence" on their children, or a failure to provide adequate connection, because of mothers' self-preoccupation and adjustment problems. My concern is that these assumptions are generally implicit and pose a hidden bias in the divorce literature whereby acceptable parental behavior is narrowly defined as well as what constitutes a "balanced" connection. For example, in Hines' (1997) review of divorce-related transitions and adolescent development she states: "If family life is stable, economic distress is minimized, relationships are supportive and intimate, affection and love are offered and reciprocated, then development can proceed along a *normal* and *unstressful* [italics added] path (p. 379)." After stating this, Hines documents the negative outcomes for adolescents associated with parental divorce in terms of mothers' financial instability, diminished parenting skills, and permissive fathering based on well worn research typically done on samples of younger children. Studies generally fail to consider the diverse and fluid nature of parent-child bonds, the *meanings* older children might attach to these changes, and how this might relate to individuation.

The purpose of this study was twofold. First, I wanted to examine, in greater depth, qualitative aspects of mother-child relationships, and consider the strengths in these relationships as they might emerge from young adult children's narratives. The data were thick with descriptions of reasons for close mother-child relationships, as well as how developmental status might contribute to conflict or closeness with mothers. A central theme in the data consisted of offsprings' accounts of boundary shifts and role behavior with their mothers. These issues are examined and explored in terms of how these phenomena were appraised by older children, and whether their recollections seemed to "fit" the clinical literature briefly summarized in the previous paragraphs.

A second purpose of the study was to give voice to young adult children's descriptions and recollections. Increasingly, scholars are becoming aware of the importance of children's perspectives and their construction of reality as significant predictors of well-being during the divorce process and beyond (Wenk, Hardesty, Morgan, & Blair, 1994). Kurdek (1993) also emphasizes this point, in commenting on the need for incorporating a developmental perspective when studying children and divorce, and reasons that often the *appraisal* of life events is more important than their mere occurrence. I proceeded on the assumption that it was worthwhile to hear directly from children (Stewart, Copeland, Chester, Malley, & Barenbaum, 1997), and consistent with a qualitative approach (Creswell, 1994), to explore young adults' subjective reality of their past and current experiences.

METHOD

Sample and Design

This study was based on data drawn from interviews conducted with 58 college students from a large mid-Atlantic state university whose parents had divorced before the time of the interview. The reader is also referred to Arditti and Prouty (1999) which was based on interview data pertaining to fathers. Purposive sampling techniques were used and the research team posted announcements throughout the university and made announcements in specific classes. A relatively equal balance of male and female participants was obtained.

Based on the 58 students participating in the larger project, the average participant in the study was 21 years old, single, and White. The age reported at the time of parental divorce ranged from 1 to 24 years with an average age of approximately 9.5 years (*SD,* 5.7 years). Thirty-two percent of the sample was male (*n* = 18) and 67% was female (*n* = 37). Twenty-nine percent of the study participants reported that their mothers had remarried; 60% reported that their fathers had remarried. The average length of time young adults in the study reported living in a single parent household was seven years (*SD,* 5.5 years). Unfortunately, demographic data was unavailable for 3 participants (indicated by an asterisk "*" in the results section).

I utilized a within-group design, similar to methodology employed by Stewart et al. (1997). I was not interested in assessing the causal impact of parental divorce on mother-child relationships. Rather, I was interested in understanding something about what parental divorce might mean in the context of mother-child relationships. While a comparative design would have allowed me to explore differences in mother-child relationships between families with and without divorces, as Stewart et al. (1997) so eloquently point out, and I affirm, "making the comparison would require the assumption that parental divorce was the only or crucial difference between the two groups (p. 31)." However, findings are considered within the larger context of parent-adolescent relationships and developmental influences. In-depth interviews were conducted with young adults from divorced homes to provide rich description for understanding the meanings of events from the participants' perspectives (Bogdan & Bilken, 1998; Snyder, 1992). Consistent with a qualitative paradigm, the interview gathered descriptive data in the participants' own words in order for me to gain insight into how young adults' interpreted various aspects of their family life (Bogdan & Bilken, 1998). My concern was not whether young adults' descriptions about their family relationships were factually accurate, but rather to elucidate the matrix of meanings associated with "thick description" (Gilgun, 1992a). Such an approach gives way to findings which are multilayered and is compatible with the coding scheme utilized in the present study. The interview questions were open-ended and designed to encourage students to discuss their relationships with their parents, their memories of their parents' divorce, and how they believed the divorce had affected their family relationships. Similar to the process detailed by Marshall and Rossman (1995), certain objectives and theoretical concepts were identified, which then guided the questions asked and the content analysis of the study. Strengths, changes, and problems of mother-child relationships were the foci of this particular article.

Coding and Interpretation

The data coding process developed over time and reflected a series of modifications based on repeated readings of the data and discussions with the research team. The team consisted of the primary researcher and three doctoral students in Family Studies and Marriage and Family Therapy who were responsible for coding the data. The team met periodically to discuss any modifications or concerns that emerged with regard to the codes utilized to organize the interview data. This approach to coding is consistent with qualitative methodology described by Strauss and Corbin (1990) and Gilgun (1992a) whereby codes are developed through knowledge of previous theory and research as well as by hypotheses developed during the process of data analysis.

Codes were developed, and interview data was analyzed using a software package, NUD*IST. NUD*IST stands for Non-numerical Unstructured Data Indexing Searching and Theorizing (Richards & Richards, 1994). Nudist provides a tree diagram format in which categories, termed as "nodes," can be developed and coded in relation to one another on hierarchical levels. Diagrammatically, these nodes are depicted in the tree as parent/child hierarchies. The use of these diagrams, along with on-line definitional and memo data, represented the initial step of theory-building and allowed for the exploration of interrelationships among various nodes (Weitzman & Miles, 1995). The coding scheme was modified throughout the research process to reflect nuances in the data and meanings that the initial tree diagram might not have reflected. The portion of the tree pertaining to strengths, problems, and changes in mother-child relationships was the basis for the content analysis of this study. After all of the interviews were collected, I then extracted text reports from these coding areas, and read the reports several times. Summary concepts were written in the margin of the text reports. These summary concepts, meant as a form of researcher shorthand, were used to summarize the participants' stories and their context. Within these reports, clear themes emerged supported by the participants. These themes provide the basis of the areas discussed in the present article: co-residence and closeness, mothers as sources of support, mothers as best friends, and developmental issues.

Confirmability

The construct of "confirmability" was utilized as the central methodological criteria to guide this study. Lincoln and Guba (1985) propose the construct of "confirmability" as an important methodological standard to evaluate qualitative research. Confirmability involves a blend of issues related to reliability and validity, and encompasses whether the findings of a study can be confirmed by another, as well as the connection between the data and the interpretations of the researcher. Hence, the concept of confirmability captures a range of issues relating to the consistency and repeatability of findings (Gilgun, 1992b); and how well the data is linked to the categories of prior theory (Miles & Huber-

man, 1993). The consistency of judgments concerning categorizations was determined by comparing results of observers working independently on the same materials (see for example Harbert, Vinick, & Ekerdt, 1992). All of the interviews were coded independently by at least two doctoral students. A "hit ratio" was calculated by determining the agreement between two observers on a block of text. A "hit" was defined as two observers coding a block of text with *exactly* the same code, hence our estimates are purposely conservative. The percentage of exact hits was 81.5% between Observer 1 and Observer 2 and 68.4% between Observer 1 and Observer 3. Overall, the hit ratio was 74.7% between two observers on at least one code for each block of text.

In addition to the hit ratio described above, the coding scheme and subsequent themes that emerged demonstrated confirmability in other ways. First, the coding scheme and thematic interpretations were informed by prior research and theory, and several readings of the data by the principal researcher. In addition, confirmability was further reflected by the convergence of major coding categories and themes defined by a separate content analysis conducted on a subsample of 21 interviews and the codes and themes independently developed and defined by the text of all 58 interviews for the present study. Ruble (1998) found in an independent analysis of the subsample that mother-child relationships were characterized by closeness and warmth.

RESULTS

Co-Residence and Closeness

There is some evidence to suggest that the nature of children's relationships with their mothers is different than with their fathers after divorce (Arditti, 1995). Aquilino (1994) notes the importance of residence in determining positive parent-child relationships for mothers and fathers after divorce. Amato and Booth (1996) also observed that divorce appeared to have a unique influence on lessening fathers' affection for their children, but not necessarily lessening mothers' affection for their children. They believe this is largely due to the fact that children usually reside with their mothers after divorce. Stories from young adults in this study confirm that living with one's parent provides an important context for closeness, availability, communication, and support.

For example:

...I think I was very close to her (before the divorce). Now I'm very close to her. She's one of my best friends. I tell her everything. I think it strengthened over the years, but that's because I lived with her. [female Family & Child Development freshman, 7 years old when parents divorced]

In response to how the divorce might have changed her relationship with her mother, this young woman's response reflected the continuity co-residence provides, "Basically the same as it is now. I live with my mom, so we've always been pretty tight." [20-year-old FCD major, one year old at the time of parental divorce]. Similarly, this male, also very young when his parents' divorced, connected living with his mother with their solid relationship:

I'm not real sure what it was like before the divorce because it was so long ago, but it's a very good relationship now. I live with her. I've lived with her ever since the divorce. I have a pretty solid relationship with my mom. We talk about a lot of stuff. There's not too much we don't talk about. [20-year-old Math major, 5 years old when parents divorced]

Co-residence, while creating closeness, was also a context for conflict. A male 21-year-old computer science student explained:

Close, I mean we live with each other. It's a little bit hard because she's out of work right now due to an injury so she's always at home when I'm home it's kind of conflicting. But we're closer than we have been in a long time. [8 years old at the time of parents' divorce]

This young woman recounted a similar experience:

I guess when my parents got divorced I was little, so I was close with my mom, and I'm still close with my mom now, but once I'm older I think I get a little more conflictual with her. But I'm real close with my mom. If anything maybe I just got closer to her after the divorce because I lived with her. [20-year-old FCD major, parents divorced when she was 8 years old]

As with fathers, geographical distance and non-residence seemed to constrain relationships between young adult children and their mothers. One young woman discussed what led up to her current separation from her mother, and how she believed it had impacted their relationship:

...I guess it (the relationship) was good before the divorce. Now, we were really, really close until like my sophomore year in high school because I was living with her and I lived with my grandmother.... She (my mother) decided to go to South America. She got sick of the nine-to-five work week here. She thought

that she couldn't spend enough time with me and she wanted to go. Supposedly our trip to South America was going to be for the summer, but she decided to stay and I hated it. We sort of separated even though we were really close up until my sophomore year. Now she lives in South America; I write to her, I talk to her, but it still isn't the same as it was before. I know it's because of the distance. [*]

This student was 5 years old when his parents divorced, and lived with his grandparents afterward:

Before the divorce, I was her baby and she took me everywhere. Although she worked and would leave me with a baby-sitter, she cared a lot about me. It's probably been eight or nine years since I've talked to her. I live with my grandparents. I moved in with my grandparents right after my parents separated. So I've lived there since I was five or six years old. [19-year-old Engineering major]

For this young man, not living with his mother after divorce for most of his life, appeared to be connected to the present disengagement between them. It is interesting to note how the young man above attributed meaning to the memory of his mother taking him "everywhere."... He interpreted the time she spent with him as evidence of her caring. The divorce necessitated a shift in residence and primary caregivers which appeared to contribute to the distance in his relationship with his mother.

Another young woman who lived with her father after divorce discussed the emotional distance between her and her mother:

Well she was my primary caregiver before the divorce, and now I'm not very close to her at all because my father raised us, my sister and I. I see my mom once every two months maybe, and she lives ten minutes away which is not a lot considering how close we had lived together. [Finance major, 1 year old when parents divorced]

It is unclear how this non-normative arrangement might be interpreted by children. Students were not explicit in equating non-residence with lack of effort and caring on the part of the mother, but it seemed to be implied by some of the comments. Not sharing a residence seemed to create emotional distance between children and mothers, unless they spent substantial time with each other. Children who were very young at the time of parental divorce, or experienced a shift in residence at an early age and had less time to establish a strong relationship with their mothers, were particularly vulnerable. To a certain extent, spending time with the non-residential parent seemed to ameliorate the impact of non-residence as reflected by the following account:

Well, for three years she lived in New Mexico and she just moved back. I saw her every summer...that she has been there. I would say it's good. I can talk to her about anything. I never had the sort of classical relationship that you see with a lot of people where the mother and daughter don't get along. I've never really fought with my mother and I don't know if that's a good thing or a bad thing...But I live with my father and I grew up with my father. So I would see my mom at least once a week...when I was in grad school it was during the week, and as I got older it was on the weekends. Usually on Sundays we would go to brunch and we'd go shopping or something. Sometimes we did real serious things, but we always spent time together. Just because we were shopping, you know doing something sort of frivolous, doesn't mean that we weren't like bonding. [24-year-old Biology major, 8 years old at the time of parental divorce]

For this student, consistent involvement and frequent visitation with her nonresidential mother enabled them to create and maintain close relations. This young woman's account supported the literature that already defined both of these factors—consistency and frequency—as important elements of nonresidential fathers' involvement (Arditti, 1995). Although residence was not synonymous with involvement, non-residential parents of either gender, appeared to be more challenged in terms of having frequent opportunity to display caring and support.

Mothers as Sources of Support/Availability

Many young adults discussed aspects of their mothers involvement before the divorce and beyond. For some young adults, mothers were seen as an important source of support. This was also connected with her perceived availability. These seemed to be essential elements of caregiving acknowledged by the participants in this study, and formed the basis of what many believed to be a "good mother." It is important to note that as discussed in the previous section, co-residence provided a context for closeness, and this could largely be because of the greater opportunities parents, who lived with their children, had to be available to their children and to provide support.

A female psychology student, who was 11 when her parents divorced, described the conti-

nuity of her mother's availability in terms of her "being there," both before and after the divorce:

Before she was always there for us. She was someone you could go to, you didn't have to hide anything from her. She was just always there for you and she's the same way now. She's really easy to get along with. You can talk to her about anything. I have a really good relationship with her.

The following two students described their relationships with their mothers before the divorce, emphasizing the importance of the time mothers spent with them and mothers' diverse involvement in various aspects of their lives:

[the relationship with my mother is] Great. She encouraged us to do things, get involved in sports. School was always important. She worked a lot of the time, but she tried to involve herself in a lot of our activities and things like that. She always tried to make herself available to us. So that was a good relationship. [22-year-old male FCD major, whose parents divorced when he entered college]

It was pretty close. My mother, she always took a lot of time with me and my two brothers. She basically just supported us in everything. Like took us to the park and everything. So she was basically doing everything before the divorce. [female Housing/Interior Design student, 14 years old at the time of parental divorce]

Unlike with fathers (see Arditti & Prouty, 1999), divorce did not dramatically alter perceptions of mothers' involvement, probably due in part to mothers' usually maintaining their role as primary caregiver. Student 1 continued, explaining his role in soliciting his mothers' involvement and expressing his feelings toward her:

> It's still like that [i.e. close] pretty much. I think as she's getting older and we're getting older…I still try to make an effort to let her know that there are still some things that she can do for me, *that I still love her, and that she's still a very big influence."* [emphasis added]

Student 2 also noted her mother's continuing involvement, after divorce and since she left for college:

> …She's basically the primary caregiver. She takes care of us, she supports us financially. If we need money, she gives it to us. If we need support, like her coming to one of our racquetball games or to borrow the car or something, she's always available.

Listening and providing guidance to children seemed to be a valued aspect of mother-child relations. This young man explained:

> …talk to my mom about them (relationships) a lot. Like if I'm having problems or whatever understanding things or something, and I'll explain to her what's going on and she'll help me out. [Management student, 2 years old when parents divorced]

Another son described a close relationship with his mother, emphasizing how much he appreciated her attitude and mentoring:

> Its (the relationship with my mother) is really, really good. Really good. I can tell her anything. I talk to her about everything. It's my first year here and I've gone through a lot of changes this year ever since high school and I've been able to talk to her and she's been great. Always positive…. She always taught us to …learn from my mistakes. I made a lot of mistakes in high school, and in my first year, but she's really taught me how to turn them around and not make them again and stuff like that. She's always really positive. [male English major, 5 years old at the time of parents' divorce]

The descriptions of mothers' behavior in this study highlight parenting strengths from children's perspectives. Little is known regarding divorced mothers' parenting practices, especially positive parental behaviors. When positive parenting behaviors have been identified, such as single mothers' talking to or reading to their children, they are framed in comparison to married mothers and based on quantitative analyses seeking to expose "differences" between families (Acock & Demo, 1994; McLanahan & Sandefur, 1994). Assumptions are then made regarding what mothers might be talking to their children about, even given an absence of descriptive data concerning what is actually being discussed between mothers and children. McLanahan & Sandefur (1994) assume more talking on the part of single mothers and their children is due to the confidante role *children* may take on after divorce. While I explore this issue in greater depth in the next section, the findings presented here give some insight regarding this issue. Mothers' supportive parenting practices, such as listening and providing guidance and advice may also account for high levels of communication with their children.

She's My Best Friend...

Mother-child relationships were generally discussed as close, and daughters seemed particularly apt to describe their mothers as their "best friend." Students varied in terms of whether the best friend status was arrived at due to their own maturity, or resulted from the divorce itself. Interestingly, such a description was rarely found in the data on fathers (Arditti & Prouty, 1999). For example: "Since then (the divorce) my mom and I have developed a lot. She's my best friend now" (21½-year-old female Family & Child Development major, age 2 at time of parents' divorce). "Before the divorce, when I was little, I remember I didn't like her. I don't know...I just didn't. Now my mom, we're more like really good friends. We have a pretty good relationship" (female Biology major, age 3 at time of divorce).

Given the young age of these two students at the time of their parents' divorce, it is uncertain how accurately they were able to recollect the pre-divorce time period. Other students who were in early adolescence at the time of their parents' divorce also referred to their mothers as their best friends:

> Being the only child I guess I had a really good relationship with both my parents. I would sit and watch my mom cook and do stuff like that with her a lot. Now of course it's a more mature relationship. My mom is probably one of my best friends. I live with my mom. So when I go home I stay with her. We have a very good relationship. [female Psychology major, 12 years old when parents divorced]

"...We're like friends; very close friends. I tell my mother everything and she tells me a lot. It's good," (Psychology major, 14 years old when parents divorced).

Although all of these students discussed their relationship with their mothers as a friendship, it was difficult to determine the exact processes that resulted in this friendship status. On the one hand, it was possible that the parental role shifts and the additional responsibilities that children take on after divorce may have contributed to these more egalitarian friendship roles. On the other hand, this status may have developed as a result of the young women reaching young adulthood—a time period that is often accompanied by increased autonomy and maturity. Regardless of the processes that lead to a friendship status, one of the most prevalent demonstrations of the friendship quality of these relationships was the level of self-disclosure that occurred between mothers and daughters.

Friendship status sometimes implied an evolution from caregiving or "mothering" activities to "friendship" activities like communicating and/or doing enjoyable things together. These changes were intertwined with students' growing maturity. For example, "It's more like we're friends. It's not really like she's my mother. She takes me out with her friends, and buys me beer, and wants me to go out with them so I'm not at home alone" (male Biology major, age 10 when parents divorced).

This young woman's response highlighted her active role in discouraging mothers' caregiving efforts and facilitating the shift to "friend":

> After the divorce it changed. She was continuing the role as caregiver, but I was a lot less receptive. But after several years and some major changes, now we're really good friends. She still is like a caregiver, but it's more on

a friend level. [Family & Child Development major, 7 years old when parents divorced]

It seemed that for young adults, caregiving implied a certain level of controlling behavior by the mother, and that friendship was equated with either fewer attempts by mothers to control them or to tell them what to do—or children's active resistance to these attempts. For example, similar to "best friend" status, this young woman described why her relationship with her mother felt like they were "sisters":

Now it's like we're sisters. That's how it (the relationship) changed when they got divorced. We started growing up together. It's like she had to start growing up all over again. Since then, it's just like we're sisters, and it makes it kind of tough when there's conflict because I don't hesitate to talk back to her which you shouldn't do with your mother. It's so different. [20-year-old student, age 6 at the time of her parent's divorce]

The above example reflects meanings about renewal and rebirth as a result of divorce. For this young woman, divorce signaled the beginning of something different with her mother.

Role shifts. Many students attributed the shift from "mother" to "best friend" to mothers' role shifts, necessitated from the divorce, and mothers' subsequent withdrawal of caregiving activities. It was not entirely clear what the implications were for children with regard to the likelihood that they may have greater independence and responsibility for household chores in single mother homes. The discourse around these issues has been predominantly negative. (See for example Wallerstein & Blakeslee's,

1989 description of the "overburdened child.") Yet in a report on single heads of households by Shore (cited in Kissman & Allen, 1993), one of the family strengths identified in this study was increased independence for parent and child. The data in this study suggested mothers' role shifts provided both benefits and difficulties for children:

Before the divorce she was more like a mother. She would take the role as a stereotypical mother like cooking and taking care of things that needed to be taken care of like signing a form for school. Now I view her as more independent—as a friend. Sometimes that's frustrating because I want someone to like cook dinner when I come home, but she doesn't. I view her more as a friend…. And I can see the weaknesses in her now, whereas before she was more like a stereotypical parent. [Psychology major, age 13 when her parents divorced]

Her perceptions around her mother's independence, a strength, as well as her vulnerabilities, have contributed to her viewing her mother as a friend.

The following woman describes changes related to her mother's return to work and her emerging understanding about the implications of the role shift:

Before my mom was like staying home completely for me and my brother, so I guess I was pretty close. She was pretty much the household mother. But when the divorce happened, she went back to work and we didn't see her as much. But we were still pretty close. Now, we're

very close. She's got to work and spends the majority of her time doing that, but now I understand it *[emphasis added]. [Family & Child Development major, 7 years old when parents divorced]*

In general, the young adults in this study expressed respect for the additional responsibilities that their mothers took on after the divorce. The role shifts that may have occurred in the post divorce time period appear to be associated with positive outcomes. In addition to facilitating the development of autonomy in the child, these role shifts also resulted in an increased respect and understanding for the mother that seemed connected to close mother-child relationships.

Emerging equality and disclosure. For some adult offspring, the evolution of friendship with mothers was marked by an emerging sense of equality. One indicator of this new equality for several students had to do with their sense of being "needed" or leaned on by their mothers for emotional support or to act as confidants. As discussed earlier in this article, the literature often discusses these phenomena in terms of generational blurring, and links such boundary ambiguity to negative psychological outcomes for children. In contrast, data from the present study revealed children's positive interpretations of their provision of support as well as their sharing intimate disclosures:

I was always close to my mom. My mother relied on me a lot, and I was almost designated as the other adult in the family. So my mother and I became close, as far as I was concerned, and we relied on each other a lot for different types of support. [22-year-old student, age 7 at the time of divorce]

This young man believed his acting as a confidante for his mother has in part created a stronger relationship since the divorce:

My relationship with my mother has always been really good. She's always been a confidante for me. I could always talk to her about things. And it really hasn't changed since the divorce. If anything, it's like strengthened our relationships because she's needed someone to lean on.... Our relationship's really good because she talks to me about the things she's going through now. [21-year-old Biochemistry major, parents divorced one year ago]

Other young adults described similar changes:

My relationship with my mother was just mediocre (before the divorce). After the divorce, things have changed in the sense that there's much more equality between the two of us. Before, it was always me crying on my mom's shoulder, and now it's me crying on my mom's shoulder and my mom cries on my shoulder. [female Psychology major, 17 years old when parents divorced]

The content of disclosures between mothers and children seemed to vary. Participants were vague regarding what kinds of things they discussed with their mothers—possibly because of the open ended nature of the interview questions (they were not specifically asked about what they talked about with either parent). Students mentioned talking to their mothers about "stuff," "things," "anything," and "everything." Of particular interest is what might be defined as "off limits." For example one young African-American woman said: "We were close. We talked a lot about girlfriends, school, and just about anything else. The only difference now (after divorce) is that I kind of like to stay away from a father subject," (22½-year-old FCD major, 19 years old when parents divorced).

On the other hand, another participant seemed not to mind discussing her father with her mother, "She was my best friend. I would go and talk to her about anything. She confided in me a lot about my dad, and a lot about their relationship," (*). The following woman echoed a similar sentiment. She interpreted her mother's sharing about her father as a sign of closeness, "So THAT'S how close we were; she would actually tell me about that...she talked to me a lot about her problems with my dad. So we were really, really close before the divorce," (Family & Child Development major, age 15 at the time of parents' divorce).

From the above examples, it seemed that young adults were not uniformly comfortable discussing their fathers, and varied in terms of how they interpreted the sharing of these confidences with mothers. The literature provides ample evidence that loyalty conflicts and triangulation negatively impacts children's well-being (Emery, 1994). Discussed in greater detail elsewhere (see Arditti & Prouty, 1999) there was also evidence from this group of participants that undermining fathers actually diminished mother-child relationships. It could be that avoiding discussion and sharing around one's father is a boundary some young adults created in order to prevent or minimize loyalty conflicts. While I found little in terms of mothers' sharing inappropriate details of their lives with their children (like for example their sex lives), it would seem that the content of disclosures between mother and offspring would have bearing on how "best friend" status was experienced, and that this may be a more idiosyncratic phenomena than previously believed.

Divorce then, became a context of change and led to closer relationships for some mothers and children. Mothers' need for emotional support and the sharing of confidences with children gave children a sense of equality which was generally interpreted positively. This runs counter to clinical/researcher interpretations which focus on mothers leaning on children as *burdensome,* rather than a path to closeness. However, these results are unclear on how the child's age at the time of the divorce, as well as the content of disclosures, may mediate the degree of burden that is experienced. For example, it is possible that younger children, who cannot yet draw clear boundaries, may have a more difficult time coping with maternal expectations of emotional support, or defining certain uncomfortable topics (such as the other parent) as "off limits."

Developmental Issues

Adolescence and maturity were salient for many young adults as they described relationship changes with their mothers. This was also the case for offspring with their fathers (Arditti & Prouty, 1999). Indeed, the literature contains much material describing conflicts between adolescents and their parents rooted in the dualism inherent in parenting during this time. Parents may be trying to encourage autonomy and control their children at the same time (Guttman, 1993). For some young adults, adolescence was associated with fighting and conflict with mothers. This student who was 6 years old when his parents divorced explained:

When I got older after the divorce, especially in high school, I lived with my mom, and there was a lot of tension. Like right before I left for college, we had a couple of pretty nasty fights, like big yelling matches. [He goes on to discuss his interpretation of the conflict between them and de-

scribed the relationship as "better now" since he has left for college.] I think a lot of it had to do with me leaving the house and my mom being by herself. And at the same time I wanted to do my own thing. I was trying to be independent, and I wasn't telling her what I was doing or where I was going. [male Engineering major]

This young woman, who seemed to still have difficulties with her mother, saw her parents' divorce as having little to do with their fighting:

…When I was in high school, all we did was fight. Now that I'm here, I talk to her once a week, but I don't have much to say…It (the divorce) didn't really change it. We fought a lot. We probably fought more after the divorce, but it was probably also because I was a teenager then. [Animal Science major, 9 years old when parents divorced]

One young man commented on how adolescence was a time of emotional distance between him and his mother:

It's hard to compare the relationship when I was eight to now in relations to the divorce. Because when I was fifteen or sixteen I kind of went apart from my mother, you know that sort of thing happens, and I still sort of am because that whole thing happens. And now I'm starting to get kind of closer again as I get older, but in terms of the divorce it really didn't make a whole lot of difference. [Biology student, 8 years old when parents divorced]

For some participants, their developing maturity gave way to growing understanding, empathy, and appreciation for their mothers. This could also be linked to Phares and Renk's (1998) finding that while younger adolescents did not appear to feel differently about their mother and their father, *older* adolescents (similar in age to this sample) appeared to have more positive feelings, and less negative feelings toward their mother than their fathers. Indeed, with a few exceptions, relationships with mothers were described in positive terms. For example:

So it's like, my relationship with my mother now is great. I mean it's like I understand, I came to understand like what she was going through and all that…so now, we get along great, we have a great understanding. [21-year-old female FCD major, 3 years old at the time of divorce]

When I was younger I was closer to my dad. But now I think especially at this age, I'm closer to my mom because I'm realizing a lot more things that she's gone through. There were three children, and she had to take us all on. I just see things better from her point of view now, so we've gotten a lot closer. [female undergraduate, 7 years old when parents divorced].

This female undergraduate, whose parents divorced when she was in high school, extended her understanding to equate the "clashing," with caring involvement from her mother, "It (the relationship) was clashing. We fought about everything like most teenage girls do from what I understand. I guess underneath it all I realized she cared."

It is important to acknowledge that children's developmental changes influence relationships with parents, making it difficult to isolate the impact divorce has on mother-child relationships. It is also unclear as to whether retrospective interviews distort or crystallize experience. Fortunately, it is not my goal to draw causal conclusions concerning the role of divorce, but rather to *describe* the nature of mother-child relationships in the context of parental divorce. Perhaps given the greater likelihood of co-residence with mothers after divorce, issues of control and conflict during adolescence and subsequent "drops" in closeness as described by Stevenson and Black (1995) are even more central to mother-child relationships (than with fathers) during early adolescence. In later adolescence, leaving home affords children the opportunity to distance from mothers' efforts to control, subsequently improving relationships. Children's growing maturity also facilitates empathy and understanding on the part of offspring, giving way to better quality relationships with their mothers. This interpretation is consistent with a developmental framework which suggests that feelings toward parents are related to cognition (Baldwin, 1992; Phares & Renk, 1998). This data also provides qualitative support for evidence that greater levels of maternal control is inversely correlated with negative affect (see also Phares & Renk, 1998).

DISCUSSION

The findings in this article highlight the benefits of maternal proximity, involvement, and support for young adults. Indeed, recent research indicates that parental support is multifaceted in nature and contributes to life satisfaction and well-being for children and young adults (Young, Miller, Norton, & Hill, 1995). Similarly, Phares and Renk (1998) note that more positive feelings toward parents, especially mothers, were associated with better psychological functioning for adolescents. It is encouraging to discover that within the context of parental divorce, young

adults felt close to their mothers, and acknowledged and appreciated aspects of their mothers' involvement and support (i.e. time spent, money spent, listening, providing support). The findings confirmed Wallerstein and Blakeslee's (1989) descriptions from adolescent children about relations with custodial mothers. They found that mother-child relationships were marked by closeness, appreciation for all she had done, and concern for their mothers' well-being. As with fathers, co-residence seems to provide an important context to provide support and be involved with one's children, even though nonresidence did not inevitably lead to disengaged relations as evidenced by one student who described a vital, close relationship with her nonresidential mother. Indeed, there has been speculation that nonresidence is less of a factor in determining closeness for mother-child relationships than for fathers. That is, noncustodial mothers are more likely to maintain contact and close relations than are noncustodial fathers (Arditti & Madden-Derdich, 1993).

It is interesting to note that the data were most "dense" with respect to strengths with mothers and problems with fathers, supporting research which finds children's relationships with mothers to be closer than those with fathers after divorce (Duran-Aydintug, 1997). Problems that were discussed concerning mothers included three students describing personality conflicts with their mothers (including one who said her mother "gave too much advice" and one who did not live with or really know her mother), one who reported an interfering stepfather, and one whose mother abused alcohol. Differences in parental relationships after divorce could largely be due to fathers' typical nonresidential status and mobility, and there was evidence that children who lived with their fathers reported very close and satisfactory relationships. Qualitative differences between mothers and fathers relationships with their children might also be, in part, due to a greater prevalence of reported "problem behavior" on the part of fathers (see Arditti & Prouty, 1999, for a detailed exploration of father-child relationships).

Role Shifts and Boundary Issues

Young adults appeared to have diverse relationships with mothers. Yet, they were predominantly described as close and satisfying. Mothers were viewed as friends, and their withdrawal from perceived efforts to control was generally welcomed. Sometimes, mothers relied on children for emotional support or advice. As noted earlier in this paper, such behavior has largely been pathologized in the literature and seen as "inappropriate." In contrast, these data suggest that mothers leaning on children for emotional support contributed to a sense of equality, being needed, closeness, shared disclosures, and friend status. These qualities appeared to be valued by the young adults in this study.

Weiss (1979, 1980, cited in Guttman, 1993) offers an alternative paradigm for understanding these changes. He noted that divorce, and the leaving of the other parent, tends to decrease the social distance between mothers and their children. Thus, boundaries between mothers and their children are characterized by an openness that is qualitatively different than in two parent households. According to Weiss, the authority structure in a two-parent household is based on the implicit coalition of two adults who are in a hierarchically more powerful position than the children. In single parent families, this hierarchy may disappear and children are "promoted." Hence, mothers may relinquish some decision-making control and relate to their children as if they were "junior partners." Although we do not have specific information on decision-making processes from participants, our data support what Stewart et al. (1997) explain as the "different" relationship a single mother might have with her children compared to married mothers.

The positive aspects of role shifts have been rarely explored. However, the data in this study confirm Simmel's (cited in Wolff, 1950) hypotheses that the decomposition of the authority structure and group size increases communication and disclosure. Indeed there is some evidence that single mother parent-child relationships are characterized by greater equality, more frequent interaction, more discussion, and greater intimacy and companionship—especially with older children who are more in touch with a parent's emotional state. (Guttman, 1993). Arditti & Madden-Derdich (1995) also confirmed the intimate connection between mothers and children. From mothers' perspectives, children were seen as a source of emotional support and this was an important buffer for dealing with stress—giving mothers a sense of continuity and purpose as they coped with the responsibilities of single parenting. In deconstructing parent-child relationships, the "best friend" status of their mothers described by many young adults in this study emerges. The closeness and intimacy described by young adults in relation to their mothers is an important example of the viability of single-mother households. Guttman emphasizes the need to conceptualize households headed by divorced mothers as a system with its "own authority structure, norms, processes of conflict management and boundary maintenance, patterns of exchange and reciprocity, and decision making rules" (p. 90). Stewart et al. (1997) echo a similar opinion based on the findings of their study. They note that firm role boundaries between mothers and children were not associated with either good or bad outcomes for children. In fact, they were actually associated with *worse* outcomes for mothers. The authors point to the complexity of issues involved in single-parent families' role structure and the importance of flexibility. Intimate disclosure and shared communication between mothers and children are manifestations of flexibility that may be beneficial to divorced households. Indeed, friendship between mothers and children provides evidence of the potential renewal divorce might bring to parenting.

The findings in this study also highlight the role shifts many children experience when their mothers become more involved in breadwinning, and subsequently may withdraw from caregiving or expect their children to be more self-reliant. As with other issues previously discussed, the discourse around these shifts have focused on predominantly detrimental outcomes for children (e.g. Hewlitt, 1991; Thurer, 1994) along with the negative implications of role overload for single mothers (McLanahan & Sandefur, 1994). Mothers' role shifts were also acknowledged in conceptualizing divorce as a "stressor" which leads to inevitable changes, felt as losses, in offsprings' relationships with parents (Stevenson & Black, 1995). Hence, mothers' return to the labor force, or even an intensification of breadwinning activities, would be viewed as a stressor associated with loss for children. While this may be true in certain instances, the data summarized in this study suggested that an alternative understanding may be needed. Young adults tended to see these changes as relatively benign, or, because of increasing maturity, understood the necessity of mothers' role shifts and enjoyed the benefits of greater independence, decision-making, and support provision. Overall, based on the available data for this study, there was a relative absence of reported difficulties associated with mothers' reliance on children.

The findings, while exploratory, lend support to the idea that processes connected to generational boundaries is "emergent" and may shift over time due to situational and developmental forces. Interpretation of how changes in boundary patterns and, roles between parents and children must be grounded in the specific contexts which they occur (i.e. intact family, clinical sample, etc.). For example, conclusions drawn in the clinical literature, regarding the implications of boundary violations and generational alliances, may not be applicable to many single mother households. The results also confirm Fish et al.'s (1991) proposition that constructs such as intergenerational boundaries (and their violation or dissolution) are difficult to operationalize and take many forms within and across age periods. It is important to acknowledge that experience may be reinvented as children mature. Hence it is possible that while mothers' role shifts or increasing emotional reliance on children after divorce might be experienced negatively at one point in time, children's later description may or may not reflect the way it was experienced then, but how it feels to them in the present.

It is also noteworthy that with the exception of one male student, students who provided excerpts relating to mothers as best friends were female, even though approximately 32% of the larger sample was male. It should also be pointed out that men were represented well in other thematic areas such as text describing father-child relationships (see Arditti & Prouty, 1999), along with other aspects of mother-child relationships. Hence, while a clear pattern did not emerge with respect to the implications of the timing of parents' divorce, the implications of children's gender seemed more obvious. Mother-daughter relationships appeared to be particularly close in this sample and daughters tended to attach positive attributions with regard to "best friend status." Indeed, two studies have documented close relationships between divorced mothers and preadolescent daughters, although conflict often ensued in later adolescence (Baumrind, 1991, cited in Hines 1997; Hetherington & Clingempeel, 1992). In addition, this finding was consistent with research indicating that adult children reported closer relationships with mothers than with fathers and that mothers report receiving more emotional support from children than fathers reported (Umberson, 1992). In cases of divorce, mothers were more likely than fathers to continue to exchange both emotional and practical support with their adult children. What remains less clear are the implications of "generational blurring" for mothers and sons. It is unknown from this study whether the dynamics described, overwhelmingly by daughters, were applicable to mother-son relationships. For example, the aforementioned studies documented greater disruption between divorced mothers and their sons (Hines, 1997). Yet, important questions remain unanswered regarding the source of difficulties between mothers and children. Are sons less inclined to act as confidants for their mothers? Are mothers less likely to solicit emotional support from their sons? Are sons less comfortable with mothers' vulnerability and intimate disclosures? Future research needs to explore, in greater depth, the role gender may play in shaping parent-child relationships after divorce, along with how gender may influence children's experience of shifting boundaries with their mothers in single parent households.

Closeness and Autonomy

Adolescence emerged as a time of turbulence for many students highlighting the importance of maturity for shaping parent-child relationships. Although beyond the scope of this paper, a similar theme was apparent when participants in this study discussed relations with their fathers. However, overall, mother-child relationships appeared to be characterized by more closeness and satisfaction than relationships with fathers, despite greater opportunities for conflict. Closeness between divorced mothers and their children has important implications with respect to the development of autonomy and progress toward individuality. An emergent view is that healthy adolescent autonomy is compatible with continued connection, rather

than at the *expense* of closeness with parents. Theorists contend that mothers and fathers of teenagers must engage in a gradual process of renegotiation of boundaries that originates in childhood and accelerates during adolescence and is rooted in connectedness (see Peterson, Bodman, Bush, & Madden-Derdich, in press, for a full review). As discussed in the previous section, it is possible that divorced mothers, because of role shifts and emotional demands, may be particularly equipped to facilitate a "letting go" during adolescence and young adulthood that is valued and experienced positively by their children. Single mothers are very *salient* to children (Arditti & Bickley, 1996). This is a potentially hidden strength in divorced households to the extent mothers are able to maintain close ties with children. The data provide evidence of mothers' availability, support, and mutual disclosure—all of which contribute to a solid foundation for the development of autonomy.

Implications for Practitioners: Capitalizing on Family Strengths

The findings of this study have important implications for family practitioners working with single-parent families and households experiencing parental divorce. Single-parent family structures are distinctly different from two-parent structures in that generally all of the responsibility for both the instrumental and emotional tasks of the family fall onto one adult. Despite this fact, single-parent families continue to be normed against two parent families at the broader societal level leading to negative attitudes about this family form. Kissman & Allen (1993) have expressed concern that negative societal expectations regarding single-mother families may bias practitioners' views regarding what constitutes normal and viable family systems. Such a bias is likely to interfere with the efficacy of intervention and to limit treatment options. Specifically, Kissman & Allen suggest that practitioners shift away from pathology and negative labeling and move toward a more holistic, problem-solving framework that helps to identify the needs that are relevant to carrying out the goals of the family.

Such a shift would require family practitioners, educators, and researchers to begin to recognize and to acknowledge the diversity of single-parent families, including their unique strengths. A strength-based approach promotes positive family functioning by first identifying family strengths and capabilities and then building interventions on what a family already does well. Family strengths become building blocks for the family to become even stronger and more capable of supporting individual and family well-being (Judge, 1998). Close mother-child relationships can be viewed as a critical building block for positive family functioning in several dimensions and serve as an important protective function. Indeed, Bogenschneider (1996) identifies that a close relationship with at least one person and the bonding to family are important protective factors for youth development. In contrast, distant, uninvolved parenting tends to be associated with ecological risk. Many young adults in this study seemed to have had the benefit of at least one involved parent, who was seen as supportive and accessible.

Furthermore, as pointed out earlier, connected parent-child relationships, along with the ability to relinquish authority over time has the potential to provide a strong foundation for the development of autonomy during adolescence. Supportive parental behavior that fosters autonomy includes encouragement, acceptance, and empathy (Peterson et al., in press). Family therapists might seek to emphasize the importance of these behaviors by mothers. The data suggest that mothers are available to their children and are already doing many things "right." In the face of other kinds of difficulties, such as economic hardship, role strain, family conflict, or perhaps even

non-residence, practitioners can emphasize strengths existing between mothers and their children; providing encouragement to their clients as they work on other possible problems.

The results of the current study also suggest other areas in which family strengths can be identified by practitioners and educators. Mutual self-disclosure may be a strength for mothers and their children. It does not appear, from the interview data, that mothers' reliance on children for emotional support or advice, precludes mothers from engaging in more traditional parenting behaviors such as providing guidance. Perhaps mutual self-disclosure allows divorced mothers to capitalize on opportunities, not only to be heard themselves, but to engage their children in discussion and listen to their concerns. Given these possibilities, practitioners working with divorced mothers may need to begin to distinguish more carefully between various types of boundary violations. Refining concepts related to boundary violation in single-mother families in a way that does not confine family members to a certain range of experiences appears to be particularly important. For example, it may be that while triangulating children into conflictual relationships with a former spouse may have detrimental effects, some forms of mutual disclosure about a former spouse may be acceptable. Similarly, increased household responsibilities. and expecting an increased level of independence in self-care may be associated with strength and resiliency as young adults. Rather than implementing structural interventions that have been developed for two-parent families, therapists need to hold a more flexible view of boundary issues.

Adopting a more holistic framework however, does not preclude careful consideration of developmental issues. Although the young adults in this research reported positive experiences with their mothers as "best friends," it is important for family practitioners to consider the developmental state of the participants in the study. It is unknown from this study how support and greater self-reliance might be experienced and explained by younger children. Furthermore, the young adult years are associated with an increased desire for individuation and independence, yet, developing a set of beliefs, values, and convictions that are separate from one's family of origin is often a struggle. In the course of this individuation process, many young adults demonstrate a staunch loyalty to family practices and beliefs. Consequently, some denial may exist surrounding unhealthy family interaction patterns and, I do not conclude from the results of this study, that the "best friend" status of mothers is inevitably in the children's best interests.

In summary, the findings of this study contribute to family practice and scholarship by providing therapists, educators, and researchers with information that affirms the viability and strengths of relationships between divorced mothers and their children. The current findings also point to the need for refining concepts related to boundary violation in single-mother families. Clinical researchers are encouraged to examine their expectations, methodology, and to design studies that seek to capture the experiences of parents and children. If the unique circumstances of single-mother families are not considered during the therapeutic process, interventions might be imposed that ignore important family strengths or protective factors already present in divorced households.

Reading 29   The Social Self as Gendered: A Masculinist Discourse of Divorce

TERRY ARENDELL*

Divorce functions as a prism, making available for examination an array of issues. Pulled into question are the shape and dictates of extra-familial institutions and practices, such as the juridical and economic; and the character of family life, parenting and domestic arrangements. Also brought into view are matters of interpersonal relations and gender identity: it is "unfamiliar situations" which call forth "taken as given identities" and present opportunities to observe the effects of identity upon behavior (Foote 1981, p. 338):

> "Establishment of one's own identity to oneself is as important in interaction as to establish it for the other. One's own identity in a situation is not absolutely given but is more or less problematic" (Foote 1981, p. 337).[1]

Thus investigation of participants' perspectives on and responses to divorce and the postdivorce situation can illumine processes not only of interactional adjustment in the context of change but also of identity maintenance and alteration.

Family and identity transitions are located within a broader sociocultural context: the gender hierarchy and belief system and gender roles are being questioned and altered, although at broadly discrepant rates (Hochschild 1989; Pleck 1985). Specifically, the conventions of masculinity—"those sets of signs indicating that a person is a 'man', or 'not a woman' or 'not a child'" (Hearn 1987, p. 137) and which are "the social reality for men in modern society" (Clatterbaugh 1990, p. 3)—are being challenged (Hearn 1987; Clatterbaugh 1990; Kimmel 1987). Indeed, Kimmel (1987, p. 153) has concluded that contemporary men, like men in other periods characterized by dramatic social and economic change, "confront a crisis in masculinity." Divorce both exemplifies and prompts a crisis in gender identity (Riessman 1990; Vaughan 1986).

Men's perspectives on, actions in, and adjustments to divorce have been relatively neglected in divorce research. Yet they are sig-

This paper is a revision of one presented at the 1991 Gregory Stone Symposium held at the University of California, San Francisco, and the research was funded in part by a PSC-CUNY grant. Appreciation is extended to Joseph P. Marino, Jr., for the many useful and provocative discussions regarding this work; Arlie R. Hochschild for her thoughtful commentary on an earlier draft; and to the anonymous reviewers for their constructive remarks on earlier drafts of the paper.

*Arendell, Terry. 1992. "The Social Self as Gendered: A Masculinist Discourse of Divorce." *Symbolic Interaction* 15(2): 151–181. Copyright 1992 by JAI Press. Reprinted by permission of University of California Press.

nificant for understanding contemporary social arrangements and processes as well as for broadening understanding of men's lives: how men define their situations and act in divorce points to their positions in a gender-structured society and to their understandings of the nature of social practices, relationships, and selves. To paraphrase an argument made with regard to the study of a gendered division of labor in families, the ways in which divorced fathers "use motive talk [Mills 1940] to account for [Scott and Lyman 1968], disclaim [Hewitt and Stokes 1975], and/or neutralize [Sykes and Matza 1957] their behavior or changes in their behavior need to be more fully explored and developed" (Pestello and Voyandoff 1991, p. 117).

METHODOLOGY

Based on data obtained through intensive interviews examining postdivorce situations, experiences, and feelings with a sample 75 divorced fathers (Arendell forthcoming), this paper explores the problem of the social self as gendered, and specifically, the nature of the masculinist self. All participants were volunteers who responded to notices and advertisements placed in newsletters, magazines, and newspapers or to referrals from other participants. The men ranged in age from 23 to 59 years with a median age of 38.5 years. Sixty-four interviewees were white, three were black, four Hispanic, two Asian-American, and two Native American. All respondents were residents of New York State, had one or more minor children, and had been divorced or legally separated for at least 18 months. The median time divorced or separated was 4.8 years. At the time they were interviewed, 18 men were remarried, 5 were living with a woman in a marital-like relationship, and the others were unmarried. Nearly half of the sample had some college education with over one-third having completed college and approx-

imately one-sixth having earned a graduate or professional degree. Occupationally, one-third of the employed respondents worked in blue-collar and two-thirds worked in white-collar positions. Six men were unemployed at the time of the interview, three by choice.

The respondents were fathers to a total of 195 children ranging in age from 2 to 25 with a median age of 9.5 years. The number of children per father ranged from one to six; the mean number of children was 2.6 and the median was 2. Child custody arrangements varied among the men: six fathers had primary physical custody, five had co- or shared physical custody with their former wives, and 64 were noncustodial fathers. Two of those categorized as noncustodial fathers actually had split custody arrangements; each had one child living with him and another two children living with their mothers. A total of eleven fathers were "absent" fathers, meaning that they had no contact with any of their children for at least the past twelve months; another four fathers were "absent" from one or more but not all of their children. The sample over-represents "involved" fathers; for example, only 15 percent were "absent" compared to the national figure of about 50 percent (Furstenberg et al. 1987) and 85 percent were noncustodial parents compared to a national figure of 90 percent (USBC 1989). Additionally, with only a few exceptions, the non-residential fathers repeatedly maintained that they desired increased access to and involvement with their children; many wished for more satisfying relations with their children.

Interviews were open-ended, tended to be long, lasting between two and five hours, and were conducted primarily in 1990 with some occurring in late 1989 and early 1991. Seven respondents participated in follow-up interviews. An interview instrument, initially developed and revised on the basis of 15 earlier interviews in another state, was used as a reference to insure that certain areas were covered during the discussions. All interviews were tape recorded and transcribed. Data were analyzed using the constant comparative method and coding paradigm developed in works on grounded theory (Glaser and Strauss 1967; Strauss 1989).

A MASCULINIST DISCOURSE OF DIVORCE

What the data in this study of divorce provide is a richly descriptive testimony of the men's perspectives on and actions in family and divorce. These divorced fathers, largely irrespective of variations in custody, visitation, marital, or socioeconomic class status, shared a set of dispositions, practices, and explanations with which they managed their identities, situations, and emotional lives. They held in common a body of *gender strategies:* plans of action "through which a person tries to solve problems at hand given the cultural notions of gender at play" and through which an individual reconciles beliefs and feelings with behaviors and circumstances (Hochschild 1989, p. 15). In similar ways, they accounted for past and present actions and described and implied intended future lines of activity, including, significantly, the probable meanings of such movement. The participants shared a *discourse*—particular "matrix of perceptions, appreciations, and actions" (Bourdieu 1987:83). More specifically, they shared a *masculinist discourse of divorce.*

That these men, with their unique personal and family histories, participated in a common divorce discourse points to its complexity. It is not simply an expression of individual men's intentions, pointing to "men we disapprove of and good guys" (Schwenger 1989, p. 101). Rather, the shared discourse points to the collective character and force of gender arrangements and identities: gender is institutionalized (Rubin 1975; Daniels 1987), buttressed by ideology (Jaggar

1983; Hochschild 1989) and internalized, a fundamental aspect of the social self (Chodorow 1978). The acting self, performance, and social stage are braced and shaded by the structures and ideologies of gender.

While very definite patterns prevailed in the men's accounts, organized around central themes and largely involving a turn to and reliance upon conventional gender definitions and practices—the processes of *traditionalization* (LaRossa and LaRossa 1989)—inconsistencies existed both within and across accounts. Having particular significance, a small group, consisting of nine fathers, varied from the others in certain actions and attitudes in largely uniform ways. Characterized as postdivorce "androgynous" fathers, these men were distinctive principally in the ways in which they had, according to their perceptions and explanations, appropriated parental behaviors and postures characterized typically as "feminine" ones, involving especially an emphasis on nurturing activities.[2] Where they perceived they could, they "departed from traditional formulations of men's lives" (Cohen 1989, p. 228).

Considered specifically in this paper are the interviewees' understandings and definitions of family, encompassing issues of gender differences and a *broken* family and the processes of devaluation of the former wife. Then examined is the related use of a rhetoric of *rights.* Following this is a brief discussion and analysis of the contrasting perspectives and actions of the divergent group, the postdivorce "androgynous" fathers. Lastly, several of the implications of the findings are specified.

DEFINITION OF FAMILY

Gender Differences

The family was shown to be a threshold of masculinity in these men's accounts; it was the primary social group (Cooley 1981) that conveyed and reinforced the constructs of gender. The family of origin served as the nursery and early classroom of gender acquisition, and the family of procreation (that formed through marriage) served as a workshop where gender identity was continuously retooled). Then, as the marriage ended and the postdivorce situation entered, the family and its changes evoked a questioning of masculine identity. Made particularly evident in the divorcing process was that beneath the jointly created and shared reality of married life (Berger and Kellner 1964) were distinctive experiences and understandings, organized according to and understood in terms of gender—the "his" and "hers" of married life (Bernard 1981; Riessman 1990). Nearly all of the respondents expressed a belief that gender differences had been at play in their marriages and divorces; while some regretted the consequences of the differences and attributed marital problems to them (see also Riessman 1990), most nonetheless expressed confidence that, compared to their former wife's, their own experiences and perceptions had been, to use their terms, the more valid, reasonable, logical, reliable, or objective ones.

Communication patterns and conversational styles in their marriages varied along gender lines, reflecting and reinforcing gender differences. The men usually expected and reported themselves to be less expressive and self-disclosing in marriage than their former wives; they also claimed to have felt pressured during marriage to be otherwise (see also Tannen 1990; Riessman 1990; Cancian 1987). One participant, in a remark about the differences between men and women which was similar in substance to most others' comments about gender differences, noted:

Men compartmentalize. It's just a different pattern of doing things, it has to do with the differences between men and women. I think men are always a few months, a few steps, be-

hind women in a relationship. And men don't talk to each other the way women do to each other so men don't know what's going on outside of the things they are already most familiar with. They are at a disadvantage, they usually don't know what's going on.

Despite its gendered and therefore problematic character, marriage, for a large majority of these men, was essential to family; indeed, family was predicated upon the enduring "successful marriage." The "successful" and desired marriage, however, was defined in a paradoxical way as being both the traditional marriage and the companionate marriage. That is, on the one hand, most of these men wanted a marital arrangement in which they were ultimately, even if largely benignly, the dominant spouse, befitting men in relationship with women according to the conventions of masculinity. On the other hand, these men wanted a relationship in which they were equal copartners, forging mutually a high degree of intimacy and seeking reciprocally to meet the other's needs and desires. This next person, a co-custodial parent who had opted to leave his marriage two years earlier but was now hoping for a marital reconciliation, explained his position:

I'm not talking about a marriage and family with a patriarchal model, but the priority of the relationship between a man and a woman as a husband and wife. I want an equal relationship, a partnership. But let me word it this way, I would like her to be able to trust me to be the leader of the family. When there are times we can't sit down at the table and make decisions cooperatively, then I will make the decisions and she will trust me. I want to be able to do that in a marriage. What I need and want is the trust from her to be able to be the leader of the family. I want her to be the first one to say: 'we've talked about it and I'll let you decide.' I guess I expect her to relinquish the control of the situation first.

The improbability, even impossibility, of having simultaneously both types of marriage was largely obscured by the gender assumptions held. By conceiving of themselves as more rational, logical, and dependable than their wives, for example, assertions repeated in various ways throughout their accounts of marriage and divorce, these men were able to make claims to both types of marriage without acknowledging the contradictions or tensions between them.

The explanation for the failure to have the desired and lasting companionate marriage was the existence of fundamental differences between themselves as *men* and their former wives as *women*. In specifying these differences, the men rehearsed and reinforced the cultural stereotypes of gender and their expectations that they be the dominant partner. The problem in achieving the companionate marriage, unrecognized by these divorced men, was summarized by Riessman (1990, p. 73):

"The realization of the core ingredients of the companionate marriage— emotional intimacy, primacy and companionship, and mutual sexual fulfillment—depends on equality between husbands and wives. Yet institutionalized roles call for differentiation: neither husbands nor wives have been socialized to be equals."

Perceiving themselves to be fundamentally dissimilar from women had enabled these men to objectify their wives during marriage, at least as their retrospective accounts indicated, and to thereby discount or reconstruct the meanings of their communications in particular ways. Although this process is not limited to husbands in divorce (Vaughan 1986), the objectification of another has distinctive configurations when done by men rather than women given their respective gender socialization and placement (Glenn 1987). Accepting the conventional beliefs in gender differences and asserting the preeminence of their levels of rationality and insight served to strengthen the respondents' identities as masculine selves. For example:

I just mostly stayed rational and reasonable during the months we considered separation but she just got crazier and crazier through the whole thing. I should have been prepared for that, I always knew during the marriage not to take her too seriously because she could be so illogical. I mean, you know, it's men's rationality that keeps a marriage together to begin with.

Likewise, having dismissed or redefined a wife's expression of marital discontent was justified through claims to basic superiority. One man noted:

She kept saying she was unhappy, that I worked too much and was never home, and that I neither listened to or appreciated her, that I didn't help out with the kids, maybe even didn't care about them. But I insisted she was just depressed because her father had died. It just made sense but I couldn't get her to see it.

By redefining a wife's expressed feelings of discontent with the marriage or him as a partner, an individual could rationalize and discount his own participation in the demise of the marriage. Through such disclaimers (Hewitt and Stokes

1981), the estranged husband reinforced his definitions of the situation and of self. Additionally, the assault on identity resulting from the perception that divorce was a personal failure made public (Arendell forthcoming; see also Riessman 1990), a view held even by those who had been the partner most actively seeking the divorce, was countered.

A wife's sentiments about and assessments of their marriage could be discounted; entering into the wife's point of view, or attempting to "take the role of the other"—defined by Mead (1934, p. 254) as a uniquely human capacity which "assumes the attitude of the other individual as well as calling it out in the other"—was not a constitutive element of a husband's range of activities in the conventional marital relationship. Women spoke a "different language," as one man summed up the differences between men and women which lead to divorce, a language not to be taken too seriously, or at least not as seriously as one's own as a *man*.[3] This posture toward a wife's perspectives and feelings carried over into the postdivorce situation where differences and conflicts of interest were typically highlighted and multiplied.

A "Broken Family"

Family, within the masculinist discourse of divorce, was understood to be a *broken family,* consisting essentially of two parts: the male-self and the wife-and-children or, as referred to, " 'me' and 'them'." Even men who had sought the divorce, about one-third of the group, and several of those who had primary or shared custody of children, understood and discussed the post-divorce family as being a *broken* one. Most of the noncustodial fathers perceived themselves to have been marginalized from the family, and nearly all felt stigmatized as divorced fathers. For instance:

You're not part of the family, part of the society anymore. You really don't

have a proper place, a place where you have input into what goes on in your life. You're treated as if you're just scum, that's what you are really.

One father, using the language of *broken* family explicitly, summed up the dilemma he faced, suggesting that with the fracturing of the family went a loss of power and authority:

I guess I'm sort of at a loss in all of this; I just don't know what to do to fix a broken family. I can't say I didn't want the divorce, it was a mutual decision. But I just hadn't understood before how it would break the family into pieces. It's really become them and me and I don't know what to do. I keep thinking of the rhyme: 'Humpty Dumpty sat on a wall, Humpty Dumpty had a great fall. All the king's horses and all the king's men, couldn't put Humpty together again.' I ran it by my ex last week and asked her if she had any Super-Glue but she didn't think it was funny.

The definition of the postdivorce family as a *broken* one had several sources, including the belief that family is predicated on the marriage. Other sources of the view were: acceptance of the conventional definition that masculinity is the measure of mature adulthood in comparison to both femininity and childhood (Broverman et al. 1970; Phillips and Gilroy 1985),[4] meaning, therefore, that men are different in distinctive ways from women and children, and of the ideology, if not the actual practice, of a traditional gender-based family division of labor: child-rearing and caretaking are the responsibilities primarily of women, whether or not they are employed, and economic providing is the responsibility primarily of men (Hochschild 1989; Cohen 1989).[5]

Another and related factor in the view that the postdivorce family consisted of 'me' and 'them' was the understanding that the respective parent–child relationships differed, a perception shared by divorced mothers as well, according to other studies (Arendell 1986; Hetherington et al. 1976). Mother–child relationships were distinctive and separate from father–child relationships. The holding of this view was independent of children's ages and was reinforced by, and arguably based in, the dominant sociocultural ethos linking children to their mothers (Chodorow 1978; Coltrane 1989) and the predominance of maternal custody after divorce (USBC 1989). In contrast to the unique and independent mother–child unit, the father–child relationship was mediated in varying ways by the wife, consistent with her marital role as emotional worker (Hochschild 1983; 1989), and so was dependent on her actions. One father, who had read extensively about the psychological effects of divorce on children, compared the outcomes of his two divorces:

I would have to say that my children's primary attachment really was with their mother. I think that's typical in families, mothers are just better trained, maybe it's an instinct for parenting. Maybe fathers just don't make the effort. Anyway, even after my first divorce, I found that my ex-wife was vital to my relationship with the child of our marriage: she thought it was important that he maintain contact with me and that I be a part of his life. So she really encouraged him to do this and so it continued to be a relationship. She ran a kind of interference between us. He's 21 now and we have a good, solid relationship, but my children of this last marriage are essentially withdrawn from me. Their mother, my second wife, never really facilitated our relationship.

The retreat by former wives from the activity of facilitating the relationship between children and their fathers after divorce was interpreted as a misuse of power, and often as an overt act of hostility or revenge. In addition to the use and misuse of their psychological power in interpersonal relations (see also Pleck 1989), former wives exercised power by interfering with visitation, denigrating them as fathers and men to their children, provoking interpersonal conflicts, being uncooperative in legal matters, and demanding additional money. Their power in the postdivorce situation was viewed as being wholly disproportionate and undue: former wives were seen as not only holding center-stage position but as directing the production, if not actually writing the script, in the postdivorce drama. Nearly all of the men had an acute sense that their own power and authority in the family had been seriously eroded through divorce (Arendell 1992, forthcoming; see also Riessman 1990). This perception was central to the crisis in gender identity and was not limited to noncustodial fathers: more than half of the primary or co-custodial fathers argued that their former wives had usurped power illegitimately and at their expense. Moreover, former spouses had attained or appropriated dominance only partly through their own actions: the judiciary and legal system and the institutional and informal gender biases of both were accomplices and even instigators.

The legal system is such a crock, I can't believe it. The legal system is so for the woman and so against the man, it's just incredible. And the result is that all of these women get to go around screwing their ex-husbands.

Another person explained:

When we went to court after the divorce was over because of disagreements over support and visitation, the court did nothing. The situation is as it is today [with the mother interfering with his visitation] because the judge did nothing except hold meeting after meeting, delay after delay. The judge even said she was an unfit mother. She violated every aspect of the agreement, she obstructed. But they let her do it.

In support of their assertions about the unjustness of the system, numerous men cited the lack of a legal presumption in favor of joint child custody in New York State. Over half of the fathers argued (erroneously) that joint custody is not allowed in New York State (*Family Law* 1990) and nearly all of the noncustodial fathers, most of whom were granted what they called the "standard visitation arrangement"—every other weekend and one evening a week—complained bitterly about their limited access to their children.

Consistent with the categorization of 'me' and 'them', the perceived centrality of the former wife, and their own limited parental involvement, children most often were talked about as if they were extensions of their mothers rather than separate, unique persons. Thus, identity as a divorced father was intermixed with identity as a former spouse, adding further ambiguity and uncertainty to their place and activities in the changed family. Further, nearly all of the noncustodial and a third of the custodial fathers viewed their children as being instruments of their mothers in the postdivorce exchanges between the parents. A case in point was this father who discussed his young-adolescent daughter's reluctance to have contact with him even though her brother continued to have regular involvement. He attributed the tensions between him and his daughter to both his former wife's actions and essential gender differences:

My daughter was always more resistant, she really didn't want to see me

and she always seemed somewhat resistant. Many instances of this kind. How to put it? She's very hard to get along with this kid. She's very bright, thinks she knows everything and she's a real pain in the ass. She's a whiner about everything and we used to get into these terrible fights, just like her mother and I used to have. I can't relate to girls as well as I can relate to boys in that I don't understand a lot of what they think. I never even understood anything about women anyway until after I was divorced. I tried to stay away from my daughter because I thought what I would do is hit her, that's what I thought I would do because I'm angry. I'm less angry now. But where the hell does this little bitch get off trying to dictate everything to her father? I mean, she's not the one who's supposed to set the terms. Obviously she's just become the stand-in for her mother: her mother can't aggravate me much, directly anyway, anymore, but her daughter sure can. I worry about them. What kind of life is that?

Fathers tended to merge their children with their former wives in other ways as well. In explaining their motives for or the consequences of actions, the majority of men frequently shifted from their children as the subject to their former wife. For instance,

I wanted the kids to have a house. So it remains as it is, with them [the kids] living in it, until the youngest is 18. But that was my biggest mistake. I should have had the house sold. Then I could have really gotten away from her [the former wife] and had no ties to her at all.

The approach of not disaggregating the children from the former wife served varying functions. On the one hand, this approach bolstered the primacy of the former spouse in the post-divorce situation, granting her a position of centrality and augmenting the charges against her, and, on the other hand, it reduced her status by categorizing her with the children. Children's experiences and feelings could be discounted more easily than if they were respected as independent persons, thus creating more emotional distance between them. Distancing themselves from unfamiliar and identity-threatening feelings was a primary mechanism for reasserting control of their situations and of themselves and was relied upon particularly by "absent" and "visiting" fathers; one outcome of this gender strategy was the common acceptance of postdivorce father absence as an acceptable line of action under certain conditions (Arendell 1992). Not surprisingly, then, fathers satisfied with their parent–child relations were the exception: they included the postdivorce "androgynous" fathers and eight others. The majority were discontented with and disconcerted by the nature of their interactions with, emotional connections to, and levels of involvement with their children. Most characterized their relations with their children as being strained or superficial, distrustful, and unfulfilling.

Devaluing a Wife's Family Activities

Most of the respondents specifically devalued the family activities done both during and after marriage by the former wife (see also Riessman 1990). Through deprecating the former partner's activities, the men were able to buttress various assertions, including that they had been the dominant spouse and had been mistreated badly by the divorce settlement. Over a third of the fathers contended that they had been exceptional men in their marriages—a "superman," as several fathers quipped, in contrast to the popularized no-tion of "superwoman"—carrying the major share of income-earning and participating equally or near equally in caretaking activities. These particular fathers especially generalized their critique of their former wife's activities to a broad indictment of women's family roles, thus further reinforcing their beliefs in male superiority. As one noncustodial father, whose career development had demanded exceptionally long work weeks and whose former wife had stayed home during the marriage with the children, said:

> After all, I was able to do it [work and family] all, while she did next to nothing, so I don't see what these women are complaining about.

The devaluing of a former wife's activities also helped sustain the perception that, at least in retrospect, her economic dependence during marriage had been unfair, as was any continued exchange of resources after divorce. The implicit marriage contract operative during marriage, involving a culturally defined and socially structured gender-based division of labor and exchange (Weitzman 1985), was to be terminated upon divorce. Child support was viewed as a continuation of support for the undeserving former spouse. Of the 57 fathers (three-quarters of the sample) who were paying child support consistently or fairly regularly, almost two-thirds were adamant in their assertions that men's rights are infringed upon by the child support system.[6] One man, in a representative statement, said:

> I, a hard-working family man, got screwed, plain and simple. The court, under the direction of a totally biased judge, dictated that she and her children, our children, can relate to me simply as a money machine: 'just push the buttons and out comes the money, no strings attached'. And

leave me without enough money even to afford a decent place to live.

"Adding insult to injury," as one irate father put it, was the demonstrated and undeniable reality that each time money defined as child support was passed to her, the former wife gained discretionary authority over its use, being accountable to neither the former husband or any institutional authority. Resentment over the child support system and the former wife's unwarranted power over his earnings was the explanation for various actions of resistance. Such common behaviors included: refusing to pay support, providing a check without funds in the bank to cover it, and neglecting to pay on time so that the former spouse was pushed into having to request the support check. Other actions were more idiosyncratic; for example, one father of three described his strategy for protesting the payment of child support:

I put the check in the kids' dirty clothes bag and send it home with them after they visit. I used to put it in the clean clothes but now I put it in the dirty clothes bag. One woman told me her husband sent back the kids' clothes with a woman's sock, then the next time a woman's bra. I won't go that far, it's too low. But I suspect even this keeps her angry and off-balance and she can't say a word to me about it. She knows I can simply withhold it, refuse to pay it.

The respondents deflned their postdivorce situations and actions primarily in terms of the former wife, and a preoccupation with her was sustained whether or not there was continued direct interaction. Contributing were overlapping factors: lingering feelings about her, characterized generally by ambivalence, frustration and anger and remaining intense for over a third of

the men (see also Wallerstein 1989); the perception that she held a position of dominance in the postdivorce milieu together with the processes of devaluing her significance; and the continuing relevance of issues pertaining to their children and finances.

A Rhetoric of Rights

A rhetoric of *rights* was interspersed throughout the men's accounts: it was basic to their understanding of family and their place in it and to their postdivorce actions, perspectives, and relationships. Attitudes held towards *rights* and its use were largely independent of particular experiences. Men satisfied with their divorce and postdivorce experiences spoke of *rights* in ways analogous to those men who were intensely dissatisfied with nearly every aspect of their divorce, the general exception being the small group characterized as "androgynous" fathers.

As used by the men in the study, the rhetoric of *rights* encompassed the ethics of individualism and autonomy and cultural views about choice, control, and authority, each of which is also central to the dominant beliefs about masculinity (Jaggar 1983; Pateman 1990). The rhetoric of *rights*, appropriated largely from political and legal theory and practice, was widely available in the culture at large. Specifically, for example, numerous respondents made reference to newspaper articles or television news spots over the course of the past several years which covered divorce-related issues (and particularly the implementation of the 1989 New York Child Support Standards Act) as ones involving rights. Attorneys were another source of the language of *rights* as was the law itself since the statutory approach to family relations, evidenced in family law codes, is one of rights and obligations (i.e., *Family Law* 1990).

That *rights* were to be secured in relation to another, and primarily the former wife, demystified the assertions and implications that what was at issue were matters of abstract principles of justice. Central among the various issues framed within the rhetoric of *rights* were the privileges of position of husband and father as held, or expected to be held, in the family prior to separation and divorce. As one father referring to the dominant pattern in which mothers receive custody and fathers pay child support pointedly said,

> *Divorce touches men in the two most vulnerable spots possible: rights to their money and rights to their children.*

The rhetoric of *rights* had a distinctive and complex connotation: that which was expected, desired, and believed to be deserved as a *man*. This person, for example, insisted repeatedly and explicitly throughout much of his account that his *rights* had been continuously violated. He had obtained primary custody of their children after "forcing my wife out of our home" and claiming that "she deserted us" in response to her request for a divorce:

> *The legal system abuses you as a man. You know: you have no rights. That is, you're treated as a nonperson or as a second, third, fourth or fifth class citizen. They look at us: you know, 'who is that guy with the mother?' Suddenly we're just sperm donators or something. We're a paycheck and sperm donators and that's our total function in society. The legal bias for the mother is incredible. You pull your hair and spend thousands of dollars and say, 'aren't I a human being?' I mean I saw on tv: gay rights, pink rights, blue rights, everybody has rights and they're all demonstrating. I said, 'don't men have rights too? Aren't these my children? Isn't*

> *this my house? Don't they bear my name?' I mean I was the first one to hold each of them when they were first born. I was there for it all. What will they do sometime later on in their lives when they are in a crisis—a divorce, job loss, whatever—and they don't have an identity? If I haven't been there to lay the foundation, what kind of identity will they have? Their foundation is to a large extent the result of my input. Don't I have a say as to their fate? I mean, did I have this thing backwards or something? You have to stop believing in the American way: truth and justice and all of that, that's not what happens. That only happens in books. And tv shows. None of my rights were protected, but had I been a woman, you can bet that if I were a female, I'd have had these things automatically, without any fight at all. I was fighting desperately for them because if I had lost my kids, I would have probably turned out to be one of those fathers who says I can't live with myself. I would have lost my identity, my self-respect, my future. I had already failed at marriage; she had insisted on ending it. I wasn't about to let them do this to me.*

This father remained locked in a power struggle with his former wife, especially as he actively resisted her involvement with the children. Like many of the men in the study and even though he was a custodial parent, his relations with his children were continuously filtered through his relations and feelings about their mother.

Threats to rights were attributed to, most commonly, the former wife and some attorneys.

Conflicts with the former spouse were common experiences among the men participating in the study irrespective of their general level of satisfaction with the postdivorce situation. Dissension involved matters carried over from the marriage as well as issues specific to the divorce settlement and the custody, living arrangements, care, and financial support of children. Resistance or disagreement from the former wife were characterized as "being intended to deny me my rights." Yet, while former wives posed the most tangible threats to their rights by their actions regarding children and finances, the challenge involved a complex meeting of family, cultural, and social changes. For example, in discussing his divorce experience, a noncustodial, "visiting" father of two referred to broader changes which had adversely affected his marriage and position in the family:

> Our [his and his former wife's] fighting is just part of the package. We're involved in gender wars here. The women's movement has wimpified men—everywhere, the family, at work. Just look at the reverse discrimination for jobs: women get onto the police force down in New York City with lower scores than men. And it's dangerous, people will die because women are less qualified. Police in New York have been wimpified by the lowering of the scores for women and minorities. There's a loss of integrity for females too. And it's a violation of the taxpayer who doesn't get what he's paid for. It's going to take an all-out assault by men to protect men, to restore men's rights. There's been too much favoring of women, it's time for the pendulum to swing back

> now. And men's rights are about custody, about visitation, about genetic ties.

Feminists were also frequently mentioned as sources of threats to rights but were only vaguely defined. Often attributed to the actions of "feminists," for example, were the development and implementation of the New York Standard Child Support Guidelines.

A large number of respondents used the language of *fathers' rights,* most often in relation to the former wife and not the children. This stance was reinforced by legal codes pertaining to divorce: children were a kind of property, over which custody was to be authorized, if the divorcing parents were in agreement, or assigned, if they were not.[7] And the determination of child custody was related to the parents' family activities. As men they were penalized in divorce for having invested their energies and efforts primarily in income-earning rather than in child-caretaking. The institutional and cultural biases against them in divorce as men in families took on even greater dimensions for them because they devaluated women's parenting activities. One custodial father explained his determination to obtain and then retain custody of his young children, who were 14 and 25 months at the time his wife left the marital home:

> They're my children, that's how I got custody. I've been challenged nine times for custody. But they're my kids. I love them. I wanted them living with me. I couldn't see living on my own without the little guys [a son and a daughter] around. You know, she's capable, I never denied that. She just wants everybody to bend to her. She wants to be boss. I didn't claim that she was an unfit mother. That's what

everybody told me to do: 'claim she's an unfit mother and maybe you've got a chance. That's what everybody does.' But I said, 'no.' I believed I was the better parent, that I was more emotionally capable at the time. My first attorney kept pointing out that she had been a full-time mother while I was working, but that was only because I had to work. Why should that make me lose my rights to my kids? If anything, it should give me more rights. I was supporting them, and her for that matter.

The notion of *fathers' rights* was used also by some men to explain their efforts to control their children's behaviors; for example, adhering to a position of inflexibility with regard to the visitation schedule:

I've made it clear to my kids that visitation is not negotiable: 'I expect you here: this is my time with you. This is our time together. I expect you here and when you're with me, this is your home.' I can be a dictator! So my kids come over. They waffle here and there, they've got stuff to do and that sort of thing, they're teenagers now with lots of activities. But they are to come and they do. It's nonnegotiable. I'm their father. These are my rights. I didn't let attorneys or social workers tell me what to do, I don't let their mother tell me what to do, and I don't let these kids tell me what to do.

Several fathers characterized the actions of their young children as having violated their *rights* as fathers; infractions included not demanding and arranging greater amounts of visitation, initiating telephone calls, or aligning with them in disagreements between the parents. But

what was primarily to be secured within the context of *fathers' rights* was a position of control and authority. This man explained his return of their child to his former wife after having fought mightily for custody:

I am a strong advocate for fathers' rights, for men's rights. I had to fight for my rights as a father; and it cost me over twenty thousand dollars to win the custody fight. But I had to show my ex that I was still in control here, that she couldn't deny me my basic rights just because she got the divorce she wanted. By winning the custody battle, I showed her that I was still in charge. But I knew all along that I would let my son go back to live with his mother once this was over.

Because *rights* were integral to identity, the securing of them was fundamentally important and entailed a process loaded with urgency. The largely adversarial character, whether implicit or explicit, of the legal divorce process reinforced their sense of being both engaged in a competition and, because of the loss of power attendant to divorce, positioned continuously on the defensive. Their response was, as one characterized it, "to go on the offensive since the best defense is a strong offense."[8] Thus, their participation in the negotiations, whether informal between the estranged spouses or formal, involving legal representation, was often intense; exaggerated demands, especially involving child custody or support issues, were made in the anticipation that less than what was being sought would actually be obtained. Seeking to intimidate the former wife was a commonly described, preferred strategy. For instance,

The truth is that whenever she brings up changing, increasing, the Child

Support Order—she'd have to go and get an Order of Modification—all I have to do is 'alright, just go ahead, and I'll be right behind you seeking a change of custody.' I will too. I'll call up my buddy, Bill, in Albany, the guy [family law attorney] who's been winning all of these cases for fathers and we'll get sole custody.

These men's relations to the legal system and assessments of their legal experiences, framed within the context of *rights,* were paradoxical. On one hand, the juridical institution was perceived as being a tool, available for their use. Men expressed pride in the aggressiveness of *their* attorneys, often referring to them by first name, and claimed to share with them, to cite one respondent, "a certain degree of rationality, efficiency, and intelligence." Such perceptions and assertions of commonality empowered them in their interactions, settlement negotiations, and self-evaluations. Legal procedures themselves were characterized as being masculine—aggressive, competitive, tough, and significant.

On the other hand, the law, attorneys, and judges were viewed with disdain and distrust. One man stated that family attorneys are "nothing but today's carpetbaggers." Another said,

I have nothing but contempt for the system. I don't give a damn what the law says, what the legal system says. I don't give a damn what their psychologists and counselors say. I know best. I know better, these are my kids. Do you know what the legal system does? It tries to emasculate you.

Legal professionals were blamed for the formal divorce-related actions of former wives; such as, efforts to secure sole child custody, obtain finan-cial support, dictate the visitation schedule, and establish the terms of the property settlement.

Thus, some attorneys and judges were allies and others were opponents, and movement between the camps was common. Attorneys were hired, directed, and fired in succession. The authority of the judiciary was conditional, to be voluntarily conceded or withheld: child support could be held back, children "snatched" from their custodial mothers (as nine fathers reported having done), and former wives harassed legally through formalized, legal procedures. Such actions were explicable within the logic of securing one's *rights* in an unjust system.

That the system inherently discriminates against men in divorce was a shared belief irrespective of personal experiences with or assessments of the legal system: whatever the extent of their actual involvement with the legal system, the men shared the beliefs that they were "bargaining in the shadow of the law" (Mnookin and Kornhauser 1979) and that the shadow was darkened with bias against them. Even the men expressing pride in their legal successes, those giving fairly innocuous assessments of their encounters with the system, and those having little direct dealings with it were convinced that women are favored in divorce law and proceedings. One father, for instance, critiqued the legal system in a representative way:

The practices of the legal system today infringe upon and revoke our rights as men to make even the most fundamental family decisions. We are systematically being displaced.

Although about a quarter of the men made references to women acquaintances who had been unjustly treated by divorce and its outcome, such cases were defined as exceptional; no one suggested that his own former wife had been treated unfairly.

The legal divorcing process was viewed as a highly charged contest, the outcome of which carried high stakes. Nearly everyone talked about the legal divorce settlement as evidence of winning or losing and military and sports metaphors, prevalent throughout their overall accounts, were particularly evident in the men's discussions of their legal experiences. *Rights* had either been secured or unjustly lost. Moreover, participation itself in the legal processes of divorce exemplified for many a loss of power and authority in their family lives; the *right* to self-determination in what were viewed as private matters prior to divorce was usurped by the legal and judicial institutions (see also Folberg and Milne 1988), and in some instances, by social service agencies operating at the direction of the judiciary. Made public, and sometimes scrutinized, were such issues as marital relations; childrearing practices and parental involvement; and earning, spending and saving patterns.

The rhetoric of *rights* then was multifaceted, consisting of complex and overlapping themes pertaining to self-identity and involving issues of personal efficacy, dominance, and control. It served to define, reaffirm, and reassert a masculine self. *Rights* was a euphemism for male privilege within the family and the stratified gender system generally, and provided a means for characterizing one's place and experiences in the social order and in divorce. *Rights* then provided a framework for defining the self in relation to others, a particularly important function in a context characterized by rapid changes and ambiguity, and for explaining the changing locus of power and various actual or threatened losses.

Adding yet further complexity to the use of *rights* was its use as a gender strategy (Hochschild 1989): framing their experiences, actions, and relationships as matters of *rights* served as a way to manage feelings and shore up self-identity. This strategy or line of activity empowered them in their assertions that they remained "in control" both of themselves and their situations, despite the unfamiliar, complicated, and usually emotionally stressful postdivorce circumstances. Fears of losing one's children and feelings of confusion, loss, and grief about either or both their children and former wife were reconstructed to be matters of *rights*. Defining a situation as a threat to or an assault on one's rights allowed the emotions experienced to be interpreted as, or to be channeled into, ones of anger (Arendell 1992). Anger was allowed, even expected, within the conventions of masculinity.

Consistent with the view that the postdivorce family was a broken family, the rhetoric of *rights* fostered an objectifying of relationships and an intensification of a perception of a self as autonomous and separate. Moreover, in its framing of relationships, actions, and feelings, *rights* promoted and reinforced competitive and aggressive lines of action even as it reaffirmed, in the unfamiliar postdivorce circumstance, a confident rather than a confused or uncertain self. The rhetoric of *rights* within the gendered divorce discourse abetted and justified their engagement in the processes of traditionalization (LaRossa and LaRossa 1989).

But gendered identity and social arrangements were not deterministic and the processes of traditionalization not universal. As with the role transitions "in becoming a husband and a father" analyzed elsewhere (Cohen 1989, p. 225), some fathers took on new responsibilities, expanded roles, and sought alternative definitions.

"ANDROGYNOUS" FATHERS

The "androgynous" fathers, 9 out of the 75 fathers in the study, differed from the majority in broadly consistent ways. Variations in postdivorce custody status alone did not account for the differences between this small group of fathers and the others. Three of these fathers had primary custody of their children and two shared custody with their former spouses (which in their cases involved dividing equally the time spent with and caring for their children). The other four men were noncustodial fathers who were extensively involved with their children. Only one had remarried, a noncustodial father.

Eight of these men, and two of the others, marveled at how they had "learned to become a father only after divorcing." Six had found it necessary to make major alterations in their behaviors and priorities in order to become involved, nurturing fathers. For example, this postdivorce "androgynous" father assumed his role as a custodial parent of three young children suddenly when his wife left:

It was terrifying at first, just terrifying. I remember the night she walked out the door. And I cried at the thought of it: I said to myself, 'how in the hell am I going to do this?' I was raised in a stereotypically way, stereotypically male. I did not cook. I did not particularly clean. I was working a lot so it was 'come home and play with the baby.' The youngest was just a year and a half, one was going towards three, and the oldest one was just about four. So it was like playtime. I didn't have any responsibility for their daily care. I'd hardly changed a diaper before. I didn't know what parenting was about, really. I mean, who teaches us how to parent? I really didn't know how to ask for help. I don't truly remember the first year. It was day by day by day. After about a year, I managed to figure out that I had my act together. But it goes

deeper than all of that. I had to learn to relate to them.

After describing in some detail his strategies for coping in the new and stressful situation, he assessed the personal changes:

I actually think I'm a better person, to be honest with you, and certainly a far better parent than I ever would have been had she not left. Not that it would be by choice [single parenting], but however you'd like it to be, I would rather have done what I've done. What happened by becoming single is that I was forced into all of this. Now I admit I lost the playtime when they were little, and that's my greatest regret, and all of that. And it's been very hard financially because I'm always limited in how much I can work and I felt I couldn't change jobs. But I've shared so much more with them than any other father I know, they just don't even know what I'm talking about. Now I can't imagine what life will be like when they're grown and leave home. I feel like I'll be starting all over. I thought I had this ball game all figured out.

The postdivorce family was not characterized as a *broken* one by these fathers. Comparatively little use was made of the language of *rights* to frame experiences, relations, or feelings, although fundamental legal issues were sometimes intrinsic to their experiences also. The postdivorce family context was not characterized as a battleground on which the struggle for *rights* was actively fought and there was no talk of divorce or gender wars. Instead, family was represented in various ways as a network of relationships which, as a result of the divorce, necessitated changes in assumptions and interactions.

The areas in which these men were particularly unique were their positive assessments of their relations with their children, overall level of sustained postdivorce parental involvement, and perceptions that the postdivorce father–child relationship depended centrally on their own actions. Interactions with the former wife were aimed primarily at fostering and maintaining cooperation and open communication; the objective was to view and relate to her primarily as the other parent, the mother of the children, and not as the former wife. Thus, issues of the relationship and interpersonal tensions between them were generally subordinated to those regarding their children's well-being and their own parenting. Unlike the majority, for example, the "androgynous" fathers had little if anything to say about postdivorce father absence other than that they neither understood it nor perceived it to be an optional line of action, regardless of the extent of tensions or differences with the former wife (Arendell 1992).

Minimizing conflict with the children's mother was viewed as essential to the fostering and protecting of a positive, stable, and sustained father-child relationship regardless of the specific residential arrangements or the nature and scope of their feelings about the former spouse. These men viewed themselves as having a particular and greater burden for preventing or reducing conflict than their former spouse. In ways similar to the other men, they believed that women have within their grasp and at their discretion the support of the legal system and divorce law generally. Primary and co-custodial fathers feared that their custody status could be revoked and noncustodial fathers feared that access to their children could be impeded.

At the same time, however, the moderate or conciliatory attitude toward the former wife went beyond a pragmatic assessment of their circumstances as divorced fathers. For example, rather than devaluing the former wife's mothering or other family activities, these men typically acknowledged the significance of her past and present efforts, even if they held some negative feelings about her in other regards. This person, for example, continued to feel some resentment, which he also characterized as betrayal, about his wife's decision to end the marriage:

> We never had a custody fight and I never threatened her with one. We were in agreement that it [maternal custody] was probably the best thing we could do. I just work too many hours, there was no way I could care for the kids all the time. The kids were too young. Why do that to the kids? I mean, 'you can see your mother ever other weekend?' And just for some reason it seemed to me that it was better, easier, that they stay with their mother at their young ages. They were just three and five years old. And she'd been a full-time mother, she hadn't been employed while I was building my career. She was always there for them. We'd been in agreement about that. And she's a good mother. There are times when I wished I could have them, I would just love to have them everyday. You know, if she would give them to me, I'd take them.

With only one exception, the postdivorce "androgynous" fathers viewed their postdivorce parenting activities as being part of a team effort, done collaboratively with the former spouse. They were part of a *parenting partnership.*[9]

Integral to these men's accounts but generally absent in the others' was the notion of parental or paternal obligation; child support, for example, was discussed primarily in terms of children's needs rather than in terms of conflicts with the former wife. Even so, these men also had some ambivalence about the relationship between child support payments and the former wife as the direct recipient. This father, for example, discussed the settlement process and his child support obligation:

So the divorce, when you come down to it, didn't involve any true battles or fights or anything. We both worked to keep it on an even keel even though we were upset. It was basically a moderate process, based on agreements and an equal division of everything, although it took longer than it probably needed to because of the slowness of the lawyers. We just had the house, the cars, some furniture, and a few monetary assets. Obviously, she wanted more child support and I would have paid less. But it's what we ended up with. It was a reasonable amount. The point is that the state guidelines were the exact amount I had been paying for two and a half years without even knowing what the formula would be. It just hit it right on the head. We sat down and worked out what seemed right. So it was just what I could afford to pay her. I have financial responsibility for the children, no doubt about that. But I had some funny feelings about it all for awhile, there was this small financial issue because I felt like 'I'm giving her a lot of money per year.' I had this tendency to think 'why

should I pay her all this money when she's probably just going to go out and marry another guy who's making money? Like where do I get my income when I'm paying for the child support?' I have no other worldly manner in my life to get additional money to cover that. But it wasn't that she didn't deserve it or anything like that. They need the money.

As suggested by this participant, the "androgynous" fathers shared with most of the men in the study the assumption that their former spouses would remarry, if they had not already, and be economically supported by another man (even though all but five of their former spouses had some kind of employment), and that this financial change would benefit their children. With the exception of issues regarding finances, however, the "androgynous" fathers viewed their children as unique persons who were distinct from their mothers and siblings and who had particular perceptions of and feelings about the family situation. Also, according to these fathers, while children's understandings and behaviors were affected by the actions and expectations of both parents, they were not determined by either of them. At the same time, both parents were obliged to forego any efforts aimed at polarizing their children.

Issues of gender identity were present, in significant ways, however, for this subset of men also. Although they raised questions about and challenged the conventions of masculinity, its constraints and consequences, they too were agents of and participants in the masculinist discourse of divorce by virtue of their gender identity, status, and experiences in a gendered-structured society. Because the postdivorce adaptive strategies and attitudes they adopted were often inconsistent with the major themes of the gendered divorce discourse, extensive intra-gender conflict was experienced (Rosenblum 1990). Reflective about and deliberately rejecting of what they perceived to be the typical behaviors and explanations of fathers after divorce, these men "paid a price" for their divergence (see also Coltrane 1989). They were beset with doubts about their actions and motives. Seeking alternative lines of action, they too, nonetheless, used as their measure of self, the norms of masculinity. One custodial father who was struggling with questions of motive and objective said,

> I just have to keep asking myself: 'Why are you doing this?' I need to constantly ask myself if I'm doing this for my child or for some other reason. Am I trying to prove something?

Self-doubt was reinforced by inexperience and a sense of isolation: they were largely unprepared for parenting in the postdivorce context and had found few, if any, adequate male role models for their situations as divorced parents. In lamenting the lack of a male role model, four of these fathers observed that their exemplar for parenting was their mother, two noted that theirs was their former wife, and another credited his sister. Persistent questions of identity confronted these men: both they and others around them defined their actions and perspectives as being appropriations of "women's activities and experiences" or "mothers' lives":

> I have tried to be a mother, tried to be the image of what their mother should be, do with them in given times what a mother would do, provide a lot of the emotions she would give them, etc., etc.

In not conforming more fully to the conventions of masculinity, the men found themselves subject to question and even ridicule, especially from male co-workers and relatives: certain performance of gender carry more status and power than others and theirs were defined as deviant. As one man noted, in describing his lingering uncertainty about his decisions "to find another way,"

> Even my father and brother told me to get on with my life, to start acting 'like a man' and to let this child go, that my involvement with him would just interfere with my work and future relationships with women. They told me that other people were going to think I was a wimp, you know, unmanly, for not standing up to my former wife.

Interpersonal and cultural pressures to conform to gender conventions were reinforced by structural practices and arrangements. The traditional gender-based division of labor, persisting not only in the domestic but also in the employment arena, hindered these fathers' attempts to act in ways generally deemed to be unconventional for men. Impediments included work schedules and demands, the gender wage gap, cultural definitions of male career success, and perceived, if not real, gender biases in the legal system as well as the culture. Individually confronting the conventions of masculinity and challenging the relevance in their situations of gender prescriptions did not alter dominant ideologies or institutionalized arrangements or constraints (see also Risman 1989; Cohen 1989).

CONCLUSION AND IMPLICATIONS

The masculinist discourse of divorce, constructed and anchored in interaction and reinforced by the stratified social order, made available a set of practices and dispositions that prescribed and reaffirmed these men's gendered identities. But the template of familial relations and interpersonal interactions offered was a restricted one, often unsuited for the ambiguous and emergent character of the postdivorce circumstance. Even as the altered, and often stressful, situation called for continued interactional adjustments, negotiations, and alignment, lines of action were aimed instead primarily at repair and reassertion of self as autonomous, independent, and controlling. Those few men who sought out and engaged in some alternative behaviors also were both agents in and constrained by the gendered divorce discourse.

The implications of the findings from this exploratory study are numerous and can only be touched on here. The perspectives on and actions in family and divorce provided by the participants in this exploratory study invite further investigation into various postdivorce paternal behaviors, including, for example: noncompliance with child support orders (USBC 1989) and limited other forms of parental support (Teachman 1991); father absence after divorce (Furstenberg et al. 1987; Furstenberg 1988); repeat child custody challenges (Weitzman 1985); and the phenomenon of "serial fathering" (Furstenberg 1988). While often counterproductive to the development and sustaining of mutually satisfying father-child relationships, these behaviors, nonetheless, may be understood by the actors as meaningful and appropriate responses given their perspectives and circumstances. The points of view, explanations, and motives underlying such behaviors warrant further investigation and analysis. So too do the findings that men typically are less satisfied with divorce than are women (Riessman 1990; Wallerstein 1989).

Clearly much more study of divorce is called for since divorce as a common event appears to be here to stay. Careful attention must be given to the voices and viewpoints of all participants in divorce—children, women, and men. A fundamental part of the research agenda needs to be consideration of the effects of gender on divorce outcomes because divorce, like marriage, is not gender neutral. But a focus on individuals' definitions of and adjustments to divorce must be coupled with investigation of the effects of institutional practices and arrangements and cultural biases.

Professionals intervening in or advising about family situations and processes in divorce must be sensitized to the effects of gender on interactions and perspectives, and to their own gender biases and identity issues. Legal processes and practices which promote and augment rather than alleviate conflict between divorced parents need to be quickly abandoned and alternatives put in their place. Mediation must be available to assist parents in working through their differences, conflicts of interest, and emotional responses to the ending of their marriage so that they can focus on the postdivorce circumstances and exigencies. Education of divorcing parents is essential: specifically, parents need to be informed of their options, prerogatives, and obligations. They need to be encouraged to seek common ground in order to develop parenting arrangements satisfactory to both and beneficial to their children. A new way of thinking and behaving after divorce needs to be promoted: that a negotiated postdivorce parenting partnership is both appropriate and necessary and, although it requires communication and good faith efforts, can take a variety of forms. Men and women need to be made aware that, although their responses may differ, they actually share many of the same fears and uncertainties in divorce, particularly with regard to their parenting status and activities (Arendell 1986; forthcoming).

Even while divorce reforms continue, and alternative, more constructive, and innovative practices and processes explored, other fundamental social reforms must proceed. As Kay (1990, p. 29) asserted, "if we have learned anything from the work of Weitzman, Marcus, and others, it is that we cannot expect to remedy the defects of marriage at the point of divorce." Specifically required, for example, are the elimination of institutional constraints on and cultural attitudes against both men's more total engagement in family life, especially in parenting and childrearing activities, and women's full and equitable participation in the employment and political arenas. Individuals, including our youth, must receive much more education about marriage and family, parenting, divorce, and gender even as a broad rethinking of these institutions, practices, and underlying ideologies occurs. The "stalled revolution" (Hochschild 1989) in transformations and related institutional reforms must be stirred; social movement must seek to insure gender justice together with the protecting of children in divorce. Called for then, in brief, are continual assessments of what is transpiring in the lives of families; a conscious revisiting of our assumptions about family and the relations between married and former spouses, and parents and children; and a recasting of society aimed at empowering individuals to move beyond the constraints of gender roles and, most significantly, the constraints of gender identity.

Reading 30   Divorce and Fatherhood

ERMA JEAN LAWSON and AARON THOMPSON*

My sons went through so much hurt and pain. I told both my sons that I will be there to help them.

—*Matt*

In this chapter, we turn to the role that fathers play as noncustodial parents, explore barriers that prevent father-child involvement, examine reactions of children to divorce, and discuss problems of noncustodial stepfathers and fathers from interracial marriages. Finally, we explore the future of Black fatherhood and propose solutions to strengthen father-child bonds.

IMPACT OF DIVORCE ON FATHERHOOD

Divorce changes the structure of fathering (Arendell, 1995; Marsiglio, 1991; Weiss, 1979). First, and most important, there are no norms for noncustodial fathering; thus, these fathers often are uncertain about their roles as disciplinarians versus weekend friends (Seltzer, 1991; Weiss, 1975). Second, divorced men no longer have wives to encourage and to facilitate father-child interactions. Third, noncustodial fathers often are unprepared to accept sole responsibility for supervising young children because mothers usually care for young children (Umberson, 1992). Studies have found that divorced fathers often disengage from parenting roles over time (Furstenberg & Nord, 1985). Approximately 23% of children 11 to 16 years of age have no contact with their fathers, and 25% have bimonthly contact with their fathers postdivorce (Furstenberg, Morgan, & Allison, 1987). Of interest, fathers who are divorced longer are more likely to be disengaged from children (Furstenberg et al., 1987).

Various explanations have been postulated as to reasons why noncustodial fathers withdraw from their children. First, postdivorce withdrawal has been related to continued antagonism with former wives (Arendell, 1995; Weiss, 1975). The lack of cooperation from ex-wives about children's education and upbringing impel men to decrease father-child interactions (Fulton, 1979; Grief, 1985; Gutmann, 1987). Second, work conflicts, inadequate incomes, and geographical distance have been associated with noncustodial father withdrawal (Arendell, 1995). Fourth, an interesting theory for the absence of noncustodial fathers has been posited by Ihinger-Tallman and Pasley (1989). These researchers suggest that withdrawal may be a response to feeling unappreciated or rejected by children, particularly older children.

CUSTODY ISSUES AND VISITATION

Approximately 53% of couples who divorce have children under 18 years of age, and in 90% of cases, the mother has custody by agreement or default (National Center for Health Statistics, 1991). According to Lamanna and Riedmann (1994), child custody has been an extension of the basic exchange principle; divorced fathers have legal responsibility for support, whereas divorced mothers continue daily child care.

The controversy has been centered on joint custody. In joint custody, both divorced parents assume equal responsibility for child rearing. However, it is difficult to maintain joint legal custody of children when one parent has sole physical custody. One problem with joint physical custody is geographic distance when children divide the year between two different communities and schools. In addition, joint custody is expensive, with each parent maintaining housing, equipment, toys, and separate clothing for children. Furthermore, research has not supported the assumption that joint custody is best for divorced parents and for children (Kline, Tschann, Johnston, & Wallerstein, 1989).

Visitation

Fathers often feel out of touch with their children because contact weekly or every other weekend does not provide the same relationship with children as does living within the same household. Consequently, noncustodial fathers experience a sense of extreme loss. Ironically, more emotionally involved fathers before their divorces visit their children *less* often (Kruk, 1991). Evidence suggests that this also applies to stepfathers and men in cohabitation relationships (Dullea, 1987).

CHILDREN'S REACTIONS TO DIVORCE

The impact of divorce on children has been documented extensively (Glenn, 1987). Children from divorced parents acquire less education, marry earlier, tend to have out-of-wedlock births, and are more likely to divorce (see, e.g., Keith & Finlay, 1988; McLanahan & Bumpass, 1988). On the other hand, Amato and Booth (1991) conclude that children of divorce are little different from children of intact marriages and that the negative impact of divorce on children might be overstated. Similarly, Spanier (1989) argues that children who experience family disruption possess a strong commitment to family life.

Nevertheless, both optimistic and pessimistic views of the impact of divorce on children often have failed to explore the impact of divorce on racial/ethnic minority children. The following discussion explores telling children of divorce.

CHILDREN AS A REASON TO REMAIN MARRIED

From the back porch, James watched his two sons play. He wanted to call them and say, "'I'm sorry I turned your world upside down.' I then felt the divorce was real." James could hear himself breathing and tears seemed suspended as he attempted to tell his children about the marital breakup. He explained, "The children seemed so happy, and I hated to upset them. I told them to obey their mother and grandmother and I would [go] away for a while. 'It's just that your mother and me can't live together anymore.'"

"Where are you going?" James's oldest son asked.

"I'll be in the next state and will see you every month. Plus, we will talk on the phone every day."

"Daddy, do you have to go? What are we supposed to do?"

These words struck James like a bullet that would remain lodged inside his chest forever. He explained, "The divorce was painful, but knowing that I had disappointed my two sons was more painful. I felt that it was important to be in their lives daily as they deal with living in White America."

As James and his children walked back to the house, a pain as sharp as that of an ax blade split his skull into two pieces. The thought of missing the precious moments of his sons' lives resulted in tears streaming softly at first and then in a gradual crescendo that seemed destined to never end. Most men indicated that they regretted their divorces because of the decreased contact with their children. They often believed that in leaving the marriages, they abandoned their children. "The divorce was hard because I hated leaving my children" was a representative comment.

The distress of divorce was heightened for the respondents because they viewed children as the brightest aspects of their marriages. Compared to their own fathers and those of earlier generations, they were extremely involved fathers. The predominant father-child relationship was nurturant, warm, and loving. Predivorce, 10 men coached sports teams and 5 taught Sunday school in which their children took part. Thus, due to geographical distance, some men complained about exclusion from opportunities to interact with their children postdivorce.

TELLING CHILDREN

Research has shown that children should be informed of divorce. For example, Wallerstein and Kelly (1979) found that children who were told that their fathers were planning to live elsewhere appeared less distraught than did those whose fathers disappeared without any explanations. Without exception, fathers reported that they informed children of the divorces through short explanations. Bernie said, "I simply told my son that his mother and I just changed so much, and it was impossible for us to live together. He seemed satisfied with that explanation." Bronson explained how he informed his biological sons and stepsons of the divorce to prevent them from adopting a negative view of marriage:

> I took my sons took to their favorite restaurant, the Pizza Hut, and after we had finished eating, I said, "Your mother and I took marriage seriously, but sometimes marriages don't work. That does not mean we love you less; if anything, we love you more. When you grow up and marry, you will make it work."

The respondents also informed their children of the divorces without discrediting their ex-wives. For example, Brent said, "I told my kids that their mother and me just had some problems we could not work out." Overall, most men emphasized that it was important to be supportive of their children's mothers and often told their children that their mothers were not to blame for the divorces. However, several respondents reported that ex-wives often defamed them in front of their children. Leon said,

> Carol told my children that I did not care about them. She also told them

that I did not want to see them. Carol tried to turn my children against me and called me derogatory names in front of them. Children pay attention to that stuff, and now I think my daughter is ashamed of me.

Barry also reported intense emotional pain because Jennifer made negative comments about him to his sons. He perceived those comments as destroying the relationship with his children:

Jennifer has always said negative things about me in front of the children. That hurts because my children have a tendency to avoid me. My son said, "Dad, Mom told me you were no good and didn't care about us." He made no effort to see or call me because he was under Jennifer's spell.

Barry struggled through tears stating that most people are unaware of the problems divorced Black men endure with ex-wives and the deep hurt they feel from missing their children. As a result, their relationships with children often were a source of pain and frustration. Whereas respondents coped with being inaccessible to their children and endured the pain that they no longer had genuine authority in their children's lives, the tendency of ex-wives to discredit and berate them to their children generated much distress and agony.

FATHERS' PERCEPTIONS OF CHILDREN'S REACTIONS

Black children also are more likely than White children to live with divorced parents. How do separation and divorce affect Black children? Experts disagree. The men in this study reported that during and, for a period of time, following

divorce, their children were depressed and anxious and displayed behavioral problems.

Preschool and School-Age Children

Fathers of preschool children reported that the children exhibited numerous behavioral problems including bed-wetting, hyperactivity, thumb-sucking, and withdrawal. Jim said, "My 5-year-old started to wet his bed and fought kids in his preschool. He was obviously affected by the divorce."

Fathers of school-age children also believed that their divorces negatively affected their children. For example, Douglas said,

My son started acting out in school. He started to fight other kids after the divorce. I had to go to his school several times to talk to teachers. Can you imagine a 6-year-old being suspended from school? He really hurt another boy in school, and I'm trying to get some help for him.

According to the respondents, school-age children appeared to experience more psychological distress than did preschool children 1 year postdivorce.

PREADOLESCENT AND ADOLESCENT CHILDREN

Children in their preadolescence and adolescence years appeared to be overwhelmed by the stresses of divorce. They also felt abandoned by their mothers, who were overwhelmed by supporting and managing households alone.

Matt described a sad story of his son's reaction to the divorce. His sons were 11 and 15 years old when he divorced. The youngest son, Dameon, immediately reacted to the divorce with a sense of detachment. Matt explained,

Dameon was going through so much hurt and pain. He was withdrawn and fighting. He started to steal, and I could not put up with it anymore. I put him in a treatment center for juveniles. The only thing I wanted him to do was to live a normal life. Dameon stayed at the center for 1 year and then went to Job Corps at age 13. He came home from Job Corps, and I was actually afraid of him. He got involved in street gangs. He did not want to do anything. I said, "You are going to school." We got into a fight. He ran out the house and returned with four other guys. They all had .25 automatics. I called my brother to come over to my house. I got my pistol. Dameon and his friends were coming toward my door shooting. I shot the gun up in the air to scare them. I just wanted to scare them away. The police came, and I explained to them the situation. I had to lock Dameon in detention for a couple of months. When he got out of detention, I told him that we could not live together. I said, "Two men can't live together. One of them must be the father, and the other must be the son, and I am not gonna be your son. I brought you into this world." He left and went back to Job Corps. He calls my mother often. He is lost, confused, and in pain, wandering through life with no hope for a better future.

Tears rolled from Matt's eyes when he described his oldest son's problems:

My oldest son, Marcus, is in prison. He was at a dangerous age at the time of the divorce.... Marcus loved his mother, you know. One day, 6 months after the divorce, Hazel was beaten and robbed. She was beaten so badly that two ribs were broken and all of her teeth were knocked out. They took her money, her clothes, and even her shoes. Marcus knew the boys who did this. One afternoon, Marcus bought a gun and shot the boys who beat his mother. He was in a state of shock and hadn't realized that he had killed them. Blood was gushing out like a waterfall as they crumpled over on the floor. Marcus suddenly felt sorry for them. Police cars were pulling up, lighting up the driveway, and the sirens and red flashing lights brought all the neighbors out. Marcus was arrested. I didn't have money to get him a good lawyer, but I paid $1,000 for the lawyers. They sentenced him to 10 years in prison. My mother sobbed in disbelief when the bailiffs led Marcus from the courtroom in handcuffs.

Matt said that the divorce contributed to his son's behavior:

My sons went through so much hurt and pain. I told both my sons that I will be there to help them. I told Marcus that it wasn't all his fault. I told him I don't know what I would do if I had been in his situation, seeing someone beat my mother. I understand that when someone disrespects your mother, a man has to do what he has to do. I didn't want to tell Marcus that if Hazel had stayed married, this probably wouldn't have happened, because I think Hazel's boyfriend instigated the whole incident.

Other men also reported that children adopted destructive behavioral patterns following their divorces. For example, Maurice reported that his teenage daughter became sexually active following the divorce and believed that she was encouraged by his dating to act on her sexual impulses. Other respondents reported that children displayed similar behavior when their ex-wives dated. As Carl explained, "When Rita started to date male friends, my 13-year-old daughter became absolutely boy crazy. She asked me if she could kiss and have a boyfriend."

There has been a lack of research on the relationship between growing up in a mother-headed household and Black female adolescent sexual development. From the respondents' perspective, preteen daughters often were more desirous of masculine attention and approval postdivorce. An interesting research question concerns the relationship, if any, between divorced mothers' dating and subsequent teenage pregnancy among Black adolescents. Men also reported that their sons became resentful of their ex-wives' dates. For example, Derek explained, "My 12-year-old son was so angry when he met Joan's boyfriend. He left home and stayed over at a friend's house because Joan was dating. My son complains that Joan's boyfriend tries to discipline him and to tell him what to do."

Men also reported that preadolescent and adolescent children were troubled by a lingering sorrow that resulted in self-destructive behavioral patterns including engaging in the drug culture, becoming pregnant, and skipping school. Some men said that their children were angry at them for disrupting their homes and believed that the divorces were childish. Wallerstein and Kelly (1979) identify this process as "precipitous de-idealization of the parent" in which the

adolescent feels disappointed and lost without moral guidance.

Perhaps the cultural pull of pseudo-macho hip-hop fads are powerful inducements for Black preadolescent and adolescent children of divorce because these children often experience the loss of daily interaction with their fathers. Indeed, there is a younger generation of Blacks who are more alienated than were previous generations. Thus, these children might be in even greater need of fathering and might be even more adversely affected by divorce than were previous generations of Black children.

CHILD CUSTODY

The respondents believed that there is a gender bias in the U.S. child custody laws due to maternal preference in custody awards. Therefore, without exception, fathers reported extreme psychological distress because courts automatically assume that women should be awarded custody of children. A case in point was Henry, who described his reaction when the judge awarded maternal custody:

> *I wanted joint custody, and the judge said because I had been separated from my spouse for 1 year, my daughter and son should live with Linda. I was sick to my stomach for months, I couldn't sleep or eat for weeks because I am a better parent than Linda. I tried to tell the judge that Linda was depressed and was not capable of being a good mother because she was being emotionally ripped apart at work by racism. But Linda was awarded sole custody.*

The men reported extreme difficulty adjusting to the reduced involvement in their children's lives. For example, Leon was exuberant at the birth of his daughter. He pointed out the stress of noncustodial parenting:

I was involved as much as possible with my daughter from birth. Because I had experienced little warmth from my father, I wanted to be the opposite of him. I attended prenatal appointments and child birth classes. I was in the delivery room when she was born. As I held my newborn daughter, nothing could prepare me for the love I felt. All of a sudden, the world changed and I wanted to protect her. When I cut the umbilical cord, I experienced the greatest moment of my life.

Leon's daughter was 3 years old when he and his wife divorced. He emphasized, "I regret not being part of my daughter's life on a daily basis. Anything that reminds me of her makes me cry, even a child on TV commercials, like the Kodak commercials with fathers and daughters." Brent also said, "The greatest stressor is not being there when my daughter returns from dates. Since I want her to marry a man like me, I want to meet her dates and be there when she returns." During the interview, Brent cried, expressing the grief he felt at leaving his daughter. He thought about buying a home "where my daughter would live when she reaches age 18." He even coached his daughter's basketball team to spend time with her and expressed considerable pain over seeing his daughter only intermittently.

For the respondents, their absence from their homes was particularly stressful given the presence of gangs and the high rates of homicides, adolescent pregnancies, and illicit drug use among Black youths. For example, they became anxious at indications that their children were succumbing to a negative teen subculture. As Anton explained,

I was afraid of the subtle changes in my son Shawn's behavior. He was becoming defiant toward his teachers and stepfather. He behaved in a way that nobody understood. He bopped liked the kids who lived in the 'hood. He started to let his baggy jeans fall lower on his behind. He suddenly resisted authority and displayed an arrogant body language that teenagers do to tell grown-ups they are the boss. It drove me up the wall that I couldn't have more influence or control over his life. I felt powerless.

Respondents also reported numerous difficulties with maintaining contact with teenage children. Kenneth expressed the intense frustration of his failed attempts to contact his daughter. He explained, "When I call my 16-year-old daughter, she's too busy to talk. She's busy with friends, at a dance class, or at the mall with her friends. It seems like she has no time for me." He also indicated that he felt abandoned when his daughter failed to acknowledge a birthday or a holiday. Kenneth tearfully stated, "My daughter didn't call to wish me happy birthday, nor did she wish me happy Father's Day. It's like she hates me. I keep telling Mary to tell my daughter to call me." In the past, Kenneth contributed to family discussions with the assurance that his viewpoint would be seriously considered. Now, he felt like an outsider. His point of view often was voiced only as a criticism of the mother's opinion.

Todd also vividly expressed the lack of influence in his daughter's life:

I am trying to make Cheryl understand and to figure out what she wants to be. Her favorite words are "my friends." Rachael lets Cheryl have her own way and to do her own

things. Rachael wants to be friends [with] Cheryl. So, what I think does not count. In the final analysis, Rachael's opinion is what counts.

Although the respondents reported that they saw their children in accordance with the divorce decrees, they underscored that these visits reminded them that they were losing influence over their children. Although they pursued independent relationships with their children, in many instances, ex-wives defined and orchestrated father-child relationships.

VISITATION AND CHILD SUPPORT

Most men retained relationships with their children, even if they lived in other geographical regions. Fathers who remained in the children's localities maintained a regular schedule of visits. However, they encountered a number of problems. One problem involved ex-wives' noncooperativeness. According to Ivan, he was allowed to see his children only when it was convenient for his ex-wife. Similar to Arendell's (1995) study, Ivan and other men frequently complained that ex-wives used visitation to pursue their activities without having to pay for babysitting.

Men indicated that although they might send child support payments to their wives, they often were viewed merely as income sources, like employers or social security. Thus, the following was a representative comment among the men: "Ex-wives often fail to recognize how valuable a father is for the development and growth of children. They see fathers only as a money source." Visitation sometimes was directly linked to child support; if men did not pay child support, then some wives would not permit visitation or contact with children. Clyde de-

scribed an incident in which Betty had him arrested because he failed to pay child support:

I called Betty and asked if I could see the children. I was really looking forward to seeing my daughters, Futima and Tamekia. I planned to take them to the children's museum and to eat pizza. I thought about all the things I wanted to ask them. Driving on the street, I noticed that the apartment was dark. I had talked with Betty a couple of hours before, so she was expecting me. Then I heard footsteps behind me. It was a policeman. I stood still and put my hands up. He shoved me into the backseat of a police car and said, "There's been a felony warrant issued for your arrest." I was in shock. Betty had arranged this so I could go to jail—and to destroy me. I had fallen behind on my $1,000-a-month child support, even though I had gotten loans, sold my car, [and] pawned all of my stereo and photography equipment to comply with child support payments.

Clyde emphasized that no one understood that he was doing his best with child support. He told his attorney about his plight, but the attorney only asked for another installment on his bill. Clyde could not understand why Betty linked child visitation rights to his child support obligations, especially considering she remained close to his family. After spending 2 days in jail, he pondered eliminating contact with his children to avoid Betty:

For a while, I stopped picking my kids up on weekends because I was so ashamed [that] I didn't have any money. I felt like less than a man. I thought of just giving up and tried to tell myself just to let them go, but I couldn't abandon my babies.

Clyde and other men considered withdrawing from children to avoid contact with ex-wives.

Coping with Noncustodial Parenting

Approximately 90% (*n* = 45) of the fathers coped with noncustodial parenting by increasing their involvement with their children. Stanley moved three blocks away from Paula and her husband to be near his children. He asserted that he participates biweekly in activities with his children including attending church and seeing movies. Willy reported that his children live with him every summer and during school vacations.

For the majority of men, spending time with their children was a priority for the following reasons. First, they were committed to raising their children. This was a representative comment: "There is absolutely nothing I would not do for my children. I want them to have a better life than I had." Second, they often received encouragement from family members to sustain contact with their children. "My mother and sister insist that they see my children every week" was another representative remark. Third, children often increased the respondents' self-esteem. Todd proclaimed, "When my daughter tells me I am a great father, and when she smiles upon seeing me, I feel 10 feet tall in a society where I am often treated as a second-class citizen."

Noncustodial fathering resulted in few benefits and little satisfaction, and it created profound emotional distress. The absence of daily interaction with children, difficulty in maintaining contact with teenage children, and conflictual postmarital relations made noncustodial fathering extremely stressful.

INTERRACIAL CHILDREN AND NONCUSTODIAL FATHERING

Men who were in interracial marriages reported particular stress with noncustodial parenting. Men often were concerned about their children's identification with a stepparent of a different race in that the children might develop serious identity problems. For example, Taylor agonized over being inaccessible to his son, who lived in another state. He explained,

> *My sons are biracial and are struggling with identity issues, and I am the only one who can help them with this. They don't even know who they are, and they are very angry and confused. They have been called racial names at school and [have] wondered why.*

Graham also voiced profound frustration at being separated from his biracial daughter:

> *My daughter is 12 years old, and when I see her during the summer months, I see how confused she is.... I feel so guilty because I can't help her sort out who she is. She is being raised by my ex-wife to be culturally White, but society treats her as Black. She is having trouble coping with racial stereotypes and prejudices. She doesn't even understand what it means to be Black in America. The hardest thing for me as a Black parent is to teach my daughter to live in a racist society.*

Graham was convinced that his daughter would experience a better life living with him. Because Tina was considering marrying a man who had concerns about raising a biracial stepdaughter, Graham believed that he could provide a more normal life for his daughter by exposing her to a Black community.

STEPFATHERS IN A NONCUSTODIAL SETTING

The cultural norms of appropriate stepfather behavior are less precise than those pertaining to biological or adoptive fathers (Marsiglio, 1991). The norms for noncustodial stepparenting are even more ambiguous in Western societies. Therefore, stepfathers face increased adjustment problems postdivorce. For example, with trembling of his hands and tears streaming softly down his face, James reported intense frustration over the lack of daily contact with his stepdaughter: "I raised Ukemia from the age of 2. She was like my own daughter, and I miss her deeply. She was so devastated by the divorce, she is staying out late at night and getting into smoking and drinking." Because mothers usually retained custody of stepchildren, the respondents experienced profound distress and a sense of loss. Contact with stepchildren usually was by phone calls; however, as time passed, the number of phone calls decreased.

Stepchildren frequently requested to live with their stepfathers. In fact, Sam waged a court battle for joint custody of his stepdaughter, even though he lived with another woman. He reported, "My stepdaughter has always been with me from age 4. Her father died, so I feel like I have as much right to her as her mother." Sam visited his stepdaughter daily after the divorce.

Of interest, stepfathers encouraged biological fathers and other family members to become involved in the lives of their stepchildren. For example, Truman said,

I saw how depressed my stepson, Ricky, was after the divorce. He'd call, cry, and tell me he was miserable. I told his biological father he needed to spend some time with him because he is at the age where he needs a father. He said he would try to call Ricky soon.

Stepfathers who married women with teenage children reported that there was no contact postdivorce. For instance, Arthur, who indicated that his stepdaughter was unwilling to accept a male authority figure said, "I don't see my stepdaughter. She left for college after the divorce, and I have not seen or heard from her. It has been 3 years." Taylor said,

My stepdaughter and I have no contact. I wonder how she is doing, but I have not talked with her since I divorced her mother. My stepdaughter is relieved her mother divorced. She did not like having a Black stepfather.

Stepfathers and Visitation

Visitation was especially problematic with stepchildren. A large number of stepfathers were unable to visit their stepchildren unless they had biological children by the mothers. For example, James married a woman with a daughter, and they later had two sons. He was able to visit his stepdaughter while he visited his biological sons. However, Larry, who married a woman with two sons and had no subsequent children, relinquished contact with his stepsons. Larry's ex-wife, Pat, regarded marriage as a package deal. She could not separate Larry's relationship with her sons from the marriage. When the marriage ended, the stepfather-stepson bond withered. The rights of stepfathers and custody of stepchildren in the event of divorce is a crucial issue. Law in this area is rapidly changing, although it is unlikely that biological fathers will be legally replaced by stepfathers.

In the next section, we turn to respondents' views of the future of fatherhood and discuss recommendations to empower Black fathers. They were profoundly concerned about the current trends that are paralyzing the Black community and that are gradually spreading to all American families that are economically disadvantaged.

THE FUTURE OF BLACK FATHERHOOD

The respondents were concerned about the high levels of marital instability and the plight of Black youths. As Maurice pointed out,

What scares me is the younger generation of Black males who are angry. Their whole rap music is about abusing women. When I grew up in the 1960s, the music I listened to was about building a stronger relationship with women. The younger generation has little respect for their own lives and the lives of others.

Although some respondents presented dismal views of the state of Black America in general and of father-child relationships in particular, they believed that Black youths have been profoundly affected by the identity crisis of White youths and that the self-rejection of the total value system in which many Black youths have been socialized has been overshadowed by "a broader culture of pathology." Unlike previous generations of Blacks who had positive self-images that shaped their destinies, some men believed that the younger generation often lacked internal resources to cope with mainstream society.

Decrease Economic Marginality and Social Discrediting

The men recommended complicated prescriptions for policymakers to alter the present situa-tion. One such solution was to offer premarital counseling and family life education with job training programs. Whereas most men stated that material resources were problematic for a large proportion of Black males, others stated that emotional resources were equally problematic. As Matt explained,

Black men face a difficult time in establishing emotional connections because their image of manhood is directly tied to their marginal economic status in America, and most don't earn enough money to support their children. Some of my friends say they get tired of hearing "We are not hiring" when they look for jobs. Even if a Black man is hired, his employment is complicated by prejudice and distrust about whether he will be a good worker. He must prove himself constantly. So, it's hard for some Black men to be emotionally responsible fathers without jobs.

Matt also said that it is difficult for Black fathers to transmit high aspirations when they live in a society that often is hostile to Black aspirations:

America treated Jesse Jackson more like an outsider than a qualified presidential candidate. They assumed that a Black man could not want to be president of the United States. They couldn't understand a Black could have the mental strength, moral conviction, and intelligence to become a president.

According to Matt, solving some of the problems of Black fatherhood is translated into changing the attitudes of Whites toward Blacks. From the perspective of most men, the disengagement of

Black fathers is the consequence of racial discrimination, cultural factors, and economic instability, which are inextricably linked. If America continues to sustain a racist culture, then there will be future generations of Black children who lack close relationships with their fathers.

Premarital and Drug Rehabilitation Programs

Several men also believed that premarital programs should be directly tied to effective drug rehabilitation programs. In their view, crack/cocaine has contributed to the deterioration of Black fatherhood. Many youths are using drugs or alcohol to escape and to remove themselves from problematic situations. Larry commented on the relationship between the use of crack and fatherhood:

> It's hard being a drug dealer, but the money is good for a man who can make $1,000 to $3,000 a day versus $5.75 per hour. It is a demanding job that takes time and energy away from anything else. It's a round-the-clock hustle. Plus, you have to act ruthless or act like you are prepared to kill your friend or family. This attitude has created a different set of values among some Black men that prevents the development of the emotional sides of themselves.

Some men indicated that the seductive pull of the underground economy offers quick and easy money because there are few available jobs paying decent salaries. Thus, a future generation of Black fathers will have the attitude that women and children are burdens and that taking care of somebody else is devalued when it means having less for oneself.

New Definitions of Black Masculinity

Other men indicated that it is important to change the definition of Black masculinity to change Black fatherhood. They believed that the socialization of Black men often emphasizes domination of women. This means that some Black men learn to function psychologically in ways to maintain their authority. Similar to White men, they suggested that Black men often strive to fit into male-dominated, hierarchically organized institutions through the adoption of aggressive behavior. Paradoxically, the socialization of Black men often is contrary to the dominant male preoccupation with power and competitiveness. As a result, Black youths often adopt an exaggerated and romanticized prototype of masculinity, which frequently is antithetical to enduring intimate relationships.

Male Support Groups

Several men emphasized the need for support groups for young Black men who are anticipating fatherhood. Such a group could assist fathers in parent-child communication and could alert them to the effects of conflictual partner relationships on the development of children. A teenage male support group also would provide an outlet for men to discuss their problems and to generate solutions or strategies for coping with prospective problems of fatherhood. As Dwayne noted,

> Men hurt, and there is nothing geared to Black men about fathering. They are disappointed and frustrated when they see the streets taking the lives of their children. Black women have magazines to help them to cope.

The respondents were concerned about the plight of future Black fathers and believed that children of involved fathers enjoyed a number of social, emotional, and intellectual advantages. They also were clear that given the competition from the media, peer groups, and a culture of drugs and violence, Black fathers can offer a unique contribution to children including love, care, and attention that promotes the optimum development of children. However, to effectively influence the future generation of Black fathers, mainstream society must tear down barriers imposed by race, erase stereotypes based on genetic background, and increase economic opportunities for Black men.

SUMMARY

Children played a central role in the lives of biological fathers as well as stepfathers. Of importance, fathers viewed children as the most important reason to remain in an unhappy marriage, and they often delayed divorce. The most significant finding is that stepchildren and biological children were viewed as equals in vying for love and affection, suggesting that some stepfathers felt more like real fathers. However, it is unknown how the quality of these relationships affects stepchildren as adults.

There were a variety of stressors associated with noncustodial parenting as men sought to maintain contact with their children. For example, visitation often was hampered by ex-wives' noncooperation, maintaining consistent contact with teenage children was difficult, and uncertainty of the role of being a good noncustodial father compounded the stress inherent in noncustodial fathering.

Stepfathers encouraged biological fathers to increase interaction with their children. This might be a race-specific behavior and points to the respondents' emphasis on nurturing Black children. Thus, encouragement of biological connections symbolized stepfathers' love and concern.

The findings of the present study both support and refute past research on Black fatherhood. Psychological strain was evident in most of the noncustodial divorced fathers, a finding consistent with other studies (Carter & Glick, 1970; Goldberg, 1979; Gutmann, 1987; Zeiss, Zeiss, & Johnson, 1980). Compared to the men in Umberson and Williams' (1993) study, respondents in our study did not experience extreme distress associated with noncustodial parenting. There are several reasons why our results differ from those of the previous studies. First, most of the fathers recognized the impact that divorce played in their children's lives and developed strategies to maintain positive relationships including establishing positive relationships with ex-spouses, even at times when they would rather not. Other methods used by fathers included making sure that children were as comfortable with them as with their mothers. In fact, some fathers furnished rooms for their children in their houses or apartments similar to those provided by the mothers.

Consistent with Goldsmith's (1981) findings, several fathers believed that ex-wives purposely erected barriers to retard regular interaction with children and became more prominent following divorce. Similar to results reported by Arendell (1995), fathers felt cheated by the court system and ex-wives because of visitation privileges. The length of time divorced influenced whether conflict with ex-wives was a frustration; men who were divorced longer were less likely to perceive their former spouses as a source of strain.

The findings concur with Wilson and Clarke's (1992) conclusions that noncustodial Black fathers are involved in the development of their children. Without exception, fathers supported their children financially and emotionally. Few stated that they had ever been late paying child support; however, it must be remembered that this was a working/middle class sample.

The socialization of Black sons was especially relevant to the men in this study. One issue involved the value of training sons to aspire to be effective fathers in the context of social discrediting. Fathers encouraged sons to be autonomous and independent. This emphasis began during the marriage and extended postdivorce.

Of interest, previous research has documented that children brought into first marriages increase marital instability (Chan & Heaton, 1989; Trent & South, 1992). In the present study, stepchildren often increased marital stability. Some stepchildren were adopted by the respondents and received child support. However, the younger the children at the time of the marriage, the stronger the relationship postdivorce, suggesting that teenage children often may be mature enough to solely think of stepfathers as their mothers' husbands rather than as their stepfathers. In addition, stepchildren who were raised by stepfathers from a young age experienced divorce-related emotional distress similar to that of biological children.

There is a perception, fostered by the sensationalism of the mass media, that the Black family is dying. This perception was shared by respondents when they discussed the future of Black fatherhood. Although some problems that respondents mentioned might be appropriately viewed as community problems rather than as problems of the Black family, they certainly have a negative effect on the functioning of Black fathers. Contemporary young Black fathers are particularly vulnerable to stress due to adherence to traditional definitions of masculinity, lack of male support groups, inadequate economic resources, and lack of drug rehabilitation programs. These factors result in delinquency and criminal behavior that occur within the family as well as in the broader society. Thus, the building of more prisons and harsher punitive measures will not erase the feelings of alienation among a large number of future Black fathers.

Reading 31   Stepparents

De Facto Parents or Legal Strangers?

MARY ANN MASON*   SYDNEY HARRISON-JAY
GLORIA MESSICK SVARE   NICHOLAS H. WOLFINGER

In most states, stepparents have little or no legal decision-making authority. Stepchildren do not receive the legal recognition as dependents that triggers a safety net in the event of death or divorce, nor do former stepparents have the legal right to visitation or custody. However, the lack of legal recognition of the stepparent role may not reflect the reality of contemporary stepfamilies. This article examines stepfamily functioning with the aim of creating a new policy orientation. We draw on both the National Survey of Families and Households and an in-depth study of 27 stepfamilies to investigate the everyday functioning of stepparents with regard to caregiving tasks, discipline, distribution of economic resources, attitudes toward legal status, and perception of parental roles. The findings support a new policy initiative that would legally recognize stepparents as de facto parents for a variety of purposes.

Stepparents are, generally speaking, legal strangers to their stepchildren (Mahoney, 1995). State laws give almost no recognition to the parental role of residential stepparents. They have no legal or decision-making authority in day care centers, schools, or other critical areas of their stepchildren's lives. Nor in most states are they required to support their stepchildren (Mason & Mauldon, 1996). Dependent benefits, including medical insurance and death benefits, sometimes exclude stepchildren. Similarly, in the event of death or divorce, there is no recognition of inheritance, visitation, or custody rights for stepparents; nor is there any obligation of

Authors' Note: *The fourth author's participation in this research was facilitated by a grant from the Bireley Foundation. An earlier version of this article was presented at the 2000 annual meeting of the American Sociological Association, Washington, DC.*

child support or continuation of dependent benefits. Federal law goes further than state law in recognizing the dependency of stepchildren in determining benefits, including social security survivor benefits. Nevertheless, federal policies are inconsistent, and most fall short of fully recognizing the stepparent/stepchild relationship (Mason & Simon, 1995). These legal shortcomings may leave stepchildren without a safety net and, in the event of divorce, with no access to their stepparent (Mason & Mauldon, 1996).

The absence of a legal status for stepparents has historical origins deeply imbedded in the issue of inheritance. Until the 19th century, only biological parentage within a marriage created legal parental rights and obligations, and only biological children would inherit (absent a will to the contrary). It was the issue of inheritance that blocked the possibility of legal adoption, which was not an option in this country until the second half of the 19th century (Grossberg, 1985).

Until recently, death and not divorce was the cause of most stepfamilies. The issue of who was the guardian of the estate and of the child was critical among the propertied classes, where there were concerns that a stepparent could gain these rights (Mason, 1994). Modern stepfamilies are most often formed following a divorce rather than a death, and we now allow inheritance from nonbiological parents through adoption, yet we have not reviewed our legal assumptions regarding stepparents. Although the rights and obligations of biological parents, particularly unwed fathers, have been greatly expanded in recent years (Mason, 1994), stepparents have received almost no attention from policy makers. Does stepfamily functioning reflect the role of *legal stranger*, the term used by many courts? Does this designation hinder the functioning of stepfamilies? Does it further the best interests of the children or of the stepparent in the event of the dissolution of the family by divorce or death?

What do stepparents and their spouses want with regard to legal protection?

We address these questions by drawing on the literature and our own data analysis. Following this, we propose a new policy initiative aimed at providing stepparents with a legal status, that of de facto parents, which we believe will better fit the reality of stepfamily functioning and better support stepfamilies.

Until recently, social science has provided us with little guidance for policy reform in this arena. Andrew Cherlin (1978) first noted that stepfamilies suffered from "lack of institutionalization" in 1978, but this work has not been followed by serious attempts to create new models or policy initiatives. More recent studies still find that the public views the stepparent role as ambiguous (Schwebel, Fine, & Renner, 1991) and that stepparents are uncertain about their own roles (Marsiglio, 1992).

Most studies of stepfamilies have focused on psychological functioning. The now-large literature emphasizes the hardships of adjustment and the emotional complexities of stepfamily life (Cherlin & Furstenberg, 1994; Coleman & Ganong, 1990; Keshet 1988; Papernow, 1988; Schwebel et al., 1991; White & Booth, 1985). These findings are complicated by the fact that parenting behavior generally changes over time. Most stepparents enter their new marriages with unrealistic expectations. They envision idealized relationships, perhaps fantasizing about what family life will be like. They may see themselves as the healers who will restore families left in upheaval by divorce (Papernow, 1988). The reality, as has been chronicled by the numerous studies of stepfamily dynamics, is very different. Frustration will set in as the "healer" discovers that good intentions often get short-circuited in an inherently difficult situation. It is only with patience and hard work that functional family relationships can be developed. Doing so seems to require the rejection of preconceived notions of family functioning in lieu of innovative compromise (Keshet, 1988; Papernow, 1988).

Although there is general recognition that the stepparent role is different than the role of a biological parent, there has been little progress in re-conceptualizing this role or discussion about the public policy desirability of doing so (Gamache, 1997). Fine (1994) suggested considering the English model, where stepparents may apply for parental rights without actually resorting to adoption. He qualified this suggestion with the caution that more research was required to determine the feasibility of such a scheme. A few scholars have written about the issues of support obligations (Riley, 1984) and the lack of recognition given to stepparents in custody proceedings (Silverman, 1992), but there have been few advances in promoting a new legal model.

The evidence on which to suggest a legal re-conceptualization of the role of stepparents has grown in recent years. A major concern of public policy is the economic support of children. The stepfamily literature reveals little about how income and other resources are shared during second marriages (Cherlin & Furstenberg, 1994). Although remarriage restores family income to nuclear family levels, economic well-being plunges drastically when a remarriage ends in divorce (Bachrach, 1983; Mason & Mauldon, 1996), an event more common than in first marriages (Sweet, Bumpass, & Call, 1988).

There is evidence that existing stepfamily policy does not match public attitudes. Ganong, Coleman, and Mistina (1995) found widespread support for the notion that residential stepparents are obliged to support their stepchildren. In the event of the dissolution of the stepfamily, there is a perception of continuing obligation but less so than for biological parents. Interestingly, this perception does not reflect the actual laws in most states, which do not require that stepparents provide support in an intact marriage or in the event of divorce.

Another type of economic contribution that stepparents may make to the family is in the form of dependent benefits. Mason and Simon (1995) explore the complex world of medical insurance and federal and state dependent-stepchildren benefits, but their major finding is the state of confusion and contradiction that characterizes eligibility requirements. Moreover, most of these benefits are terminated summarily in the event of divorce or death, which is not the case with biological families.

Another major public policy concern is the strengthening of families. Currently, the law gives no recognition to the parenting performed by stepparents: They have no authority in the child's world; in most states, they cannot legally sign a field trip permission slip or authorize teeth cleaning. Studies of parental caregiving for the most part have focused on rule setting and enforcement. We know from these studies that the biological parent, particularly the mother, is more likely to take the lead in rule setting and discipline, at least in the beginning (Heatherington & Clingempeel, 1992). One study found that stepparents were actively engaged in child rearing and became increasingly involved over a 4-year period (Ganong & Coleman, 1994). The literature does not, however, reveal much about the allocation of specific caregiving tasks, such as helping with homework or providing transportation. Finally, there has been little research on the attitudes of stepparents and their spouses about stepparents' legal rights or obligations. As with all families, legal issues are more likely to assume prominence in times of family crises such as divorce or death. Still, attitudes toward the everyday issues of legal authority and support obligations have been largely overlooked, as have stepparents' attitudes toward adoption and continued access to stepchildren in the event of divorce.

The purpose of this article is threefold. First, we present new findings that illuminate the gap between the legal conception of stepparents as strangers and the actual role that residential stepparents play, as well as their understanding of that role. Our study is directed particularly at hitherto ignored issues. These include an examination of everyday parenting tasks such as helping with homework, transporting children, giving advice, and administering discipline. We also look at how stepfamilies allocate their resources, determine which parent provides children with medical and other benefits, and decide which parent declares children dependents for income tax purposes. Second, we query stepparents about their knowledge of legal rights and what concerns they may have about them. These findings focus on questions of economic support, adoption, visitation in case of divorce, and authority in the public realm. Third, based on the results of this study and others, we evaluate the inadequacies of the current legal-stranger model and present a new legal model for consideration, a de facto parent model.

METHOD

Two sources of data are employed for this study. The first source is an in-depth qualitative study of 27 stepfamilies with minor children, and the second is the first wave of the National Survey of Families and Households (NSFH). The NSFH provides quantitative measures of behaviors and attitudes from a nationally representative sample. Our in-depth interviews offer rich qualitative data not available in a large sample survey.

In-Depth Interviews

We conducted in-depth interviews with 27 married couples in which at least one partner had children from a former relationship. We interviewed only married couples because they have a legal relationship. Subjects were recruited using convenience and snowball techniques. Husbands and wives were interviewed separately; interviews were semistructured, including questions about parental involvement in caregiving activities and discipline, the financial dependence of the stepchild(ren) on their stepparent, and knowledge of the legal rights and responsibilities of stepparents. Interviewers encouraged participants to respond to the open-ended questions with examples. Respondents were also queried about demographic information. Interviews lasted from 1 to 3 hours and were tape-recorded.

Description of In-Depth Interview Sample

All but three of the study couples had dependent children who were still living in their home at the time of the interviews. The children of the remaining three couples had left home recently. Of the 54 participants, 42 (78%) were Caucasian. The largest number of participants (20; 37% of sample) were professionals (lawyers, professors, psychologists). The second-largest group (15; 28%) worked in other white-collar jobs. There were also four business owners, two blue-collar workers, four retirees, and three students. The remaining six respondents (10%) were not working by choice. The ages of the participants varied from 29 to 76, with a median age of 45. The children of the respondents ranged widely in age, with the youngest child 6 months and the oldest children grown and living independently. In 16 of the couples (59%), the residential stepparent was the father. In California, joint custody is relatively common. As a result, many of the children of the couples interviewed were involved in joint custody arrangements but were living at least half of the time in the family interviewed.

NSFH

The NSFH is a national sample survey of American adults 19 and older (Sweet et al., 1988). In

1987 and 1988, 13,008 respondents were interviewed. These include a main sample of 9,643 respondents plus an oversample of minorities, newlyweds, single parents, individual parents in stepparent families, and individuals in cohabiting unions. Case weights supplied with the NSFH are used so the data constitute a nationally representative sample.

The NSFH contains numerous items on parenting attitudes and behavior. We report percentages based on stepparents' responses; elsewhere, we contrast the responses of biological and stepparents. Questions asked only of stepparents have sample sizes ranging from 1,038 to 1,050; items directed to both step- and biological parents have sample sizes ranging from 2,228 to 2,346, with about 32% hailing from stepfamilies. Supplementary analyses revealed that results were not an artifact of ethnicity, education, or respondent age.

FINDINGS: PARENTAL ACTIVITIES

NSFH

The NSFH data indicate that stepfamilies function very much like biological families on important parental caregiving tasks such as helping with homework and having private talks with children. About 43% of parents in both biological and stepfamilies said they frequently had private talks with their children. As for helping with homework, 51% of parents in biological families said they frequently helped with homework, as compared to 48% of those in stepfamilies.

In-Depth Interviews

Our in-depth interviews support the NSFH results and offer insight into the small differences between biological families and stepfamilies. On average, stepparents and biological parents put in a similar number of hours per week on parental tasks such as transporting children (3.0 hours for stepparents, 3.0 for biological parents) and helping with homework (2.6 hours for stepparents, 3.0 for biological parents). This and other small disparities may have more to do with the exigencies of everyday life than with a differentiation of the parent and stepparent roles. For transportation issues, it is largely a question of the parents' work schedules. As one stepfather commented, "Getting these kids out in the morning is a shared business. My wife usually makes breakfast, but I gather them together and drive them to school on my way to work." Help with homework was often provided by the parent who was considered more knowledgeable, something that could change over time. One stepfather noted, "When they were in grade school [my wife] did most of it. Now that [my stepdaughter] is doing algebra, she comes to me, I guess because I do it in my work."

FINDINGS: DISCIPLINE AND ADVICE

NSFH

The NSFH data suggest that discipline is a complex and seemingly contradictory topic for stepfamilies. About 66% stated that raising stepchildren was hard because they are used to different rules. On the other hand, 61% said it was just as easy to discipline stepchildren as biological children.

In-Depth Interviews

There is greater role differentiation in the establishment and enforcement of rules than in other parenting tasks. Both parents are about as likely to participate in setting rules for the children as the biological parent alone. In 13 families, both parents set the rules, and in 10 families, only the biological parent did so. Both parents are also likely to enforce the rules, with biological parents only slightly more apt to do so. However, stepparents by themselves are unlikely to be the chief rule makers or the chief enforcers. This occurred in only two families.

Another instance of role differentiation concerns advice seeking. Children are far more likely to turn to their biological mother than their stepparent or their biological father (in 12 families, the children sought the advice of their biological mother first). There is, however, a qualitative difference based on the advice sought. Stepparents are often considered as specialists, looked to for specific advice on academic subjects such as math or on personal matters in which the gender of the stepparent is important. As one stepfather put it, "Just last year, when she started going to dances, she started asking me about what guys might be thinking, like, when they just hang out against the wall."

FINDINGS: PERCEPTION OF PARENTAL ROLE

Although it is useful to understand how parental tasks are allocated in stepfamilies, it is even more important to ascertain whether the stepparents consider themselves to be actual parents.

NSFH

The majority of NSFH stepparents (57%) believe it is false to state that "stepparents don't have the full responsibility of being a parent" Moreover, one half (50%) believe that stepchildren are just as satisfying as biological children.

In-Depth Interviews

We asked stepparents and their spouses if the stepparent is considered a parental figure. (We devised this question wording carefully: We did not ask if stepparents considered themselves the equivalent of the biological parents). Strikingly, both partners in all but three stepfamilies inter-

viewed considered the stepparent to be a parental figure. In two of the three families where this was not the case, the couple was engaged in a bitter dispute with an ex-wife. Only three of the stepparents qualified their parental status with a caveat about not taking the place of the other biological parent. As one stepmother put it, "When they come back from their mom's on Sunday night, I want to cry. They treat me different[ly]. They want me to know I am not their real mom."

FINDINGS: ECONOMIC ARRANGEMENTS

In-Depth Interviews

The NSFH lacks data on the management and sharing of resources within families, but our in-depth interviews allow us to address this topic. The majority of families in our sample (15) are one-pot families. For most, this means that all the income brought in by either spouse is put into a common pool from which all family expenses are paid. In some cases, this arrangement is not so straightforward. A few families among the 15 offer modified versions of the one-pot practice: Most common is the biological parent who receives child support from an ex-spouse and keeps it separately for some of the expenses of that child, or the stepparent who pays out support money for a nonresident child before he or she deposits money in the common pool. Fewer than 30% of our one-pot stepfamilies receive support from a noncustodial parent, but in all these families, the money is kept separate for that child's expenses. Sometimes, this includes payment for lessons or private schools that the family could not otherwise afford. One mother said,

> I don't have a separate account. We do have a joint second checking account, but it's where I deposit her child support checks. That money is

*just saved up, and I pay school tu-
ition with that, and so we don't use
that money for anything else, but it's
still a joint account.*

Among the separate pot families, the fact
that a stepparent maintains a separate pot by no
means indicates that he or she is not helping to
support the stepchild. No matter how much is
held back as separate, all families share common
household expenses. One father, whose wife was
the stepmother and the secondary earner, described their system:

*We've set up a household budget,
and we've allocated a share of how
much each other pays toward the
budget determined by what share
each of us—I don't know how to describe this—but what share each of us
make proportionate with our income.*

The arrangements dealing with medical
benefits are far more complex. In the first place,
employee-based medical plans differ widely
with regard to who is considered a dependent
child. In most cases, residential stepchildren are
covered (Mason & Simon, 1995). When stepchildren are covered, expediency appears to be
the greatest decision maker. Children receive
medical benefits from whichever parent has the
more generous plan, or any plan at all. Sometimes, it is the noncustodial parent who offers
this advantage, and in one case, it was the cohabiting girlfriend of the noncustodial parent whose
plan somehow included the nonresidential children of her partner. Still, a number of stepchildren have currently or at some point in the past
been considered dependents of their stepparents
for these purposes.

Expediency may also determine who declares
children as dependents for income tax purposes.

Most trade off yearly with noncustodial parents.
This may reflect a settlement agreement or the fact
that joint custody is common in California.

FINDINGS: LEGAL STATUS

In-Depth Interviews

The NSFH does not address legal issues or questions relating to the stepparents' status with regard
to outside institutions, such as the children's
schools. In our interviews, we queried respondents about the legal rights and responsibilities
of stepparents and asked them what they thought
law and society could do to support them better.
Questions about adoption were also asked of
both spouses. Finally, the subject of whether the
stepparent would want to pursue contact in the
event of divorce or the death of the biological
parent was addressed.

Not surprisingly, stepparents and biological
parents, even those who are lawyers, were generally unclear about the legal rights and responsibilities of stepparents, although the great majority
realized there were not many. None of them said
legal considerations played a significant role in
their decision to marry, although a few had discussed the issue. In response to what the law
could do to improve their current situation, there
were three patterns. A large group believed stepparents should have more authority with regard to
the outside world: the right, for instance, to be involved in school conferences or to authorize legal
permission. One biological father, engaged in an
ongoing custody battle with his ex-wife, said, "It
would empower my [current] wife to be considered as a parent by the school and by the courts."
A second group called for more public awareness
and education in the schools about the situation of
stepfamilies and/or support and counseling for
stepfamilies. A third group believed that their
problems were their own and that the law could
do nothing to help.

As to the specific question of whether the stepparent would like to continue contact with the stepchild in the event of divorce or death, the almost universal response was yes. Explanations of this sentiment varied considerably. One position was represented by the stepfather who said, half jokingly, that if he and his wife were to separate, he would want his stepson to live with him. In this case, the stepfather had known the teenage son from the time he was 2 years old. On the other end of the continuum was the stepfather who said that if the couple were to divorce, he would like to continue to see the children, but that the reality was that he would probably leave the area, making future contact difficult. That couple had been together for only about a year. Other stepparents pointed to the wishes of the stepchildren as determining the extent of contact to be maintained if the marriage ended. Only one stepparent indicated that she would not want to continue contact.

In contrast to the almost unanimous wish for continued contact with stepchildren, no stepparent wanted primary custody in the event of a divorce. However, most said they would consider it if their spouse died. Almost all stepparents qualified this response by referring to the nonresident biological parent. In only one case would both spouses definitely want the stepparent to seek custody of the stepchild in the event of the death of the biological parent. This couple had a mutual biological child, while the nonresident biological parent of the stepchild lived out of the area, and neither he nor his family had frequent contact with that child. In the only case where the other biological parent was deceased, the stepparents did not think the child would agree to it. The child was an older teen and had close relationships with relatives.

As for legal adoption of the stepchild, the majority of stepparents had at least considered the idea but rejected it because of the existence of the nonresident biological parent. In a few cases, there was concern about the name change, particularly where there were grandparents who would be unhappy (possibly because of inheritance issues). "They couldn't get around the name thing," explained one stepfather who had suggested the idea of adoption to his in-laws. Some believed the children would not want it. For others, it simply did not feel like the right decision.

DISCUSSION

It is not a secret that the emotional relationship between the stepparent and stepchild is different from that of a biological parent with his or her child. Less acknowledged or understood are the caregiving and economic support provided by stepparents. Nevertheless, most stepparents see themselves as parental figures, as do their spouses. The findings of this study, highlighting several important aspects of stepfamily functioning and relationships, have policy implications for strengthening the legal role of stepparents and protecting the interests of their stepchildren.

Stepparents serve as primary caregivers. Our findings show that on important everyday tasks, they perform the yeoman work of helping with homework and shuttling the children back and forth, just as the biological parents do. On the more delicate issues of giving advice and setting and enforcing rules, they are less often the leaders, but they are still active participants. Stepparents also make a major difference to the economic well-being of their stepchildren, given that remarriage generally restores family income to predivorce levels (Bachrach, 1983; Mason & Mauldon, 1996). In contrast, absent biological parents rarely provide much financial assistance. On average, only 25% of all stepfamilies receive some form of child support, and that is likely to be far below what it costs to raise a child (Mason & Mauldon, 1996).

Stepparents may provide other material benefits. Although a minority of children in our in-depth interviews were listed as dependents on their stepparents' medical insurance, this may not always be the case. In times of family breakdown, dependent benefits can be even more critical. Other research has shown there is a great deal of contradiction in how stepchildren are considered for the purposes of dependent benefits. Many federal programs, including social security, recognize the dependent role of stepchildren for benefits, whereas state laws generally do not (Mason & Simon, 1995). State laws also do not recognize stepchildren as natural heirs in the event of the death of the stepparent, nor do most work-related life insurance plans. Neither do work-related medical benefits uniformly recognize stepchildren as dependents.

Our results show that many stepparents and their spouses would like more outside recognition of the stepparent's parental role, and nearly all stepparents express a desire to continue contact with their stepchildren if the marriage should end through death or divorce. Ambivalence about adoption is complex. Most do not consider it a possibility because of the existence of the nonresident biological parent. Others see themselves as lacking full parental status. Also, most stepparents are at least a little wary of yet another divorce. For all these reasons, legal adoption may not seem attractive to most stepparents.

POLICY IMPLICATIONS AND POLICY INITIATIVES

Stepparents perform parental duties, contribute to the support of their stepchildren, and consider themselves parental figures. Nevertheless, public opinion and state law offer little recognition of what stepparents do for their stepchildren. This lack of recognition can have negative con-

sequences in intact families and even more so in the event of the dissolution of the stepfamily.

In intact stepfamilies, the authority of the stepparent may be seriously undermined in his or her dealings with the outside world. The inability to be recognized as a legitimate parental authority by schools, courts, camps, hospitals, and other institutions that deal with children may impair effective parenting, a concern that was expressed by many stepparents in our in-depth interviews. This lack of legal standing may have repercussions within the family and the extended family as well. Just as we depend on legal marriage to define our roles to the outside world and extended family—and to some extent within the nuclear family as well—the absence of legal recognition can influence public and private perception. The "incomplete institutionalization" of the stepparent role (Cherlin, 1978) is surely affected by the absence of legal recognition. More critically, in the event of the dissolution of the stepfamily, the lack of continuing rights and obligations may jeopardize the well-being of the stepchildren, who have been dependent, economically and otherwise. Unlike divorce in a biological family, divorce in a stepfamily offers no safety net of child support or benefits, and there is no expectation of continuing access to the nonbiological parent. In the event of the death of the stepparent, the stepchild is not considered a natural heir for purposes of inheritance and is not considered an automatic beneficiary on life insurance (Mason & Simon, 1995).

It is time, given the rapid increase of stepfamilies and our growing knowledge about their needs, to reconsider the stepparent/stepchild relationship. One possibility would be to create a new parental category, that of a de facto parent, which would legally recognize stepparents as parental authorities but not cut off the rights of nonresident biological parents and not continue indefinitely in the event of divorce. The concept of de facto parent is currently used loosely in the law with respect to those caring for children, but it has not taken on full form, with clearly delineated rights and responsibilities. Moreover, there is no consistency in the courts as to its use.

For the purposes of federal and state policy, a de facto parent could be treated virtually the same as a biological parent during the marriage. The same rights, obligations, and presumptions would attach vis-à-vis their stepchildren, including the obligation of support. These rights and duties would continue in some form, based on the length of the marriage, following divorce or the death of either the biological or the de facto parent. In the event of divorce, the stepparent would have standing to seek custody or visitation, but the stepparent could also be obligated for child support of a limited duration, perhaps half the length of the marriage. This support could extend to medical and other benefits on which the stepchildren rely. On the death of a stepparent, a minor dependent stepchild—but not necessarily an adult stepchild—would be treated like a biological child for purposes of inheritance and benefits.

Creating a de facto parent category for stepparents would not invalidate the existing rights and obligations of the biological parent who does not live with the child. Rather, this proposal would empower a stepparent as an additional parent. Multiple parenting is the barrier on which many family law reform schemes have foundered (Bartlett, 1984), including efforts to reformulate the role of stepparents. Working out the details is critical to the acceptance of such a concept. For instance, an important aspect of multiple parenting is legal authority. If stepparents are required to accept support obligations, fairness dictates that they must also be given parental rights. As noted above, a stepparent generally has no legal authority over a stepchild, even to authorize a field trip. If stepparents were

given de facto status, teachers, doctors, camp directors, the courts, and other important people and institutions in the stepchild's life could look to the stepparent as well as the biological parents for consultation and approval. The parental role of the stepparent would be recognized as normative. When the biological parents have shared legal custody, the law could recognize the parental rights of three parents, rather than two. Although this sounds unusual, in practical terms, it is an accurate reflection of how many families now raise their children.

The model of de facto parent could be used for other classes of parental figures, such as long-term cohabitors who are not legally married to the biological parent (but who are referred to as stepparents). These parent figures, however, vary widely in their long-term commitment to the children or to the biological parent, to whom they have no legal tie. For these parent figures, an application process might be appropriate, as well as consent by the biological parent.

CONCLUSION

This study suggests that stepparents see themselves as parental figures, relied on by their stepchildren. Yet, public and legal recognition is ambiguous at best. The lack of legal clarification can have negative effects on the stepparent/stepchild relationship, both during the marriage and in the event of its dissolution. Limited legal recognition is particularly relevant when stepchildren are left with no economic safety net after a divorce. We suggest a new legal conceptualization of stepparents as de facto parents with most of the same rights and obligations as biological parents, but with a limited duration in the event the marriage ends. A new legal status could also promote a more complete social institutionalization of the stepparent role in society.

Reading 32   Family Law in the New Millennium

For Whose Families?

MARY ANN MASON*   MARK A. FINE
SARAH CARNOCHAN

In this article, the authors review changes in family law over the past 30 years in the following areas: marriage, divorce, child custody, remarriage and stepfamilies, unwed fathers, third-party visitation, nontraditional partnerships, assisted reproduction, and adoption. The authors also discuss the role that the social sciences have had in the family law revolution. Finally, the authors speculate about future changes in family law and the role that the social sciences will play in these legal reforms.

Marriage and family have historically played an important role in U.S. society. According to one judge in a 1939 divorce case,

> *one of the foundation pillars of our government is the sanctity of the marriage relation and the influences of the home life, where the holy bond of wedlock is looked upon with profound reverence and respect, and where the marriage vows are sedulously observed. (Fania v. Fania, 1939, p. 373)[1]*

Marriage remains a cherished institution; 93% of Americans rate a happy marriage as one of their most important life goals (Gallagher & Waite, 2000). However, Americans are marrying less often and for shorter periods (Nagourney, 2000). In the last part of the 20th century, family law has focused on redefining the legal institution of marriage and, at the same time, recognizing other family and childrearing forms.

Although there is not a consensual definition, for the purposes of this article, *family law* is defined as the branch of law that addresses issues pertaining to romantically involved partners

Authors' Note: We acknowledge the assistance of Nicole Zayac with this article.

*Mason, Mary Ann, Mark A. Fine, and Sarah Carnochan. "Family Law in the New Millennium: For Whose Families?" *Journal of Family Issues* Vol. 22, No. 7, October 2001 pp. 859–881. Copyright 2001 Sage Publications, Inc. Reprinted by permission of Sage Publications, Inc.

(e.g., marriage, divorce, and domestic partnerships) and children (e.g., child custody following divorce, assisted reproduction, and adoption). Changes in family law have typically lagged behind societal changes; the law struggles to come to terms with new social realities (e.g., domestic partnerships, unwed fathers, and alternative reproduction) by either incorporating or reacting against those changes. However, in some instances, such as no-fault divorce statutes, changes in the law have served to facilitate social change. Finally, some family issues of great social importance are virtually neglected in family law, most strikingly, the role of stepparents.

Most issues in family law are decided state by state. Therefore, wide variations exist among states in fundamental issues, such as the division of property following divorce. Nonetheless, it is possible to recognize trends that cross all or most state lines. Although several federal laws have had substantial effects, family law remains solidly within states' jurisdiction.

Another part of the revolution in family law is the role played by the social sciences. Both legal rhetoric and judicial reasoning have been greatly influenced in some parts of family law by professionals in mental health and related social science disciplines. Judges often refer to research in their opinions regarding the best interests of the child, and mental health experts are routinely called on in familial disputes. Still, the application of the social sciences is uneven and uncertain, and there are many areas in which research is routinely ignored or manipulated.

TRENDS IN FAMILY LAW

Marriage

Although marriage remains a central cultural paradigm, substantial changes have occurred in marriage as a legal institution over the past 30 years. During most of U.S. history, a married couple was regarded as having a single legal identity. Although married women made significant progress in the 19th century in obtaining the right to own and manage their own property through the passage of property legislation, women were still largely considered dependents of their husbands. Husbands were responsible for the families' financial well-being, and women who worked were eligible for lesser benefits than their male counterparts based on the assumption that they were not the household's primary wage earner. Prenuptial agreements were not honored by the courts, and the obligations at divorce differed for men and women—only women could receive alimony. Debts incurred by women were their husbands' responsibility, but women had no corresponding responsibility for their husbands' debts (Regan, 1999). Moreover, there was no tort liability between spouses, spouses could not testify against one another in court, and police were hesitant to intervene in cases of domestic violence. For example, in *Ennis v. Donovan* (1960), a Maryland court held that "a married woman had no common-law right to sue her husband for injuries suffered by her as the result of his negligence, and, the Legislature has not yet seen fit to grant her such a right" (p. 543). Despite changes in women's position throughout the past century, the rhetoric of a unitary spousal identity—"husband and wife as 'a single person, represented by the husband'"—remained in judicial discourse into the 1970s (*Lewis v. Lewis,* 1976).

In the last three decades of the 20th century, this paradigm of dependence shifted toward a partnership model in which marriage is more like a contractual relationship between two individuals. Under the new model, a husband and wife are considered equal partners contracting in a marriage, and both retain an independent legal existence. The current law relating to marriage views "the marital relationship as one constituted by personal choice, the natural character of which is rooted in the desire of individuals to seek happiness through intimate association with another" (Regan, 1999, p. 652). With this shift, the nature of marriage has undergone a fundamental alteration. Spouses now hold mutual rights and responsibilities with respect to one another (*Queen's Medical Center v. Kagawa,* 1998). The presumption of the husband as breadwinner and the wife the homemaker has been replaced with the partnership concept. Spouses are now perceived as creating their own marital roles. This perception led courts to uphold and enforce the validity of prenuptial agreements upon divorce (*McHugh v. McHugh,* 1980). Under the partnership model, these agreements presumably do not weaken marriage by making divorce more desirable; they secure the rights of the individuals entering marriage against future disputes. Support obligations and responsibility for a spouse's debts are now placed equally on men and women, and contributions that women outside of the workforce make to the family are gaining recognition.

The push for equal treatment between men and women in marriage, and ultimately in divorce and child custody, was driven primarily by the movement to obtain equal rights for women (Mason, 1988). In addition to the recognition of the contributions that women make to a marriage, this feminist attentiveness has resulted in an increasing awareness that women often suffer when there are marital problems. As a result, law enforcement and the courts are now more likely to intervene when there are problems within a marriage. Domestic violence and marital rape are given more attention, and men and women now have the right to decide whether they will testify against their spouses in federal court (*Trammel v. United States,* 1980). Moreover, tort liability between spouses now exists in most states, albeit at a

higher standard than between legal strangers (*Lewis v. Lewis,* 1976). These changes reflect recognition that legal institutions have a role to play in enforcing the rights and responsibilities created by marriage while also respecting the independent identity' of each spouse.

Changes in reproductive laws also have affected the spousal relationship. U.S. Supreme Court decisions such as *Roe v. Wade* (1973) have given women more reproductive choices, and they have empowered them to make those choices independent of their husbands. Although married women could take few actions independent of husbands under the dependent marriage model, under the partnership model, women can make important reproductive decisions (e.g.; to have an abortion) independently, even against their husbands' objections. This change reflects the increasing recognition of each spouse's independent identity and rights within marriage.

Divorce

The shift to a partnership model of marriage was accompanied by a change in how the partnership could be dissolved. The past 30 years ushered in what has been termed a *divorce revolution*. Drastic changes in divorce law rendered divorce a unilateral decision not based on fault. This made divorce far easier to obtain and in most states created a fundamentally different framework for the distribution of property and the allocation of support following divorce. Following the lead of California's revolutionary Family Law Act of 1969, all states by 1985 offered some form of no-fault divorce (Krause, 1986). In some states, one party had only to complain that the marriage had reached a point of "irretrievable breakdown" with no requirement of proof; in other states, "incompatibility" or "irreconcilable differences" had to be demonstrated if one party objected, but if one partner chose to live separately for a period of time, that was also seen as proof of marital breakdown. There are debates about how much changes in divorce law contributed to rising divorce rates; some claim the rise was an extension of earlier increases that were temporarily reversed in the 1950s. Regardless of the reasons for the increase, demographic trends clearly reveal that the divorce rate doubled between 1966 and 1976. By the 1980s, it was predicted that half of all marriages would end in divorce (Cherlin, 1992).

The basic assumption underlying the changes in divorce and custody law was that men and women should be treated equally before the law. This was a sharp departure from the beliefs in the era of dependent marriage and fault-based divorce. Family law had then perhaps favored women (and children) by making divorce hard to obtain and by allowing extended support for wives and children after divorce, in the belief that wives were less able to take care of themselves economically than were husbands. A maternal presumption in custody, established by the early 20th century, also favored mothers, reflecting beliefs that they were more nurturing than fathers.

The assumption that men and women should be treated equally had serious consequences for the distribution of property and on alimony. Unless the woman was at fault, alimony or spousal support was routinely granted for life in most states, but collection and enforcement rates were low. As divorce law changed to reflect the equality of partners, the concept of alimony came under negative scrutiny. The Uniform Marriage and Divorce Act (UMDA) moved that alimony only be used when the spouse could not take care of herself and that fault in the divorce should not be a consideration. Fault also was deemed an inappropriate consideration in determining property division. UMDA did, however, pursue a substantial change, allowing women to have a claim to the equitable distribution of property in common law states where the person who held title, typically the husband, was usually granted the property.

The shift toward easy-to-obtain divorce has not gone unchallenged. One aspect of this backlash is the recent passage of "covenant marriage" statutes (Louisiana Act 1380, 1977; Ariz. Rev. Stat. Ann. § 25-901-906, 1998). These laws allow couples to enter into a marriage that can be ended only on statutorily specified grounds. Proponents argue that covenant marriage increases respect for marriage as an institution and will reduce the divorce rate. Supporters of covenant marriage also believe "that no-fault divorce is responsible for the high divorce rate and for other societal problems that are correlated with divorce and single-parent homes" (Pearson, 1999, p. 633). Opponents claim these statutes are both too restrictive (they may trap an individual in a bad marriage) and not restrictive enough (they are voluntarily entered and may be invalidated with the consent of both spouses). At their strongest, statutory covenant marriages eliminate only one aspect of the no-fault divorce statutes—absent wrong-doing, one spouse in a covenant marriage cannot unilaterally demand and be granted a divorce (Wardle, 1999).

Child Custody

Unlike previous eras where child custody issues ordinarily involved orphans or children of parents who could not care for them, the majority of child custody matters in the modern era are the product of divorce. Although under the jurisdiction of courts, most child custody determinations are made by the parties rather than by a judge at trial (Mason, 1994). In addition to increased volume, the substantive rules that the courts used to determine custody shifted drastically. This shift followed in the wake of radical divorce reforms and reflected the new emphasis on egalitarian marriage.

The simple fact of being a mother does not by itself indicate a capacity or willingness to render a quality of care different from that which the father can provide (*State ex red. Watts v. Watts,* 1973). With this statement, a New York court challenged nearly a century of a judicial presumption in favor of mothers. Not all courts were as outspoken in reducing the importance of mothers; nevertheless, the presumption that the interest of a child of tender years is best served in the custody of the mother was legally abolished or demoted to a "factor to be considered" in nearly all states between 1960 and 1990. By 1982, only seven states gave mothers a custody preference over fathers for children of tender years (Atkinson, 1984). Rather, most states mandate that custody decisions be based on a consideration of the "best interests of the child," a standard that is far less clear and specific than the maternal preference standard. In an attempt to address this ambiguity, state legislatures drafted statutes to direct judges left with the task of applying the elusive best interests standard. Most legislatures also suggested joint custody as an alternative to awarding custody to one parent, giving fathers as much time with children as mothers, and thereby avoiding the problem of having to choose between legally equal parents. Some states adopted a primary caretaker preference, providing custody to the parent who spent the most time with the child (Mason, 1994).

California led the way in custody initiatives, as it had in no-fault divorce, by introducing a preference for joint legal custody in 1980. By 1988, 36 states had followed California's lead. Legislatures, and sometimes courts, produced several variations on the joint custody theme. Joint physical custody dictated that parents should share their time with the child as equally as possible. Joint legal custody, on the other hand, allowed a more traditional sole custody arrangement with visitation for the non-custodial parent. Both parents retained equal input into decisions affecting the child, such as choosing medical treatment and schools. By the end of the century, joint legal and physical cus-

tody was the preference in most states (Mason, 2000).

Remarriage and Stepfamilies

Because most partners who divorce eventually remarry, the dramatic increase in divorce resulted in a steep rise in the number of stepfamilies (Seltzer, 1994). Although changes in law and practice relating to marriage and divorce have led to more stepfamilies, little has changed with respect to the legal status of stepparents. Stepparents who do not adopt their stepchildren remain in an ambiguous role with no legal identity (Mahoney, 1994). Their rights and duties toward their stepchildren are largely undefined, and when they are defined, a consistent understanding of their role in the family is not reflected (Mason, 1998). The American Law Institute (2000) addressed some of the legal issues surrounding stepfamilies by defining de facto parents and parents by estoppel (i.e., individuals who are considered parents because they have presented themselves as parents and because it would be inequitable for them to later deny that role) and allowing them to petition for custody of children at divorce. Many stepparents would meet the requirements of these rules. However, even this measure is limited in its applicability because it only indirectly defines stepparent rights and responsibilities to stepchildren during marriage. For example, stepparents are often unable to consent to medical treatment or sign a school permission slip for their stepchildren (*State v. Miranda,* 1997). Generally, stepparents do not have a legal obligation to support their stepchildren, and those who take on such an obligation by acting in loco parentis (i.e., in the place of the parent) do so voluntarily and may end their obligation unilaterally at any time (*Niesen v. Niesen,* 1968). Nonetheless, some federal and state welfare programs take a stepparent's income into account when determining a child's eligibility, whereas others do not.

Stepchildren face legal obstacles in most states that prevent them from filing wrongful death suits on behalf of their stepparents or inheriting when a stepparent dies intestate (i.e., without a will) (*Champagne v. Mcdermott, Inc.,* 1992). Despite the confusion this ambiguity may cause for families, courts and legislatures have been hesitant to address the problem and define a legal role for stepparents. Thus, the changes that are occurring in the law relating to stepparent relationships come slowly and indirectly through changes designed to benefit others. For example, some stepparents are having success in obtaining visitation with their stepchildren following divorce. To a large extent, this success results from states' general third-party visitation statutes, which allow stepparents (and others) to petition for visitation when there is disruption in the family but do not create for stepparents the presumptive right to visitation that exists for biological parents.

Unwed Fathers

Through much of the 20th century, unwed fathers were largely invisible in family law. In the past 25 to 30 years, however, as the number of children born to unmarried parents has risen (McLanahan & Sandefur, 1994), substantial changes have occurred with regard to the legal consequences of "illegitimacy" and the paternity, custody, and child support rights and obligations of unwed fathers. It is difficult to determine the precise number of unwed fathers; they are frequently not listed on birth certificates, and when not involved in the child's life, they do not come into contact with the agencies that maintain data on families (Blank, 1997). However, the increase in unwed mothers over the past 30 years has clearly been accompanied by an increase in the number of unwed fathers. A number of high-profile cases has involved unmarried fathers seeking custody of their children, but these fathers as a group do not play a consistent parenting role for their children. Ler-

man (1993) estimated the number of unwed fathers who were not supporting their children at 1.6 million. Still, the rights and obligations of unwed fathers are increasingly recognized and enforced.

Beginning in the late 1960s, courts and state legislatures began offering rights and protections to "illegitimate" children comparable to those of nonillegitimate children (Sugarman, 1998). As the rights of illegitimate children began to be recognized, so did the rights and obligations of their fathers. Under the Uniform Parentage Act, based on common law tradition and adopted in numerous states, the husband of the child's mother is presumed to be the father. Historically, this presumption has barred an unwed father from claiming paternity to preserve intact families, protect the child, and ensure child support. The U.S. Supreme Court affirmed this presumption as recently as 1989, ruling that the biological unwed father's interest did not outweigh the state's interest in preserving an intact family (*Michael H. v. Gerald D.,* 1989). However, numerous state courts and legislatures have overridden the presumption, granting unwed fathers the right to claim paternity even when the mother is married to another. For example, the California Supreme Court granted an unwed father the right to establish paternity, arguing that the child was conceived before the mother married (Mason, 2000).

With the increasing recognition of an unwed father's right to claim paternity, courts and legislatures have begun to recognize rights in custody disputes and cases in which the mother has decided to relinquish the child for adoption. In *Stanley v. Illinois* (1971), the U.S. Supreme Court first recognized the custodial rights of an unwed father, ruling that an unwed father who had acted as a parent was entitled to a fitness hearing after the mother's death before the children were made wards of the court. However, the custody rights of an unwed father are not automatic. In subsequent decisions, the U.S. Supreme Court ruled that the biological link of an unwed father may be insufficient to confer rights and required that he acts as a father and participates in childrearing (*Caban v. Mohammed,* 1979; *Lehr v. Robertson,* 1983). State courts, however, have granted unmarried fathers rights comparable to those of married fathers (Mason, 2000).

Finally, as the number of children living in single-parent households has increased, policy initiatives in the past quarter century have focused on enforcing child support obligations. In 1985, only about 13% of never-married mothers reported receiving support from the fathers of their children (Lerman, 1993). In 1975, the Federal Office of Child Support Enforcement was created, with state agency counterparts, to increase child support collection. Subsequently, the Family Support Act of 1988 set stricter standards for state child support enforcement, resulting in increased enforcement among the Aid to Families with Dependent Children population. Despite enforcement efforts, the frequency and amount of child support awards and payments remain low (Mason, 2000). However, welfare reform, with time-limited benefits for parents to receive aid, has made the enforcement of child support a critical issue. As pressure grows to collect child support from both unmarried and formerly married fathers, remaining legal distinctions between them are likely to disappear.

Third-Party Visitation

Unwed fathers are not the only group that has won increased protection of their interests in maintaining a relationship with a child. As a result of the loosening hold of marriage, any number of adults, related and unrelated, are raising children with little or no legal backing. State legislatures and a number of courts have begun to recognize the roles of these multiple parties by expanding visitation rights to individuals other than parents. Third-party visitation statutes have been enacted in all states, granting a right to petition for visitation to certain categories of petitioners that may include stepparents, grandparents (upon the death or divorce of their child), unmarried parents, or in the broadest conception, any interested party (Elrod, Spector, & Atkinson, 1999). These statutes usually grant such rights because of family disruption, although some statutes are broadly worded to allow third-party visitation petitions any time.

Third-party visitation statutes have been challenged on constitutional grounds in a number of states with varied results. The state of Washington enacted one of the broadest statutes, allowing any person to petition for visitation at any time and authorizing courts to grant visitation on a showing of best interest. In *Troxel v. Granville* (2000), one of the few examples of U.S. Supreme Court intervention in a visitation dispute, the mother and unmarried father had two children before the father died. The paternal grandparents sought more extensive visitation than the mother desired and prevailed in the trial court. The state supreme court overruled the lower court, holding that the statute unconstitutionally infringed on parents' fundamental right to raise their children. The U.S. Supreme Court upheld this decision on the grounds that the statute was too broad and gave no weight to the parent's judgment regarding the children's best interest. The court refrained from deciding whether all third-party statutes require a showing of harm or potential harm if visitation were not awarded as a condition of granting visitation. The court's ruling displayed an explicit recognition of the important role played by third parties in children's lives, particularly when the traditional family model is not involved.

In contrast, a number of state courts have upheld third-party visitation statutes against constitutional challenges. For example, in *West v. West* (1998), the appellate court ruled that the Illinois statute did not violate the "long-recognized constitutionally protected interest of parents to raise their children without undue State influence" and affirmed the state's interest in maintaining relationships found to be in the child's best interest. In *Williams v. Williams* (1998), the court upheld Virginia's law, interpreting it to require a finding of harm if visitation were not granted. In a contrary holding, the Georgia Supreme Court found the state's grandparent visitation statute to be unconstitutional on the grounds that it did not clearly promote the welfare of the child and did not require a showing of harm (*Brooks v. Farkerson,* 1995). It is likely that the decisions affirming third-party visitation statutes will stand (*Troxel v. Granville,* 2000).

Nontraditional Partnerships

While the rise of single-parent households has been well documented and has received attention from policy makers and researchers, there has been a simultaneous increase in nontraditional or nonmarital partnerships, including cohabitation, same-sex marriage, and domestic partnerships. These nontraditional relationship forms raise legal issues relating to property division and support obligations following termination of the relationship, access to the legal benefits conferred on spouses, and parental rights issues such as custody, visitation, and second-parent adoption (i.e., the partner who is the nonbiological parent adopts the child).

Perhaps the most well-known case dealing with the rights of cohabiting partners is *Marvin v. Marvin* (1976), in which the California Supreme Court allowed the woman to sue her male partner for compensation following termination of the relationship on contractual grounds. The court held that when there is an explicit or implied contract between mutually assenting individuals in a nonmarital relationship, a court may use principles of equity to divide property at the termination of the relationship. Such a reading of a cohabitation relationship reflects a partnership rather than a dependency model. Subsequent decisions in other states have been more restrictive, however, requiring proof of a contract of cohabitation and refusing to enforce agreements based on sexual obligations or promises. Recently, a Massachusetts court upheld the validity of a written cohabitation agreement (*Wilcox v. Trautz,* 1998). However, although a contractually based right to compensation may be recognized by the courts, cohabitation does not entitle participants to other benefits of marriage, such as social security benefits (Katz, 1999).

The issue of same-sex marriage has been far more controversial than the rights of cohabiting heterosexual couples. In the early 1970s, several cases challenging state marriage laws were rejected (Chambers & Polikoff, 1999). In the early 1990s, the issue gained national prominence when the Hawaiian Supreme Court set forth a presumption that the legislative ban on same-sex marriage violated the state's constitutional provision granting equal protection and barring sex-based discrimination (*Baker v. Lewin,* 1993). Legislative responses to the decision have been almost uniformly negative. Hawaii passed a constitutional amendment limiting marriage to heterosexual couples, 29 states had enacted laws barring recognition of same-sex marriage by mid-1999, and the U.S. Congress enacted the Defense of Marriage Act, declaring that states have the right to refuse recognition to same-sex marriages from other states and defining marriage as heterosexual unions for federal law purposes (Chambers & Polikoff, 1999).

Most recently, Vermont passed a civil union statute, taking effect in July 2000, that grants to partners in civil unions, including same-sex partners, the benefits and responsibilities afforded to married couples under state laws. The legislature acted in response to the Vermont Supreme Court's decision in *Baker v. State of Vermont* (1999), holding that the state is constitutionally required to extend to same-sex couples the benefits and protections afforded to married couples, either through inclusion in the marriage laws or in an equivalent statutory alternative. It remains to be seen how these unions are treated by other states or by federal law (Bonauto, 2000). The Vermont civil union statute provides more benefits than the domestic partnership laws, which permit unmarried partners to register their relationships and/or provide benefits to partners of employees of the city, county, or state enacting the law. Numerous cities and counties have enacted such laws, and by 1999, Hawaii, New York, Oregon, and Vermont provided partner benefits to employees.

In contrast to the flurry of legislative activity relating to same-sex marriage and domestic partnership, states have for the most part declined to enact statutes regulating the rights of gay and lesbian parents in custody and visitation disputes, leaving the courts to develop the law in this area. Since the first cases arose in the 1970s, courts have ruled both for and against gay and lesbian parents in determining the best interests of the child but have more frequently denied gay and lesbian parents custody of their children. As recently as the late 1990s, state supreme court decisions in the South and Midwest have restricted visitation rights or transferred custody away from a gay or lesbian parent (*Marlow v. Marlow,* 1998; *Pulliam v. Smith,* 1998). Some states have acted on adoption or foster parenting by gay men or lesbians. The first was Florida, where a law prohibiting adoption by lesbians and gay men was enacted in 1977. However, in many other states, gay men and lesbians have been allowed to adopt in second-parent adoptions (Chambers & Polikoff, 1999).

Assisted Reproduction

The National Center for Health Statistics (NCHS) reported in 1995 that 6.1 million women between the ages of 15 and 44 experienced an impaired ability to have children; the number of infertile married couples was estimated at 2.1 million. NCHS (1995) further estimated that 9 million women had used infertility services by 1995. The development of medical technologies enabling infertile women and couples to bear children has presented legal and ethical challenges. Perhaps because of the rapidity of the developments, or perhaps due to the complexity of the relationships established by these new techniques, adequate legal and ethical structures or systems to guide participants in assisted reproduction have not been developed. As use of these technologies becomes more prevalent, courts and legislatures will be increasingly pressured to respond. This is already beginning; the National Conference of Commissioners on Uniform State Laws' 1998 Draft Revision of the Uniform Parentage Act includes provisions relating to assisted reproduction. These revisions are in discussion, and it may be years before the project is complete and states can consider adopting it.

Infertility treatment may include relatively uncontroversial procedures such as artificial insemination with a husband's sperm or ovarian stimulation to enhance the chances of conception. Other methods (e.g., in vitro fertilization and ovum donation) raise complex legal issues by introducing additional parties contributing genetic material or biological support to the reproductive process or by creating unprecedented decision-making options at each stage of the process. The involvement of a third parry in a couple's efforts to create a family is not itself a new event. Donor sperm conception has long been available, as it does not require advanced medical intervention. Similarly, traditional surrogacy, in which a woman agrees to conceive and bear a child for a couple using the man's sperm, has also been historically available. The increasing range of treatment options, however, creates pressure for the law to respond.

Although the law is underdeveloped in the area of assisted reproduction, we can identify several issues that may require legal resolution. First, the standard in vitro fertilization process using the sperm and eggs of a couple seeking to conceive creates preembryos that exist outside of the uterus and can be frozen for an undetermined period. Consequently, disputes over the custody and control of the preembryos may arise between the partners, as in *Davis v. Davis* (1992), where the Tennessee Supreme Court ruled that both spouses had a right regarding procreation, but the father's desire not to procreate outweighed the mother's interest in donating the embryos. Second, with ovum donation, the donor may also claim an interest in decisions about the pregnancy, the embryos, or a child born of the process. Finally, with gestational and traditional surrogacy, disputes over decisions regarding pregnancy, embryos, or children may develop among the individuals intending to act as parents, the donors of genetic material, and the surrogate carrying the fetus. In the case of Baby M. (*In the Matter of Baby M.,* 1988), the court held that the surrogacy contract was void because it was contrary to public policy. Treating the case as a custody dispute between the biological surrogate mother and the biological father, the court granted custody to the father with limited visits for the surrogate mother. Claims by donors and surrogates challenge the law to address the interests of parties outside the marital or partnership relationship.

Federal and state legislation governing disputes between participants in assisted reproduction is rare, so the courts are playing the most significant role. Judges are relying on varying legal concepts and doctrines in resolving disputes, including property law, contract law, child custody law, and constitutional law (Triber, 1998). The more novel concept of intent to parent was articulated in a California Court of Appeals case where the court ruled that individuals who intend to and act to create a child through assisted reproduction technology become legally responsible for the resulting child, even where there is no genetic relationship to the child (*In re Marriage of Buzzanca,* 1998).

Adoption

Adoption is not a new phenomenon in family law. However, the following three trends merit attention: transracial, intercountry, and open adoptions. Intercountry and transracial adoptions are criticized on the grounds that parents whose racial, ethnic, or cultural identity differs from that of their children cannot provide an essential element of parenting in a society where racial and ethnic discrimination exists. Open adoption gives rise to a different controversy— the potential conflict between adopted children who seek information about and possible contact with birth parents and birth parents who may want to maintain anonymity.

The issue of transracial adoption arises primarily in the adoption of children in the foster care system whose parents' rights have been terminated by the state. In 1999, the United States Department of Health and Human Services estimated there were 117,000 children in the foster care system seeking adoption. Of these, 51% were African American, 32% were White, and 11% were Hispanic. The groups most likely to adopt include childless women, women with fecundity impairments, White women, and women with higher levels of income and education (Mosher & Bachrach, 1996). The number of transracial adoptions is unknown, but estimates range from 1% to 11% of all children in foster care (Avery & Mont, 1994). With the majority of foster children ready for adoption being African American and with White women seeking to adopt more frequently, the benefits and problems of transracial adoption deserve attention.

The federal government has enacted legislation to facilitate transracial adoption in the foster care system. The Howard Metzenbaum Multiethnic Placement Adoption Act of 1994 had the stated purpose of preventing discrimination in placement decisions on the basis of race, color, or national origin. In 1996, another federal law repealed and replaced the Multiethnic Placement Act with stronger provisions barring the use of race as a criterion in decisions about foster care or adoption placements (1996b). For those who question "whether white adoptive parents can raise Black children to be well-adjusted productive adults with a positive sense of racial identity" (Perry, 1999, p. 470), the federal government's promotion of transracial adoption is problematic. Others may view the federal government's response to the increasing number of African American children awaiting placement as consistent with a broader trend toward interracial marriage and partnerships, resulting in an increase in interracial parenting without adoption (Census Bureau, 1999).

Intercountry adoption also raises the question of parental competency when the parents' and the child's race, ethnicity, or culture differ. Over the past 10 years or so, the number of children adopted in the United States from other countries has more than doubled, from 8,102 in 1989 to 16,396 in 1999 (U.S. Department of State, 2000). On October 6, 2000, President Clinton signed the Inter-Country Adoption Act, ratifying the Hague Adoption Convention, which is designed to encourage intercountry adoption.

Open adoption, in which adopted children are provided with information about and in some cases the choice to contact birth parents, are another example of society's recognition that families can include more parties than two spouses and their biological children. Although adopted children may desire information about or a relationship with their birth parents, birth parents may want anonymity. Adoption laws changed from relatively open records to sealed records by the mid-1960s (Cahn & Singer, 1999). In the 1970s, adoptees began challenging sealed adoption records, seeking access to birth certificates through the courts. Rejected by the courts, adoptees pursued legislative remedies with success. Most states now provide nonidentifying information about birth parents and have established procedures for contact when there is mutual consent. The first state laws making original birth records fully accessible passed in 1999, with efforts underway in other states. The Oregon statute was challenged, but the U.S. Supreme Court denied a motion to not allow it to go into effect (Roseman, 2000).

SOCIAL SCIENCE AND FAMILY LAW

Social scientists have increasingly played a role in legal processes pertaining to families (Mason, 1994), although this increase has been sporadic. This is partly due to the complex relation between social science and law and because many factors must be considered in formulating policy, not just the results of social science research. There is debate about the extent to which social science research has influenced family policy decisions (Bogenschneider, 2000). One reason for the limited influence of social science is that many of the shifts in family law were initiated by social forces rather than by research findings (e.g., divorce reform and third-party visitation rights). Actually, social science has had more of a role in assessing the consequences of these changes (e.g., child custody decisions after divorce) than in initiating them.

Roles of Social Scientists in the Legal Process

Social scientists' influence on law is often traced to the beginning of the 1900s, as empirical research gradually overtook the reliance on "natural" or "divine" law as informers of legal decision making (Mason, 1994). However, it was not until the last, third of the 20th century that social science researchers had an explicit and substantial effect on legal processes in at least the following three ways: (a) informing public policy and legal reform, (b) developing interventions that were integrated into legal processes, and (c) serving as expert witnesses in court. Because the law tends to be more involved when families are undergoing transitions (e.g., divorce and adoption), the influence of social scientists has been greatest during these periods of change.

Informing public policy and law. In the 1970s, social science theories became particularly influential in child custody after divorce (Mason, 1994). In fact, theories have had perhaps as great an effect as research. For example, one of the influential early social scientific works was by Goldstein, Freud, and Solnit (1973), who introduced the notion of the psychological parent as the individual with whom the child is most closely attached and by extension, the individual who should have complete (and possibly exclusive) custody rights. Although this was a concept rooted in attachment theory rather than one that emerged from systematic empirical study, Goldstein et al. presented it as if it were empirically supported. Despite the lack of support, the notion of the psychological parent was frequently used by courts to choose which parent should be granted custody following divorce and/or to defeat a joint custody arrangement (Mason, 1994). It was also influential in justifying gender-neutral child custody decisions after divorce because the psychological parent could be either parent (Mason, 2000).

As findings accumulated, social science research was increasingly influential in court decisions. For example, research on the potential benefits of joint custody (Johnston, Kline, & Tschann, 1989) was used to justify policies that made joint custody the preferred custodial arrangement, and research on the well-being of children raised by gay and lesbian couples has informed court decisions regarding adoption rights for gay and lesbian couples (Patterson, 2000).

Research-informed interventions. A second way that social scientists have influenced legal processes affecting families is that social science interventions have become part of court proceedings. Two examples are mediation and parent education programs for divorcing parents. Divorce mediation attempts to help spouses negotiate divorce settlements in nonadversarial ways and has become popular, even mandated, in many jurisdictions. The elimination of fault-based divorce laws and a growing sense that the adversarial process leads to long-term negative outcomes contributed to the growth in mediation (Mason, 1994). There is evidence that mediation leads to positive outcomes, including lower relitigation rates, greater compliance with mediated agreements, and high rates of satisfaction with the process (Emery, 1995).

Mediation is not without critics. Feminists argue that mediation favors men because men have more power than women and because mediation is based on the assumption that fault should be left out of the process, which advantages men who may have oppressed their wives (e.g., spousal abuse) and/or who had benefited from support provided by their wives in their careers (Emery, 1995; Mason, 1994). Conversely, noting that women are more satisfied than are men with both litigated and mediated settlements, Emery (1995) suggested that it is not that women fare poorly in mediation but rather that men are disadvantaged in litigation. Thus, men gain more in mediation than in litigation, which leads them to be more satisfied with mediated agreements. By contrast, women typically fare as well in both types of settlements, perhaps explaining why women have similar levels of satisfaction with each approach.

Parenting education programs attempt to help divorcing parents more effectively help their children cope with the stressful divorce process. Even prior to the accumulation of data supporting their efficacy, these programs were mandated in almost half of the counties in the United States (Blaisure & Geasler, 1999).

Social scientists as expert witnesses. Social scientists have become more frequent fixtures in legal proceedings as expert witnesses. Although there have been changes in standards used to determine if expert testimony is admissible, the most common states that to be admissible, evidence must be based on peer-accepted scientific methods, and the scientific evidence must be directly applicable to the issues in the specific trial (Siegel, 2000).

Social scientists as expert witnesses have probably had their greatest influence in the child custody determination process. As the best interests of the child criterion replaced maternal preference child custody laws, mental health professionals were called on to provide evaluations regarding the parent with whom the child should reside. Furthermore, because judges had more discretion than they did under maternal preference laws, they were more likely to call on experts to assist them in their decision making (Mason, 1994).

Limits of Social Science's Influence on the Legal Process

Legal professionals not understanding social science research. Courts, lawyers, and policy makers are not typically sophisticated consumers of social scientific research. They may not understand the limitations of research and may misinterpret the meaning of research findings. Consequently, social scientists must be careful to clarify the limitations of and the appropriate uses of their research and to educate legal and policy experts.

Believing social science research. Many legal professionals question the validity of social science research. Fueling the skepticism are disagreements among social scientists regarding certain issues (e.g., father's importance to children's development and in which custody situations children fare best), the likelihood that two experts can reach diametrically opposing conclusions regarding the same case, and the tendency among some social scientists to prematurely advance a position in legal venues before it has support in the social scientific community. For example, parental alienation syndrome, which involves a child becoming estranged from a parent, has recently been used in custody hearings (Warshak, 2000). Although there is abundant research suggesting that children can experience deteriorations in the quality of their relationships with parents after divorce, there is no compelling evidence to justify elevating this phenomenon to a syndrome. Social scientists who advance untested syndromes and disorders magnify underlying doubts about the integrity of social science research, at least partly because premature pronouncements in court settings inevitably are accompanied by critics of unsupported claims.

Expecting clear findings. Policy makers, lawyers, and judges expect research to provide clear, unambiguous, and objective answers to questions, which is often referred to as a *positivist approach.* However, social science research does not typically lead to unambiguous and unqualified findings. To some extent, social science and the law have opposing foundations. Most social scientists now adopt some variant of a postpositivist approach, which includes the premises that research is not objective and value free, knowledge is not absolute but is context dependent (i.e., the context in which research is conducted and in which participants live affects findings in known and unknown ways), and the views of researchers and other outsiders may differ from those of study participants. Thus, there is tension between the legal professionals' desire for absolute and clear answers and most social scientists' disinclination to provide such answers. This tension and others have led some to argue that social scientists should limit their involvement in legal proceedings, claiming that social scientific theories and research are sufficiently imprecise that experts, for example, could not accurately determine which parent would best serve the interests of the child (Weithorn & Grisso, 1987).

Research results can be selectively reviewed to advance political or ideological positions. For example, differing value stances affect how researchers (and others) interpret research on the effects of divorce on children and parents (Fine & Demo, 2000). Occasionally, research is misinterpreted to support a particular policy preference (Fine & Fine, 1994). For example, findings suggesting that children's well-being was greater when they were in their mothers' custody than when they were in mandatory joint custody arrangements (Johnston et al., 1999) were misleadingly used to justify the claim that joint custody, whether mandatory or voluntary, was inferior to sole custody for children.

Distinguishing between theory and data. Many legal professionals justify their arguments and decisions by using social science theoretical constructs that make intuitive sense to them. However, many concepts lack empirical evidence and therefore can easily be challenged. For example, the claim that children will fare better with their psychological parent can be challenged by the competing claim that children will fare better living with two caring parents actively involved in their lives. Thus, legal reliance on theories to the exclusion of empirical research often contributes to criticisms that social science is soft, inconclusive, and ideological.

Differing units of interest. Social science research is generally designed to make generalizations about groups (albeit within the specific contexts in which they live) and tends to place less emphasis on exceptions (some qualitative research is an exception to this). Although policy makers need to base their decisions on soundly derived group generalizations, judges need to make decisions in individual cases. No matter how well any piece of research has been done or how sound the conclusions, generalizations do not necessarily fit any specific individual. Therefore, research is necessarily limited in its ability to inform courts.

Differing timetables. Social science research takes time to complete. However, there are instances when policy makers and the court cannot afford to wait to make decisions regarding legislation and perhaps more importantly, individual cases. Thus, decisions need to be made with or without sound research, and social scientists may be tempted to convey greater confidence in preliminary findings or the efficacy of interventions than is warranted.

LOOKING TO THE FUTURE

It is possible to develop optimistic hypotheses about family law in the new millennium. In regard to marriage, divorce, and nontraditional relationship forms, it seems clear that the partnership model will continue to prevail over the earlier dependence model. The underlying economic and social changes relating to the role of women in society are not likely to be reversed. Alternative relationships, such as those between same-sex couples, will slowly receive recognition as society strives to create structures that support stable relationships in which children can thrive. However, resistance to nontraditional families and relationships will continue to generate legislative responses such as the Defense of Marriage Act and covenant marriage statutes. Child custody laws and laws relating to unwed fathers will continue to promote fathers' parenting role, motivated in part by a desire to impose financial responsibility for child support. Similarly, nonparents will continue to gain access to children with whom they have close relationships; laws will still struggle to mediate varying interests in stepfamilies.

The legal ambivalence toward gay or lesbian parents should gradually fade if evidence of their children's well-being continues to accumulate. For families created through assisted reproduction technology and for stepfamilies, the courts and legislatures will continue to struggle with the interests of multiple parties. Recent reforms favoring transracial adoption may not endure—the pendulum could swing back in favor of same-race placements as Americans continue to struggle with race relations and racism. However, intercountry adoption seems unlikely to disappear. Individual countries may limit adoptions or make the adoption process more difficult, but economic pressures are likely to prevail.

Future Involvement of Social Science in the Law

As in the past century, shifts in family law are likely to be driven by demographic and social changes. Nevertheless, it is likely that social scientists will continue to influence legal processes. The factors that contributed to the increasing,

role of social science—more judicial flexibility, greater legitimacy of social science research, greater likelihood of courts requiring intervention programs, more need for expert testimony, and others—are likely to continue to expand social scientists' roles in legal proceedings. We support the use of social science research to inform and guide the development of the law. To maximize the extent to which research influences the process of legal reform, social scientists need to appropriately qualify and explain their findings so that professionals not trained in research methods can understand their work. Social scientists may need to educate legal professionals regarding the limits of research and the difficulties inherent in drawing generalizations that apply across contexts. However, it is unlikely that the role of social science will dramatically increase in the next century.

In which areas of family law are social scientists likely to make their greatest contributions? Divorce, remarriage, adoption, and in general, issues surrounding parenting and parent-child relationships will be in the forefront of social science contributions. For example, issues such as how children's time will be allocated among divorced parents and the effect of parenting plans will be of great interest. In addition, as technologies change how families are formed (e.g., surrogate childbearing), social science research may be helpful in working through the delicate issues related to the roles, rights, and responsibilities of the multiple parties involved in these family processes. Overall, in the future, we can expect a continuing revolution in family law as the ways in which families are formed and maintained continue to evolve. We can also expect that both law and social science will be seriously challenged to keep up with the changes.

Notes and References

IMMIGRANT FAMILIES IN THE CITY—MARK HUTTER

References

Anderson, Michael. 1971. *Family Structure in Nineteenth Century Lancashire.* Cambridge: Cambridge University Press.

Archdeacon, Thomas. 1983. *Becoming American: An Ethnic History.* New York: The Free Press.

Hareven, Tamara K. 1975. "Family Time and Industrial Time: Family and Work in a Planned Corporation Town, 1900–1924." *Journal of Urban History* 1 (May): 365–389.

Jones, Maldwyn Allen. 1960. *American Immigration.* Chicago: University of Chicago Press.

Metzker, Isaac (ed.) 1971. *A Bintel Brief.* New York: Ballatine Books.

Riis, Jacob A. 1957/1890. *How the Other Half Lives: Studies Among the Tenements of New York.* New York: Hill and Wang.

Seller, Maxine. 1977. *To Seek America: A History of Ethnic Life in the United States.* Englewood, New Jersey: Jerome S. Ozer, Publisher.

Yancey, William L., Eugene P. Ericksen, and Richard N. Juliani. 1976. "Emergent Ethnicity: A Review and Reformulation." *American Sociological Review* 4 (June): 391–402.

Yans-McLaughlin, Virginia. 1971. "Patterns of Work and Family Organization." Pp. 111–126 in *The Family in History: Interdisciplinary Essays,* edited by Theodore K. Rabb and Robert I. Rotberg. New York: Harper Torchbooks.

INTERPRETING THE AFRICAN HERITAGE IN AFRO-AMERICAN FAMILY ORGANIZATION —NIARA SUDARKASA

References

Agbasegbe, B. (1976) "The Role of Wife in the Black Extended Family: Perspectives from a Rural Community in Southern United States," pp. 124–138 in D. McGuigan (ed.) *New Research on Women and Sex Roles.* Ann Arbor: Center for Continuing Education of Women, University of Michigan.

———. (1981) "Some Aspects of Contemporary Rural Afroamerican Family Life in the Sea Islands of Southeastern United States." Presented at the Annual Meeting of the Association of Social and Behavioral Scientists, Atlanta, Georgia, March 1981.

Allen, W. R. (1978) "The search for Applicable Theories of Black Family Life." *Journal of*

Marriage and the Family 40 (February): 117–129.

———. (1979) "Class, Culture, and Family Organization: The Effects of Class and Race on Family Structure in Urban America." *Journal of Comparative Family Studies* 10 (Autumn): 301–313.

Aschenbrenner, J. (1973) "Extended Families Among Black Americans." *Journal of Comparative Family Studies* 4: 257–268.

———. (1975) *Lifelines: Black Families in Chicago.* New York: Holt, Rinehart & Winston.

———. (1978) "Continuities and Variations in Black Family Structure," pp. 181–200 in D. B. Shimkin, E. M. Shimkin, and D. A. Frate (eds.) *The Extended Family in Black Societies.* The Hague: Mouton.

——— and C. H. Carr. (1980) "Conjugal Relationships in the Context of the Black Extended Family." *Alternative Lifestyles* 3 (November): 463–484.

Bender, D. R. (1967) "A Refinement of the Concept of Household: Families, Co-residence, and Domestic Functions." *American Anthropologist* 69 (October): 493–504.

Billingsley, A. (1968) *Black Families in White America.* Englewood Cliffs, NJ: Prentice-Hall.

Blassingame, J. W. (1979) *The Slave Community.* New York: Oxford University Press.

Colson, E. (1962) "Family Change in Contemporary Africa." *Annals of the New York Academy of Sciences* 96 (January): 641–652.

DuBois, W. E. B. (1969) *The Negro American Family.* New York: New American Library. (Originally published, 1908).

Elkins, S. (1963) Slavery: A Problem in American Intellectual Life. New York: Grosset and Dunlap. (Originally published, 1959).

English, R. (1974) "Beyond Pathology: Research and Theoretical Perspectives on Black Families," pp. 39–52 in L. E. Gary (ed.) *Social Research and the Black Community: Selected Issues and Priorities.* Washington, DC: Institute for Urban Affairs and Research, Howard University.

Fortes, M. (1949) *The Web of Kinship among the Tallensi.* London: Oxford University Press.

———. (1950) "Kinship and Marriage Among the Ashanti," pp. 252–284 in A. R. Radcliffe-Brown and D. Forde (eds.) *African Systems of Kinship and Marriage.* London: Oxford University Press.

———. (1953) "The Structure of Unilineal Descent Groups." *American Anthropologist* 55 (January–March): 17–41.

Frazier, E. (1966) *The Negro Family in the United States.* Chicago: University of Chicago Press. (Originally published, 1939).

Furstenberg, F., T. Hershbert, and J. Modell (1975) "The Origins of the Female-headed Black Family: The Impact of the Urban Experience." *Journal of Interdisciplinary History* 6 (Autumn): 211–233.

Genovese, E. D. (1974) *Roll Jordan Roll: The World the Slaves Made.* New York: Random House.

Goody, J. (1976) *Production and Reproduction: A Comparative Study of the Domestic Domain.* Cambridge: Cambridge University Press.

Gutman, H. (1976) *The Black Family in Slavery and Freedom: 1750–1925.* New York: Random House.

Herskovits, M. J. (1958) *The Myth of the Negro Past.* Boston: Beacon. (Originally published, 1941).

Johnson, C. S. (1934) *Shadow of the Plantation.* Chicago: University of Chicago Press.

Kerri, J. N. (1979) "Understanding the African Family: Persistence, Continuity, and Change." *Western Journal of Black Studies* 3 (Spring): 14–17.

Landman, R. H. (1978) "Language Policies and Their Implications for Ethnic Relations in the Newly Sovereign States of Sub-Saharan Africa," pp. 69–90 in B. M. duToit (ed.) *Ethnicity in Modern Africa.* Boulder, CO: Westview Press.

Linton, R. (1936) *The Study of Man.* New York: Appleton-Century-Crofts.

Lloyd, P. C. (1968) "Divorce Among the Yoruba." *American Anthropologist* 70 (February): 67–81.

Maquet, J. (1972) *Civilizations of Black Africa.* London: Oxford University Press.

Marshall, G. A. [Niara Sudarkasa] (1968) "Marriage: Comparative Analysis," in *International Encyclopedia of the Social Sciences, Vol. 10.* New York: Macmillan/Free Press.

Murdock, G. P. (1949) *Social Structure.* New York: Macmillan.

Nobles, W. (1974a) "African Root and American Fruit: The Black Family." *Journal of Social and Behavioral Sciences* 20: 52–64.

———. (1974b) "Africanity: Its Role in Black Families." *The Black Scholar* 9 (June): 10–17.

———. (1978) "Toward an Empirical and Theoretical Framework for Defining Black Families." *Journal of Marriage and the Family* 40 (November): 679–688.

Okediji, P. A. (1975) "A Psychosocial Analysis of the Extended Family: The African Case." *African Urban Notes, Series B,* 1(3): 93–99. (African Studies Center, Michigan State University).

Onwuejeogwu, M. A. (1975) *The Social Anthropology of Africa: An Introduction.* London: Heinemann.

Oppong, C. (1974) *Marriage among a Matrilineal Elite: A Family Study of Ghanaian Senior Civil Servants.* Cambridge: Cambridge University Press.

Owens, L. H. (1976) *This Species of Property: Slave Life and Culture in the Old South.* New York: Oxford University Press.

Perdue, C. L., Jr., T. E. Barden, and R. K. Phillips [eds.] (1980) *Weevils in the Wheat: Interviews with Virginia Ex-Slaves.* Bloomington: Indiana University Press.

Powdermaker, H. (1939) *After Freedom: A Cultural Study in the Deep South.* New York: Viking.

Radcliffe-Brown, A. R. (1950) "Introduction," pp. 1–85 in A. R. Radcliffe-Brown and D. Forde (eds.) *African Systems of Kinship and Marriage.* London: Oxford University Press.

——— and D. Forde [eds.] (1950) *African Systems of Kinship and Marriage.* London: Oxford University Press.

Rivers, W. H. R. (1924) *Social Organization.* New York: Alfred Knopf.

Robertson, C. (1976) "Ga Women and Socioeconomic Change in Accra, Ghana," pp. 111–133 in N. J. Hafkin and E. G. Bay (eds.) *Women in Africa: Studies in Social and Economic Change.* Stanford: Stanford University Press.

Shimkin, D. and V. Uchendu (1978) "Persistence, Borrowing, and Adaptive Changes in Black Kinship Systems: Some Issues and Their Significance," pp. 391–406 in D. Shimkin, E. M. Shimkin, and D. A. Frate (eds.) *The Extended Family in Black Societies.* The Hague: Mouton.

Shimkin, D., E. M. Shimkin, and D. A. Frate [eds.] (1978) *The Extended Family in Black Societies.* The Hague: Mouton.

Shorter, E. (1975) *The Making of the Modern Family.* New York: Basic Books.

Smith, R. T. (1973) "The Matrifocal Family," pp. 121–144 in J. Goody (ed.) *The Character of Kinship.* Cambridge: Cambridge University Press.

Stack, C. (1974) *All Our Kin.* New York: Harper & Row.

Staples, R. (1971) "Toward a Sociology of the Black Family: A Decade of Theory and

Research." *Journal of Marriage and the Family* 33 (February): 19–38.

———. [ed.] (1978) *The Black Family: Essays and Studies.* Belmont, CA: Wadsworth.

Stone, L. (1975) "The Rise of the Nuclear Family in Early Modern England: The Patriarchal Stage," pp. 13–57 in C. E. Rosenberg (ed.) *The Family in History.* Philadelphia: University of Pennsylvania Press.

Sudarkasa, N. (1973) Where Women Work: A Study of Yoruba Women in the Marketplace and in the Home. *Anthropological Papers* No. 53. Ann Arbor: Museum of Anthropology, University of Michigan.

———. (1975a) "An Exposition on the Value Premises Underlying Black Family Studies." *Journal of the National Medical Association* 19 (May): 235–239.

———. (1975b) "National Development Planning for the Promotion and Protection of the Family." *Proceedings of the Conference on Social Research and National Development,* E. Akeredolu-Ale, ed. The Nigerian Institute of Social and Economic Research, Ibadan, Nigeria.

———. (1976) "Female Employment and Family Organization in West Africa," pp. 48–63 in D. G. McGuigan (ed.) *New Research on Women and Sex Roles.* Ann Arbor: Center for Continuing Education of Women, University of Michigan.

———. (1980) "African and Afro-American Family Structure: A Comparison." *The Black Scholar* 11 (November–December): 37–60.

———. (1981) "Understanding the Dynamics of Consanguinity and Conjugality in Contemporary Black Family Organization." Presented at the Seventh Annual Third World Conference, Chicago, March 1981.

Tilly, L. A. and J. W. Scott (1978) *Women, Work, and Family.* New York: Holt, Rinehart & Winston.

Uchendu, V. (1965) *The Igbo of South-Eastern Nigeria.* New York: Holt, Rinehart & Winston.

Ware, H. (1979) "Polygyny: Women's Views in a Transitional Society, Nigeria 1975." *Journal of Marriage and the Family* 41 (February): 185–195.

Woodson, C. G. (1936) *The African Background Outlined.* Washington, DC: Association for the Study of Negro Life and History.

SETTING THE CLOCK FORWARD OR BACK? COVENANT MARRIAGE AND THE "DIVORCE REVOLUTION" —LAURA SANCHEZ ET AL.

References

Abramowitz, M. (1988). *Regulating the lives of women.* Boston: South End.

Baehr et al. v. Lewin, No. 15689, Supreme Court of Hawaii, 74 Haw. 645; 852 P.2d 44; 1993 Haw. LEXIS 30, May 27, 1993, May 27, 1993, Filed, Reported at: 852 P.2d 44 at 74. Available: web.lexis-nexis.com/universe

Buehler, C. (1995). Divorce law in the United States. *Marriage and Family Review, 21,* 99–120.

Carbone, J. R. (1994). A feminist perspective on divorce. *Children and Divorce, 4,* 183–209.

Cohen, S., & Katzenstein, M. F. (1988). The war over the family is not over the family. In S. M. Dornbusch & M. H. Strober (Eds.), *Feminism, children, and the new families* (pp. 25–46). New York: Guilford.

Davidson, N. (1990). Life without father: America's greatest social catastrophe. *Policy Review, 51,* 40–44.

Donovan, B. (1998). Political consequences of private authority: Promise Keepers and the transformation of hegemonic masculinity. *Theory and Society, 27,* 817–843.

Folbre, N. (1984). The pauperization of motherhood: Patriarchy and public policy in the United States. *Review of Radical Political Economics, 16,* 72–88.

Folbre, N. (1994). *Who pays for the kids? Gender and the structures of constraint.* London: Routledge.

Fraser, N. (1989). *Unruly practices: Power discourse and gender in contemporary theory.* Minneapolis: University of Minnesota Press.

Fraser, N., & Gordon, L. (1994). A genealogy of dependency: Tracing a keyword of the U.S. welfare state. *Signs, 19,* 309–336.

Gilder, G. (1989). The myth of the role revolution. In N. Davidson (Ed.), *Gender sanity* (pp. 227–244). New York: University Press of America.

Glenn, N. D. (1991). The recent trend in marital success in the United States. *Journal of Marriage and the Family, 53,* 261–270.

Goldberg, S. (1989). The universality of patriarchy. In N. Davidson (Ed.), *Gender sanity* (pp. 129–145). New York: University Press of America.

Goldscheider, F. K., & Waite, L. J. (1991). *New families, no families? The transformation of the American home.* Los Angeles: University of California Press.

Hochschild, A. (1997, April 20). There's no place like work. *New York Times Magazine,* pp. 51–84.

hooks, b. (1984). *Feminist theory: From margin to center.* Boston: South End.

Howard, C. (1993). The hidden side of the American welfare state. *Political Science Quarterly, 108,* 403–437.

Hunt, J. G., & Hunt, L. L. (1982). The dualities of careers and families: New integrations or new polarizations? *Social Problems, 29,* 499–510.

Kass, L. R. (1997). The end of courtship. *The Public Interest, 126,* 39–63.

Kozol, W. (1995). Fracturing domesticity: Media, nationalism, and the question of feminist influence. *Signs, 20,* 646–667.

Krause, H. D. (1995). *Family law in a nutshell* (3rd ed.). St. Paul, MN: West.

Loving v. Virginia, No. 395, 388 U.S. 1; 87 S. Ct. 1817; 18 L. Ed. 2d 1010; 1967 U.S. LEXIS 1082, April 10, 1967, Argued, June 12, 1967, Decided. Available: http://web.lexis_nexis.com/universe

Mattox, W. R., Jr. (1995). Why aren't conservatives talking about divorce? *Policy Review, 73,* 50–54.

McIntyre, L. J. (1995). Law and the family in historical perspective: Issues and antecedents. *Marriage and Family Review, 21,* 5–30.

Okin, S. M. (1989). *Justice, gender, and the family.* New York: Basic Books.

Popenoe, D. (1993). American family decline, 1960–1990. *Journal of Marriage and the Family, 55,* 527–555.

Popenoe, D., Elshtain, J. B., & Blankenhorn, D. (1996). *Promises to keep: Decline and renewal of marriage in America.* Lanaham, MD: Rowman and Littlefield.

Stacey, J. (1990). *Brave new families: Stories of domestic upheaval in late 20th century America.* New York: Basic Books.

Stacey, J. (1993). Good riddance to "the family": A response to David Popenoe. *Journal of Marriage and the Family, 55,* 545–547.

Stacey, J. (1996). *In the name of the family: Rethinking family values in the postmodern age.* Boston: Beacon.

U.S. Bureau of the Census. (1990). (Database C90STFIA). Available: http://venus.census.gov/cdrom/lookup/1002655918

Weisberger, J. M. (1986). Marital property discrimination: Reform for legally excluded women. *Ethology and Sociobiology, 7,* 353–365.

Whitehead, B. D. (1997). *The divorce culture.* New York: Knopf.

Wilkinson, S. (1998). Focus groups in feminist research: Power, interaction, and the co-construction of meaning. *Women's Studies International Forum, 21,* 111–125.

THE FEMALE WORLD OF CARDS AND HOLIDAYS: WOMEN, FAMILIES, AND THE WORK OF KINSHIP —MICAELA di LEONARDO

Notes

1. Acknowledgment and gratitude to Carroll Smith-Rosenberg for my paraphrase of her title, "The Female World of Love and Ritual: Relations between Women in Nineteenth-Century America," *Signs: Journal of Women in Culture and Society* 1, no. 1 (August 1975): 1–29. [*Signs: Journal of Women in Culture and Society,* 1987, vol. 12, no. 3] © 1987 by The University of Chicago. All rights reserved 0097-9740/87/1203-0003$01.00.

2. Ann Landers letter printed in *Washington Post* (April 15, 1983); Carol Gilligan, *In a Different Voice* (Cambridge, Mass.: Harvard University Press, 1982), 17.

3. Heidi I. Hartmann, "The Family as the Locus of Gender, Class, and Political Struggle: The Example of Housework," *Signs* 6, no. 3 (Spring 1981): 366–94; and Christopher Lasch, *Haven in a Heartless World: The Family Besieged* (New York: Basic Books, 1977).

4. Representative examples of the first trend include Joann Vanek, "Time Spent on Housework," *Scientific American* 231 (November 1974): 116–20; Ruth Schwartz Cowan, "A Case Study of Technological and Social Change: The Washing Machine and the Working Wife," in *Clio's Consciousness Raised,* ed. Mary Hartmann and Lois Banner (New York: Harper & Row, 1974), 245–53; Ann Oakley, *Women's Work: The House-*

wife, Past and Present (New York: Vintage, 1974); Hartmann; and Susan Strasser, *Never Done: A History of American Housework* (New York: Pantheon Books, 1982). Key contributions to the second trend include Louise Lamphere, "Strategies, Cooperation and Conflict among Women in Domestic Groups," in *Women, Culture and Society,* ed. Michelle Zimbalist Rosaldo and Louise Lamphere (Stanford, Calif.: Stanford University Press, 1974), 97–112; Mina Davis Caulfield, "Imperialism, the Family and the Cultures of Resistance," *Socialist Revolution* 20 (October 1974): 67–85; Smith-Rosenberg; Sylvia Junko Yanagisako, "Women-centered Kin Networks and Urban Bilateral Kinship," *American Ethnologist* 4, no. 2 (1977): 207–26; Jane Humphries, "The Working Class Family, Women's Liberation and Class Struggle: The Case of Nineteenth Century British History," *Review of Radical Political Economics* 9 (Fall 1977): 25–41; Blanche Weisen Cook, "Female Support Networks and Political Activism: Lillian Wald, Crystal Eastman, Emma Goldman," in *A Heritage of Her Own,* ed. Nancy F. Cott and Elizabeth H. Pleck (New York: Simon & Schuster, 1979); Temma Kaplan, "Female Consciousness and Collective Action: The Case of Barcelona, 1910–1918," *Signs* 7, no. 3 (Spring 1982): 545–66.

5. On this debate, see Jon Weiner, "Women's History on Trial," *Nation* 241, no. 6 (September 7, 1985): 161, 176, 178–80; Karen J. Winkler, "Two Scholars' Conflict in Sears Sex-Bias Case Sets Off War in Women's History," *Chronicle of Higher Education* (February 5, 1986), 1, 8; Rosalind Rosenberg, "What Harms Women in the Workplace," *New York Times* (February 27, 1986); Alice Kessler-Harris, "Equal Employment Opportunity Commission vs. Sears Roebuck and Company: A Personal Account," *Radical History Review* 35 (April 1986): 57–79.

6. Portions of the following analysis are reported in Micaela di Leonardo, *The Varieties of*

Ethnic Experience: Kinship, Class and Gender among California Italian-Americans (Ithaca, N.Y.: Cornell University Press, 1984), chap. 6.

7. Clearly, many women do, in fact, discuss their paid labor with willingness and clarity. The point here is that there are opposing gender tendencies in an identical interview situation, tendencies that are explicable in terms of both the material realities and current cultural constructions of gender.

8. Papanek has rightly focused on women's unacknowledged family status production, but what is conceived of as "family" shifts and varies (Hanna Papanek, "Family Status Production: The 'Work' and 'Non-Work' of Women," *Signs* 4, no. 4 ([Summer 1979]: 775–81).

9. Selma Greenberg, *Right from the Start: A Guide to Nonsexist Child Rearing* (Boston: Houghton Mifflin Co., 1978), 147. Another example of indirect support for kin work's gendered existence is a recent study of university math students, which found that a major reason for women's failure to pursue careers in mathematics was the pressure of family involvement. Compare David Maines et al., *Social Processes of Sex Differentiation in Mathematics* (Washington, D.C.: National Institute of Education, 1981).

10. Larissa Adler Lomnitz and Marisol Pérez Lizaur, "The History of a Mexican Urban Family," *Journal of Family History* 3, no. 4 (1978): 392–409, esp. 398; Matthews Hamabata, *For Love and Power: Family Business in Japan* (Chicago: University of Chicago Press, in press); Sylvia Junko Yanagisako, "Two Processes of Change in Japanese-American Kinship," *Journal of Anthropological Research* 31 (1975): 196–224; Maila Stivens, "Women and Their Kin: Kin, Class and Solidarity in a Middle-Class Suburb of Sydney, Australia," in *Women United, Women Divided,* ed. Patricia Caplan and Janet M. Bujra (Bloomington: Indiana University Press, 1979), 157–84.

11. Carol B. Stack, *All Our Kin: Strategies for Survival in a Black Community* (New York: Harper & Row, 1974). These cultural constructions may, however, vary within ethnic/racial populations as well.

12. Elizabeth Bott, *Family and Social Network,* 2d ed. (New York: Free Press, 1971); Michael Young and Peter Willmott, *Family and Kinship in East London* (London: Routledge & Kegan Paul, 1957); and idem, *Family and Class in a London Suburb* (London: Routledge & Kegan Paul, 1960). Classic studies that presume this class difference are Herbert Gans, *The Urban Villagers: Group and Class in the Life of Italian-Americans* (New York: Free Press, 1962), and Mirra Komarovsky, *Blue-Collar Marriage* (New York: Random House, 1962). A recent example is Ilene Philipson, "Heterosexual Antagonisms and the Politics of Mothering," *Socialist Review* 12, no. 6 (November–December 1982): 55–77. Edward Shorter, *The Making of the Modern Family* (New York: Basic Books, 1975), epitomizes the pessimism of the "family sentiments" school. See also Mary Lyndon Shanley, "The History of the Family in Modern England: Review Essay," *Signs* 4, no. 4 (Summer 1979): 740–50.

13. Stack, *All Our Kin,* and Brett Williams, "The Trip Takes Us: Chicano Migrants to the Prairie" (Ph. D. diss., University of Illinois at Urbana-Champaign, 1975).

14. David Schneider and Raymond T. Smith, *Class Differences and Sex Roles in American Kinship and Family Structure* (Englewood Cliffs, N.J.: Prentice-Hall, Inc., 1973), esp. 27.

15. See Nelson Graburn, ed., *Readings in Kinship and Social Structure* (New York: Harper & Row, 1971), esp. 3–4.

16. The moral mother/cult of domesticity is analyzed in Barbara Welter, "The Cult of True Womanhood, 1820–1860," *American Quarterly* 18, no. 2 (Summer 1966): 151–74; Nancy Cott, *The Bonds of Womanhood: "Women's Sphere"*

in *New England, 1780–1835* (New Haven, Conn.: Yale University Press, 1977); and Ruth Bloch, "American Feminine Ideals in Transition: The Rise of the Moral Mother, 1785–1815," *Feminist Studies* 4, no. 2 (June 1978): 101–26. The description of the general political-economic shift in the United States is based on Harry Braverman, *Labor and Monopoly Capital: The Degradation of Work in the Twentieth Century* (New York: Monthly Review Press, 1974); Peter Dobkin Hall, "Family Structure and Economic Organization: Massachusetts Merchants, 1700–1850," in *Family and Kin in Urban Communities, 1700–1950,* ed. Tamara K. Hareven (New York: New Viewpoints, 1977), 38–61; Michael Anderson, "Family Household and the Industrial Revolution," in *The American Family in Social-Historical Perspective,* ed. Michael Gordon (New York: St. Martin's Press, 1978), 38–50; Tamara K. Hareven, *Amoskeag: Life and Work in an American Factory City* (New York: Pantheon Books, 1978); Richard Edwards, *Constested Terrain: The Transformation of the Workplace in the Twentieth Century* (New York: Basic Books, 1979); Mary Ryan, *The Cradle of the Middle Class: The Family in Oneida County, New York, 1790–1865* (Cambridge: Cambridge University Press, 1981); Alice Kessler-Harris, *Out to Work: A History of Wage-earning Women in the United States* (New York: Oxford University Press, 1982).

17. Ryan, *Cradle of the Middle Class,* 231–32.

18. Sylvia Junko Yanagisako, "Family and Household: The Analysis of Domestic Groups," *Annual Review of Anthropology* 8 (1979): 161–205.

19. See Donald J. Treiman and Heidi I. Hartmann, eds., *Women, Work and Wages: Equal Pay for Jobs of Equal Value* (Washington, D.C.: National Academy Press, 1981).

20. Lamphere (n. 4 above); Jane Fishburne Collier, "Women in Politics," in Rosaldo and Lamphere, eds. (n. 4 above), 89–96.

21. Nancy Folbre and Heidi I. Hartmann, "The Rhetoric of Self-Interest: Selfishness, Altruism, and Gender in Economic Theory," in *The Consequences of Economic Rhetoric,* ed. Arjo Klamer and Donald McCloskey (New York: Cambridge University Press, forthcoming).

MEXICAN AMERICAN WOMEN GRASSROOTS COMMUNITY ACTIVISTS: "MOTHERS OF EAST LOS ANGELES"—MARY PARDO

Notes

On September 15, 1989, another version of this paper was accepted for presentation at the 1990 International Sociological Association meetings to be held in Madrid, Spain, July 9, 1990.

1. See Vicky Randall, *Women and Politics, An International Perspective* (Chicago: University of Chicago Press, 1987), for a review of the central themes and debates in the literature. For two of the few books on Chicanas, work, and family, see Vicki L. Ruiz, *Cannery Women, Cannery Lives, Mexican Women, Unionization, and the California Food Processing Industry, 1930–1950* (Albuquerque: University of New Mexico Press, 1987), and Patricia Zavella, *Women's Work & Chicano Families* (Ithaca, N.Y.: Cornell University Press, 1987).

2. For recent exceptions to this approach, see Anne Witte Garland, *Women Activists: Challenging the Abuse of Power* (New York: The Feminist Press, 1988); Ann Bookman and Sandra Morgan, eds., *Women and the Politics of Empowerment* (Philadelphia: Temple University Press, 1987); Karen Sacks, *Caring by the Hour* (Chicago: University of Illinois Press, 1988). For a sociological analysis of community activism among Afro-American women see Cheryl Townsend Gilkes, "Holding Back the Ocean with a Broom," *The*

Black Woman (Beverly Hills, Calif.: Sage Publications, 1980).

3. For two exceptions to this criticism, see Sara Evans, *Born for Liberty, A History of Women in America* (New York: The Free Press, 1989), and Bettina Aptheker, *Tapestries of Life, Women's Work, Women's Consciousness, and the Meaning of Daily Experience* (Amherst: The University of Massachusetts Press, 1989). For a critique, see Maxine Baca Zinn, Lynn Weber Cannon, Elizabeth Higginbotham, and Bonnie Thornton Dill, "The Costs of Exclusionary Practices in Women's Studies," *Signs* 11, no. 2 (Winter 1986).

4. For cases of grassroots activism among women in Latin America, see Sally W. Yudelman, *Hopeful Openings, A Study of Five Women's Development Organizations in Latin American and the Caribbean* (West Hartford, Conn.: Kumarian Press, 1987). For an excellent case analysis of how informal associations enlarge and empower women's world in Third World countries, see Kathryn S. March and Rachelle L. Taqqu, *Women's Informal Associations in Developing Countries, Catalysts for Change?* (Boulder, Colo.: Westview Press, 1986). Also, see Carmen Feijoó, "Women in Neighbourhoods: From Local Issues to Gender Problems," *Canadian Woman Studies* 6, no. 1 (Fall 1984) for a concise overview of the patterns of activism.

5. The relationship between Catholicism and political activism is varied and not unitary. In some Mexican American communities, grassroots activism relies on parish networks. See Isidro D. Ortiz, "Chicano Urban Politics and the Politics of Reform in the Seventies," *The Western Political Quarterly* 37, no. 4 (December 1984): 565–77. Also, see Joseph D. Sekul, "Communities Organized for Public Service: Citizen Power and Public Power in San Antonio," in *Latinos and the Political System,* edited by F. Chris Garcia (Notre Dame, Ind.: University of Notre Dame Press, 1988). Sekul tells how COPS members challenged prevailing patterns of power by working for the well-being of families and cites four former presidents who were Mexican American women, but he makes no special point of gender.

6. I also interviewed other members of the Coalition Against the Prison and local political office representatives. For a general reference, see James P. Spradley, *The Ethnographic Interview* (New York: Holt, Rinehart and Winston, 1979). For a review essay focused on the relevancy of the method for examining the diversity of women's experiences, see Susan N. G. Geiger, "Women's Life Histories: Method and Content," *Signs* 11, no. 2 (Winter 1982): 334–51.

7. During the last five years, over 300 newspaper articles have appeared on the issue. Frank Villalobos generously shared his extensive newspaper archives with me. See Leo C. Wolinsky, "L.A. Prison Bill 'Locked Up' in New Clash," *Los Angeles Times,* 16 July 1987, sec. 1, p. 3; Rudy Acuña, "The Fate of East L.A.: One Big Jail," *Los Angeles Herald Examiner,* 28 April 1989, A15; Carolina Serna, "Eastside Residents Oppose Prison," *La Gente UCLA Student Newspaper* 17, no. 1 (October 1986): 5; Daniel M. Weintraub, "10,000 Fee Paid to Lawmaker Who Left Sickbed to Cast Vote," *Los Angeles Times,* 13 March 1988, sec. 1, p. 3.

8. Cerrell Associates, Inc., "Political Difficulties Facing Waste-to-Energy Conversion Plant Siting," Report Prepared for California Waste Management Board, State of California (Los Angeles, 1984): 43.

9. Jesus Sanchez, "The Environment: Whose Movement?" *California Tomorrow* 3, nos. 3 & 4 (Fall 1988): 13. Also see Rudy Acuña, *A Community Under Siege* (Los Angeles: Chicano Studies Research Center Publications, UCLA, 1984). The book and its title capture the sentiments and the history of a community that bears an unfair burden of city projects deemed undesirable by all residents.

10. James Vigil, Jr., field representative for Assemblywoman Gloria Molina, 1984–1996, Personal Interview, Whittier, Calif., 27 September 1989. Vigil stated that the Department of Corrections used a threefold strategy: political pressure in the legislature, the promise of jobs for residents, and contracts for local businesses.

11. Edward J. Boyer and Marita Hernandez, "Eastside Seethes over Prison Plan," *Los Angeles Times,* 13 August 1986, sec. 2, p. 1.

12. Martha Molina-Aviles, currently administrative assistant for Assemblywoman Lucille Roybal-Allard, 56th assembly district, and former field representative for Gloria Molina when she held this assembly seat, Personal Interview, Los Angeles, 5 June 1989. Molina-Aviles, who grew up in East Los Angeles, used her experiences and insights to help forge strong links among the women in MELA, other members of the coalition, and the assembly office.

13. MELA has also opposed the expansion of a county prison literally across the street from William Mead Housing Projects, home to 2,000 Latinos, Asians, and Afro-Americans, and a chemical treatment plant for toxic wastes.

14. The first of its kind in a metropolitan area, it would burn 125,000 pounds per day of hazardous wastes. For an excellent article that links recent struggles against hazardous waste dumps and incinerators in minority communities and features women in MELA, see Dick Russell, "Environmental Racism: Minority Communities and Their Battle against Toxics," *The Amicus Journal* 11, no. 2 (Spring 1989): 22–32.

15. Miguel G. Mendívil, field representative for Assemblywoman Lucille Roybal-Allard, 56th assembly district, Personal Interview, Los Angeles, 25 April 1989.

16. John Garcia and Rudolfo de la Garza, "Mobilizing the Mexican Immigrant: The Role of Mexican American Organizations," *The West-ern Political Quarterly* 38, no. 4 (December 1985): 551–64.

17. This concept is discussed in relation to Latino communities in David T. Abalos, *Latinos in the U.S., The Sacred and the Political* (Indiana: University of Notre Dame Press, 1986). The notion of transformation of traditional culture in struggles against oppression is certainly not a new one. For a brief essay on a longer work, see Frantz Fanon, "Algeria Unveiled," *The New Left Reader,* edited by Carl Oglesby (New York: Grove Press, Inc, 1969): 161–85.

18. Karen Sacks, *Caring by the Hour.*

19. Juana Gutiérrez, Personal Interview, Boyle Heights, East Los Angeles, 15 January 1988.

20. Erlinda Robles, Personal Interview, Boyle Heights, Los Angeles, 14 September 1989.

21. Mina Davis Caulfield, "Imperialism, the Family, and Cultures of Resistance," *Socialist Revolution* 29 (1974): 67–85.

22. Erlinda Robles, Personal Interview.

23. Ibid.

24. Juana Gutiérrez, Personal Interview.

25. Frank Villalobos, architect and urban planner, Personal Interview, Los Angeles, 2 May 1989.

26. The law student, Veronica Gutiérrez, is the daughter of Juana Gutiérrez, one of the cofounders of MELA. Martín Gutiérrez, one of her sons, was a field representative for Assemblywoman Lucille Roybal-Allard and also central to community mobilization. Ricardo Gutiérrez, Juana's husband, and almost all the other family members are community activists. They are a microcosm of the family networks that strengthened community mobilization and the Coalition Against the Prison. See Raymundo Reynoso, "Juana Beatrice Gutiérrez: La incansable lucha de una activista comunitaria," *La Opinion,* 6 Agosto de 1989, Acceso, p. 1, and Louis Sahagun, "The Mothers of East L.A. Transform Themselves and Their Community," *Los Angeles Times,* 13 August 1989, sec. 2, p. 1.

27. Frank Villalobos, Personal Interview.

28. Father John Moretta, Resurrection Parish, Personal Interview, Boyle Heights, Los Angeles, 24 May 1989.

29. The Plaza de Mayo mothers organized spontaneously to demand the return of their missing children, in open defiance of the Argentine military dictatorship. For a brief overview of the group and its relationship to other women's organizations in Argentina, and a synopsis of the criticism of the mothers that reveals ideological camps, see Gloria Bonder, "Women's Organizations in Argentina's Transition to Democracy," in *Women and Counter Power,* edited by Yolanda Cohen (New York: Black Rose Books, 1989): 65–85. There is no direct relationship between this group and MELA.

30. Aurora Castillo, Personal Interview, Boyle Heights, Los Angeles, 15 January 1988.

31. Aurora Castillo, Personal Interview.

32. Erlinda Robles, Personal Interview.

33. Ibid.

34. Reynoso, "Juana Beatriz Gutiérrez," p. 1.

35. For historical examples, see Chris Marín, "La Asociación Hispano-Americana de Madres Y Esposas: Tucson's Mexican American Women in World War II," *Renato Rosaldo Lecture Series 1: 1983–1984* (Tucson, Ariz.: Mexican American Studies Center, University of Arizona, Tucson, 1985) and Judy Aulette and Trudy Mills, "Something Old, Something New: Auxiliary Work in the 1983–1986 Copper Strike," *Feminist Studies* 14, no. 2 (Summer 1988): 251–69.

36. Mina Davis Caulfield, "Imperialism, the Family and Cultures of Resistance."

37. Aurora Castillo, Personal Interview.

38. As reconstructed by Juana Gutiérrez, Ricardo Gutiérrez, and Aurora Castillo.

39. Aurora Castillo, Personal Interview.

40. Juana Gutiérrez, Personal Interview.

41. Lucy Ramos, Personal Interview, Boyle Heights, Los Angeles, 3 May 1989.

42. Ibid.

43. For an overview of contemporary Third World struggles against environmental degradation, see Alan B. Durning, "Saving the Planet," *The Progressive* 53, no. 4 (April 1989): 35–59.

44. John Logan and Harvey Molotch, *Urban Fortunes* (Berkeley: University of California Press, 1988). Logan and Molotch use the term in reference to a coalition of business people, local politicians, and the media.

45. Mike Davis, "Chinatown, Part Two? The Internationalization of Downtown Los Angeles," *New Left Review,* no. 164 (July/August 1987): 64–86.

46. Paul Ong, *The Widening Divide, Income Inequality and Poverty in Los Angeles* (Los Angeles: The Research Group on the Los Angeles Economy, 1989). This UCLA-based study documents the growing gap between "haves" and "have nots" in the midst of the economic boom in Los Angeles. According to economists, the study mirrors a national trend in which rising employment levels are failing to lift the poor out of poverty or boost the middle class; see Jill Steward, "Two-Tiered Economy Feared as Dead End of Unskilled," *Los Angeles Times,* 25 June 1989, sec. 2, p. 1. At the same time, the California prison population will climb to more than twice its designed capacity by 1995. See Carl Ingram, "New Forecast Sees a Worse Jam in Prisons," *Los Angeles Times,* 27 June 1989, sec. 1, p. 23.

47. The point that urban land use policies are the products of class struggle—both cause and consequence—is made by Don Parson, "The Development of Redevelopment: Public Housing and Urban Renewal in Los Angeles," *International Journal of Urban and Regional Research* 6, no. 4 (December 1982): 392–413. Parson provides an excellent discussion of the working-class struggle for housing in the 1930s, the counterinitiative of urban renewal in the 1950s, and the inner city revolts of the 1960s.

48. Louise Tilly, "Paths of Proletarianization: Organization of Production, Sexual Division of Labor, and Women's Collective Action," *Signs* 7, no. 2 (1981): 400–17; Alice Kessler-Harris, "Women's Social Mission," *Women Have Always Worked* (Old Westbury, N.Y.: The Feminist Press, 1981): 102–35. For a literature review of women's activism during the Progressive Era, see Marilyn Gittell and Teresa Shtob, "Changing Women's Roles in Political Volunteerism and Reform of the City," in *Women and the American City,* edited by Catharine Stimpson et al. (Chicago: University of Chicago Press, 1981): 64–75.

49. Karen Sacks, *Caring by the Hour,* argues that often the significance of women's contributions is not "seen" because they take place in networks.

50. Aurora Castillo, Personal Interview.

MUSCOGEE WOMEN'S IDENTITY DEVELOPMENT —BARBARA B. KAWULICH

References

Bartram, W. (1987). Observations on the Creek and Cherokee Indians, 1789 (1853). In Sturtevant, W. C. (Ed.), *A Creek source book.* New York: Garland Publishing, Inc.

Bataille, G. M. & Sands, K. M. (1991). *American Indian women: A guide to research.* New York: Garland.

Champagne, D. (1992). *Social order and political change: Constitutional governments among the Cherokee, the Choctaw, the Chickasaw, and the Creek.* Stanford, CA: Stanford University Press.

Debo, A. (1942). *The road to disappearance.* Norman, OK: The University of Oklahoma Press.

Deegan, M. J. (1987). Symbolic interaction and the study of women: An introduction. In Deegan, M. J. & Hill, M. R. (Eds.), *Women and symbolic interaction.* Boston: Allen & Unwin, Inc.

Deloria, V. Jr. (1992). American Indians. In Ratner, L. A. & Buenker, J. D. *Multiculturalism in the United States,* (pp. 31–52). New York: Greenwood Press.

Dinnerstein, L., Nichols, R. L. & Reimers, D. M. (1990). *Natives and strangers: Blacks, Indians, and immigrants in America.* New York: Oxford University Press, Inc.

Fitzgerald, T. K. (1974). *Social and cultural identity: Problems of persistence and change.* Athens, GA: University of Georgia Press.

Foreman, G. (1972). *Indian removal.* Norman, OK: University of Oklahoma Press.

Green, R. (1983). *Native American women: A contextual bibliography.* Bloomington, IN: Indiana University Press.

Green, M. K. (1995). Cultural identities: Challenges for the twenty-first century. In Green, M. K. (Ed.), *Issues in Native American cultural identity.* New York: Peter Lang Publishing, Inc.

Greenman, N. (1996). More than a mother: Some Tewa women reflect on Gia. In Etter-Lewis, G. & Foster, M. (Eds.), *Unrelated kin: Race and gender in women's personal narratives.* New York: Routledge.

Hagan, W. T. (1961). *American Indians.* Chicago: The University of Chicago Press.

Hill, B., Vaughn, C. & Harrison, S. B. (1995). Living and working in two worlds: Case studies of five American Indian women teachers. *The Clearing House, 69 (1),* pp. 42–49.

Jacobson-Widding, A. (Ed.) (1983). Introduction. In *Identity: Personal and sociocultural: A symposium,* (pp. 13–32). Stockholm: Almquist & Wiksell International.

Josselson, R. (1987). *Finding herself: Pathways to identity development in women.* San Francisco: Jossey-Bass.

King, A. R. (1974). A stratification of labyrinths: The acquisition and retention of cultural identity in modern culture. In Fitzgerald, T. K. (Ed.), *Social and cultural identity: Problems of persistence and change.* Athens, GA: University of Georgia Press.

Kleinfeld, J. & Kruse, J. A. (1982). Native Americans in the labor force: Hunting for an accurate measure. *Monthly Labor Review, 105 (7),* pp. 47–51.

LaFramboise, T. D., Heyle, A. M. & Ozer, E. J. (1990). Changing and diverse roles of women in American Indian cultures. *Sex Roles, 22 (7/8),* pp. 455–476.

Lincoln, Y. S. & Guba, E. G. (1985). *Naturalistic Inquiry.* Newbury Park, CA: Sage Publications.

Lynn, S. (1992). *Progressive women in conservative times: racial justice, peace, and feminism, 1945 to the 1960s.* New Brunswick, NJ: Rutgers University Press.

Medicine, B. (1983). Indian women: Tribal identity as status quo. In Low, M. & Hubbard, R. (Eds.), *Women's nature: Rationalizations of inequality.* New York: Pergamon Press, 63–73.

Miles, M. B. & Huberman, A. M. (1994). *Qualitative Data Analysis: An Expanded Sourcebook.* (Second edition) Thousand Oaks, CA: Sage Publications.

Morris, M. H., Davis, D. L. & Allen, J. W. (1994). *Journal of International Business Studies, 25 (1),* pp. 65–89.

Nunez, T. A., Jr. (1987). Creek nativism and the Creek War of 1813–1814 (Part 2). In Sturtevant, W. C. (Ed.), *A Creek source book.* New York: Garland Publishing, Inc.

O'Brien, S. (1989). *American Indian tribal governments.* Norman, OK: University of Oklahoma Press.

Paredes, J. A. (1987). Kinship and descent in the ethnic reassertion of the eastern Creek Indi-

ans. In Sturtevant, W. C. (Ed.), *A Creek source book.* New York: Garland Publishing, Inc.

Patterson, S. J., Sochting, I. & Marcia, J. E. (1992). The inner space and beyond: Women and identity. In Adams, G. R., Gullotta, T. P. & Montmayor, R. (Eds.), *Adolescent identity formation.* Newbury Park, CA: Sage Publications.

Sattler, R. A. (1995). Women's status among the Muskogee and Cherokee. In Klein, L. F. & Ackerman, L. A. (Eds.), *Women and power in native North America.* Norman, OK: University of Oklahoma Press.

Strauss, A. & Corbin, J. (1990). *Basics of qualitative research: Grounded theory procedures and techniques.* Newbury Park, CA: Sage Publications.

Swanton, J. R. (1987). Modern square grounds of the Creek Indians (1931). In Sturtevant, W. C. (Ed.), *A Creek source book.* New York: Garland Publishing, Inc.

Urban, G. (1994). The social organizations of the southeast. In DeMallie, R. J. & Ortiz, A. (Eds.), *North American Indian Anthropology: Essays on society and culture.* Norman, OK: University of Oklahoma Press, 172–193.

LONG DISTANCE COMMUNITY IN THE NETWORK SOCIETY: CONTACT AND SUPPORT BEYOND NETVILLE —KEITH N. HAMPTON AND BARRY WELLMAN

Notes

1. Authors' Notes: This research was supported by the Social Science and Humanities Research Council of Canada and Communication and Information Technologies Ontario. At the University of Toronto, we have benefitted from

our involvements with the Centre for Urban and Community Studies, the Department of Sociology, and the Knowledge Media Design Institute. We thank a host of people for their comments, assistance, and support. At the University of Toronto: Dean Behrens, Nadia Bello, Sivan Bomze, Bonnie Erickson, Todd Irvine, Kristine Klement, Emmanuel Koku, Alexandra Marin, Dolly Mehra, Nancy Nazer, Christien Perez, Grace Ramirez, Janet Salaff, Richard Stren, Carlton Thorne, and Jeannette Wright. Others: Ross Barclay, Donald Berkowitz, Damien De Shane-Gill, Jerome Durlak, Herbert Gans, Paul Hoffert, Timothy Hollett, Thomas Jurenka, Marc Smith, Liane Sullivan, and Richard Valentine. Our greatest debt is to the residents of Netville who have given their time and patience, allowing us into their homes and answering many questions. Portions of this work are reprinted from Keith Hampton's doctoral dissertation, © Copyright Keith Neil Hampton 2001. For more papers on the Netville project please visit www.mysocialnetwork.net and www.chass.utoronto.ca/~wellman.

2. "Affordances" is a term widely used in the study of human computer interaction (Gaver, 1996; Norman, 1999). Erin Bradner (2000), writing for computer scientists, coined the term "social affordances" to emphasize the social as well as individual possibilities of computer networks.

3. This study is limited by the conventional wiring of Netville residents non-neighborhood social ties.

4. Neighborhood ties are an exception in Netville and are treated as a special case in Hampton, 2001a and a forthcoming Hampton and Wellman article.

5. For more details, see Hampton (2001b), Hampton (2001a), Hampton (1999), and Hampton & Wellman (1999).

6. "Netville" and the "Magenta Consortium" are pseudonyms.

7. "Always on" Internet access refers to a property of most high-speed Internet services which allows users to be connected to the Internet whenever the computer is turned on, without performing any special tasks, manually starting any additional programs, or "dialing up" to the Internet.

8. This agreement was only lightly enforced and often forgotten by the residents. No resident was ever denied service for refusing to participate, and no data were ever collected without the residents' knowledge.

9. Magenta never clarified why some Netville homes were connected and others were not. The two most likely causes were the Consortium's limited access to resources for completing home installations, and miscommunications with the housing developer in identifying homes that had been occupied.

10. Some caution should be taken in the interpretation of this data taking into account that participants were not asked to indicate if they had ties at the specified distances both pre and post move. Participants who responded that they did not have social ties at a given distance were coded as having the "same" level of contact or support pre and post move. Participants may have experienced no change in contact as a result of not having ties at the specified distance, or report change as a result of not having network members at the specified distance either pre-move or post-move. However, there is no indication that this limitation in the data should significantly effect the results as they are presented here.

11. Cronbach's alpha, a measure of internal consistency and reliability among scale items shows that all scales (except one) have a satisfactory alpha above 0.7. The exception, the scale for chance in contact with non-neighborhood network members living within 50 km, is retained because the significant correlation of 0.32 of the

two variables comprising it validates the underlying consideration in scale construction that participants respond consistently across scale constructs.

12. Our research about neighboring in Netville is reported more fully in an article being prepared by Hampton & Wellman; and in Hampton, 2001b.

13. The lack of variation in the support scale for wired residents suggests that some caution should be taken in interpreting the results of the regression analysis.

14. The lack of variation in the contact scale for wired residents suggests that some caution should be taken in interpreting the results of the regression analysis.

15. Regression analysis with a dependent variable that is extremely light-tailed, as is the scale for change in support at more than 500 km, violates the assumption of equal variance. The results of the regression reported in Table 4 for ties at this distance should be interpreted with caution.

References

Bradner, E. (2000). *Understanding Groupware Adoption: The Social Affordances of Computer-Mediated Communication among Distributed Groups.* Working Paper, Department of Information and Computer Science, University of California, Irvine, February.

Clark, S. D. (1966). *The Suburban Society.* Toronto: University of Toronto Press.

Ekos Research Associates (1998). *Information Highway and the Canadian Communications Household.* Ottawa, Canada: Ekos Research Associates.

Fischer, C. (1982). *To Dwell Among Friends.* Berkeley: University of California Press.

Fischer, C. (1984). *The Urban Experience.* Orlando, FL: Harcourt Brace Jovanovich.

Fox, R. (1995). Newstrack. *Communications of the ACM, 38(8),* pp. 11–12.

Gans, H. (1967). *The Levittowners.* New York: Pantheon.

Gaver, W. (1996). Affordances for Interaction: The Social is Material for Design. *Ecological Psychology, 8,* pp. 111–129.

Hampton, K. N. (1999). Computer Assisted Interviewing: The Design and Application of Survey Software to the Wired Suburb Project. *Bulletin de Méthode Sociologique, 62,* pp. 49–68.

Hampton, K. N. (2001a). Broadband Neighborhoods Connected Communities. In J. Jacko and A. Sears (Eds.), *CHI 2001 Extended Abstracts.* ACM Press.

Hampton, K. N. (2001b). *Living the Wired Life in the Wired Suburb: Netville, Glocalization and Civil Society.* Doctoral Dissertation, Department of Sociology, University of Toronto.

Hampton, K. N. (2001c). Grieving For a Lost Network: Collective Action in a Wired Suburb. *Mobilization,* Forthcoming.

Hampton, K. N., & Wellman, B. (1999). Netville Online and Offline: Observing and Surveying a Wired Suburb. *American Behavioral Scientist, 43(3),* pp. 475–492.

Hawley, A. (1986). *Human Ecology.* Chicago: University of Chicago Press.

Haythornthwaite, C., & Wellman, B. (1998). Work, Friendship and Media Use for Information Exchange in a Networked Organization. *Journal of the American Society for Information Science 49(12),* pp. 1101–1114.

Homans, G. (1961). *Social Behavior: Its Elementary Forms.* New York: Harcourt Brace Jovanovich.

Kraut, R., Lundmark, V., Patterson, M., Kiesler, S., Mukopadhyay, T., & Scherlis, W. (1998). Internet paradox: A social technology that reduces social involvement and psychological well-being? *American Psychologist, 53(9),* pp. 1017–1031.

Nie, N. (2001). Sociability, Interpersonal Relations, and the Internet: Reconciling Conflicting Findings. *American Behavioral Scientist, 45,* this issue.

Nie, N., & Erbring, L. (2000). *Internet and Society: A Preliminary Report.* Stanford, CA: Stanford Institute for the Quantitative Study of Society: Stanford University.

Norman, D. (1999). Affordance, Conventions, and Design. *Interactions 6(3),* pp. 38–44.

Oldenburg, R. (1999). *The Great Good Places: Cafés, Coffee Shops, Book Stores, Bars, Hair Salons and other Hangouts at the Heart of a Community.* New York: Marlow.

Patton, P. 1986. *Open Road.* New York: Simon and Schuster.

Rheingold, H. (2000). *The Virtual Community* (revised ed.). Cambridge, MA: MIT Press.

Smith, M., & Kollock, P., (Eds.) (1999). *Communities in Cyberspace.* London: Routledge.

Sproull, L., & Kiesler, S. (1991). *Connections.* Cambridge, MA: MIT Press.

Stein, M. (1960). *The Eclipse of Community.* Princeton, NJ: Princeton University Press.

Walther, J. B., Anderson, J., & Park, D. (1994). Interpersonal effects in computer-mediated interaction: a meta-analysis of social and antisocial communication. *Communication Research, 21(4),* pp. 460–487.

Wellman, B. (1997). An Electronic Group is Virtually a Social Network. In Kiesler, S. (Ed.), *Culture of The Internet,* pp. 179–205. Hillsdale, NJ: Lawrence Erlbaum.

Wellman, B. (Ed.) (1999). *Networks in the Global Village.* Boulder, CO: Westview Press.

Wellman, B. (2001). Physical Place and Cyber Place: the Rise of Networked Individualism. *International Journal of Urban and Regional Research, 25:* forthcoming.

Wellman, B., Carrington, P., & Hall, A. (1988). Networks as Personal Communities. In Wellman, B., and Berkowitz, S. D. (Eds.), *Social Structures: A Network Approach,* pp. 130–184. Cambridge: Cambridge University Press.

Wellman, B., & Frank, K. (2001). Network Capital in a Multi-level World: Getting Support in Personal Communities. In Lin, N., Cook, K., and Burt, R. (Eds.), *Social Capital: Theory and Research,* pp. 233–273. Chicago, IL: Aldine DeGruyter.

Wellman, B., & Gulia, M. (1999). Net Surfers Don't Ride Alone: Virtual Communities as Communities. In Wellman, B. (Ed.), *Networks in the Global Village,* pp. 331–367. Boulder, CO: Westview Press.

Wellman, B., & Leighton, B. (1979). Networks, Neighborhoods and Communities. *Urban Affairs Quarterly 14,* pp. 363–390.

Wellman, B., Quan, A., Witte, J., & Hampton, K. N. (2001). Does the Internet Increase, Decrease, or Supplement Social Capital: Social Networks, Participation, and Community Commitment. *American Behavioral Scientist, 45,* this issue.

Wellman, B., & Tindall, D. (1993). Reach out and touch some bodies: how telephone networks connect social networks. *Progress in Communication Science, 12,* pp. 63–94.

Wellman, B., & Wortley, S. (1990). Different strokes from different folks: community ties and social support. *American Journal of Sociology 96,* pp. 558–588.

DATING ON THE NET: TEENS AND THE RISE OF "PURE" RELATIONSHIPS —LYNN SCHOFIELD CLARK

Notes

1. I serve as Associate Researcher on the Lilly Endowment funded project, "Media, Meaning, and the Lifecourse," which is under the direction

of Stewart M. Hoover at the Center for Mass Media Research, University of Colorado. I gratefully acknowledge the funding for the research in this chapter, which has been provided by the Lilly Endowment and by a dissertation fellowship from the Louisville Institute.

2. I paid each of the leaders $25 for their efforts and paid each of the participants they recruited $8. I also provided money for pizza, which the leader purchased at the conclusion of the discussion.

3. For an illustration of warnings in the popular press, see, for example, Rozen, L. (1997, November). Undercover on the Internet. *Good Housekeeping,* pp. 76–78, 82.

4. It should be noted, however, that while the teens in my study by and large noted preferences for the teen chat rooms, many of them had experimented with the more racy adult chat rooms, as well.

References

Austen, J. (1989). *Sense and sensibility.* New York: Signet. (Original work published 1795)

Bailey, B. (1988). *From front porch to back seat.* Baltimore, MD: Johns Hopkins University Press.

Baym, N. (1995). The emergence of community in computer-mediated communication. In S. G. Jones (Ed.), *CyberSociety: Computer-mediated communication and community* (pp. 138–163). Thousand Oaks, CA: Sage.

Blumer, H. (1933). *The movies and conduct.* New York: Macmillan.

Brown, L., & Gilligan, C. (1992). *Meeting at the crossroads. Women's psychology and girls' development.* Cambridge, MA: Harvard University Press.

Erickson, E. (1968). *Identity: Youth and crisis.* New York: W. W. Norton.

Fass, P. (1977). *The damned and the beautiful: American youth in the 1920s.* New York: Oxford University Press.

Friend, R. (1993). Choices, not closets: Heterosexism and homophobia in schools. In L. Weis & M. Fine (Eds.), *Beyond silenced voices: Class, race, and gender in United States schools* (pp. 209–235). Albany: State University of New York Press.

Giddens, A. (1991). *Modernity and self-identity: Self and society in the late modern age.* Palo Alto, CA: Stanford University Press.

Illouz, E. (1997). *Consuming the romantic Utopia: Love and cultural contradictions of capitalism.* Berkeley: University of California Press.

Jones, S. (1995). Understanding community in the information age. In S. G. Jones. (Ed.), *CyberSociety: Computer-mediated communication and community* (pp. 10–35). Thousand Oaks, CA: Sage.

Kliesler, S., Siegel, J., & McGuire, T. (1984). Social psychological aspect of computer-mediated communication. *American Psychologist, 39*(10), 1123–1134.

Kramarae, C. (1995). A backstage critique of virtual reality. In S. G. Jones (Ed.), *CyberSociety: Computer-mediated communication and community* (pp. 36–56). Thousand Oaks, CA: Sage.

Modell, J. (1989). *Into one's own: From youth to adulthood in the United States 1920–1975.* Berkeley: University of California Press.

Rakow, L. (1988). Gendered technology, gendered practice. *Critical Studies in Mass Communication, 5(1),* 57–70.

Rakow, L., & Navarro, V. (1993, June). Remote mothering and the parallel shift: Women meet the cellular telephone. *Critical Studies in Mass Communication, 10*(2),144–157.

Rheingold, H. (1991). *The virtual community: Homesteading on the electronic frontier.* Reading, MA: Addison-Wesley.

Rozen, L. (1997, Nov.). Undercover on the Internet. *Good Housekeeping, 225*(10), 76–78, 82.

Seabrook, J. (1997). *Deeper: My two-year odyssey in cyberspace.* New York: Simon & Schuster.

Yin, R. (1994). *Case study research: Design and methods* (2nd ed.). Thousand Oaks, CA: Sage.

GETTING A MAN OR GETTING AHEAD: A COMPARISON OF WHITE AND BLACK SORORITIES —ALEXANDRA BERKOWITZ AND IRENE PADAVIC

Notes

1. The notion of scripts for social life stems from symbolic interaction theory, which describes how sexual scripts—plans or blueprints that designate culturally appropriate answers to the who, what, when, where, and whys of sexuality—are formed and how they are internalized (Simon and Gagnon 1986; see also Lorber 1994). Scripts are learned through interactions and are influenced by the larger society and by peer groups.

2. College youth of both sexes (particularly at predominantly black colleges) were strongly encouraged to use their education to better the community ("Privilege must always be translated into terms of responsibility, or else it will become shackles to your feet and chains to your hands," Howard University students were told in 1910 [Shaw 1996, 91–92]).

3. Their grandmothers' motivation may have differed, however. As Spain and Bianchi (1996) noted, a decision to earn the fabled "Mrs." degree and attach oneself to a husband's career prospects was a sound economic decision in the face of extremely limited career opportunities for women.

4. The two women who reported no date functions were in a small chapter at the predominantly white university. The chapter's size is probably the main reason that the group does not host such an event.

5. The small size of African American collegiate sorority chapters—between 10 and 30 members, compared to about 120 members for white sororities—promoted a "family feeling" that extended to relations with the graduate chapter, whose members often act as quasi-mothers. This support system of peers and elders was especially important to women who attended the predominantly white university.

References

Amott, T., and J. Matthaei. 1991. *Race, gender and work: A multicultural economic history of women in the United States.* Boston: South End.

Anderson, E. 1990. *Streetwise: Race, class, and change in an urban community.* Chicago: University of Chicago Press.

Andersen, M. L., and P. Collins. 1992. *Race, class, and gender: An anthology.* Belmont, CA: Wadsworth.

Barnett, B. M. 1993. Invisible southern black women leaders in the civil rights movement: The triple constraints of gender, race, and class. *Gender & Society* 7:162–82.

Barrett, M., and A. Phillips. 1992. *Destabilizing theory: Contemporary feminist debates.* Cambridge: Polity.

Blumstein, P., and P. Schwartz, 1989. Intimate relationships and the creation of sexuality. In *Gender in intimate relationships: A miciostructural approach,* edited by B. J. Risman and P. Schwartz, 120–29. Belmont, CA: Wadsworth.

Cancian, F. M. 1989. Love and the rise of capitalism. In *Gender in intimate relationships: A microstructural approach,* edited by B. J. Risman and P. Schwartz, 12–25. Belmont, CA: Wadsworth.

Cherlin, A. S. 1992. *Marriage, divorce, remarriage.* Cambridge, MA: Harvard University Press.

Collins, P. H. 1990. *Black feminist thought: Knowledge, consciousness, and the politics of empowerment.* Boston: Unwin Hyman.

———. 1991. The meaning of motherhood in black culture and black mother-daughter relationships. In *Double stitch: Black women write about mothers and daughters,* edited by P. Bell-Scott, B. Guy-Sheftall, J. J. Royster, J. Sims-Wood, M. DeCosta-Willis, and L. P. Fultz, 42–60. New York: Harper Perennial.

Corsaro, W. A. 1997. *The sociology of childhood.* Thousand Oaks, CA: Pine Forge.

Corsaro, W. A., and K. B. Rosier. 1992. Documenting productive-reproductive processes in children's lives: Transition narratives of a black family living in poverty. In *Interpretive approaches to children's socialization, new directions for child development, No. 58,* edited by W. Corsaro and P. J. Miller, 67–91. San Francisco: Jossey-Bass.

Cowie, C., and S. Lees. 1981. Slags or drags. *Feminist Review* 9:17–31.

Davis, A. 1981. *Women, race and class.* New York: Random House.

Davis, K., and S. Fisher. 1993. Power and the female subject. In *Negotiating at the margins: The gendered discourses of power and resistance,* edited by S. Fisher and K. Davis, 3–22. New Brunswick, NJ: Rutgers University Press.

Davis, M. 1982. *Contributions of black women to America,* vol. 2. Columbia, SC: Kenday Press.

Dill, B. T. 1979. The dialectics of black womanhood. *Signs* 4:543–55.

———. 1988. Our mothers' grief: Racial ethnic women and the maintenance of families. *Journal of Family History* 13:425–31.

Fass, P. 1977. *The damned and the beautiful: American youth in the 1920s.* New York: Oxford University Press.

Franklin, C. W., II. 1992. Black male-female conflict: Individually caused and culturally structured. In *Men's lives,* edited by M. Kimmel and M. Messner, 341–49. New York: Macmillan.

Giddings, P. 1988. *In search of sisterhood: The history of Delta Sigma Theta Sorority, Inc.* New York: Morrow.

Glover, C. C. 1993. Sister Greeks: African-American sororities and the dynamics of institutionalized sisterhood at an Ivy League university. Paper presented at the Eastern Sociological Society Meeting, Boston.

Handler, L. 1995. In the fraternal sisterhood: Sororities as gender strategy. *Gender & Society* 9:236–55.

Higginbotham, E., and L. Weber. 1992. Moving up with kin and community: Upward social mobility for black and white women. *Gender & Society* 6:416–40.

Holland, D. C., and M. A. Eisenhart. 1990. *Educated in romance: Women, achievement, and college culture.* Chicago: University of Chicago Press.

hooks, b. 1981. *Ain't I a woman: Black women and feminism.* Boston: South End.

———. 1989. *Talking back: Thinking feminist, thinking black.* Boston: South End.

Horowitz, H. L. 1987. *Campus life: Undergraduate cultures from the end of the eighteenth century to the present.* New York: Knopf.

Jackson, R., and R. C. Winkler. 1964. A comparison of pledges and independents. *Personnel and Guidance Journal* (December): 379–82.

Jones, J. 1985. *Labor of love, labor of sorrow: Black women, work, and the family from slavery to the present.* New York: Basic Books.

Kalof, L., and T. Cargill. 1991. Fraternity and sorority membership and gender dominance attitudes. *Sex Roles* 25:417–23.

King, D. 1988. Multiple jeopardy, multiple consciousness: The context of black feminist ideology. *Signs* 19:42–72.

Ladner, J. 1971. *Tomorrow's tomorrow: The black woman.* New York: Doubleday.

Lees, S. 1986. *Losing out: Sexuality and adolescent girls.* London: Hutchinson.

Lerner, G. 1979. *The majority finds its past: Placing women in history.* New York: Oxford.

Lorber, J. 1994. *Paradoxes of gender.* New Haven, CT: Yale University Press.

Lord, M. J. 1987. The Greek rites of exclusion. *The Nation* (4 July):10–13.

Machung, A. 1989. Talking career, thinking job: Gender differences in career and family expectations of Berkeley seniors. *Feminist Studies* 15:35–58.

Martin, P. Y., and R. A. Hummer. 1989. Fraternities and rape on campus. *Gender & Society* 3:457–73.

Modell, J. 1989. *Into one's own: From youth to adulthood in the U.S. 1920–1975.* Berkeley: University of California Press.

Mullings, L. 1997. *On our own terms: Race, class, and gender in the lives of African American women.* New York: Routledge.

Reskin, B. F., and I. Padavic. 1994. *Women and men at work.* Newbury Park, CA: Pine Forge Press.

Rice, T. W., and D. L. Coates. 1995. Gender role attitudes in the southern United States. *Gender & Society* 6:744–56.

Risman, B. J. 1982. College women and sororities: The social construction and reaffirmation of gender roles. *Urban Life* 11:231–52.

Saluter, A. 1992. Marital status and living arrangements: March 1992. *Current Population Reports,* Series P-20-468 (December), p. xiii.

Sanday, P. R. 1990. *Fraternity gang rape: Sex, brotherhood, and privilege on campus.* New York: New York University Press.

Shaw, S. 1996. *What a woman ought to be and to do: Black professional women workers during the Jim Crow era.* Chicago: University of Chicago Press.

Simon, W., and J. H. Gagnon. 1986. Sexual scripts: Permanence and change. *Archives of Sexual Behavior* 15:97–120.

Spain, D., and S. M. Bianchi. 1996. *Balancing act: Motherhood, marriage, and employment among American women.* New York: Russell Sage.

Stack, C. 1974. *All our kin: Strategies for survival in a Black community.* New York: Harper & Row.

Stombler, M., and I. Padavic. 1997. Sister acts: Resisting men's domination in black and white fraternity little sister programs. *Social Problems* 44:257–75.

Strong, B., and C. DeVault. 1994. *Human sexuality.* Mountain View, CA: Mayfield.

Treichler, P. 1985. Alma mater's sorority: Women and the University of Illinois 1890–1925. In *For alma mater: Theory and practice in feminist scholarship,* edited by P. A. Treichler, C. Kramarae, and B. Stafford, 5–61. Champaign: University of Illinois Press.

West, C., and S. Fenstermaker. 1995. Doing difference. *Gender & Society* 9:8–37.

MARRIAGES—ARRANGED, SEMI-ARRANGED OR LOVE? —JOHANNA LESSINGER

References

Agarwal, Priya. 1991. *Passage From India: Post-1965 Indian Immigrants and Their Children.* Palos Verdes, CA: Yuvati Publications.

Luthra, Rashmi. 1989. "Matchmaking in the Classifieds of the Immigrant Indian Press." In *Making Waves: An Anthology of Writings By and About Asian American Women.*

Asian Women United of California, eds. Boston: Beacon Press.

Narayan, Shoba. 1995. "When Life's Partner Comes Pre-Chosen." *New York Times,* May 4: C1, C8.

THE FEMINIZATION OF LOVE —FRANCESCA M. CANCIAN

Notes

1. The term "feminization" of love is derived from Ann Douglas, *The Feminization of Culture* (New York: Alfred A. Knopf, 1977).

2. The term "androgyny" is problematic. It assumes rather than questions sex-role stereotypes (aggression is masculine, e.g.); it can lead to a utopian view that underestimates the social causes of sexism; and it suggests the complete absence of differences between men and women, which is biologically impossible. Nonetheless, I use the term because it best conveys my meaning: a combination of masculine and feminine styles of love. The negative and positive aspects of the concept "androgyny" are analyzed in a special issue of *Women's Studies* (vol. 2, no. 2[1974]), edited by Cynthia Secor. Also see Sandra Bem, "Gender Schema Theory and Its Implications for Child Development: Raising Gender-aschematic Children in a Gender-schematic Society," *Signs: Journal of Women in Culture and Society* 8, no. 4 (1983): 598–616.

3. The quotations are from a study by Ann Swidler, "Ideologies of Love in Middle Class America" (paper presented at the annual meeting of the Pacific Sociological Association, San Diego, 1982). For useful reviews of the history of love, see Morton Hunt, *The Natural History of Love* (New York: Alfred A. Knopf, 1959); and Bernard Murstein, *Love, Sex and Marriage through the Ages* (New York: Springer, 1974).

4. See John Bowlby, *Attachment and Loss* (New York: Basic Books, 1969), on mother-in-

fant attachment. The quotation is from Elaine Walster and G. William Walster, *A New Look at Love* (Reading, Mass.: Addison-Wesley Publishing Co., 1978), 9. Conceptions of love and adjustment used by family sociologists are reviewed in Robert Lewis and Graham Spanier, "Theorizing about the Quality and Stability of Marriage," in *Contemporary Theories about the Family,* ed. W. Burr, R. Hill, F. Nye, and I. Reiss (New York: Free Press, 1979), 268–94.

5. Mary Ryan, *Womanhood in America,* 2d ed. (New York: New Viewpoints, 1979), and *The Cradle of the Middle Class: The Family in Oneida County, N.Y, 1790–1865* (New York: Cambridge University Press, 1981); Barbara Ehrenreich and Deirdre English, *For Her Own Good: 150 Years of Experts' Advice to Women* (New York: Anchor Books, 1978); Barbara Welter, "The Cult of True Womanhood: 1820–1860," *American Quarterly* 18, no. 2(1966): 151–74; Carl N. Degler, *At Odds* (New York: Oxford University Press, 1980).

6. Alternative definitions of love are reviewed in Walster and Walster, Clyde Hendrick and Susan Hendrick, *Liking, Loving and Relating* (Belmont, Calif.: Wadsworth Publishing Co., 1983); Ira Reiss, *Family Systems in America,* 3d ed. (New York: Holt, Rinehart & Winston, 1980), 113–41; Margaret Reedy, "Age and Sex Differences in Personal Needs and the Nature of Love" (Ph.D. diss., University of Southern California, 1977).

7. Abraham Maslow, *Motivation and Personality,* 2d ed. (New York: Harper & Row, 1970), 182–83.

8. Zick Rubin's scale is described in his article "Measurement of Romantic Love," *Journal of Personality and Social Psychology* 16, no. 2 (1970): 265–73; Lillian Rubin's book on marriage is *Intimate Strangers* (New York: Harper & Row, 1983), quote on 90.

9. The emphasis on mutual aid and instrumental love among poor people is described in Lillian Rubin, *Worlds of Pain* (New York: Basic Books, 1976); Rayna Rapp, "Family and Class

in Contemporary America," in *Rethinking the Family,* ed. Barrie Thorne (New York: Longman, Inc., 1982), 168–87; S. M. Miller and F. Riessman, "The Working-Class Subculture," in *Blue-Collar World,* ed. A. Shostak and W. Greenberg (Englewood Cliffs, N.J.: Prentice-Hall, Inc., 1964), 24–36.

10. Francesca Cancian, Clynta Jackson, and Ann Wysocki, "A Survey of Close Relationships" (University of California, Irvine, School of Social Sciences, 1982, typescript).

11. Swidler.

12. *Webster's New Collegiate Dictionary* (Springfield, Mass.: G. C. Merriam Co., 1977).

13. Paul Rosencrantz, Helen Bee, Susan Vogel, Inge Broverman, and Donald Broverman, "Sex Role Stereotypes and Self-Concepts in College Students," *Journal of Consulting and Clinical Psychology* 32, no. 3 (1968): 287–95; Paul Rosencrantz, "Rosencrantz Discusses Changes in Stereotypes about Men and Women," *Second Century Radcliffe News* (Cambridge, Mass., June 1982), 5–6.

14. Nancy Chodorow, *The Reproduction of Mothering* (Berkeley: University of California Press, 1978), 169. Dorothy Dinnerstein presents a similar theory in *The Mermaid and the Minotaur: Sexual Arrangements and Human Malaise* (New York: Harper & Row, 1976). Freudian and biological dispositional theories about women's nurturance are surveyed in Jean Stockard and Miriam Johnson, *Sex Roles* (Englewood Cliffs, N.J.: Prentice-Hall, Inc., 1980).

15. Carol Gilligan, *In a Different Voice* (Cambridge, Mass: Harvard University Press, 1982), 32, 159–61; see also L. Rubin, *Intimate Strangers.*

16. Talcott Parsons and Robert F. Bales, *Family, Socialization and Interaction* (Glencoe, Ill., Free Press, 1955). For a critical review of family sociology from a feminist perspective, see Arlene Skolnick, *The Intimate Environment* (Boston: Little, Brown & Co., 1978). Radical feminist theories also support the feminized con-

ception of love, but they have been less influential in social science, see, e.g., Mary Daly, *Gyn/Ecology; The Metaethics of Radical Feminism* (Boston: Beacon Press, 1979).

17. I have drawn most heavily on Ryan, *Womanhood,* (n. 5 above), Ryan, *Cradle* (n. 5 above), Ehrenreich and English (n. 5 above), Welter (n. 5 above).

18. Ryan, *Womanhood,* 24–25.

19. Similar changes occurred when culture and religion were feminized, according to Douglas (n. 1 above). Conceptions of God's love shifted toward an image of a sweet and tender parent, a "submissive, meek and forgiving" Christ (149).

20. On the persistence of women's wage inequality and responsibility for housework, see Stockard and Johnson (n. 14 above).

21. Jean Baker Miller, *Toward a New Psychology of Women* (Boston: Beacon Press, 1976). There are, of course, many exceptions to Miller's generalization, e.g., women who need to be independent or who need an attachment with a woman.

22. In psychology, the work of Carl Jung, David Bakan, and Bem are especially relevant. See Carl Jung, "Anima and Animus," in *Two Essays on Analytical Psychology: Collected Works of C. G. Jung* (New York: Bollinger Foundation, 1953), 7:186–209; David Bakan, *The Duality of Human Existence* (Chicago: Rand McNally & Co., 1966). They are discussed in Bem's paper, "Beyond Androgyny," in *Family in Transition,* 2d ed., ed. A. Skolnick and J. Skolnick (Boston: Little, Brown & Co., 1977), 204–21. Carl Rogers exemplifies the human potential theme of self-development through the search for wholeness. See Carl Rogers, *On Becoming a Person* (Boston: Houghton Mifflin Co., 1961).

23. Chodorow (n. 14 above) refers to the effects of the division of labor and to power differences between men and women, and the special effects of women's being the primary parents are widely acknowledged among historians.

24. The data on Yale men are from Mirra Komarovsky, *Dilemma of Masculinity* (New York: W. W. Norton & Co., 1976). Angus Campbell reports that children are closer to their mothers than to their fathers, and daughters feel closer to their parents than do sons, on the basis of large national surveys, in *The Sense of Well-Being in America* (New York: McGraw-Hill Book Co., 1981), 96. However, the tendency of people to criticize their mothers more than their fathers seems to contradict these findings; e.g., see Donald Payne and Paul Mussen, "Parent-Child Relations and Father Identification among Adolescent Boys," *Journal of Abnormal and Social Psychology* 52 (1956): 358–62. Being "closer" to one's mother may refer mostly to spending more time together and knowing more about each other rather than to feeling more comfortable together.

25. Studies of differences in friendship by gender are reviewed in Wenda Dickens and Daniel Perlman, "Friendship over the Life Cycle," in *Personal Relationships,* vol. 2, ed. Steve Duck and Robin Gilmour (London: Academic Press, 1981), 91–122, and Beth Hess, "Friendship and Gender Roles over the Life Course," in *Single Life,* ed. Peter Stein (New York: St. Martin's Press, 1981), 104–15. While almost all studies show that women have more close friends, Lionel Tiger argues that there is a unique bond between male friends in *Men in Groups* (London: Thomas Nelson, 1969).

26. Komarovsky, *Blue-Collar Marriage* (New York: Random House, 1962), 13.

27. Daniel Levinson, *The Seasons of a Man's Life* (New York: Alfred A. Knopf, 1978), 335.

28. The argument about the middle-aged switch was presented in the popular book *Passages,* by Gail Sheehy (New York: E. P. Dutton, 1976), and in more scholarly works, such as Levinson's. These studies are reviewed in Alice Rossi, "Life-Span Theories and Women's Lives," *Signs* 6, no. 1 (1980): 4–32. However, a survey by Claude Fischer and S. Oliker reports an increasing tendency for women to have more close friends than men beginning in middle age, in "Friendship, Gender and the Life Cycle," Working Paper no. 318 (Berkeley: University of California, Berkeley, Institute of Urban and Regional Development, 1980).

29. Studies on gender differences in self-disclosure are reviewed in Letitia Peplau and Steven Gordon, "Women and Men in Love: Sex Differences in Close Relationships," in *Women, Gender and Social Psychology,* ed. V. O'Leary, R. Unger, and B. Wallston (Hillsdale, N.J.: Lawrence Erlbaum Associates, 1985), 257–91. Also see Zick Rubin, Charles Hill, Letitia Peplau, and Christine Dunkel-Schetter, "Self-Disclosure in Dating Couples," *Journal of Marriage and the Family* 42, no. 2 (1980): 305–18.

30. Working-class patterns are described in Komarovsky, *Blue-Collar Marriage.* Middle-class patterns are reported by Lynne Davidson and Lucille Duberman, "Friendship: Communication and Interactional Patterns in Same-Sex Dyads," *Sex Roles* 8, no. 8 (1982): 809–22. Similar findings are reported in Robert Lewis, "Emotional Intimacy among Men," *Journal of Social Issues* 34, no. 1 (1978): 108–21.

31. Rubin et al., "Self-Disclosure."

32. These studies, cited below, are based on the self-reports of men and women college students and may reflect norms more than behavior. The findings are that women feel and express affective and bodily emotional reactions more often than do men, except for hostile feelings. See also Jon Allen and Dorothy Haccoun, "Sex Differences in Emotionality," *Human Relations* 29, no. 8 (1976): 711–22; and Jack Balswick and Christine Avertt, "Gender, Interpersonal Orientation and Perceived Parental Expressiveness," *Journal of Marriage and the Family* 39, no. 1 (1977): 121–128. Gender differences in interaction styles are analyzed in Nancy Henley, *Body*

Politics: Power, Sex and Non-verbal Communication (Englewood Cliffs, N.J.: Prentice-Hall, Inc., 1977). Also see Paula Fishman, "Interaction: The Work Women Do," *Social Problems* 25, no. 4 (1978): 397–406.

33. Gender differences in leisure are described in L. Rubin, *Worlds of Pain* (n. 9 above), 10. Also see Margaret Davis, "Sex Role Ideology as Portrayed in Men's and Women's Magazines" (Stanford University, typescript).

34. Bert Adams, *Kinship in an Urban Setting* (Chicago: Markham Publishing Co., 1968), 169.

35. Marjorie Lowenthal and Clayton Haven, "Interaction and Adaptation: Intimacy as a Critical Variable," *American Sociological Review* 33, no. 4 (1968): 20–30.

36. Joseph Pleck argues that family ties are the primary concern for many men, in *The Myth of Masculinity* (Cambridge, Mass.: MIT Press, 1981).

37. Gender-specific characteristics also are seen in same-sex relationships. See M. Caldwell and Letitia Peplau, "Sex Differences in Same Sex Friendship," *Sex Roles* 8, no. 7 (1982): 721–32; see also Davidson and Duberman (n. 30 above), 809–22. Part of the reason for the differences in friendship may be men's fear of homosexuality and of losing status with other men. An explanatory study found that men were most likely to express feelings of closeness if they were engaged in some activity such as sports that validated their masculinity (Scott Swain, "Male Intimacy in Same-Sex Friendships: The Impact of Gender-validating Activities" [paper presented at annual meeting of the American Sociological Association, August 1984]). For discussions of men's homophobia and fear of losing power, see Robert Brannon, "The Male Sex Role," in *The Forty-nine Percent Majority,* ed. Deborah David and Robert Brannon (Reading, Mass.: Addison-Wesley Publishing Co., 1976), 1–48. I am focusing on heterosexual relations, but similar gender-specific differences may characterize homosexual relations. Some studies find that, compared with homosexual men, lesbians place a higher value on tenderness and verbal self-disclosure and engage in sex less frequently. See e.g., Alan Bell and Martin Weinberg, *Homosexualities* (New York: Simon & Schuster, 1978).

38. Unlike most studies, Reedy (n. 6 above) did not find that women emphasized communication more than men. Her subjects were upper-middle-class couples who seemed to be very much in love.

39. Sara Allison Parelman, "Dimensions of Emotional Intimacy in Marriage" (Ph.D. diss., University of California, Los Angeles, 1980).

40. Both spouses thought their interaction was unpleasant if the other engaged in negative or displeasureable instrumental or affectional actions. Thomas Wills, Robert Weiss, and Gerald Patterson, "A Behavioral Analysis of the Determinants of Marital Satisfaction," *Journal of Consulting and Clinical Psychology* 42, no. 6 (1974): 802–11.

41. L. Rubin, *Worlds of Pain* (n. 9 above), 147.

42. See L. Rubin, *Worlds of Pain;* also see Richard Sennett and Jonathon Cobb, *Hidden Injuries of Class* (New York: Vintage, 1973).

43. For evidence on this point, see Morton Hunt, *Sexual Behavior in the 1970s* (Chicago: Playboy Press, 1974), 231; and Alexander Clark and Paul Wallin, "Women's Sexual Responsiveness and the Duration and Quality of Their Marriage," *American Journal of Sociology* 21, no. 2 (1965): 187–96.

44. Interview by Cynthia Garlich, "Interviews of Married Couples" (University of California, Irvine, School of Social Sciences, 1982).

45. For example, see Catharine MacKinnon, "Feminism, Marxism, Method, and the State: An Agenda for Theory," *Signs* 7, no. 3 (1982): 515–44. For a thoughtful discussion of this issue from a historical perspective, see Linda Gordon

and Ellen Dubois, "Seeking Ecstacy on the Battlefield: Danger and Pleasure in Nineteenth Century Feminist Thought," *Feminist Review* 13, no. 1 (1983): 42–54.

46. Reedy (n. 6 above).

47. William Kephart, "Some Correlates of Romantic Love," *Journal of Marriage and the Family* 29, no. 3 (1967): 470–74. See Peplau and Gordon (n. 29 above) for an analysis of research on gender and romanticism.

48. Daniel Yankelovich, *The New Morality* (New York: McGraw-Hill Book Co., 1974), 98.

49. The link between love and power is explored in Francesca Cancian, "Gender Politics; Love and Power in the Private and Public Spheres," in *Gender and the Life Course,* ed. Alice S. Rossi (New York: Aldine Publishing Co., 1984), 253–64.

50. See Jane Flax, "The Family in Contemporary Feminist Thought," in *The Family in Political Thought,* ed. Jean B. Elshtain (Princeton, N.J.: Princeton University Press, 1981), 223–53.

51. Walter Gove, "Sex, Marital Status and Mortality," *American Journal of Sociology* 79, no. 1 (1973): 45–67.

52. This follows from the social exchange theory of power, which argues that person A will have a power advantage over B if A has more alternative sources for the gratifications she or he gets from B than B has for those from A. See Peter Blau, *Exchange and Power in Social Life* (New York: John Wiley & Sons, 1964), 117–18.

53. For a discussion of the devaluation of women's activities, see Michelle Rosaldo, "Woman, Culture and Society: A Theoretical Overview," in *Woman, Culture and Society,* ed. Michelle Rosaldo and Louise Lamphere (Stanford, Calif.: Stanford University Press, 1973), 17–42.

54. Gilligan (n. 15 above), 12–13.

55. Inge Broverman, Frank Clarkson, Paul Rosenkrantz, and Susan Vogel, "Sex-Role Stereotypes and Clinical Judgments of Mental Health," *Journal of Consulting Psychology* 34, no. 1 (1970): 1–7.

56. Welter (n. 5 above).

57. Levinson (n. 27 above).

58. L. Rubin, *Intimate Strangers* (n. 8 above); Harold Rausch, William Barry, Richard Hertel, and Mary Ann Swain, *Communication, Conflict and Marriage* (San Francisco: Jossey-Bass, Inc., 1974). This conflict is analyzed in Francesca Cancian, "Marital Conflict over Intimacy," in *The Psychosocial Interior of the Family,* 3d ed., ed. Gerald Handel (New York: Aldine Publishing Co., 1985), 277–92.

"THAT'S OUR KIND OF CONSTELLATION" LESBIAN MOTHERS NEGOTIATE INSTITUTIONALIZED UNDERSTANDINGS OF GENDER WITHIN THE FAMILY—SUSAN E. DALTON AND DENISE D. BIELBY

Notes

1. In California, if the husband is either fertile and living with his wife or infertile but consents to his wife's impregnation, his father status is considered unrebuttable (see the Uniform Parentage Act in *Deerings California Codes* 1996).

2. The traditional single-parent adoption requires that a child's existing legal parents relinquish all rights to the child before the adopting parent may legally acquire those rights. In a two-parent lesbian family, this would require the biological mother to lose her motherhood status so that her partner could acquire that status.

3. *Buzzanca v Buzzanca,* 61 Cal. App. 4th 1410, 69 Cal. Rptr. 2d 280 (1998).

4. *Re. Guardianship of ZCW and KGW,* 71 Cal. App. 4th 524, Daily Journal D.A.R. 3668 (1999).

5. The respondents for this study are a subset of a larger sample that includes both lesbian mothers and gay fathers who have entered California's legal arena to either establish themselves as legal parents or to fight for custody of their children, attorneys who routinely represent lesbian and gay parents in custody matters, social workers who are often called upon to investigate these families and report their findings to the court, and superior court judges who routinely preside over these cases. The subset of gay fathers who were interviewed for this study does not include enough gay men who are active co-parents to provide a comparison to the lesbian mothers reported on here.

6. A second-parent adoption severs the legal relationship between the biological father and the child, thus protecting the nonbiological mother from claims made by him or his relatives.

7. "Yes donors" are men who donate their sperm to a sperm bank and who answer yes to the question, "Are you willing to be contacted by any resulting children after they have turned 18 years of age?"

8. Known donors are different from "yes donors" in that "yes donors" donate their sperm directly to sperm banks, and their identities are not revealed until the children reach 18 years of age. Known donors are men who agree to assist lesbian couples in achieving pregnancy, and their identities are known by the couples.

9. In this case, the mother is referring to the donor's parents and siblings.

10. For heterosexual-headed families, these protections come through either biological reproduction or marriage. An unmarried man and a woman may gain co-parental rights by jointly producing a child. A nonreproductive male, on the other hand, may gain parental rights simply by being married to a reproductive female. Also, men and women who marry spouses with children may adopt those children through stepparent

adoption, a form of adoption that is not available to lesbian and gay couples (Dalton, 1999).

11. *West v. Superior Court,* 59 Cal. App. 4th 302, 69 Cal. Rptr. 2d 160 (1997).

12. It is important to keep in mind that while some of these protections, such as the right to be legally recognized as a parent, are attached to marriage, others, including access to a parent's health care coverage, are class based and remain unavailable to poor heterosexual-headed families as well.

13. We thank the special issue editors for this insight.

14. This does not mean that women and men who biologically reproduce children will necessarily be divested of their parental status. Indeed, one may "parent" a fetus by taking steps to ensure its physical well-being and to prepare for its birth.

References

Benkov, Laura. 1994. *Reinventing the family.* New York: Crown.

Berk, Sarah Fenstermaker. 1985. *The gender factory: The apportionment of work in American households.* New York: Plenum.

Bielby, W. T., and D. D. Bielby. 1989. Family ties: Balancing commitments to work and family in dual earner households. *American Sociological Review* 54:76–89.

Blumstein, P., and P. Schwartz. 1983. *American couples.* New York: William Morrow.

Bolak, Hale Cihan. 1997. When wives are major providers: Culture, gender, and family work. *Gender & Society* 11:409–33.

Brines, Julie. 1993. The exchange value of housework. *Rationality and Society* 5:367–74.

Burch, Beverly. 1997. *Other women: Lesbian/ bisexual experience and psychoanalytic views of women.* New York: Columbia University Press.

Cherlin, Andrew. 1978. Remarriage as an incomplete institution. *American Journal of Sociology* 84:634–50.

Dalton, Susan. 1999. We are family: Understanding the structural barriers to the legal formation of lesbian and gay families. Ph.D. diss., University of California, Santa Barbara.

Deering's California codes. Family code, annotated. 1996. San Francisco: Bancroft-Whitney.

DiMaggio, Paul, and Walter Powell. 1991. Introduction. In *The new institutionalism in organizational analysis,* edited by W. Powell and P. DiMaggio. Chicago: University of Chicago Press.

Emirbayer, M., and A. Mische. 1998. What is agency? *American Journal of Sociology* 4:962–1023.

Erickson, Rebecca. 1993. Reconceptualizing family work: The effect of emotion work on perceptions of marital quality. *Journal of Marriage and the Family* 55:888–900.

Ferree, Myra Marx. 1990. Beyond separate spheres. *Journal of Marriage and the Family* 52:866–84.

Goffman, Erving. 1977. The arrangement between the sexes. *Theory and Society* 4:301–31.

Kurdek, Lawrence. 1993. The allocation of household labor in gay, lesbian, and heterosexual married couples. *Journal of Social Issues* 49:127–39.

Luxton, M. 1991. *More than a labor of love: Three generations of women's work in the home.* Toronto, Canada: Women's Press.

McCandlish, Barbara. 1992. Against all odds: Lesbian mother family dynamics. In *Lesbians and child custody: A casebook,* edited by Delores J. Maggiore. New York: Garland.

McWhirter, D. P., and A. M. Mattison. 1984. *The male couple: How relationships develop.* Englewood Cliffs, NJ: Prentice Hall.

Osmond, Marie. 1987. Feminist theories: The social construction of gender in families and society. In *Sourcebook of family theories and methods,* edited by Pauline Boss. New York: Plenum.

Patt, Emily C. 1987–88. Second parent adoption: When crossing the marital barrier is a child's best interest. *Berkeley Women's Law Journal* 3:96–133.

Patterson, Charlotte. 1995. Families of the lesbian baby boom: Parents' division of labor and children's adjustment. *Developmental Psychology* 31:115–23.

Peplau, Letitia A., and S. D. Cochran. 1990. A relational perspective on homosexuality. In *Homosexuality/heterosexuality: Concepts of sexual orientation,* edited by D. P. McWhirter, S. A. Sanders, and J. M. Reinisch. New York: Oxford University Press.

Pyke, K., and S. Coltrane. 1996. Entitlement, obligation, and gratitude in family work. *Journal of Family Issues* 17:60–82.

Ricketts, W., and R. Achtenberg. 1990. Adoption and foster parenting for lesbians and gay men: Creating new traditions in family. In *Homosexuality and family relations,* edited by F. W. Bozett and M. B. Sussman. New York: Harrington Park.

Risman, Barbara J. 1998. *Gender vertigo: American families in transition.* New Haven, CT: Yale University Press.

Sewell, William H. Jr. 1992, A theory of structure: Duality, agency, and transformation. *American Journal of Sociology* 98:1–29.

Slater, Suzanne. 1995. *The lesbian family life cycle.* New York: Free Press.

Sullivan, Maureen. 1996. Rozzie and Harriet? Gender and family patterns of lesbian coparents. *Gender & Society* 10:747–67.

Thompson, Linda. 1993. Conceptualizing gender in marriage: The case of marital care. *Journal of Marriage and the Family* 55:557–69.

West, C., and S. Fenstermaker. 1995a. Doing difference. *Gender & Society* 9:8–37.

———. 1995b. Reply: (Re)doing difference. *Gender & Society* 9:506–13.

West, C., and D. Zimmerman. 1987. Doing gender. *Gender & Society* 1:125–51.

Weston, Kath. 1991. *Families we choose.* New York: Columbia University Press.

Zucker, Lynn. 1991. The role of institutionalization in cultural persistence. In *The new institutionalism in organizational analysis,* edited by W. Powell and P. DiMaggio. Chicago: University of Chicago Press.

Zuckerman, Elizabeth. 1986. Comment: Second parent adoption for lesbian parented families: Legal recognition of the other mother. *University of California, Davis Law Journal* 19:729–59.

ISLAMIC FAMILY IDEALS AND THEIR RELEVANCE TO AMERICAN MUSLIM FAMILIES—BAHIRA SHERIF

Notes

1. Veiling has too long and complicated a history to explore here. The custom varies in degree and type across groups, classes, and historical periods.

2. Gil'adi (1992) has translated parts of several important Islamic works on children.

3. The word is derived from the same Arabic root as *hidn,* or breast; in law, child care and custody are strongly associated with the mother and the other females in the maternal line.

References

Barakat, H. (1985). "The Arab Family and the Challenge of Social Transformation," in E. W. Fernea (Ed.), *Women and the Family in the Middle East, New Voices of Change,* Austin, TX: University of Texas Press.

Bates, D. and A. Rassam. (1983). *Peoples and Cultures of the Middle East.* Englewood Cliffs, NJ: Prentice-Hall.

Beck, L. and N. Keddie. (1980). "Introduction," in Lois Beck and Nikki Keddie (Eds.), *Women in the Muslim World.* Cambridge, MA: Harvard University Press.

Esposito, John. (1982). *Women in Muslim Family Law.* Syracuse, NY: Syracuse University Press.

Fernea, E., ed. (1985). *Women and the Family in the Middle East: New Voices of Change.* Austin, TX: University of Texas Press.

Fernea, E. and B. Bezirgan, eds. (1977). *Middle Eastern Muslim Women Speak.* Austin, TX: University of Texas Press.

Fluehr-Lobban, C. (1987). *Islamic Law and Society in the Sudan.* London: Frank Cass.

Gil'adi, A. (1992). *Children of Islam: Concepts of Childhood in Medieval Muslim Society.* New York: St. Martin's Press.

Haddad, Y. and J. Smith (1996). "Islamic Values Among American Muslims." In B. Aswad and B. Bilge (Eds.), *Family and Gender Among American Muslims,* pp. 19–40. Philadelphia: Temple University Press.

Hermansen, M. (1991). "Two-Way Acculturation: Muslim Women in America between Individual Choice and Community." In Y. Haddad (Ed.), *The Muslims of America,* pp. 188–204. Oxford: Oxford University Press.

Hoffman-Ladd, V. (1987). "Polemics on the Modesty and Segregation of Women in Contemporary Egypt," in *International Journal of Middle East Studies 19*(1) pp. 23–50.

Kolars, C. (1994). "Masjid ul-Mutkabir: The Portrait of an African American Orthodox Muslim Community." In Y. Haddad and J. Smith (Eds.), *Muslim Communities in North America,* pp. 475–500. Albany, NY: State University of New York Press.

Liebesny, Herbert. (1975). *The Law of the Near and Middle East: Readings, Cases, & Materials.* Albany, NY: State University of New York Press.

Macleod, A. (1991). *Accommodating Protest: Working Women, the New Veiling and Change in Cairo.* New York: Columbia University Press.

Marcus, J. (1992). *A World of Difference. Islam and Gender Hierarchy in Turkey.* London: Zed Press.

Mernissi, F. (1987). *Beyond the Veil—Male-Female Dynamics in Modern Muslim Society.* Rev. ed. Bloomington, IN: Indiana University Press.

Minai, N. (1981). *Women in Islam.* London: John Murray.

Nasir, J. (1990). *The Status of Women Under Islamic Law and Under Modern Islamic Legislation.* London: Graham and Trotman.

Pickthall, M. (1976). *The Glorious Koran: Text and Explanatory Translation* (trans). Albany, NY: State University of New York Press.

Rugh, A. (1984). *Family in Contemporary Egypt.* Syracuse, NY: Syracuse University Press.

Schacht, J. (1964). *An Introduction to Islamic Law.* Oxford: Clarendon Press.

Stone, C. (1991). "Estimate of Muslims in America." In Y. Haddad (Ed.), *The Muslims of America,* pp. 25–36. New York: Oxford University Press.

Wikan, U. (1984). "Shame and Honour, A Contestable Pair," *Man 19(4),* pp. 635–51.

World Almanac and Book of Facts. (1998). Mahwah, N.J.: World Almanac Books.

Youssef, N. (1973). "Cultural Ideals, Feminine Behaviour and Family Control." *Comparative Studies in Society and History, 15(3),* pp. 326–47.

GENDER, CLASS, FAMILY, AND MIGRATION: PUERTO RICAN WOMEN IN CHICAGO —MAURA I. TORO-MORN

References

Acosta-Belen, Edna. 1986. *The Puerto Rican woman: Perspectives on culture, history, and society.* New York: Praeger.

Boyd, Monica. 1986. Immigrant women in Canada. In *International Migration: The femal experience,* edited by R. Simon and C. Brettell. Totowa, NJ: Rowman and Allanheld.

Dietz, James L. 1986. *Economic history of Puerto Rico: Institutional change and capitalist development.* Princeton, NJ: Princeton University Press.

Diner, Hasia R. 1983. *Erin's daughters in America: Irish immigrant women in the nineteenth century.* Baltimore: Johns Hopkins University Press.

Ewen, Elizabeth. 1983. *Immigrant women in the land of dollars: Life and culture on the lower east side, 1890–1925.* New York: Monthly Review Press.

Falcon, Luis M. 1990. Migration and development: The case of Puerto Rico. In *Determinants of emigration from Mexico, Central America, and the Caribbean,* edited by S. Diaz-Briquets and S. Weintraub. Boulder, CO: Westview.

Fernandez-Kelly, Maria. 1983. *For we are sold, I and my people: Women and industry in Mexico's frontier.* Albany: State University of New York Press.

Garcia-Castro, Mary. 1985. Women versus life: Colombian women in New York. In *Women and change in Latin America,* edited by J. Nash and H. Safa. South Hadley, MA: Bergin and Garvey.

Glenn, Evelyn N. 1986. *Issei, Nisei, War Bride: Three generations of Japanese women in domestic service.* Philadelphia: Temple University Press.

Glenn, Evelyn N. 1987. Women, labor migration and household work: Japanese American women in the pre-War period. In *Ingredients for women's employment policy,* edited by C. Bose and G. Spitae. Albany: State University of New York Press.

History Task Force. 1979. *Labor migration under capitalism: The Puerto Rican experience.* New York: Monthly Review Press.

Hondagneu-Sotelo, Pierrette. 1992. Overcoming patriarchal constraints: The reconstruction of gender relations among Mexican immigrant women and men. *Gender & Society* 6:393–415.

Juarbe, Ana. 1988. Anaatasia's story: A window into the past, a bridge to the future. *Oral History Review* 16:15–22.

Kibria, N. 1990. Power, patriarchy, and gender conflict in the Vietnamese immigrant community. *Gender & Society* 4:9–24.

Lamphere, Louise. 1987. *From working daughters to working mothers: Immigrant women in a New England industrial community.* Ithaca, NY. Cornell University Press.

Morokvasic, M. 1983. Women in migration: Beyond the reductionist outlook, in *One way ticket: Migration and female labor,* edited by A. Phizacklea. London: Routledge and Kegan Paul.

Pantojas-Garcia, Emilio. 1990. *Development strategies as ideology: Puerto Rico's export-led industrialization experience.* Boulder, CO: Lynne Rienner.

Pedraza, Sylvia. 1991. Women and migration: The social consequences of gender. *Annual Review of Sociology* 17:303–25.

Prieto, Yolanda. 1986. Cuban women and work in the United States: A New Jersey case study. In *International migration: The female experience,* edited by R. Simon and C. Brettell. Totowa, NJ: Rowman and Allanheld.

Rodriguez, Clara. 1989. *Puerto Ricans: Born in the U.S.A.* Boston: Unwin Hyman.

Safa, Helen. 1984. Female employment and the social reproduction of the Puerto Rican working class. *International Migration Review* 18:1168–87.

Sanchez-Ayendez, Melba. 1986. Puerto Rican elderly women: Shared meanings and informal supportive networks. In *All-American women: Lines that divide, ties that bind,* edited by Johnnetta Cole. New York: Free Press.

Sanchez-Korrol, Virginia. 1983. *From colonia to community: The history of Puerto Ricans in New York City, 1917–1948.* Westport, CT: Greenwood.

———. 1986. The forgotten migrant: Educated Puerto Rican women in New York City, 1920–1940. In *The Puerto Rican woman: Perspectives on culture, history and society,* edited by E. Acosta-Belen. New York: Praeger.

Sassen-Koob, S. 1984. Notes on the incorporation of Third World women into wage-labor through immigration and off-shore. *International Migration Review* 18:1144–67.

Simon, Rita, and Caroline Brettell. 1986. *International migration: The female experience.* Totowa, NJ: Rowman and Allanheld.

Simon, Rita, and Margo Corona DeLey. 1986. Undocumented Mexican women: Their work and personal experiences. In *International migration: The female experience,* edited by R. Simon and C. Brettell. Totowa, NJ: Rowman and Allanheld.

Sullivan, Teresa. 1984. The occupational prestige of women immigrants: A comparison of Cubans and Mexicans. *International Migration Review* 18:1045–62.

Tienda, Marta, Leif Jensen, and Robert L. Bach. 1984. Immigration, gender, and the process of occupational change in the United States, 1970–80. International Migration Review 18:1021–43.

Tyree, Andrea, and Katharine Donato. 1986. A demographic overview of the international migration of women. In *International migration: The female experience,* edited by R. Simon and C. Brettell. Totowa, NJ: Rowman and Allanheld.

Weinberg, Sydney Stahl. 1988. *The world of our mothers: The lives of Jewish immigrant women.* New York: Schocken Books.

BASEBALL WIVES: GENDER AND THE WORK OF BASEBALL —GEORGE GMELCH AND PATRICIA MARY SAN ANTONIO

Notes

1. Several wives (e.g., Garvey 1989; Hargrove and Costa 1989; Torrez 1983) have published memoirs about their experiences being married to ballplayers, and two graduate students (Crute 1981; Powers 1990) have produced dissertations about the role of wives among professional athletes generally.

2. Team media relations directors often help arrange the interviews. We are especially grateful to Kevin Kalal, Steve Copses, Sam Kennedy, and Ethan Wilson.

3. The time varied depending on whether they accompanied their husbands to spring training (most minor league wives do not go along) and winter ball. The geography of the league also influenced how long their husbands were away. Long road trips are less frequent in minor leagues where teams are less spread out.

4. To protect the wives from abusive and gawking fans, major league teams are increasingly sitting the wives and children in a special section, with security and shielded from the other patrons.

References

Abu-Lughod, L. 1993. *Writing women's worlds.* Berkeley: University of California Press.

Ardell, J. 1994. A letter from spring training. *Nine* 2 (2): 361–67.

Bosco, J. 1989. *Look at the boys who would be called Cubs.* New York: Morrow.

Bouton, B., and N. Marshall. 1983. *Home games.* New York: St. Martin's.

Burstyn, V. 1999. *The rites of men: Manhood, politics, and the culture of sport.* Toronto, Canada: University of Toronto.

Coser, L. 1974. *Greedy institutions.* New York: Free Press.

Crute, B. 1981. Wives of professional athletes: An inquiry into the impact of professional sport on the home and family. Ph.D. diss., Boston College.

Davis, L. 1997. *The swimsuit issue and sport: Hegemonic masculinity in* Sports Illustrated. Albany: State University of New York.

Disch, Lisa, and Mary Jo Kane. 2000. When a looker is really a bitch. In *Reading sport: Critical essays on power and representation,* edited by S. Birrell and M. McDonald, 108–43. Boston: Northeastern University Press.

Ferrante, K. 1994. Baseball and the social construction of gender. In *Women, media and sport: Challenging gender values,* edited by P. Creedon, 238–56. Thousand Oaks, CA: Sage.

Fine, G. 1987. *With the boys: Little League baseball and preadolescent culture.* Chicago: University of Chicago Press.

Fireovid, S., and M. Weingardner. 1991. *The 26th man.* New York: Macmillan.

Garvey, C. 1989. *The secret life of Cyndy Garvey.* New York: Doubleday.

Gmelch, G., and P. San Antonio. 1998. Groupies in American baseball. *Journal of Sport and Social Issues* 22 (1): 32–45.

Golenbock, P. 1991. *The forever boys.* Secaucus, NJ: Carol.

Gooden, D., and R. Woodley. 1985. *Rookie.* Garden City, NY: Doubleday.

Hargrove, S., and R. Costa. 1989. *Safe at home: A baseball wife's story.* College Station: Texas A&M University Press.

House, T. 1989. *The jock's itch.* Chicago: Contemporary.

Jordan, P. 1975. *A false spring.* New York: Dodd Mead.

McKenzie, B. 1999. Retiring from the sideline: Becoming more than hockey's daughter and football's wife. In *Inside sports,* edited by J. Coakley and P. Donnelly, 232–36. New York: Routledge.

Menon, S. 1996. Male authority and female autonomy: A study of the matrilineal nayars of Kerala, South India. In *Gender, kinship, power,* edited by M. J. Maynes, A. Waltner, B. Soland, and U. Strasser, 131–48. New York: Routledge.

Moore, H. 1988. *Feminism and anthropology.* Minneapolis: University of Minnesota Press.

Powers, A. 1990. Psychological and sociological effects of professional sports on the wives and families of athletes. Ph.D. thesis, Ann Arbor, MI. Microfilm: Ohio State University.

Ripken, C., and M. Brian. 1997. *The only way I know.* New York: Penguin.

Rogers, S. 1975. Female forms of power and the myth of male dominance: A model of female/male interaction in peasant society. *American Ethnologist* 2 (4): 727–62.

———. 1991. *Shaping modern times in rural France: The transformation and reproduction of an Aveyronnais community.* Princeton, NJ: Princeton University Press.

Sanday, P. 1981. *Female power and male dominance: On the origins of sexual inequality.* Cambridge, UK: Cambridge University Press.

Sirman, N. 1995. Gender roles and female strategies among the nomadic and semi-nomadic Kurdish tribes of Turkey. In *Women in modern Turkish society: A reader,* edited by S. Tekeli, 219–30. London: Atlantic Highlands.

Thompson, W. 1999. Wives incorporated: Marital relationships in professional ice hockey. In *Inside sports,* edited by J. Coakley and P. Donnelly, 180–89. New York: Routledge.

Torrez, D. 1983. *High inside: Memoirs of a baseball wife. New* York: G. P. Putnam's Sons.

Trujillo, N. 2000. Hegemonic masculinity on the mound: Media representations of Nolan Ryan and American sports culture. In *Reading sport: Critical essays on power and representation,* edited by S. Birrell and M. McDonald, 14–39. Boston: Northeastern University.

Voigt, D. 1978. Sex in baseball: Reflections of changing taboos. *Journal of Popular Culture* 12 (3): 389–403.

SINGLE MOTHERS BY CHOICE —VALERIE S. MANNIS

References

Allen, K. R. (1989). *Single women/family ties: Life histories of older women.* Newbury Park: Sage.

Allen, K. R., & Pickett, R. S. (1987). Forgotten streams in the family life course: Utilization of qualitative retrospective interviews in the analysis of lifelong single women's family careers. *Journal of Marriage and the Family, 49,* 517–526.

Anderson, C. M., & Stewart, S. (1994). *Flying solo: Single women midlife.* New York: W. W. Norton & Company.

Atkinson, P. (1992). *Understanding ethnographic texts.* Newbury Park: Sage.

Bengtson, V., & Allen, K. (1993). The life course perspective applied to families over time. P. G. Boss, W. J. Doherty, R. LaRossa, W. R. Schumm, & S. K. Steinmetz (Eds.), *Sourcebook of family theories and methods: A contextual approach.* New York: Plenum.

Bertaux, D. (1981). From the life-history approach to the transformation of sociological practice. D. Bertaux (Ed.), *Biography and society.* Beverly Hills: Sage.

Blankenthorn, D. (1995). *Fatherless America: Confronting our most urgent social problem.* New York: Basic.

Briggs, C. L. (1992). *Learning how to ask: A sociolinquistic appraisal of the role of the interview in social science research.* New York: Cambridge University Press.

Burns, A., & Scott, C. (1994). *Mother-headed families and why they have increased.* Hillsdale, NJ: Lawrence Erlbaum Associates.

Cowan, P. A. (1993). The sky is falling, but Popenoe's analysis won't help us do anything about it. *Journal of Marriage and the Family, 55,* 542–544.

Farnesworth, E. B., & Allen, K. R. (1996). Mothers' bereavement: Experiences of marginalization, stories of change. *Family Relations, 45,* 360–368.

Fineman, M. A. (1995). *The neutered mother, the sexual family and other twentieth century tragedies.* New York: Routledge.

Featherman, D. L. (1983). Life-span perspectives in social science research. P. B. Baltes & O. G. Brim, Jr. (Eds.), *Life-span development and behavior* (Vol. 5, pp. 1–59). New York: Academic Press.

Foster, E. M., Jones, D., & Hoffman, S. D. (1998). The economic impact of nonmarital childbearing: How are older, single mothers faring? *Journal of Marriage and the Family, 60,* 163–174.

Garfinkel, I., & McLanahan, S. (1986). *Single mothers and their children: A new American dilemma.* Washington, D.C.: Urban Institute Press.

Gerson, K. (1985). *Hard choices: How women decide about work, career, and motherhood.* Berkeley: University of California Press.

Gerson, K. (1993). *No man's land: Men's changing commitments to family and work.* New York: Basic.

Gerson, K. (1997). The social construction of fatherhood. T. Arendell (Ed.), *Contemporary parenting: Challenges and issues.* Thousand Oaks: Sage.

Glenn, N. D. (1993). A plea for objective assessment of the notion of family decline. *Journal of Marriage and the Family, 55,* 542–544.

Groze, V. (1991). Adoption and single parents. *Child Welfare, 70,* 321–332.

Hertz, R., & Ferguson, F. I. T. (1997). Kinship strategies and self-sufficiency among single mothers by choice: Post modern family ties. *Qualitative Sociology, 20,* 187–209.

Kane, S. (1993). The movement of children for international adoption: An epidemiological perspective. *Social Science Journal, 30,* 323–339.

Kornfein, M. (1985). *Motherhood without marriage: A longitudinal study of elective single mothers and their children* (Doctoral dissertation, University of California-Los Angeles, 1985). Dissertation Abstracts International 46, 07A, 2075 (University Microfilms No. 85-19117).

Lather, P. (1991). *Getting smart: Feminist research and pedagogy with/in the postmodern.* New York: Routledge.

Leslie, M. R. (Ed.). (1994). *The single mother's companion.* Seattle, WA: Seal Press.

Linn, R. (1991). Mature unwed mothers in Israel: Socio-moral and psychological dilemmas. *Lifestyles: Family and Economic Issues, 12,* 145–170.

Ludtke, M. (1997). *On our own: Unmarried motherhood in America.* New York: Random House.

Mattes, J., C. S. W. (1994). *Single mothers by choice: A guidebook for single women who are considering or have chosen motherhood.* New York: Random House.

McCartney, C. F. (1985). Decision by single women to conceive by artificial donor insemination. *Journal of Psychosomatic Obstetrics and Gynecology, 4,* 321–328.

McGuire, M., & Alexander, N. J. (1995). Artificial insemination of single women. *Fertility and Sterility,* 182–184.

McKaughan, M. (1987). *The biological clock: Balancing marriage, motherhood and career.* New York: Penguin.

McLanahan, S., & Booth, K. (1989). Mother-only families: Problems, prospects, and politics. *Journal of Marriage and the Family, 51,* 557–580.

McLanahan, S., & Sandefur, G. (1994). *Growing up with a single mother: What hurts, what helps.* Cambridge, MA: Harvard University Press.

Merritt, S., & Steiner, L. (1984). *And baby makes two.* New York: Franklin Watts.

Miller, N. (1992). *Single parents by choice: A growing trend in family life.* New York: Plenum.

Osmond, M. W., & Thorne, B. (1993). Feminist theories and methods: A contextual approach. P. G. Boss, W. J. Doherty, R. LaRossa, W. R. Schumm, & S. K. Steinmetz (Eds.), *Sourcebook of family theories and methods: A contextual approach* (pp. 591–623). New York: Plenum.

Pakitzegi, B. (1990). Emerging family forms: Single mothers by choice-demographic and psychological variables. *Maternal-Child Nursing Journal, 19,* 1–19.

Polokow, V. (1993). *Lives on the edge: Single mothers and their children in the other America.* Chicago: The University of Chicago Press.

Popenoe, D. (1993). American family in decline, 1960–1990: A review and appraisal. *Journal of Marriage and the Family, 55,* 542–544.

Potter, A. E., & Knaub, P. K. (1988). Single motherhood by choice: A parenting alternative. *Lifestyles: Family and Economic Issues,* 240–249.

Renovise, J. (1985). *Going solo: Single mothers by choice.* London: Routledge.

Richardson, L. (1994). Writing: A method of inquiry. In N. K. Denzin & Y. S. Lincoln (Eds.), *Handbook of qualitative research* (pp. 516–529). New York: Sage.

Richardson, L. (1995). Narrative and sociology. J. Van Maanen (Ed.), *Representation in ethnography.* New York: Sage.

Rice, J. (1994). Reconsidering research on divorce, family life cycle, and the meaning of family. *Psychology of Women Quarterly, 18,* 559–584.

Rubin, H. J., & Rubin, I. S. (1995). *Qualitative interviewing: The art of hearing data.* Thousand Oaks: Sage.

Saffron, L. (1994). *Challenging conceptions: Planning a family by self-insemination.* London, England: Villiers House.

Stacey, J. (1990). *Brave new families.* New York: Basic.

Stacey, J. (1993). Good riddance to "The Family": A response to David Popenoe. *Journal of Marriage and the Family, 55,* 542–544.

Stacey, J. (1996). *In the name of the family: Rethinking family values in the postmodern age.* Boston: Beacon Press.

Strauss, A., & Corbin, J. (1990). *Basics of qualitative research: Grounded theory procedures and techniques.* New York: Sage.

Thompson, E. H., Jr., & Gongla, P. (1983). Single parent families: In the mainstream of American society. E. D. Macklin & R. H. Rubin (Eds.), *Contemporary families and alternative lifestyles: Handbook on research and theory* (pp. 97–124). New York: Sage.

U.S. Bureau of Census. (1996). Statistical abstracts of the U.S.: 1996 (116th edition). Washington, D.C.: U.S. Government Printing Office.

Ward, L. (1983). *Innovative female identity: Experiential antecedents of the capacity for nontraditional childbearing choices.* Dissertation Abstracts International 44, 05B (University Microfilm No. 83-19947).

Wolcott, H. F. (1994). *Transforming qualitative data: Description, analysis, and interpretation.* Thousand Oaks: Sage.

SHIFTING THE CENTER: RACE, CLASS, AND FEMINIST THEORIZING ABOUT MOTHERHOOD —PATRICIA HILL COLLINS

Notes

1. In this essay, I use the terms "racial ethnic women" and "women of color" interchangeably. Grounded in the experiences of groups who have been the targets of racism, the term "racial ethnic" implies more solidarity with men involved in the struggles against racism. In contrast, the term "women of color" emerges from a feminist background where racial ethnic women committed to feminist struggle aimed to distinguish their history and issues from those of middle-class, white women. Neither term captures the complexity of African-American, Native American, Asian-American and Hispanic women's experiences.

2. Positivist social science exemplifies this type of decontextualization. In order to create scientific descriptions of reality, positivist researchers aim to produce ostensibly objective generalizations. But because researchers have widely differing values, experiences, and emotions, genuine science is thought to be unattainable unless all human characteristics except rationality are eliminated from the research process. By following strict methodological rules, scientists aim to distance themselves from the values, vested interests, and emotions generated by their class, race, sex, or unique situation. By decontextualizing themselves, they allegedly become detached observers and manipulators of nature. Moreover, this researcher decontextualization is paralleled by comparable efforts to re-move the objects of study from their contexts (Jaggar 1983).

3. Dominant theories are characterized by this decontextualization. Boyd's (1989) helpful survey of literature on the mother-daughter relationship reveals that while much work has been done on motherhood generally, and on the mother-daughter relationship, very little of it tests feminist theories of motherhood. Boyd lists two prevailing theories, psychoanalytic theory and social learning theory, that she claims form the bulk of feminist theorizing. Both of these approaches minimize the importance of race and class in the context of motherhood. Boyd ignores Marxist-feminist theorizing about motherhood, mainly because very little of this work is concerned with the mother-daughter relationship. But Marxist-feminist analyses of motherhood provide another example of how decontextualization frames feminist theories of motherhood. See, for example, Ann Ferguson's *Blood at the Root: Motherhood, Sexuality, and Male Dominance* (1989), an ambitious attempt to develop a universal theory of motherhood that is linked to the social construction of sexuality and male dominance. Ferguson's work stems from a feminist tradition that explores the relationship between motherhood and sexuality by either bemoaning their putative incompatibility or romanticizing maternal sexuality.

4. Psychoanalytic feminist theorizing about motherhood, such as Nancy Chodorow's groundbreaking work, *The Reproduction of Mothering* (1978), exemplifies how decontextualization of race and/or class can weaken what is otherwise strong feminist theorizing. Although I realize that other feminist approaches to motherhood exist, see Eisenstein's (1983) summary for example, I have chosen to stress psychoanalytic feminist theory because the work of Chodorow and others has been highly influential in framing the predominant themes in feminist discourse.

5. The thesis of the atomized individual that underlies Western psychology is rooted in a much larger Western construct concerning the relation of the individual to the community (Hartsock 1983). Theories of motherhood based on the assumption of the atomized human proceed to use this definition of individual as the unit of analysis, and then construct theory from this base. From this grow assumptions based on the premise that the major process to examine is one between freely choosing rational individuals engaging in bargains (Hartsock 1983).

6. The narrative tradition in the writings of women of color addresses this effort to recover the history of mothers. Works from African-American women's autobiographical tradition, such as Ann Moody's *Coming of Age in Mississippi,* Maya Angelou's *I Know Why the Caged Bird Sings,* Linda Brent's *Narrative in the Life of a Slave Girl,* and Marita Golden's *the Heart of a Woman* contain the authentic voices of Black women centered on experiences of motherhood. Works from African-American women's fiction include Sarah Wright's *This Child's Gonna Live,* Alice Walker's *Meridian,* and Toni Morrison's *Sula* and *Beloved.* Asian-American women's fiction, such as Amy Tan's *The Joy Luck Club* and Maxine Kingston's *Woman Warrior,* and autobiographies such as Jean Wakatusi Houston's *Farewell to Manzanar* offer a parallel source of authentic voice. Connie Young Yu (1989) entitles her article on the history of Asian-American women "The World of Our Grandmothers," and proceeds to recreate Asian-American history with her grandmother as a central figure. Cherrie Moraga (1979) writes a letter to her mother as a way of coming to terms with the contradictions of her racial identity as a Chicana. In *Borderlands/La Frontera,* Gloria Anzaldua (1987) weaves autobiography, poetry and philosophy together in her exploration of women and mothering.

7. Notable examples include Lutie Johnson's unsuccessful attempt to rescue her son from the harmful effects of an urban environment in Ann Petry's *The Street;* and Meridian's work on behalf of the children of a small Southern town after she chooses to relinquish her own child, in Alice Walker's *Meridian.*

8. Noticeably absent from feminist theories of motherhood is a comprehensive theory of power and explanation of how power relations shape theories. Firmly rooted in an exchange-based marketplace, with its accompanying assumptions of rational economic decision-making and white, male control of the marketplace, this model of community stresses the rights of individuals, including feminist theorists, to make decisions in their own self-interests, regardless of the impact on larger society. Composed of a collection of unequal individuals who compete for greater shares of money as the medium of exchange, this model community legitimates relations of domination by denying they exist or by treating them as inevitable but unimportant (Hartsock, 1983).

References

Allen, Paula Gunn. 1986. *The Sacred Hoop: Recovering the Feminine in American Indian Traditions.* Boston: Beacon.

Andersen, Margaret. 1988. "Moving Our Minds: Studying Women of Color and Reconstructing Sociology." *Teaching Sociology* 16 (2), pp. 123–132.

Anzaldua, Gloria. 1987. *Borderlands/La Frontera: The New Mestiza.* San Francisco: Spinsters.

Awiakta, Marilou. 1988. "Amazons in Appalchia." In Beth Brant, ed., *A Gathering of Spirit.* Ithaca, NY: Firebrand, pp. 125–130.

Boyd, Carol J. 1989. "Mothers and Daughters: A Discussion of Theory and Research." *Journal of Marriage and the Family* 51, pp. 291–301.

Brant, Beth, ed. 1988. *A Gathering of Spirit: A Collection by North American Indian Women.* Ithaca, NY: Firebrand.

Brown, Elsa Barkley. 1989. "African-American Women's Quilting: A Framework for Conceptualizing and Teaching African-American Women's History." *Signs* 14 (4), pp. 921–929.

Chodorow, Nancy. 1978. *The Reproduction of Mothering.* Berkeley, CA: University of California Press.

———, and Susan Contratto. 1982. "The Fantasy of the Perfect Mother." In Barrie Thorne and Marilyn Yalom, eds., *Rethinking the Family: Some Feminist Questions.* New York: Longman, pp. 54–75.

Coleman, Willi. 1987. "Closets and Keepsakes." *Sage: A Scholarly Journal on Black Women* 4 (2), pp. 34–35.

Collins, Patricia Hill. 1990. *Black Feminist Thought: Knowledge, Consciousness and the Politics of Empowerment.* New York: Unwin Hyman/Routledge.

de la Cruz, Jessie. 1980. "Interview." In Studs Terkel, ed., *American Dreams: Lost and Found.* New York: Ballantine.

Davis, Angela Y. 1981. *Women, Race, and Class.* New York: Random House.

Dill, Bonnie Thornton. 1988. "Our Mothers' Grief: Racial Ethnic Women and the Maintenance of Families." *Journal of Family History* 13 (4), pp. 415–431.

Eisenstein, Hester. 1983. *Contemporary Feminist Thought.* Boston: G. K. Hall.

Ferguson, Ann. 1989. *Blood at the Root: Motherhood, Sexuality, and Male Dominance.* New York: Unwin Hyman/Routledge.

Flax, Jane. 1978. "The Conflict between Nurturance and Autonomy in Mother-Daughter Relationships and within Feminism." *Feminist Studies* 4 (2), pp. 171–189.

Glenn, Evelyn Nakano. 1985. "Racial Ethnic Women's Labor: The Intersection of Race, Gender and Class Oppression." *Review of Radical Political Economics* 17 (3), pp. 86–108.

———. 1986. *Issei, Nisei, War Bride: Three Generations of Japanese American Women in Domestic Service.* Philadelphia: Temple University Press.

Green, Rayna. 1990. "The Pocahontas Perplex: The Image of Indian Women in American Culture." In Ellen Carol Dubois and Vicki Ruiz, eds., *Unequal Sisters.* New York: Routledge, pp. 15–21.

Hartsock, Nancy. 1983. *Money, Sex and Power.* Boston: Northeastern University Press.

Jordan, June. 1985. *On Call.* Boston: South End Press.

LaDuke, Winona. 1988. "They always come back." In Beth Brant, ed., *A Gathering of Spirit.* Ithaca, New York: Firebrand, pp. 62–67.

Lerner, Gerda. 1972. *Black Women in White America.* New York: Pantheon.

Moraga, Cherrie. 1979. "La Guera." In Cherrie Moraga and Gloria Anzaldua, eds., *This Bridge Called My Back: Writings by Radical Women of Color.* Watertown, MA: Persephone Press, pp. 27–34.

Noda, Kesaya E. 1989. "Growing Up Asian in American." In Asian Women United of California, eds., *Making Waves: An Anthology of Writings By and About Asian American Women.* Boston: Beacon, pp. 243–250.

Rich, Adrienne. 1986 [1976]. *Of Women Born: Motherhood as Institution and Experience.* New York: W. W. Norton.

Shanley, Kate. 1988. "Thoughts on Indian Feminism." In Beth Brant, ed., *A Gathering of Spirit.* Ithaca, NY: Firebrand, pp. 213–215.

Smith, Dorothy E. 1990. *The Conceptual Practices of Power: A Feminist Sociology of Knowledge.* Boston: Northeastern University Press.

Spelman, Elizabeth V. 1988. *Inessential Woman: Problems of Exclusion in Feminist Thought.* Boston: Beacon Press.

Tajima, Renee E. 1989. "Lotus Blossoms Don't Bleed: Images of Asian Women." In *Asian Women United of California, eds., Making Waves: An Anthology of Writings by and about Asian American Women.* Boston: Beacon, pp. 308–317.

Terborg-Penn, Rosalyn. 1986. "Black Women in Resistance: A Cross-Cultural Perspective." In Gary Y. Okhiro, ed., *In Resistance: Studies in African, Caribbean and Afro-American History.* Amherst: University of Massachusetts Press, pp. 188–209.

Wright, Sarah. 1986. *This Child's Gonna Live.* Old Westbury, NY: Feminist Press.

Yamoto, Jenny. 1988. "Mixed Bloods, Half Breeds, Mongrels, Hybrids…" In Jo Whitehorse Cochran, Donna Langston and Carolyn Woodward, eds., *Changing Our Power: An Introduction to Women's Studies.* Dubuque, IA: Kendall/Hunt, pp. 22–24.

Yu, Connie Young. 1989. "The World of Our Grandmothers." In Asian Women United of California, eds., *Making Waves: An Anthology of Writings by and about Asian American Women.* Boston: Beacon, pp. 33–41.

BLACK TEENAGE MOTHERS AND THEIR DAUGHTERS: THE IMPACT OF ADOLESCENT CHILDBEARING ON DAUGHTERS' RELATIONS WITH MOTHERS —ELAINE BELL KAPLAN

Note

1. The mothers of teen mothers (including those who themselves were teenage mothers) will be referred to as adult mothers.

References

Allen, Lind, and Darlene Britt
1984   "Black women in American society." In *Social Psychological Problems of Women,* eds. A. G. Rickel, M. Gerrard, and I. Iscoe, 33–47. New York: Hemisphere.

Apfel, Nancy H., and Victoria Seitz
1991   "Four models of adolescent mother-grandmother relationships in Black inner-city families." *Family Relations* 40:421–429.

Bell Kaplan, Elaine
Forthcoming   *'Not Our Kind of Girl:' Black Teenage Motherhood: Realities Hiding Behind the Myths.* University of California Press, June 1997.

Brewer, Rose
1995   "Gender, poverty, culture, and economy: Theorizing female-led families." In *African American Single Mothers,* ed. Bette J. Dickerson, 164–178. Beverly Hills, Calif.: Sage, Inc.

Burton, Linda M., and Vern L. Bengston
1985   "Black grandmothers." In *Grand Parenthood,* eds. Vern Bengston and J. Roberston, 75–110. Beverly Hills, Calif.: Sage, Inc.

Collins, Patricia H.
1987   "The meaning of motherhood." Sage 2:32–46.
1990   *Black Feminist Thought.* New York: Routledge.

Elliott, Marta, and Lauren J. Krivo
1991   "Structural determinants of homelessness in the United States." *Social Problems* 38:113–131.

Fischer, Lucy R.
1986   *Linked Lives.* New York: Harper & Row.

Furstenberg, Frank, Jr.
1980   "Burdens and benefits." *Journal of Social Issues* 36:64–87.

George, Susan M., and Bette J. Dickerson
1995 "The role of the grandmother in poor single-mother families and households." In *African American Single Mothers,* ed. Bette I. Dickerson, 146–163. Beverly Hills, Calif.: Sage.

Geronimus, Arline T.
1990 "Teenage birth's new conceptions." *Insight* 30:11–13.

Gilligan, Carol
1990 In *Making Connections,* eds. Carol Gilligan, Nona P. Lyons, and Trudy J. Hanmer, 6–29. Cambridge: Harvard University Press.

Goffman, Erving
1963 *Stigma.* Englewood Cliffs, NJ.: Prentice-Hall, Inc.

Hardy, Janet B., and Laurie S. Zabin
1991 *Adolescent Pregnancy in an Urban Environment.* Washington, D.C. The Urban Institute.

Ladner, Joyce, and Ruby M. Gourdine
1984 "Intergenerational teenage motherhood." Sage 1:22–24.

MacLeod, Jay
1987 *Ain't No Makin' It.* Boulder, Colo.: Westview Press.

Mayfield, Lorraine P.
1994 "Early parenthood among low-income adolescent girls." In *Black Family, 4th Edition,* ed. Robert Staples, 230–242. Belmont, Calif.: Wadsworth Publishing Co.

McGrory, Mary
1994 "What to do about parents of illegitimate children." *The Washington Post,* February 15:25.

Mills, C. Wright
1956 *The Sociological Imagination.* New York: Oxford University Press.

Moynihan, Daniel P.
1965 *The Negro Family: The Case for National Action.* U.S. Department of Labor: Washington, D.C.

Musick, Judith S.
1987 "The high-stakes challenge of programs for adolescent mothers." A report for the Ounce of Prevention Fund, 1–4. Chicago, Ill.: Department of Children and Family Services.

Myers Wright, Lena
1980 *Black Women: Do They Cope Better?* Englewood Cliffs, NJ.: Prentice-Hall.

Oakland City Council Report
1988 "Women and children in Oakland, September, 1988." Unpublished report.

Reinharz, Shulamit
1992 *Feminist Methods in Social Research.* New York: Oxford University Press.

Rich, Sharon
1990 "Daughters' views of their relationships with their mothers." In *Making Connections,* eds. Carol Gilligan, Nona P. Lyons, and Trudy J. Hanmer, 258–273. Cambridge: Harvard University Press.

Rogers, Earline, and Sally H. Lee
1992 "A comparison of the perceptions of the mother-daughter relationship: Black pregnant and nonpregnant teenagers." *Adolescence* 107:554–564.

Russo, Nancy F.
1976 "The motherhood mandate." *Journal of Social Issues* 32:143–153.

Stack, Carol
1974 *All Our Kin.* New York: Random House.

Staples, Robert
1994 "The family." In *The Black Family,* ed. Robert Staples, 1–3. Belmont, Calif.: Wadworth.

Stokes, Randall, and John P. Hewitt
1976 "Aligning actions." *American Sociological Review* 41:838–849.

Wilson, William J.
1987 *The Truly Disadvantaged.* Chicago: University of Chicago Press.

THE CHANGING CULTURE OF FATHERHOOD IN COMIC-STRIP FAMILIES: A SIX-DECADE ANALYSIS —RALPH LAROSS ET AL.

References

Atkinson, M. P., & Blackwelder, S. P. (1993). Fathering in the 20th century. *Journal of Marriage and the Family, 55,* 975–986.

Berger, P., & Luckmann, T. (1966). *The social construction of reality: A treatise in the sociology of knowledge.* New York: Anchor/Doubleday.

Brabant, S. (1976). Sex role stereotyping in the Sunday comics. *Sex Roles, 2,* 331–337.

Brabant, S., & Mooney, L. A. (1986). Sex role stereotyping in the Sunday comics: Ten years later. *Sex Roles, 14,* 141–148.

Brabant, S., & Mooney, L. A. (1997). Sex role stereotyping in the Sunday comics: A twenty year update. *Sex Roles, 37,* 269–281.

Chavez, D. (1985). Perpetuation of gender inequality: A content analysis of comic strips. *Sex Roles, 13,* 93–102.

Coltrane, S. (1996). *Family man: Fatherhood, housework, and gender equity.* New York: Oxford University Press.

Coltrane, S., & Allan, K. (1994). "New" fathers and old stereotypes: Representations of masculinity in 1980s television advertising. *Masculinities, 2,* 43–66.

Day, R. D., & Mackey, W. C. (1986). The role image of the American father: An examination of a media myth. *Journal of Comparative Family Studies, 3,* 371–388.

Furstenberg, F. F., Jr. (1988). Good dads—bad dads: Two faces of fatherhood. In A. J. Cherlin (Ed.), *The changing American family and public policy* (pp. 193–218). Washington, DC: Urban Institute Press.

Goulart, R. (1995). *The funnies: 100 years of American comic strips.* Holbrook, MA: Adams Publishing.

Griswold, R. L. (1993). *Fatherhood in America: A history.* New York: Basic Books.

Griswold, W. (1994). *Cultures and societies in a changing world.* Thousand Oaks, CA: Sage.

Harrison, R. P. (1981). *The cartoon: Communication to the quick.* Beverly Hills, CA: Sage.

Inge, M. T. (1979). Introduction. *Journal of Popular Culture, 12,* 631–639.

Inge, M. T. (1990). *Comics as culture.* Jackson, MS: University Press of Mississippi.

Kasen, J. H. (1979). Exploring collective symbols: America as a middle-class society. *Pacific Sociological Review, 22,* 348–381.

Kasen, J. H. (1980). Whither the self-made man? Comic culture and the crisis of legitimation in the United States. *Social Problems, 28,* 131–148.

Kinnaird, C. (1963). Cavalcade of funnies. In D. M. White & R. H. Abel (Eds.), *The funnies: An American idiom* (pp. 88–96). New York: Free Press. (A revision of an article that appeared in *The Funnies, Annual No. 1,* 1959, King Features Syndicate, Inc.)

LaRossa, R. (1988). Fatherhood and social change. *Family Relations, 37,* 451–457.

LaRossa, R. (1997). *The modernization of fatherhood: A social and political history.* Chicago: University of Chicago Press.

LaRossa, R., Gordon, B. A., Wilson, R. J., Bairan, A., & Jaret, C. (1991). The fluctuating image of the 20th century American father. *Journal of Marriage and the Family, 53,* 987–997.

Macionis, J. J. (1989). What makes something funny? In J. J. Macionis & N. V. Benokraitis (Eds.), *Seeing ourselves: Classic, contemporary, and cross-cultural readings in sociology* (pp. 109–113). Englewood Cliffs, NJ: Prentice-Hall.

Mooney, L., & Brabant, S. (1987). Two martinis and a rested woman: "Liberation" in the Sunday comics. *Sex Roles, 17,* 409–420.

Mooney, L., & Brabant, S. (1990). The portrayal of boys and girls in six nationally-syndicated comic strips. *Sociology and Social Research, 74,* 118–126.

Mukerji, C., & Schudson, M. (Eds.). (1991). *Rethinking popular culture: Contemporary perspectives in cultural studies.* Berkeley, CA: University of California Press.

Mulkay, M. (1988). *On humor: Its nature and its place in modern society.* Oxford, England: Basil Blackwell.

Pleck, J. H. (1997). Parental involvement: Levels, sources, and consequences. In M. E. Lamb (Ed.), *The role of the father in child development* (pp. 66–103). New York: John Wiley.

Radway, J. (1984). *Reading the romance: Women, patriarchy, and popular literature.* Chapel Hill, NC: University of North Carolina Press.

Rogosa, D. (1995). Myths and methods: "Myths about longitudinal research" plus supplemental questions. In J. M. Gottman (Ed.), *The analysis of change.* Mahwah, NJ: Erlbaum.

Simonds, W. (1992). *Women and self-help culture: Reading between the lines.* New Brunswick, NJ: Rutgers University Press.

Strecker, E. (1946). *Their mothers' sons: The psychiatrist examines an American problem.* Philadelphia: Lippincott.

Swidler, A. (1986). Culture in action: Symbols and strategies. *American Sociological Review, 51,* 273–286.

Ward, B. (1993, May 9). The changing face of Mother's Day. *Atlanta Journal and Constitution,* p. C3.

Wilson, C. (1979). *Jokes: Form, content, use and function.* London: Academic Press.

Wood, A. (1987). *Great cartoonists and their art.* Gretna, LA: Pelican.

Wylie, P. (1942). *Generation of vipers.* New York: Holt, Rinehart, & Winston.

Zerubavel, E. (1991). *The fine line: Making distinctions in everyday life.* New York: Free Press.

Zerubavel, E. (1997). *Social mindscapes: An invitation to cognitive sociology.* Cambridge, MA: Harvard University Press.

"THE NORMAL AMERICAN FAMILY" AS AN INTERPRETIVE STRUCTURE OF FAMILY LIFE AMONG GROWN CHILDREN OF KOREAN AND VIETNAMESE IMMIGRANTS—KAREN PYKE

References

Abel, E. K. (1991). *Who cares for the elderly?* Philadelphia: Temple University Press.

Ambert, A., Adler, P., Adler, P., & Detzner, D. (1995). Understanding and evaluating qualitative research. *Journal of Marriage and the Family, 57,* 879–893.

Bellah, R. N., Madsen, R., Sullivan, W. M., Swidler, A., & Tipton, S. (1985). *Habits of the heart.* San Francisco: Harper & Row.

Berger, P. L., & Luckmann, T. (1966). *The social construction of reality.* New York: Doubleday.

Bernades, J. (1985). "Family ideology": Identification and exploration. *Sociological Review, 33,* 275–297.

Bernades, J. (1993). Responsibilities in studying post-modern families. *Journal of Family Issues, 14,* 35–49.

Blankenhorn, D. (1995). *Fatherless America.* New York: Basic Books.

Brown, D., & Bryant, J. (1990). Effects of television on family values and selected attitudes and behaviors. In J. Bryant (Ed.), *Television and the American family* (pp. 253–274). Hillsdale, NJ: Erlbaum.

Cancian, F. M. (1986). The feminization of love. *Signs, 11,* 692–708.

Cancian, F. M. (1987). *Love in America.* New York: Cambridge University Press.

Caplan, N., Choy, M. H., & Whitmore, J. K. (1991). *Children of the boat people: A study of educational success.* Ann Arbor: University of Michigan Press.

Cha, J. (1994). Aspects of individualism and collectivism in Korea. In U. Kim, H. C. Triandis, Ç. Kâǧitçibaşi, S. Choi, & G. Yoon (Eds.), *Individualism and collectivism: Theory, methods, and applications* (pp. 157–174). Thousand Oaks, CA: Sage.

Chung, D. K. (1992). Asian cultural commonalities: A comparison with mainstream American culture. In S. Furuto, R. Biswas, D. Chung, K. Murasc, F. Ross-Sheriff (Eds.), *Social work practice with Asian Americans* (pp. 27–44). Newbury Park, CA: Sage.

Coltrane, S. (1996). *Family man.* New York: Oxford University Press.

Coontz, S. (1992). *The way we never were.* New York: Basic Books.

Dilworth-Anderson, P., Burton, L. M., & Turner, W. L. (1993). The importance of values in the study of culturally diverse families. *Family Relations, 42,* 238–242.

Espiritu, Y. L. (1997). *Asian American women and men.* Thousand Oaks, CA: Sage.

Fineman, M. A. (1995). *The neutered mother, the sexual family, and other twentieth century tragedies.* New York: Routledge.

Freeman, J. M. (1989). *Hearts of sorrow: Vietnamese-American lives.* Stanford, CA: Stanford University Press.

Gerbner, G., Gross, L., Morgan, M., & Signorielli, N. (1980). *Media and the family: Images and impact.* Washington, DC: White House Conference on the Family, National Research Forum on Family Issues. (ERIC Document Reproduction Service No. ED 198 919).

Glaser, B. G., & Strauss, A. L. (1967). *The discovery of grounded theory.* New York: Aldine.

Gold, S. J. (1993). Migration and family adjustment: Continuity and change among Vietnamese in the United States. In H. P. McAdoo (Ed.), *Family ethnicity* (pp. 300–314). Newbury Park, CA: Sage.

Greeley, A. (1987, May 17). Today's morality play: The sitcom. *New York Times,* p. H1.

Greenberg, B. S., Hines, M., Buerkel-Rothfuss, N., & Atkin, C. K. (1980). Family role structures and interactions on commercial television. In B. S. Greenberg (Ed.), *Life on television: Content analyses of U.S. TV drama* (pp. 149–160). Norwood, NJ: Ablex.

Gubrium, J. F., & Holstein, J. A. (1997). *The new language of qualitative method.* New York: Oxford University Press.

Holstein, J. A., & Gubrium, J. F. (1995). Deprivatization and the construction of domestic life. *Journal of Marriage and The Family, 57,* 894–908.

Holstein, J. A., & Miller, G. (1993). Social constructionism and social problems work. In J. A. Holstein & G. Miller (Eds.), *Reconsidering social constructionism* (pp. 151–172). New York: Aldine De Gruyter.

Huber, G. A., & Espenshade, T. J. (1997). Neoisolationism, balanced-budget conservatism, and the fiscal impacts of immigrants. *International Migration Review, 31,* 1031–1054.

Hurh, W. M. (1998). *The Korean Americans.* Westport, CT: Greenwood Press.

Kibria, N. (1993). *The family tightrope: The changing lives of Vietnamese Americans.* Princeton, NJ: Princeton University Press.

Kibria, N. (1997). The construction of 'Asian American': Reflections on intermarriage and ethnic identity among second-generation Chinese and Korean Americans. *Ethnic and Racial Studies, 20,* 523–544.

Kim, U., & Choi, S. (1994). Individualism, collectivism, and child development: A Korean perspective. In P. Greenfield & R. Cocking (Eds.), *Cross-cultural roots of minority child development* (pp. 227–257). Hillsdale, NJ: Erlbaum.

Kurz, D. (1995). *For richer, for poorer.* New York: Routledge.

Maharaj, D. (1997, July 8). E-mail hate case tests free speech protections. *Los Angeles Times,* pp. A1, A16.

Maharidge, D. (1996). *The coming white minority: California eruptions and America's future.* New York: New York Times Books.

Min, P. G. (1995). Major issues relating to Asian American experiences. In P. G. Min (Ed.), *Asian Americans* (pp. 38–57). Thousand Oaks, CA: Sage.

Min, P. G. (1998). *Changes and conflicts: Korean immigrant families in New York.* New York: Allyn and Bacon.

Nakao, A. (1996, November 17). Asians' political image marred: Fund-raising probes' timing "unfortunate." *The San Francisco Examiner,* p. A1.

Omi, M., & Winant, H. (1994). *Racial formation in the United States.* New York: Routledge.

Oropesa, R. S., & Landale, N. S. (1995). *Immigrant legacies: The socioeconomic circumstances of children by ethnicity and generation in the United States.* (Working Paper 95–01R.) Population Research Institute, The Pennsylvania State University, State College.

Pettengill, S. M., & Rohner, R. P. (1985). Korean-American adolescents' perceptions of parental control, parental acceptance–rejection and parent–adolescent conflict. In I. R. Lagunes & Y. H. Poortinga (Eds.), *From a different perspective: Studies of behavior across culture* (pp. 241–249). Berwyn, IL: Swets North America.

Popenoe, D. (1993). American family decline, 1960–1990: A review and appraisal. *Journal of Marriage and the Family, 55,* 527–555.

Popenoe, D. (1996). *Life without father: Compelling new evidence that fatherhood and marriage are indispensable and for the good of the children and society.* New York: Martin Kessler/Free Press.

Pyke, K. D. (1999). The micropolitics of care in relationships between aging parents and adult children: Individualism, collectivism, and power. *Journal of Marriage and the Family, 61,* 661–672.

Pyke, K. D., & Bengtson, V. L. (1996). Caring more or less: Individualistic and collectivist systems of family eldercare. *Journal of Marriage and the Family, 58,* 379–392.

Pyke, K. D., & Johnson, D. (1999, November). *Between two faces of gender: The incongruity of home and mainstream cultures among sons and daughters of Asian immigrants.* Paper presented at the Annual Meeting of the National Council of Family Relations, Irvine, CA.

Rohner, R. P., & Pettingill, S. M. (1985). Perceived parental acceptance-rejection and parental control among Korean adolescents. *Child Development, 56,* 524–528.

Rumbaut, R. G. (1994). The crucible within: Ethnic identity, self-esteem and segmented assimilation among children of immigrants. *International Migration Review, 28,* 748–794.

Rumbaut, R. G. (1997). Assimilation and its discontents: Between rhetoric and reality. *International Migration Review, 31,* 923–960.

Shaner, J. (1982). Parental empathy and family role interactions as portrayed on commercial television. *Dissertation Abstracts International, 42,* 3473A.

Skill, T. (1994). Family images and family actions as presented in the media: Where we've been and what we've found. In D. Zillmann, J. Bryant, & A. C. Huston (Eds.), *Media, children, and the family* (pp. 37–50). Hillsdale, NJ: Erlbaum.

Skolnick, A. (1991). *Embattled paradise: The American family in an age of uncertainty.* New York: Basic Books.

Smith, D. E. (1993). The standard North American family: SNAF as an ideological code. *Journal of Family Issues, 14,* 50–65.

Stacey, J. (1998). The right family values. In K. Hansen & A. Garey (Eds.), *Families in the U.S.* (pp. 859–880). Philadelphia: Temple University Press.

Strauss, A., & Corbin, J. (1990). *Basics of qualitative research.* Newbury Park, CA: Sage.

Sue, S., & Morishima, J. K. (1982). *The mental health of Asian Americans.* San Francisco: Jossey-Bass.

Sweet, J. A., & Bumpass, L. (1987). *American families and households.* New York: Russell Sage Foundation.

Thorne, B., & Yalom, M. (1992). *Rethinking the family: Some feminist questions.* Boston: Northeastern University.

Tran, T. V. (1988). The Vietnamese American family. In C. H. Mindel, R. W. Habenstein, & R. Wright, Jr. (Eds.), *Ethnic families in America: Patterns and variations* (pp. 276–299). New York: Elsevier.

Tsui, P., & Schultz, G. (1985). Failure of rapport: Why psychotherapeutic engagement fails in the treatment of Asian clients. *American Journal of Orthopsychiatry, 55,* 561–569.

Uba, L. (1994). *Asian Americans: Personality patterns, identity, and mental health.* New York: The Guilford Press.

U.S. Immigration and Naturalization Service (1997). *Statistical yearbook of the immigration and naturalization service, 1995.* Washington, DC: U.S. Government Printing Office.

Waters, M. C. (1996). The intersection of gender, race, and ethnicity in identity develop-ment of Caribbean American teens. In M. C. Waters (Ed.), *Urban girls: Resisting stereotypes, creating identities* (pp. 65–81) New York: New York University Press.

Wolf, D. (1997). Family secrets: Transnational struggles among children of Filipino immigrants. *Sociological Perspectives, 40,* 457–482.

Zhou, M. (1997). Growing up American: The challenge confronting immigrant children and children of immigrants. *Annual Review of Sociology, 23,* 63–95.

Zhou, M., & Bankston, III, C. (1998). *Growing up American: How Vietnamese children adapt to life in the United States.* New York: Russell Sage Foundation.

Zinn, M. B. (1994). Feminist rethinking of racial–ethnic families. In M. B. Zinn & B. T. Dill (Eds.), *Women of color in U.S. society* (pp. 303–314). Philadelphia: Temple University Press.

THE BATTERER'S VIEW OF THE SELF AND OTHERS IN DOMESTIC VIOLENCE—SARAH GOODRUM, DEBRA UMBERSON, AND KRISTIN L. ANDERSON

Endnotes

This article is a revised version of a paper presented at the 1998 meeting of the American Sociological Association, San Francisco, California. This study is from a larger project funded by the Hogg Foundation for Mental Health (Principal Investigator, Debra Umberson). We thank Mark C. Stafford, Kristi Williams and anonymous reviewers for their comments on an earlier draft of this paper.

1. A batterer is a person who uses physical violence against an intimate partner. We use masculine pronouns to refer to batterers because our study focuses on male perpetrators and because

men perpetrate the majority of repetitive, severe acts of domestic violence in the United States.

References

Athens, Lonnie. 1997. *Violent Criminal Acts and Actors Revisited.* Chicago: University of Illinois.

———. 1995. "Dramatic Self-Change." *Sociological Quarterly* 36:571–86.

———. 1994. "The Self as Soliloquy." *Sociological Quarterly* 35:521–32.

———. 1992. *The Creation of Dangerous Violent Criminals.* Urbana: University of Illinois Press.

Baker, Phyllis. 1996. "Doin' What It Takes to Survive: Battered Women and the Consequences of Compliance to a Cultural Script" *Studies in Symbolic Interactionism* 20:73–90.

Blumer, Herbert. 1969. *Symbolic Interactionism: Perspective and Method.* Englewood Cliffs, NJ: Prentice Hall.

Carden, Ann D. 1994. "Wife Abuse and the Wife Abuser." *The Counseling Psychologist* 22:539–73.

Denzin, Norman K. 1984. "Toward a Phenomenology of Domestic, Family Violence." *American Journal of Sociology* 90:483–513.

Dobash, R. Emerson, and Russell Dobash. 1979. *Violence Against Wives: A Case Against Patriarchy.* New York: The Free Press.

Forte, James A., David D. Franks, Janett A. Forte, and Daniel Rigsby. 1996. "Asymmetrical Role-Taking: Comparing Battered and Nonbattered Women." *Social Work* 41:59–73.

Franks, David D. 1986. "Role-taking, Social Power and Imperceptiveness: The Analysis of Rape." *Studies in Symbolic Interactionism* 6:229–59.

Gelles, Richard J. 1980. "Violence in the Family: A Review of Research in the Seventies." *Journal of Marriage and the Family* 42:873–85.

Gondolf, Edward. 1985. *Men Who Batter: An Integrated Approach to Stopping Wife Abuse.* Holmes Beach, FL: Learning Publications.

Goodman, Richard A., James A. Mercy, Peter M. Layde, and Stephen B. Thacker. 1988. "Case-control Studies: Design Issues for Criminological Applications." *Journal of Quantitative Criminology* 4:71–84.

Hirschel, J. David, Ira W. Hutchison III, and Charles W. Dean. 1992. "The Failure of Arrest to Deter Spouse Abuse." *Journal of Research in Crime and Delinquency* 29:7–34.

Holtzworth-Munroe, Amy, and Gregory L. Stuart. 1994. "Typologies of Male Batterers: Three Subtypes and the Differences Among Them." *Psychological Bulletin* 116:476–97.

Lempert, Lora Box. 1994. "A Narrative Analysis of Abuse: Connecting the Personal, the Rhetorical, and the Structural." *Journal of Contemporary Ethnography* 22:411–41.

Loftin, Colin, and David McDowall. 1988. "The Analysis of Case-control Studies in Criminology." *Journal of Quantitative Criminology* 4:85–98.

Mead, George Herbert. 1934. *Mind Self and Society.* Chicago: The University of Chicago Press.

Pate, Anthony M., and Edwin E. Hamilton. 1992. "Formal and Informal Deterrents to Domestic Violence: The Dade County Spouse Assault Experiment." *American Sociological Review* 57:691–97.

Pence, Ellen, and Michael Paymar. 1993. *Education Groups for Men Who Batter: The Duluth Model.* New York, NY: Springer Publishing Co.

Ptacek, James. 1988. "Why do Men Batter their Wives?" Pp. 133–57 in *Feminist Perspectives on Wife Abuse,* edited by Kersti Yllo and Michele Bogard. Beverly Hills, CA: Sage.

Schlesselman, James J. 1982. *Case-control Studies: Design, Conduct, Analysis.* New York: Oxford University Press.

Scully, Diana. 1990. *Understanding Sexual Violence: A Study of Convicted Rapists.* Boston: Unwin Hyman.

Sherman, Lawrence W., Janell D. Schmidt, Douglas A. Smith, and Dennis Rogan. 1992. "Crime, Punishment, and Stake in Conformity: Legal and Informal Control of Domestic Violence." *American Sociological Review* 57:680–91.

Stark, Evan, and Anne Flitcraft. 1996. *Women at Risk: Domestic Violence and Women's Health.* Thousand Oaks, CA: Sage.

Stets, Jan E. 1988. *Domestic Violence and Control.* New York, NY: Springer-Verlag.

Straus, Murray A. 1979. "Measuring Intrafamily Conflict and Violence: The Conflict Tactics Scale." *Journal of Marriage and the Family* 41:75–88.

———. 1978. "Wife Beating: How Common and Why?" *Victimology* 2:443–58.

Straus, Murray A., Richard J. Gelles, and Suzanne K. Steinmetz. 1980. *Behind Closed Doors: Violence in the American Family.* Garden City, NY: Transaction Publishers.

Strauss, Anslem. 1987. *Qualitative Analysis for Social Scientists.* New York: Cambridge University Press.

Walker, Lenore E. 1979. *The Battered Woman.* New York, NY: Harper & Row.

Yllo, Kersti A. 1993. "Through a Feminist Lens: Gender, Power and Violence." Pp. 47–62 in *Current Controversies on Family Violence,* edited by Richard Gelles and Donileen Loseke. Thousand Oaks, CA: Sage Publications, Inc.

Zawitz, Marianne W. 1994. *Domestic Violence.* Washington, DC: Department of Justice, Office of Justice Programs, Bureau of Justice Statistics.

TEN MYTHS THAT PERPETUATE CORPORAL PUNISHMENT —MURRAY A. STRAUS

Notes

1. The average age is eight because almost no one remembers anything specific about what happened at ages two and three the actual peak years for corporal punishment... Even at age eight, memory for specific details is poor. So the figure of an average of six times is almost certainly much lower than the actual number of times these students were hit when they were eight years old.

2. Charts 22–1 and 22–2 are based on data from Sears, Maccoby, and Levin (1957).

References

Alvy, Kirby T., and Marilyn Marigna. 1987. *Effective Black Parenting.* Studio City, CA: Center For the Improvement of Child Caring.

Bavolek, Stephen J. 1992. *The Nurturing Programs.* City Utah: Family Development Resources.

Calvert, Robert. 1974. "Criminal and Civil Liability in Husband-Wife Assaults." Chapter 9 in *Violence in the Family,* edited by S. K. Steinmetz and M. A. Straus. New York: Harper and Row.

Crozier, Jill and Roger C. Katz. 1979. "Social Learning Treatment of Child Abuse." *Journal of Abnormal Child Psychology.* 10: 213–20.

Day, Dan E. and Mark W. Roberts. 1983. "An analysis of the Physical Punishment Component of a Parent Training Program." *Journal of Abnormal Child Psychology* 11:141–52.

Deley, Warren W. 1988. "Physical Punishment of Children: Sweden and the USA." *Journal of Comparative Family Studies.* 19:419–31.

Dinkmeyer Sr., Don and Gary D. McKay. 1989. *Systematic Training for Effective Parenting.* Circle Pines, MN: American Guidance Service.

Gordon, Thomas. 1975. *Parent Effectiveness Training.* New York: New American Library.

Haeuser, Adrienne A. 1988. *Reducing Violence Towards U.S. Children: Transferring Positive Innovations from Sweden.* Milwaukee WI: Department of Social Welfare, University of Wisconsin, Milwaukee.

Higgins, E. Tory and John A. Bargh. 1987. "Social Cognitions and Social Perception." *Annual Review of Psychology* 38:369–425.

Hirschi, Travis. 1969. *The Causes of Delinquency.* Berkeley and Los Angeles: University of California Press.

Kadushin, Alfred and Judith A. Martin. 1981. *Child Abuse: An Interactional Event.* New York: Columbia University Press.

Larzelere, Robert E. 1986. "Moderate Spanking: Model or Deterrent of Children's Aggression in the Family?" *Journal of Family Violence* 1–27–36.

Larzelere, Robert E. 1994. "Empirically Justified Uses of Spanking: Toward a Discriminating View of Corporal Punishment." *Journal of Psychology and Theology.*

LaVoie, Joseph C. 1974. "Type of Punishment as a Determination of Resistance To Deviation." *Developmental Psychology.* 10: 181–89.

Matteson, Margaret E., Earl S. Pollack, and Joseph W. Cullen. 1987. "What Are the Odds that Smoking Will Kill You?" *American Journal of Public Health* 77:425–31.

Newson, John and Elizabeth Newson. 1963. *Patterns of Infant Care in an Urban Community.* Baltimore: Penguin Books.

Patterson, Gerald R. 1982. "A Social Learning Approach to Family Intervention." *Coercive Family Process.* Eugene, OR: Castalia.

Reed, William H., Edward K. Morris and Jerry A. Martin. 1975. "Effects of Positive and Negative Adult-Child Interactions on Children's Social Preference." *Journal of Experimental Child Psychology* 19:153–64.

Rosemond, John K. 1981. *Parent Power: A Common Sense Approach to Raising Your Children in the '80s.* Charlotte, NC: East Woods Press.

Sears, Robert R., Eleanor C. Maccoby, and Harry Levin. 1957. *Patterns of Child Rearing.* Evanston, IL: Row, Peterson, and Company.

Stern, Daniel. 1977. *The First Relationship: Mother and Infant.* Cambridge, MA: Harvard University Press.

Tannatt, Lupita Montoya and Kirby T. Alvy. 1989. *Los Ninos Bien Educados Program.* Studio City, CA: Center for the Improvement of Child Caring.

Webster-Stratton, Carolyn, Mary Kolpcoff, and Terri Hollinsworth. 1988. "Self-Administered Videotape Therapy for Families with Conduct-Problem Children: Comparison with Two Cost-Effective Treatments and a Control Group." *Journal of Consulting and Clinical Psychology* 56:558–66.

Webster-Stratton, Carolyn. 1990. "Enhancing the Effectiveness of Self-Administered Videotape Parent Training for Families with Conduct-Problem Children." *Journal Abnormal Child Psychology* 18:479–92.

DIVORCE CULTURE: A QUEST FOR RELATIONAL EQUALITY IN MARRIAGE —KARLA B. HACKSTAFF

Notes

1. Glenn (1987) refers to this conflict between family scholars as either "concerned" or "sanguine." I refer to these groups as pessimists and optimists because I see both groups as concerned. Pessimists represent those who see mostly problems and little promise in new patterns of marital and family life and optimists see the valuable facets in these new patterns. Also,

there could be cause to describe these different viewpoints as liberal or conservative. However, some pessimistic scholars, such as Hewlett and West (1998) are liberal in their political orientations, and many of the political solutions advanced by pessimists concern government regulations, which are often considered anathema to conservatives.

2. Taking a more economistic view of marriage, Burggraf (1997) also argues for the importance of an exit option in *The Feminine Economy and Economic Man*.

3. Because these samples are not representative, these frequencies are only indicative of widespread changes. However, it might be useful for future researchers to have a report of the changing ideological patterns. While 73 percent of the older spouses believed in marriage culture, this was down to 61 percent for the younger spouses. Among those who talked marriage culture, those who believed in male dominance had declined by a 17 percentage-point difference (from 46 among the '50s spouses to 29 percent among the '70s spouses), while those who believed in equality had increased by a 5 percentage-point difference (from 27 to 32 percent). Further, those spouses who believed in divorce culture had increased by an 11 percentage-point difference (from 27 to 38 percent). Beliefs in a male-dominated divorce culture were more often part of men's hidden agendas. Those who believed in equality and divorce culture increased by a 19 percentage-point difference (from 19 to 38 percent).

The '70s wives were more likely than husbands to espouse the virtues of egalitarianism and slightly more likely to embrace the premises of divorce culture. These patterns and the qualitative text suggest wives are changing faster; however, this small and unrepresentative sample cannot be generalized. Among the older couples, wives constituted half of those sharing beliefs in marriage culture and male dominance; wives constituted 57 percent of those believing in marriage culture and equality and 60 percent of those believing in divorce culture and equality (note that this represents 3 out of 5 spouses). Among the younger couples, wives constituted 55 percent of those believing in marriage culture and equality (6 out of 11 spouses) and 54 percent of those believing in divorce culture and equality (7 out of 13 spouses). Younger wives only made up 40 percent of the traditionalists embracing marriage culture and male authority (4 out of 10), whereas they constituted 50 percent of traditionalists among the older couples (6 out of 12).

4. It should be noted, however, that husbands rated "joint conflict over roles" second, while women found alcohol, untrustworthiness and immaturity, and extramarital sex slightly more important complaints than joint conflict over roles. In many ways these reveal relational concerns that have prevailed in traditional marriage culture.

5. This was a re-evaluation of Weitzman's (1985) figures based on a California sample that overestimated women's downward mobility upon divorce. A conservative estimate from a nationally representative sample following five thousand families found that intact families had a 21 percent increase in standard of living, divorced men had a slightly retarded increase of 17 percent; divorced women had a 7 percent decrease in their standard of living over a seven-year period (Hoffman and Holmes 1976, cited in Weitzman 1985, 337).

6. Historically, marriage represented social commitment and duty for both women and men, however, for women it has also represented a livelihood. As Christopher Jencks has observed: "As long as most American men and women married and pooled their economic resources, as they traditionally did, the fact that men received 70 percent of the nation's income had little effect

on women's material well-being" (cited in Weitzman 1985, 355).

7. While still higher than female wages, male wages have stagnated significantly. Hewlett and West (1998, 173) report that "wages are down 25 percent for men twenty-five to thirty-four years of age." They also report that: "Over the last twenty years, the tide has risen (real per capita GNP went up 29 percent between 1973 and 1993), yet 80 percent of the boats have sunk. Equalizing trends of the period from 1930 to 1970 reversed sharply in the early 1980s, and the gap between the haves and have-nots is now greater than at any time since 1929" (174).

8. Hewlett and West (1998, 180) go on to argue: "The fact is, we don't need a bigger crackdown—we need a new approach." They propose "A Parents' Bill of Rights" with an array of commendable and problematic policies addressing structural and cultural impediments to families—notably missing is any attention to the gender equalities in marriage addressed here.

9. For example, Wilson (1987) has argued that declining marriage in African-American communities is related to the declining numbers of "marriageable males," that is, young men who are not jobless, dying, or incarcerated. Lack of education and job opportunities combine to severely restrict marriage as an option for men. Material means to marriage remain important for it to be an option one embraces or repudiates. Still, "marriageability" in this analysis rests on constructing "husband/father" ideals in terms of the male provider role; clearly, poor women are parenting and providing at once. In this context the female-headed household can be understood as a strategy to contend with the lack of a marriage option (Baca Zinn 1989). While some have blamed welfare for displacing fathers, female-headed households have been increasing across the class system and in industrialized nations throughout the world with policies very different from our own.

10. Blankenhorn (1995a) describes the historically diminishing role of fathers as the shrinking of fatherhood, and the more recent noninvolvement and absence of fathers (including being reduced to their sperm in sperm banks) as the fragmentation of fatherhood. While I agree with Blankenhorn that fathers' participation has diminished and should be expanded and made more robust, I do not agree that we need to return to the role of fatherhood that implies patriarchal authority or biological primacy.

11. These assertions reflect the research that found that marriage generally improves men's well-being more than women's (Hu and Goldman 1990). It also suggests that "his" marriage has generally been better than "hers" (Bernard 1982).

12. As Skolnick (1997a, 94) observed: "It is hard to find a liberal or feminist who argues that a loving, harmonious, two-parent family is not preferable to a post-divorce single or recombined family. But that's beside the point. Loving, harmonious families are unlikely to break up." As Skolnick notes, this echoes the "Just Say No" campaign against drug abuse.

13. More recent research questions the degree to which fathers' relationships with children are mediated by mothers, particularly in stepfamilies. (See Lynn White's paper on "Affective Relationships between Parents and Young Adult Children: Stepfamilies, Gender, and Context." Paper presented at the annual meeting of the American Sociological Association, August 21, 1998.)

14. As Faludi (1991, 457) discovered upon analyzing survey data, being a good provider continues to be the leading trait of masculinity recognized by women and men. Blankenhorn (1995) also found that men still highlight the good provider role in defining manhood.

15. Research shows that some fathers are increasing their parental participation within egalitarian marriages—though this is not the

prevailing pattern (Blaisure and Allen 1995; Coltrane 1998; Hochschild with Machung 1989; Gerson 1993). For example, about one-fifth of Hochschild and Machung's sample of working married parents shared the second shift of housework and child care equally.

16. While those who believe in divorce as a last resort often base this on the sake of the children—the "children's sake" is still being determined by adults' perceptions and interests and is framed as "staying together" rather than "parting" for the children's sake.

17. The hidden benefits of a contested rather than a hegemonic marriage culture may be reflected in recent research. Amato (1994, 149) notes that compared to older research, recent research shows less disparity in adjustment between continuously married and divorced families for both children and adults; he reasons that this probably reflects reduced stigma, less acrimony due to no-fault divorce, and, finally, the sum total of divorces may be constituted by relatively fewer desperate, highly conflicted, and violent divorces.

18. Giddens (1991, 180) has described therapy as "an expression of generalised reflexivity" that "exhibits in full the dislocations and uncertainties to which modernity gives rise."

19. The 1993 Family and Medical Leave Act provides only 12 weeks of *unpaid* leave for family responsibilities like childbirth or adoption—if the worker is employed by a business with 50 or more workers. About one-third of adults are simply not covered by this policy—and many more cannot afford the unpaid leave. As Hewlett and West (1998) point out, not only is this leave policy anemic compared to most European nations—which provide at least twice the leave time and offer pay—but we would need an overhaul of government and corporate policies to manifest the support for families that we express. See Hewlett and West's comprehensive "A Parents' Bill of Rights," which concludes their book.

20. Such ethnocentrism is apparent in the definitions of family and household used by the U.S. Census Bureau. For example, the rate of out-of-wedlock births is very high among the Navajo, yet formalized or legal marriage is not "the" magic linchpin; what might be labeled single parenthood and a lack of family values by outsiders represents a high regard for motherhood and commitment to the community in the context of matrilineal support networks for many Navajo (Deyhle and Margonis, 1995). As other researchers have observed, African-Americans have a tradition of relying upon extended family for shared parenting, as well as a greater acceptance of single parenthood (Fine and Schwebel 1988; Stack 1974; Taylor, Chatters, and Tucker 1990). The marital relationship may be important, but it is not the only relationship in which one can accomplish committed support. This may also explain why African-American children of divorced or single parents may manifest fewer problems than European-American children of divorce in some research on self-esteem (Fine and Schwebel 1988). Peters and McAdoo (1983) made a point about two-job married couples that is relevant to the new family forms brought by divorce; when this pattern became widespread among European-Americans it was decreasingly perceived as "pathological" and increasingly perceived as "alternative." Further, Crosbie-Burnett and Lewis (1999) observe that for centuries African-American family life has required role flexibility, relations across households, bicultural socialization, and contended with a "deviant" label. They argue that postdivorce Euro-American families could learn a great deal about nontraditional families from African-Americans.

21. Increasing cohabitation among heterosexual couples and the rise of domestic partnership

laws have probably reduced the marginality of gay and lesbian couples and families. Many lesbian and gay couples choose to marry ceremonially and make commitments through legal contracts. Through the language of choice, the premises of divorce culture are, in some sense, "friendlier" than marriage culture toward gay and lesbian couples (Weston 1991). Choosing to participate in wedding ceremonies or to draw up contracts are activities shaped by structural obstacles to legal marriage. While not all lesbian and gay scholars promote legal marriage (Sherman 1992), many were thrilled in 1993 when Hawaii's Supreme Court was the first state in the country to rule (in *Baehr v. Lewin*) that denying marriage to lesbians and gays is unconstitutional because it violates the equal-protection clause through gender discrimination (F. Johnson 1996). Congress and state legislatures reacted by securing the frayed borders of the old tapestry. The Defense of Marriage Act, passed by Congress in 1997, retains rights and benefits for male-female unions only and grants states the right to refuse to recognize marital unions in other states. By questioning the heterosexual imperative (Rich 1980), lesbian and gay marriages may be a more radical challenge to the old tapestry. Same-sex marriages challenge the threads of heterosexuality and institutionalized male authority that have been sustained through religious and secular laws and economic arrangements, while affirming the threads of monogamy and commitment. However, if the resistance to same-sex marriage were overcome, it could help undo the enduring, if ever-changing, gender stratification that has defined marriage (Blumstein and Schwartz 1983; Arendell 1995).

Appendix

1. I also relied upon exploratory interviews with and observation of "experts" in marriage and divorce (including clergy, attorneys, psychologists, and mediators), attended a workshop on divorce mediation, and collected and analyzed products of popular culture on marriage and divorce; all of this is considered supplementary data.

2. After 1969, the Guidance Study was merged with another longitudinal study at the Institute of Human Development, the Oakland Growth Study.

3. The 1958 interviews are referred to as the Adult-I follow-up, the 1969–1971 interviews are the Adult-II follow-up, and the 1981–1982 interviews are known as the Adult-III follow-up. These multiple interview schedules and guides for the Longitudinal Studies are not reproduced here, but can be obtained from the Institute of Human Development at the University of California, Berkeley.

4. These scores include self-report as well as ratings by clinicians on the basis of the Adult-III data. I am indebted to Dr. Arlene Skolnick at the Institute for Human Development for allowing me to use these ratings to select my sample.

Bibliography

Ahrons, Constance R., and Roy H. Rodgers. 1987. "The Remarriage Transition." Arlene Skolnick and Jerome Skolnick, eds., *Family In Transition,* 9th ed. New York: Longman, 1997, pp. 185–96.

Amato, Paul R. 1994. "Life-Span Adjustment of Children to Their Parents' Divorce." *The Future of Children: Children and Divorce* 4(1): 143–64.

Amato, Paul R., and Alan Booth. 1995. "Changes in Gender Role Attitudes and Perceived Marital Quality." *American Sociological Review* 60: 59–66.

Amato, Paul R., and B. Keith. 1991. "Parental Divorce and the Well-Being of Children: A Meta-Analysis." *Psychological Bulletin* 100: 26–46.

Amato, Paul R., L. S. Loomis, and Alan Booth. 1995. "Parental Divorce, Marital Conflict, and Offspring Well-Being During Early Adulthood." *Social Forces* 73: 895–915.

Arendell, Terry. 1986. *Mothers and Divorce: Legal, Economic and Social Dilemmas.* Berkeley, CA: University of California Press.

———. 1995. *Fathers and Divorce.* Thousand Oaks, CA: Sage.

———. 1997. "Divorce and Remarriage." In Terry Arendell, ed., *Contemporary Parenting: Challenges and Issues.* Thousand Oaks, CA: Sage Publications, pp. 154–95.

Arendell, Terry, and Demie Kurz. 1999. "Divorce, Gender, and Violence." Paper presented at Women's Worlds International, 1999. Tromo, Norway. June 1999.

Baca Zinn, Maxine. 1989. "Family, Race, and Poverty in the Eighties." In Arlene Skolnick and Jerome Skolnick, eds., *Family In Transition,* 9th ed. New York: Longman, 1997, pp. 316–29.

Bellah, Robert N., Richard Madsen, William M. Sullivan, Ann Swidler, and Steven M. Tipton. 1985. *Habits of the Heart.* Berkeley, CA: University of California Press.

Bernard, Jessie. 1981. "The Good-Provider Role: Its Rise and Fall." In Arlene Skolnick and Jerome Skolnick, eds., *Family In Transition,* 9th ed. New York: Longman, 1997, pp. 99–119.

Blaisure, Karen R., and Katherine R. Allen. 1995. "Feminists and the Ideology and Practice of Marital Equality" *Journal of Marriage and the Family* 57: 5–19.

Blankenhorn, David. 1995a. *Fatherless America: Confronting Our Most Urgent Social Problem.* New York: Basic Books.

Block, J., J. H. Block, and P. E. Gjerde. 1986. "The Personality of Children Prior to Divorce: A Prospective Study." *Child Development* 57: 827–40.

Blumstein, Philip, and Pepper Schwartz. 1983. *American Couples.* New York: William Morrow and Company, Inc.

Brewer, Rose M. 1988. "Black Women in Poverty: Some Comments on Female-Headed Families." *Signs: Journal of Women and Culture in Society* 13(2): 331–39.

Burggraf, Shirley P. 1997. *The Feminine Economy and Economic Man.* New York: Addison-Wesley.

Campbell, James L., and Brent M. Snow. 1992. "Gender Role Conflict and Family Environment as Predictors of Men's Marital Satisfaction." *Journal of Family Psychology* 6(1): 84–87.

Cancian, Francesca. 1987. *Love in America: Gender and Self-Development.* New York: Cambridge University Press.

Cherlin, Andrew. 1981. *Marriage, Divorce, Remarriage.* Cambridge, MA: Harvard University Press.

Coltrane, Scott, and Neal Hickman. 1992. "The Rhetoric of Rights and Needs: Moral Discourse in the Reform of Child Custody and Child Support Laws." *Social Problems* 39: 400–420.

———. 1998. *Gender and Families.* Thousand Oaks, CA: Pine Forge Press.

Coontz, Stephanie. 1992. *The Way We Never Were: American Families and the Nostalgia Trap.* New York: Basic Books.

Cowan, Philip, and Carolyn Pape Cowan. 1998. "New Families: Modern Couples as New Pioneers." In Mary Ann Mason, Arlene Skolnick, and Stephen D. Sugarman, eds., All *Our Families: New Policies for a New Century.* New York: Oxford University Press, pp. 169–92.

Crosbie-Burnett, Margaret, and Edith A. Lewis. 1993. "Use of African-American Family Structures and Functioning to Address the Challenges of European-American Postdivorce Families." In Stephanie Coontz,

Maya Parson, and Gabrielle Raley, eds. *American Families: A Multicultural Reader.* New York: Routledge, 1999, pp. 455–68.

DeVault, Marjorie. 1987. "Doing Housework: Feeding and Family Life." In Naomi Gerstel and Harriet Engle Gross, eds., *Families and Work.* Philadelphia: Temple University Press, pp. 178–91.

Deyhle, Donna, and Frank Margonis. 1995. "Navajo Mothers and Daughters: Schools, Jobs, and the Family." *Anthropology and Education Quarterly* 26(2): 135–67.

di Leonardo, Micaela. 1987. "The Female World of Cards and Holidays: Women, Families, and the Work of Kinship." *Signs: Journal of Women and Culture in Society* 12(3): 440–53.

Durkheim, Emile. 1951. *Suicide.* New York: The Free Press.

Ehrenreich, Barbara. 1984. *The Hearts of Men: American Dreams and the Flight from Commitment.* Garden City, NY: Anchor Books.

Faludi, Susan. 1991. *Backlash: The Undeclared War Against American Women.* New York: Crown Publishers.

Fine, Mark, and A. Schwebel. 1988. "An Emergent Explanation of Different Racial Reactions to Single Parenthood." *Journal of Divorce* 11(2): 1–15.

Furstenberg, Frank. 1988. "Good Dads–Bad Dads: Two Faces of Fatherhood." In Arlene Skolnick and Jerome Skolnick, eds., *Family in Transition,* 9th ed. New York: Longman, 1997, pp. 221–41.

Furstenberg, Frank, and Andrew Cherlin. 1991. "Children's Adjustments to Divorce." in Arlene Skolnick and Jerome Skolnick, eds., *Family In Transition,* 9th ed. New York: Longman, 1997, pp. 267–77.

Gelles, Richard, and Murray Straus. 1988. "Profiling Violent Families." In Arlene Skolnick and Jerome Skolnick, eds., *Family in Tran-*

sition, 9th ed. New York: Longman, 1997, pp. 445–62.

Gerson, Kathleen. 1993. "Dilemmas of Involved Fatherhood." In Susan J. Ferguson, ed., *Shifting the Center: Understanding Contemporary Families.* Mountain View, CA: Mayfield Publishing Company, 1998, pp. 355–71.

Giddens, Anthony. 1979. *Central Problems in Social Theory.* Berkeley, CA: University of California Press.

Glenn, Norval D. 1987. "Continuity Versus Change, Sanguineness Versus Concern." *Journal of Family Issues* 8(4): 348–54.

———. 1996. "Values, Attitudes, and the State of American Marriage." In David Popenoe, Jean Bethke Elshtain, and David Blankenhorn, eds., *Promises to Keep: Decline and the Renewal of Marriage in America.* Lanham, MD: Rowman and Littlefield, pp. 15–33.

Glenn, Norval D., and Kathryn B. Kramer. 1987. "The Marriages and Divorces of the Children of Divorce." *Journal of Marriage and the Family* 49: 811–25.

Goldscheider, Frances K., and Linda J. White. 1991. *New Families, No Families?* Berkeley, CA: University of California Press.

Goode, William J. 1956. *After Divorce.* Glencoe, IL: The Free Press.

Gottman, John, James Coan, Sybil Carrere, and Catherine Swanson. 1998. "Predicting Marital Happiness and Stability from Newlywed Interactions." *Journal of Marriage and the Family* 60: 5–22.

Hetherington, E. Mavis, Tracy C. Law, and Thomas G. O'Connor. 1993. "Divorce: Challenges, Changes, New Chances." In Arlene Skolnick and Jerome Skolnick, eds., *Family In Transition,* 9th ed. New York: Longman, 1997, pp. 176–85.

Hewlett, Sylvia Ann, and Cornel West. 1998. *The War Against Parents: What We Can Do for*

America's Beleaguered Moms and Dads. New York: Houghton Mifflin Company.

Hochschild, Arlie R. 1983. *The Managed Heart: The Commercialization of Human Feeling.* Berkeley, CA: University of California Press.

———. 1997. *The Time Bind. When Work Becomes Home and Home Becomes Work.* New York: Metropolitan Books.

Hochschild, Arlie R., with Anne Machung. 1989. *The Second Shift: Working Parents and the Revolution at Home.* New York: Viking Press.

Hoffman, Saul, and John Holmes. 1976. "Husbands, Wives, and Divorce." In *Five Thousand American Families—Patterns of Economic Progress.* Ann Arbor, MI: Institute for Social Research.

Holden, George W., Robert A. Geffner, and Ernest N. Jouriles. 1998. *Children Exposed to Marital Violence: Theory, Research, and Applied Issues.* Washington, DC: American Psychological Association.

Hu, Y., and N. Goldman. 1990. "Mortality Differentials by Marital Status: An International Comparison." *Demography* 27(2): 233–50.

Johnson, Colleen Leahy. 1988. *Ex-Familia.* New Brunswick, NJ: Rutgers University Press.

Johnson, Fenton. 1996. "Wedded to an Illusion: Do Gays and Lesbians Really Want the Right to Marry?" *Harpers Magazine,* November 1996, pp. 43–50.

Kelly, Joan Berlin. 1982. "Divorce: The Adult Perspective." In Arlene Skolnick and Jerome Skolnick, eds., *Family in Transition,* 5th ed. Boston: Little, Brown and Company, 1986, pp. 304–37.

———. 1988. "Longer-Term Adjustment in Children of Divorce: Converging Findings and Implications for Practice." *Journal of Family Psychology* 2(2): 119–40.

Kitson, Gay C., and William Holmes. 1992. *Portrait of Divorce: Adjustment to Marital Breakdown.* New York: The Guilford Press.

Kurz, Demie. 1989. "Social Science Perspectives on Wife Abuse." *Gender & Society* 3(4): 489–505.

Landis-Kleine, Cathy, Linda A. Foley, Loretta Nall, Patricia Padgett, and Leslie Walters-Palmer. 1995. "Attitudes Toward Marriage and Divorce Held by Young Adults." *Journal of Divorce and Remarriage* 23(33): 63–73.

Lasch, Christopher. 1979. *The Culture of Narcissism.* New York: W. W. Norton and Company.

Maccoby, Eleanor E., and Robert H. Mnookin. 1992. *Dividing the Child: Social and Legal Dilemmas of Custody.* Cambridge, MA: Harvard University Press.

Mason, Mary Ann, Arlene Skolnick, and Stephen D. Sugarman, eds. 1998. *All Our Families: New Policies for a New Century.* New York: Oxford University Press.

McLanahan, Sara S., and Larry L. Bumpass. 1988. "Intergenerational Consequences of Family Disruption. *American Journal of Sociology* 94: 130–52.

McLanahan, Sara S., and Gary Sandefur. 1994. *Growing Up with a Single Parent.* Cambridge, MA: Harvard University Press.

Mullings, Leith. 1986. "Anthropological Perspectives on the Afro-American Family." *American Journal of Social Psychiatry* 6: 11–16.

Oliker, Stacey. 1989. *Best Friends and Marriage.* Berkeley, CA: University of California Press.

Peters, Marie F., and Harriette P. McAdoo. 1983. "The Present and Future of Alternative Lifestyles in Ethnic American Cultures." In Eleanor D. Macklin and Roger H. Rubin, eds., *Contemporary Families and Alternative Lifestyles.* Beverly Hills, CA: Sage Publications, pp. 288–307.

Peterson, R. 1996. "Statistical Errors, Faulty Conclusions, Misguided Policy: Reply to Weitzman." *American Sociological Review* 61(3): 539–42.

Popenoe, D. 1988. *Disturbing the Nest: Family Change and Decline in Modern Societies.* New York: Aldine De Gruyter.

Popenoe, David, Jean Bethke Elshtain, and David Blankenhorn, eds. 1996. *Promises to Keep: Decline and Renewal of Marriage in America.* Lanham, MD: Rowman & Littlefield Publishers, Inc.

Rich, Adrienne. 1980. "Compulsory Heterosexuality and Lesbian Existence." In Elizabeth Abel and Emily Abel, eds., *The Signs Reader: Women, Gender, and Scholarship.* Chicago: University of Chicago Press, pp. 139–68.

Riessman, Catherine Kohler. 1990. *Divorce Talk: Women and Men Make Sense of Personal Relationships.* New Brunswick, NJ: Rutgers University Press.

Scanzoni, J. 1979. "A Historical Perspective on Husband-Wife Bargaining Power and Marital Dissolution." In George Levinger and Oliver Moles, eds., *Divorce and Separation: Context, Causes and Consequences.* New York: Basic Books, pp. 20–36.

Sherman, Suzanne, ed. 1992. *Lesbian and Gay Marriage: Private Commitments, Public Ceremonies.* Philadelphia: Temple University Press.

Skolnick, Arlene. 1991. *Embattled Paradise.* New York: Basic Books.

———. 1997a. "Family Values: The Sequel." *The American Prospect* 32(May–June 1997): 86–94.

Spanier, Graham B. 1989. "Bequeathing Family Continuity." *Journal of Marriage and the Family* 51: 3–13.

Stacey, Judith. 1988. "Can There Be a Feminist Ethnography?" *Women's Studies International Forum* 11: 21–27.

Stack, Carol. 1974. *All Our Kin: Strategies for Survival in a Black Community.* New York: Harper and Row.

Stewart, Abigail J., Anne P. Copeland, Nia Lane Chester, Janet E. Malley, and Nicole B. Barenbaum. 1997. *Separating Together: How Divorce Transforms Families.* New York: Guilford Press.

Straton, Jack C. 1994. "The Myth of the 'Battered Husband Syndrome.'" In Maxine Baca Zinn, Pierrette Hondagneu-Sotelo, and Michael A. Messner, eds., *Through the Prism of Difference: Readings in Sex and Gender.* Boston: Allyn and Bacon, 1997, 118–20.

Sugarman, Stephen. 1998. "Single-Parent Families." Mary Ann Mason, Arlene Skolnick, and Stephen D. Sugarman, eds., *All Our Families: New Policies for a New Century.* New York: Oxford University Press, pp. 13–38.

Taylor, Robert J., Linda M. Chatters, and Belinda Tucker. 1990. "Developments in Research on Black Families: A Decade Review." *Journal of Marriage and the Family* 52: 993–1014.

Thompson, Linda. 1991. "Family Work: Women's Sense of Fairness." *Journal of Family Issues* 12(2): 181–96.

Thompson, Linda, and Alexis Walker. 1989. "Gender in Families: Women and Men in Marriage, Work, and Parenthood." *Journal of Marriage and the Family* 51: 844–71.

U.S. Department of Commerce, Bureau of the Census. 1992. *Marriage, Divorce, and Remarriage in the 1990's.* In Current Population Reports, Series P23-180. Washington, DC: U.S. Government Printing Office.

———. 1995a. *Child Support for Custodial Mothers and Fathers: 1991.* In Current Population Reports, Series P60-187. Washington, DC: U.S. Government Printing Office.

Wallerstein, Judith, and Sandra Blakeslee. 1989. *Second Chances: Men, Women and Children a*

Decade After Divorce—Who Wins, Who Loses and Why. New York: Ticknor and Fields.

Wallerstein, Judith, and Joan Berlin Kelly. 1980. *Surviving the Breakup: How Children and Parents Cope with Divorce.* New York: Basic Books.

Weitzman, Lenore. 1985. *The Divorce Revolution.* New York: The Free Press.

Weston, Kath. 1991. *Families We Choose: Lesbians, Gays, Kinship.* New York: Columbia University Press.

Whitehead, Barbara Dafoe. 1993. "Dan Quayle Was Right." *The Atlantic,* April.

Wilson, William Julius. 1987. *The Truly Disadvantaged: The Inner City, The Underclass, and Public Policy.* Chicago: University of Chicago Press.

RETHINKING RELATIONSHIPS BETWEEN DIVORCED FATHERS AND THEIR CHILDREN: CAPITALIZING ON FAMILY STRENGTHS —JOYCE A. ARDITTI

References

Acock, A., & Demo, D. (1994). *Family diversity and well-being.* Thousand Oaks, CA: Sage.

Amato, P. R., & Booth, A. (1996). A prospective study of divorce and parent-child relationships. *Journal of Marriage and the Family, 58,* 356–365.

Aquilino, W. S. (1994). Impact of childhood family disruption on young adults' relationships with parents. *Journal of Marriage and the Family, 56,* 295–313.

Arditti, J. A. (1995). Noncustodial parents: Emergent issues of diversity and process. *Marriage and Family Review, 20,* 283–304.

Arditti, J. A., & Bickley, P. (1996). Fathers' involvement and mothers' parenting stress postdivorce. *Journal of Divorce & Remarriage, 26,* 1–23.

Arditti, J. A., & Madden-Derdich, D. (1995). No regrets: Custodial mothers' accounts of the difficulties and benefits of divorce. *Contemporary Family Therapy, 17,* 229–248.

Arditti, J. A., & Madden-Derdich, D. (1993). Noncustodial mothers: Developing strategies of support. *Family Relations, 42,* 305–314.

Arditti, J. A., & Prouty, A. (1999). Change, disengagement, and renewal: Relationship dynamics between young adults with divorced parents and their fathers. *Journal of Marital and Family Therapy, 25,* 61–81.

Baldwin, M. W. (1992). Relational schemas and the processing of social information. *Psychological Bulletin, 112,* 461–484.

Bogdan, R. C., & Bilken, S. K. (1998). *Qualitative research in education: An introduction to theory and methods* (3rd ed.). Boston: Allyn & Bacon.

Bogenschneider, K. (1996). An ecological risk/protective theory for building prevention programs, policies, and community capacity to support youth. *Family Relations, 45,* 127–138.

Capaldi, D. M., & Patterson, G. R. (1991). Relation of parental transitions to boys' adjustment problems: I. A linear hypothesis. II. Mothers at risk for transitions and unskilled parenting. *Developmental Psychology, 3,* 489–504.

Creswell, J. W. (1994). *Research design: Qualitative and quantitative approaches.* Thousand Oaks, CA: Sage.

Duran-Aydintug, C. (1997). Children of divorce revisited: When they speak up. *Journal of Divorce and Remarriage, 27,* 71–84.

Emery, R. E. (1994). *Renegotiating family relationships: Divorce, child custody, and mediation.* New York: The Guilford Press.

Fish, M., Belsky, J., & Youngblade, L. (1991). Developmental antecedents and measurement of intergenerational boundary violation in a nonclinic sample. *Journal of Family Psychology, 4,* 278–297.

Forehand, R., Thomas, A. M., Wierson, M., Brody, G., & Fauber, R. (1990). Role of maternal functioning and parenting skills in adolescent functioning following parental divorce. *Journal of Abnormal Psychology, 99,* 278–283.

Gilgun, J. F. (1992a). Definitions, methodologies, and methods in qualitative family research. In J. Gilgun, K. Daly, & G. Handel (Eds.), *Qualitative methods in family research* (pp. 22–39). Thousand Oaks, CA: Sage.

Gilgun, J. F. (1992b). Observations in a clinical setting: Team decision-making in family incest treatment. In J. Gilgun, K. Daly, & G. Handel (Eds.), *Qualitative methods in family research* (pp. 236–259). Thousand Oaks, CA: Sage.

Guttman, J. (1993). *Divorce in a psychosocial perspective.* Hillsdale, NJ: Lawrence Erlbaum Associates.

Harbert, E. M., Vinick, B. H., & Ekerdt, D. J. (1992). Analyzing popular literature: Emergent themes on marriage and retirement. In J. Gilgun, K. Daly, & G. Handel (Eds.), *Qualitative methods in family research,* pp. 263–278. Newbury Park, CA: Sage.

Hetherington, E. M. (1989). Coping with family transitions: Winners, losers, and survivors. *Child Development, 60,* 1–14.

Hetherington, E. M., & Clingempeel, W. G. (1992). Coping with marital transitions: A family systems perspective. *Monographs of the Society for Research in Child Development, 57,* 1–34.

Hewlitt, S. A. (1991). *When the bough breaks: The cost of neglecting our children.* New York: Basic Books.

Hines, A. M. (1997). Divorce-related transitions, adolescent development, and the role of the parent-child relationships: A review of the literature. *Journal of Marriage and the Family, 59,* 375–388.

Jacobvitz, D. B., & Bush, N. F. (1996). Reconstruction of family relationships: Parent-child alliances, personal distress, and self-esteem. *Developmental Psychology, 32,* 732–743.

Johnston, J. (1993). Family transitions and children's functioning: The case of parental conflict and divorce. In P. Cowan, D. Field, D. Hansen, A. Skolnick, G. Swanson (Eds.), *Family, self, and society: Toward a new agenda for family research* (pp. 197–234). Hillsdale, NJ: Lawrence Erlbaum Associates.

Judge, S. (1998). Parental coping strategies and strengths in families of young children with disabilities. *Family Relations, 47,* 263–268.

Kerr, M., & Bowen, M. (1988). *Family evaluation.* New York: Norton.

Kissman, K., & Allen, J. (1993). *Single-parent families.* Beverly Hills, CA: Sage.

Kurdek, L. A. (1993). Issues in proposing a general model of the effects of divorce on children. *Journal of Marriage and the Family, 55,* 39–45.

Lincoln, Y., & Guba, E. (1985). *Naturalistic inquiry.* Beverly Hills, CA: Sage.

Marshall, C., & Rossman, G. B. (1995). *Designing qualitative research.* Thousand Oaks, CA: Sage.

McLanahan, S., & Sandefur, G. (1994). *Growing up with a single parent: What hurts, what helps.* Cambridge: Harvard University Press.

Miles, M. B., & Huberman, A. M. (1994). *Qualitative data analysis: An expanded sourcebook* (2nd ed.). Thousand Oaks, CA: Sage.

Minuchin, S. (1974). *Families and family therapy.* Cambridge: Harvard University Press.

Peterson, J. L., & Zill, N. (1986). Marital disruption, parent-child relationships, and behavior problems in children. *Journal of Marriage and the Family, 48,* 295–307.

Peterson, G. W., Bodman, D. A., Bush, K. R., & Madden-Derdich, D. (in press). Gender and parent-child relationships. In D. H. Demo, K. R. Allen, & M. A. Fine (Eds.), *Handbook of family diversity.* New York: Oxford University Press.

Phares, V., & Renk, K. (1998). Perceptions of parents: A measure of adolescents' feelings about their parents. *Journal of Marriage and the Family, 60,* 646–659.

Richards, T., & Richards, L. (1994). Using computers in qualitative analysis. In N. Denzin & Y. Lincoln (Eds.), *Handbook of qualitative research* (pp. 445–462). Thousand Oaks, CA: Sage.

Richards, L. N., & Schmiege, C. J. (1993). Problems and strengths of single-parent families: Implications for practice and policy. *Family Relations, 42,* 277–285.

Ruble, S. (1998). Relationship paradigms and parental divorce: Investigating the experiences of adult children from divorced families. Unpublished Masters' Thesis, Virginia Polytechnic Institute and State University, Blacksburg, VA.

Satir, V. (1967). *Conjoint family therapy.* Palo Alto, CA: Science and Behavior Books.

Snyder, S. E. (1992). Interviewing college students about their constructions of love. In J. Gilgun, K. Daly, & G. Handel (Eds.), *Qualitative methods in family research,* (pp. 43–65). Thousand Oaks, CA: Sage.

Stevenson, M. R., & Black, K. N. (1995). *How divorce affects offspring: A research approach.* Madison, WI: Brown and Benchmark.

Stewart, A. J., Copeland, A. P., Chester, N. L., Malley, J. E., & Barenbaum, N. B. (1997). *Separating together: How divorce transforms families.* New York: Guilford.

Strauss, A., & Corbin, J. (1990). *Basics of qualitative research: Grounded theory procedures and techniques.* Newbury Park, CA: Sage.

Thurer, S. L. (1994). *The myths of motherhood.* New York: Houghton Mifflin Co.

Umberson, D. (1992). Relationships between adult children and their parents: Psychological consequences for both generations. *Journal of Marriage and the Family, 54,* 664–674.

Wallerstein, J., & Blakeslee, S. (1989). *Second chances: Women, men, and children a decade after divorce.* New York: Ticknor & Fields.

Weitzman, E. A., & Miles, M. B. (1995). *Computer programs for qualitative data analysis.* Thousand Oaks, CA: Sage.

Wenk, D., Hardesty, C., Morgan, C., & Blair, S. (1994). The influence of parental involvement on the well-being of sons and daughters. *Journal of Marriage and the Family, 56,* 229–234.

Wolff, K. (1950). The sociology of George Simmel. New York: Macmillan. Young, M. H., Miller, B. C., Norton, M. C., Hill, E. J. (1995). The effect of parental supportive behaviors on life satisfaction of adolescent offspring. *Journal of Marriage and the Family, 57,* 813–822.

THE SOCIAL SELF AS GENDERED: A MASCULINIST DISCOURSE OF DIVORCE —TERRY ARENDELL

Notes

1. Although still largely untapped in this regard, the paradigm of human behavior offered by the tradition of symbolic interaction offers rich ground for theoretical exploration of gender relations and gender identity, its acquisition and alteration. Perinbanayagam—in his contemporary works which seek to develop "a workable synthesis of various perspectives on language, self, and action" (Perinbanayagam 1985b, p. xv)

and which newly "locate a theoretical tradition," that is, symbolic interaction (Davis 1985, p. ix)—briefly acknowledges the engenderment of identity in his broad treatment of human agency:

> "A self then has an identity as well as a disidentity, albeit an implicit one most of the time. The identity is *to begin with* [italics mine] based on gender: boys and girls have to be helped to identify their own categories and identify with them as well" (Perinbanayagam 1985a, pp. 318–319).

The concept of *program,* especially as elaborated by Perinbanayagam (1985) has particular salience for investigation of gender identity.

2. Because these fathers saw themselves as having integrated masculine and feminine traits and behaviors in their adjustments to the postdivorce situation, the term "androgynous" is used to characterize them. According to Lindsay (1990, p. 13), "The concept of *androgyny* refers to the investigation of characteristics defined as feminine with those defined as masculine. A new model emerges which maintains that it is possible, and desirable, for people to express both masculine and feminine qualities since they exist in varying degrees within each of us anyway [Bern, 1974; 1975; Kaplan and Bean, 1976]. Androgyny allows for flexibility in the statuses we possess and gives us greater adaptability to the variety of situations we must confront. Ideally, androgyny eliminates the restrictions imposed by gender roles and increases opportunities to develop to our fullest potential. Although the concept of androgyny has been criticized for its ambiguity and lack of definitional rigor [Trebilcot, 1977; Locksley and Colten, 1979; Morgan, 1982a], it at least provides an alternative to images of men and women based on traditional gender roles." See also Deaux and Kite (1987).

3. That most of the participants readily asserted that the superiority of their perceptions and definitions gave them the prerogative to dismiss the wife's point of view is consistent with various theoretical arguments regarding the effects of stratification and differential socialization on interactions (Chodorow 1978; Harding 1983; and Gilligan 1982). Glenn (1987, p. 356), for example, noted:

> "It can be readily observed in a variety of situations that subordinates (women, servants, racial minorities) must be more sensitive to and responsive to the point of view of superordinates (men, masters, dominant racial groups) than the other way around."

4. Goffman (1975, p. 5), for example, early on observed that "ritually speaking, females are equivalent to subordinate males and both are equivalent to children" in depictions of gender in advertisements. He suggested that relations between men and women are based on the parent–child complex.

5. For a relevant analysis of gender division of labor in families which uses the meso domain or mesostructural approach, see Pestello and Voyandoff (1991). Although not utilized, the meso domain or mesostructural approach could be applied to the data obtained in this study; see, for example Maines (1979; 1982) and Hall (1987; 1991).

6. The recently implemented New York State Child Support Standards Act of 1989 (referred to usually by the fathers in the study as the new Child Support Guidelines) was held almost unanimously by these fathers to be grossly unjust and biased against non-custodial parents, primarily fathers; the extensive media coverage given to the Support Guidelines had reinforced many men's sense of being victimized by divorce. Moreover, according to the men in the study, the New York State Child Support Standards Act leads fathers to conclude that they should seek sole custody in order to avoid paying the mandated levels of child support.

7. That children are a form of property which belongs to the father who then is granted custody at the time of separation or divorce has a long history: "This was an unequivocal paternal right" (Polikoff 1983). Even though traditional "father right" has undergone considerable challenge and change, contemporary divorce law and procedures tend to reinforce the stance that children are objects over which to be fought.

8. Despite efforts in every state over the course of the last two decades to reform divorce law and to reduce the level of acrimony involved, the adversarial approach to adjudicating matters of child custody, child support and spousal maintenance, and property settlements persists (Weitzman 1985; Emery 1988). Marcus (1989) details the divorce law reforms in New York State specifically.

9. I am using the term *parenting partnership* rather than shared parenting or co-parents because it suggests a greater flexibility than do the other two terms. An array of types of parenting partnerships is available. For example, divorced parents could choose and develop a distant partnership in which the parents have relatively infrequent communication between them. Most probably, such a parenting partnership would be one in which one parent does most of the childcare and childrearing, even if the other sees the children regularly. On the other hand, the partnership could be a tight-knit and even friendly one in which the parents routinely and frequently communicate about a range of issues concerning their children. Most typically, but not exclusively, in this kind of parenting partnership arrangement both parents would be highly involved in the caring and rearing of their children, even to the point of sharing parental responsibilities equally as was the case for several of the participants in the study who had negotiated and developed such postdivorce partnerships with their former wives. Those worked out by the participants in the present study were flexible arrangements and had been privately, not legally, negotiated and worked out. The term is also more appropriate for the postdivorce situation than shared parenting or co-parents because the latter are commonly used in reference to parenting activities done in the context of marriage.

References

Arendell, Terry. 1986. *Mothers and Divorce: Legal, Economic and Social Dilemmas.* Berkeley: University of California Press.

———. 1992. "After Divorce: Investigations into Father Absence." *Gender & Society.* December, forthcoming.

———. Forthcoming. *Fathers and Divorce* (Tentative title). Berkeley: University of California Press.

Bernard, Jessie. 1981. "The Good-Provider Role: Its Rise and Fall." *American Psychologist* 36:1–12.

Berger, Peter and H. Kellner. 1964. "Marriage and the Social Construction of Reality." *Diogenes* 46:1–25.

Blumer, Herbert. 1969. *Symbolic Interactionism: Perspective and Method.* Englewood Cliffs, NJ: Prentice-Hall.

Bordo, Susan. 1990. "Feminism, Postmodernism, and Gender-Scepticism." Pp. 147–159 in *Feminism/Postmodernism,* edited by Linda J. Nicholson. New York: Routledge.

Bourdieu, Pierre. 1987. *Outline of a Theory of Practice.* Cambridge: Cambridge University Press.

Broverman, I., M. Broverman, F. Clarkson, P. Rosenkrantz, and S. Vogel. 1970. "Sex-Role Stereotypes and Clinical Judgments of Mental Health." Journal of Consulting and Clinical Psychology 34:1–7.

Cancian, Francesca. 1987. *Love in America: Gender and Self Development.* New York: Cambridge University Press.

Chodorow, Nancy. 1978. *The Reproduction of Mothering.* Berkeley: University of California.

Clatterbaugh, Kenneth. 1990. *Contempory Perspectives on Masculinity: Men, Women and Politics in Modern Society.* Boulder, CO: Westview Press.

Cohen, Theodore. 1989. "Becoming and Being Husbands and Fathers: Work and Family Conflict for Men." Pp. 220–234 in *Gender in Intimate Relationships: A Microstructural Approach,* edited by Barbara J. Risman and Pepper Schwartz. Belmont, CA: Wadsworth Publishing Company.

Coltrane, Scott. 1989. "Household Labor and the Routine Production of Gender." *Social Problems* 36:473–490.

Cooley, Charles. 1981. "Self as Sentiment and Reflection." Pp. 169–174 in *Social Psychology Through Symbolic Interaction* (2nd edition), edited by Gregory Stone and Harvey Farberman. New York: John Wiley and Sons.

Daniels, Arlene Kaplan. 1987. "Invisible Work." *Social Problems* 34:403–415.

Davis, Fred. 1985. "Foreword." Pp. ix–xi in *Signing Acts: Structure and Meaning in Everyday Life,* by Robert Perinbanayagam. Carbondale: Southern Illinois University Press.

Deaux, Kay and Mary E. Kite. 1987. "Thinking About Gender." Pp. 92–177, in *Thinking About Gender: A Handbook of Social Science Research.* Newbury Park, CA: Sage Publications.

Emery, Robert. 1988. *Marriage, Divorce, and Children's Adjustment.* Newbury Park, CA: Sage Publications.

Family Law of the State of New York. 1990. Flushing, NY: Looseleaf Law Publications.

Flax, Jane. 1989. "Postmodernism and Gender Relations in Feminist Theory. Pp. 51–74 in *Feminist Theory in Practice and Process,* edited by Micheline Maslon, Jean O'Barr, Sarah Westphal-Wihl, and Mary Wyer. Chicago: The University of Chicago Press.

Folberg, Jay and Ann Milne. 1988. *Divorce Mediation: Theory and Practice.* New York: Guilford Press.

Foote, Nelson. 1981. "Identification as the Basis for a Theory of Motivation." Pp. 333–342 in *Social Psychology Through Symbolic Interaction* (2nd edition), edited by Gregory Stone and Harvey Farberman. New York: John Wiley and Sons.

Furstenberg, Frank. 1988. Good Dads-Bad Dads: Two Faces of Fatherhood. Pp. 193–207 in *The Changing American Family and Public Policy,* edited by Andrew Cherlin. Washington, DC: Urban Institute.

Furstenberg, Frank, S. Philip Morgan, and Paul Allison. 1987. "Parental Participation and Children's Well-Being After Marital Dissolution." *American Sociological Review* 52:695–701.

Gilligan, Carol. 1982. *In a Different Voice: Psychological Theory and Women's Development.* Cambridge: Harvard University Press.

Glaser, Barney and Anselm Strauss. 1967. *The Discovery of Grounded Theory.* New York: Aldine.

Glenn, Evelyn Nakano. 1987. "Gender and the Family." Pp. 348–380 in *Analyzing Gender,* edited by Beth Hess and Myra Marx Ferre. Beverly Hills: Sage Publications.

Goffman, Erving. 1975. *Gender Advertisements.* New York: Harper and Row.

Hall, Peter. 1987. "Interactionism and the Study of Social Organization." *The Sociological Quarterly* 28:1–22.

———. 1991. "in Search of the Meso Domain: Commentary on the Contributions of Pestello and Voydanoff." *Symbolic Interaction* 14(2):129–134.

Harding, Sandra. 1983. "Why Has the Sex/Gender System Become Visible Only Now?" Pp. 311–324 in *Discovering Reality: Feminist Perspectives on Epistemology,*

Metaphysics, Methodology, and Philosophy of Science, edited by Sandra Harding and Merrill Hintikka. Dordrecht, Holland: D. Reidel Publishing.

Hearn, Jeff. 1987. *The Gender of Oppression: Men, Masculinity and the Critique of Marxism.* New York: St. Martin's Press.

Hetherington, Elizabeth, Mavis Cox, and Richard Cox. 1976. "Divorced Fathers." *The Family Coordinator* 25:417–428.

Hochschild, Arlie. R. 1983. *The Managed Heart: Commercialization of Human Feeling.* Berkeley: University of California Press.

Hochschild, Arlie R. with Anne Machung. 1989. *The Second Shift.* New York: Viking Press.

Jaggar, Allison. 1983. Feminist Politics and Human Nature. Totowa, NJ: Rowman and Allenheld.

Kay, Herma Hill. 1990. "Beyond No-Fault: New Directions in Divorce Reform." Pp. 6–36 in *Divorce Reform at the Crossroads,* edited by Stephen D. Sugarman and Herma Hill Kay. New Haven: Yale University Press.

Kimmel, Michael. 1987. "The Contemporary Crisis of Masculinity in Historical Perspective." Pp. 121–154 in *The Making of Masculinities: The New Men's Studies,* edited by Harry Brod. Boston: Allen and Unwin.

LaRossa, Ralph and Maureen Mulligan LaRossa. 1989. "Baby Care: Fathers vs. Mothers." Pp. 138–154 in *Gender in Intimate Relationships: A Microstructural Approach,* edited by Barbara J. Risman and Pepper Schwartz. Belmont, CA: Wadsworth Publishing Company.

Lindsay, Linda. 1990. *Gender Roles: A Sociological Perspective.* New York: Prentice-Hall.

Maines, David. 1979. "Mesostructure and Social Process." *Contemporary Sociology* 8: 524–527.

———. 1982. "in Search of Mesostructure: Studies in the Negotiated Order." *Urban Life* 11:267–279.

Marcus, P. 1989. "Locked In and Locked Out: Reflections on the History of Divorce Law Reform in New York State." *Buffalo Law Review* 37:374–395.

Mead, George H. 1934. Mind, Self and Society. Chicago: University of Chicago Press.

Mnookin, Robert and L. Kornhauser. 1979. "Bargaining in the Shadow of the Law." *Yale Law Journal* 88(950):952–958.

Mnookin, Robert, Eleanor E. Maccoby, Catherine R. Albiston, and Charlene E. Depner. 1990. "Private Ordering Revisited: What Custodial Arrangements Arc Parents Negotiating?" Pp. 37–74 in *Divorce Reform at the Crossroads,* edited by Stephen D. Sugarman and Herma Hill Kay. New Haven: Yale University Press.

Pateman, Carol. 1990. *The Disorder of Women: Democracy, Feminism, and Political Theory.* Stanford: Stanford University Press.

Perinbanayagam, Robert. 1985a. "How to Do Self with Things." Pp. 315–340 in *Beyond Goffman,* edited by S. Riggins. Berlin: Mouton-de Gruyter.

———. 1985b. *Signifying Acts: Structure and Meaning in Everyday Life.* Carbondale: Southern Illinois University Press.

Pestello, Frances and Patricia Voyandoff. 1991. "In Search of Mesostructure in the Family: An Interactionist Approach to Division of Labor." *Symbolic Interaction* 14(2):105–128.

Phillips, Roger and Faith Gilroy. 1985. "Sex-Role Stereotypes and Clinical Judgments of Mental Health: The Broverman's Findings Reexamined." *Sex Roles* 12(1–2):179–193.

Pleck, Joseph. 1985. *Working Wives Working Husbands.* Beverly Hills: Sage Publications.

———. 1989. Men's Power with Women, Other Men, and Society: A Men's Movement

Analysis. Pp. 21–29 in *Men's Lives,* edited by Michael Kimmel and Michael Messner. New York: Macmillan Press.

Polikoff, Nancy. 1983. "Gender and Child-Custody Determinations: Exploding the Myths." Pp. 183–202 in *Families, Politics, and Public Policy,* edited by Irene Diamond. New York: Longman.

Riessman, Catherine. 1990. *Divorce Talk: Women and Men Make Sense of Personal Relationships.* New Brunswick, NJ: Rutgers University Press.

Risman, Barbara. 1989. "Can Men 'Mother'? Life as a Single Father." Pp. 155–164 in *Gender in Intimate Relationships: A Microstructural Approach,* edited by Barbara J. Risman and Pepper Schwartz. Belmont, CA: Wadsworth Publishing Company.

Risman, Barbara and Pepper Schwartz. 1989. "Being Gendered: A Microstructural View of Intimate Relations." Pp. 1–9 in *Gender in Intimate Relationships: A Microstructural Approach,* edited by Barbara J. Risman and Pepper Schwartz. Belmont, CA: Wadsworth Publishing Company.

Rosenblum, Karen. 1990. "The Conflict Between and Within Genders: An Appraisal of Contemporary Femininity and Masculinity." Pp. 193–202 in *Families in Transition,* edited by Arlene Skolnick and Jerome Skolnick. Glenview, IL: Scott, Foresman, and Company.

Rubin, Gayle. 1975. "The Traffic in Women: Notes on the Political Economy of Sex." In *Toward An Anthropology of Women,* edited by R. Reiter. New York: Monthly Review Press.

Schwenger, Peter. 1989. "The Masculine Mode in Speaking of Gender." Pp. 101–113 in *Speaking of Gender,* edited by Elaine Showalter. New York: Routledge.

Spanier, Graham and Linda Thompson. 1984. *Parting: The Aftermath of Separation and Divorce.* Beverly Hills: Sage Publications.

Stone, Gregory. 1981. "Appearance and the Self: A Slightly Revised Version." Pp. 187–202 in *Social Psychology Through Symbolic Interaction* (2nd edition), edited by Gregory Stone and Harvey Farberman. New York: John Wiley and Sons.

Strauss, Anselm. 1989. *Qualitative Analysis in the Social Sciences.* Cambridge: Cambridge University Press.

Tannen, Deborah. 1990. *You Just Don't Understand: Men and Women in Conversation.* New York: Ballantine Books.

Teachman, Jay. 1991. "Contributions to Children by Divorced Fathers." *Social Problems* 38(3):358–371.

United States Bureau of the Census. 1989. *Statistical Abstracts of the United States, 1988. National Data Book and Guide to Sources.* Washington, DC: U.S. Government Printing Office.

Vaughan, Diane, 1986. *Uncoupling: Turning Points in Relationships.* New York: Oxford University Press.

Wallerstein, Judith and Sandra Blakeslee. 1989. *Second Chances: Men, Women, and Children a Decade After Divorce.* New York: Ticknor and Fields.

Weitzman, Lenore. 1985. The Divorce Revolution. *The Unexpected Social and Economic Consequences for Women and Children in America.* New York: Free Press.

DIVORCE AND FATHERHOOD —ERMA JEAN LAWSON AND AARON THOMPSON

References

Amato, P. R. & Booth, A. (1991). The consequences of divorce for attitudes toward divorce and gender roles. *Journal of Family Issues, 12,* 306–322.

Arendell, T. (1995). *Fathers and divorce.* Thousand Oaks, CA: Sage.

Carter, H., & Glick, J. (1970). *Marriage and divorce: A social and economic study.* Cambridge, MA: Harvard University Press.

Chan, L., & Heaton, T. (1989). Demographic determinants of delayed divorce. *Journal of Divorce, 13,* 97–112.

Dullea, G. (1987, March 18). Divorces spawn confusion over stepparents' rights. *Omaha World-Herald,* p. A1.

Fulton, J. A. (1979). Parental reports of children's post-divorce adjustment. *Journal of Family Issues, 35,* 126–140.

Furstenberg, F. F., Jr., Morgan, P., & Allison, P. (1987). Parental participation and children's well-being after marital dissolution. *American Sociological Review, 52,* 695–701.

Furstenberg, F. F., Jr., & Nord, C. W. (1985). Parenting apart: Patterns of childrearing after marital dissolution. *Journal of Marriage and the Family, 47,* 893–904.

Glenn, N. D., (1987), Continuity versus change, sanguineous versus concern: Views of the American family in the late 1980s. *Journal of Family Issues, 8,* 348–354.

Goldberg, H. (1979). *The new male: From macho to sensitive but still all male.* New York: William Morrow.

Goldsmith, J. (1981). The relationship between former spouses: Descriptive findings. *Journal of Divorce, 4,* 1–20.

Grief, G. (1985). *Single fathers.* Lexington, MA: D.C. Heath.

Gutmann, D. (1987). *Reclaimed powers: Towards a new psychology of men and women in later Life.* New York: Basic Books.

Ihinger-Tallman, M., & Pasley, K. (1989). *Remarriage.* Newbury Park, CA: Sage.

Keith, V. M., & Finlay, B. (1988). The impact of parental divorce on children's educational attainment, marital timing, and likelihood of divorce. *Journal of Marriage and the Family, 51,* 797–809.

Kline, M., Tschann, J. M., Johnston, J. R., & Wallerstein, J. S. (1989). Children's adjustment in joint and sole physical custody families. *Developmental Psychology, 25,* 430–438.

Kruk, E. (1991). Discontinuity between pre- and post-divorce father–child relationships: New evidence regarding parental disengagement. *Journal of Divorce and Remarriage, 16,* 195–227.

Lamanna, M. A., & Riedmann, A. (1994), *Marriages and families: Making choices and facing change* (5th edition). Belmont, CA: Wadsworth.

Marsiglio, W. (1991). Stepfathers with minor children living at home. *Journal of Family Issues, 13,* 195–214.

McLanahan, S. S., & Bumpass, L. (1988). Intergenerational consequences of family disruption. *American Journal of Sociology, 94,* 130–152.

National Center for Health Statistics. (1995). *Health, United States, 1994.* Hyattsville, MD: Public Health Service.

Seltzer, J. (1991). Legal custody arrangement and children's economic welfare. *Journal of Marriage and the Family, 53,* 79–101.

Spanier, G. B. (1989). Bequeathing family continuity. *Journal of Marriage and the Family, 51,* 3–13.

Trent, K., & South, S. (1992). Sociodemographic status, parental background, childhood family structure, and attitudes toward family formation. *Journal of Marriage and the Family, 54,* 427–439.

Umberson, D. (1992). Relationships between adult children and their parents: Psychological consequences for both generations. *Journal of Marriage and the Family, 54,* 664–674.

Umberson, D., & Williams, C. (1993). Divorced fathers: Parental role strain and psychological distress. *Journal of Family Issues, 14,* 378–400.

Wallerstein, J. S., & Kelly, J. B. (1979). Divorce counseling: A community service for families in the midst of divorce. *American Journal of Orthopsychiatry, 47,* 4–22.

Weiss, R. S. (1973). *Marital separation.* New York: Basic Books.

Weiss, R. S. (1979). *Going it alone.* New York: Basic Books.

Wilson, B. F., & Clarke, S. C. (1992). Remarriages: A demographic profile. *Journal of Family Issues, 13,* 123–141.

Zeiss, A. M., Zeiss, R. H., & Johnson, S. M. (1980). Sex differences in initiation and adjustment to divorce. *Journal of Divorce 4,* 21–33.

STEPPARENTS: DE FACTO PARENTS OR LEGAL STRANGERS—MARY ANN MASON ET AL.

References

Bachrach, C. (1983). Children in families: Characteristics of biological, step-, and adopted children. *Journal of Marriage and the Family, 45,* 171–79.

Bartlett, K. (1984). Rethinking parenthood as an exclusive status: The need for alternatives when the premise of the nuclear family has failed. *Virginia Law Review, 70,* 879–903.

Cherlin, A. (1978). Remarriage as an incomplete institution. *American Journal of Sociology, 84,* 634–650.

Cherlin, A., & Furstenberg, A. F. (1994). Stepfamilies in the United States: A reconsideration. *Annual Review of Sociology, 20,* 359–381.

Coleman, M., & Ganong, L. (1990). Remarriage and stepfamily research in the 1980s: Increased interest in an old family form. *Journal of Marriage and the Family, 52,* 925–240.

Fine, M. (1994). Social policy pertaining to stepfamilies: Should stepparents and stepchildren have the option of establishing a legal relationship? In A. Booth & J. Dunn (Eds.), *Stepfamilies: Who benefits, who does not?* Hillsdale, NJ: Lawrence Erlbaum.

Gamache, S. (1997). Confronting nuclear family bias in stepfamily research. *Marriage and Family Review, 26,* 41–69.

Ganong, L., & Coleman, M. (1994). *Remarried family relationships.* Thousand Oaks, CA: Sage.

Ganong, L. H., Coleman, M., & Mistina, D. (1995). Normative beliefs about parents' and stepparents' financial obligations to children following divorce and remarriage. *Family Relations: Journal of Applied Family and Child Studies, 44,* 306–315.

Grossberg, M. (1985). *Governing the health: Law and family in nineteenth century America.* Chapel Hill: University of North Carolina Press.

Heatherington, E. M., & Clingempeel, W. G. (1992). Coping with marital transitions. *Monographs of the Society for Research in Child Development, 57,* 1–242.

Keshet, J. K. (1988). The remarried couple: Stresses and successes. In W. R. Beer (Ed.), *Relative strangers: Studies of stepfamily processes* (pp. 29–53). Totowa, NJ: Rowman & Littlefield.

Mahoney, M. (1995). *Stepfamilies and the law.* Ann Arbor: University of Michigan Press.

Marsiglio, W. (1992). Stepfathers with minor children living at home: Parenting perceptions and relationship quality. *Journal of Family Issues, 13,* 195–214.

Mason, M. A. (1994). *From fathers' property to children's rights: A history of child custody in America.* New York: Columbia University Press.

Mason, M. A., & Mauldon, J. (1996). The new stepfamily requires a new public policy. *Journal of Social Issues, 52,* 11–27.

Mason, M. A., & Simon, D. (1995). The ambiguous stepparent: Federal legislation in search of a model. *Family Law Quarterly, 3,* 445–483.

Papernow, P. L. (1988). Stepparent role development: From outsider to intimate. In W. R. Beer (Ed.), *Relative strangers: Studies of stepfamily processes* (pp. 54–82). Totowa, NJ: Rowman & Littlefield.

Riley, J. M. (1984). Symposium: Family law: Stepparents' responsibility of support. *Louisiana Law Review, 44,* 1753–1784.

Schwebel, A. I., Fine, M. A., & Renner, M. A. (1991). A study of perceptions of the stepparent role. *Journal of Family Issues, 12,* 43–57.

Silverman, S. (1992). Stepparent visitation rights: Toward the best interests of the child. *Journal of Family Law, 30,* 943–982.

Sweet, J. A., Bumpass, L. L., & Call, V. R. A. (1988). *The design and content of the National Survey of Families and Households* (NSFH Working Paper No. 1). Madison: University of Wisconsin, Center for Demography and Ecology.

White, L. K., & Booth, A. (1985). The quality and stability of remarriages: The role of stepchildren. *American Sociological Review, 50,* 689–698.

FAMILY LAW IN THE NEW MILLENNIUM FOR WHOSE FAMILIES—MARY ANN MASON, MARK A. FINE, AND SARAH CARNOCHAN

Note

1. References for all cases and legal statutes may be obtained from the second author; e-mail: finem@missouri.edu.

References

American Law Institute. (2000). *Principles of the law of family dissolution: Analysis and recommendations* (Tentative Draft No. 4). Philadelphia: Author.

Atkinson, J. (1984). Criteria for deciding custody in the trial and appellate courts. *Family Law Quarterly, 18,* 11–32.

Avery, R. J., & Mont, D. M. (1994). *Special needs adoption in New York State: Final report on adoptive parent survey* (DHHS Contract No. 90CW1012). Washington, DC: Department of Health and Human Services.

Blaisure, K., & Geasler, M. (1999, July). *Divorce education across the U.S.* Paper presented at the Coalition for Marriage, Family and Couples Education Conference, Washington, DC.

Blank, R. M. (1997). *It takes a nation.* New York: Russell Sage.

Bogenschneider, K. (2000). Has family policy come of age? A decade review of the state of U.S. family policy in the 1990s. *Journal of Marriage and the Family, 62,* 1136–1159.

Bonauto, M. (2000). *Civil union update* [Online]. Available: www.glad.org

Cahn, N., & Singer, J. (1999). Adoption, identity, and the constitution: The case for opening closed records. *University of Pennsylvania Journal of Constitutional Law, 2,* 150–194.

Census Bureau. (1999). *Interracial married couples: 1960 to present* [Online]. Available: www.census.gov/population/socdemo/ms-la/tabms-3.txt

Chambers, D. L., & Polikoff, N. D. (1999). Family law and gay and lesbian family issues in the twentieth century. *Family Law Quarterly, 33,* 523–542.

Cherlin, A. (1992). *Marriage, divorce, remarriage.* Cambridge, MA: Harvard University Press.

Elrod, L. D., Spector, R. G., & Atkinson, J. (1999). A review of the year in family law: Children's issues dominate. *Family Law Quarterly, 32,* 661–717.

Emery, R. E. (1995). Divorce mediation: Negotiating agreements and renegotiating relation-ships. *Family Relations, 44,* 377–383.

Fine, M. A., & Demo, D. (2000). Divorce: Societal ill or normative transition? In R. Milardo & S. Duck (Eds.), *Families as relationships* (pp. 135–156). Chichester, UK: Wiley.

Fine, M. A., & Fine, D. (1994). An examination and evaluation of recent changes in divorce laws in five Western countries: The critical role of values. *Journal of Marriage and the Family, 56,* 249–263.

Gallagher, M., & Waite, L. (2000). *The case for marriage.* New York: Doubleday.

Goldstein, J., Freud, A., & Solnit, A. (1973). *Beyond the best interests of the child.* New York: Free Press.

Johnston, J., Kline, M., & Tschann, J. (1989). Ongoing postdivorce conflict: Effects on children of joint custody and frequent access. *American Journal of Orthopsychiatry, 59,* 576–592.

Katz, S. N. (1999). Establishing the family and family-like relationships: Emerging models for alternatives to marriage. *Family Law Quarterly, 33,* 663–675.

Krause, H. (1986). *Family law* (2nd ed.). St. Paul, MN: West.

Lerman, R. L. (1993). A national profile of young unwed fathers. In R. L. Lerman & T. J. Ooms (Eds.), *Young unwed fathers* (pp. 35–39). Philadelphia: Temple University Press.

Mahoney, M. (1994). *Stepfamilies and the law.* Ann Arbor: University of Michigan.

Mason, M. A. (1988). *The equality trap.* New York: Simon & Schuster.

Mason, M. A. (1994). *From father's property to children's rights.* New York: Columbia.

Mason, M. A. (1998). The modern American stepfamily: Problems and possibilities. In M. A. Mason, A. Skolnick, & S. D. Sugarman (Eds.), *All our families* (pp. 95–116). New York: Oxford University Press.

Mason, M. A. (2000). *The custody wars.* New York: Basic Books.

McLanahan, S., & Sandefur, G. (1994). *Growing up with a single parent.* Cambridge, MA: Harvard University Press.

Mosher, W. D., & Bachrach, C. A. (1996). Understanding U.S. fertility: Continuity and change in the National Survey of Family Growth, 1988–1995 [13 pages]. *Family Planning Perspectives* [Online serial], *28*(1). Available FTP: Hostname: agi-usa.org Directory: pubs/journals/2800496.html

Nagourney, E. (2000, February 15). Study finds families bypassing marriage. *The New York Times,* p. F8.

National Center for Health Statistics. (1995). *Fertility/infertility* [Online]. Available FTP: Hostname: cdc.gov Directory. nchslf-astatslfertile.htm

Patterson. C. J. (2000). Family relationships of lesbians and gay men. *Journal of Marriage and the Family, 62,* 1052–1069.

Pearson, J. (1999). Domestic and international legal framework of family law: Court services: Meeting the needs of twenty-first century families. *Family Law Quarterly, 33,* 617–635.

Perry, T. L. (1999). Race matters: Change, choice, and family law at the millennium. *Family Law Quarterly, 33,* 461–474.

Regan, M. C., Jr. (1999). Establishing the family and family-like relationships: Marriage at the millennium. *Family Law Quarterly, 33,* 647–662.

Roseman, E. (2000, Fall). OPEN 2000: Are you ready for open records? *Resolve of Northern California Quarterly Newsletter,* 6.

Seltzer, J. (1994). Intergenerational ties in adulthood and childhood experience. In A. Booth

& J. Dunn (Eds.), *Stepfamilies* (pp. 89–96). Hillsdale, NJ: Lawrence Erlbaum.

Siegel, A. J. (2000). Note: Setting limits on judicial scientific, technical, and other specialized fact-finding in the new millennium. *Cornell Law Review, 86,* 167.

Sugarman, S. (1998). Single-parent families. In M. A. Mason, A. Skolnick, & S. Sugarman (Eds.), *All our families* (pp. 13–38). New York: Oxford University Press.

Triber, G. A. (1998). Growing pains: Disputes surrounding human reproductive interests stretch the boundaries of traditional legal concepts. *Seton Hall Legislative Journal, 23,* 103–140.

U.S. Department of State. (2000), *Hague convention on intercountry adoptions* [Online].

Available: www.travel.state.gov/adoption_ info_sheet.html

Wardle, L. D. (1999). Reorganizing the family: Divorce reform at the turn of the millennium: Certainties and possibilities, *Family Law Quarterly, 33,* 783–800.

Warshak, R. A. (2000). Remarriage as a trigger of parental alienation syndrome. *American Journal of Family Therapy, 28,* 229–241.

Weithorn, L. A., & Grisso, T. (1987). Psychological evaluations in divorce custody: Problems, principles, and procedures. In L. Weithom (Ed.), *Psychology and child custody determinations: Knowledge, roles, and expertise* (pp. 157–181). Lincoln: University of Nebraska Press.